FRENCH SECRET PROJECTS 2

FRENCH SECRET PROJECTS 2

Bombers, Patrol and Assault Aircraft

JEAN-CHRISTOPHE CARBONEL

Publisher's note
Research has brought to light many contemporary and rare photographs and drawings of varying quality. They are reproduced and have been enhanced as far as possible.

First published in 2017 by Crécy Publishing

A CIP record for this book is available from the British Library

Printed in Malta by Melita Press

ISBN 9781910809006

Crecy Publishing Ltd
1a Ringway Trading Est, Shadowmoss Rd
Manchester M22 5LH
TEL (+44) (0)161 499 0024
www.crecy.co.uk

FRONT COVER AND TITLE PAGEBACK COVER **Specially commissioned artwork by Daniel Uhr depicting a strategic missile separating from its Nord-Aviation "mother" aircraft as part of the Minerve long-range strategic bomber programme.**

TOP **Breguet Br 941 prototype flying above the Alps in 1964.** *Philippe Ricco*

MIDDLE **Desk-model of the proposed Dassault Minerve VIB strategic bomber.** *Dassault photograph*

BOTTOM **NC271-01, flying scale model of the proposed NC270 jet bomber, still attached to its SE 161 Languedoc carrier.** *José Fernandez*

Contents

Introduction ... 6
Acknowledgements ... 14
Glossary ... 15

Chapter One – The First Jet Bombers ... 18
Chapter Two – A More Reasonable Approach:
Heavy Fighters and Strike Aircraft (Up to Vautour) ... 27
Chapter Three – The Quest for the Supersonic Bomber ... 44
Chapter Four – The Minerve Programme ... 60
Chapter Five – Strike and Training (ECAT) ... 87
Chapter Six – In the Field (Baroudeur) ... 107
Chapter Seven – COIN is Minted ... 123
Chapter Eight – Low-Speed VTOL ... 141
Chapter Nine – Helicopters ... 161
Chapter Ten – Assault Transports ... 184
Chapter Eleven – Maritime Patrol and Anti-Submarine ... 213
Chapter Twelve – Atomic Power ... 234
Chapter Thirteen – I Dreamt of Saucers ... 237
Chapter Fourteen – Strange Ways ... 245

Reference Sources and Bibliography ... 255
Index ... 256

Introduction

ABOVE Models of the jet-propelled flying wing aircraft proposed by Heinrich Hertel to the French air ministry in 1945. None were built. *José Fernandez*

The first volume of French Secret Projects dealt with fighter types and associated aircraft, so now in this second volume we will deal with machines that were intended to act against enemy ground and naval forces. This will naturally cover bombers *sensu stricto*, but also ground attack and counter-insurgency machines, maritime patrol aircraft and even assault transports.

Contrary to their British and US counterparts, the French Air Force had no real tradition of big and heavy bombers, no Bomber Command and no Eighth Air Force, and the country just could not afford large machines such as this. Therefore it engaged enthusiastically in the design of versatile medium bombers, the initial end product of this being the SO 4050 Vautour.

At the same time, another major factor that affected the path that would be followed in the development of an offensive air force, and which was prevalent during the whole period from the end of the Second World War to the early 1960s, was the various difficult conflicts into which France became entangled relating to decolonisation. These led to the development of various light attack and counter-insurgency aircraft but all of these emerged as being too specialised for their task. The same mindset of creating an aerial force directed to supporting the ground forces led to the design of various aircraft intended to repulse a communist invasion in a devastated central Europe. Two results of this thinking were the Baroudeur, intended to operate from any patch of grass or other surface, and the Potez 75, an anti-tank aircraft developed outside any official requirement (a sure way to get it shelved).

The Suez operation of 1956 led to the perception by the French government that to be a country independent from the two superpowers, the USA and the Soviet Union, it was necessary to possess *la Bombe* (nuclear weapons) and the long-range vehicle to deliver it. Before land- or submarine-launched missiles could be designed, the first such vehicle was to be the Dassault Mirage IV strategic bomber. However, the type, although a prominent and dissuasive spearhead, was found by many people, including the French political powers, to be somewhat short-legged. Consequently, a highly confidential programme under the codename Minerve (the ancient Roman goddess of war) was launched to replace or continue the Mirage IV with a concept where a large missile was carried aloft and launched from an aircraft. This programme certainly generated some of the most advanced aircraft and missile projects designed in France up to that time.

Helicopter design was a specialised field that also emerged in France after the war and which has now put the country among the leaders on the world stage (even if all effort is now agglomerated into a pan-European company). From light battlefield reconnaissance machines to a large flying crane, plus assault and attack helicopters, French rotary aircraft achieved considerable success on the world market, although those that will appear in the following pages had difficulty lifting themselves from the drawing boards! To complement the helicopters came various attempts to produce more exotic VTOL-type machines, from flying saucers to 'flying armoured cars', but out of this menagerie of wonderful (or not so wonderful) designs only the Ludion one-man flying device actually made it into the air.

On top of all of this, France's aircraft designers produced various assault transport and large reconnaissance aircraft designs, some of which were flown. And limited production

ABOVE The He 274 prototype accompanied by other French aircraft of German design. *Philippe Ricco*

did not always prohibit operational use, for example in the case of the Hurel-Dubois aircraft that saw operations with the *Service de Documentation Extérieure et de Contre-Espionnage* (SDECE) – today the DGSE or *Direction Générale de la Sécurité Extérieure*, the French equivalent to MI6 or the CIA.

Maritime patrol aircraft were also part of the output, but here the results were rather the opposite of what would happen with the VTOL studies – the designs produced were often successful and that limited the creation of weird projects. Finally, the coverage of French aircraft research would not be complete without a look at advanced but not altogether realistic designs including nuclear-powered aircraft or man-made flying saucers.

The German Input into French Aeronautical Research

French aeronautical research met German aeronautical research twice! During the war French bureaux d'études (design offices) were 'invited' to help in the design of a few aircraft types of German origin, some of which formed part of the collaboration sponsored by the French Vichy Government. While the Germans did not have enough confidence in French aircraft designers to entrust them with the detailed design of new high performance aircraft (and with good reason!) they did require, as part of the 'support' for planned long-range stratospheric bombers, various transport aircraft and a 'flying crane' type of helicopter. The catch was that there was little in terms of technology transfer, and most notably none of these machines featured the new-fangled jet engines. In 1944 French designer Henri Coanda boasted that Willy Messerschmitt had invited him to witness a flight of one of the early Me 262s, but all that Coanda got out of this was a sojourn in a Paris prison on the grounds of 'collaboration with the enemy'. And when a joint British and American Combined Intelligence Objectives Sub-Committee (CIOS) team visited him and his Paris laboratory during the autumn of 1944, it found nothing of interest and labelled him as just an amateur inventor.

The following are the German aircraft in which French designers became involved.

Arado Ar 396

The successful Ar 96 trainer was evolved into the Ar 296, but the difficult supply situation in Germany meant that before the latter could fly a redesign was in order using as little strategic material as possible. The task was turned over to SIPA in occupied France. Prototypes were built in France by SIPA but in view of the war situation (i.e. the success of the Allied invasion of Normandy) the Germans decided to transfer production to Letov in Prague. The first flight of the new aircraft took place on 29 December 1944 and after the war was over SIPA produced 232 examples for use by the French Air Force as the SIPA S.10, and later as the S.11, S.111, S.12 (which returned to a full metal structure as originally envisioned for the Ar 296) and S.121.

Blohm & Voss Bv 144

The Bv 144 was a project initiated by Blohm & Voss against an order from Lufthansa. The German *Reichsluftfahrtministerium* (RLM), or Ministry of Aviation, was intrigued by the variable incidence system to be incorporated in the aircraft but felt that, since it was intended to be purely a civilian aircraft, it would detract from the German war effort to have Blohm & Voss

BELOW Front view of the Blohm & Voss Bv 144 as built in France. The variable incidence wing was seemingly of minimal interest for the RLM, and of no interest at all to the STAé. *via J. Fernandez*

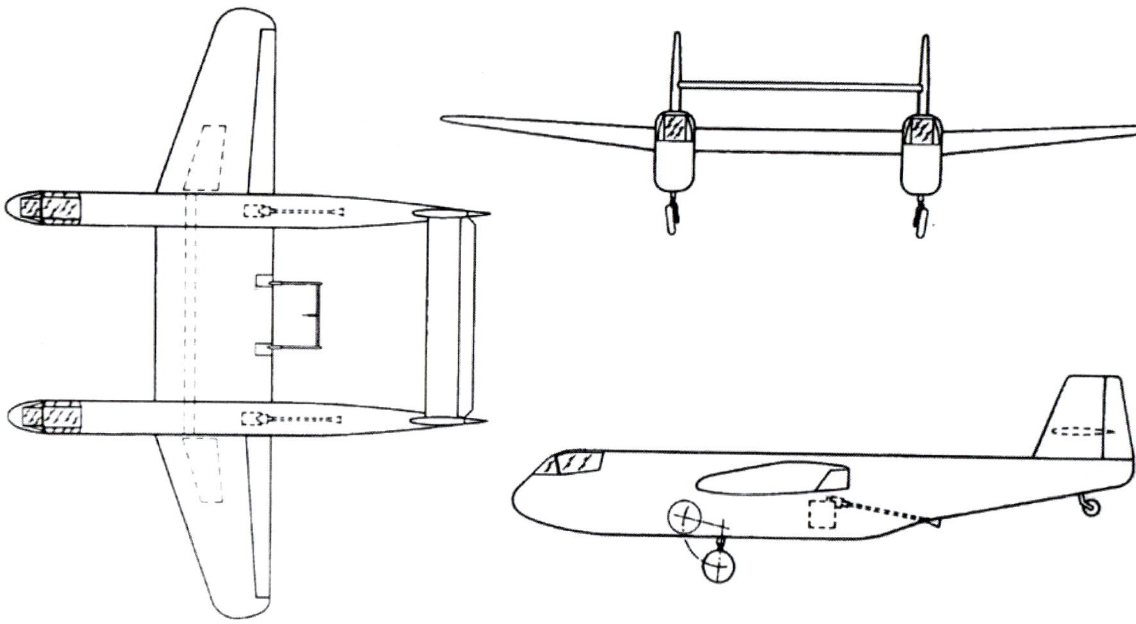

ABOVE **A sketch of the mysterious DFS 332, of which two prototypes were built by Caudron. Both disappeared without a trace in 1944.** *Author's collection*

undertake the full design. Consequently, the project was transferred to the Breguet factory in Anglet near Bordeaux and a Blohm & Voss team was sent there to work with the French *bureau d'études*. As might be expected, the design and assembly progressed slowly and only the first of the two prototypes had been completed by the time the factory was liberated in January 1945. Three flights were made with this machine during the spring of 1945 before it was abandoned. In addition to this project, Louis Breguet undertook a few other low-key jobs for the Germans in a (successful) bid to keep his *bureau d'études* employed during the war.

DFS 332

The DFS 332 was an odd twin-boom aircraft built to test aerofoil profiles in full scale. It was to be powered two Walther rocket engines and a contract was signed between DFS and Société Caudron in 1943. It was intended to have two aircraft produced in just four months but bottlenecks with the supply of materials meant that the first machine was not ready until June 1944. Having been loaded on to a train pointing in the direction of Ainring in Bavaria in Germany on 12 July 1944, the aircraft is presumed to have been destroyed while still aboard. The second (incomplete?) airframe never left the Caudron factory … but it never appeared in any 'war booty' list either.

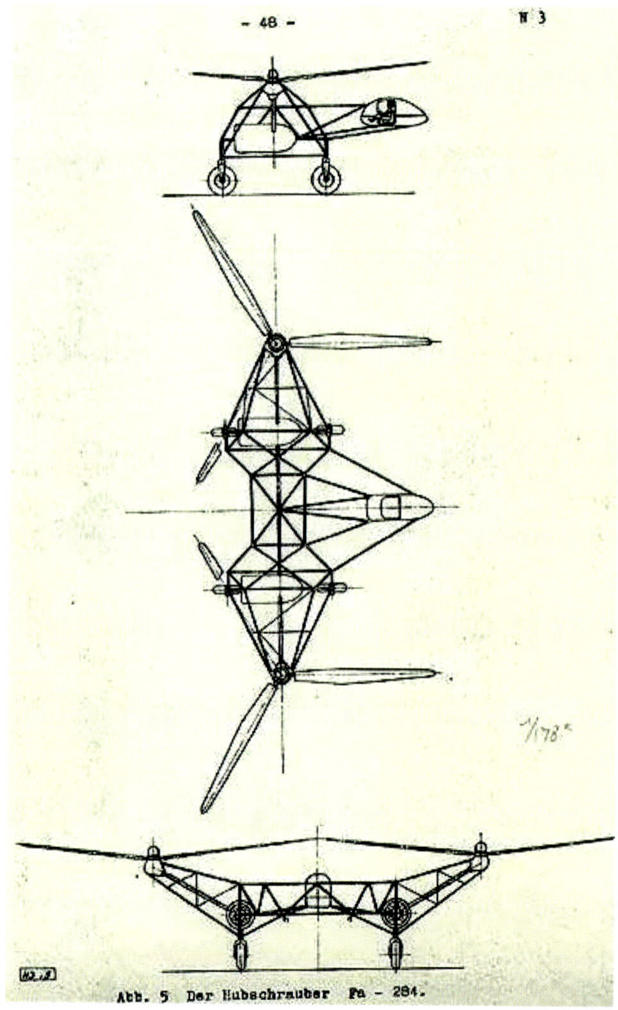

RIGHT **German drawing of the revised Fa 284 'flying crane' that was to have been built by Breguet.** *Author's collection*

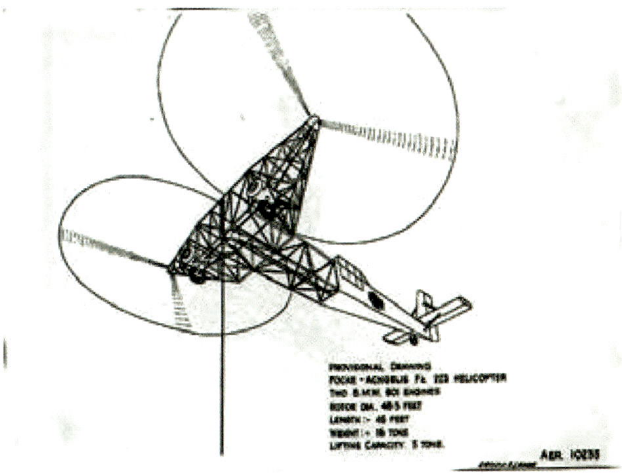

ABOVE The Fa 284 as described by Breguet personnel to a visiting British technical intelligence unit, which was led by rotary wing expert Captain Liptrot. *Author's collection*

Focke-Achgelis Fa 284

The Fa 284 was originally a large assault helicopter designed to carry loads or personnel in a large pod fitted underneath the boom-like fuselage, although a version was also proposed that was intended to carry large loads (such as engineer's bridges) on a sling. Development of what could be termed an austere version was transferred to Breguet Montaudran in 1942 and the design was simplified considerably by the French team, with a square truss structure replacing the original round fuselage. When the CIOS team investigating the former French-occupied factories visited Breguet in late 1944, all the Fa 284 documentation was reported to have been destroyed in a bombing raid on the factory. Development of the Fa 284 was not pursued after the Liberation, but shades of this design could still be found in the flying crane projects by Nord and Sud Aviation in the mid-1960s (see Chapter Nine).

Focke-Wulf Ta 400

This was among the many long-range bombers studied by the German manufacturers during the mid-war period, at a time when they no longer had enough resources to devote to such studies. For this reason, the detailed design of this machine, under the name Fw 300A, was entrusted to the Chatillon factory of SNCAN. Nothing came out of this project and no technology transfer could have resulted from it, except, maybe the remote-controlled turrets.

Heinkel He 274

Another Amerika-Bomber competitor whose detailed design was carried out by the French was the Heinkel He 274, this time by the *Société Anonyme des Usines Farman* (SAUF) in Rue Poissonière in the centre of Paris, with two prototypes built in Suresnes. The *bureau d'études* of SAUF was, as was revealed after the war, expert in finding causes to delay its work with the end result that the two aircraft were not complete when the Paris area was freed from German control in August 1944. The retreating Germans attempted to sabotage the engines and wreck the airframes while carrying away all the blueprints, but in the end the damage to the aircraft proved to be minimal (a set of undamaged engines was found in another part of the factory) and the blueprints were redrawn far more quickly than they had been done originally under German control. The first prototype was completed in September 1945 (just a year later!) and a wall of the factory had to be taken down to extract the completed aircraft from it. The machine was then transferred by road to Orléans Bricy airfield, where the first flight took place on 30 December 1945. The second prototype did not fly until 22 December 1947 and both machines proved to be very delicate to handle at low altitude, having been designed as stratospheric bombers. Neither was used in its intended role but they played an important part as carrier aircraft (motherships) for the SO M1 and NC 271 manned flying models and the full-size Leduc 016 (see Volume 1 for the Leduc and Chapter One of the present volume for the SO M1 and NC-271). The He 274's pressure cabin and supercharged engines were studied closely by French engineers.

TOP The fuselage of the first prototype He 274 showing the state it had reached by about September 1944. This view was formed by the merging of two separate photos. *Author's collection*

ABOVE The second prototype was less well advanced. The factory itself was in bad shape, and in particular all the glass panels in the roof had been blown out during bombing raids. *Author's collection*

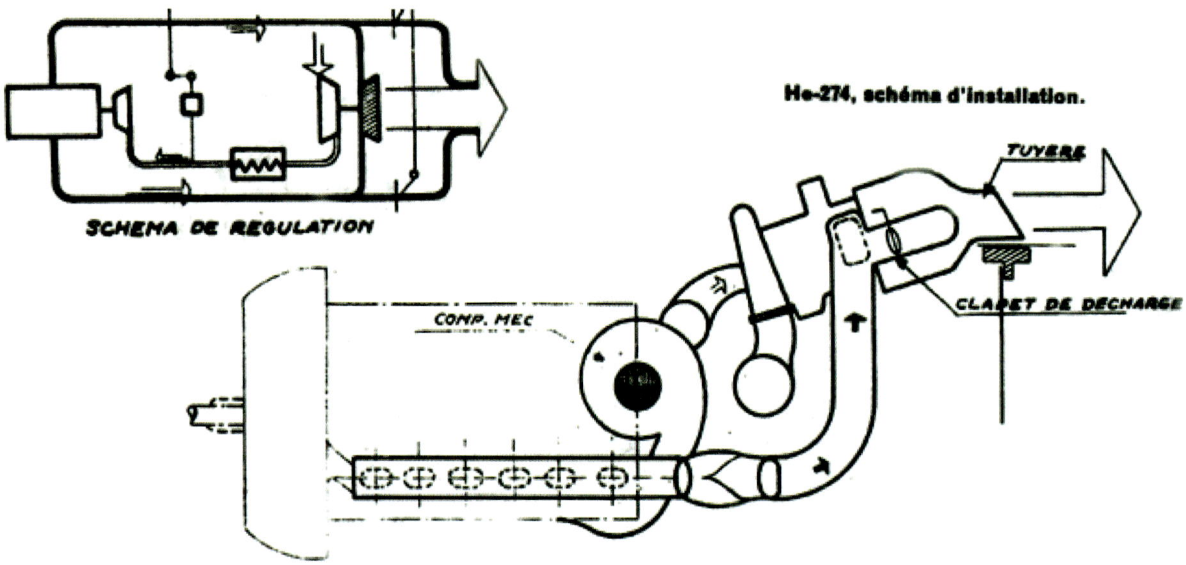

ABOVE **French schematic drawings of the compressor used on the He 274's engines. French engineers were interested in the high-altitude equipment used on the He 274.** *Author's collection*

Junkers Ju 488

The Ju 488 was an ultra-long-range bomber derivative of the Junkers Ju 88 family and was also intended for ocean patrol duties. It did not feature any advanced technology and the assembly of two prototypes, a pre-series of four aircraft and later the construction of the Ju 488A production series, was subcontracted to a Latécoère factory near Toulouse. In the aftermath of D-Day, the Germans tried to send the first two nearly complete prototypes to Germany by train, but the French Résistance managed to damage one machine when it was still in the factory while components of the second were 'mislaid' along various sidings of the railway stations around Toulouse.

Messerschmitt Me 164

Messerschmitt transferred the design and construction of the Me 164 prototype, a twin-engined transport aircraft, to

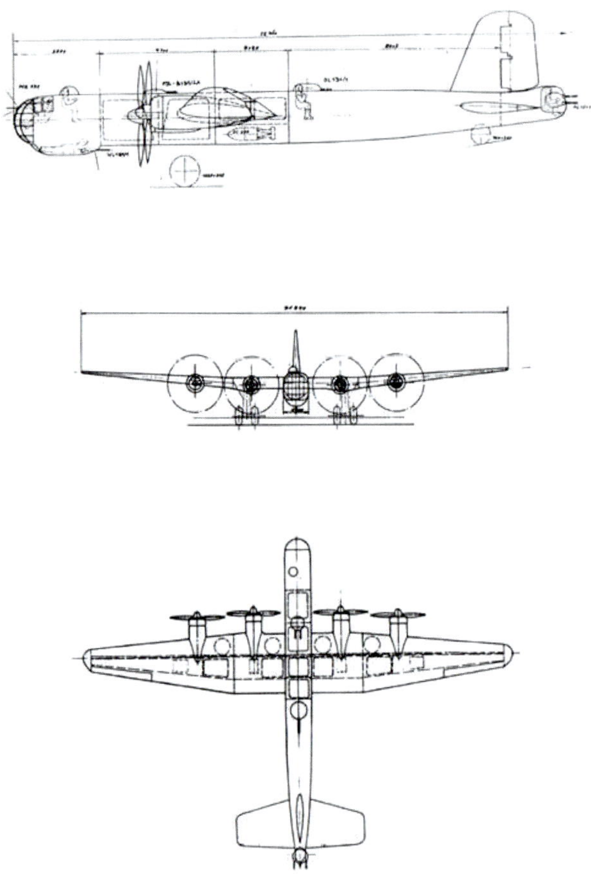

ABOVE **Three-view drawing of the intended appearance of the Heinkel He 274. The prototypes were built without armament.** *Heinkel document, Author's collection*

RIGHT **The Junkers Ju 488 in the Montaudran factory.** *Author's collection*

ABOVE Another view of the Ju 488, here showing the damaged fuselage section following French Résistance sabotage. *Author's collection*

Caudron. The machine had no distinguishing features and it appears that it never went beyond the RLM Typenblatt three-view drawing.

Messerschmitt Me 208

From 1941 SNCAN *bureau d'études* at Sartrouville was tasked by Messerschmitt to help in the design of an improved version of the famous Bf 108 Taifun. By 1942 the French company had produced a full set of blueprints and a wooden mock-up of the Me 208, and then the initial Argus-powered design was reworked with a French engine, a Renault 6Q. For once the two prototypes (GK+RZ and KR+BZ) were completed before the Libération but the first of these was destroyed when the factory was bombed.

The surviving second prototype took off under French markings and became the prototype of the Nord 1100 Noralpha (the military versions were called the Nord Ramier).

Zeppelin ZSO 523

Zeppelin was given the job of developing a large transport aircraft to carry heavy vehicles, rather like the earlier Messerschmitt Me 323. Since this was a low-priority programme for the Germans they transferred the work to SNCASO near Paris, which, like the other French companies co-operating with the enemy, worked hard to progress as little as possible. By the time the factory had returned to French control the ZSO 523 project had only reached the status of a wooden mock-up of the front fuselage, and it progressed no further.

The Dornier Do 24, Fieseler Fi 156, Focke-Wulf Fw 190A, Junkers Ju 52 and Siebel 204 were also produced or repaired in France but this work did not involve the bureaux d'études. It should be noted that none of the programmes outlined above brought any direct technological transfer from Germany (which was not the intention of the Germans anyway!), but it did allow those French companies that became involved to preserve their bureaux d'études and to allow their personnel (engineers, draughtsmen, factory workers) to dodge the *Service du Travail Obligatoire* (STO), or Compulsory Work Organisation, a forced labour programme imposed by the Germans upon the French to force them to work in Germany in direct support of the Nazi war effort).

Like the other Allies, the French were keen to obtain German aeronautical and technological secrets and after the war scientific investigation teams were sent into Germany to find and acquire aircraft, rockets, equipments and documentation. The following aircraft were obtained:

Dornier Do 335B (flown)
Fieseler Fi 103
Focke-Achgelis Fa 61 (rotor only)
Focke-Achgelis Fa 223 (parts)
Focke-Achgelis Fa 330 (flown)
Heinkel He 162 (flown)
Henschel Hs 293
Messerschmitt Me 163B
Messerschmitt Me 262A (flown)
Messerschmitt Enzian
Peenemünde A4 (V2)
Peenemünde Wasserfall
Ruhrstahl X-4 (flown)
Ruhrstahl X-7 (flown?)
Ruhrstahl Fritz X (flown ?)

Also after the war, several German specialists were persuaded to work in France, including the following:

ABOVE A Heinkel He 162 in French colours. This type was not flown very much because an early flight had ended in a fatal crash. *Philippe Ricco*

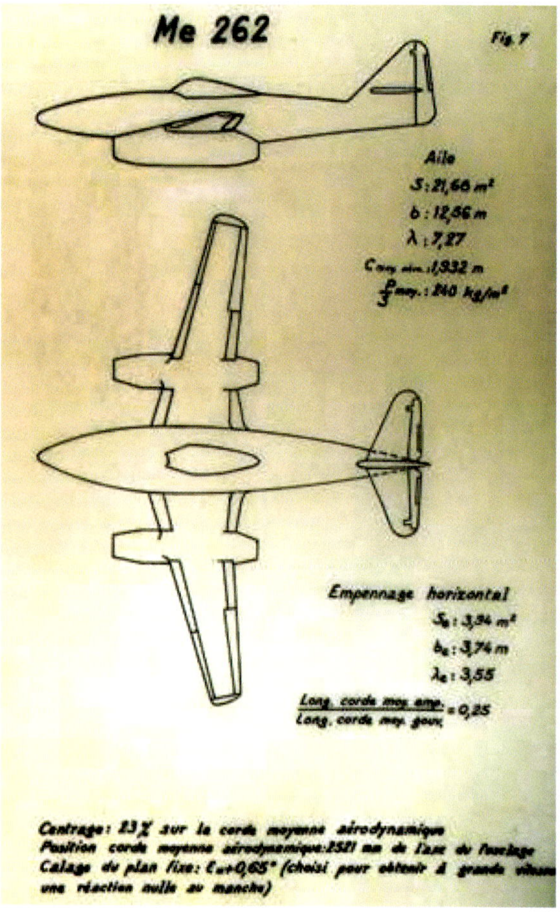

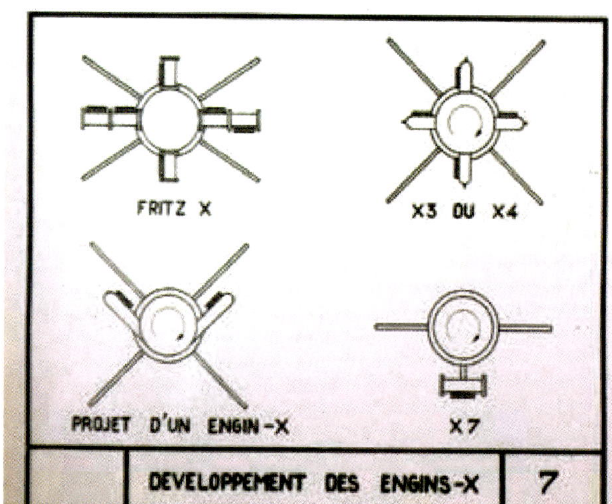

ABOVE French document describing the features and data relating to the wing of the Messerschmitt Me 262. *Author's archive*

ABOVE RIGHT A Messerschmitt Enzian missile upended in the Nord Aviation Châtillon factory. *Author's collection*

RIGHT Taken from a BTZ report, this schematic drawing of Ruhrstahl missiles illustrates the control devices. *Zborowski's Archives*

Heinrich Focke, formerly of Focke-Achgelis

One of Germany's leading experts in rotary wings and in fact a pioneer in this domain. His Fw 61 is generally regarded as the first truly operable helicopter, while the Fa

ABOVE **Theodor Laufer was a major player in the conception of the SO 1221 Djinn helicopter.** *Philippe Ricco*

223 was a large helicopter that was slowly entering service with the Luftwaffe as the war ended. In 1945 the French army obtained a lot of spares, engines and documentation at Ochsenhausen (although some had been destroyed by French soldiers), the main establishment of the Focke-Achgelis company. Originally it was planned to build ten Fa 223s (the military version) and ten Fa 266 (a civilian version) but this was soon increased to thirty aircraft. A factory was established at Argenteuil near Paris for their construction as the SE 3000, but Focke did not fit in well with the French and by mid-1948 he had left France and abandoned the project (and an unrealised larger SE 3100) to the French team. The SE 3000 itself was not a success but paved the way to the future achievements of SNCASE in rotary wing aircraft (see Chapter Nine).

Theodor Laufer, formerly of Doblhoff

Laufer was the mathematician in Doblhoff's jet helicopter team. He found work with SNCASO in May 1946 and was instrumental in the development of the SO 1100 Ariel and later SO 1221 Djinn helicopters (see Chapter Nine).

Hermann Oestrich, formerly of BMW

Oestrich was the manager of the jet engine branch at BMW. Almost as soon as the war was over he began working with the French and even had a unit named after him, the Groupe O, which had the job of developing jet engines. He proposed the development of the BMW 018 advanced jet engine and the BMW 028 turbo propeller in various forms, and as head manager of the *Atelier Technique Aéronautique de Rickenbach* he designed the ATAR 101 and ATAR 103 (which had little in common with the later ATAR 101B); he even proposed a series of flying wing aircraft of various types including a four-engined bomber and a six-engined transport. Later, Oestrich joined SNECMA and with the ATAR series was instrumental in giving France a series

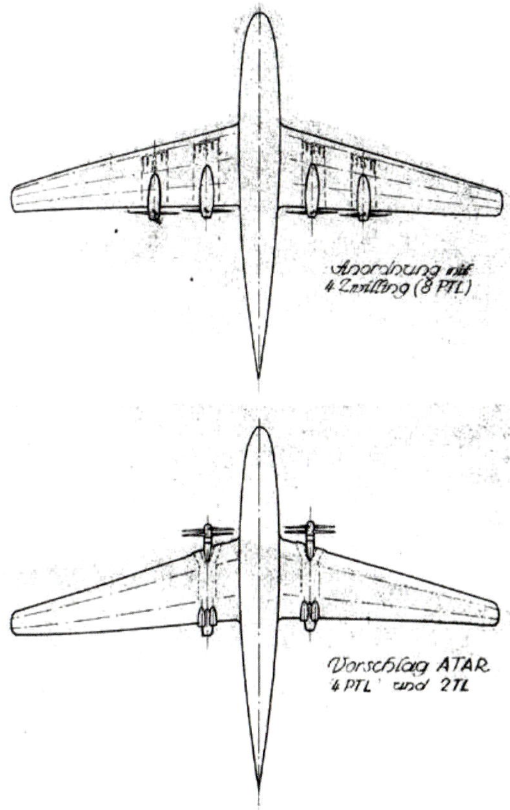

ABOVE **A proposal by Herman Oestrich to install jet engines or turboprops on the projected SNCASO SO 5000 large transport airplane project of 1945-46.** *Author's collection*

of nationally designed and built jet engines to power the military aircraft that would equip the revived *Armée de l'Air*.

Eugen Sänger

Sänger was a pure scientist who worked on ramjets and rocket engines. None of his designs was developed into a complete aircraft but he came to prominence when his most ambitious proposal, the Antipodal Bomber, was discovered after the war. The Soviets are even supposed to have mounted a failed kidnapping operation to get hold of him! Instead, he worked for *l'Arsenal Aéronautique*, a state organisation created before the war and tasked with translating and evaluating captured German documents. *L'Arsenal Aéronautique* specialised in ramjets and also tried to reconstruct the supersonic DFS 346 research aircraft (which the Russians had acquired). Reputedly Sänger's input was quite limited but he certainly provided an impulse to French supersonic research (see Volume I).

Helmut von Zborowski, formerly of BMW

Helmut von Zborowski was the head manager of the BMW engine factory but also the head of the special development section of this company, working mostly on rocket engines.

ABOVE **Scale Model of the *Charançon* missile (drone) proposed by von Zborowski.** *via Isolde Zborowski*

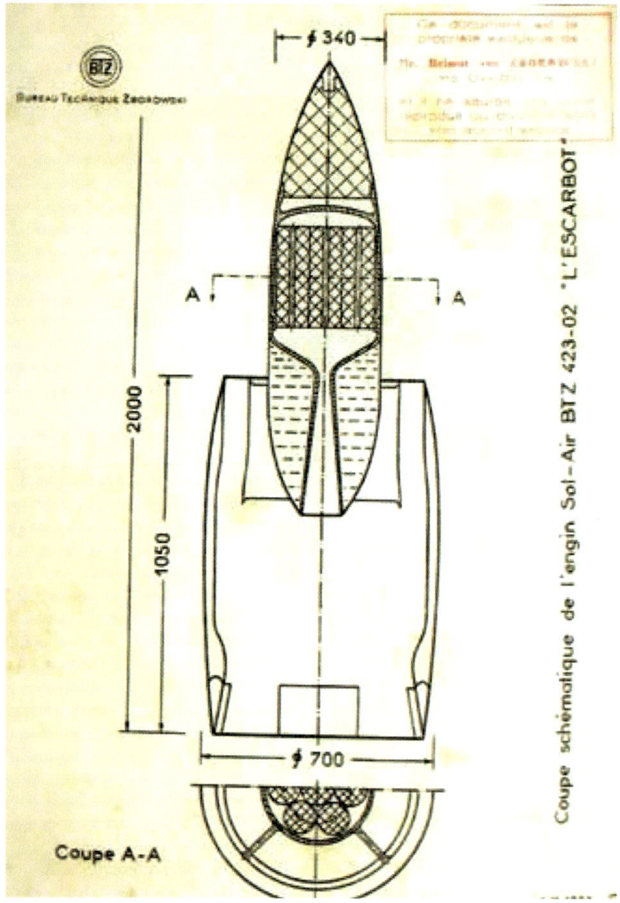

ABOVE **Taken from the Zborowski archives, this is a drawing of the Escarbot rocket missile. Like all Zborowski designs, its name came from an insect belonging to the coleopterae family of beetles. In this case Escarbot is an old French word for the Cetonia aurata, the rose chafer also known as the Goldsmith beetle. The dimensions are indicated in millimetres.** *Archives Zborowski*

In some way he was Germany's expert in smaller booster rockets, while Wernher von Braun was the expert in much larger missiles. From 1948 he worked in France but never became directly involved with a big company, instead carrying out his research while based in a mansion near Paris. However, through his former colleague Herman Oestrich he became consultant to SNECMA for the Coleoptère project (Volume 1).

J.C. Carbonel 2016

Acknowledgements

I would like to thank the following people for their contribution in collecting the material on which this book is based:

A special thank you first should be made to Philippe Ricco, long-time collector of everything related to French aviation, who helped me trace the more (and the less) obscure designs in this book, and also to José Fernandez, who supplied many photographs of real aircraft.

On the industry side special thanks should also go to Luc Berger at Dassault Aviation, who helped me to discover nuggets in the cavernous company archive room, to Philippe van Lierde of Association Patrimoine Aérospatiale (EADS), who gave me access to the Nord archives, and to Dominique Prot at Espace Patrimoine Safran/SNECMA, who was always ready to answer my numerous requests for photographs and documents pertaining to SNECMA.

And as usual to Tony Buttler for his very thorough reviews that helped in tracking down many mistakes, including sometimes in the source material.

Then the following people contributed by their help to access specific material:

Mrs. Isolde von Zborowski, who gave me access to the archives of her father; M. Jean-François Clervoy, ESA; M. Paul Gauge, expert in everything Trident; M. Henri Lacaze, who helped me regarding the Morane designs and the advanced Sud designs; M. Renaud Mangallon, who owns and designs Sharkit models.

Glossary

Note: although fully state-owned companies, the series of *Sociétés Nationales de Constructions Aéronautiques* (SNCA) manufacturers were operated as private concerns.

AAM Air-to-air missile.
Anhedral Downward slope of wing from root to tip.
Angle of Attack The angle at which the wing is inclined relative to the airflow.
Angle of Incidence Angle between the chord line of the wing and the fore and aft datum line of the fuselage.
appui tactique Ground support (by aircraft).
Area Rule Principal law for keeping transonic drag to a minimum. States that cross-section areas of an aeroplane plotted from nose to tail on a graph should form a smooth curve.
Armée de l'Air French Air Force.
Arsenal Aéronautique An agency set up in 1936 together with the Air Ministry for the triple purpose of firstly allowing the technical staff of the Ministry to get hands-on experience in the design of aircraft and thereby giving them a better capability and understanding in the evaluation of manufacturer's cost proposals, second to do advanced or confidential research that could not be done by the industry, and third to train technical staff in advanced technology and techniques. After the war it was tasked with exploiting captured German technology. Reorganised in 1952 as the SFECMAS company (qv).
ASM Air-to-surface missile.
ASMP *Air Sol Moyenne Portée* – air-to-ground, medium-range missile. A French air-launched cruise missile type weapon that entered service during the 1980s.
Aspect Ratio Ratio of wingspan to mean chord, calculated by dividing the square of the span by the wing area.
ASW Anti-submarine warfare.
ATAR *Atelier Aéronautique de Rickenbach.* An organisation set up in Germany in 1945 by SNECMA (qv) to receive those ex-BMW German engineers who had decided to work for France. Transferred to Decizes in France, then to SNECMA's HQ at Melun Villaroche (south of Paris) in 1947.
avion d'armes Combat aircraft.
BAC British Aircraft Corporation.
Balancines In French parlance, 'arms' with light wheels or skids usually installed near an aircraft's wingtips or in wing engine nacelles to stabilise the airframe when the main landing gears were placed on the centreline.
Biréacteur Aircraft fitted with two turbojets.
BTZ *Bureau Technique Zborowski.*
Bundesluftwaffe Post-war German Air Force created in 1956.
***Bureaux d'Études* or BE** Design offices.
CAPRA *Compagnie Anonyme de Production et Réalisation Aéronautique.* A private company incorporated in 1937 that would become MATRA (qv) in 1941.
CEAM *Centre d'Expériences Aériennes Militaires* (Centre for Military Aerial Experimentation). While the CEV (qv) tested an aircraft's airworthiness and general flying qualities, CEAM validated and assessed how the new type could or would be used by the Armée de l'Air. The CEAM is part of the French Air Force and located on BA 118 Mont de Marsan.
CEV *Centre d'Essais en Vol* (Flight Test Centre). Attached to the French Defence Ministry in charge of testing and approving military and, on a more limited basis, civil aircraft. Had numerous bases, the main ones at *Bretigny sur Orge* (near Paris) and Istres (near Marseilles).
Chord Distance between centres of curvature of wing leading and trailing edges when measured parallel to the longitudinal axis.
CIOS Combined Intelligence Objectives Sub-Committee.
CofG Centre of gravity.
COIN Counter-insurgency (aircraft).
Coléoptère A type of aircraft invented by Helmut von Zborowski and characterised by an annular wing.
Conseil Supérieur de la Marine French Navy's 'High Council'.
CPE *Centre de Perspective et d'Évaluation* (Centre for Evaluation and [long-term] Perspective). A research committee set up in 1964 by the French Defence Ministry to investigate long-term defence and weapon systems.
Critical Mach Number Mach number at which an aircraft's controllability is first affected by compressibility, i.e. point at which shock waves first appear.
CTOL Conventional Take-off and Landing.
DEFA *Direction des Études et Fabrications d'Armement* (French Defence Ministry Directorate for Study and Manufacturing of Armament), the grouping of the various '*arsenaux*', i.e. the army weapon factories, from 1945. DEFA later became GIAT and was privatised during the 1990s. Today the company is named Nexter.
Délégué Ministériel à l'Armement Ministry Delegate to Armament. From 1961 this was the branch of the French Defence Ministry in charge of defining and procuring weapons for the services. Became the

Direction Générale de l'Armement (General Directorate for Armament) (qv) in 1977.

DERS *Développement, Études et Réalisations Spéciales* (Special Studies, Developments and Realisations). Company incorporated in 1952 to enable von Zborowski to set up a team of engineers and technicians and develop his 'ring-wing' concepts. This structure later led to the formation of BTZ (qv).

Deutsche Forschungsanstalt für Segelflug German Research Institute for Gliding Flight. One of the many aircraft research establishments set up by Nazi Germany.

Diabolo In French parlance, the type of landing gear where two wheels share the same axle, usually with the landing leg attached to the axle between the two wheels.

Dihedral Upward slope of wing from root to tip.

Direction Générale de l'Armement General Directorate for Armament. From 1977 the replacement for the *Délégué Ministériel à l'Armement* (qv).

DTI *Direction Technique et Industrielle* (Technical and Industrial Directorate of the French Defence Ministry). Also known as DTIA (*Direction Technique et Industrielle Aéronautique*). Until 1961 the entity in charge of defining and ordering French military aircraft programmes.

ECM Electronic countermeasures.

Ecole Supérieure de l'Aéronautique Superior School of Aeronautics.

Etat-Major Staff.

Fête Nationale de l'Air National Air Feast. In 1950 the Paris Air Show was split into two parts: a static display in the Grand Palais (a large Victorian-style hall situated at the bottom of the *Champs Élysées* in Paris) and the flying display in Orly, named the Fête Nationale de l'Air.

Fiche Programme Call for Proposals by the French Air Ministry.

Flèche Sweep: Aile en fleche – swept wing.

Flutter A high frequency oscillation of an aircraft's structure induced by both aerodynamic and aeroelastic forces.

Flotille Naval unit. Similar to squadron for an air force.

Forces Aériennes Stratégiques Strategic Air Forces. The air component of the French *Forces de Dissuasion*. Created in 1964, their role is to carry and if required deliver France's nuclear weapons. Originally established with the Mirage IVA bomber, it now uses Rafale fighters.

Force de frappe Strike Force. From 1961 became *Force de Dissuasion*.

Groupe de Bombardement Bomber wing. Became Escadron de Bombardement during the 1950s through the similarity with the use of 'squadron' among NATO allies.

Groupe de Chasse Fighter wing.

Groupe de Reconnaissance Reconnaissance wing.

Gross Weight Usually signifies maximum weight with internal fuel plus all equipment/weapons aboard, but not external drop tanks.

IFR In-flight refuelling.

Ing *Ingénieur* (engineer).

JATO Jet Assisted Take-Off.

Mach Number Ratio of aeroplane's speed to that of sound in the surrounding medium – expressed as a decimal.

Marine Nationale French Navy.

MATRA *Mécanique Aviation TRAction*. From 1941 the new name of the company originally incorporated as CAPRA (qv).

Ministère de l'Air French Air Ministry. A sub-division of the Defense Ministry until 1947. From then until 1957 it was the *Sous-Secrétariat d'État à l'Air* (qv).

Monobloc Gouvernes – one-piece control surfaces.

Musée de l'Air Today the *Musée de l'Air et de l'Espace* (Air and Space Museum) situated on Le Bourget airfield, north of Paris. It is partially housed in the historic buildings of *Le Bourget* airport, including its control tower.

NACA National Advisory Committee for Aeronautics (in USA).

NATO North Atlantic Treaty Organisation.

NIDA *Nid d'abeilles* or honeycomb structure.

nm Nautical mile.

NBMR NATO Basic Military Requirement. NBMR.3 dealt with VTOL fighters and ground support aircraft, NBMR.4 with transport aircraft.

NOTAR No tail rotor.

ONERA Office *Nationale d'Etude et de Recherches Aéronautiques* (National Agency for Aerospace Studies and Research). The French aerodynamic research establishment that undertakes work for the country's aircraft manufacturers, notably with its numerous wind tunnels.

Porte Aéronefs Aircraft carrier.

Propellor-Turbo-Lader Turbopropeller (German designation).

RAE Royal Aircraft Establishment (UK).

RAF Royal Air Force.

RATO Rocket-Assisted Take-Off (replaced JATO when rocket permanently adopted to give extra take-off thrust).

Ravitailleur Refueller aircraft.

RLM German *Reichsluftfahrtministerium*.

Salon de l'Aéronautique de Paris Paris Air Show.

SANCEM *Société Aéronavale de Construction et d'Entretien de Moteurs*. Company for building and maintaining aircraft and ship engines. Incorporated on 20 June 1946 by Marius Girodin and Aimé Evrard, two engineers from the famed *Arts et Métiers* school. Although set up to develop aircraft prototypes from

Girodin's patents, it ended up being a major supplier of compressors for the French, German and Italian navies. The company is still trading today as Girodin-Sauer.

SAR Search and Rescue.

Saut de puce In French parlance a flea jump. Here refers to a take-off followed immediately by a landing, the 'brief hop' often performed by test pilots during taxying trials prior to the official maiden flight of a prototype.

SDECE *Service de Documentation Extérieure et de Contre-Espionnage.*

Secrétariat d'État à l'Air Sub-division of the French Defence Ministry from 1948 to 1957.

Secrétaire d'Etat aux Forces Armées Secretary of State for the Armed Forces.

SEM *Super Etendard Modernisé.*

SEPR *Société d'Études de la Propulsion par Réaction* (Company for the Study of Reaction Propulsion). Specialist and major supplier of rocket engines during the 1950s until its amalgamation with the rocket division of SNECMA in 1969.

SEREB *Société pour l'Etude et la Réalisation d'Engins Balistiques.*

SFECMAS *Société Française d'Etude et de Construction de Matériels Aéronautiques Spéciaux.* In 1955 SFECMAS merged with SNCAN as SNCAN Nord.

s.l Sea level.

SIPA *Société Industrielle pour l'Aéronautique* (Industrial Company for Aeronautics). One of the French aircraft manufacturers of the post-war era.

SOCEMA *Société de Constructions et d'Équipements Mécaniques pour l'Aviation* (Company for Mechanical Equipment and Fittings for Aircraft). Proposed a jet engine design in the immediate post-war era, but without success.

Société Française du Gyroplane French Gyroplane Company. The company incorporated to develop R. Dorand's helicopter concepts.

Souris Mice. Conical bodies that moved in or out of a jet engine's intake to regulate the flow of air. This in/out movement was likened by Dassault's engineers to mice coming out of their holes.

SNA *Système de Navigation et d'Attaque* (Combat and Navigation System). The navigation and weapon control part of an aircraft's avionics.

SNCAC *Société Nationale de Constructions Aéronautiques du Centre.* Also known as *Aérocentre.* Integrated as part of SNCAN in June 1949http://en.wikipedia.org/wiki/SNCAN.

SNCAM *Société Nationale de Constructions Aéronautiques du Midi.* One of the French aircraft manufacturers of the post-war era.

SNCAN *Société Nationale de Constructions Aéronautiques du Nord.* One of the French aircraft manufacturers of the post-war era.

SNCASE *Société Nationale de Constructions Aéronautiques du Sud-Est.* Post-war French aircraft manufacturer.

SNCASO *Société Nationale de Constructions Aéronautiques du Sud-Ouest.* Post-war French aircraft manufacturer.

SNECMA *Société Nationale d'Étude et de Construction de Moteurs d'Aviation.* Post-war engine manufacturer which developed the ATAR series of turbojets. Today forms part of Groupe SAFRAN.

SST Supersonic Transport.

STAé *Service Technique de l'Aéronautique* (Technical Department of Aeronautics).The Department of the Defense Ministry in charge of defining the Air Force's technical requirements and evaluating proposals from industry.

Statoréacteur ramjet.

STOL Short Take-Off and Landing.

STOVL Short Take-Off and Vertical Landing.

TALP Tactique, longue portée.

t/c Thickness/chord ratio.

Tous-temps All-weather.

Transonic Flight The speed range either side of Mach 1.0 where an aircraft has both subsonic and supersonic airflow passing over it at the same time.

Triebflugel Propulsive wing. German VTOL concept invented by von Halem in 1944 and developed by Focke-Wulf later on. A large, massive rotor that enabled an aircraft to take off and provided part of the lift during horizontal flight. The rotor was to be rotated through small egg-shaped wingtip ramjets designed by Otto Pabst. This should not be confused with a Lippisch concept of the same name in which the whole inside of a wing became a ramjet, the trailing edge becoming the exhaust nozzle.

vg Variable geometry.

V/STOL Vertical/Short Take-Off and Landing.

VTOL Vertical Take-Off and Landing.

VTO Vertical Take-Off.

Chapter One
The First Jet Bombers

ABOVE An odd period picture showing a model of the SO 4000 superimposed over a North American-style city line. *José Fernandez*

Immediately after the Second World War the French looked at the question of the creation of a new heavy bomber force. Two heavy bomber prototypes had actually survived the war – a German design called the Heinkel He 274 and the French Breguet Br 482.

The Heinkel He 274 was to have been a stratospheric bomber designed to attack the east coast of the USA. After the prototypes had been sabotaged by the retreating Germans, it was found that the sabotage had only dealt with the engines and stocks of these existed elsewhere in the factory. Therefore the two prototypes, renamed AAS-1 (*Ateliers Aéronautiques de Suresnes*), were 're-ordered' by the new Ministère de l'Air but only as experimental machines since they were considered outdated as pure bomber designs. The AAS-1's major contribution to our story was to become a mothership for various other French projects and programmes.

The French aircraft had been a pre-war design. The Br 482 was the only survivor of a programme to provide the *Armée de l'Air* with a long-range four-engined bomber and two prototypes had been built before the 1940 Armistice. One was evacuated to French North Africa, where it was subsequently destroyed, but the other had been kept hidden near Biarritz during the Occupation and resurfaced, intact, after the Libération. However, handicapped by its intended Hispano-Suiza 12Z engines (which could have been replaced by just two 24Z), the Br 482 never made it to the status of a true 'bomber' and it was soon relegated to the role of engine test bed. Officials toyed with the idea of also using it as a mothership for the Leduc ramjets covered in Volume I, but this job was already taken by the AAS-1. After its twentieth and last flight on 13 September 1950 the Br 482 went to the scrapyard.

The Last Piston-Engined Bomber Programme

During the last months of 1944 a new bomber programme was established called the B6/R6. This showed a direct continuity to the pre-war programmes (the B4) but was now bigger ('B' for bombardier/bomber with 4 or 6 indicating the number of crew required).

Arsenal

L'Arsenal de l'Aéronautique modified a proposal for a transatlantic airliner into a bomber project. Nothing else is known about either of these designs!

Breguet

Of course, Breguet had its own champion for this programme, the

ABOVE **France's 'current' design for a heavy bomber was represented by the Breguet Br 482 prototype, which in reality was a carry-over from the pre-war years and was outdated when it first flew on 28 November 1947. This in-flight picture of the Breguet Br 482 was taken after the war by Jean Dieuzaide, the factory photographer for the Breguet Montaudran plant near Toulouse.** *Philippe Ricco collection*

already discussed Br 482. However, it was regarded as being too big for use as a medium bomber and too small for the new B6/R6 programme. On 13 January 1945 the *Armée de l'Air* wrote to Breguet stating that it had *'no use'* for this aircraft.

Nord 1800

Nord received a letter of intent in February 1945 ordering the construction of a prototype within the B6/R6 programme. From what has survived it appears the Nord 1800 was inspired somewhat by the Boeing B-29, with a canopy fully integrated within the nose cone (something that had also been proposed many times for the pre-war B4 programme by Amiot and Breguet in particular) plus a defensive armament composed of remote-operated turrets. German influence was present (from both the Heinkel He 177 and He 274) in that the project was offered with both coupled and separate engines, but it was cancelled in September 1945 when opinion turned decidedly in favour of jet-powered aircraft. However, that did not stop Nord offering a 'B version' of about 100 tons flight weight and powered by turboprop engines (turboprops were at that stage thought to offer 'the best of both worlds' by bringing together jet performance and propeller endurance). This design may also have been influenced by the Germans because several of their design offices had in 1945 hoped to produce high-performance fighters based on the new 'Propellor-Turbo-Lader' (PTL) engines, and by the autumn of 1945 translated German documents were beginning to disseminate inside the French industry. Not that this new version fared any better (lengthy delays in producing working turboprops did not help) and it was finally cancelled in May 1947 under Cancellation Contract N° 3392/47. Nord then proposed a version boosted by jet engines, historian Jean Cuny noting that this may have been the first project to propose the use of ATAR jet engines.

SNCAC (Centre)

It seems that the SNCAC entry in this programme was a continuation of the unbuilt NC 110 design of 1940. A prototype was ordered through a letter of intent dated 18 April 1945 under the name 'NC 200' (although this designation has also been attributed to a two-seater fighter). It seems that a mock-up was produced, but by September of the same year an order was given by the *Service Technique de l'Aéronautique* (STAé) to abandon all work on this design. The company was told that it should now focus on jet aircraft.

SNCASE (Sud-Est)

The SNCASE offered a land derivative of its giant SE 200 seaplane, a project about which nothing has survived.

SNCASO (Sud-Ouest) SO 71

This company offered a variant of an earlier four-engined transatlantic airliner, two prototypes of this SO 70 having been under contract in 1943 and 1944. The bomber derivative was the SO 71, which differed mostly by its new fuselage (which was to incorporate not only a wide bomb bay but also a number of defensive turrets), its powerplant (the Gnôme-Rhône 18R giving 2800hp [2,088kW] at take-off instead of the Hispano-Suiza 24Z or 48Z) and its armour, which was placed around the crew positions, the engines and the fuel tanks (in addition the main spars were specially reinforced to give better resistance against bullets).

The original proposal featured two turrets each with four 13mm machine guns in the nose and in the tail, two side and upper turrets with twin 13mm, and two 'long-range' turrets each fitted with two 20mm cannon. The two larger turrets were retractable, another carry over from pre-war practice. Since all this weaponry would have required more than six crew members just to man the guns, it was suggested that some of them should be remote-operated (something that was totally unknown in France and would have required reverse-engineering of US or German equipment). The bomb bay could accommodate up to 35,273lb (16,000kg) of bombs with single projectiles of up to 5.4 tons (that is the RAF's 12,000lb/5,443kg bombs). The landing gear was of

SNCASO SO 71	
Status	project
Span	139ft 1in (42.40m)
Length	109ft 11in (33.50m)
Gross wing area	2,226sq ft (207sq m)
Gross weight	109,458 to 119,290 lb (49,650 to 54,110kg)
Powerplant	four Gnôme-Rhône 18R 2,800hp (2,088kW)
Maximum speed/Height	369mph at 16,405ft? (593km/h at 5,000m)
Armament	Up to 16,000kg (35,273lb) bombs, various guns in turrets

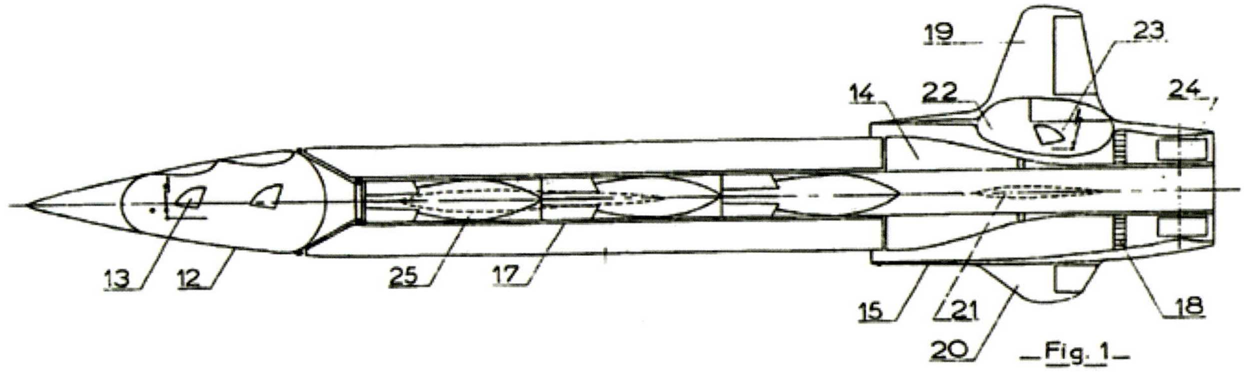

ABOVE **Rather sketchy side view of the Matra bomber project showing the tubular bomb bay inside the fuselage and the two-seat cockpit in the nose cone.** *Author's collection/Robert's patent*

tricycle configuration and the range was estimated to be 1,865 miles (3,000km) with 13,228lb (6,000kg) of bombs aboard, 622 miles (1,000km) with the full load and up to 4,350 miles (7,000km) when the bomb bay was fitted with extra fuel tanks for the reconnaissance role. The SO 71 as a whole looked a generation late and it was not developed.

The First Jet Bomber Studies

By September 1945 all the remaining piston-engined bomber projects had been cancelled and on 4 September the *Etat-Major de l'Armée de l'Air* issued a new programme. This required the design of a 28 ton-class bomber powered by two Rolls-Royce Nene jet engines or similar to carry 5 tons of ordnance at a speed of 559mph (900km/h) and with a range of 1,865 miles (3,000km). In March 1946 prototype contracts were awarded to both SNCAC (Centre) and SNCASO (Sud-Ouest) for two prototypes each of their proposals (the NC 270 and SO 4000). However, these were soon caught up by the financial constraints from which the country was suffering at the time and by December 1947 everything had once again been cancelled: the Etat-Major (Air Staff) wrote: '*Bombers must not be pursued with, not because the General Headquarters no longer believe in the importance of a bomber force in combat but because the means they require in equipment, personal, and material are way over the present or future financial capabilities of this Country*.'[1]

Matra

In around 1947 the ever-inventive Roger Robert designed a very unusual jet bomber aircraft. Its long tubular fuselage was traversed by a cylindrical shaft that contained the bombs (which if needed could be self-propelled projectiles), and at the rear of the fuselage a large ramjet was supposed to propel the aircraft at 994mph (1,600km/h) at an operational height of between 19,685ft and 39,370ft (6,000m and 12,000m). The general architecture of the aircraft was quite similar to the R 130 fighter (see Chapter 14 of Volume I) but on a much bigger scale. The crew of three was located in two pressure cabins. In the nose sat the pilot and a second crew member (probably a navigator), while at the rear, under the upper fin and rudder assembly, a second pressure cabin housed the bombardier.

Robert described the operation of the aircraft in this way: '*When nearing the target, the aircraft follows a strongly ascendant trajectory, so that the acceleration thus created can be born safely by the aircraft and its crew, considering that those could be either seated or reclining and equipped with special suits. At the end of its climb, the*

Matra bomber	
Status	project
Span	-
Length	75ft 5.5in (c. 23.00m)
Gross wing area	-
Gross weight	-
Powerplant	One ramjet
Maximum speed/Height	994mph at 39,370ft (1,600km/h at 12,000m)
Armament	three bombs

1 Quoted by Jean Cuny in *Les Avions de Combat Français 1944-1960* Volume II.

BELOW **The smaller version of the NC270 retained a gun turret for defence from the rear, in fact a German type fitted with a quartet of 13mm guns.** *Jacques Moulin*

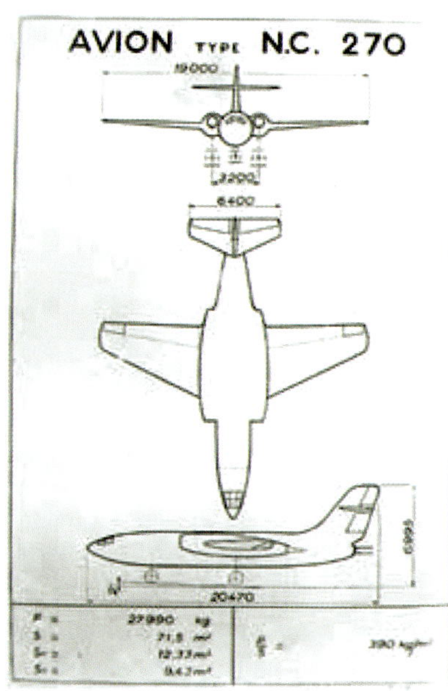

ABOVE **The first NC 270 being built in the Centre factory. The aircraft was never completed.** *José Fernandez*

aircraft's horizontal speed is decreasing and its vertical trajectory is more or less straight above the target. From that time, the bombardier in his cabin at the rear assumes control of the aircraft and, through a sighting device similar to the one used on fighter craft, he releases the bombs which drop through the central shaft straight at the target. The pilot can then retake control of the aircraft and bring it back to a horizontal attitude for its return flight.'

Nothing was done with this highly original (but unnamed) design and it is dubious as to whether it was ever presented to the *Armée de l'Air* authorities.

BELOW **The larger version of the NC 270 dispensed with the rear turret and gained a T-tail. This is the version upon which the uncompleted prototype was based.** *Jacques Moulin*

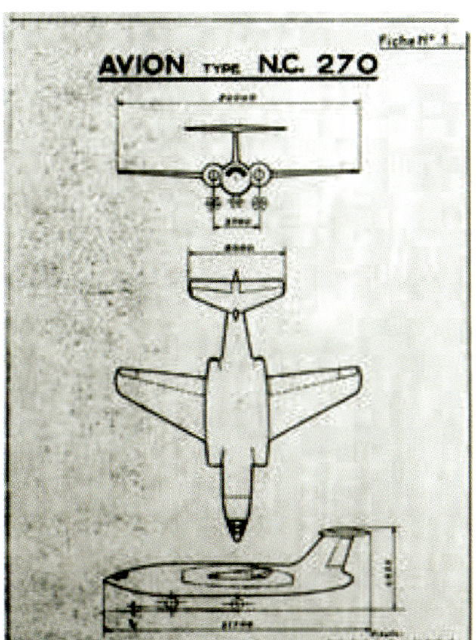

SNCAC NC 270

Through a letter of intent dated 23 May 1946 an order was given to Centre to proceed with the construction of a prototype of its NC 270, to supply parts for a second prototype and to build two 1:2.5 scale flying models. The NC 270 design, by Maxime Robin, was an aesthetically pleasing shoulder wing monoplane with two large jet nacelles (necessary through the use of centrifugal-flow engines) attached directly to the spindle-shaped fuselage; the fuselage itself was dominated by a T-tail. The upper half of the centre fuselage was allocated to the fuel tanks and the lower half to the bomb bay, which could hold 11,023lb (5,000kg) of bombs. The cockpit was fully faired into the nose cone (this section could be detached in case of emergency) and was accessed via a ventral hatch (which was hydraulically operated to create a depression to help the egress of the crew in case of an emergency exit during flight). The landing tricycle gear used 'diabolos' (twin wheels) in all positions to support the machine's weight, and for flight the nose leg retracted into the fuselage just behind the nose cone while the main gear retracted into the engine nacelles.

Construction of the prototype was begun eagerly at Centre's Boulogne-Billancourt factory. As originally designed, it was thought that the wing loading was excessive and therefore the dimensions were enlarged slightly, the span being increased by 3ft 3.5in (1m)

SNCAC NC 270 (1st stage)	
Status	project
Span	62ft 4in (19.00m)
Length	67ft 2in (20.47m)
Gross wing area	768.8sq ft (71.5sq m)
Gross weight	61,706lb (27,990kg)
Powerplant	two Hispano Suiza (Rolls-Royce licence) Nene 5,000lb (22.2kN)
Maximum speed/Height	603mph at 29,530ft (970km/h at 9,000m)
Armament	11,023lb (5,000kg) bombs and rear turret with four 15mm machine guns

SNCAC NC 270 (2nd stage)	
Status	prototype
Span	65ft 6.5in (20.00m)
Length	71ft 2in (21.70)
Gross wing area	835.5sq ft (77.7sq m)
Gross weight	55,115lb (25,000kg)
Powerplant	two Hispano Suiza (RR licence) Nene 5,000lb (22.2kN)
Maximum speed/Height	539mph at 29,530ft (867km/h at 9,000m)
Armament	11,023lb (5,000kg) bombs and rear turret with four 15mm machine guns

ABOVE Although the NC 270 was cancelled, the NC 271-01 flew a dozen times aboard a Languedoc and three times in free flight. *José Fernandez*

LEFT The NC 271-01 was exhibited at the Paris Air Show. *Author's collection*

BELOW LEFT Three-view drawing showing the first flying model NC 271-01 as flown. *Jacques Moulin*

BELOW RIGHT Drawing of the NC 271-02. Note the complete redesign of the rear section with the T-tail and the rocket engine exhaust. *Jacques Moulin*

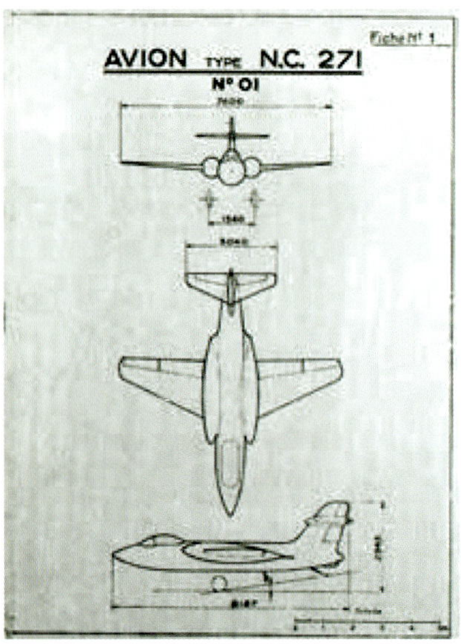

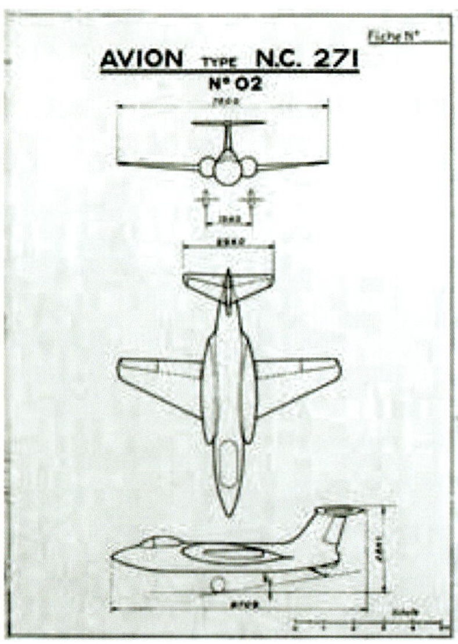

along with the overall length. Also, a remote-operated turret of German origin, armed with a quartet of 13mm guns, was to be installed at the rear of the fuselage. This was tested during the prototype's assembly but it was finally decided not to install it for the first flight. The rear tail assembly from now on incorporated the T-tail and it may have appeared prudent to dispense with any excess weight. Indeed, it soon appeared that the design office had been overly optimistic in the NC 270's weight/performance calculations.

In the NC 270's weight/performance calculations. In addition, some elements of the design had never been finalised (for example the sighting for the rear turret – to be done using radar or by television?). Finally, although having the canopy faired integrally into the fuselage shape was both aerodynamically and aesthetically pleasing, it gave almost no forward view to the crew, so it had to be stepped up slightly to improve the pilot's vision forward. When the *Armée de l'Air* was informed of the problems in February 1947 it hesitated a few months before cancelling the bomber prototype outright in October. However, the scale model aircraft were spared.

NC 271

The first scale test aircraft, the NC 271-01, had already been flown piggyback on its Sud-Est SE 161 Languedoc mothership and, after a dozen composite flights, the first separation occurred on 28 January 1949, followed by two more in February and March. These flights were intended to test the low-speed characteristics of the now stillborn NC 270. The NC 271-02, however, was fitted with an HWK 109-509 rocket engine (saved from one of three German Me 163B Komet rocket fighters obtained by France after the war) because this aircraft was destined to investigate the high-speed features of the projected bomber.

It has long been thought that only the NC 271-01 ever flew, but the fourth addition to the original construction contract (which effectively liquidated the programme and the Nord Centre company) claimed that both flying models had flown. The NC 271-01 reflected the original design of the NC 270 but the NC 271-02 introduced

SNCAC NC 271-02	
Status	flying model
Span	24ft 11in (7.60m)
Length	26ft 8.5in (8.14m)
Gross wing area	123.0sq ft (11.44sq m)
Gross weight	7,496lb (3,400kg)
Powerplant	HWK 109-509A 3,750lb (16.7kN)
Maximum speed/Height	559mph (900km/h)
Armament	None

the redesigned T-tail. According to historian Pierre Gaillard, who had worked for Nord Centre and actually seen these machines, the first NC 271 was painted brown and looked '*like a pleasure boat with brass fittings*' while the second was red.

The end of the NC 270 also brought the end of SNCA Centre. The company was liquidated in October 1948 with the factory being closed in June 1949 (note: although they were fully state-owned companies, the various *Sociétés Nationales de Constructions Aéronautiques* organisations were operated as private firms).

SO 4000-01	
Status	prototype
Span	58ft 7in (17.86m)
Length	64ft 9.5in (19.75m)
Gross wing area	806.5sq ft (75sq m)
Gross weight	48,501lb (22,000kg)
Powerplant	two Hispano Suiza (Rolls-Royce licence) Nene 22.2kN (5,000lb)
Maximum speed/Height	528mph (850km/h) at ground level
Armament	11,023lb (5,000kg) bombs and two barbettes with two 15mm machine guns

SNCASO SO 4000

On 25 May 1946 SNCASO received a similar letter of intent relating to the study, construction and delivery for flight testing of two experimental scale model jet aircraft called the SO M1 and SO M2 respectively, a full-size SO 4000-01 bomber prototype '*for the experimental study of a jet bomber of high performance*' and the delivery of material for a second SO 4000-02. The SO 4000 that came out of Jean-Charles Parot's design office was again a very clean aircraft. It had a spindle-shaped fuselage with a clear nose cone housing two crew members in tandem in heavily armoured seats (this section was pressurised), long air intakes along the bomb bay and with the fuel tanks above the bay, and finally an engine section that also supported a conventional fin and rudder assembly (a V-tail was also envisaged). The wing was swept 31° and the tricycle landing gear was slightly unusual in that the main legs were duplicated. A weakness in the undercarriage design was in fact revealed when it collapsed during taxiing trials on 23 April 1950! Considering that the design of this landing gear had taken some 40,000 man hours of study and 75,000 man hours for its construction (according that is to a reference in the contemporary *Aviation Magazine*), this cast some doubts on the abilities of the SNCASO design office!

The other unusual feature of the SO 4000's design was its defensive weapons: two rear-facing barbettes in wingtip pods each containing a doublet of 15mm machine guns with 1,000 rounds for each weapon (in fact these were never installed). The avionics was quite comprehensive for the time, using the Gee-H navigation system introduced by the RAF (an Ames Type 100 radio-navigation system) associated with an H2S bombing radar in the underside of the nose and a 'Rebecca' IFF (identification friend or foe). In addition, an unspecified radar system was used for sighting the defensive barbettes. During construction the SO 4000's cockpit configuration was revised with the two ejector seats being installed back to back and with the pilot slightly higher than his colleague, and all under a bubble canopy. The extreme nose was then passed over entirely to the radar antenna. Many variants of the SO 4000 were proposed:

SO 4000 'Sapphire'	
Status	bomber project
Span	58ft 7in (17.86m)
Length	65ft 11.5in (20.11)
Gross wing area	806.5sq ft (75sq m)
Gross weight	61,728lb (28,000kg)
Powerplant	two Sapphire 7,150lb (31.8kN)
Maximum speed/Height	609mph (980km/h) at ground level
Armament	11,023lb (5,000kg) bombs and two barbettes with two 15mm machine guns

British Engines (SO 4000 Sapphire)

SNCASO also offered the SO 4000 with either Armstrong Siddeley Sapphire or Rolls-Royce Avon axial turbojets. In 1951 the Avon-powered version was expected to reach 559mph (900km/h) at an altitude of 29,528ft (9,000m).

SO 4000 Reconnaissance Version

In this version the bomb bay was replaced by a reconnaissance bay with six to eight cameras mounted inside.

SO 4000 All-Weather Fighter

SNCASO wanted to compare the SO 4000 to the English Electric Canberra (to its advantage of course) and, taking inspiration from the latter, offered an all-weather fighter version. However, this 1950 proposal was turned down by the *Armée de l'Air* because it thought that the machine was too big and too costly for a fighter.

The national budgetary problems had the same effects on this programme as they did on the NC 270, and the SO 4000 bomber was cancelled in May 1950. Only one flight was carried out, in fact on 15 March 1951 and at the company's expense, and during this sortie test pilot Daniel Rastel found the bomber unstable and its controls heavy. Although SNCASO tried to get sufficient financing to perform further flights (because the machine seemed useful for the testing of '*bulky equipment*'), the firm's requests were constantly rejected. The contract as a whole was terminated in December 1951 and the prototype was sent to the Bourges artillery range for testing the effects of ordnance on modern airframes. Throughout the

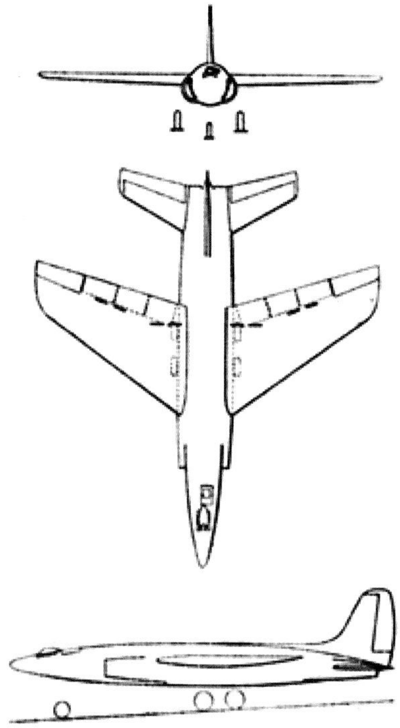

ABOVE **A period three-view drawing of the SO 4000 strategic bomber.** *Author's collection*

TOP RIGHT **In the usual way, a full size mock-up of the SO 4000 was built to assess how to fit the crew, avionics, fuel tanks and engines inside the fuselage.** *José Fernandez*

ABOVE RIGHT **In the end, the prototype of the SO 4000 did fly, albeit very briefly.** *José Fernandez*

RIGHT **The SO 4000 being serviced by mechanics, probably before its first and only flight.** *Philippe Ricco*

BELOW **A nice side view of the single SO 4000 prototype showing the curious landing gear.** *Author's collection/ SNCASO document*

ABOVE Two flying scale models flew in support of the SO 4000 programme. This is the unpowered SO M1 glider. *José Fernandez*

year, *Aviation Magazine* campaigned for its resurrection, or at least the continuation of SO 4000 flying, on the basis that France urgently needed a medium jet bomber, but this was all to no avail.

SO M1

This was a half-scale flying model that was flown aboard and later launched from two motherships (the Heinkel He 274 and Sud-Est/Bloch 161 Languedoc); the first captive flight, aboard a Languedoc, taking place on 6 April 1948 and the first free flight after release from the mothership on 26 September 1949. During these glide flights the M1 reached a speed of 373mph (600km/h), but at this speed it experienced heavy ailerons. A plan to install an HWK 109-509 rocket engine was not fulfilled and, just like its full-size counterpart, the SO M1 ended its days as a target on an artillery range.

SO M1	
Status	flying model
Span	29ft 9.5in (9.08m)
Length	32ft 4in (9.85m)
Gross wing area	189.8sq ft (17.65sq m)
Gross weight	6,316lb (2,865kg)
Powerplant	None
Maximum speed/Height	450mph (724km/h)
Armament	None

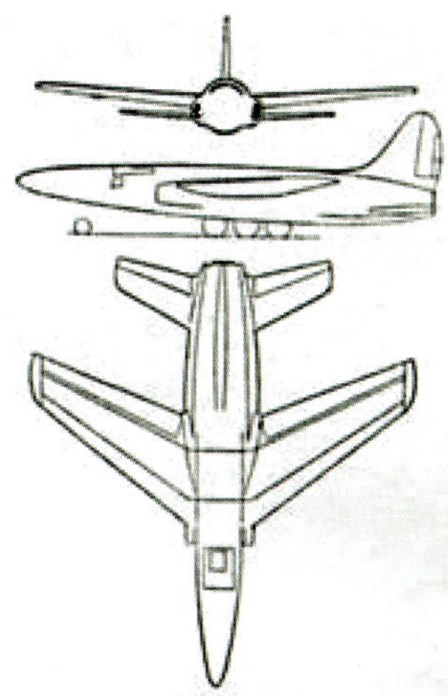

LEFT A period three-view drawing of the SO M2. *Author's collection*

SO M2

While generally similar to its sister ship, the SO M2, was, from the beginning, powered by a Rolls-Royce Derwent 5 jet installed in the rear of the fuselage. So, unlike the M1, which required a mothership, the M2 was able to take-off by itself, which it did for the first time on 13 April 1949. While this aircraft was again difficult to handle at high speeds due to heavy controls, it did become the first French aircraft to break the 622mph (1,000km/h) barrier in a shallow dive

SO M2	
Status	flying model
Span	29ft 9.5in (9.08m)
Length	32ft 6in (9.90m)
Gross wing area	189.8sq ft (17.65sq m)
Gross weight	Up to 10,362lb (4,700kg)
Powerplant	one Derwent V 3,200lb (14.3kN), later Derwent 8 3,500lb (15.5kN)
Maximum speed/Height	590mph (950km/h)
Armament	None

RIGHT The SO M2 on display at the 1946 Paris Salon. It was powered by a Rolls-Royce Derwent engine. *José Fernandez*

ABOVE The SO M2 displays its curious 'monotrace' landing gear. Unlike the SO M1, which had to be carried aloft by a mothership, the M2 could take off under its own power. *José Fernandez*

(flown by David Rastel on 9 May 1949) and without encountering any compressibility problems. However, it was appreciated that this machine was underpowered and so in April 1951 the Derwent 5 was replaced by a more powerful Derwent 8. An important point was the use for the first time in France of hydraulically assisted controls on an aircraft.

Rocket boosters were incorporated into an improved post-April 1951 SO M2, but during the first ground test these broke the tether cables and damaged the airframe. A later flight test using smaller rockets (on 8 October 1952) was described as '*brutal*' by the test pilot. Had the need arisen, the pilot would have had an escape route through a jettisonable panel under the fuselage. The landing gear was of the bicycle type that was often used in France during the 1950s, here with a nose wheel, three main wheels in a line and then skids at the wingtips. Consideration was given for some time towards the development of a fighter based on the SO M2, but as the SNCASO company already had its own major fighter project (the SO 9000 and 9050 Trident) this idea was not pursued. And so the SO M2 joined its sister on the artillery range.

Neither the 1946 programme, nor the revised '1946-1951' plans of 1947, proved to be particularly clear in regard to bombers. For example, although the SO 4000 and NC 270 were in the minds of the Air Ministry decision-makers, at the start they felt it was too early to give a precise estimation of the numbers of new bombers that would be required ... and of which type. The need was estimated to be around sixty aircraft, but this was never clarified. In the end, there was no production at all of any of these early jet bomber designs.

BELOW The M2 cockpit. *José Fernandez*

BELOW A Topps postcard of the M2. *Author's collection*

Chapter Two
A More Reasonable Approach: Heavy Fighters and Strike Aircraft (Up to Vautour)

ABOVE **The winner of the competition was to be the SO 4050 Vautour, here represented by the first prototype.** *Author's collection/ SNCASO*

Heavy Fighters and Strike Aircraft (Up to Vautour)

As explained in the previous chapter, after a few inclinations toward possessing a heavy bomber force just after the end of the Second World War, *the Etat-Major de l'Armée de l'Air* wisely decided it just could not afford a force of such complex and costly machines (both to develop and then to operate). However, that did not mean it relinquished all thoughts towards 'aggressive weapons'. If large bombers were 'out' then heavy fighters, which could double as medium bombers, were 'in'. It is also quite probable that this change of mind was due to the continued emphasis placed, from 1945 onwards, on France getting its very own nuclear weapon. Who in this context really still needed a mass of 'Flying Fortress' type machines (even if they were jet-powered) if a single Mosquito-type aircraft could do the job? That must have been the thoughts from the late 1940s, which explains why, from this point, much more emphasis was placed on medium-size aircraft that could take on multiple roles from heavy fighter to strike aircraft. Thus, in 1945 a programme was established for an '*appareil d'appui aérien*' (a close support aircraft), which was a kind of German Me 262 'à la Française'. This was to be a twin-jet aircraft carrying four 30mm guns and forty unguided rockets.

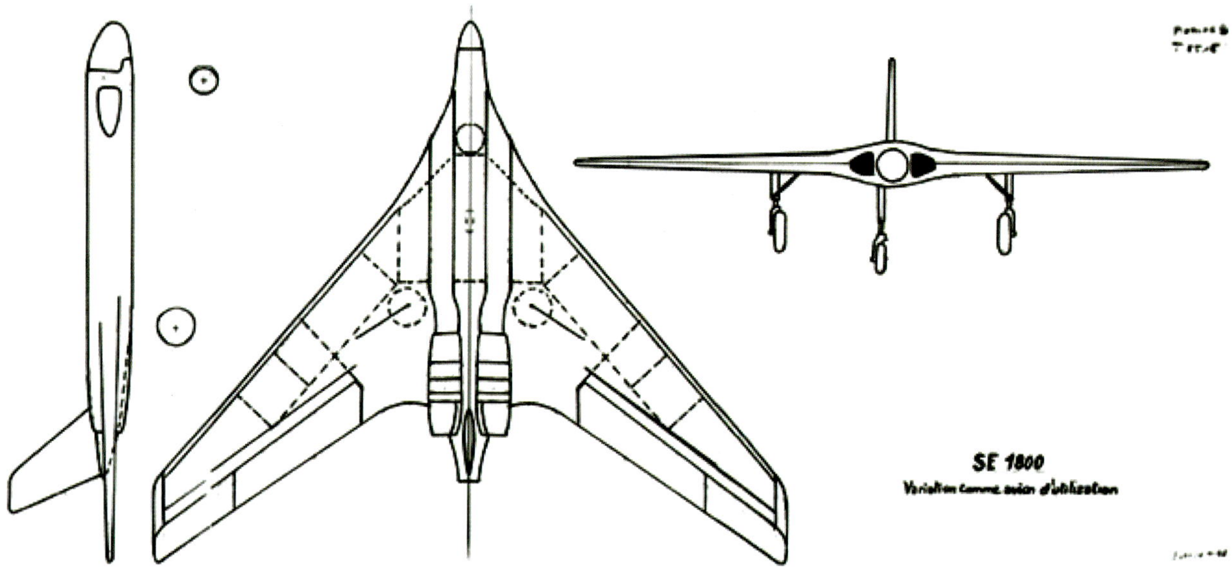

ABOVE A rare example of flying wings among the French designs was the SE 1800 bomber. *Author's from a SNCASE document*

SE 1801/SE 1802	
Status	project
Span	55ft 9in (17.00m)
Length	43ft 0in (13.10m)
Gross wing area	784.95sq ft (73sq m)
Gross weight	33,069lb (15,000kg)
Powerplant	two Nene 5,000lb (22.2kN) or ATAR 101 5,625lb (24kN)
Maximum speed/Height	Over 622mph (1,000km/h) Mach 0.85
Armament	?

Dream for a Flying Wing

Behind the scenes, France carried out it own 'Paperclip' project, the acquisition of documents and materials from the archives of various German wartime companies (Messerschmitt, BMW, etc.) and also secured the assistance of several German aircraft and engine designers. Among them was Heinrich Hertel, formerly of Heinkel and Junkers, who was assigned to the SNCASE Marignane factory. There Hertel promoted flying wing designs, among them some 'jumbo jet'-size transports of either 617,284lb or 330,688lb (280,000kg or 150,000kg) weight. The larger designs were obviously far too big for the capability and technology of the times and

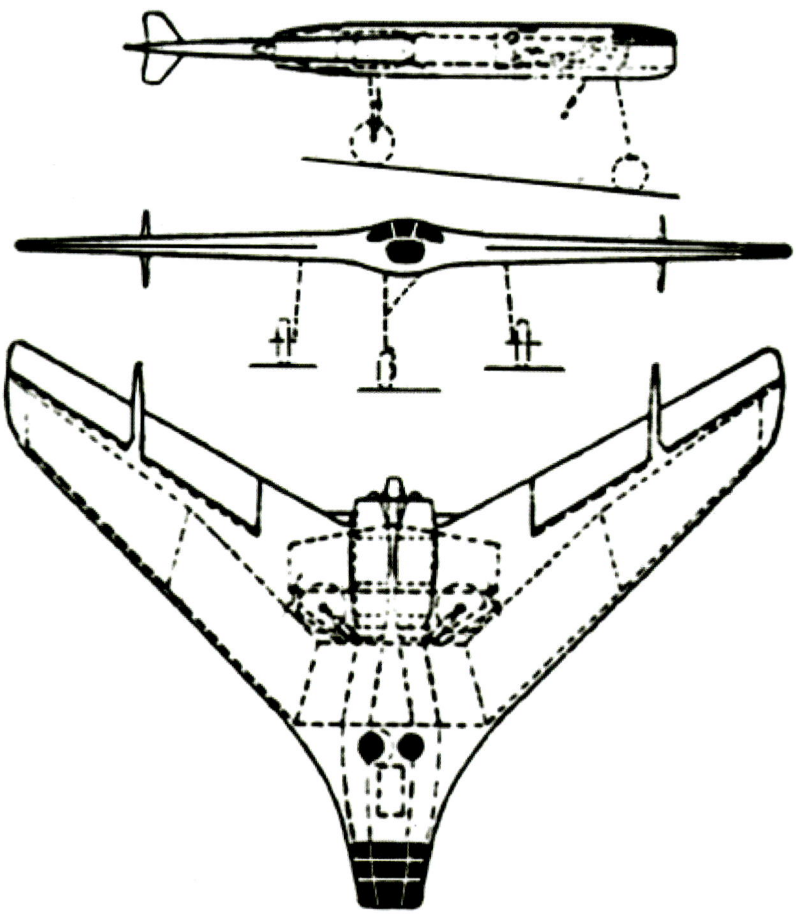

ABOVE The definitive SE 1801 bomber would have been somewhat different from the proof-of-concept SE 1800. Of note is the nose intake going through the cockpit. *Author's collection*

someone suggested that Hertel should limit his ambitions to a smaller 150-ton aircraft. His transport was to be a flying wing and for this he was criticised considerably by Charles Fauvel, the French specialist in this type of aircraft (and who was probably quite vexed not to have been financed by the French government himself). Fauvel declared: '*Since their defeat, the German engineers are looked upon as winners in the design offices of the Big Four [nations that won the Second World War]. It is now confirmed that a French national company is about to build the flying wing design of one of those winners who adorned himself with Lippisch's feathers while he never built by himself a flying wing before getting into France where he was given a design office, documentation and test facilities, contrary to French designers who have in the past actually built flying wings and to whom the information obtained by the Allies in Germany has been denied.*'[1] Hertel's transport projects were certainly too ambitious and indeed destroyed his credibility in the eyes of the STAé.

Fauvel may have been disappointed, but he was certainly correct concerning the lack of Franco-German experience with flying wings. Then a letter of intent was sent to SNCASE on 30 April 1947 asking for the construction of an '*experimental aircraft*' powered by two jet engines. The resulting flying wing project had a single pilot accommodated in the prone position and, even stranger, a flight engineer/test equipment operator seated behind him where the wing was thicker. The said '*experimental aircraft*', now named SE 1800, was proposed in early 1948 as a heavy fighter and, as was often the case at this time, uncertainty regarding the availability of the jet powerplant led to two options being offered: the SE 1801 powered by two ATAR 101s of 5,625lb (24kN) thrust each or the SE 1802, which used the 5,000lb (22.2kN) Rolls-Royce Nene.

1 Les Ailes Volantes by Charles Fauvel in *Forces Aériennes Françaises*, March 1948.

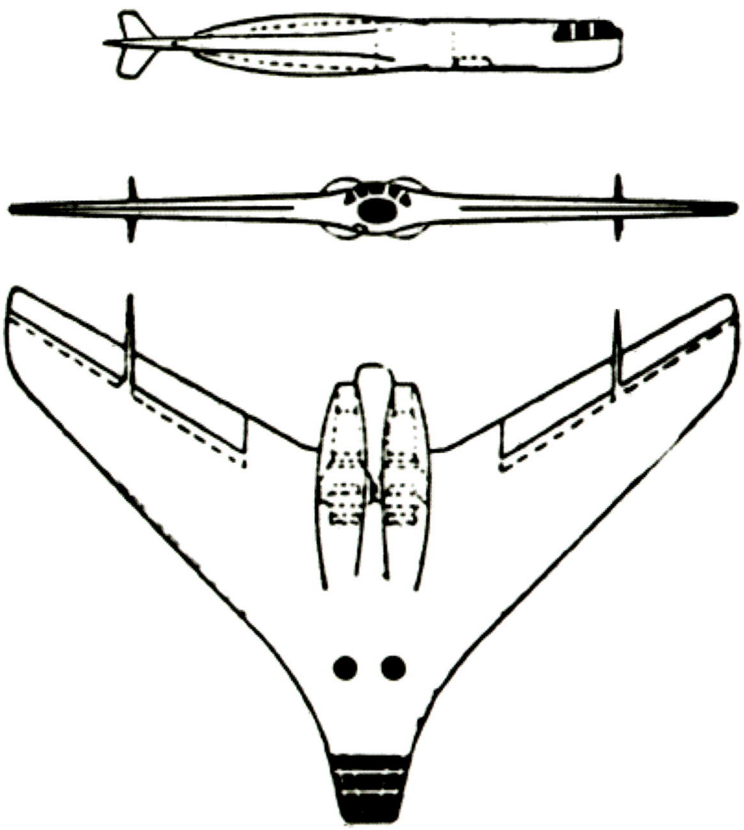

ABOVE The SNCASE SE 1802 differed from the SE 1801 in being powered by the Rolls-Royce Nene instead of the ATAR 101. The significance of the two black discs in the centre fuselage is unknown. *Author's collection*

As might be expected, the SE 1802 had a somewhat longer wing centre section with more prominent engine nacelles. From the surviving illustration it was obvious that the Nene option was a nod to reality (because the Nene was readily available) but the engine would have produced pronounced bulges to the fuselage lines. The ATAR was much more plausible in terms of size and was probably the favoured choice of Hertel, considering it was designed by his compatriot Hermann Ostrich. The prone pilot configuration was also a mainstay of Hertel's designs for small aircraft and he also promoted it later on when he worked as consultant on the Coléoptère (see Volume I). At this time the SE 1800 was supposed to have a range of 1,865 miles (3,000km), given a flight time of one hour thirty minutes at 497mph (800km/h) and 26,245ft (8,000m), and a cruise speed of 603mph (970km/h). The armament was unspecified but could have been a quartet of guns. As noted, the experimental flying wing was ordered on 30 April 1947 under Letter of Intent N° 07776 but was then cancelled (indeed with the whole flying wing contract) on 1 December 1948, although Hertel continued to work on it until he left SNCASE to return in Germany in April 1949.

The Appareil d'Appui Aérien 1946-1950

SNCASE Grognard

While the SNCASE SE 1800 had been proposed as an offshoot of a giant transport project, for this programme SNCASE replied with a completely new fighter proposal fitted with two SOCEMA TGAR-1008 axial-flow jets. On 30 November 1945 a study contract was officially signed with SNCASE for the development of this machine.

SE 2400	
Status	project
Span	-
Length	-
Gross wing area	-
Gross weight	-
Powerplant	two TGAR-1008 4,500lb (20kN)
Maximum speed/Height	-
Armament	none

The first proposal to be made by Pierre Sartre's design office had been a simple one-seat machine with straight wings and the engines in pods underneath them. The only concession to modern times was its tricycle undercarriage. If the German-led design office was too ambitious, the French-led design office was too wary and this too mundane proposal was rejected by STAé.

BELOW **A three-view drawing of an early wind tunnel model of the future SE 2410 Grognard. The cockpit and the dorsal intake are faired over in this drawing, something normal on a test model that is not representative of the final appearance of the aircraft. Drawing dated 11 December 1948.** *Philippe Ricco*

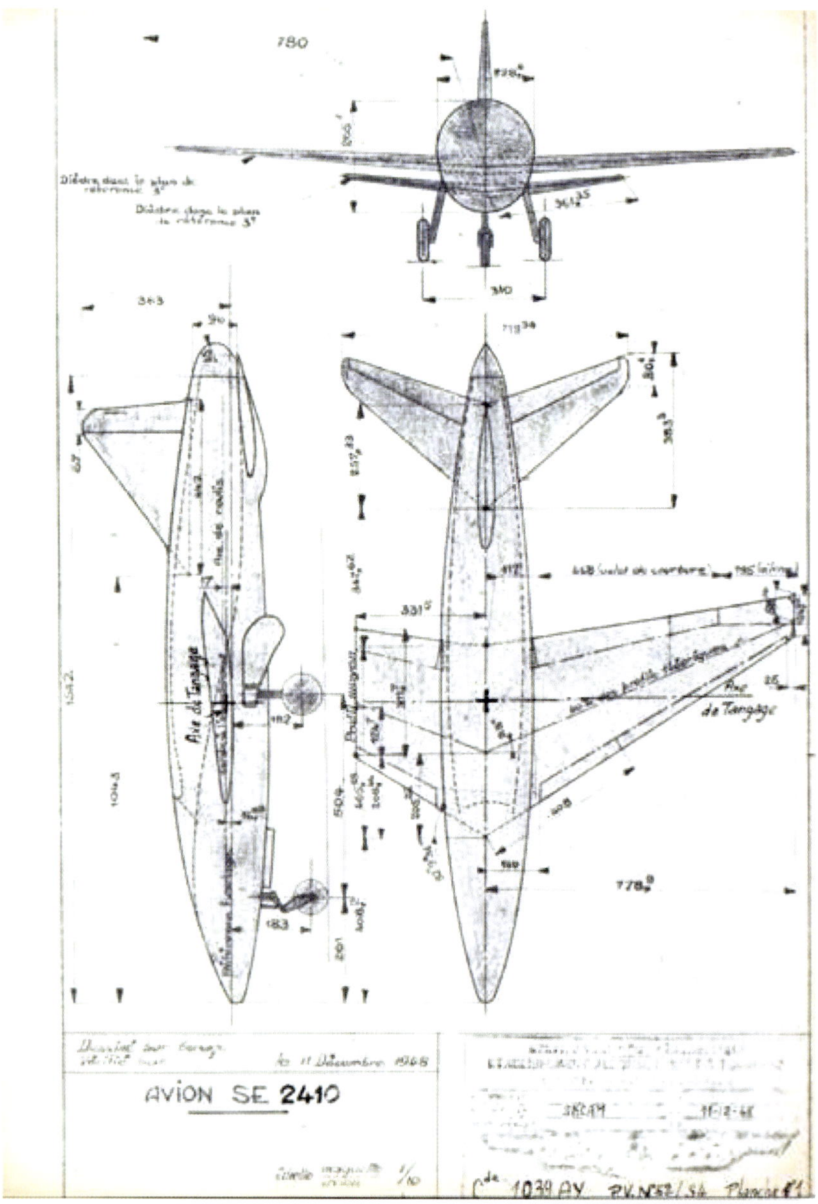

A new project was designed in January 1946 that incorporated both new design elements (a swept wing) and old (the dorsal intake from the piston-powered SE 580 (see Volume I). The two jet engines were to be set one above the other in the extreme rear fuselage rather like in the later British English Electric Lightning, although initially the two turbojets should have been installed side by side. A patent filed in 1946 actually presented the two options: '*Both propulsion units are disposed within the fuselage, symmetrically with respect to the central longitudinal plane of the later*,' which described the side-by-side arrangement. But the same patent claimed: '*In the case of the propulsive means being turbine jet engines, it is desirable to use the arrangements diagrammatically shown in figures 6 and 7. The turbine jet engines, which are two in number are arranged one above the other and are offset in a fore and aft direction so that the maximum cross-section of the fuselage be kept down to minimum.*'

Thus the final choice was the staggered configuration fed by a large common dorsal intake. The 1946 patent also explained the choice of the dorsal intake: '*The arrangement of the normal air intake to the propulsion units at the top of the fuselage is particularly desirable because, firstly it frees entirely the lower part of the fuselage and the part of the fuselage connecting with the swept-back wings and secondly it does not restrict the visibility of the pilot whose cockpit is located in the fore part of the connecting section of the fuselage with the swept-back wings. The lower part of the fuselage may thus, in a military craft, be used to house bomb-releasing gear with dropping doors, or various armament devices.*' Indeed as described in the patent, the pilot sat under a large canopy completely faired into the fuselage shape in the extreme nose of the machine.

In 1948 the SE 1400 project, a 'flying model' of the larger SE 2400, was accepted by the *Armée de l'Air* and

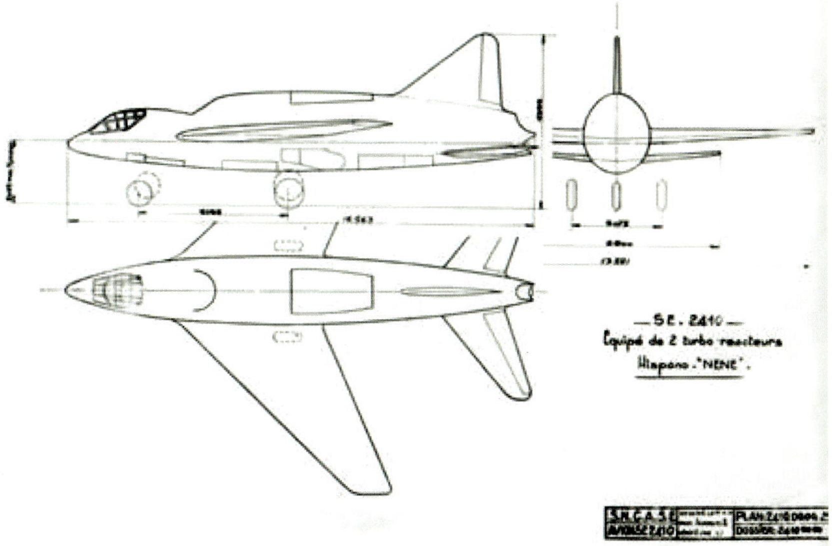

ABOVE **A SNCASE drawing from June 1951 that represents the Grognard as built.** *Author's collection*

this allowed it to be designed under contract 2155/48. The SE 1400 would have been powered by a single Rolls-Royce Derwent turbojet, though an SE 1410 variant powered by a German HWK 109-509 rocket engine was also proposed but not taken up. Actually, neither the SE 1400 nor the SE 1410 would be built.

In the original 1946 contract the *Armée de l'Air* had ordered three prototypes: the SE 2400 experimental aircraft fitted with SOCEMA jet engines, the SE 2410 with the Rolls-Royce Nene (as a guarantee in case the French-designed jet engine proved disappointing), and the SE 2411 with full military equipment (and also fitted with Nene, which seems to suggest nobody had much hope for the SOCEMA engine). At that time the requirement was expected to be around 300 machines in 1950 (to equip eight *groupes de chasse*) with the production order being placed in 1948 (once the prototypes would had flown).

Construction of the wings was started in Marignane (near Marseilles) while the remainder of the airframes were prepared in Toulouse. Unfortunately an over-optimistic view of the building abilities of the prototype workshops coupled with plain bad management (which put the company on the brink of calling in receivership in 1947) delayed the completion of the first prototype until 1950. Naturally, and in parallel, all sorts of other troubles reared their ugly heads as well. First off, the French jet engine proved a failure and SOCEMA wanted to get out of this activity, while STAé was getting worried by the too high take-off speed and urged SNCASE to redesign the wing of the second prototype. In 1948 the whole project was considered '*too audacious*' and by September the SOCEMA-powered SE 2400 had been abandoned. Two months later the SE 2411 followed suit, to be replaced by a two-seat all-weather fighter called the SE 2415.

SE 2410	
Status	project
Span	-
Length	-
Gross wing area	-
Gross weight	-
Powerplant	two Nene 5,100lb (22.7kN)
Maximum speed/Height	-
Armament	none

SE 2411	
Status	-
Span	-
Length	-
Gross wing area	-
Gross weight	-
Powerplant	two Nene 5,100lb (22.7kN)
Maximum speed/Height	-
Armament	four 30mm guns and twenty-four HVAR

SE 2410-01 Grognard I

The wing of the SE 2410 was swept at an angle of 42°7', the fuselage began with a heavily armoured (800kg/1,764lb in total) and pressurised cockpit for the single pilot, then came the nose gear bay, the weapon bay (ballasted only on the -01), fuel tanks, the HVAR rocket bay (which could be fitted with an extra fuel tank of 284gal/1,290lit if

SE 2410-01	
Status	prototype
Span	44ft 6.5in (13.58m)
Length	50ft 7.5in (15.43m)
Gross wing area	496.1sq ft (46.14sq m)
Gross weight	39,683lb (18,000kg)
Powerplant	two Nene 5,100lb (22.7kN)
Maximum speed/Height	645mph (1,038km/h)
Armament	none installed

BELOW **The first prototype of the SE 2410 Grognard on display at the Paris Air Show, probably in 1951. Note the heavily framed canopy, more evocative of a Second World War aircraft than of modern jet types.** *Philippe Ricco*

required), the main gear bay and, at the extreme rear, the two turbojets. Brake and anti-spin parachutes were also provided. In 1952 Georges Héreil, the then president of SNCASE, was clearly very happy about his aircraft stating that: '*The SE Grognard displays performances which are above the contract requirements. Its speed has reached 1,038km/h (645mph).*'

SE 2415-01 Grognard II

This version was redesigned as a two-seater with a more streamlined but more prominent canopy and to enable this to be done the overall length had been extended by 4ft 7in (1.40m). The wing was also modified. Due to recurrent complaints about high landing speeds, the wings had been repositioned and the sweepback reduced to only 27°7'. This second Grognard prototype received its full suite of weapons and in particular was much involved in the testing of the Matra retractable unguided rocket launcher. It first flew on 14 February 1951 at Toulouse but, despite having the second seat, in truth it never flew with more than just the one crewman on board!

SE 2415-01	
Status	prototype
Span	51ft 1in (15.57m)
Length	55ft 2.5in (16.83m)
Gross wing area	475.6sq ft (44.23sq m)
Gross weight	39,683lb (18,000kg)
Powerplant	two Nene 5,100lb (22.7kN)
Maximum speed/Height	597mph (960km/h)
Armament	four 30mm guns and twenty-four HVAR

SE 2416

Single-seat strike aircraft based on the 2415 airframe with two Nene engines, four Hispano-Suiza HS 603 30mm guns, Matra rocket rack and bomb attachment points for armament.

TOP Side view of the SE 2410 showing to advantage the bulky fuselage and its curious rear end with the two nozzles, one atop the other. *José Fernandez*

ABOVE For comparison, a side view of the second prototype SE 2415 Grognard II with the revised bubble canopy (above a nominal two-seat cockpit), and the cleaned up tail end. *José Fernandez*

BELOW The Grognard II had an elongated fuselage and revised wings. *José Fernandez*

SE 2417 II

This was the SE 2415 re-engined with Tay or Verdon turbojets and with no fewer than eight (!) 20mm guns.

SE 2418

This design mated the highly swept wings of the 2410 with a 2415 fuselage (but with a single pilot) and two Tay turbojets. Two 30mm guns (other sources indicate 20mm), rocket rack and attachment points under the wings were intended to provide the armament for this variant. Optimised for ground attack duties, when it was put forward in 1950 this machine was perceived as the 'definitive' Grognard.

Grognard 'bi-ATAR'

This was the SE 2418 with two ATAR 101F engines mounted side by side and giving 4,950lb (22kN) of thrust dry and 9,675lb (43kN) with reheat.

SE 2419

This was a direct adaptation of the SE 2418 with two Rolls-Royce Nene turbojets. Two 30mm guns (other sources indicate 20mm), rocket rack and attachment points under the wings were the intended armament.

SE 2420

The SE 2420 was based on the third Grognard prototype on which construction had been stopped in 1948. It was to be fitted with the 'thin' wings of the SE 2415 and two Tay engines. A British AI.Mk.17 intercept radar was to be installed in the nose and the aircraft would also have incorporated two rocket engines of 2,755lb (12.2kN) thrust each to enable it to climb quickly to its interception altitude. The design was presented by SNCASE as the 'series' Grognard or Grognard III (three) ... which it was if one counts the airframes. Unfortunately this proved to be another false start and construction of the prototype was stopped in December 1950, definitively this time, when it was 80% complete.

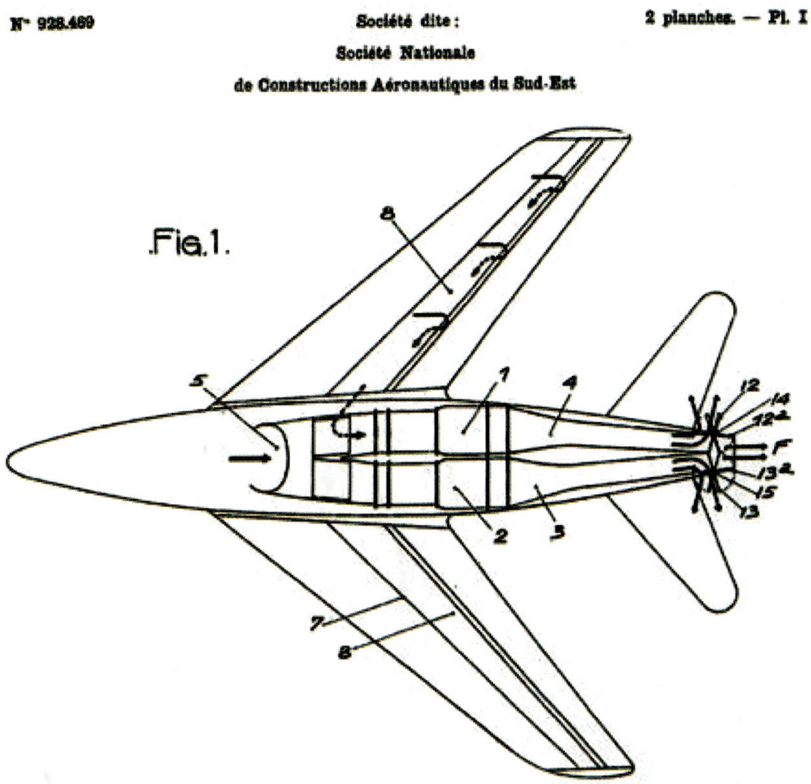

ABOVE **The SNCASE Grognard bi-ATAR variant had the two engines mounted side-by-side instead of one on top of the other.** *Author's collection/SNCASE Patent*

BELOW **Two-view drawing of the proposed SE 2420, which would have been built using parts for the third Grognard prototype.** *Philippe Ricco*

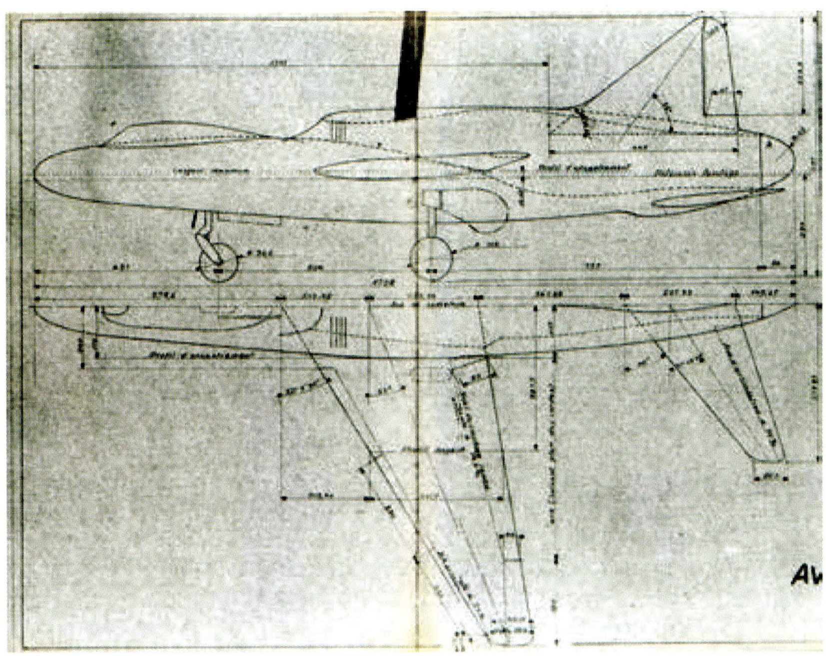

SE 2421

A two-seat, long-range, all-weather fighter variant, similar to the 2420 but with provision for drop tanks and the use of the 'thicker' 2410 wings.

SE 2422

This project was a single-seat strike aircraft that would use the 'thin' wing but would also feature a revised air intake (less bulky but wider). In the strike aircraft role it could carry a missile.

SE 2422R

The reconnaissance version of Grognard with cameras in place of the gun bay.

SE 2423

This design mated the fuselage of the 2418 variant with the wings of the 2415.

SE 2424

Another variation using the SE 2418 airframe but with a SNECMA Vulcain P-150 engine with 'post combustion', which was expected to give 14,330lb (63.7kN) of thrust. With this engine a speed of Mach 0.965 at 36,090ft (11,000m) was predicted, but the Vulcain engine never materialised.

SE 2450

A 'simplified SE 2400' was even proposed as the SE 2450. Actually this so-called SE 2450 had been born as the SE 1400 but it now had a two-seat cockpit. The two pilots sat in a pressurised cockpit on ejector seats

SE 2450	
Status	project
Span	67ft 3in (20.50m)
Length	64ft 11.5in (19.80m)
Gross wing area	752.7sq ft (70sq m)
Gross weight	44,974lb (20,400kg)
Powerplant	two Nene 5,100lb (22.7kN)
Maximum speed/Height	567mph at 13,125ft (912km/h at 4,000m)
Armament	four 30mm guns and twenty-four HVAR

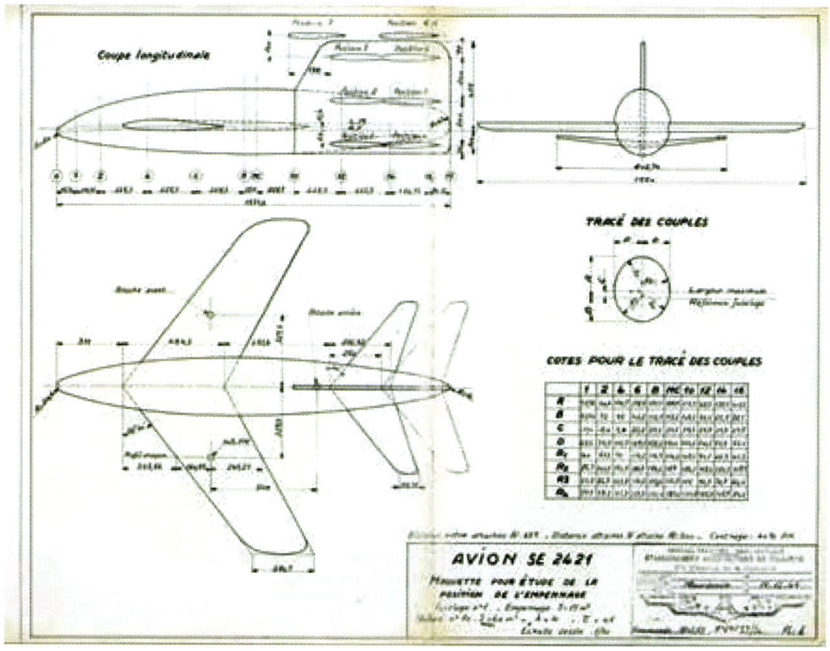

ABOVE **The revised SE 2421 would have received thicker wings and new tail surfaces. This three-view drawing from 19 December 1949 depicts a wind tunnel model designed to study the location of the horizontal tail surfaces.** *Philippe Ricco*

placed side by side under a bubble canopy and a pursuit radar ('*radar for pursuit under zero visibility*') was to be fitted in the nose. The armament, as required by the *Armée de l'Air*, was to be a quartet of guns and a bunch of unguided rockets. The landing gear could be either a conventional tricycle or a monotrace with side balancines, and the airframe itself was strictly conventional with the two jet engines fitted at the roots of the wings. The very classicism of this project killed it.

The first Grognard test flights revealed a need for some aerodynamic cleaning up of the airframe to get rid of dangerous vibration that had appeared at speeds between 342mph and 373mph (550km/h and 600km/h). As a result, the horizontal tail surfaces were redesigned, the wing was reinforced, the rear fuselage was made airtight and walls were installed in the large dorsal air intake, these modifications proving successful. Test pilots thought that flying the Grognard was easy, especially on the 2410-01, which had received assisted (powered) controls. Performance was good with all of the speed, range and take-off distance requirements being exceeded. So one may wonder why there were no production Grognards? It was even expected to improve the breed by fitting a more powerful engine, to the point where the airframe of the abandoned first (SOCEMA-powered) prototype had been retained with the hope of producing a SE 2420 fitted with Tay or Verdon turbojets.

The following reasons have been put forward regarding the cancellation of the whole programme:

1. First of all, there was the problem of the high take-off and landing speeds, and test pilots had serious reservations regarding the ability of this aircraft to operate by night or with reduced visibility.
2. The inability to obtain either from French industry or from foreign suppliers the up-to-date radar required for the operation of these all-weather fighters.
3. Future heavy strike aircraft were by now expected to be equipped with missiles, the role of attacking with guns and unguided rockets

being given to smaller, single-engine aeroplanes.

4. A third development prototype was needed, to prove that the low-speed characteristics of the SE 2415 could finally be mated with the required high performance. This would probably delay the programme sufficiently to put it behind the SNCASO candidate (the Vautour).

5. The development of the Grognard series would need replacement of the centrifugal flow turbojets by axial-flow engines (read: the French ATAR). However, while this could have improved the performance it also would have required a major redesign of the fuselage.

6. The airframe has been conceived using older technology and was thought to be more costly to put into production than more modern competitors. The two years lost through bad management between 1947 and 1948 had in effect put the whole Grognard project off track.

The Nord Entries

Nord 1600/1601

The Nord 1600 design was a rather smaller aircraft than the SNCASE projects. Proposed in July 1945, it was to be fitted with another soon-to be a failure French turbojet project called the Rateau SRA-1 giving 3,750lb (16.6kN) thrust. One of these large diameter centrifugal-flow engines was mounted in large pods in each wing root, the tail was of the then fashionable T-arrangement and the wings had 35° of sweep. Two prototypes of the 1600 were ordered under Contract 5324/46 dated 27 January 1947 and the first flight of this then purely experimental aircraft was planned for 30 April 1948.

However, the inability of Rateau to deliver a flightworthy engine condemned this and some other projects. The contract for the Nord 1600 prototypes was cancelled in 1949 and replaced in 1950 by an order for a single prototype powered by two of the rather less powerful Derwent V units giving only 3,500lb (15.5kN) thrust. During the transition from Rateau to Rolls-Royce the airframe was refined but lost its T-tail and another difference was that the engine pods were now slung under the wing instead of being positioned in a completely symmetrical way in regard to the wing. This was intended to *'retain the purity of lines of the wings, especially of the top surfaces'*, to reduce the frontal area of the engines and allow them to be attached to the strongest part of the airframe. In the earlier designs it had been intended to have an experimental flight engineer posted just behind the pilot but, in the aircraft as built, the second crew member was replaced by an equipment bay with flight recorders.

The Nord 1601 first flew on 24 January 1950, although the contract for its procurement was confirmed only on 15 September of the same

ABOVE Period postcard illustrating the Nord 1601 as it would have appeared during one of its flights. *Author's collection*

Nord 1601

Status	prototype
Span	40ft 8in (12.40m)
Length	38ft 1.5in (11.62m)
Gross wing area	324.95sq ft (30.22sq m)
Gross weight	14,770lb (6,700kg)
Powerplant	two Derwent 5 3,600lb (16kN)
Maximum speed/Height	625mph (1,005km/h) at ground level
Armament	none

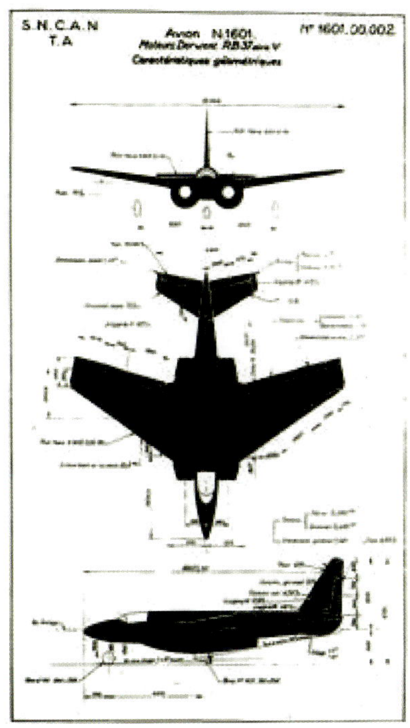

RIGHT SNCAN three-view drawing indicating the dimensions of the Nord 1601 in millimetres with two digits behind the dot! *Author's collection /Nord Aviation*

TOP **The Nord 1601 was exhibited at the 1951 Paris Air Show after only three flights had been made in the previous year.** *Author's collection*

ABOVE **Well known but excellent view of the Nord 1601 prototype.** *Author's collection*

BELOW **Poor quality art nonetheless illustrating the appearance of the Nord 1620 derivative of the Nord 1600.** *Author's collection/Nord Aviation*

year. According to the magazine *Les Ailes*, reporting on the early flights of the 1601, '*The goals of the flight testing of the Nord 1601 were as follows:*

(i) *research on swept-back wings and how it affected landing flaps and other lift augmentation devices* '(lateral control assisted by spoilers was apparently a prominent new feature on this aircraft and warranted a full page of explanation in *Les Ailes);*
(ii) *research on how stability was affected by swept-back wings*;
(iii) *research on the comportment (behaviour) of laminar profiles in high-subsonic speeds*;
(iv) *research on control efficiency and manoeuvrability*;
(v) *research on the design of engine air intakes*.'

It was also planned to study the forces and loads supported by the airframe and the distortion generated by them. While *Les Ailes* was very optimistic regarding the contribution of the Nord 1601 to aeronautical research, the first three flights revealed that the aircraft was difficult to control! Airbrakes were to be added in the rear fuselage to improve the landing characteristics and this new sequence of modifications delayed the return of the Nord 1601 to flight condition. When it finally did so in March 1952 it had become hopelessly outdated, and all the features it was supposed to investigate had been tested successfully on other machines. The contract was officially cancelled on 12 April 1952.

However, tests were carried out at ONERA that concluded that it was necessary to install assistance (power) on all three controls, to remove the dihedral, and to improve the interaction between fuselage and engine pods. Nothing was done to implement these modifications and, although the aircraft was kept airworthy until 1953, no one dared bring it back into the air. In September Nord itself suggested that it could be scrapped.

Nord 1620

In 1948, while everything felt good about this project, STAé asked Nord to design a combat aircraft based on the Nord 1601. It was to be fitted with Nene engines (at least these were trustworthy) and the wing and tail surfaces were to be straight, without any sweepback at all. The landing gear was of the monotrace type, with two (front and main) diabolos, but this project was quickly forgotten.

The 'Biréacteur d'Appui'

In June 1950, based on the experiences (or failures?) of the various projects it had previously sponsored and on the successful use of former Second World War aircraft such as the American Douglas B-26, the STAé issued a call for proposals for a new '*biréacteur d'appui*' (twin-jet close support aircraft) for which it strongly recommended the use of axial-flow turbojets for the powerplant. It seems that this specification led to the nickname used at the time of 'the ATAR twin'. It also required that both a night fighter and a reconnaissance aircraft could be derived from the basic close support airframe.

Following the submission of the SNCASO proposal, a new requirement was issued in June 1951 that appeared to have been tailored to the SNCASO project and highlighted a one-seat, twin-engine attack aircraft with a weight of 14 tons. ATAR 101E engines were specified, along with heavy armour for the pilot, an up-to date navigation system and the ability to carry either bombs or missiles; the fixed armament was to be two 37mm HS 606 guns. In term of performance, a maximum speed above 622mph (1,000km/h) at ground level and a flight endurance of about two hours were requested. The new programme also required the separate development of air-to-ground guided missiles, which were to be the armament of choice for the new aircraft.

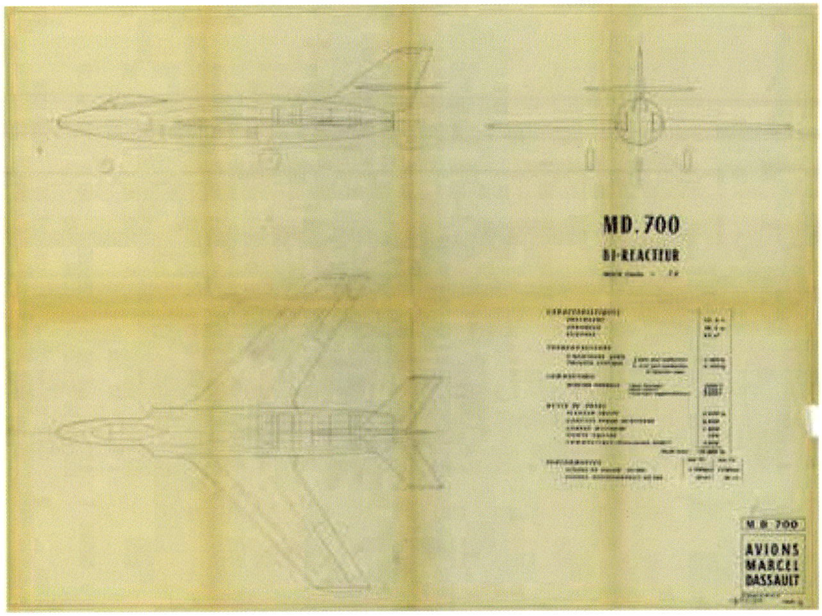

ABOVE Dassault's entry in the '*biréacteur d'appui*' competition was the MD 700. This drawing is dated 20 December 1951. *Dassault*

Nord 2900

This was the Nord response to the call for proposals. This machine, of which no illustration is known to exist, was based on the research carried out on the Nord 1601 and notably a feature that proved to be the downfall of the earlier machine, the interference between fuselage and engine (in this case ATAR turbojets). To limit the risk the engines were now fully podded and slung under the wing on short faired pylons, rather like some American projects such as the Douglas B-66. The Nord 2900 project was presented to STAé on 13 April 1951 but not pursued.

Dassault MD 700

Dassault offered its MD 700 design in several versions, each of which was more or less tailored to one of the expected missions. In February 1951 a study contract was awarded to Dassault (N°2044/51) to develop these proposals further.

MD 700 with 6-ton thrust turbojets

This was a large aircraft with a moderately swept-back wing (30°) set in the middle of the fuselage. This allowed the installation of a bomb bay 16ft 1in (4.9m) in length and a wide-section fuselage that enabled the designers to fit everything into the airframe with ease from the main landing gear to the two 'Super-ATAR' power units (these engines were known later as the Vulcain and were never actually put into production, despite giving 10,125lb [45kN] of thrust dry or 13,500lb [60kN] with 'post-combustion' [reheat]). The internal tanks contained 1,540gal (7,000 litres) of fuel and the two crew members were seated in ejector seats under a long bubble-type canopy. Despite having a large bomb bay, this design was also offered as a night fighter.

MD 700/6-ton thrust	
Status	project
Span	51ft 2in (15.60m)
Length	66ft 7in (20.30m)
Gross wing area	688.2sq ft (64sq m)
Gross weight	35,273lb (16,000kg)
Powerplant	two SNECMA Vulcain 13,500lb (60kN)
Maximum speed/Height	746mph (1,200km/h) at ground level
Armament	bombs and guns

MD 700 with 4-ton thrust turbojets

Dassault also offered a smaller machine fitted with two ATAR 101s (6,750lb/30kN dry and 9,000lb/ 40kN with reheat) and the wing had more sweepback with an angle of 42°, but otherwise the airframe was of similar shape to its bigger brethren.

MD 700/4-ton thrust	
Status	project
Span	45ft 3in (13.80m)
Length	58ft 4.5in (17.80m)
Gross wing area	526.9sq ft (49sq m)
Gross weight	27,116lb (12,300kg)
Powerplant	two ATAR 101 9,000lb (40kN)
Maximum speed/Height	746mph (1,200km/h) at ground level
Armament	?

MD 700 'Mix 'n' Match'

Dassault also suggested mating the large fuselage of the first prototype with the more sharply swept wing of the smaller version, a move that was expected to improve the range.

MD 700 mix	
Status	project
Span	51ft 2in (15.60m)
Length	63ft 11.5in (19.50m)
Gross wing area	688.2sq ft (64sq m)
Gross weight	33,069lb (15,000kg)
Powerplant	two SNECMA ATAR 101 9,000lb (40kN)
Maximum speed/Height	715mph (1,150km/h) at ground level
Armament	?

STAé turned down all three proposals, arguing that, in terms of ease of the maintenance, having the two engines fitted close together in the rear fuselage was hardly the optimal solution (earlier experiences had obviously discouraged any engine configuration except underslung pods), while grouping the fuel tanks, engines, crew, etc., all within the fuselage brought vulnerability in terms of the MD 700's combat resilience.

SNCASO Proposals

When it became apparent that the SO 4000 (see Chapter One) was a failure, SNCASO's design office under Jean-Charles Parot revised its views about fitting existing turbojets into new designs.

SO 4010

The first new project was the SO 4010. The design's moderately swept-back (35°) shoulder wing had its turbojet engines (of known and proven type, either the SNECMA ATAR 101 or Rolls-Royce Avon) housed either in pods attached to faired struts or attached directly under the wing. The long fuselage would have been adaptable to a variety of missions and a long bomb bay, 18ft 0.5in (5.5m) in length, was a fixed feature that would have taken either iron bombs, missiles, rocket racks or additional tanks. Further additional fuel could be carried in non-droppable wingtip tanks and the SO 4010 would have been crewed either by a single pilot or by a pilot and bombardier all under an elongated canopy. The most unusual feature of this project was its use of a bicycle type landing gear with twin diabolos and side balancines (which retracted into the wingtip nacelles). This landing gear configuration was tested on an example of the SO 93 Corse civil transport aircraft.

SO 4010	
Status	project
Span	48ft 6in (14.78m)
Length	62ft 3in (18.98m)
Gross wing area	483.9sq (45sq m)
Gross weight	-
Powerplant	two ATAR 101 9,000lb (40kN)
Maximum speed/Height	-
Armament	-

SO 4015

This was step two in the effort to bring back realism in the design of a bomber, initiated during the winter of 1950-51. Here, not only were the engines proven types, Nene or ATAR 101,

SO 4015/Nene	
Status	project
Span	44ft 5in (13.54m)
Length	53ft 4in (16.25m)
Gross wing area	-
Gross weight	23,810lb (10,800kg)
Powerplant	two Nene 5,100lb (22.7kN)
Maximum speed/Height	680mph (1,094km/h) at ground level
Armament	variable depending on intended role

SO 4015/ATAR	
Status	project
Span	44ft 5in (13.54m)
Length	53ft 4in (16.25m)
Gross wing area	-
Gross weight	24,416lb (11,075kg)
Powerplant	two ATAR 101B 5,400lb (24kN)
Maximum speed/Height	677mph (1,089km/h) at ground level
Armament	variable depending on intended role

SO 4015/TB 1500	
Status	project
Span	44ft 5in (13.54m)
Length	53ft 4in (16.25m)
Gross wing area	-
Gross weight	22,156lb (10,050kg)
Powerplant	two SOCEMA TB 1500 4,275lb (19kN)
Maximum speed/Height	692mph (1,114km/h) at ground level
Armament	variable depending on intended role

although the TB1500 was still being considered (perhaps in an effort to placate the authorities, which were still very keen to see this French turbojet design being put to use), but the whole airframe had been reduced in size to better adapt it to the power provided by these engines.

SO 4050 A

Following submission of the SO 4015, the *Armée de l'Air* refined its programme in June 1951. In reply, Jean-Charles Parot's team submitted the SO 4050A (A for *appui* or close support) and, under Contract N° 4026/52 of January 1952, Contract N° 2132/53 and later Contract N° 2215/53, the *Armée de l'Air* ordered three prototypes and a static test airframe for what became the Vautour.

The Vautour Prototypes

SO 4050-001

With its two-man crew seated in tandem and powered by two SNECMA ATAR 101B2 (later C) engines, the prototype SO 4050 first flew on 16 October 1952 with Jacques Guignard at the controls. Although it could have been equipped as an all-weather fighter, this remained an experimental machine. It had a short fuselage and was used mostly for aerodynamic testing. After more than 300 flights, SO 4050-001 crashed near Melun on 16 May 1956, its pilot, René Bigand, ejecting successfully.

SO 4050-002

The prototype for the single-seat ground attack (*appui*) version, powered by two SNECMA ATAR 101Ds, 002 first flew on 16 December 1953 crewed by test pilot Charles Goujon. This was still a short fuselage version but as the armament test aircraft it was equipped with two 37mm HS 606 guns and various rocket racks.

SO 4050-003

SO 4050-03 was the prototype for the two-seat medium bomber Vautour in which the bombardier was seated under a glass nose. It was powered by two Armstrong Siddeley Sapphire turbojets and the aircraft was used for aerodynamic and armament testing, and for the development of the Derveaux bombsight. However, its major contribution to the Vautour saga was the development of the one-piece (monobloc) horizontal surface/controls.

SO 4050-004

A two-seat medium bomber prototype with ATAR D2 engines. First flown 18 March 1955.

SO 4050-005

Single-seat attack version prototype with ATAR E3 engines. First flown 17 June 1955.

SO 4050-006

Prototype for the two-seater night fighter version with ATAR E3 engines and which first flew on 17 June 1955. It was used mostly for the development of the CSF DRAC 25A chase (interception) radar.

SO 4050-007

Single-seat attack prototype with ATAR E3 engines. This was first flown on 11 February 1956.

SO 4050-008

The two-seat night fighter version prototype with ATAR E3 engines and flown for the first time on 1 March 1956. This was the first airframe fitted with the complete armament and equipment for the N-series (below), and it was used mostly for armament trials.

SO 4050-009

A two-seat night fighter prototype fitted with Rolls-Royce Avon RA41 engines. This new power unit was a requirement of the Royal Belgian Air Force, which was interested in buying the Vautour. The aircraft was mostly used for the development of the later DRAC 32A chase radar.

With the results of the test flying using these prototypes, the following modifications were incorporated into production aircraft – cambered leading edges and wing fences, vortex generators, 'monobloc' (one-piece) horizontal tailplanes, and 'gun muzzles' in the form of squarish fairings around the gun tube openings (flight experience had shown that there was a risk of engine flame out when unfaired guns were fired).

Vautour Variants

Due to budgetary restrictions, the number of production machines was somewhat reduced from the original Vautour orders. On top of this a number of proposed variants were not produced. These included the Vautour IV Series (SO 4054 'Super Vautour') which would have featured more advanced turbojets, a revised thinner and more swept-back wing (the 'M4' wing with 44° of sweepback), or revised and enlarged wings for high-altitude operations. The chosen turbojets would have been the ATAR 101G-32 (9,900lb/44kN with reheat) for fighter versions and ATAR E-3 (7,875lb/35kN) for the bomber types. Later ATAR 8 (9,260lb/41.15kN

BELOW **A prototype SO 4050 A exhibited at the Paris Air Show. On the right can be seen the mysterious SNCASO B.10 glide bomb that was under consideration at the time.** *José Fernandez*

thrust), Avon or Sapphire turbojets would have been retrofitted, and the designers even toyed with the idea of fitting the Bristol Olympus rated at 16,315lb (72.50kN) thrust!

Vautour A (V II A)

This was the *appui* (close support) version. Thirty machines were produced from an initial planned total of 170. Armament 4 × 30mm DEFA 551 (later 552) guns with 100 shells each. Twenty were sold to Israel with the remainder retained for training and trials flying.

SO 4050 II A	
Status	production
Span	49ft 6.5in (15.10m)
Length	56ft 11.5in (17.36m)
Gross wing area	483.9sq ft (45sq m)
Gross weight	up to 42,549lb (19,300kg)
Powerplant	two ATAR 101E3 or E5 7,875lb (35kN)
Maximum speed/Height	Mach 0.92 at 39,370ft (12,000m)
Armament	four DEFA 552 30mm guns and bombs or rocket racks

Vautour B (V II B)

This medium bomber two-seat version fitted with a Norden M9B bombsight was produced in forty units from an initial plan of eighty-five. Joining *Armée de l'Air* squadrons somewhat late, these aircraft were soon outclassed by the Dassault Mirage IV and so were converted to non-bomber roles. Three examples were sold to Israel.

SO 4050 II B	
Status	production
Span	49ft 6.5in (15.10m)
Length	57ft 11in (17.65m)
Gross wing area	483.9sq ft (45sq m)
Gross weight	up to 42,549lb (19,300kg)
Powerplant	two ATAR 101E3 or E5 7,875lb (35kN)
Maximum speed/Height	Mach 0.92 at 39,370ft (12,000m)
Armament	11,023lb (5,000kg) bombs

Vautour BR

Two prototypes only produced (4050-003 and 4050-009). The production version would have been similar to the Vautour B but with a Derveaux radar bombsight.

Vautour BRA

Three machines modified to investigate nuclear clouds as part of the programme of nuclear testing held at Mururoa during the late 1960s.

Vautour V IV B

This was the advanced bomber version fitted with ATAR E-3 and a revised wing giving a speed of Mach 0.98. The Derveaux radar-bombsight would have been fitted systematically as in the BR version. It was intended to add defensive weapons ranging from rather old-fashioned rear-firing 30mm fixed guns to more exotic gliding missiles or even gliding mines.

SO 4054 IV B	
Status	project
Span	65ft 2in (19.87m)
Length	-
Gross wing area	629.0sq ft (58.50sq m)
Gross weight	36,949lb (16,760kg)
Powerplant	two ATAR 8 9,450lb (42kN)
Maximum speed/Height	Mach 0.97 at 39,370ft (12,000m)
Armament	-

BELOW Drawings from a SNCASO advertisement illustrating the different variants of the Vautour. *Author's collection/SNCASO*

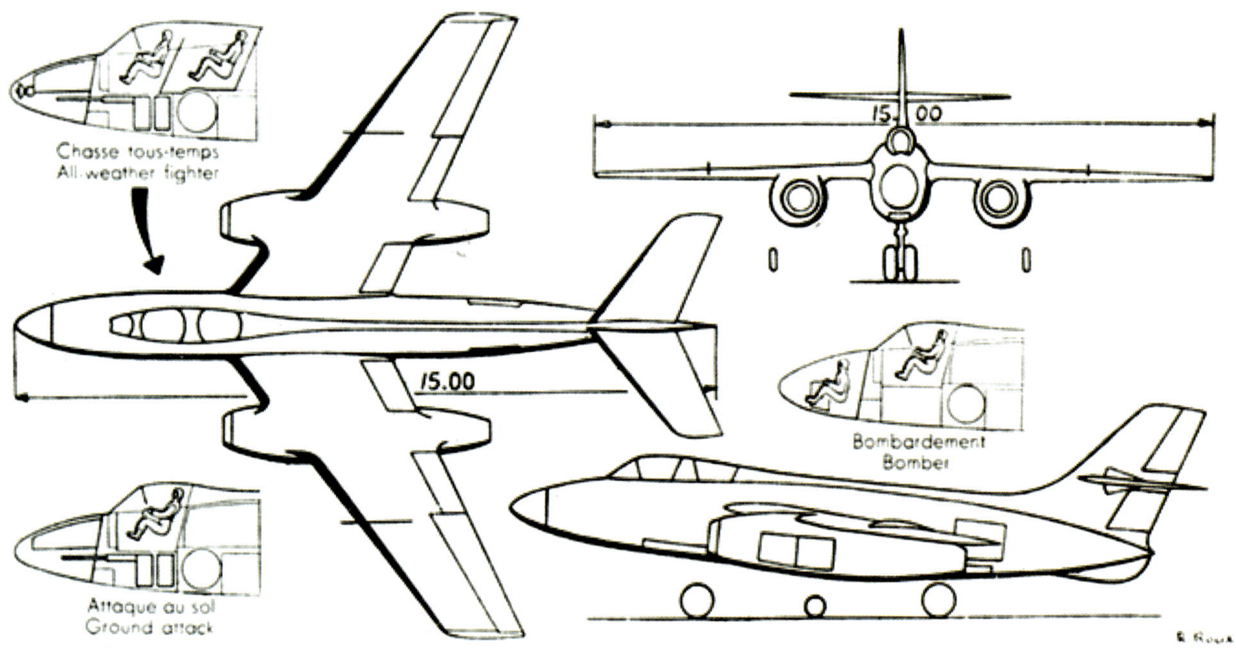

However, experience from the 1956 Suez campaign suggested that high-altitude bombing with iron bombs was not very efficient and this more or less killed this advanced Vautour bomber (although it was intended to carry nuclear ordnance as well).

Vautour N (V II N)

This was the two-seat night fighter version. A total of seventy machines were produced from an initial intention of 300. Armament comprised four 30mm DEFA 551 (later 552) guns with 100 shells each. Four or five were sold to Israel, and Belgium wanted to buy forty of this version but re-engined with Avon turbojets. The Vautours were selected over the British Javelin but NATO objected to the use of 'offshore' financing to buy a pure European-designed aircraft, so in the end Belgium bought some Canadian CF-100 heavy fighters. It seems the Netherlands Air Force was also interested in the Vautour N but that plan also failed through the same politico-financial problems. About ten V II Ns were fitted with electronic warfare equipment for the *Forces Aériennes Stratégiques*.

SO 4050 II N	
Status	production
Span	49ft 6.5in (15.10m)
Length	57ft 11in (17.65m)
Gross wing area	483.9sq ft (45sq m)
Gross weight	up to 42,549lb (19,300kg)
Powerplant	two ATAR 101E3 or E5 7,875lb (35kN)
Maximum speed/Height	Mach 0.92 at 39,370ft (12,000m)
Armament	four DEFA 552 30mm guns and rocket racks

Vautour NPP

Five further Vautours modified for sampling the radioactive clouds generated by the nuclear tests carried out in Mururoa.

Vautour V IV N

This variant was fitted with the new M4 fighter wing. The DRAC 32 radar was the base equipment but it was expected that this would be replaced with more advanced avionics and an improved combat computer. Armament would have been missiles and rockets only and this version would have been slightly supersonic (Mach 1.01 at 32,800ft/10,000m). It was not produced.

SO 4054 IV N	
Status	project
Span	44ft 11in (13.70m)
Length	-
Gross wing area	537.6sq ft (50sq m)
Gross weight	-
Powerplant	two ATAR 8 9,450lb (42kN)
Maximum speed/Height	Mach 1.02 at 39,370ft (12,000m)
Armament	-

Vautour R

No examples of this reconnaissance Vautour were produced, despite an estimated requirement for twenty-four aircraft. These would have been fitted with either three cameras (for day reconnaissance) or two cameras with flares. In the end, twelve B Series Vautours were adapted for the day reconnaissance role by installing cameras in the bomb bay and, with utter disregard for logic, these were known as the 'BR' version!

Vautour Ravitailleurs

It was planned to adapt the Vautour as an in-flight refuelling tanker by fitting Douglas refuelling pods to A or B version aircraft. However, with France's acquisition of the Boeing

BELOW Plan view of the SO 4055, which would have been fitted with a crescent-shaped wing. *Author's from Cuny*

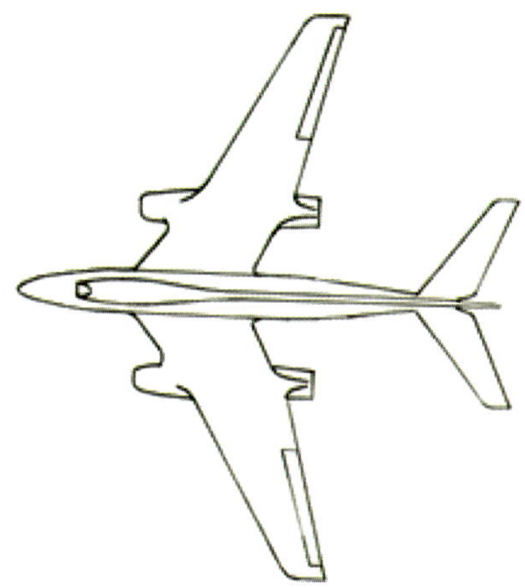

BELOW The SO 4054 Super Vautour was not produced. It would have featured improved engines and a revised and more swept-back wing. *Author's from Cuny*

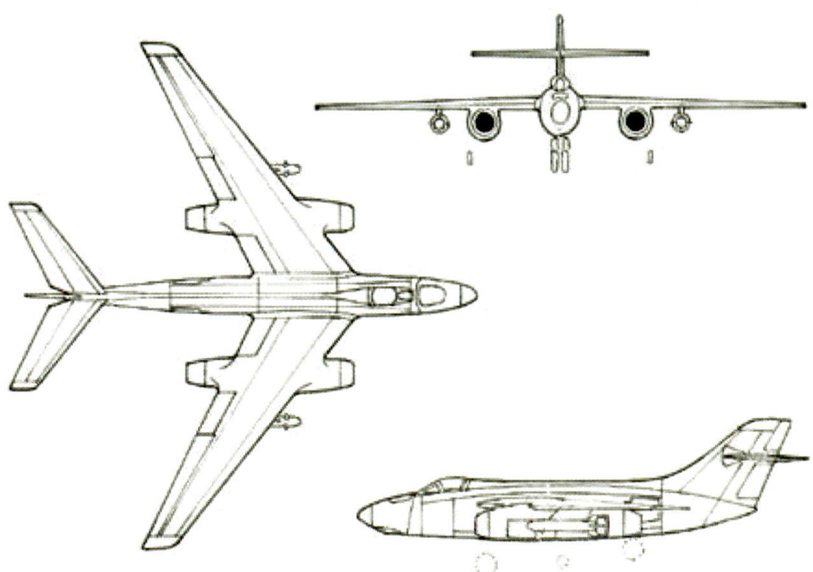

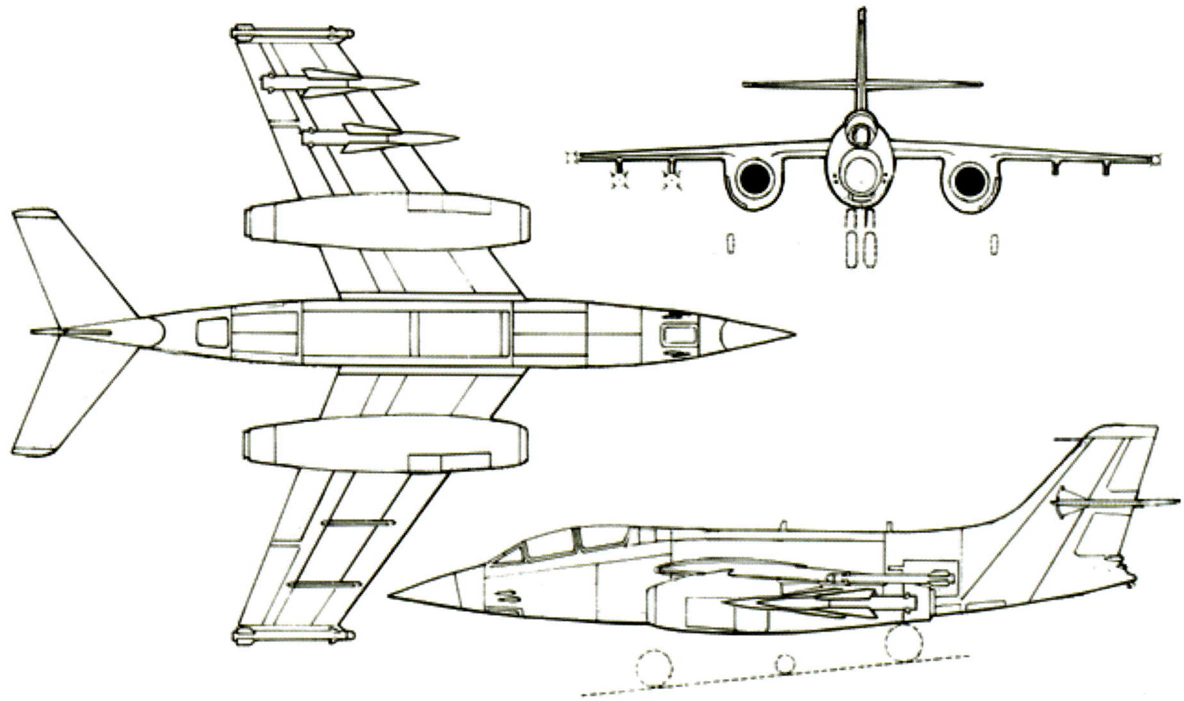

ABOVE The last effort to expand the Vautour line was made in 1964 with the 'Cyclone'. By that time SNCASO had been amalgamated into Sud Aviation. *Author's from Cuny*

KC-135, only airframe 4050-008 was converted as part of its prototype duties.

Further Vautour Derivatives

SO 4055

This was to be a development of the SO 4054 with yet another type of wing. Various wing planforms were tested in model form in wind tunnels during 1955, including 'crescent' wings.

SO 4055 crescent wing	
Status	project
Span	65ft 2in (19.87m)
Length	-
Gross wing area	629.0sq ft (58.50sq m)
Gross weight	-
Powerplant	?
Maximum speed/Height	-
Armament	-

SO 4060

Another derivative of the basic SO 4054. See next chapter.

SO 4050 'Robot'

During 1957 and 1958 SNCASO offered to use the Vautour airframe to create a cruise missile in the style of the American Martin Matador. The crew positions, some equipment and the landing gear would have been dispensed with and the space thus created would have been filled with extra fuel. Additional wingtip tanks, underwing tanks and even 'conformal' tanks (but not yet named as such) on the fuselage would have doubled the fuel tankage when compared to the manned version (the conformal tanks would have offered the added advantage of artificially creating a 'wasp' profile that would have conformed better to the Whitcomb area rule). Launched from a wheeled booster, this aircraft would have been remote-controlled during the early phase of its flight and then flown on autopilot. An 'obstacle avoidance' radar was to be installed enabling low-level attacks to be carried out, while the warhead was just 'announced' as being 5,510lb (2,500kg) in size, but in fact it may have been the French A-bomb, which was in development at that time. It was expected that the 4060 would have been adapted in the same way.

Sud Aviation Cyclone

One would have imagined that the story of the Vautour might have faded away during the 1950s, but in 1964 the press began writing about a 'Supersonic Vautour'. The idea was to improve the aircraft's speed and range to enable it to carry the French atomic bomb, and the following modifications to existing airframes were suggested:

(i) adding fairings on the fuselage to provide area ruling,
(ii) redesign the wing leading edge to give it a laminar profile,
(iii) redesign the engine pods and
(iv) if possible fit more powerful engines.

In fact, following some experiments conducted by Israel, the manufacturer, now part of Sud Aviation, was already working on a new development called the Cyclone, which was based on the Vautour airframe. This was revealed

Sud Cyclone	
Status	project
Span	45ft 4in (13.82m)
Length	61ft 3.5in (18.68m)
Gross wing area	532.3sq ft (49.50sq m)
Gross weight	up to 55,115lb (25,000kg)
Powerplant	two RB.168-1 11,610lb (51.60kN)
Maximum speed/Height	Mach 0.93
Armament	four DEFA 552 30mm guns and four Nord AS30 missiles or four Matra AS37 missiles and Sidewinder AAMs (for defence)

publicly in 1965 and the following modifications were expected:

1. A revised, thinned but shorter wing with integral fuel tanks and with missile launching rails on the wingtips; also attachment points for ordnance or drop tanks.
2. An elongated fuselage with a Cyrano interception radar inside a pointed nose cone. The navigation electronics would have been upgraded and the two-place cockpit was located just behind the radar nose, which made space for an extra fuel tank in the fuselage. The rear body fin was to be eliminated and replaced by an arrestor hook and the landing gear would have been beefed up and catapult launch hooks added. The control systems would have been revised.
3. New larger vertical and horizontal rudders would have been introduced.
4. Rolls-Royce RB168-1 Spey turbojets would have been fitted giving 11,610lb (51.60kN) of thrust.

These measures would have made the Cyclone much more capable, with the ability to carry up to 16,093lb (7,300kg) of ordnance in total, and to deliver more than 6,614lb (3,000kg) of bombs at a distance of more than 622 miles (1,000km) from its take-off base. At one stage the Cyclone was seen as a back-up to the Dassault Mirage F2 then in development (Volume I) but it was ultimately dropped because of its purely subsonic performance. Israeli might have been interested as well but a French arms embargo imposed on that country in 1967 cut the wings off the idea.

This project, which quite probably was never actually offered to any military agency, is known only through a patent

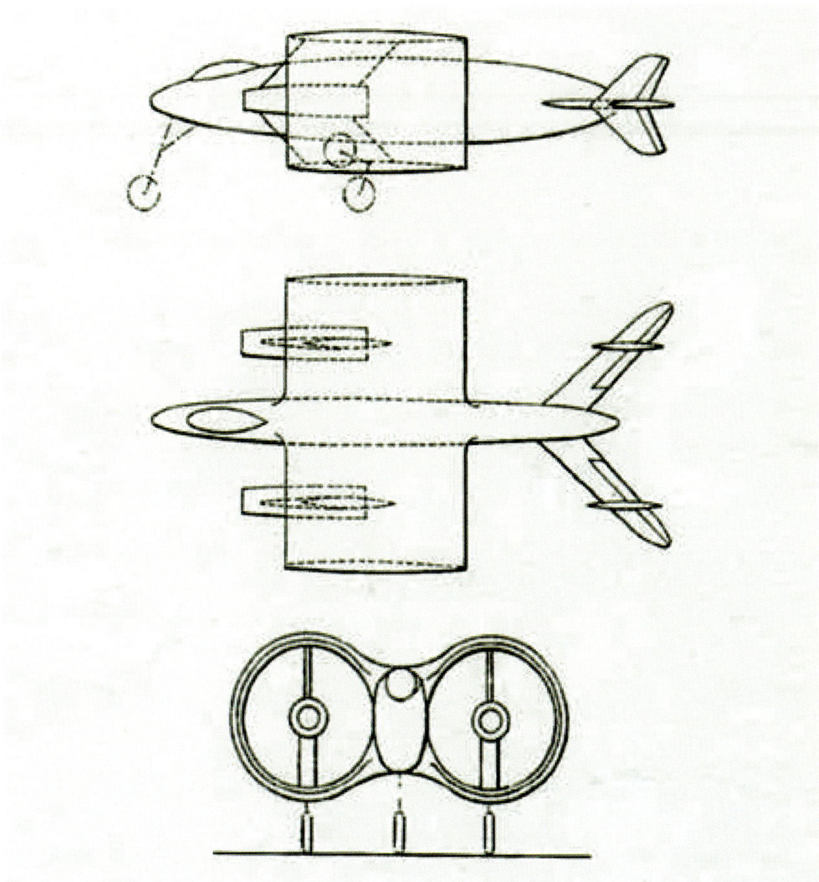

ABOVE **The unusual twin-cylindrical wing bomber design by Société REP.** *Author's collection/REP Patent*

REP Bomber with Cylindrical Wings

issued in 1954. 'Somewhere close to the Vautour' seems to be the best way to describe it. This very unusual machine featured a deep fuselage, which *'could house in its lower part a bomb bay or* [in a recess?] *a very large bomb, the upper part being allocated to the crew position'.* The fuselage was flanked by two cylindrical wings each containing a turbojet engine along its axis. The patent was applied for on 19 October 1953, at a time when the Zborowski Coléoptère had not yet been revealed to the aeronautical world.

An oddity of the whole project (beyond its unusual appearance) lies in the REP company. REP refers to '*Recherches Études Production*' which was in no way related to the better known Robert Esnault-Pelleterie (an aviation pioneer who died in 1957). So this REP appears, through its assignee René Lucien (his full name was actually René Lucien Lévy), to be an offshoot of the specialist aircraft undercarriage company Société Messier, and quite logically all of the other patents produced by Société REP relate to landing gears. What could the reason have been behind this company designing a complete aircraft, and one in which its original features do not in any way relate to its landing gear?

Chapter Three
The Quest for the Supersonic Bomber

ABOVE **The first prototype of the Mirage IV flew for the first time on 19 August 1959.** *Author's collection/Dassault photo*

Studies for a future bomber to follow the Vautour began in 1955, although in the shadow of an ongoing debate regarding the possible replacement of manned aircraft by unmanned intercontinental missiles. While these were being developed in foreign countries (the USA and USSR) it was soon realised that some of the necessary technology for unmanned projects, notably for the avionics and navigation systems, was just not available within the indigenous French industry, and it would take time to develop them. The future manned bomber was likely to encounter the same problem, but here it was expected that the crew would be able to perform some of the tasks that the avionics of that time were just not able to do. Since the new aircraft was to be designed as the vector for the future French nuclear

SNCASE X-223 (1955)	
Status	project
Span	34ft 5.5in (10.50)
Length	72ft 2in (22.00m)
Gross wing area	645.2sq ft (60sq m)
Gross weight	89,683lb (40,680kg)
Powerplant	two ATAR 9 13,050lb (58kN)
Maximum speed/Height	Mach 2.3
Armament	2,204lb (1,000kg) of stores

SNCASE X-223 (1957)	
Status	project
Span	29 6ft in (c. 9.00)
Length	59ft 8.5in (18.20m)
Gross wing area	322.6sq ft (30sq m)
Gross weight	55,115lb (25,000kg)
Powerplant	one ramjet
Maximum speed/Height	Mach 3
Armament	2,204lb (1,000kg) of stores

deterrent, it was just impossible for French decision-makers to use foreign equipment in its conception that might in due course be embargoed or neutralised. This position, already latent before it, was reinforced by the USA's attitude during the 1956 Suez Crisis. To have a truly independent diplomacy, France needed to have a completely self-designed and self-operated defence force, including an indigenously developed nuclear bomb that could be delivered by an indigenously developed system. This would lead eventually to the design by France alone of nuclear-powered submarines with ballistic missiles, of ground-to-ground ballistic missiles, and of long-range bombers, and all of these were expected to carry a French-designed nuclear weapon.

In October 1956 the *Armée de l'Air* issued a call for proposals for a new Mach 2 bomber having the following features:

(i). A cruise speed of Mach 1.8. This was a limit imposed by the operating temperatures of the materials (the metals) to be used in the airframe's construction. At higher speeds a conventional airframe would become too hot due to air friction and that would create complex problems.

(ii). A range of 930 miles (1,500km) without refuelling, of which half had to be performed at supersonic speed.

(iii) A 2,205lb (1,000kg) military load carried in a 'container' (weapon bay) 18ft 0.5in (5.5m) long and 2ft 1.5in (0.65m) wide.

(iv). Take-offs from runways made in under 6,560ft (2,000m).

(v). Choice of engines to be either ATAR 8 or 9.

(vi). Delivery of first series (production) aircraft in 1962.

Three manufacturers responded, Nord Aviation, SNCASO and Dassault, though it seems Dassault was at first not consulted. Jean Cabrière, of the Dassault *bureau d'études,* explained in 1989 how '*the* [original] *definition of the* [Mirage III follow-up] *evolved quickly: its wing surface grew from 43 to 50sq m then 55sq m* [462 to 538sq ft then 591sq ft]. *Then leaks* [of information] *occurred and, while the STAé still talked about a heavy fighter, we at last understood that the request from the State engineers had tried to define a bomber for which our company had not been consulted.*'

TOP & ABOVE Model of the Nord Mach 2 Bomber. *George Cox via Tony Buttler*

Before moving to the proposals, it must be noted that in 1955 SNCASE had designed a '*bombardier robot*', the X-223, and it tried to relaunch the concept in 1957. However, since the official statement had described a 'manned bomber', these proposals were not studied by the *Armée de l'Air*. The X-223 was originally a delta winged twin-turbojet machine with a long and thin 'spindle' fuselage housing fuel, avionics and a 2,205lb (1,000kg) warload. In its 1957 incarnation it had changed considerably: the fuselage was now tubular and housed a single ramjet (how the aircraft would be brought to the ramjet's activation speed was not specified) and the wings were slightly smaller, but the military load was still 2,205lb (1,000kg).

Nord Bombardier Supersonique

As might be expected, the Nord entry was based on a combination of two ATAR 9 turbojets in the fuselage and two 6.3in (1.60m) diameter ramjets at the tips of short straight wings. Another feature common to many Nord proposals from the 1950s was the use of canard surfaces. Beneath the fuselage of the main aircraft was hung a large missile, again powered by a ramjet. Nord predicted a speed of Mach 2.5 with a range of 1,800 miles (2,900km) at a height of 82,020ft (25,000m). On assessment this proposal was judged to be optimistic in terms of its weight and not well thought out in terms of heat dissipation, which was expected to cause trouble, not only for the ATAR engine but for the airframe itself. Nord replied with a smaller machine designed around a delta wing, a bit like a stretched Nord Gerfaut (Volume I). For propulsion this layout had two ATAR 9s grouped at the rear of the fuselage and fed via a ventral intake. There was no ramjet in this project, except for the missile that appears (from the drawings) to have been carried over from the previous project. It should be noted that Nord also had its own robot bomber project, propelled by two ramjets, although it was a design that was completely overlooked by everyone in authority.

Nord Bombardier Supersonique (large)	
Status	project
Span	28ft 10.5in (8.80m)
Length	79ft 4.5in (24.20m)
Gross wing area	645.2sq ft (60sq m)
Gross weight	66,138lb (30,000kg)
Powerplant	two ATAR 9 13,050lb (58kN) and two Nord ramjets
Maximum speed/Height	Mach 2.5 at 82,020ft (25,000m)
Armament	-

Nord Bombardier Supersonique (small)	
Status	project
Span	33ft 9.5in (c. 10.30)
Length	64ft 0in (c. 19.50)
Gross wing area	-
Gross weight	-
Powerplant	two ATAR 9 13,050lb (58kN)
Maximum speed/Height	Mach 1.5
Armament	-

SNCASO SO 4060

In 1953, after thinking about a Vautour follow-up, the SNCASO design office came up with the SO 4060. In its early iterations this project had much in common with the Vautour itself but gradually, over time, the shape changed considerably to reflect more modern thinking, the designs even taking in a delta wing. The result was a twin-ATAR-powered heavy fighter

BELOW **The prototype SO 4060 being built. Two prototypes were started but neither flew.** *Alain Marchand via Tony Buttler*

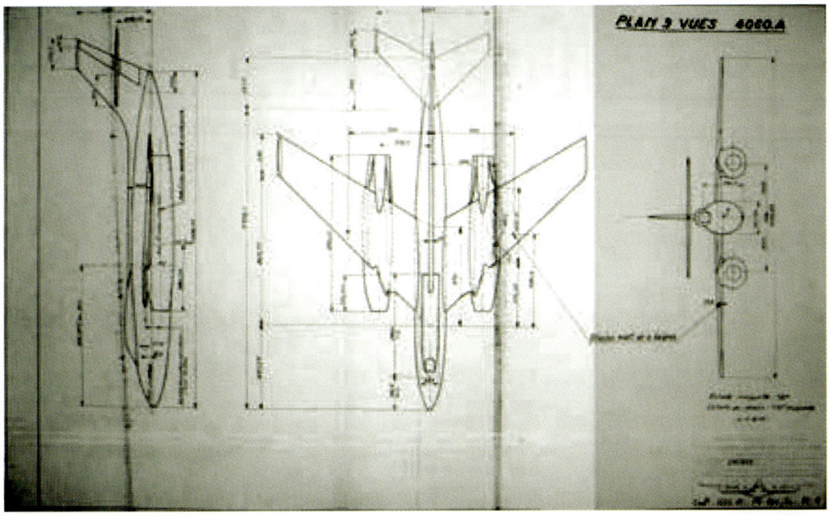

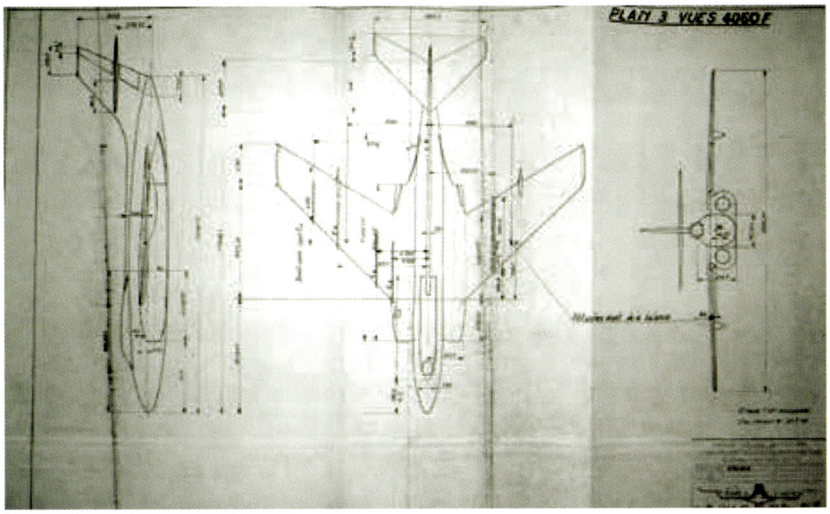

TOP **That the SO 4060 originally belonged to the Vautour family is clear in this drawing of the SO 4060A, dated 6 October 1953.** *Philippe Ricco*

ABOVE **With each separate study the SO 4060 moved away from the original Vautour architecture. In this slightly earlier SO 4060F drawing from 23 September 1953 the engine pods are adjacent to the main fuselage.** *Philippe Ricco*

SNCASO SO 4060-01	
Status	prototype (uncompleted)
Span	38ft 6in (11.73m)
Length	17.96 (58 11)
Gross wing area	537.6sq ft (50sq m)
Gross weight	33,399lb (15,150kg)
Powerplant	two ATAR 101G-1 9,675lb (43kN) and one SEPR rocket 6,525lb (29kN)
Maximum speed/Height	Mach 1.5
Armament	two missiles

SNCASO SO 4060-02	
Status	prototype (uncompleted)
Span	38ft 6in (11.73m)
Length	58ft 11in (17.96m)
Gross wing area	537.6sq ft (50sq m)
Gross weight	36,574lb (16,590kg)
Powerplant	two ATAR 9 13,050lb (58kN)
Maximum speed/Height	Mach 1.7
Armament	two missiles

SNCASO SO 4060-02B	
Status	project
Span	38ft 6in (11.73m)
Length	62ft 4in (19.00m)
Gross wing area	537.6sq ft (50sq m)
Gross weight	52,138lb (23,650kg)
Powerplant	two ATAR 25 14,175lb (63kN)
Maximum speed/Height	Mach 2
Armament	2,204lb (1,000kg) of stores

SNCASO SO 4060-03B	
Status	project
Span	42ft 0in (12.80m)
Length	65ft 3.5in (19.90m)
Gross wing area	591.4sq ft (55sq m)
Gross weight	58,576lb (26,570kg)
Powerplant	two ATAR 26 16,425lb (73kN)
Maximum speed/Height	Mach 2
Armament	2,204lb (1,000kg) of stores

with its wings swept sharply to an angle of 43° 24'. The wing was very thin and built around two main spars, and on the first prototype the space between the two spars was filled with NIDA (for *Nid D'Abeille* or honeycomb material), but in later aircraft this space would have been used for fuel. The wingtips pivoted to act as ailerons, the centre of the fuselage held fuel tanks positioned near the centre of gravity to help balance the aircraft, and the two ATARs placed at the rear of the slab-sided fuselage were fed via large intakes. Two Matra 511 missiles were positioned underneath the fuselage while the front part of the body contained the two-seat pressure cockpit (based on the type used in the Vautour) and in the extreme nose a DRAC 32A radar.

This design caught the attention of the authorities and two prototypes were ordered under Contract 4003/56 dated 18 January 1956 and confirmed in July 1956. Initially the powerplant was to be two 9,450lb (42kN) ATAR 101Gs and these would go in the first prototype along with a 6,525lb (29kN) thrust SEPR rocket motor installed under the fuselage. However, the rear fuselage was modified for the second machine and lengthened to take 11,700lb (52kN) ATAR 9s and so the rocket was dispensed with. The third prototype was to be a bomber

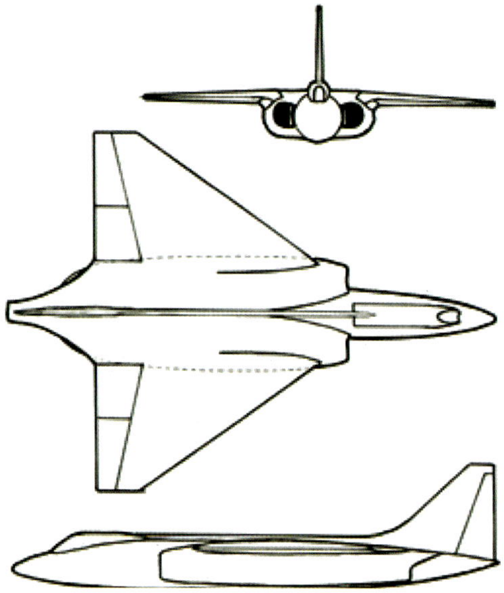

ABOVE **The next SO 4060 iteration had the engines fully integrated into the fuselage while the wing showed a clipped delta planform.** *Author's from Cuny*

BELOW **The final appearance of the SO 4060.** *Author's collection/SNCASO document*

SNCASO SO 4060M	
Status	project
Span	38ft 6in (11.73m)
Length	62ft 10.5in (19.16m)
Gross wing area	537.6sq ft (50sq m)
Gross weight	37,335lb (16,935kg)
Powerplant	two Super-ATAR 18,675lb (83kN) at 26,250ft (8,000m)
Maximum speed/Height	Mach 2
Armament	-

SNCASO SO 4061	
Status	project
Span	45ft 11in (c. 14.00m)
Length	77ft 1in (c. 23.50m)
Gross wing area	774.2sq ft (72sq m)
Gross weight	79,365lb (36,000kg)
Powerplant	Super-ATAR 18,675lb (83kN) at 26,250ft (8,000m)
Maximum speed/Height	Mach 2
Armament	2,204lb (1,000kg) of stores

SNCASO SO 4062	
Status	project
Span	34ft 5in (10.49m)
Length	57ft 7.5in (17.56m)
Gross wing area	430.1sq ft (40sq m)
Gross weight	?
Powerplant	two Super-ATAR 14,175lb (63kN) at 26,250ft (8,000m)
Maximum speed/Height	Mach 2
Armament	-

version and the fourth a single-seat fighter. SNCASO was able to announce publicly: '*After the Vautour, the company is now building the prototype of a twin-jet aircraft to tackle the heat barrier. With an important autonomy, the latest radar equipment, it will be a strike fighter, and like its forerunner independent of any heavy support infrastructure. With the ability to carry a powerful atomic weapon, it could become a redoubtable offensive weapon.*' In fact, only the construction of the first two airframes was started and neither of these was flown because the defence budget had in the meantime swung away from the attack/heavy interceptor category towards pure bomber types.

One aspect of this came during the design process. SNCASO had been reluctant to add vortex cones at the mouth of the air intakes, arguing they were not needed at the flight speeds expected when using this aircraft. When SNCASO finally accepted the need to add these, it requested a huge payment to fit them on the already well advanced -01 prototype. This was a bad move at a time when the *Armée de l'Air* was cutting its funding on many development aircraft, and it contributed to the cancellation of the whole programme in October 1957.

However, SNCASO had faith in its design and tried hard to save the project, which by this time was well advanced. It tried to sell the aircraft to the Navy (the *Marine Nationale*) as the SO 4060M, a navalised version featuring the addition of an arrestor hook, a folding nose and tail wheel (the latter a protective measure for landings made at too high an angle). This single-seat naval fighter-bomber would have carried a missile or a large nuclear store semi-recessed under the fuselage. However, it was not possible to use the new ATAR 9 engine in the 4060-01 airframe, so a redesign based on the second prototype was proposed as the SO 4062. Sadly for SNCASO, all of this effort failed to generate much interest from the *Marine Nationale*.

Let us not forget the third prototype. This was submitted to the 1956 *Armée de l'Air* bomber competition as the SO 4060B and would have been quite similar to its fighter brothers except for the nose, which had been redesigned to take a bombardier's position just behind the radome; however, in general appearance the aircraft still looked like a single-seater. The bombing equipment would have been a 'Derveaux sight' which mated a Norden-type optical sight with millimetre-wave radar. However, this equipment proved difficult to design and in addition was not really needed if the load was a single nuclear bomb. Therefore, the aircraft was redesigned with a tandem cockpit similar to the heavy fighters and carried a single bomb slightly recessed under the fuselage. The engines would have been ATAR 9s, but this aircraft fell short of the range requirements and no SO 4060B prototype was to be ordered; neither was a slightly larger machine, which was to have been powered by an improved version of the ATAR 9.

In 1958, after the choice of the Dassault proposal had been made known, and after SNCASO and SNCASE had merged to form Sud Aviation, the company tried to sell an even bigger version to be powered by two of the new 18,000lb (80kN) Super ATAR engines. The project was named the SO 4061 and offered a range of 1,243 miles (2,000km), but once again it was not pursued. Jean Cabrière, busy at Dassault on the Mirage IV during this period, claimed '*secrecy on the atomic bomber carrier was very strict at that time and we* [at Dassault] *were not aware of* [SNCASO work]'.

Undaunted, Sud Aviation continued to develop unmanned versions of its base airframe, as it had done with the Vautour. These machines would have been remote-controlled on the first leg of their flight path, then control would have shifted to an inertial platform with two automated sextants. Basing the aircraft's control on terrain recognition was at one stage also investigated, and all of these unmanned studies were carried out between 1957 and 1958.

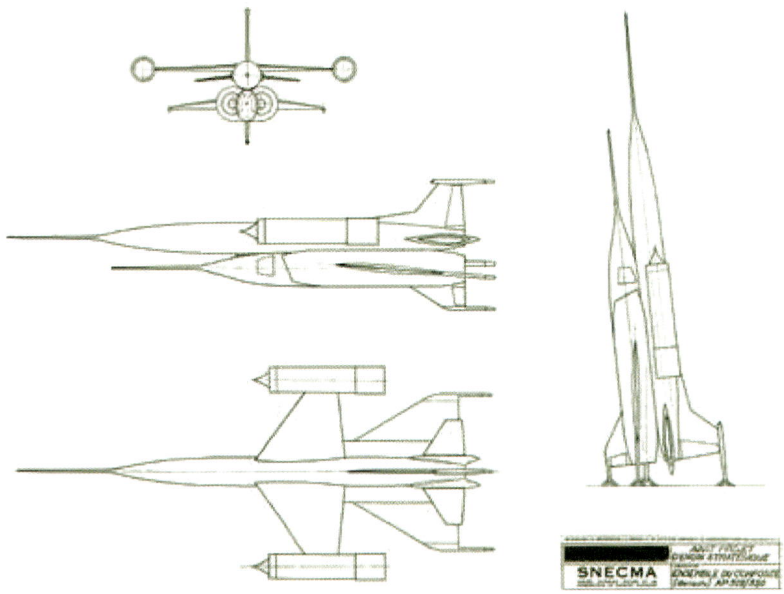

ABOVE The combination of SNECMA's AP 508 and AP 550 was intended to operate as a long-range strategic missile taking off vertically on the back of a manned carrier aircraft. *Safran, GDA - Espace Patrimoine, Fonds SNECMA*

An Early Outsider
SNECMA AP 508/AP 550/AP 551

This two-stage design was created by Gerhard Eggers, Raoul Dumez and Gunther Ernst, and was contemporary to the Coléoptère (1956) (see Volume 1). The manned AP 508, powered by two ATAR engines of an undisclosed type, was to serve as a booster for the AP 550 strategic missile. A piloted version named AP 551 was derived from the original missile but it seems to have been a purely experimental machine. There does not appear to be room for a camera bay in this design.

SNECMA AP 508	
Status	booster (project)
Span	17ft 1in (5.20m)
Length	32ft 2in (9.80m)
Gross wing area	?
Gross weight	?
Powerplant	ATAR (type unspecified)
Maximum speed/Height	?
Armament	none

SNECMA AP 550	
Status	missile
Span	17ft 1in (5.20m) without engines
Length	?
Gross wing area	?
Gross weight	?
Powerplant	two ramjets
Maximum speed/Height	?
Armament	warhead

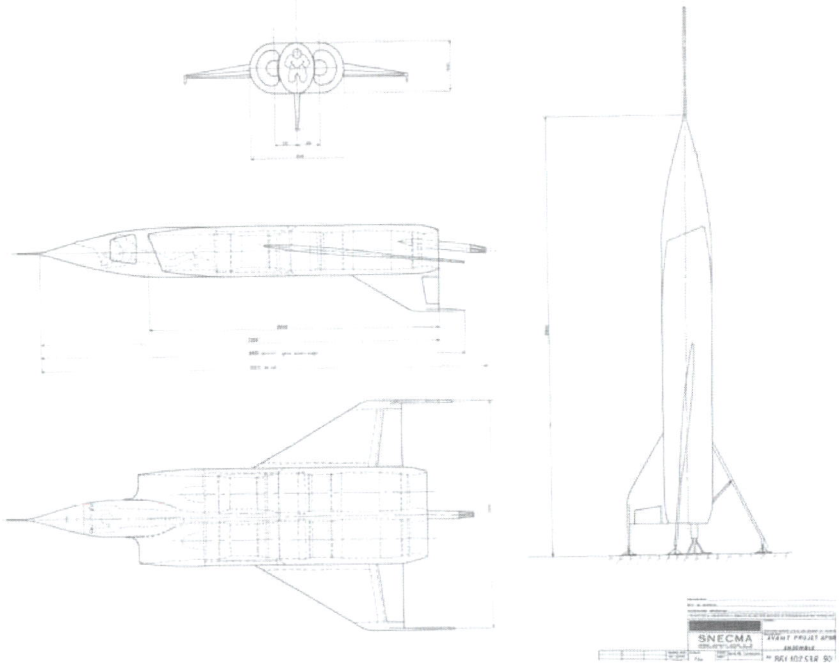

LEFT The manned AP 508 carrier was positioned vertically on the ground while the combined AP 508 and AP 550 had been angled slightly from the vertical to ensure that the engine thrust from both aircraft passed through the ensemble's centre-of-gravity. *Safran, GDA - Espace Patrimoine, Fonds SNECMA*

BELOW The AP 551 was a manned long-range reconnaissance aircraft derived from the AP 550 missile. *Safran, GDA - Espace Patrimoine, Fonds SNECMA*

BOTTOM LEFT & RIGHT Two views of a model of the AP 508/AP 550 combination. In the first picture the two types are shown together on the ground while in the second the AP 550 has separated from the AP 508 and flies alone. *Safran, GDA - Espace Patrimoine, Fonds SNECMA*

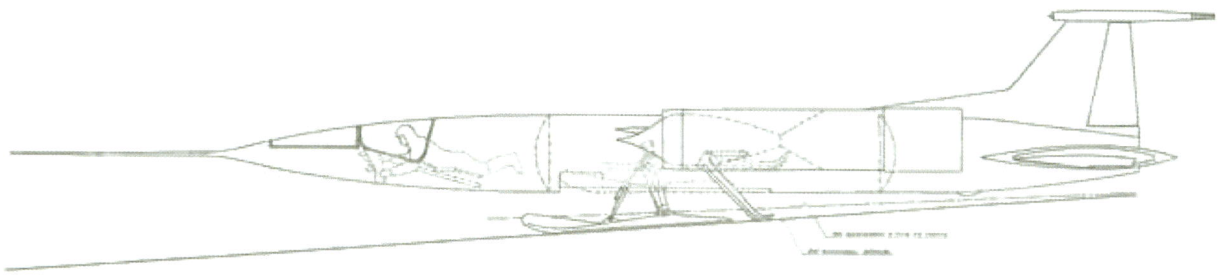

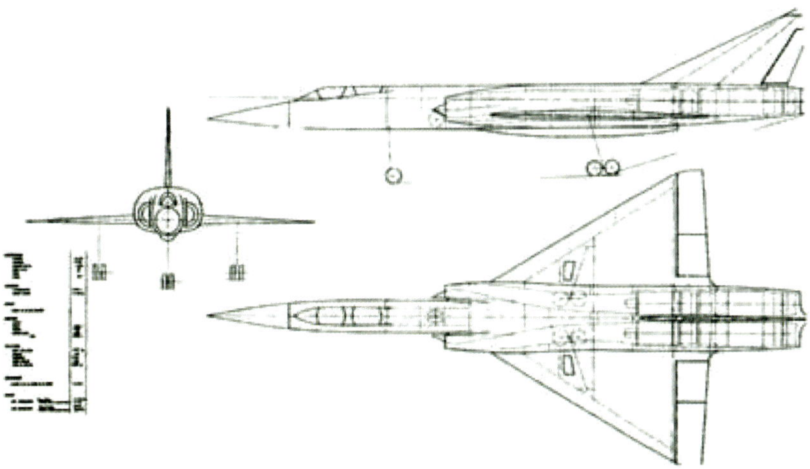

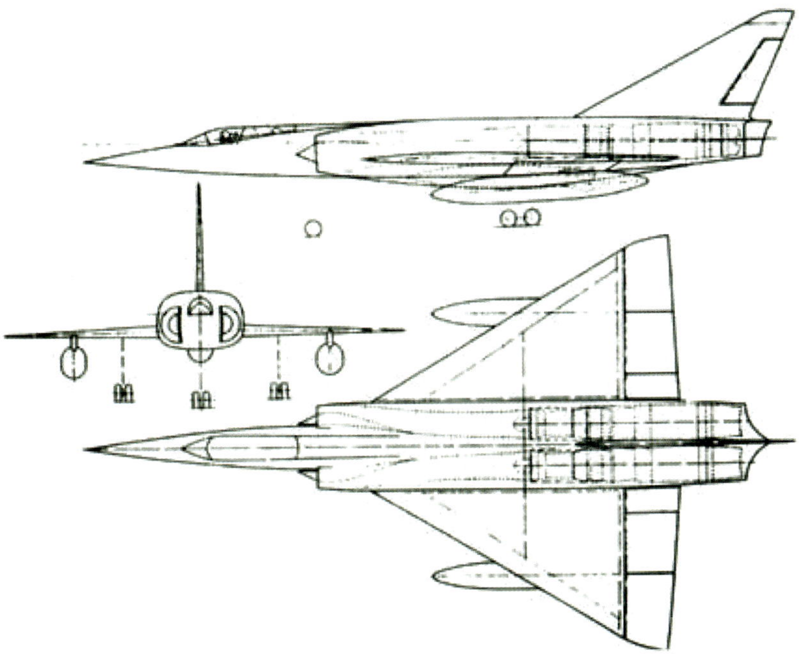

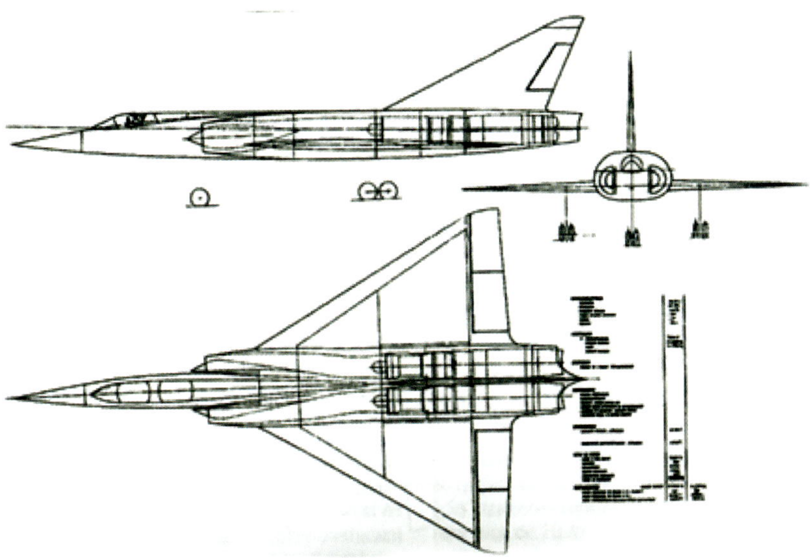

Dassault Projects

In 1953 Dassault was reported to be working on a three-engined bomber called the MD 900, but at the time it was the company's fighter designs that received by far the most attention. Initially Dassault had studied various projects for heavy interceptors that, since they were seen as the successors to the Mirage III then in development (Volume I), were labelled Mirage IV.

At that time the STAé had not made known that it was looking for a delivery system for the future nuclear bomb, but when the *Armée de l'Air* issued its call for proposals the Dassault team selected the largest of these studies, the Mirage IVC, a twin-engined delta-winged fighter-bomber, for its submission. However, this design was too small to fit and fill the demands and in the following month a larger version was proposed. On 28 November 1956 a single prototype of this new design was ordered, which was made official in April 1957 with a full contract. Jean Cabrière noted that, following a meeting in November in which the new bomber was ordered: *'I was happy with this information which would enable us to advance toward*

Dassault Mirage IV C 1956

Status	project
Span	38ft 6.5in (11.75m)
Length	68ft 1i (20.75m)
Gross wing area	752.7sq ft (70sq m)
Gross weight	52,469lb (23,800kg)
Powerplant	two ATAR 9 13,050lb (58kN)
Maximum speed/Height	Mach 2
Armament	2,205lb (1,000kg) or one nuclear bomb

TOP LEFT An early projected variant of the Mirage IV with two ATAR 9C. *Dassault archives*

MIDDLE LEFT As a bomber the Mirage IV acquired a second crew member. *Dassault Aviation*

BOTTOM LEFT The next step in the evolution was this 'bombardier léger' (light bomber) study. *Dassault Aviation*

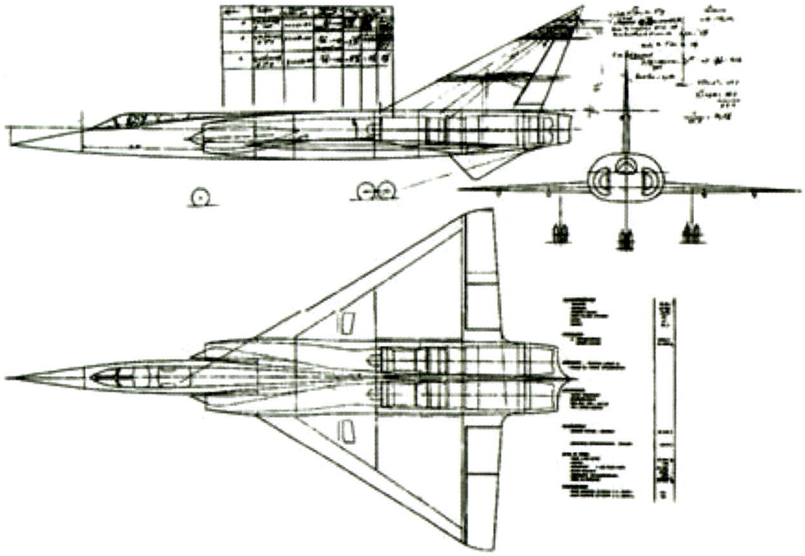

ABOVE **The same drawing but modified by Marcel Dassault himself to show the reduced height of the tail fin.** *Dassault Aviation*

the construction of an operational aircraft, and most importantly to see us winning two contracts [Mirage III fighter and Mirage IV bomber] *instead of one. But Marcel Dassault was more sombre, he certainly regretted the great twin-engined fighter which, he was certain, would have largely surpassed the American* [F-4 Phantom], *and he expected the political turmoil that would be generated by the programme for the future French A-bomb.*' The contract was at this stage kept vague in regard to the definition of the weapon to be carried – either 2,205lb or 6,614lb (1,000kg or 3,000kg) in weight and to be delivered over a range of 1,865 or 1,243 miles (3,000km or 2,000km).

The Mirage IV

The Mirage IV prototype -01 made its maiden flight on 17 June 1959 in the hands of test pilot Roland Glavany. On its third flight it participated in the air display at that year's Paris Air Show and at that time there was speculation that the Mirage IVA was only a flying mock-up for a much larger Mach 3.0 machine. This was claimed by *RAF Flying Review* magazine, which wrote: '*The Mirage IVA was originally to have been powered by the highly secret SNECMA Super ATAR which has been designed for operating in the vicinity of Mach 3.0 and to carry a French atomic bomb. However, the Super ATAR engine is still some way off and the present atomic bomb is too cumbersome to be carried by the Mirage IVA. The present machine will, therefore, be employed as a development vehicle for a larger Mach 3.0 bomber of the same basic configuration.*' If the Mirage IV-01 was really only an experimental aircraft destined to explore the problems encountered by the continuous operation of an aircraft at speeds around Mach 2 then it should have been labelled -001, in the same way the Dassault Balzac prototype had been for the equivalent VTOL fighter programme.

The Mirage IV had a delta wing that was quite similar to the Mirage III fighter but it was larger and housed both fuel tanks and landing gear. The fuselage, from the rear to the front, housed the two ATAR 9 turbojets, the main fuel tanks, the compartment for two crew seated in tandem and an elongated nose cone. In fact, this long nose caused trouble during flight testing, which forced the designers to enlarge the vertical fin. But as the latter grew in size it also grew in height and that brought fears of flutter. Dassault, ONERA and STAé argued about this problem until Marcel Dassault himself decided to cut it down by 2ft 3.5in (0.70m); at the same time the rudder

LEFT **A picturesque photograph of the Mirage IV prototype 01.** *Dassault Aviation*

actuator arm was moved up to the middle section of the rudder instead of its original base position. An unusual element of the Mirage IV-01 story was its tyres. Jean Cabrière remembered: '*We were not able to find either in France or abroad tyres suitable for the expected take-off speeds at full weight, which it reached at 200 knots* [371km/h]; *therefore, before receiving tyres specially created for it, the Mirage IV-01 did its first flights wearing tyres designed for the American* [Navaho] *missile*.' This was the only foreign element in the aircraft except for the hydraulic pumps, which also had to be procured from the USA. The military avionics, designated *Système de Navigation et de Bombardement* (SNB), or Bombing and Navigation System, were in some ways more difficult to define than the airframe. According to Jean Cabrière: '*The SNB was the critical path of the whole programme*.' Originally it had been planned to use the Derveaux sighting device, combining an optical sight and radar as described above, but this proved difficult to design and was eventually dropped. SNCASO, after the trouble it had with the Derveaux equipment (experienced first-hand with the Vautour and SO 4060), offered another system that made use of television for ground-following and astronomical navigation through the use of an early electronic computer. This very interesting proposal generated a lot of attention and appeared very promising, but it was also very complex and costly, and it fell out of favour rather quickly.

The Dassault proposal remained alone. It also relied heavily on its radars and early computers, but at least these were existing pieces of equipment that did not require separate development efforts. Dassault even proposed to buy and adapt the systems installed on the American Republic F-105 (which at the time was of considerable interest to the *Armée de l'Air*). In the end, the Mirage IV system used a Doppler radar and associated computer made by Marconi and a ground-mapping radar converted from the equipment used on the Breguet Alizé anti-submarine aircraft (see Chapter Eleven). This last item resulted in a very noticeable saucer-shaped radome placed underneath the Mirage IV's centre fuselage. At some point, to provide the aircraft with a low-level penetration capability, the installation of a Cyrano (interception) radar was considered to go under the nose radome. An additional problem associated with the avionics was that none of it was rated for operation at temperatures above 70°C, so each item had to be tested individually dependent on its location in the airframe! Since there was no optical sight in front of the pilot, the windshield could be made as a 'Vee' which was expected to improve the aerodynamics.

On 20 February 1960 the first Mirage IVA prototype flew to Istres from Melun Villaroche in just eighteen minutes and thirty seconds, the whole trip being made at a speed of Mach 1.8. Then, in September of that year, the new aircraft claimed two closed circuit speed records – figures of 1,225mph (1,971km/h) over 311 miles (500km) and 1,132mph (1,822km/h) over 622 miles (1,000km). In view of these high speeds, it is notable that the Mirage IV

BELOW **A version was also investigated powered by two Rolls-Royce RB 142 turbojets.** *Dassault Aviation*

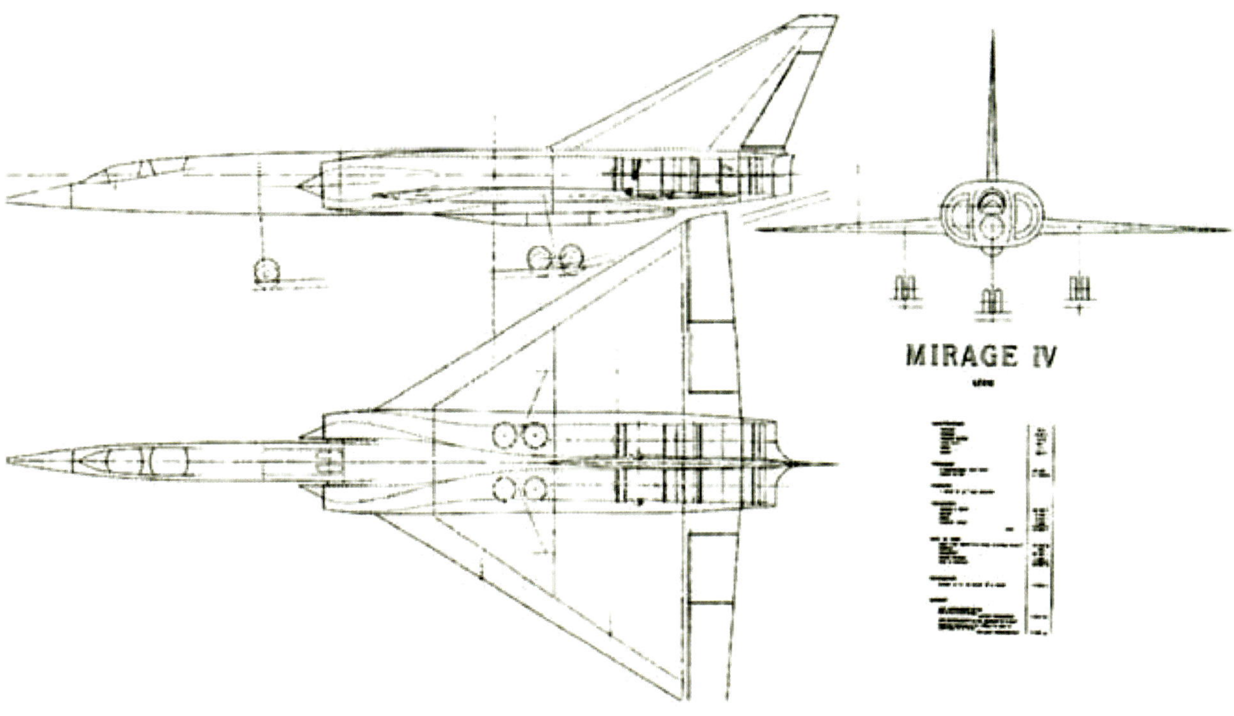

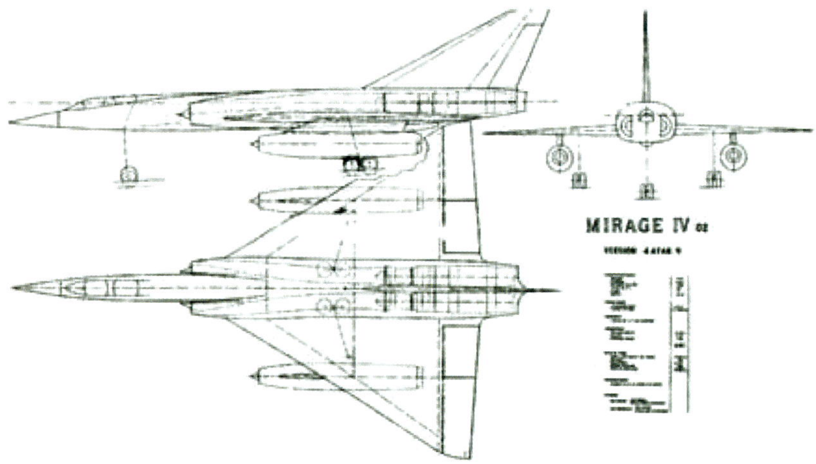

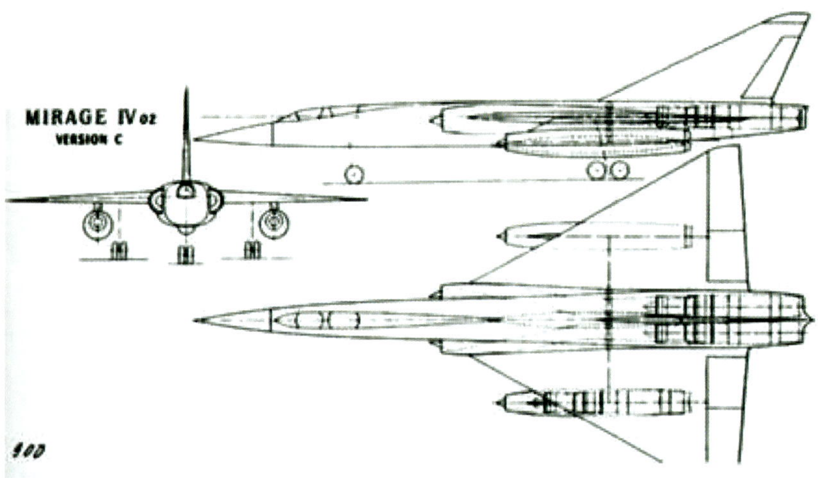

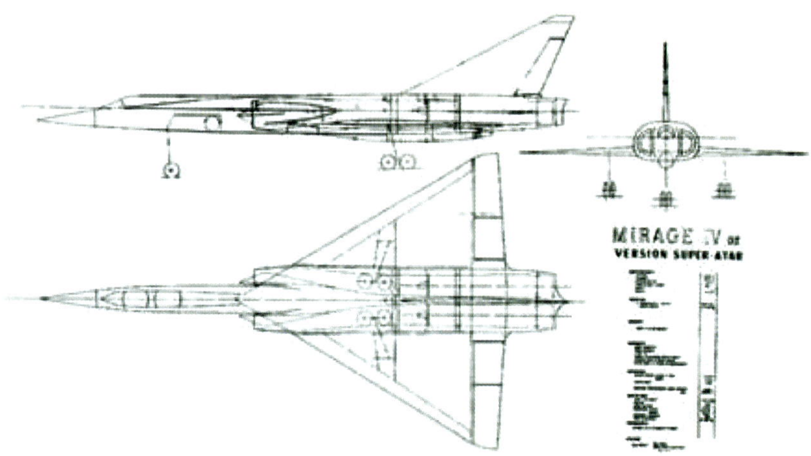

LEFT Versions of the Mirage IV were drawn with four ATAR engines, two of which were housed in underwing pods. This is an early form, and note the high tail in the front on view. *Dassault Aviation*

MIDDLE A later version with short tail and, unusually for a Mirage, near shoulder wings. *Dassault Aviation*

BOTTOM An alternative option was to use two Super ATAR units instead of four ATAR 9s. *Dassault Aviation*

was built in conventional aluminium alloys, steel and titanium being employed just in the very hot areas around the turbojets. The drawback of this structure was that the outer skin temperature was limited to 120°C (a red light came on in the cockpit to warn the pilot if he had exceeded this figure).

Unfortunately, prototype 01 crashed on 13 February 1963 but, however good the aircraft had proved to be, it was obvious that it could not fulfil all of the requirements, and in particular the requested range limits. It was not that the Dassault team had not tried. Beginning with the Mirage IVC fighter, it had stretched the fuselage by 8ft 2.5in (2.5m) and enlarged the wing again to 752.7sq ft (70sq m). The wing thickness was reduced to 3.5%, making it the thinnest ever used for such a large aircraft, and the nuclear bomb had been semi-faired into the body.

The wing was very low on the Mirage IV and the fuselage belly was mated into the wing, but from an aerodynamic point of view this was seen as not particularly good. So with the bomb bulging out of the fuselage just where the wing was, Dassault hoped that the nuclear bomb fairing would act as an area rule bulge and actually improve the aerodynamics, and that this improved aerodynamics performance would compensate for the increased drag).

Finally, the pilot could control which fuel tanks were to be used first, and in doing so he could then alter the pitch of the aircraft and hence reduce its supersonic drag. While the Mirage IV-01 was about twice the size of the Mirage III, it carried three times as much fuel! But this was not sufficient: STAé required that the range should be doubled while keeping the other mission parameters the same.

Consequently, Dassault envisioned an even bigger version called the Mirage IVB and this was to be fitted with either two 22,950lb (102kN) thrust Bristol Olympus 14R engines,

Dassault Mirage IV-01

Status	prototype
Span	36ft 7.5in (11.16m)
Length	65ft 3.5in (19.90m)
Gross wing area	752.7sq ft (70sq m)
Gross weight	57,914lb (26,270kg)
Powerplant	two ATAR 9 13,050lb (58kN)
Maximum speed/Height	Mach 2.1 (cruise Mach 1.7 at 16,500 (54,135)
Armament	none

Mirage IV B 'Super ATAR'

Status	project
Span	43ft 7.5in (13.30m)
Length	75ft 5.5in (23.00m)
Gross wing area	967.7sq ft (90sq m)
Gross weight	69,444lb (31,500kg)
Powerplant	two Super-ATAR 19,800lb (88kN)
Maximum speed/Height	Mach 2+
Armament	2,205lb (1,000kg) or one nuclear bomb

Mirage IV V 'P & W'

Status	project
Span	52ft 6in (16.00m)
Length	91ft 2.5in (27.80m)
Gross wing area	1,397.8sq ft (130sq m)
Gross weight	123,457lb (56,000kg)
Powerplant	two J75 31,500lb (140kN)
Maximum speed/Height	Mach 2.2
Armament	2,205lb (1,000kg) or one nuclear bomb

two 22,500lb (100kN) Rolls-Royce RB142Rs, two Canadian Orenda Iroquois 2 giving 26,100lb (116kN) thrust with reheat, or two 31,950lb (142kN) Pratt & Whitney J75s. Politically, however, none of those solutions would be satisfactory because it was just not acceptable to power the carrier aircraft for the French nuclear bomb with foreign engines. So Dassault went back to the drawing board with the goal of using French turbojets.

The first 'all-French' option would have been to use four ATAR 9 turbojets and versions were designed with two of the engines in pods. However, this affected the aerodynamics of the aircraft very considerably and would have required a specific prototype, which resulted in the idea being dropped. Jean Cabrière explained how '*it led to a configuration too different from the Mirage IV-01 and we would have lost the benefit of the experience on this aircraft*'. The second 'all-French' option would have been to use two Super ATARs, which were then being developed, but this would have meant more delays and more cost, and the Super ATAR-powered aircraft was expected to have a lower performance than the foreign-engined versions. In the end, the J75 version was selected with SNECMA expected to produce the engine under licence.

Three Mirage IVB prototypes were ordered in March 1959 while SNECMA bought ten Pratt & Whitney J75 engines and acquired the licence rights. It was planned to produce four variants of the base airframe, the IVB (*Bombardier* – the basic bomber), IVE (*Électronique* – an ECM aircraft for use both for electronic intelligence gathering and counter-measures), an unnamed a tanker variant, and the IVR or IVP (Reconnaissance or Photo, to operate as a strategic reconnaissance aircraft), but the three-seat IVE was soon dropped in view of the expected cost of its equipment (Note: unusually the suffix E was employed here for the electronic warfare type, when more usually in France the E was used for '*Ecole*' – training). To begin with it was planned to buy eighty Mirage IVs, of which fifty-three would be of the B type while twenty-seven would be IVEs. The first thirty-two machines were expected to be flying by the first half of 1965, a very tight schedule.

Work began immediately at Dassault on the design and construction of a new prototype and by August 1959 a mock-up had been built and the first metal was cut. However, on 3 September the *Armée de l'Air*, realising the cost of those large aircraft was way beyond what it could afford, pulled the plug on the Mirage IVB while at the same time ordering Dassault to go back to the drawing board to try and come up with a smaller aeroplane. A reduction in cost for the equipment was also required. Dassault had no option but to try to improve on the earlier designs based directly on the short-legged 01 prototype – the Mirage IVA. In March 1960 a new order was placed, once again for three prototypes but here labelled A-02 to A-04, and by the mid-1960s they had been joined by contracts for sixty-two series aeroplanes. The electronic warfare and tanker versions were both abandoned, but variants for the tactical strike role were toyed with for several months.

It should be noted that the Mirage IV was ordered by the French government against strong opposition from the *deputés* (the French National Assembly). During the presentation to the *Assemblée Nationale* of the planned law relating to military spending, MP M. Frederic-Dupont claimed that: '*It is questionable to build 50 Mirage IV which are to cost 100 billion* [francs] *and it will not satisfy many of the members of the National Defence Commission. That being said, the Marine Nationale … will, with the Etendard, we have been told, be able by 1964 to carry an atomic bomb 1,500km (932 miles) away from its aircraft carrier. This would give us an interim weapon and a capability nearly as good as the Mirage IV, and at a much reduced cost.*' His colleague, MP Marc Lauriol, later added: '*Because of its performance and its vulnerability the Mirage IV will not be up to task. About its performance, we will stick to what its manufacturer says. The results of this is that the Mirage has exactly the endurance to go to the target and return home plus one kilometre at a speed which is, in our hypothesis* [of a war between nuclear armed nations] *comparable to that of a snail, a speed which will expose it to all the interceptors launched against it by the enemy.*'[1]

Working from the original Mirage IV-01 airframe, the Dassault

1 Archives of the *Assemblée Nationale*.

team incorporated the following modifications:

(i). The replacement of the original engines by ATAR 9Ds, which gave a 15% increase in thrust at height. This led also to a modification of the rear fuselage.
(ii). An increase in the overall size of the airframe: the wing surface was enlarged by 86sq ft (8sq m) while the fuselage was stretched by 5ft 7in (1.70m) in front of the wing, which permitted an increase in the fuel capacity of 30%.
(iii). The vertical tail surface, while outwardly identical to the truncated tail of prototype 01, was redesigned to house an extra fuel tank.
(iv). The nose cone now housed a 'probe and drogue' in-flight refuelling system.

ABOVE **A trial rocket-assisted take-off is performed with Mirage IV 01.** *Dassault Aviation*

Mirage IVA-02

The first of the new prototypes was first flown by René Bigand on 12 October 1961. It was used for aerodynamic testing in all configurations (with and without the bomb under the fuselage and/or drop tanks under the wings) and also participated in refuelling experiments.

Mirage IV A	
Status	production
Span	38ft 10in (11.84m)
Length	77ft 1in (23.50m)
Gross wing area	838.7sq ft (78sq m)
Gross weight	72,751lb (33,000kg)
Powerplant	two ATAR 9K 13,050lb (58kN)
Maximum speed/Height	Mach 2+
Armament	2,205lb (1,000kg) or one nuclear bomb

Mirage IVA-03

This first flew on 1 June 1962 and was used mostly to test the avionics (the 'SNB'). Future famous aviation historian Jean Cuny was recruited specifically for this task.

Mirage IVA-04

The third prototype first flew on 23 January 1963 fitted with the improved ATAR 9K engine. It was used for performing take-offs boosted by the use of JATO rockets (six units of 1,000lb/4.4kN thrust each fixed under each wing).

BELOW **Three-view drawing of the definitive Mirage IVA.** *Author's collection/Dassault document*

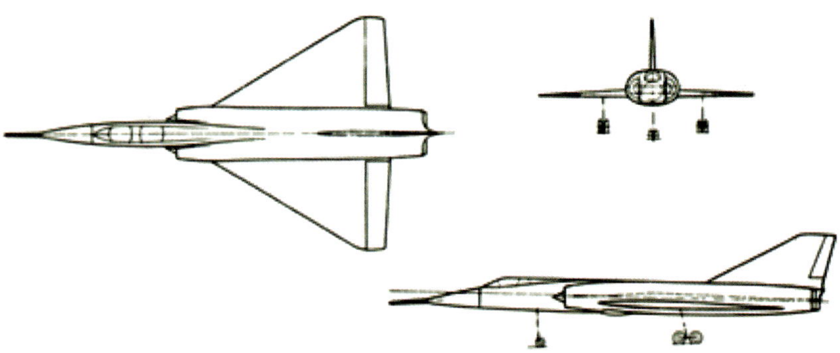

Mirage IVR

This variant was offered to the export market without any nuclear capability after many countries had shown an interest in the Mach 2 bomber. Great Britain was the first country to look closely at Dassault's aircraft; in fact as early as 1959 Air Marshall Kyle, head of the Operational Requirement (OR) division of the RAF, came to Paris to learn about the Mirage IV. In January 1963 *RAF Flying Review* reported a talk that had taken place the previous October between Peter Thorneycroft, the then British Secretary of State for Defence, and Pierre Messmer, the French Ministry of Defence regarding '*the formation of a joint Anglo-French nuclear bombing force*'. Since one cannot imagine Avro Vulcans in the *Armée de l'Air*, an 'RAF Mirage' must have been the subject of discussion!

This interest continued until 1965, when the British Aircraft Corporation (BAC) teamed with Dassault to offer a Rolls-Royce Spey-engined version of the Mirage IV to the RAF. This aircraft would have been built, in part, in Great Britain: BAC would have produced the front and rear fuselages while the engines would, obviously, have been provided by Rolls-Royce. There was also talk of using the avionics developed for the BAC TSR.2 strike aircraft, which was considered by the RAF to be more advanced than the original French SNB. From the outside the aircraft would have been distinguished from its French counterpart by a different rear fuselage and enlarged air intakes. Cost estimates were based on the production of 108 aircraft (another source quoted £2 million per aircraft if seventy-five airframes were ordered). An RAF evaluation team was sent to France and was very impressed by the performance of the prototypes, one RAF pilot claiming: *'I flew more time at Mach 2 in this aircraft than during my whole time on the Lightning in the RAF.'* At that year's Paris Air Show, Marcel Dassault told *RAF Flying Review* that: *'The installation of the Spey 25R, conferring a substantial performance improvement on the aircraft, would only require some redesign of the rear fuselage, and should an RAF order materialise then BAC-built fuselages would be married with French built wings and tail surfaces.'* In fact, the major modifications (apart from the engines) would have been a fuselage stretched by 1ft 11.5in (0.60m) and deepened by 2.99in (76mm), enlarged air intakes and new avionics based on those designed for the British F-4K Phantom and the Hawker Siddeley Kestrel (the future Harrier). The Dassault Antilope terrain-following and ground mapping radar would have been retained and it was estimated that the performance would have been equal to that of TSR.2 at low altitude; at high altitude the Mirage IV Spey would have reached Mach 2.2 and have a 30% increase in range over the TSR.2. The project was presented to the British Ministry of Aviation and a delegate of the Ministry of Defence on 25 July 1965. In early 1966 it was planned, rather optimistically in the author's view, to have the first prototype flying by 1967 and to begin deliveries to the RAF in 1969. However, all of these efforts were cut short when the British Government decided against the Spey Mirage in early 1966. (Note: The TSR.2 was cancelled in 1965 by the new British Government, which had been elected the previous year.)

From 1959 Australia showed some interest and then in 1961 contracted for the delivery of twelve Mirage IV Avon-powered bombers. However, by 1962 the order had been expanded to include a long-range reconnaissance variant to which Dassault replied with a version powered by the Pratt & Whitney TF106. The Australians, while considering the only aircraft comparable to the Mirage IV was the TSR.2, would have liked to see their missile-carrying version (intended to carry four AS-30 missiles) also ordered by the *Armée de l'Air*, but this was not to be. In 1963 Australia came out in favour of the standard (non-nuclear) Mirage IVA since it had much in common with the Mirage IIIO that the Australian Air Force had just

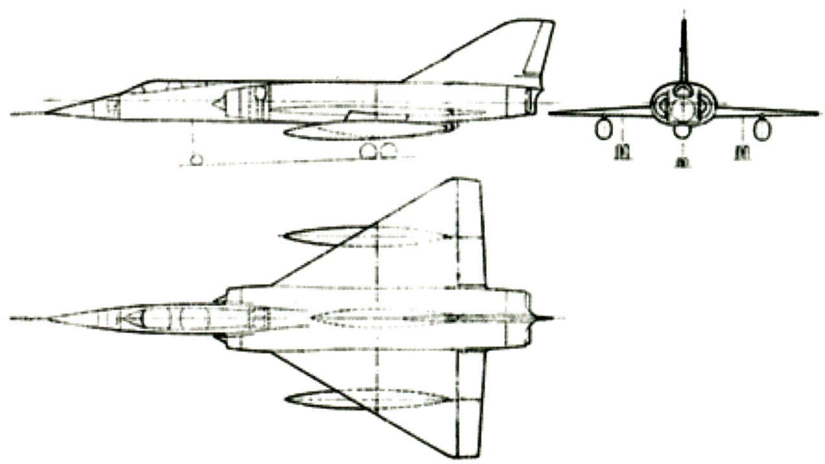

ABOVE A non-nuclear armed version was proposed as the Mirage IVR. *Dassault Aviation*

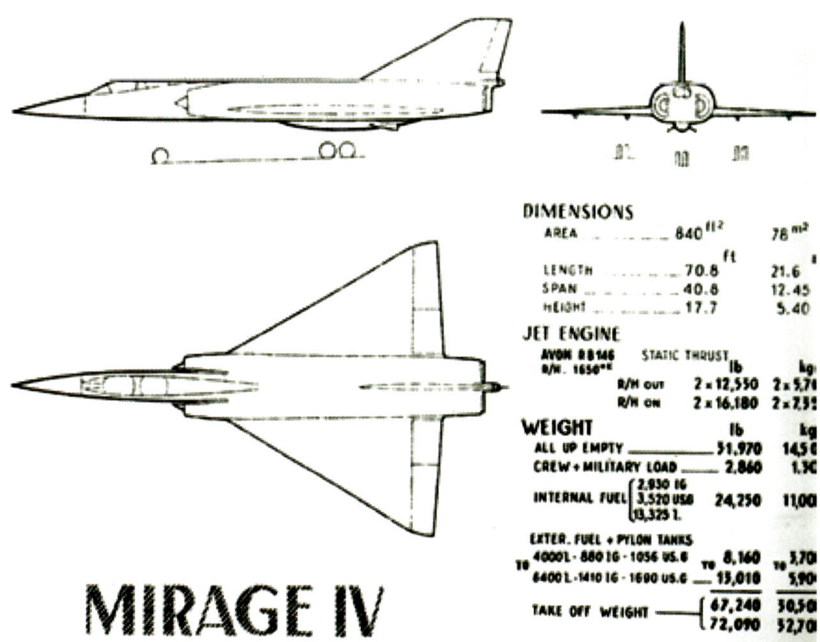

BELOW An export Mirage IV powered by two Rolls-Royce Avon turbojets. *Dassault Aviation*

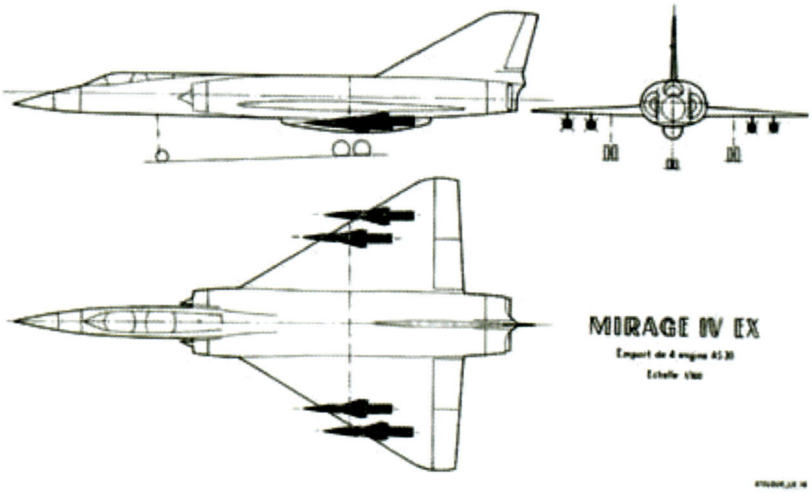

LEFT **Also with an eye on the export market, a variant was fitted out to carry four AS-30 missiles and designated Mirage IVEX.** *Dassault Aviation*

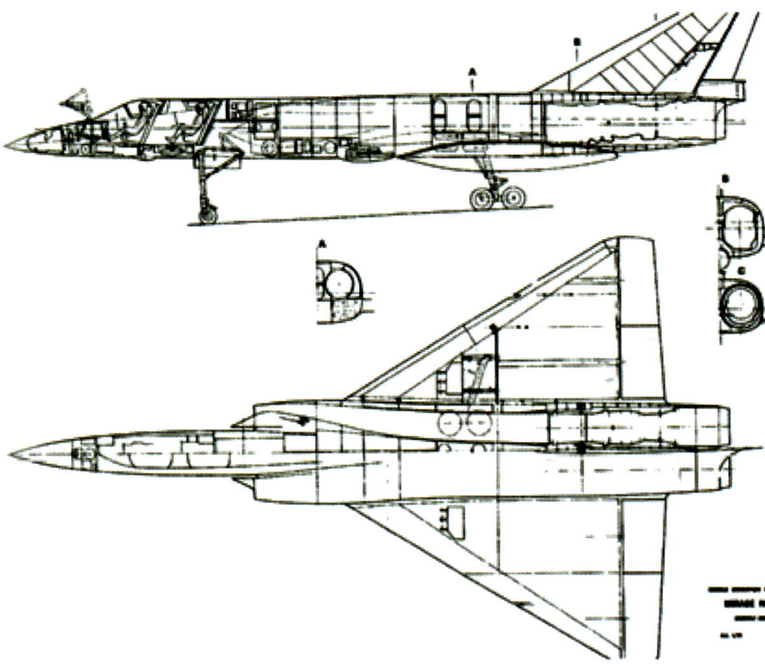

MIDDLE **This illustrates the appearance of the Mirage IV as it was offered to the RAF, the aircraft having been re-engined with two Spey turbojets. The date appears to be November 1963.** *Dassault archives*

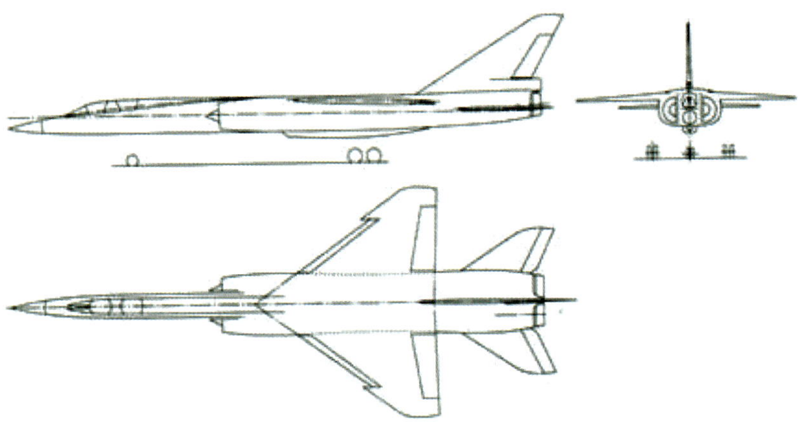

BOTTOM **In parallel with the research on swept wings initiated with the Series F on the Mirage III fighter, a similar programme was undertaken with the Mirage IV. This is the Mirage IVF2 of 1964, which is described in Volume I.** *Dassault Aviation*

ordered. The intention was to acquire twenty-four examples but in the end the order was never confirmed and the American F-111 was bought instead.

In 1963 the Luftwaffe toyed with the idea of buying the Mirage IVR powered by General Electric J79 engines. The plan was to licence-produce the aircraft locally if that would prove feasible economically, but nothing came of this. On 23 July 1964 Israel ordered fifteen Mirage IVRJ aircraft fitted out to carry four AS-30s but these were never delivered (alternative sources indicate that Israel did not finalise its order because the aircraft was too large and costly for its needs). Other countries that evaluated the Mirage IV with the object of buying it were South Africa, New Zealand and India.

The Bomb

To ease the development and production of the new aircraft, Dassault was named as the lead subcontractor for the complete weapon system. This in particular involved designing the (in)famous 'A-bomb'. Cabrière explains: '*While the specifically nuclear part was designed by the CEA* [State Commissariat for Nuclear Studies], *from the end of 1959 the weapon division of STAé (which was managing the development of the weapon for the State) contracted Dassault to design the outer casing and the equipment for the unpropelled missile which was to be the bomb.'* This involved the aerodynamic design, the release system, its fuses (time fuse, radar fuse, impact fuse), control system, and nuclear security systems. A special 'top secret' team to do the work was established in the St Cloud design office under Maurice Viel.

For the record, the chronology of French nuclear bomb testing is as follows:

13 February 1960: Gerboise Bleue, Atom A-bomb 65 kilotons (kt);
1961 to 1966: underground tests (with gemstone code names) – 2 July 1966: first test in the Pacific Range 'Aldébaran' 28kt; 24 August 1968: first hydrogen H-bomb 'Canopus' 2 megatons (Mt).

The nuclear weapons that became operational were:

- ANM 11 (Arme Nucléaire Mirage or Nuclear Weapon for the Mirage): 1964-65, nominal yield 50kt;
- ANM 21: 1965-66, nominal yield 70kt.
- ANM 22: same as ANM 21 but with an added brake parachute for 'Low Altitude Drop Delivery' 1967-88, nominal yield 70kt.
- AN-52: 1973-91, nominal yield 25kt (this was not used on the Mirage IV but on the Mirage IIIE, Jaguar and Etendard).
- ASMP (Air Sol Moyenne Portée or Air to Ground, middle range – a cruise missile with a nuclear warhead): 1986-2010 (which takes it outside the range of this book), H-bomb warhead, yield not revealed but estimated to be 300kt.

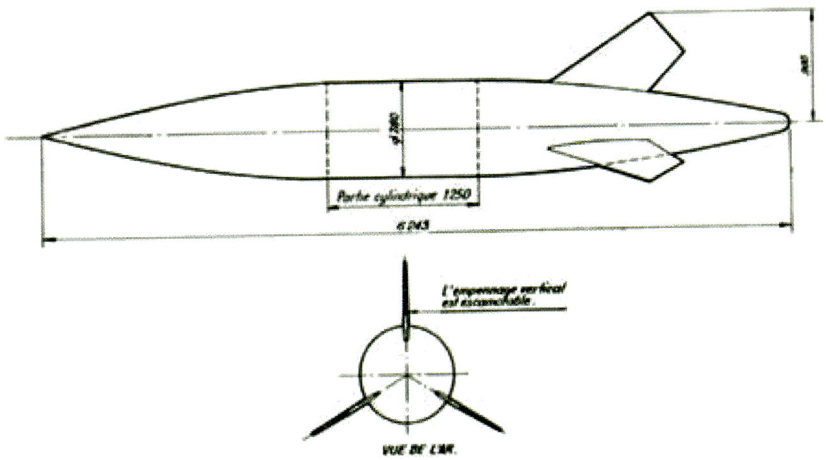

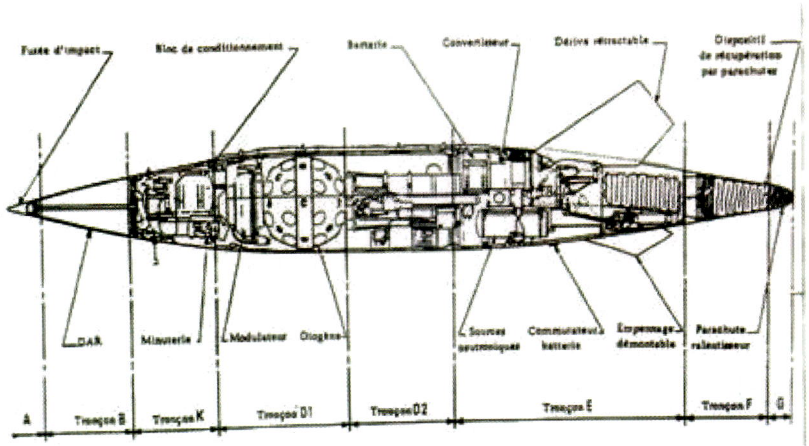

TOP The French 'Arme Spéciale', the A-bomb around which the Mirage IV was designed. *Dassault Aviation*

ABOVE Cutaway drawing of the Arme Nucléaire AN-11 weapon carried beneath a Mirage IV. *Authors' collection*

Later Mirage IV Variants

The first ideas for in-flight refuelling had been to design a specific Mirage IV variant. Later consideration was given to installing a special refuelling belly pod under a Mirage IV or even under a Vautour, but in the end the solution was to buy twelve Boeing C-135F tankers.

Other weapon loads also investigated including using the Mirage IV as a conventional bomber with eight STRIM 882lb (400kg) bombs and fuel tanks under the wings, for strategic reconnaissance by fitting a CT 52 pod equipped with optical cameras, or for electronic warfare using the CT 51 pod. All sixty-two production Mirage IV aircraft were built, the first fifty having been ordered in May 1962 with twelve more added in November 1965. In July 1966 production aircraft N° 9 performed a live drop of an atomic bomb over France's Pacific test area around Mururoa Atoll.

Mirage IVP

During the 1980s eighteen Mirage IVs were reconfigured at AIA Clermont-Ferrand by replacing their SNB with the new SAGEM system and an Iguane panoramic radar made by Thomson. In addition, this variant no longer carried a semi-recessed bomb but instead there was a new ramjet-powered nuclear missile, the ASMP, designed by Aérospatiale and loaded on a deep centerline pylon. The first prototype for what was called the Mirage IVP (P for Penetration) flew on 12 October 1982.

Chapter Four
The Minerve Programme

ABOVE **A desk model of the Dassault Minerve VIB.** *Author's collection / Dassault pictures*

If there was ever a secret 'Black' programme in French aeronautics then Minerve was the one. Even today it is still unknown what 'Minerve' actually stands for, but it may have been an acronym with the 'Mi' standing for 'missile'? Minerva was the Roman goddess of wisdom, medicine, arts, commerce and trade, and also for strategy and war, which makes the name particularly appropriate to a programme aimed at delivering the French nuclear bomb through a combination of a carrier aircraft and a long-range missile fitted with an atomic warhead. Interestingly, the steering committee for the entire French military nuclear weapons programme was called Athena, appropriate since the goddess Athena was in ancient Greek mythology the equivalent to Minerva.

The Minerve Programme

From its beginning in 1959 the Athena Committee established and developed three main weapon classes for the nuclear defence of France:

1. Silo-launched strategic ballistic missiles, eventually fielded at the plateau d'Albion from 1971 to 1997.
2. Submarine-launched strategic ballistic missiles. This project was headed by the 'Coelacanth Committee' and led to the deployment of the *Force Océanique Stratégique* (the Strategic Oceanic Force) of four nuclear-powered submarines carrying sixteen missiles each.
3. The *Forces Aériennes Stratégiques* (Strategic Air Forces) with the Mirage IV. This air component of the *Force de Dissuasion* (Dissuasion Force) was thought to be the easier to develop of the three, but it was realised very quickly that the Mirage IV was somewhat short-legged. Consequently, it was decided that the Mirage IV should have a refuelling capability and American C-135 transport aircraft were ordered fitted with special in-flight equipment that would enable them to act as tankers.[1]

A replacement for the Mirage IV was sought immediately and it seems that designing this new system around a large mother ship aircraft carrying a strategic missile was inspired by an air-to-ground missile then in development in the USA, the Douglas GAM-87 Skybolt. According to *La Force de Dissuasion Française Genèse et Evolution* (*Docavia* N° 26 by Jacques Villain, 1987): '*In February 1962 the possibility was studied of putting into service a force of air-to-ground strategic ballistic missiles launched from the belly*

1 These were ordered in the 1962 budget and delivered in 1964. Note that the French aircraft, although used as tankers, were nominally C-135F transport aircraft, not the KC-135 variant. This may have been done for political reasons since tankers would have obviously been linked to the *Force de Frappe* when transports were not, but these subtleties escaped the Sud engineers, who named them KC-135s.

of an aircraft like the American Skybolt missile which had a range of 1,800km (1,120 miles). *The research on this system was carried out over the next three years. As for the SSBS and MSBS* [SSBS is *Sol-Sol Balistique Stratégique*, ground-to-ground ballistic strategic missile, and MSBS is *Mer-Sol Balistique Stratégique*, submarine-launched ballistic strategic missile] *a* [separate] *steering committee was set up. The research showed that to give to this force sufficient survivability it was necessary to keep a key number of aircraft in the air constantly, so the operating costs were going to be high. Besides, there was an important technical question to be solved regarding the navigation of the mother ship and the guidance of the missile, especially the co-ordination of both just before the launch of the missile. These technical and financial difficulties, coupled with the growing disinterest of the USAF in Skybolt, led to the abandonment of the French programme.*' In fact, the steering committee to supervise the ground-to-ground missile was called the *Comité Athena* and was created on 29 May 1964, while the *Comité Coelacanthe* (created on 21 June 1962) covered the submarine-launched missiles and the *Comité Minerve* was established for the composite aircraft + missile only.

And that is where the certainty about Minerve ends in terms of the programme itself, its goals and its place in the French nuclear weapon programme. All of the material that follows is either reconstructed (the chronology) or comes from manufacturer documentation. Basically what there is here is the manufacturer's view with nothing of the 'customer' side, and even the manufacturer side is certainly incomplete. For example, the information covering the Sud entries is based on articles on the X-series missiles, while the missions (which is the best source available for providing what could be described as a specification) came from a Breguet brochure, and not from an *Armée de l'Air* document.

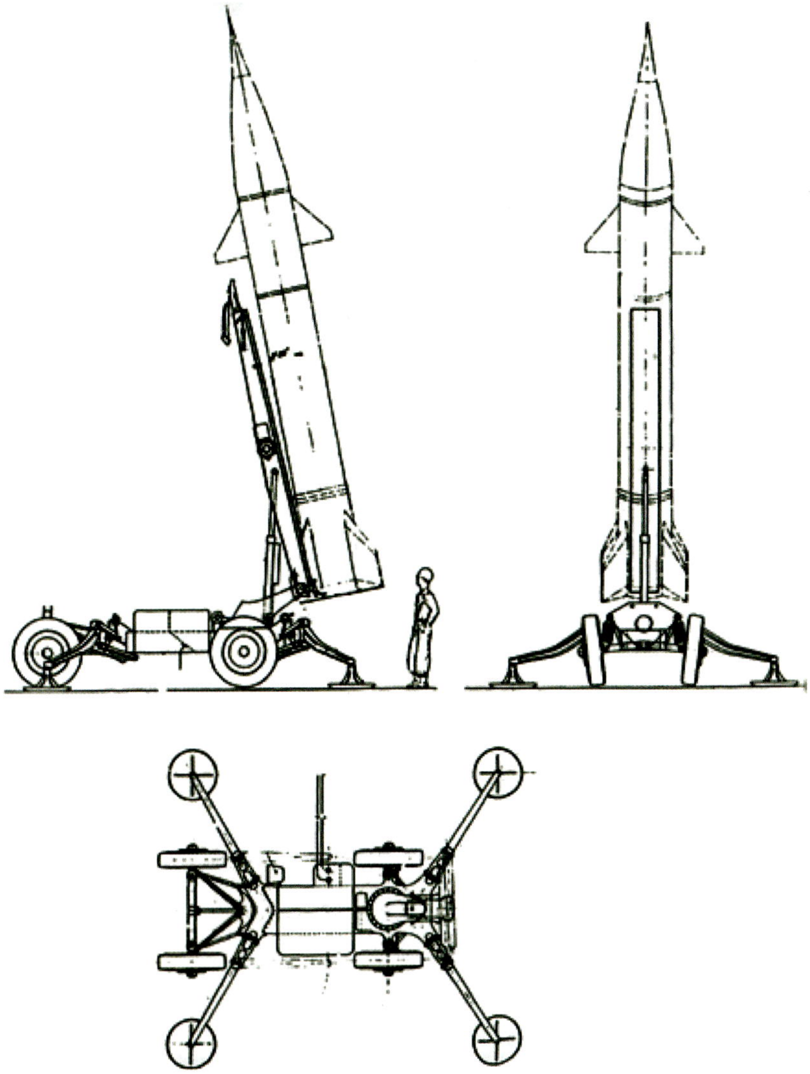

ABOVE The *Casseur* was an early ground-to-ground strategic missile proposal by Sud Aviation. *Sud Aviation*

Chronology

Very little concrete information has emerged on the Minerve project through historical research and even the chronology of the affair is uncertain, with much of it unconfirmed. However, the following is pretty certain:

12 November 1958: The French Defence Council validated the principle of a *Force de Frappe* – a Strike Force.

17 March 1959: the French Government under General de Gaulle decided that '*top priority will be given to the building of the Force de Frappe, to the design of the atomic bomb and to the launch of the production of the Mirage IV which will be its early vehicle, and to the study of the ballistic missile which will be its later vehicle.*'[2]

June 1959: Sud Aviation proposed a ground-to-ground ballistic missile with a range of 62 miles (100km). Its weight was 7,716lb (3,500kg), length 28ft 6.5in (8.70m) and diameter 2ft 7.5in (0.805m) and propulsion was provided through a 'plastolite' block with a six-point star-shaped central

2 Quoted in *La Force de Dissuasion Française Genèse et Evolution* by Jacques Villain, *Docavia* N° 26, 1987.

channel. This missile was named *Casseur* (Buster) and was never built, but its geometry appears to have guided or influenced the design of some of the later Minerve entries.

17 September 1959: Establishment of the *Société pour l'Etude et la Réalisation d'Engins Balistiques* (SEREB). This was to be the company that would undertake the study and construction of ballistic missiles, including the design of the propulsion units for French rocket missiles.

19 October 1960: In a reply to the criticism that the Mirage IV had 'short legs', debates at the *Assemblée Nationale* looked at the Mirage IV and noted '*in a few years a gliding bomb will expand its range by about 350km* (218 miles) *and increase its survivability by avoiding having to fly over the target.*'[3] This suggested that the concept was already in existence at the time, although in a limited form (an unpowered missile), because it was acknowledged by no less than Prime Minister Michel Debré, who said: '[France's] *lag in missile design was more important than in nuclear weapon design.*'[4]

13 February 1960: Using the codename *Gerboise Bleue* (Blue Gerbil) the first French-designed atom bomb was exploded successfully in the Reggane oasis, in the Sahara desert (today Algeria).

1961: The *Direction Technique et Industrielle* (DTI – the Technical and Industrial Directorate of the French Defence Ministry) issued a requirement for a ballistic missile with a range of 186 miles (300km) to be carried under a Mach 2 aircraft.

January 1961: Dassault drew a Mirage IV with a Gamma missile designed in co-operation with Matra.

19 May 1961: Dassault replied to the DTI requirement with the Mirage IV/Gamma II pairing.

3 *Assemblée Nationale* archives.

4 Reported by Joël Le Theule, rapporteur of the *Assemblée Nationale* Defence Committee on 18 October 1960.

1 October 1961: General Stehlin (*Armée de l'Air* Chief of Staff) wrote about mother ship/missile combinations to the French Ministry of Defence, declaring that: '*The Super Caravelle is the best solution on both technical and operational point of views.*'

16 December 1961: Roger Béteille, technical director of SNCASE's Cannes branch, wrote a note offering a high-speed, long-range, terrain-following missile. This would today be called a cruise missile.

April 1962: Dassault designed the Mirage IVC2 carrying the Gamma IV missile.

16 May 1962: A letter of intent (1220 DNA/P) was issued asking industry for proposals. It would appear logical that a Minerve committee would have been set up a short time before the issuing of this specification to validate it and then to review the responses. The few references to Minerve that the author has seen in historical publications (Comaéro, *Docavia* N° 26) suggest that the Minerve Committee was set up in either February or May 1962. The four missions that had to be fulfilled by the submissions were a high-altitude, high-Mach number launch of an aerodynamic flying missile (up to Mach 2, with separation of the missile from the aircraft occurring at Mach 1.5 – this was called Minerve 1a), the same operation but with a ballistic missile (Minerve 1b), carriage of a ballistic missile with separation at low altitude and Mach 1.5 (Minerve 2), and finally an aerodynamic flying missile with a low altitude separation at Mach 0.5 (Minerve 2b).

The missiles themselves were intended to be of two types: either the ground-hugging version proposed by Roger Béteille or a ballistic version designed by Matra. However, Dassault also proposed many other combinations featuring Dassault-designed ballistic missiles. Although Béteille's note may not have been a catalyst in formalising the programme at state level, it is obvious that it had an impact on the call for proposals, probably inducing the committee to include a turbojet-powered ground-hugging missile among the options when the original thinking had been (up to that point) for a rocket-powered ballistic missile only. Yet it does not seem to have impressed the aircraft manufacturers. In particular, Mission 2b (cruise missile launched at low altitude by a high performance platform) does not seem to have appealed to the industry. Breguet, for example, in its Br 1180 brochure, stated bluntly: '*The non ballistic vehicle flying at very low altitude has not been retained for lack of a suitable engine.*' Dassault studied only latterly (in the summer of 1963) the carriage of an X-411S weapon under a Mirage IVA, and in doing so found a lot of difficulties. The views of Nord on the problem have not been found.

The widely differing missions meant that, due to the two separation speeds specified, each aircraft manufacturer had to reply with two separate mother ship proposals. Breguet offered the Br 1190/BR 1191 variant of the Atlantic maritime patrol aircraft (see Chapter Eleven) and also a specifically designed supersonic Br 1180. Nord followed suit with a variant of the C-160 Transall transport (see Chapter Ten) and a supersonic bomber, while Dassault worked on from the Mirage IVA and IVC and, thanks to its links with Boeing, also offered the KC-135 for the low-speed platform (but it does seem dubious that an American-designed and produced aircraft should have been seriously considered for carrying an element of the French *Force de Frappe*).

Returning to the Chronology

10 June 1962: Sud replied to the call for proposals with its X-416 and the X-417 missiles. Their mother ship was to be an adaptation of the

Super Caravelle supersonic transport (known as the TCS for *Transport Civil Supersonique*, the Civilian Supersonic Transport). The TCS design was at this time not yet frozen and so three variants were considered – the base Super Caravelle (which was to evolve into the Concorde), another design with a high shoulder wing and even a VTOL aircraft with ten lift engines. This last variant may have been pushed by Sud's designer Lucien Servanty, who was also in favour of the VTOL option for the pure civilian SST (it seems that this proposal, which was probably much smaller than the TCS and more comparable in size to a Mirage, was also derived from Sud's aborted X-600 VTOL fighter proposal. See Volume I).

June 1962: The Dassault Mirage IV C30 was designed.

July 1962: A brochure for the Nord carrier aircraft was issued.

9 July 1962: The Matra M 600 missile was finalised by Matra.

September 1962: Probable date of issue of the Br 1180 brochure (the document itself is undated).

22 September 1962: Breguet and Matra entered into an agreement regarding the M 600 missile to be carried under the Breguet Minerve proposals.

31 October 1962: Under letter 3724 DTIA/STA/A of this date, the Ministry asked Sud to provide details of its missile designs to Dassault, Nord Aviation and Breguet.

November 1962: Specifications for the X-416A (low-speed separation, with two rocket boosters) and X-416B (high-speed separation) were communicated to Nord and Breguet, but for Dassault a top-level meeting (between Marcel Dassault and General Puget at that time CEO of Sud-Aviation) was required to clear things up before the documents could be passed to the company. Sud at this time saw Dassault as a competitor for the missile component of Minerve, and it had grounds for such a judgement since Dassault had previously worked on large missiles to go underneath its Mirage IV derivatives. It had also worked on some 'Minerve' missiles, including the Minerve E5, which appears to be a winged copy of the X-411 and had a range of 622 miles (1,000km) at Mach 2.

Dassault E5	
Status	project
Diameter	-
Length	-
Gross weight	18,078lb (8,200kg)
Powerplant	turbojet
Maximum speed/Height	Mach 2
Carrier aircraft	-

9 December 1962: Dassault issued a brochure for the Super Mirage II, which is believed to be its first proposal to the Minerve programme.

1962 (undated): Brochure for Dassault Mirage IVC22 Minerve issued.

January 1963: Brochures for the Breguet Br 1190 and 1191 issued.

31 January 1963: The Dassault Minerve IV bomber was designed.

March 1963: Dassault proposed its Minerve VB and VIB designs.

June 1963: The model of the Dassault Minerve VIB was photographed, which suggests that the design was still 'live' at that time.

27 July 1963: Dassault proposed fitting a Sud X-411S missile underneath a Mirage IV.

31 October 1963: Consideration was given to propelling the X-417 missile using an ONERA ramjet.

November 1963: The Minerve programme evolved with the abandonment of specifically designed airframes in favour of variants of known aircraft – the Breguet Br 1190/91, the Dassault Mirage IV, the Sud PSS (*Plate-forme Super Sonique*: the new name adopted for the military variant of the TCS), and the C-160 Transall from Nord Aviation.

1964: The X-422 demonstrator missile was designed.

14 January 1964: Decree 64-46 signed by Président Charles de Gaulle created the '*Forces Aériennes Stratégiques*' equipped with the Mirage IVA fitted with a refuelling probe. It is still not known just when the Minerve programme was finally cancelled, but this move was certainly the final nail in its coffin.

29 January 1967: First flight of the X-422 missile.

In the end, budgetary considerations prevailed and the whole concept of a large bomber to be used as mother ship for a large ballistic or cruise missile was abandoned. France chose to invest in nuclear missile-launching submarines and could not afford an air force programme for the same mission. In 1997 Béteille gave his own view of what killed this programme which, in truth, had been carried successfully to its end. He explained that: '*The two reasons for stopping this project were, probably:*

> *1. political: this weapon was not able to be fired "all around" because, at the time, it was not technically feasible* [and]*, at the top level of the State, it was required that dissuasion could be aimed toward any target, not just to the East or to the South;*
> *2. from a financial and industrial point of view, priority of the available funding must be allocated to the ballistic missiles which had already been selected.*'[5]

Minerve is one of the few French programmes to be kept entirely under wraps, with only occasional snippets of information appearing in the press. Putting this chronology together also shows clearly that the idea of using a large aircraft to carry a missile began to be studied during 1960 and 1961, the effort reached a peak during the second half of 1962 and the first half of 1963, and then later on all the aircraft

5 Roger Béteille, *Pégase* N° 87.

manufacturers involved in the work wound down their efforts. In the end, all that was left was the Sud Aviation ramjet-powered missile studies, which were themselves halted in 1967.

Minerve Missions

A more detailed breakdown of the various missions specified for the Minerve aircraft is as follows:

For the high-speed aircraft (taken from Br 1180 brochure):

Mission 1a

Take-off and acceleration
Climb and cruise at economy speed and without afterburning for 932 miles (1,500km)
Climb to 59,055ft (18,000m) and cruise at Mach 2 at this altitude over a distance of 311 miles (500km)
Separation of the missile
Return on the same course
Land.

Mission 1a waiting for an alert

Take-off and acceleration climb on the most fuel efficient path, wait at thc most economical speed at the optimal height in terms of range (giving the longest loitering time)
In-flight refuelling near the take-off base, then a flight similar to the one described under 1a.

Mission 1b

Take-off and acceleration
Climb and cruise at economy speed, without afterburning for 932 miles (1,500km)
Climb to 59,055ft (18,000m) and cruise at Mach 2 at this altitude on a distance of 311 miles (500km)
Separation of the missile
Loiter as long as possible before second refuelling
In-flight refuelling
Return on the same course.

Mission 2

Take-off and acceleration
Climb and economical cruise for 1,243 miles (2,000km)
In-flight refuelling
Descend and cruise for 497 miles (800km) at an upper height of 985ft (300m), the last 93 miles (150km) to be flown at Mach 1.2
Separation of the missile
Return path of 497 miles (800km) on the same course travelled during the outbound flight
Loiter as long as possible before second refuelling
In-flight refuelling
1,243 miles (2,000km) return flight on the same course travelled during the outbound flight
Land.

For the low-speed aircraft (taken from the Br 1191 brochure):

Take-off
Outbound flight during 1,243 miles (2,000km) at a height of 985ft (300m)
Separation of the missile
Return flight on the same course as the outbound flight.

The Missiles

Dassault

Dassault proposed a number of rocket-propelled missile variants to carry underneath its Mirage IV developments and Minerve entries. Their details are sketchy and have been summarised in the data table.

Matra 600	
Status	project
Diameter	3ft 5.5in (1.05m)
Length	29ft 6.5in (9.00m)
Gross weight	18,519lb (8,400kg)
Powerplant	rocket
Maximum speed/Height	Mach 2 at 59,055ft (18,000m)
Carrier aircraft	Breguet Br 1180

Matra Nuclear Martel	
Status	project
Diameter	0.40 (1 3.5)
Length	-
Gross weight	-
Powerplant	rocket 'Cassandre'
Maximum speed/Height	-
Carrier aircraft	-
Based on Matra Martel data.	

RIGHT Detail view of the Gamma IV missile. *Dassault Aviation*

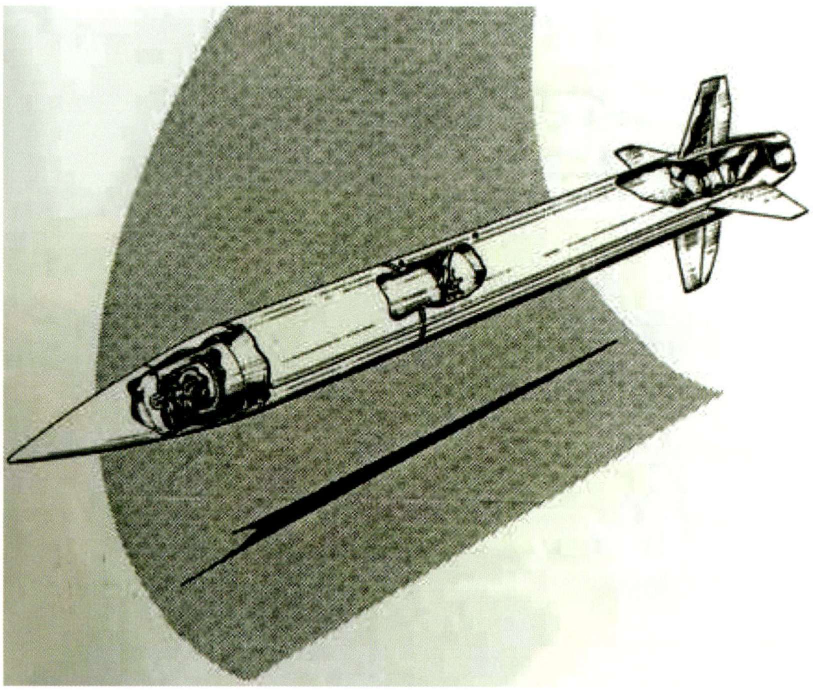

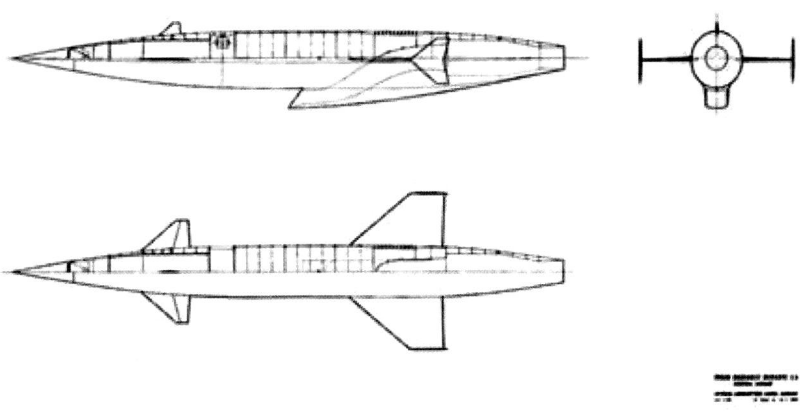

LEFT Unlike the other aircraft manufacturers that entered the Minerve competition, Dassault also made proposals for the missile component. Here is the E5, with 'E' most likely standing for '*engin*' which is the French military term for missile. Note the considerable similarity with the Sud X-411S, except that the Dassault design is winged while the X-411S was a pure lifting body. *Dassault Aviation*

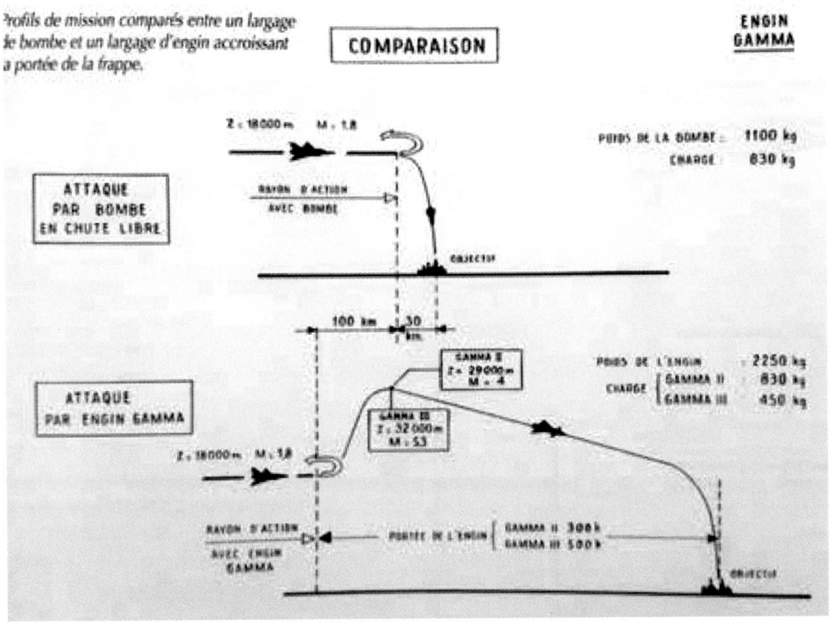

BELOW LEFT Comparison mission profile for a steel bomb and a Gamma II or III missile. *Dassault Aviation*

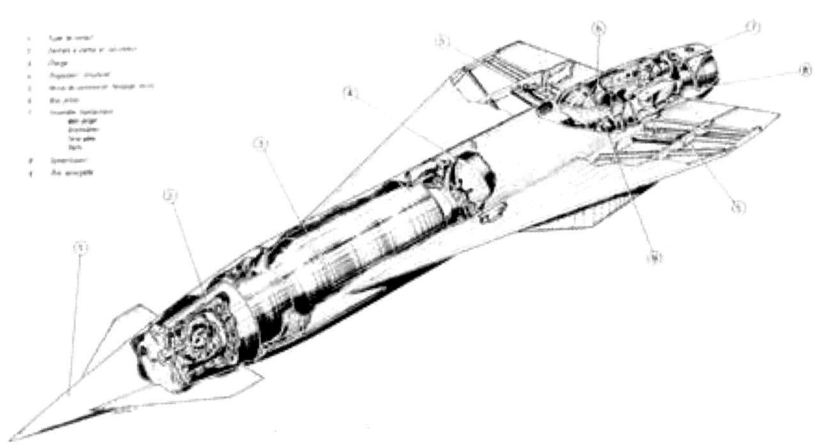

ABOVE Detail view of the Gamma II missile. *Dassault Aviation*

Matra Ballistic Missile M 600

While Sud provided the X-4xx family for the 'robot' option, Matra offered its Matra 600 missile to fill the ballistic role. Matra had earlier worked with Dassault on the later Gamma missile and the name Matra 600 came from documentation produced by the aircraft manufacturers. This may have been a cover-up because the designator Matra 600 should refer to the production version of the sixth missile designed by Matra. However, the experimental R 06, a missile weighing about 2,205lb (1,000kg) and intended to be carried by the SO 4050 Vautour, is supposed to have been started in 1950, that is according to an internal history of the company titled *Il Etait Une Fois Matra*. A few tests with mock-ups may have been carried out in 1952 before the project was cancelled in 1953. Of interest is the following from this document which states that: '*This missile had a configuration with three wings* [fins?] *which was thought to be especially useful if it was to be carried recessed into the fuselage of the carrier plane*.'[6] This happens to be exactly the configuration of the missile described in the Breguet material! A live test of the R 062 missile may have taken place on 15 October 1953, again before the programme was cancelled. But was it actually cancelled?

6 Letter from Matra historian to the author referring to this document, 21 November 2013.

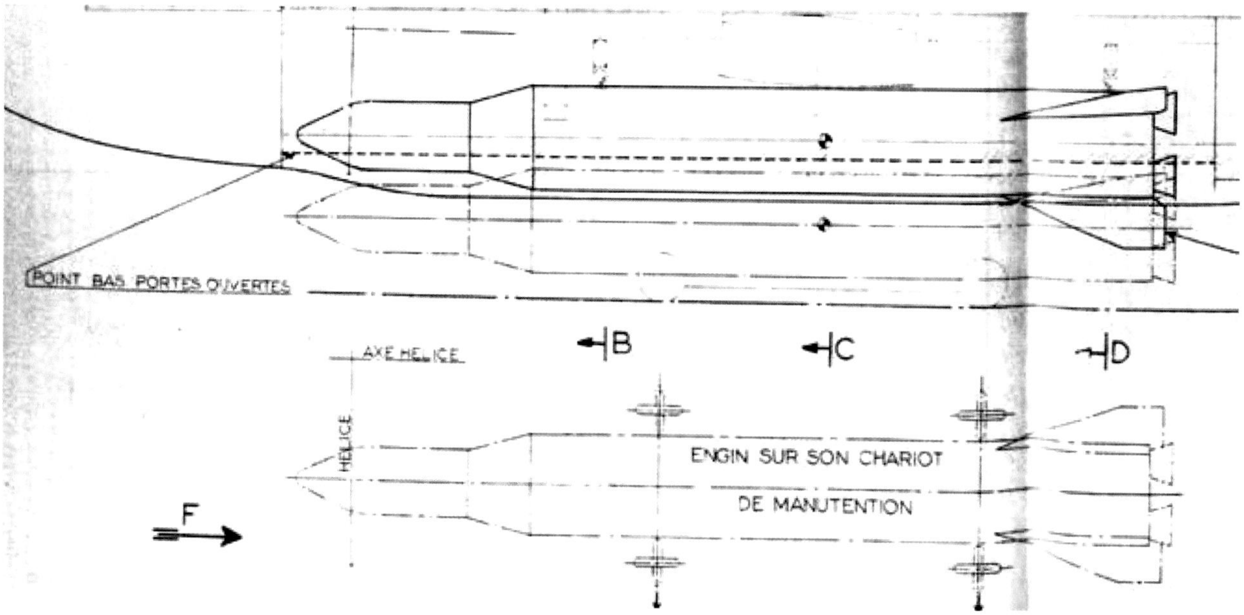

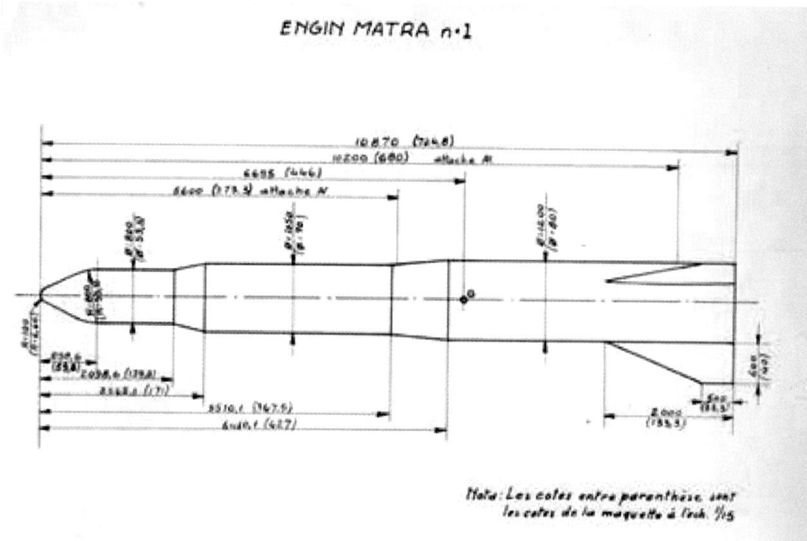

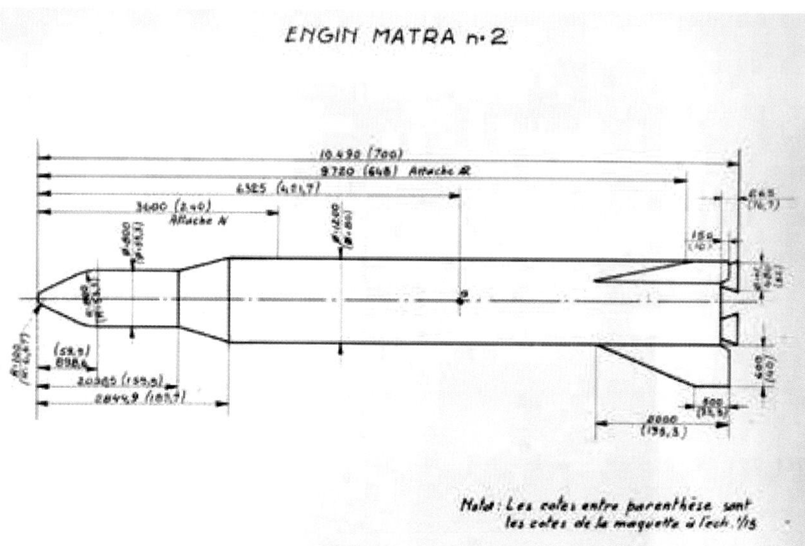

ABOVE & BELOW The Matra 600 missile was the base competitor for the ballistic missile option in the early Minerve studies. *Breguet document*

LEFT The first version of the Matra M 600. *Breguet document*

BELOW LEFT The second version of the Matra M 600. *Breguet document*

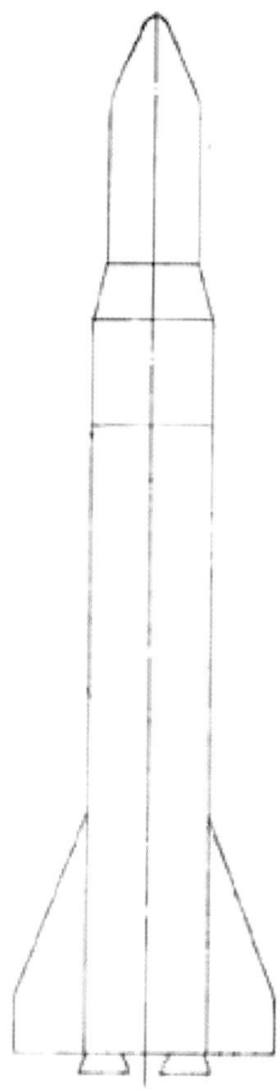

The Br 1180 brochure provides some information on the missile – '*Ballistic single-stage missile with aerodynamic stabilisation coming from fixed tail surfaces and control by orientation of the nozzles, with navigation through an inertial platform and a digital computer. Azimuth navigation setting is by astronomical sighting and in height by Doppler link*.' The Matra 600 as described in Breguet documents was a large, single-stage, rocket-powered vehicle weighing 17,634lb (8,000kg) and having a length of 29ft 6in (9.00m). Control was achieved by gimballing (rotation about a single axis) of the four rocket nozzles with guidance by an inertial computer. The warhead weighed 2,205lb (1,000kg) and when launched at 59,055ft (18,000m) the weapon had a range of 1,232 miles (1,982km) while flying at Mach 2; at low altitude its speed was reduced to Mach 1.2 and its range came down to between 622 and 746 miles (1,000km and 1,200km). A smaller version of about half the overall weight may also have been designed.

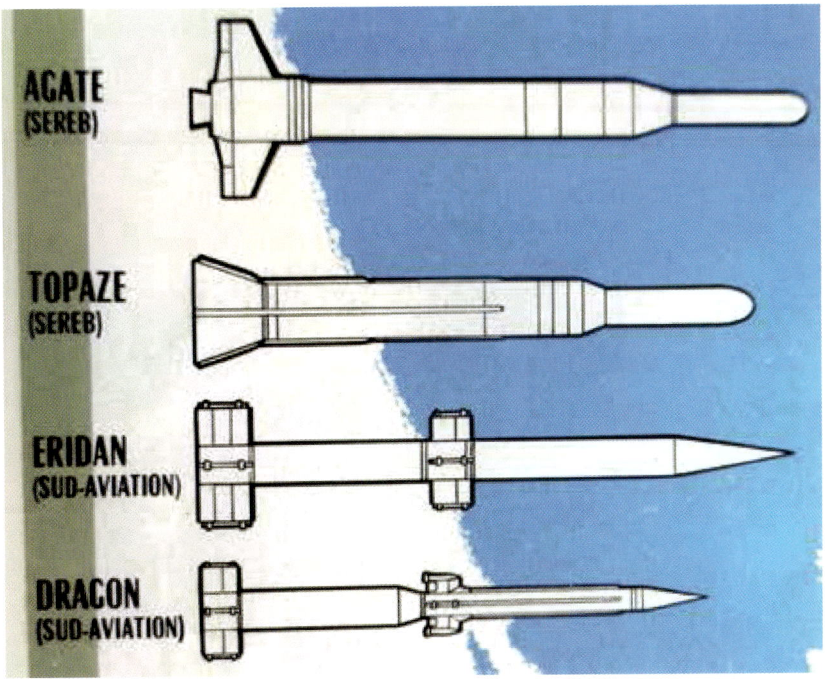

ABOVE In an illustration taken from an USIAS publication, the SEREB Topaze is pictured with other French rockets of the early 1960s. Its dimensions and data were not available at the time, but today they are known to be length 23ft 2.5in (7.07m), diameter 2ft 7.5in (0.80m) and weight 6,393lb (2,900kg). The similarity in geometry and in dimensions (but not in weight) with the so-called M 600 missile are most striking. USIAS, *Author's collection*

The Br 1180 document went on to describe the launch sequence for the M600:

'*For the high-altitude mission, the launch manoeuvre begins at about 40km* [25 miles] *before the launch and takes 1.5 minutes. The navigation correction is to be carried as near as possible as the point where the manoeuvre begins, the aircraft flying at 18,000m* [59,055ft] *at Mach 2 in the direction of the target. The missile rail is lowered and the aircraft begins a slow descent along at an angle of 10%.* [note: in France the angle of flight with the horizontal is expressed as a percentage, and here means that the aircraft height drops 33ft (10m) for every 330ft (100m) of flight]. *After a flight of 36km* [22 miles] *(about 60 seconds) the aircraft reaches a speed of Mach 2.25 at 14,400m* [47,245ft], *it then climbs with load factor of 2 and after 26 seconds it should have reached 18,000m [59,055ft] at a speed of Mach 2 and a climb angle of 25°. The launch is automated and takes place when these conditions are reached.*'

Naturally a procedure was also designed for the low-altitude launch: '*For the low altitude mission, different manoeuvres could be carried out depending on the tactical conditions. In any case, the climb to reach the launch attitude [pitch/speed] begins with a stabilised horizontal flight at low altitude. Before that the aircraft must be accelerated with all its power until it has reached Mach 1.3. If the objective is to never go over 1,000m* [3,280ft], *the launch position can be reached with a climb at 20° under an acceleration of 3g or with a climb of 25° under an acceleration of 4g. If the objective is to never accelerate over 2g then the final altitude will be 2,000m* [6,560ft]. *While the missile has not been designed to survive a strong acceleration during prolonged periods, there is no problem with it reaching 4g on one occasion for a few seconds*.'

A development of the Anglo-French Martel missile may also have been considered. Design of the Martel had begun in 1962 but it seems that the version with a nuclear warhead was only developed after 1967. At that time it was a joint Anglo-French project, with Matra and Hawker Siddeley as the two co-contractors for a medium-range (34 to 100 miles /55km to 161km) British TV-guided or French radar-homing weapon. Although the first flight took place in 1965, its delivery to operational units did not arrive until 1970. The very idea of using this jointly developed missile as a nuclear weapon upset the British, *RAF Flying Review* commenting: '*It could be argued that British money was going to support de Gaulle's nuclear policy*.' Possibly for this reason the idea was not pursued (however, on the British side a 'Megaton Martel' was also on the development line although, just like the French nuclear version, it was not built). It should be noted that

ABOVE **Launch of a Topaze rocket from the Hammaguir ground base (which today is in Algeria).** *SEREB, Author's collection*

in *Matra La Volonté d'Entreprendre* by Claude Carlier, published in 2003, there is no reference to the Matra 600 missile, although it is indicated that the *Commissariat à l'Energie Atomique* (the French Atomic Energy Agency, in charge of everything nuclear in France) ordered a few Matra 637/638 missiles in 1965 to serve as probes for the upcoming live nuclear testing of the Mirage IV air-dropped bomb in the Pacific. These may have been 'white' programmes, that is to serve as a cover for the 'dark world' Martel nuclear weapon.[7]

The author would like to point out that the M 600 missile has more than a passing resemblance to the first *Pierres Précieuses* (precious stones) gallery of rockets tested by SEREB at that time (and note: if one looks at the publications issued by USIAS – the *Union Syndicale des Industries Aéronautiques et Spatiales* – SEREB is not listed among the French aeronautical companies until 1965).

This is especially true of the VE 111 Topaze, which was the first French rocket to be controlled via a quartet of gimballed nozzles (an arrangement it shared with the Matra M 600). The VE 111 Topaze was first flown on 19 December 1962, and between December 1962 and May 1965 fourteen Topaze were flown, out of which only one was a failure. The Topaze propulsion system used the *soleil* (sun) block of isolane propellant, which gave a thrust of 27,000lb (120kN) for thirty-nine seconds and four variants were trialled:

(i). VE 111C (C for 'court' or short length – 23ft 3.5in [7.1m] long for a weight of 3,373lb [1,530kg]). Six flights in 1962-63.
(ii). VE 111CI ('court-instable' – short unstable). Four flights in 1964.
(iii). VE 111L (L for 'long' – length 26ft 3in [8.00m], weight 4,960lb [2,250kg]). Two flights in 1963-64.
(iv). VE 111LG ('long guidage' – long with inertial guidance). Two more flights in 1965.

Although the weights differ widely, the outward appearance of the casing and the control nozzle system were quite similar between the drawing board M 600 military missile and the flown test rocket VE 111.

Matra was not known to have designed any large missile comparable in size to the M 600, so to solve the apparent contradiction of the Matra historian not knowing about the M 600 sixty years after the fact, and Breguet claiming at the time to have a contract with Matra for the M 600, the author proposes the theory that Matra was not the actual designer of the M 600 but merely an integrator (a link) bridging the gap between the true but hidden designer (SEREB) and the aircraft manufacturer. The reason behind this would be to cover up any aspect of technology that would have been shared between the Minerve missile (perceived as an interim weapon system before the definitive weapon system, the missile-armed nuclear submarine, became operational) and the ground-based and submarine-based strategic missiles. Hopefully, one day we might know the answer.

Sud-Aviation 'Cruise' Missiles

In his December 1961 note Roger Béteille claimed many advantages for the terrain-following missiles: for example when flying at low altitude the missile would evade radar detection, while the launch from a mother plane would extend the range of the carrier. For the mother ship role he saw two possible alternatives, the Mirage IV and the Super Caravelle. Béteille's team was focused on missile development so it is not surprising that his note described missiles more than their launch platforms. The X-411 was powered by a SNECMA M36 turbojet, the X-412 and X-413 were similar but adapted for launch from a ground launcher with the addition of rocket boosters, the X-414 was a larger version of the X-411 with extended range, and the X-415 and X-416 were the corresponding short-range/long-range versions of the X-411 and X-414 but powered by rocket engines instead of turbojets (which is odd since the rockets certainly could not provide the

7 The author uses this very modern and American terminology consciously, but the notion of 'black programmes' is conspicuously absent from the French aeronautical press of these times!

X-411	
Status	project
Diameter	2ft 7in (0.78m)
Length	27ft 1.5in (8.27m)
Gross weight	5,952lb (2,700kg)
Powerplant	SNECMA M36
Maximum speed/Height	Mach 2
Carrier aircraft	Mirage IVC

X-411S	
Status	project
Diameter	-
Length	32ft 10in (10.00m) (approx)
Gross weight	-
Powerplant	ramjet from SE 4400 missile
Maximum speed/Height	Mach 3.6
Carrier aircraft	Mirage IVA/Mirage IIIV

X-414	
Status	project
Diameter	-
Length	42ft 10in (13.05m)
Gross weight	14,330lb (6,500kg)
Powerplant	SNECMA M36
Maximum speed/Height	Mach 2
Carrier aircraft	TCS

X-415	
Status	project
Diameter	2ft 7in (0.78m)
Length	27ft 3in (8.3m)
Gross weight	7,716lb (3,500kg)
Powerplant	rocket
Maximum speed/Height	-
Carrier aircraft	Mirage IVC

X-416	
Status	project
Diameter	3ft 3.5in (1.00m)
Length	42ft 8in (13.00m)
Gross weight	18,960lb (8,600kg)
Powerplant	rocket
Maximum speed/Height	-
Carrier aircraft	TCS

X-417 (At May 1962)	
Status	project
Diameter	-
Length	-
Gross weight	11,023lb (5,000kg)
Powerplant	turbojet (unspecified)
Maximum speed/Height	-
Carrier aircraft	TCS

X-417 (At November 1962)	
Status	project
Diameter	-
Length	52ft 6in (16.00m)
Gross weight	20,282lb (9,200kg)
Powerplant	turbojet (unspecified)
Maximum speed/Height	-
Carrier aircraft	TCS/Br 1191

X-419	
Status	project
Diameter	-
Length	65ft 7.5in (20.00m)
Gross weight	-
Powerplant	SNECMA M36
Maximum speed/Height	-
Carrier aircraft	?

X-422	
Status	prototype
Diameter	2ft 7.5in (0.80m)
Length	32ft 10in (10.00m)
Gross weight	4,189lb (1,900kg)
Powerplant	Sud 6C ramjet
Maximum speed/Height	Mach 1.7
Carrier aircraft	Ground launch

same range and flexibility as the jet).

In January 1962 the X-417 was added to the family powered by a turbojet of unspecified type but providing 5 tons of thrust. To increase the range a fuel called Cherchar, produced by Charbonnages de France, was specified since it promised an increase in range of 10% compared to JP5 fuel. Note that at this time both short-range (236 miles/380km) and long-range (1,119 miles/1,800km) missiles were proposed.

Considerable effort would be expended over the following years to solve the numerous difficulties raised by this concept, notably for example on the resistance of the nose cone to a long duration flight at Mach 2 (at this speed even raindrops were a worry because of the damage they could inflict). The radome was made of steel and housed an 'obstacle detection'

BELOW Another proposal using the Mirage IV as mother ship, this time to carry the Sud X-415 ,which was a rocket-propelled missile. *Philippe Ricco*

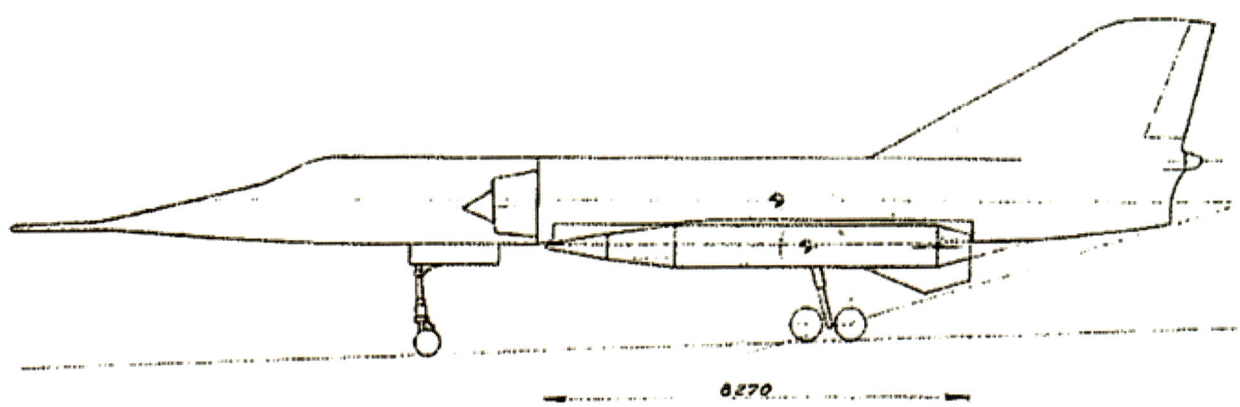

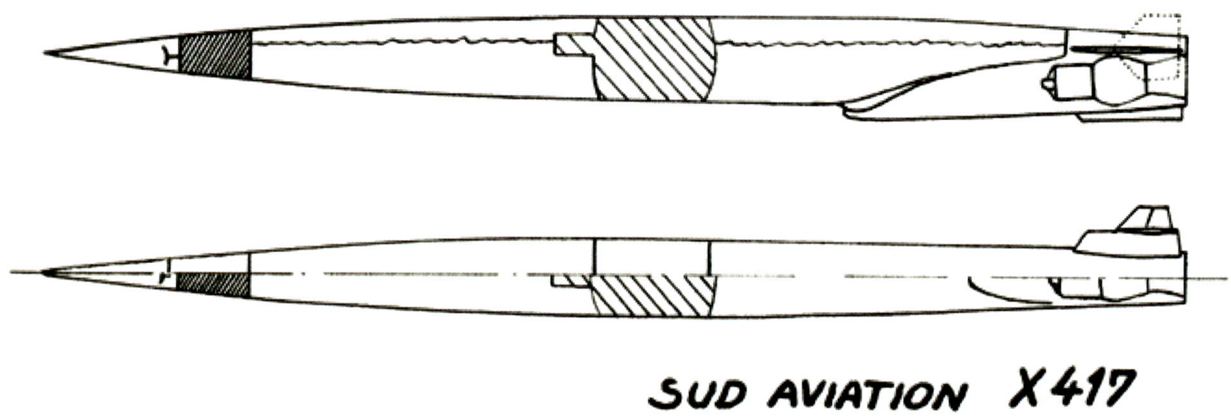

ABOVE Sud Aviation X-417 missile. *Sud Aviation document*

radar, while course tracking used inertial guidance designed by SAGEM but which required recalibration during the flight through a technique called 'clinosynthesis'. This required a good knowledge of the terrain to be overflown, something that France had at the time but which no other NATO country (not even the USA) possessed. The secret came from: '*The availability of topographical maps drawn by German topographers between 1942/44 and seized in 1945 by the French Army, which allowed a choice between many "recalibration" areas applicable to "dissuasion" targets in the USSR up to the Ural Mountains.*'[8]. The effectiveness of the system would have been demonstrated by the ability of the 'robot' (as the terrain-hugging missile was named when compared to the ballistic missile) to successfully cross over the Esterel Mountains (a range between Cannes and the Alps). However, trials over France may not have been performed that would have covered all of the parameters: for example the designers claimed that, independent of the effect of the warhead, the shockwave caused by the simple flight of the missile at tree top level (165ft to 330ft/50m to 100m) and at Mach 2 would have a devastating effect on the countryside!

It was planned to have the first X-417 flying by July 1968 and for the mother ship prototypes to begin their flight trials in July 1966 (Breguet), with the PSS flying only in October 1967. A ground-launched tactical variant was also designed called the X-418, but a major problem appeared when SNECMA ran into trouble designing the turbojet intended for the X-417. As a result, Béteille offered the X-417S powered by a yet-to-be-designed ramjet (S for statoréacteur). At the end of the year the X-411S, in its low level (X-411SB) and high altitude (X-411SH) form, was now considered to be the 'reference' flying missile for Minerve, instead of the Matra 600 ballistic missile. Its ramjet was thought to be based on the one fitted to the

BELOW Sud Aviation X-419 missile. *Sud Aviation document*

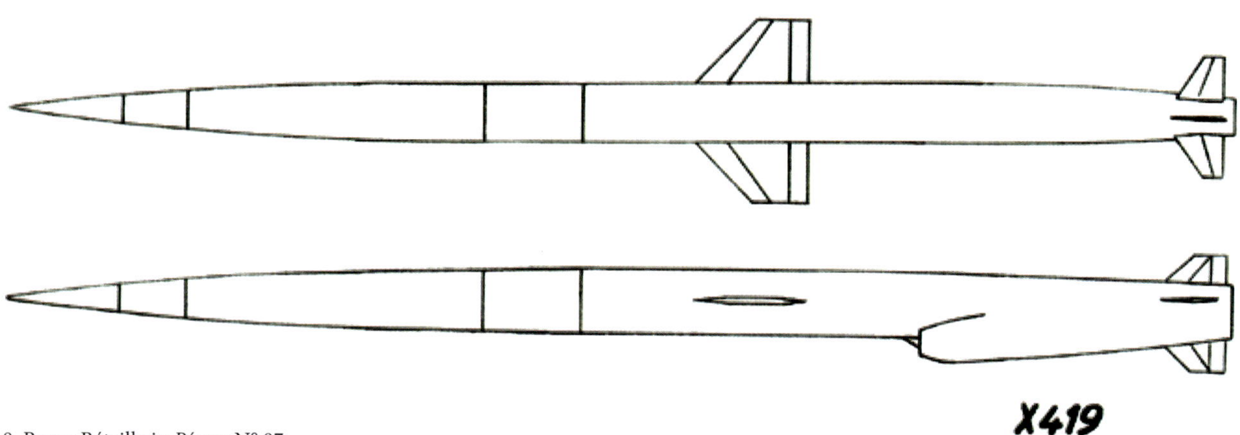

8 Roger Béteille in *Pégase* N° 87.

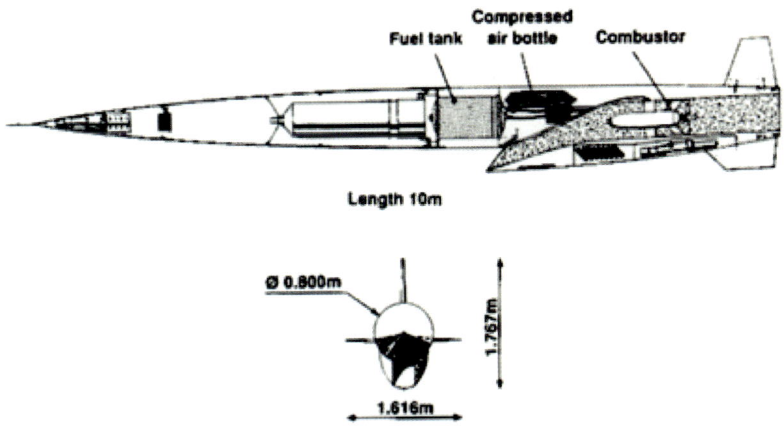

TOP Sectional and front view of the X-422, the reduced-scale demonstrator for the X-4xx series of Minerve missiles proposed by Sud Aviation. *Sud Aviation document*

MIDDLE ABOVE One of the X-422 prototype missiles. The X-422 proved to be the only material output from the Minerve programme. *Philippe Ricco*

ABOVE An X-422 is launched. *Philippe Ricco*

successful Sud Est SE 4400 ground-to-air missile.

On 31 October 1963 the Béteille team met with ONERA to discuss the possibility of using their ramjet, which had just taken the Stataltex experimental missile to Mach 5. A new ground-launched design, the X-420, was to have received this ramjet. Also, during this year the possibility was investigated of carrying the X-411S on the Mirage IIIV V/STOL fighter (Volume I). By 1964 the decision had been made to build a demonstrator based on the X-417 and called the X-422.

Substantial wind tunnel testing was carried out during that year to investigate once again the resistance of the nose cone to continued flight at Mach 2, but also to define the best ventral air intake arrangement. In January 1965 the SE 4400's ramjet was selected for the X-422 over the ONERA Statex 500 and a Nord proposal.

On 29 January 1967 the first X-422 flew successfully from the Hammaguir test range, followed on 16 March by the second prototype. The third prototype flew on 20 June 1967 from the Levant test range, by which time the Hammaguir base had been given back to Algeria.

The Aircraft

Breguet Minerve

Breguet Br 1190 / Br 1191

In reply to the low-speed Minerve requirements, Breguet chose to develop a subsonic platform from the Atlantic maritime aircraft. Basically, all the avionics and associated protuberances needed for the anti-submarine role would have been removed and the bomb bay would have been enlarged with slightly bulged doors. Advanced avionics for navigation would have been fitted to enable the platform to fly nap of the earth (very low level) missions and to launch its missile at the appropriate point. Two types of missiles were considered, the Matra

Breguet Br 1190	
Status	project
Span	119ft 1in (36.30m)
Length	92ft 11in (28.33m)
Gross wing area	1,290.3sq ft (120.00sq m)
Gross weight	up to 99,206lb (45,000kg)
Powerplant	two Tyne 20
Maximum speed/Height	399mph (642km/h)
Armament	Matra 600

Breguet Br 1191	
Status	project
Span	119ft 1in (36.30m)
Length	98ft 5in (30.00m)
Gross wing area	1,290.3sq ft (120.00sq m)
Gross weight	up to 99,206lb (45,000kg)
Powerplant	two Tyne 20
Maximum speed/Height	399mph (642km/h)
Armament	X 411

600, which flew a ballistic trajectory, and a Sud Aviation design (possibly the X-417). Breguet indicated that two variants of the Sud missiles had been taken into consideration – the *'engin léger'* and *'engin lourd'*, which would weigh 22,090lb (10,020kg) and 25,176lb (11,420kg) respectively. However, the Breguet aircraft brochure referred to the missile brochures for more in-depth descriptions and the author has been unable to locate these. The type of missile carried influenced the construction of the carrier plane because the Sud Aviation weapon was larger than the Matra design and required an extension of the bomb bay with a redesign of the mother ship's nose section: hence the two type numbers with the Br 1190 carrying the Matra missile and the Br 1191 the Sud model. In-flight refuelling was planned for both types, yet without this facility the Breguet mother ships could still fly independently for twelve hours. For loitering missions Breguet promoted the operation of the aircraft in pairs, one of the machines transferring its extra fuel to the other before returning to its base.

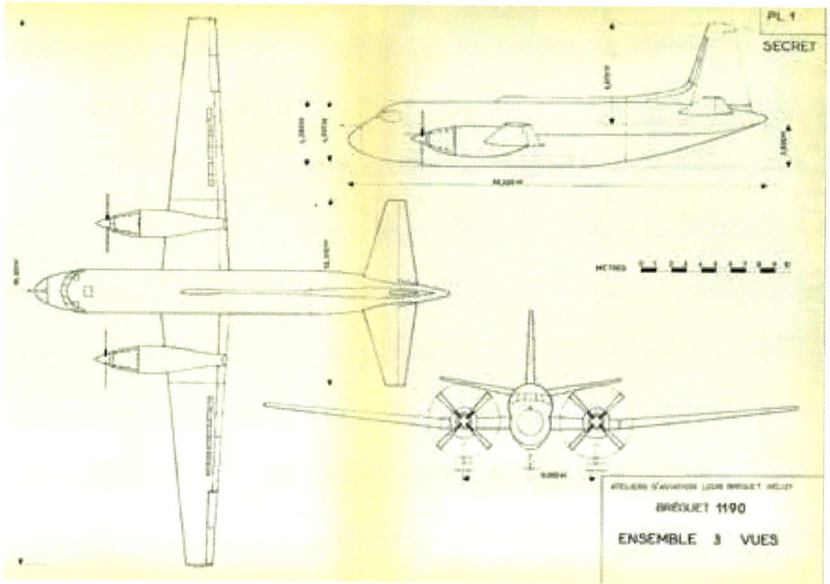

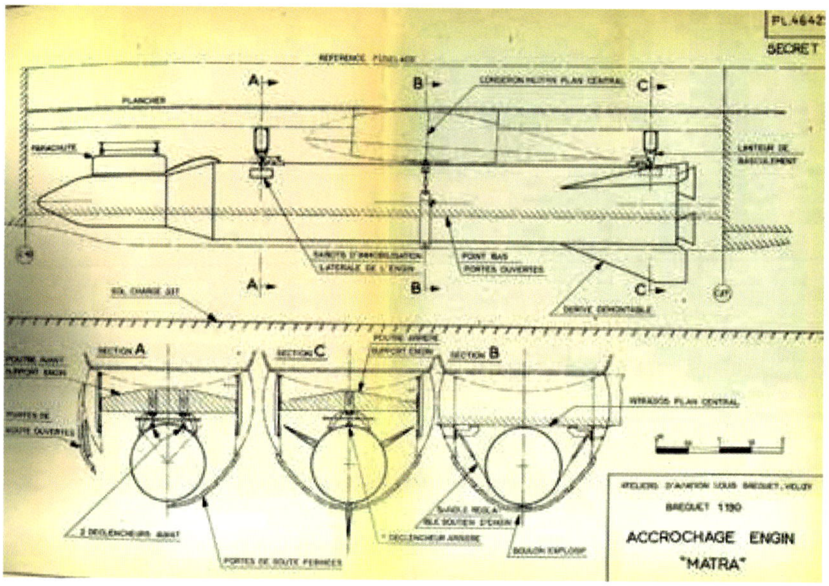

TOP The Breguet Br 1190 was the equivalent of the Br 1191 to serve as the carrier of the Matra M 600 missile. The wide difference in size and operation between the two missiles required Breguet to develop two different aircraft to carry them. *Dassault Aviation*

ABOVE Close-up of the M 600 missile installation onboard the Br 1190. *Dassault Aviation*

A lot of consideration was given to navigation, with twelve pages of both the Br 1190 and Br 1191 brochures being given to this topic. For the development of its Minerve aircraft, Breguet required wind tunnel testing for its general shape and also for the missile/mother ship separation.

The front fuselage was redesigned and the landing gear beefed up. Development of the Br 1191 carrying the Sud missile began in 1962 and continued until 1963. The larger missile required a more extensive redesign of the basic Atlantic airframe, again with a new nose similar to the Br 1190 but also with a 'lift' for extracting the missile from the weapon bay. This was because the ignition system for the missile's propulsion (the Sud Aviation

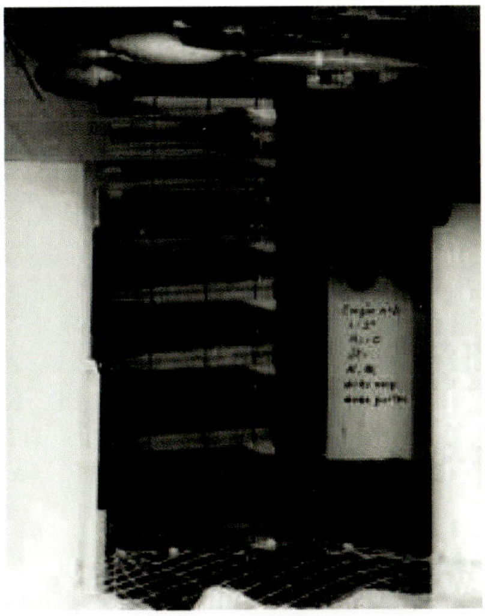

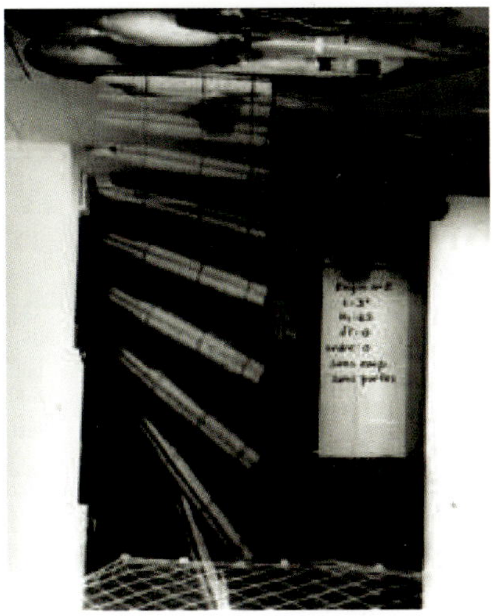

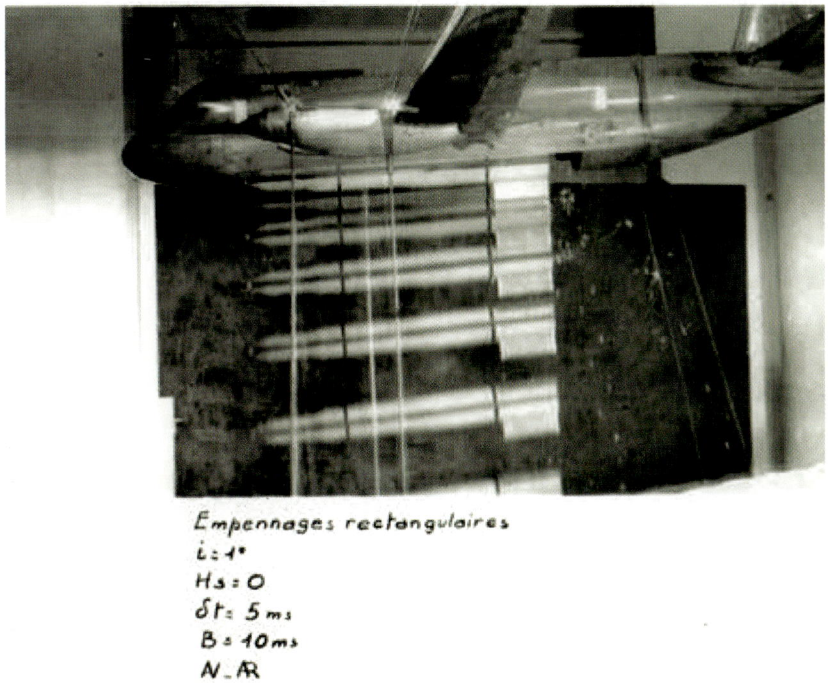

ABOVE Breguet undertook a lot of wind tunnel separation tests for the Br 1190/M 600 weapon system. Here the missile is described as being the 'first type with rectangular fins'. *Breguet*

TOP LEFT Another separation test, this time with missile N° 2 with fins. The Br 1190 weapon bay doors are fitted. *Breguet*

LEFT A final example of a separation test. Missile N° 2 is now without fins and the Br 1190 bay doors have been removed. *Breguet*

design appeared to be fitted with side boosters in addition to its own engine) could only be carried outside the aircraft, and the navigation system required that the link between the mother ship's navigation equipment should be connected to the missile navigation computer until separation. The Br 1191 brochure stated: '*This requirement necessitates a complex mechanism to lower the missile-rail ensemble because, when in the up position, the missile needs to be rigidly and precisely positioned to permit the correct operation and to reset the inertial platform.*' The loading of the missile would have been carried out with the rail in the down position, the missile being wheeled in on a special carriage that approached the aircraft from the rear.

Breguet suggested that two prototypes would have been enough to validate the design and it was stated that both would fly by July 1966 if an order was issued in July 1963. The planned programme also noted that the Matra missile would be tested and then mated to a prototype Br 1190 in 1967. Breguet hoped to have the weapon system validated by late 1967 with the first production machines rolling out from 1 June 1968 onwards, the last of a base order of fifty machines being delivered in April 1971. Breguet estimated that with forty-eight aircraft procured it would be possible to have sixteen aircraft airborne simultaneously, along with a possibility of having twenty-four airborne simultaneously for periods not exceeding two to three weeks. The total cost of the programme was given as 1,368,042,000 francs (1,907,957,928 €) for the Br 1191 and 1,257,783,000 francs (1,754,1837,51 €) for the Br 1190. Strangely for a *Dissuasion Nucléaire* programme, Breguet offered the option to share the work with other unspecified European nations. Breguet was a great promoter of European co-operation but this reference to a

Breguet Br 1180

Breguet Br 1180	
Status	project
Span	64ft 3.5in (19.60m)
Length	108ft 3in (33.00m)
Gross wing area	1,182.8sq ft (110.00sq m)
Gross weight	up to 132,275lb (60,000kg)
Powerplant	two Brstol Siddeley 593/3 41,625lb (185kN) in reheat
Maximum speed/Height	Mach 2
Armament	Matra 600

RIGHT Breguet offered the Br 1191, a somewhat modified Breguet Atlantic, as the carrier of the Sud X-417 missile. *Dassault Aviation*

BELOW RIGHT Internal detail of the Br 1191's fuselage. *Dassault Aviation*

BOTTOM RIGHT Installation of the Sud X-417 missile into the Br 1191 fuselage. *Dassault Aviation*

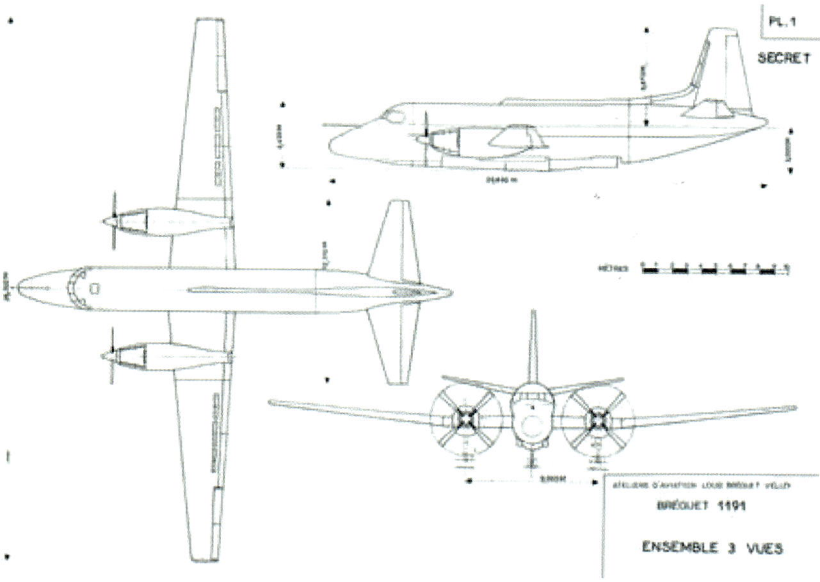

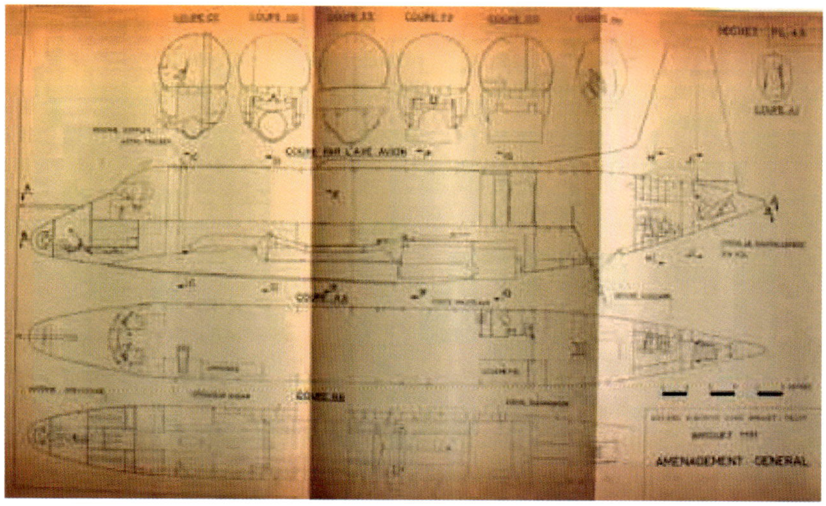

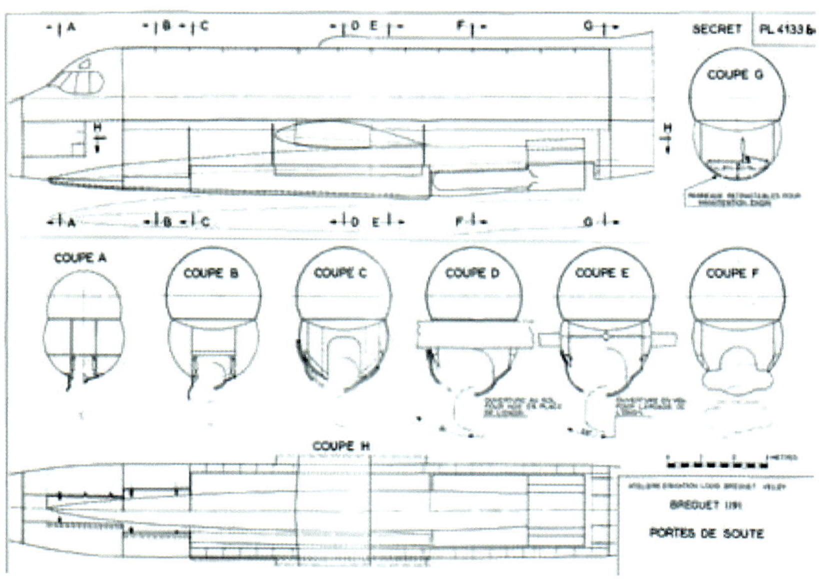

production programme with other countries may have been a lapse from the Breguet accounting department.

Breguet also offered an all-new high-performance platform for Minerve, the Br 1180. This aircraft was proposed in 1962 (so in parallel with the Br 1190) and it would have carried the Matra 600 missile like its subsonic counterpart, but Breguet claimed that it would difficult to operate the *'low-level non ballistic vehicle'* (read Sud X-4xx family) *from a Mach 2 aircraft'*.

The Br 1180 was a large three-seat aeroplane powered by two Bristol Siddeley turbojets. It was designed to incorporate a large complement of avionics for navigation and counter-measures and the manufacturer intended to fit a retractable refuelling probe in the nose, between the radar bay and the cockpit. It was also intended that Br 1180s could be fitted with a large fuel tank in their weapon bay (instead of the missile) to act as refuelling tankers for their missile-carrying colleagues. The general appearance of the airframe had been extrapolated from the Br 1001 Taon covered in Volume I and the brochure claimed that: '*Derived from the Br 1001 Taon in its aerodynamic shape and construction, it will benefit from the experience acquired*' from the earlier aircraft. However, it also warned that: '*The design of the airframe will be adjusted so as to maximise the effect of area rule at Mach 1.4, thereby obtaining a good airflow at Mach 1.2 as well as at Mach 2.0*.' From this it is pretty clear that the design of the Br 1180 airframe was far from being frozen.

Of interest is this comment also taken from the brochure: '*Carrying*

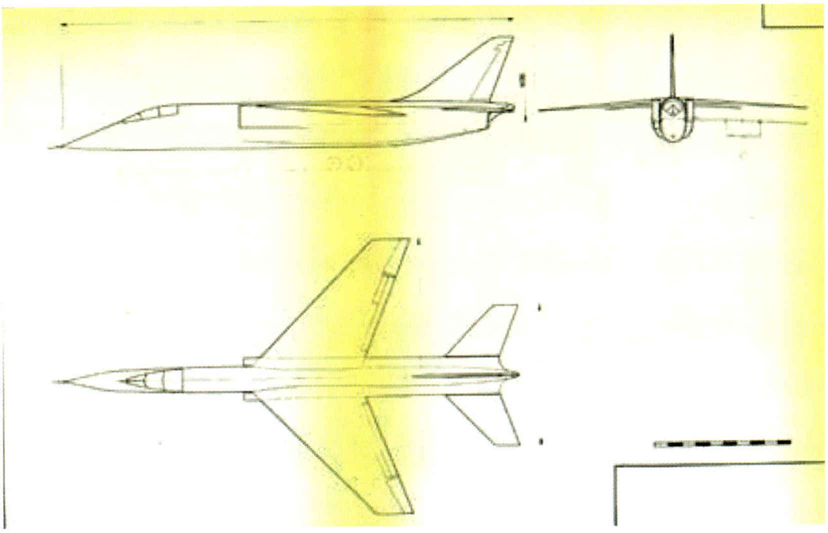

LEFT To cover all options Breguet also offered the supersonic BR 1180. *Dassault Aviation*

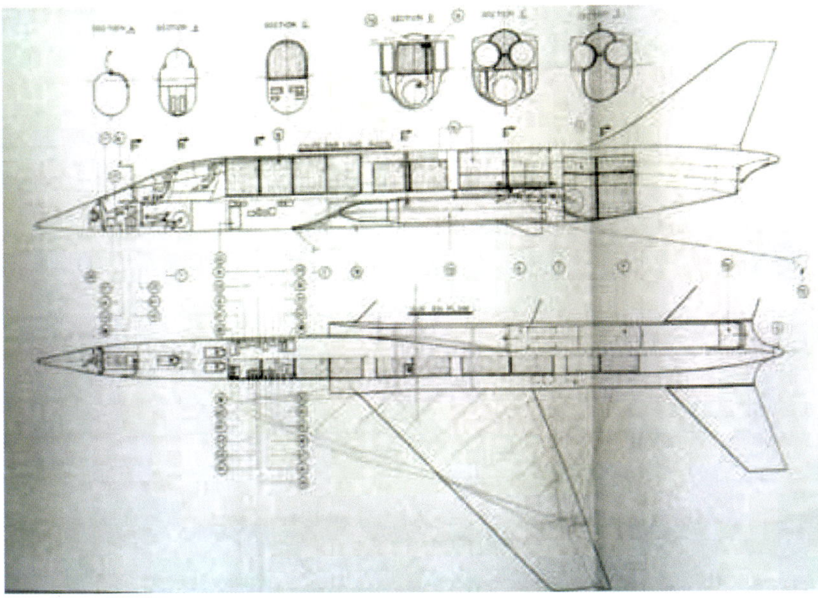

LEFT Cross-section of the Br 1180 fuselage. Note that the drawing has been modified by hand using a lead pencil and major visible modifications include a delta wing and the missile installed in a recessed fairing underneath the fuselage (instead of a closed bay). *Dassault Aviation*

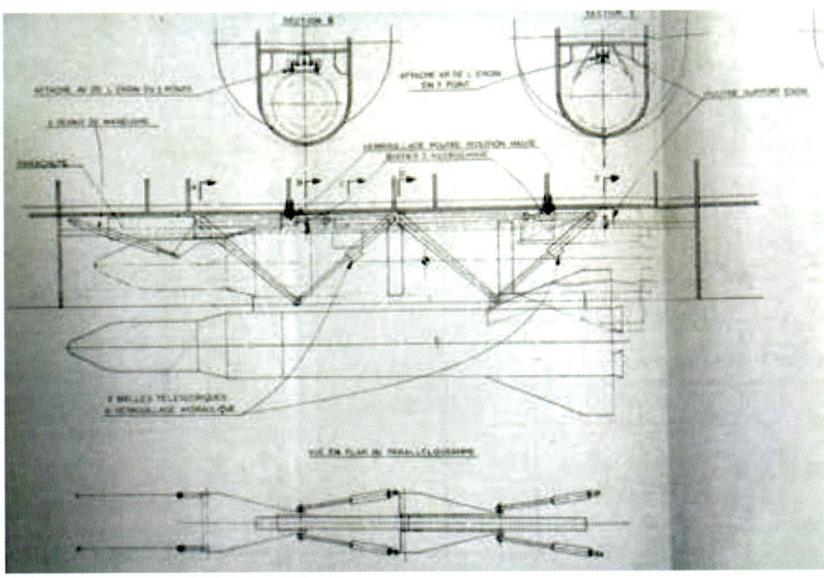

LEFT The M 600 missile fitted inside the bay of the Br 1180. *Dassault Aviation*

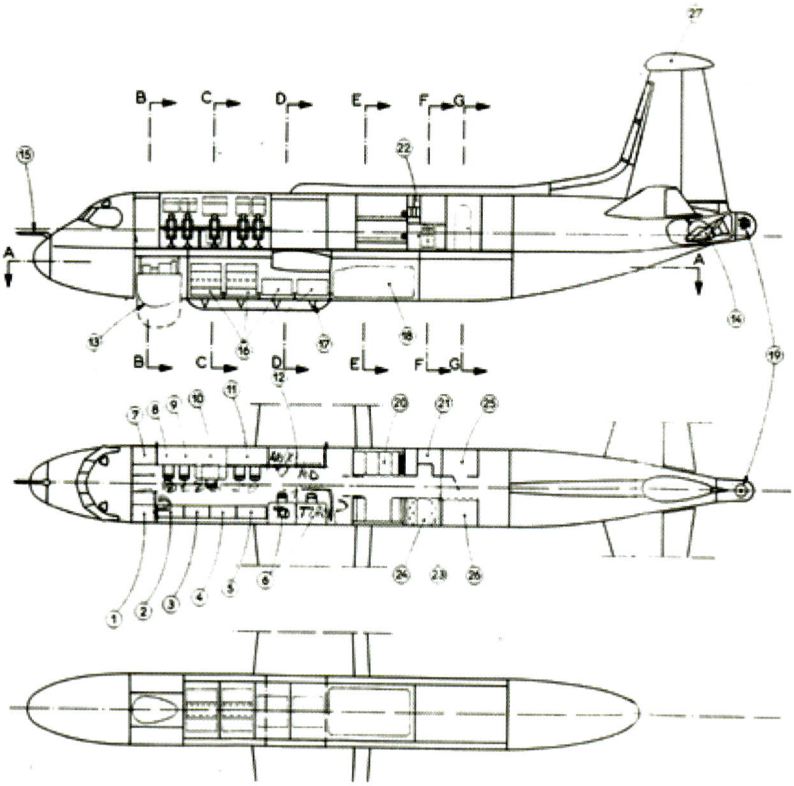

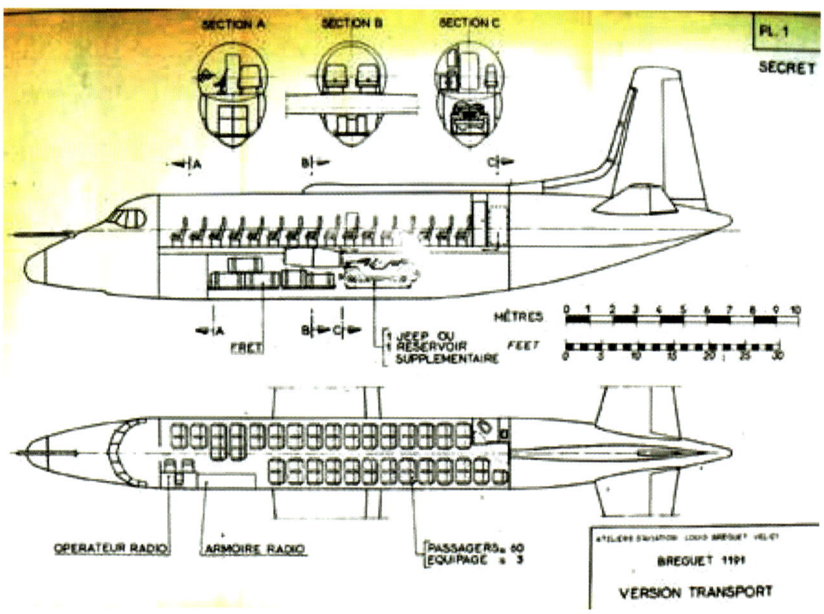

TOP **Beside its Minerve variant the Br 1190 was also offered as an electronic warfare aircraft.** *Dassault Aviation*

ABOVE **Far from its nuclear mission, the Br 1191 was also offered by Breguet as a transport aircraft.** *Dassault Aviation*

the missile can be done either outside the carrier aircraft or inwardly. The first option is not compatible with the requirements in terms of air-conditioning, avionics docking ports, and in a smaller way aerodynamics (additional drag).' In promoting the carriage of the large missile in an internal bay, Breguet took the opposite path to the one selected by Nord Aviation and Sud Aviation. In September 1962 Sud, Nord, Breguet and Matra reached an agreement to respond to the Minerve requirements.

Dassault Minerve

Dassault Mirage IV/ Gamma II

However, it appears that the Br 1180's development did not extend beyond that month.

An early project to mate the Dassault Gamma II missile to the Mirage IV was presented in January 1961, and so was probably pre-Minerve. This work was done at the request of the *Direction Technique et Industrielle de l'Armement*. The Gamma II was an air-to-ground winged missile propelled by a solid fuel rocket, it was 19ft 8in (6.0m) long and had a diameter of 2ft 7in (0.78m), but in 1962 it was superseded by the Gamma IV, which was to be fitted under a Mirage IVC2.

Dassault Mirage IV/Gamma II	
Status	project
Span	80ft 8.5in (24.60m)
Length	63ft 0in (19.20m)
Gross wing area	365.6sq ft (34.00sq m)
Gross weight	107,099lb (48,580kg)
Powerplant	two TF106 19,800lb (88kN) in reheat
Maximum speed/Height	-
Armament	Gamma II

Dassault Mirage IVC2/ Gamma IV

Appearing in April 1962, this Mirage IV design was powered by two SNECMA TF106 units giving it a maximum speed of Mach 2.2 at 36,090ft (11,000m). Maximum range was 1,243 miles (2,000km) at low altitude, of which 112 miles (180km) was attributed to the missile flying alone, or 1,367 miles (2,200km) at high altitude (at presumably 36,090ft/11,000m) of which the missile

Dassault Mirage IVC2/Gamma IV	
Status	project
Span	45ft 7in (13.90m)
Length	78ft 5.5in (23.92m)
Gross wing area	1,053.8sq ft (98.00sq m)
Gross weight	91,049lb (41,300kg)
Powerplant	two TF106 19,800lb (88kN) in reheat
Maximum speed/Height	-
Armament	Gamma IV 7,275lb (3,300kg)

Dassault Mirage IV C22	
Status	project
Span	50ft 0.5in (15.25m)
Length	92ft 4.5in (28.15m)
Gross wing area	1,397.8sq ft (130.00sq m)
Gross weight	132,275lb (60,000kg)
Powerplant	two Olympus 22R 30,600lb (136kN) in reheat
Maximum speed/Height	Mach 2.0
Armament	Missile 17,637lb (8,000kg)

covered 249 miles (400km) alone. The Gamma IV missile was developed in an association between Dassault and Matra and consisted of six parts – the nose cone with the firing devices, the rear of the cone, an instrument case housing the navigation equipment, the military load (bomb) in the centre section of the fuselage, the rocket engine and (at the extreme rear) the battery. The motor was a solid fuel rocket that could burn for thirty seconds, enough to take the missile up to a supersonic maximum speed.

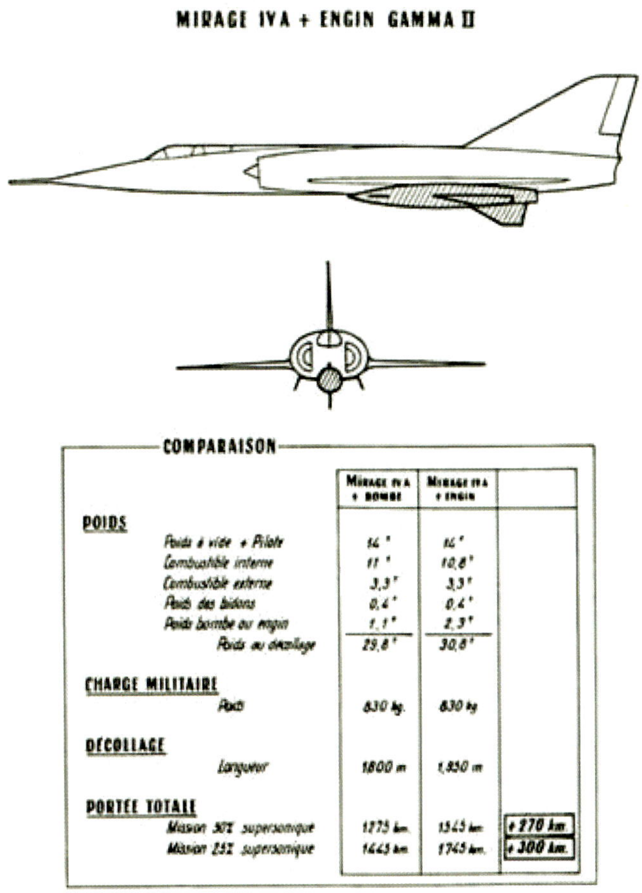

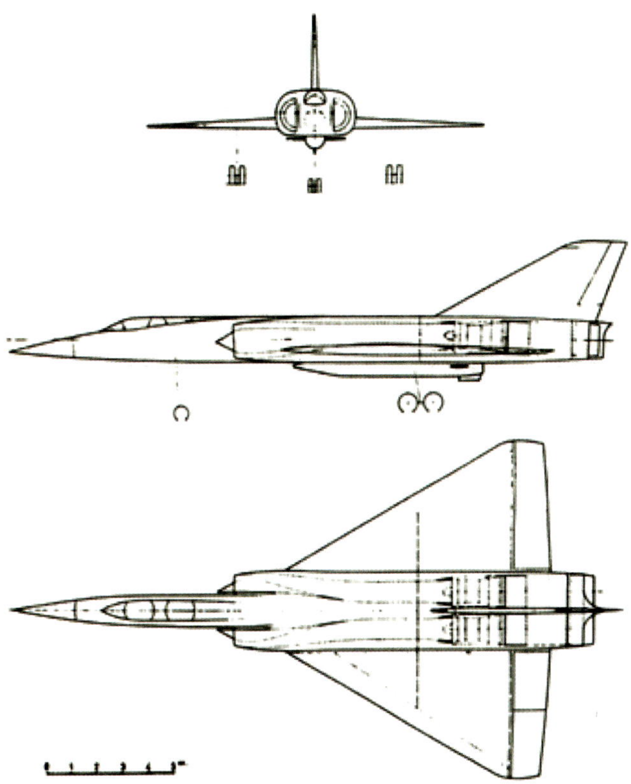

TOP RIGHT A 1961 concept had the Mirage IVA fitted with a Dassault Gamma II missile underneath the fuselage. *Dassault-Aviation*

RIGHT This variant of the Mirage IVA carries the Dassault Gamma IV missile. *Dassault Aviation*

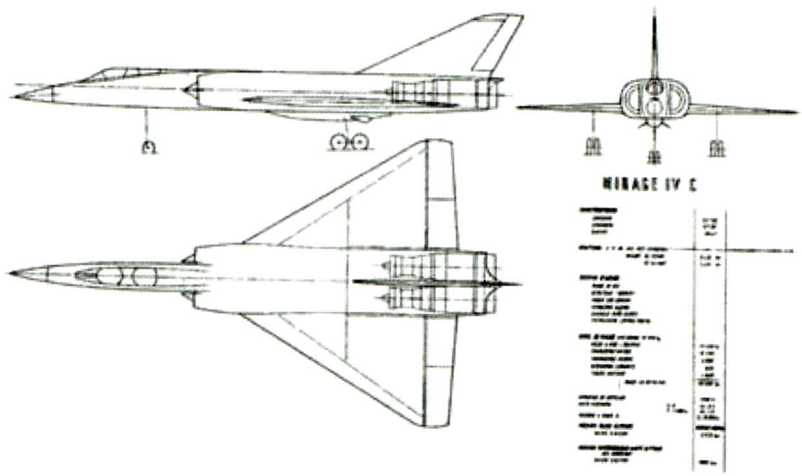

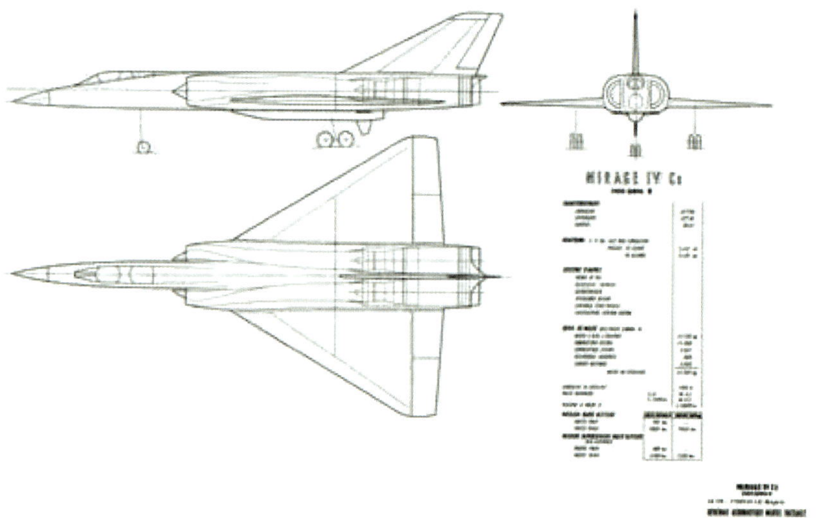

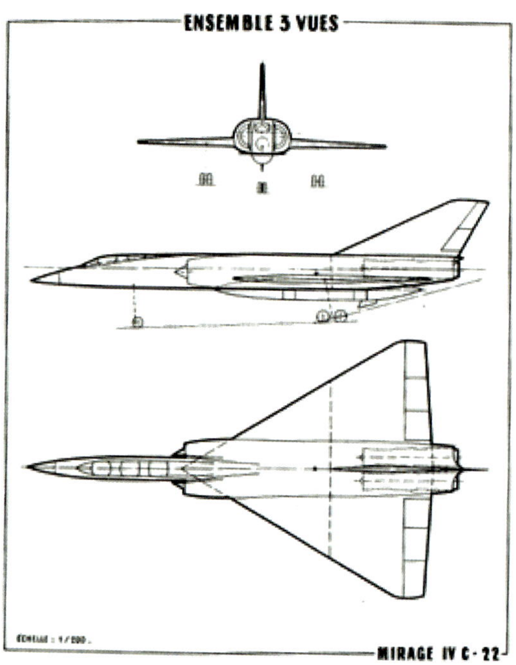

LEFT, BELOW LEFT & BOTTOM LEFT
These three drawings illustrate the development progress from an enlarged Mirage IV fitted with a nuclear drop bomb called the Mirage IVC (as then planned for the Mirage IVA), to a direct adaptation of the Mirage IV airframe with a semi-recessed missile (the Mirage IVC2, 9 April 1962), and finally the Mirage IVC22 (an early reply from Dassault to the Minerve call for proposals), which had a crew of three in a stretched fuselage. *Dassault Archives*

Dassault Mirage IVC22

The Mirage IVC22 design was proposed in late 1962 to response to the Minerve 1b and Minerve 2 missions. The C22 was a direct extrapolation of the Mirage IVA and enlarged so that it would be able to carry a warload increased to *'seven times'* that of the series Mirage IVA. Beside an unnamed Dassault-designed ballistic missile weighing 17,637lb (8,000kg), the C22 could carry either one or two *'Mirage IVA-type nuclear bombs'* or seven 1,000lb (454kg) conventional bombs (the ceiling of the recessed bomb bay would have been adapted depending on the intended load). Based on the facts that the aircraft aerodynamics were extrapolated from the Mirage IVA and that *'the aircraft is propelled by two Bristol Olympus 22R turbojets intended for the British TSR.2 bomber and already flight-tested'*, Dassault expected a quick development. The brochure also claimed that *'considering a development time of 2 years for the first prototype, testing could begin at the end of 1964 and the first production aircraft should be available*

Dassault Mirage IV C22	
Status	project
Span	50ft 0.5in (15.25m)
Length	92ft 4.5in (28.15m)
Gross wing area	1,397.8sq ft (130.00sq m)
Gross weight	132,275lb (60,000kg)
Powerplant	two Olympus 22R 30,600lb (136kN) in reheat
Maximum speed/Height	Mach 2.0
Armament	Missile 17,637lb (8,000kg)

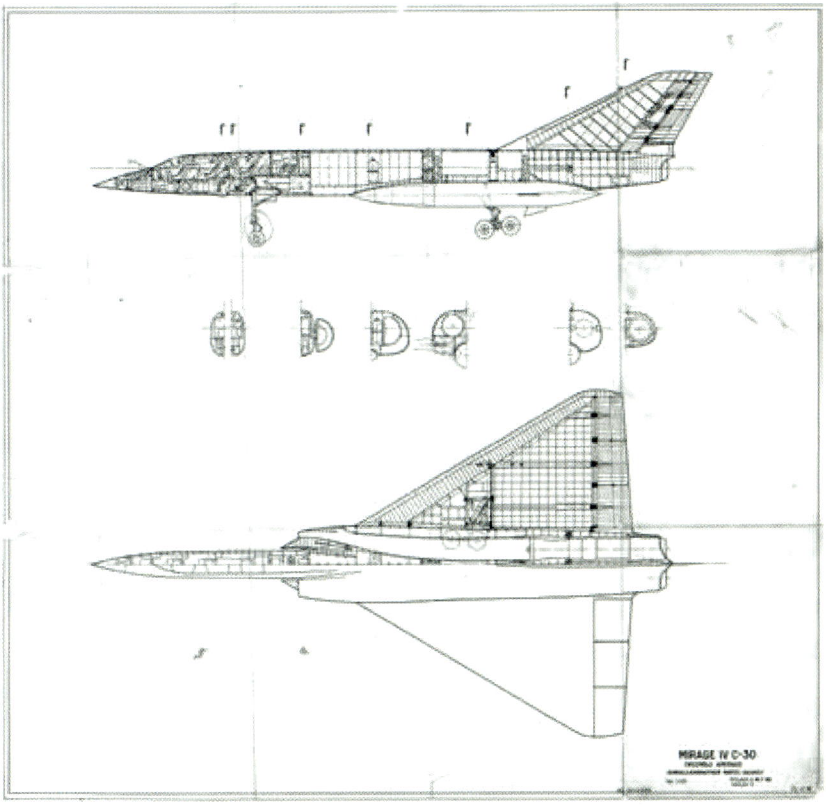

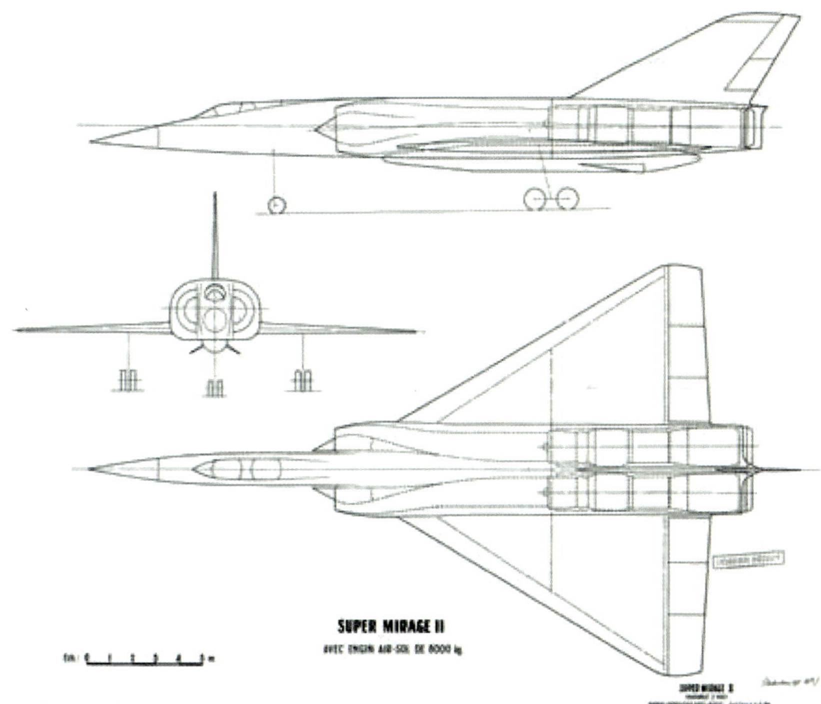

TOP **A beautifully detailed drawing of the Mirage IVC30 dated 10 July 1962, another iteration of the three-seat Mirage IV.** *Dassault Aviation*

ABOVE **The Super Mirage II, seen on a drawing dated 9 December 1961, was based on an enlarged Mirage IV that could carry a 8,000kg (17,637lb) missile.** *Dassault Aviation*

in 1967. This design was among the first offered with a three-man crew of pilot, navigator and electronic counter-measures (ECM) specialist; in fact, this configuration with a crew member dedicated to jamming enemy detection equipment was a first for a French bomber aircraft and Dassault was the only manufacturer to take electronic counter-measures sufficiently seriously to devote equipment and a crew member to it.

Dassault Mirage IVC30

Mirage IVC30 was another enlarged Mirage IVA with three crew and was intended to fill the basic requirement of being able to carry an 17,637lb (8,000kg) missile. It was designed in July 1962 and would have been fitted with a refuelling probe.

Super Mirage II

Super Mirage II was one of Dassault's initial entries in the Minerve competition and was dated 9 December 1962. A twin-engine bomber extrapolated from the Mirage IV and

Dassault Mirage IVC30	
Status	project
Span	55ft 5.5in (16.90m)
Length	-
Gross wing area	-
Gross weight	-
Powerplant	two TF106 19,800lb (88kN) in reheat
Maximum speed/Height	-
Armament	Missile 17,637lb (8,000kg)

Dassault Super Mirage II	
Status	project
Span	55ft 9in (17.00m)
Length	98ft 5in (30.00m)
Gross wing area	1,720.4sq ft (160.00sq m)
Gross weight	165,344lb (75,000kg)
Powerplant	two TF106 19,800lb (88kN) in reheat
Maximum speed/Height	Mach 2.2 at 36,090ft (11,000m)
Armament	X 411?

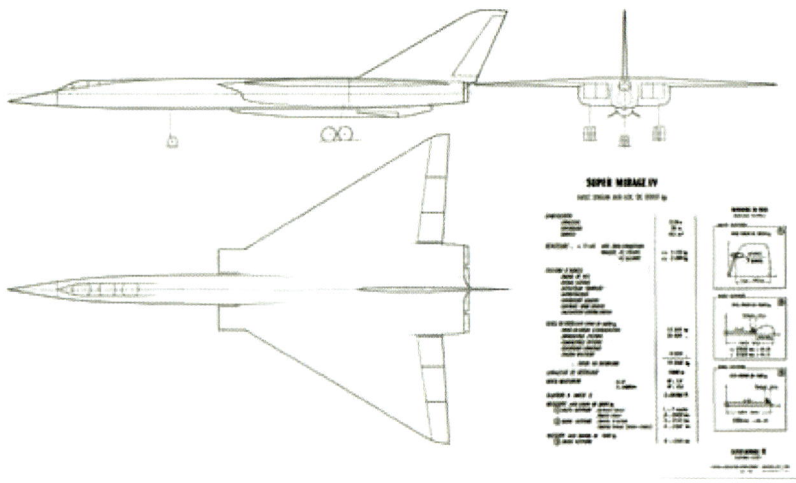

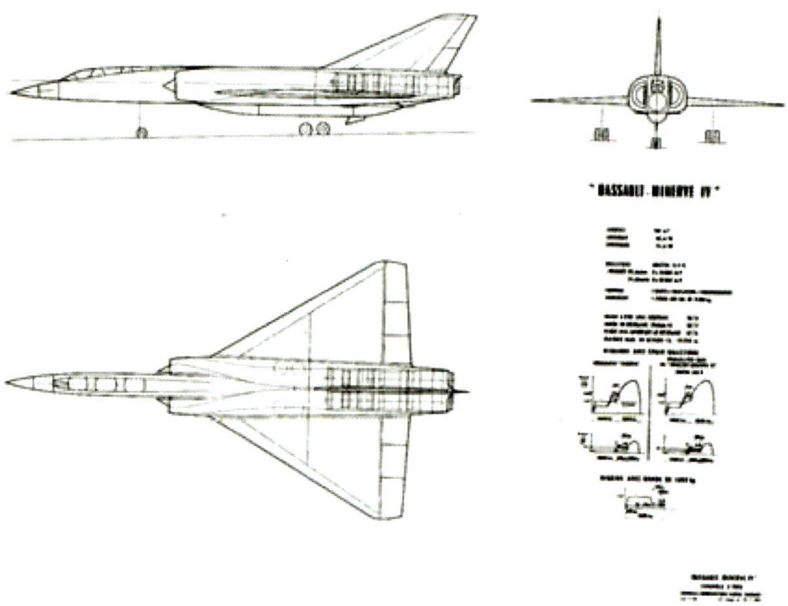

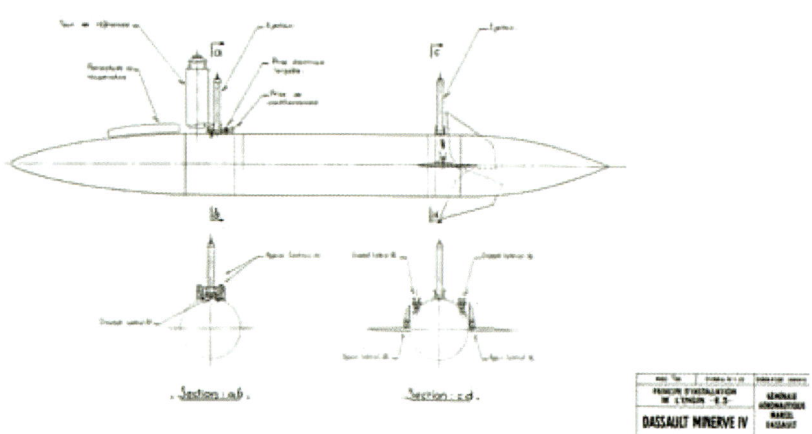

LEFT Going even further from the Mirage IV formula, the Super Mirage IV was a four-engined design that was probably too large to be really affordable within a French military budget. *Dassault Aviation*

BELOW LEFT When the Minerve programme was launched Dassault offered this larger Minerve IV design, another rare example in French jet bomber design to feature a three-man crew. The drawing is dated 31 January 1963. *Dassault Aviation*

BOTTOM LEFT Detailed drawing showing the installation of the E3 missile on the Minerve IV mother ship. *Dassault Aviation*

fitted with TF106 engines, it was to be capable of flying low- or high-altitude penetration missions. Initially the press designated it the 'Mirage IV-106' but in 1963 it was finally identified as the Minerve. The airframe was to be built in steel and titanium and its span would have been around 55ft 9in (17m). For a production run of fifty aircraft the cost was estimated to be 210 billion francs.

Dassault Super Mirage VI

This big four-engine bomber was designed between February and early March 1962. It would have received a large complement of avionics including nose and side radar sets, Doppler scanner, astrotracker, a 'slave hyposcope' (a sighting device), gyroscopic controller and a digital computer. Able to operate both in the low- and high-altitude mission profiles, powered by four TF106s and

Dassault Super Mirage VI	
Status	project
Span	65ft 7.5in (20.00m)
Length	109ft 11in (33.50m)
Gross wing area	1,989.2sq ft (185.00sq m)
Gross weight	174,162lb (79,000kg)
Powerplant	four TF106 19,800lb (88kN) in reheat
Maximum speed/Height	Mach 2.2 at 36,090ft (11,000m)
Armament	Missile 17,637lb (8,000kg)

Dassault Minerve IV	
Status	project
Span	-
Length	-
Gross wing area	-
Gross weight	-
Powerplant	-
Maximum speed/Height	-
Armament	Dassault E3

Dassault E3	
Status	project
Diameter	4ft 1.5in (1.26m)
Length	40ft 4.5in (12.30m)
Gross weight	-
Powerplant	rocket
Maximum speed/Height	Mach 2 at 59,055ft (18,000m)
Carrier aircraft	Dassault Minerve

with a loaded weight of 174,162lb (79,000kg) including the missile, this project was in the American Convair B-58 class and way beyond the financial capabilities of the French budget … so much so that it remains a mystery why it was designed in the first place!

Following an agreement made with Sud Aviation in 1962, on 31 January 1963 Dassault offered the Minerve IV project powered by two Bristol Olympus 593R turbojets, which were to be the powerplants for the Concorde. This aircraft was to be the mother ship for a 20,944lb (9,500kg) air-to-ground missile called the E3 and three crew were needed to operate it – pilot, navigator/bomber and ECM specialist.

Dassault Minerve VB

The Minerve VB was a smaller design powered by two Bristol Olympus 22R turbojets but with the same capabilities as the Minerve IV. It also had a crew of three with a dedicated ECM officer, and was offered in March 1963.

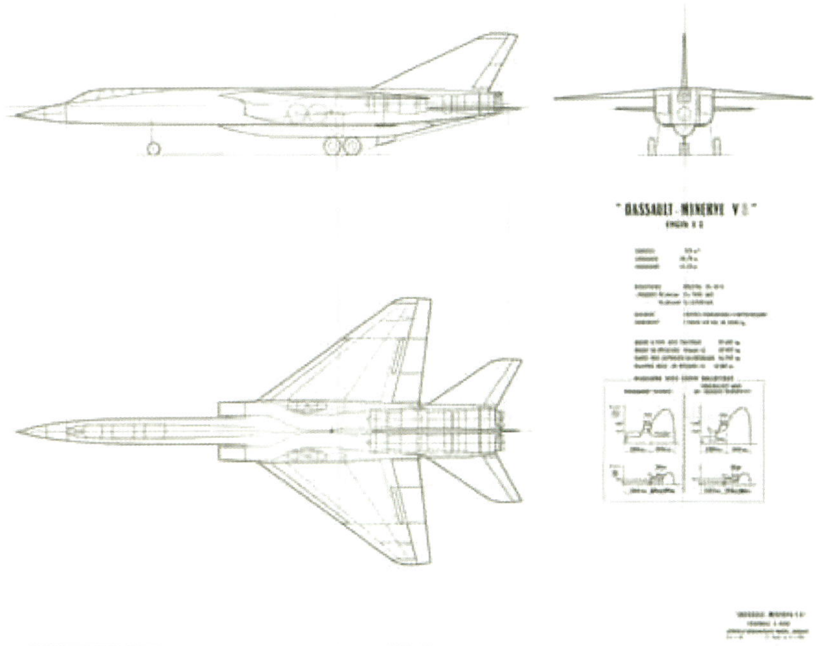

ABOVE The Minerve VB of 13 March 1963 differed from the previous Minerve IV in that it was only a two-seat aircraft. *Dassault Aviation*

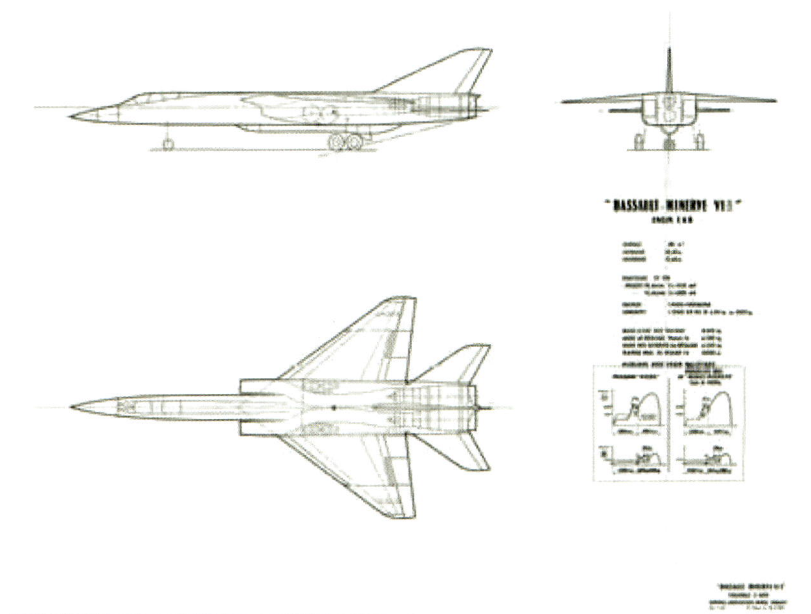

ABOVE The Dassault Minerve VI, dated 14 March 1963, was (as far as is known) the final variant of the Mirage IV to be offered in response to Minerve. With a crew of two and of reduced size, it was considered to be more financially compatible with the Armée de l'Air budget. It is shown with an E-6B missile. *Dassault Aviation*

Dassault Minerve VIB	
Status	project
Span	43ft 11.5in (13.40m)
Length	86ft 7.5in (26.40m)
Gross wing area	860.2sq ft (80sq m)
Gross weight	98,325lb (44,600kg)
Powerplant	two TF106, dry 11,355lb (50.5kN), 19,840lb (88.2kN) reheat
Maximum speed/Height	Mach 2+
Armament	Dassault E6B or E3 9,039lb (4,100kg) or 20,944lb (9,500kg)

Dassault E6B	
Status	project
Diameter	-
Length	27ft 10.5in (8.50m) (approx)
Gross weight	20,944lb (9,500kg)
Powerplant	rocket
Maximum speed/Height	-
Carrier aircraft	Mirage IVC

Dassault Minerve VIB

This March 1963 design seems to have been the winner inside the company because it is the only one for which we have evidence of a presentation being made to Marcel Dassault himself. With two seats and two engines it went back into the budget-acceptable designs after the huge Super Mirage of the preceding year. It also displayed an evolution in Dassault's line of thought with smaller swept wings (which would see fruition in the Mirage F family) and box-shaped air intakes similar in outward appearance to those of the North American A-5 Vigilante (although these were never adopted on a built Dassault aircraft). The Minerve VIB could carry either the E6B or the E3 missile, both of which were Dassault designs.

In the end, none of Dassault's aircraft designs appears to have survived past the winter of 1962-63, although the Minerve IV seems to have influenced the Mirage IVF series.

Mirage IV with X-411S

On 27 July 1963 Dassault studied the possibility of fitting a non-Dassault

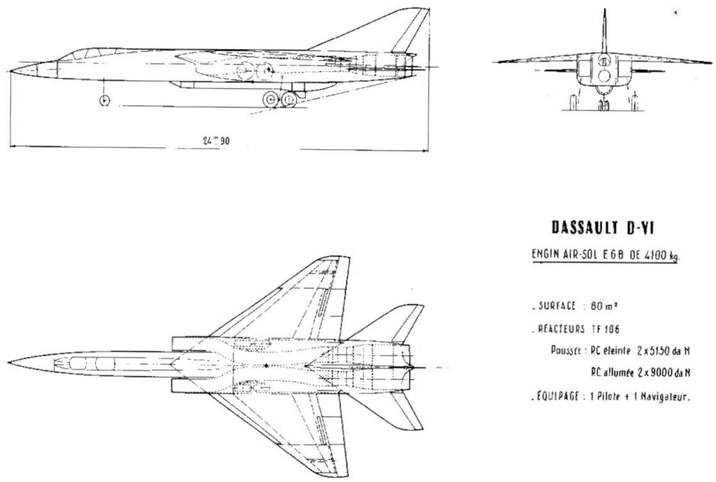

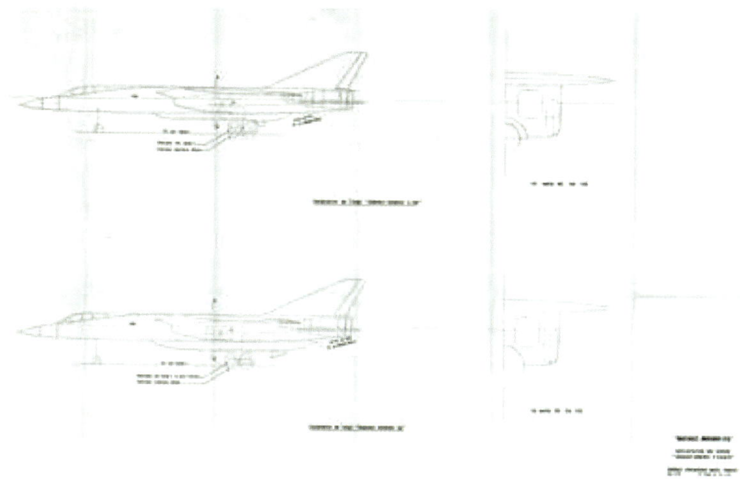

TOP **Although labelled 'D VI' on the document, this design is identical to the Minerve VI proposal from Dassault.** *Dassault Aviation*

ABOVE **A drawing from 19 March 1963 showing the installation of the E-6B and E3 missile on the Minerve VIB mother ship.** *Dassault Aviation*

BELOW **Based on this drawing, which is dated 22 July 1963, it seems Dassault had difficulties in fitting the rather large Sud-designed X-411S missile underneath a Mirage IVA.** *Philippe Ricco*

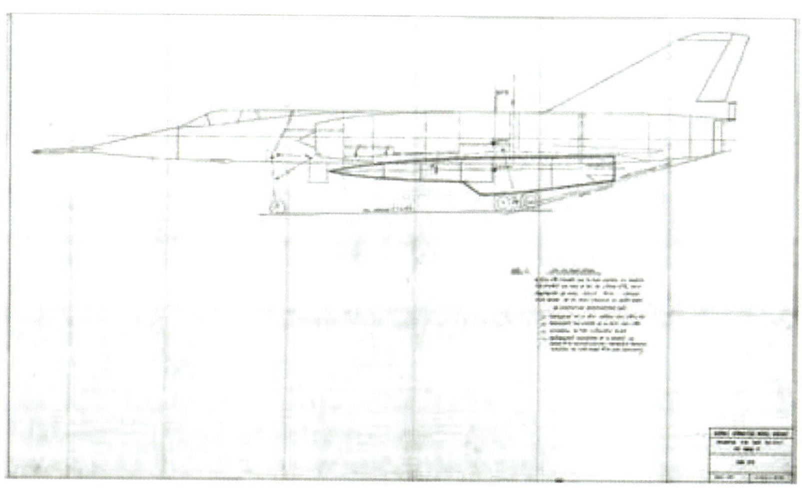

ABOVE This model has previously and erroneously been identified as a 'Mirage IVF', and then as the still unknown 'Mirage VI' thanks to the rudder marking 'M VI'. However, it appears that the true identity of this design is the Minerve VIB. *Author's collection, Dassault photos*

missile, the Sud X-411S, on to the Mirage IV. This would have required a larger weapon bay (sized originally to fit the French nuclear bomb casing) and a redesign of the front airframe with enlarged fuel tanks and ECM equipment in the dorsal equipment bay. Against this, all radar equipment would have been dropped.

Nord Aviation Minerve

Nord Aviation Minerve	
Status	project
Span	63ft 11.5in (19.50m)
Length	111ft 6.5in (34.00m)
Gross wing area	2,096.8sq ft (195.00sq m)
Gross weight	119,048lb (54,000kg)
Powerplant	two TF106 19,800lb (88kN) with reheat or two BS 593/3
Maximum speed/Height	Mach 2 at 36,090ft (11,000m)
Armament	Missile 8,600kg (18,959lb)

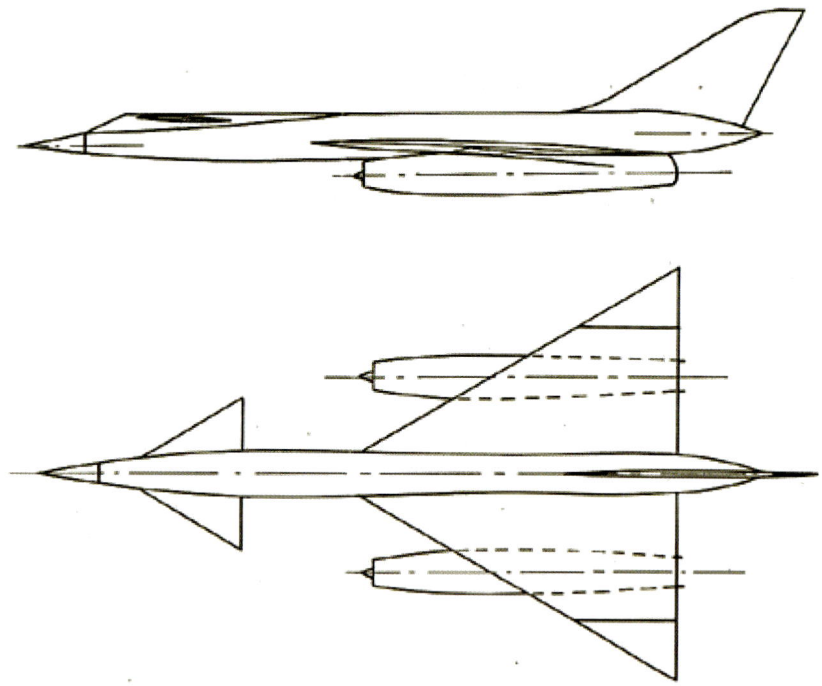

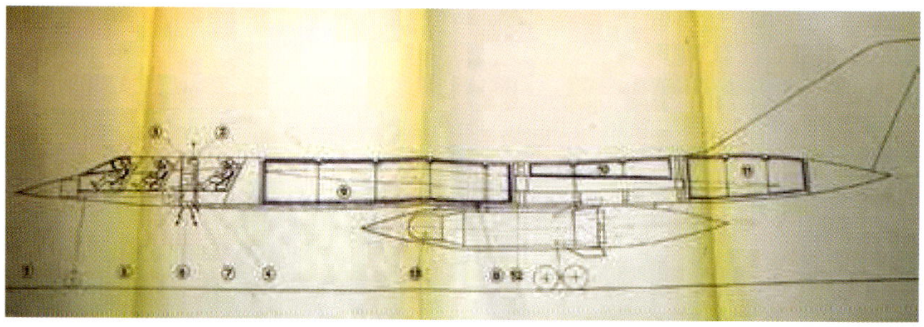

TOP **Nord Aviation made this supersonic proposal to the Minerve competition.** *Philippe Ricco*

ABOVE **Section drawing of the Nord Minerve bomber's fuselage showing the three crew positions, and the M 600(?) missile in a faired container underneath the fuselage.** *Philippe Ricco*

Nord Minerve bomber

Nord's high-speed Minerve aircraft was a large delta with engines podded under the wing that were to be probably either TF106s or Olympus 593/3s (curiously they were not turbo-ramjets although this was a speciality of Nord). The Nord team designed a fairing to carry the missile underneath the fuselage but whether the weapon was to be a Matra M 600 is not known; however, the shape was similar and the aircraft was also to be able to carry the Sud X-416/X-417 missile. The three crew members would probably include an ECM operator and, looking at the surviving drawing, only the pilot appeared to benefit from a view outside. Speed was intended to be Mach 1.2 at sea level for the approach cruise, with Mach 2.0 then being reached while the aircraft climbed to 6,090ft (11,000m) for its combat flight

The Nord design featured anti-gust devices and was, therefore, the only proposed design to specifically take into account the more difficult wind conditions encountered in the low-altitude mission. The full cost for fifty aircraft including five prototypes was estimated by Nord to be 1.4 billion francs, but this price would have included provision for ten ground simulators and servicing equipment. However, the documents noted that: '*For the lack of certain data, the cost of operating the weapon system has not been evaluated: airfields, communication network, maintenance workshops. Neither has the cost of support systems: refueller aircraft, satellite navigation system.*' Interestingly, the highest price in the budget quoted for the prototype phase was given to the development of the navigation system. The brochure was issued in July 1962, with supplements for the BS.593/3 version added on 9 October. Since Nord did not produce the missile the brochure indicated that the weapon to be carried could weigh either 20,613lb or 21,164lb (9,350kg or 9,600kg) dependent on the improvements that could be made to the Bristol Siddeley engine's reheat system. This is consistent with what is known about the X-416 missile, but the Nord Minerve design also appears to have been abandoned before 1963.

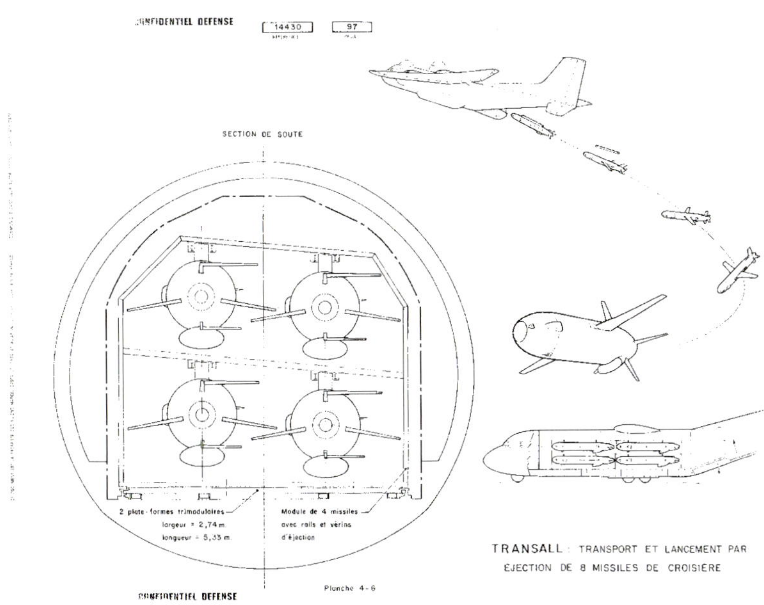

ABOVE No illustration has yet surfaced of the Transall Minerve. However, this later drawing of a Transall adapted to carry Dassault's cruise missile project may give an idea of what it looked like. *Dassault Aviation*

Transall Minerve

Nothing has so far emerged regarding the missile carrier based on the Transall, although it appears to have survived in the minds of the Minerve Committee for much longer than did the supersonic platform. It is also known that later on the Transall was considered again as a platform for the Exocet missile (Exocet was itself a follow-up to the X-4xx family), and even later as the carrier of an octet of Dassault-designed cruise missiles.

Sud Aviation Minerve

Sud Aviation PSS	
Status	project
Span	78ft 0in (23.78m)
Length	170ft 0in (51.81m)
Gross wing area	3,333.3sq ft (310.00sq m)
Gross weight	220,459lb (100,000kg)
Powerplant	four Olympus 29,250lb (130kN)
Maximum speed/Height	Mach 2
Armament	two X-414 missiles or one X-416 missile
Based on the civilian Super Caravelle as of early 1963.	

Sud Aviation Super Caravelle Minerve

To begin with, Sud Aviation responded with a variant of the SE 210 Caravelle fitted with four turbojets (which it called the Super Caravelle), but the designers soon discovered the SE 210 was too small to carry the rather large missile then under consideration (in the 17,637lb to 22,046lb [8,000kg to 10,000kg] class). Sud also studied a foreign-designed aircraft, the Boeing KC-135, which may have been topical in that the type was being considered to provide longer range for the Mirage IV. However, as stated already, using the American KC-135 as a major element of the *Force de Frappe* would have been difficult politically.

In the end it was another Super Caravelle that was selected, the *Transport Civil Supersonique* (Civilian Supersonic Transport) or TCS. This was a variant of the initial project from which the Concorde was developed and the idea of mating the X-225 Super Caravelle with a long-range missile was acknowledged by Ministre des Armées (Armed Forces Minister) Pierre Messmer during the preparation of the 1963 defence budget. As reported by *Aviation Magazine* in its 1 August 1962 issue, he said: '*Speaking of this aircraft* [the Super Caravelle], *one must take into account that beyond the first generation of dissuasion weapon systems based on Mirage IV carrying nuclear bombs, a second generation is currently being studied which could feature platforms based on the Supersonic Transport, from which would be launched ballistic air-to-ground missiles carrying thermonuclear warheads.*' Messmer also indicated that: '*Concerning this weapon system, a decision* [to proceed] *could be taken in the coming two years.*' This was also noted by *RAF Flying Review* in October with a report that said: '*A supersonic launching platform for thermonuclear missiles based on the Super Caravelle* [is] *now being studied.*'

However, it proved difficult to adapt the Super Caravelle/Concorde to military needs because of the way it had been designed: for example the aircraft's ogee wing was so well integrated with the fuselage that it would have been impossible to create a recess in it, let alone a bomb bay, to house the big missile. This was unfortunate because otherwise the aircraft looked perfectly adapted for the role, and the 19,841lb (9,000kg) missile would have weighed about as much as the passengers in the airliner. Launched 1,554 miles (2,500km) from its base, at 39,370ft (12,000m) altitude, the missile would have carried a 1,543lb (700kg) warhead. If the project had been given the go-ahead in July 1963 Sud had hoped to have its *Plate-forme Super Sonique* (PSS), carrying two X-417s, flying in prototype form by October 1967. An order for thirty-four machines was outlined with deliveries beginning in July 1969. As noted earlier, alternative versions studied in parallel with the future Concorde were also assessed as military mother ships, including a VTOL type.

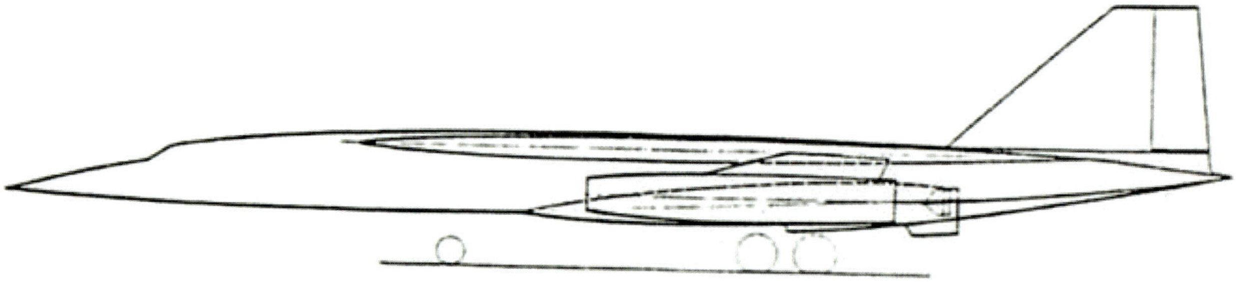

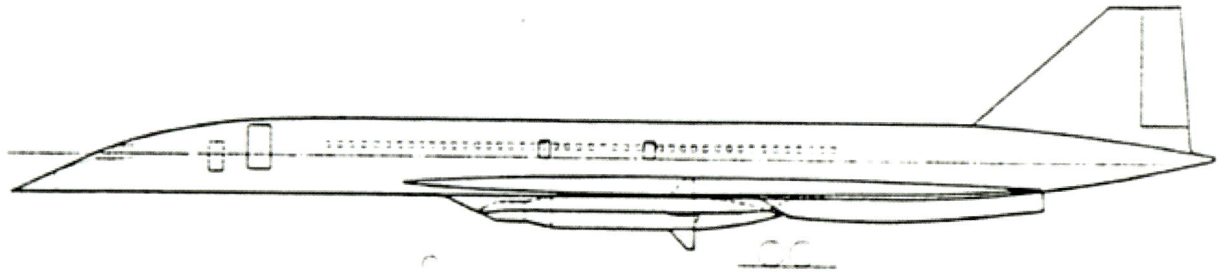

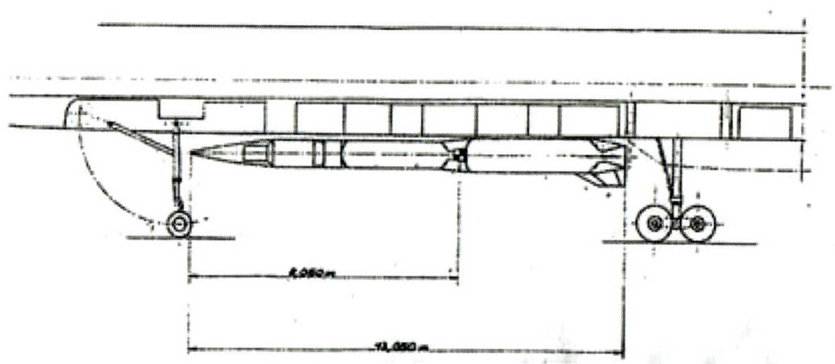

TOP One of the variants of the Sud Supersonic Transport adapted to carry the X-417. *Sud Aviation*

ABOVE The Super Caravelle SST (the future Concorde) was adapted to carry a X-416 rocket-propelled missile. *Sud Aviation*

RIGHT Detail for the attachment point of the X-416 underneath a Super Caravelle. Sud Aviation

BELOW RIGHT As an option the Super Caravelle could have be designed to carry the X-414 turbojet powered 'robot' missile. *Author from a Sud Aviation drawing*

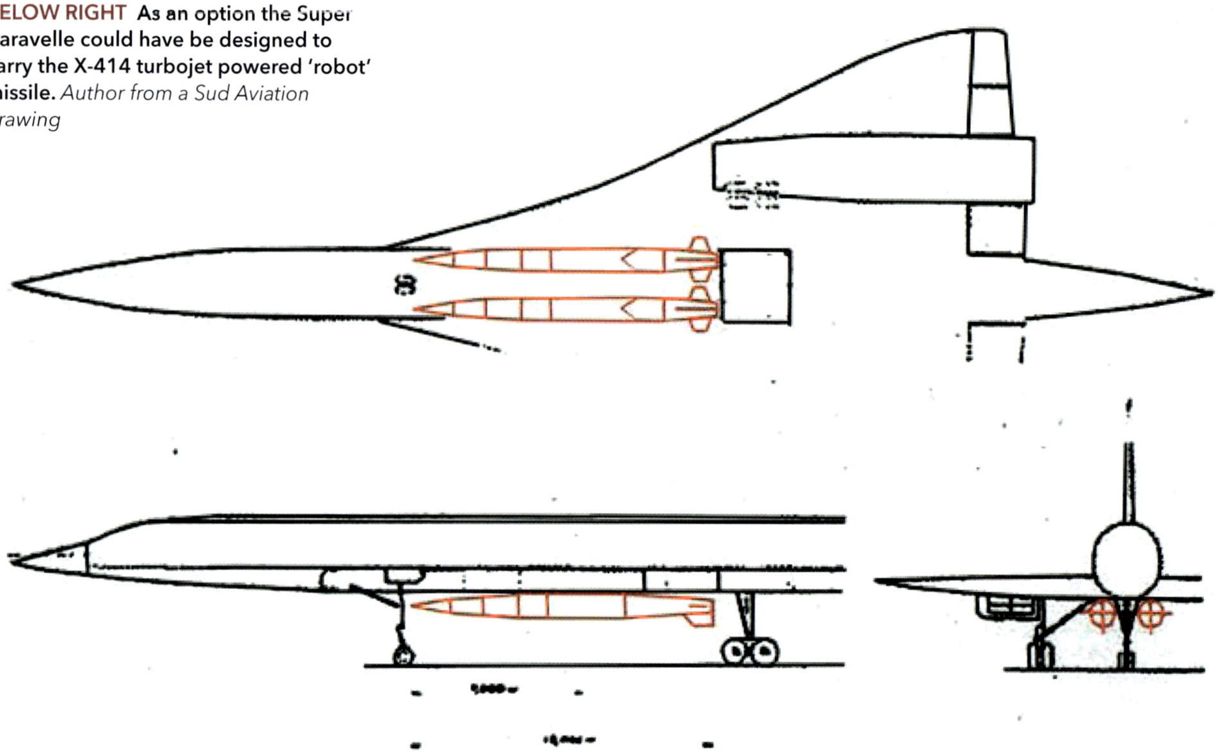

Chapter Five
Strike and Training (ECAT)

ABOVE The first three prototype Jaguars, E01, E02 and A03. All of them attended the 1969 Paris Show, where the single-seater was flown by Bernard Witt of Breguet and the two-seaters were handled by BAC's Paul Millet and Jimmy Dell. *Author's collection*

This chapter brings together a variety of strike and trainer aircraft types from several manufacturers and in particular looks at the *Ecole de Combat et Appui Tactique* (ECAT) story.

The Original Strike/ Trainer Aircraft

The Fouga Magister Family

The Fouga company was founded by Gaston Fouga in 1920.

CM 130

The CM 130 was a twin-engined trainer aircraft designed by Pierre Mauboussin and Robert Castello (hence the type names CM) as a replacement for the Morane Saulnier MS 470 Vanneau, at the time the primary trainer for the *Armée de l'Air*. With two Turboméca Palas turbojets giving 350lb (1.6kN) of thrust this design was found to be underpowered, so an enlarged version was produced instead fitted with Marboré jets.

CM 170

The CM 170 was the base version of the Fouga Magister, of which 445 units were produced. The cockpit was enlarged from the initial design after the mock-up inspection made by STAé in 1951. After the crash of the first prototype on 3 November 1952 a brief investigation was made towards fitting conventional tail surfaces rather than the V-tail. However, the accident report proved that the V-tail was not responsible for the crash and so the standard tail, which would have increased the aircraft's overall weight, was not pursued further.

CM 170R

This model was the first basic twin-jet trainer to enter service anywhere in the world, in 1956. Before that ten pre-production machines had been produced and an initial order was placed for ninety-five production aircraft, increased later in 1956 to 325.

CM 160

This was a planned lighter version of the CM 170 proposed in 1955. It weighed only 5,895lb (2,674kg) and could operate from grass fields.

CM 170M Esquif

In 1955 the Fouga Company began the development of a naval variant of the Magister adapted for deck landings. Two prototypes were built fitted with an arrester hook, catapult spools and a reinforced undercarriage and were known as the CM 170M (M for Marine). Esquif means a skiff or light boat.

CM 170-2 Super Magister

A new version with 1,060lb (4.7kN) thrust Turboméca Marboré VI turbojets was called the Super Magister and 544 examples were produced.

CM 170-3 Super Magister

This improved version first flew in 1963 with a redesigned nose housing a fire-direction radar such as the CSF Cyrano (which was also used on Mirage fighters). New Martin-Baker ejector seats were installed and the fuel capacity was increased.

CM 170 Pamplemousse

A special variant of the CM 170 was fitted experimentally with a silencer nozzle instead of the usual Marboré II nozzles. This silencer nozzle, named '*Pamplemousse*' (Grapefruit) because of its spherical shape, was designed by Jean Bertin as a sideline to his '*trompes*' (injector) work. On 7 December 1960 a demonstration of the device was held for the benefit of the press in which a noise reduction of 10db was recorded; however, the system was not generalized.

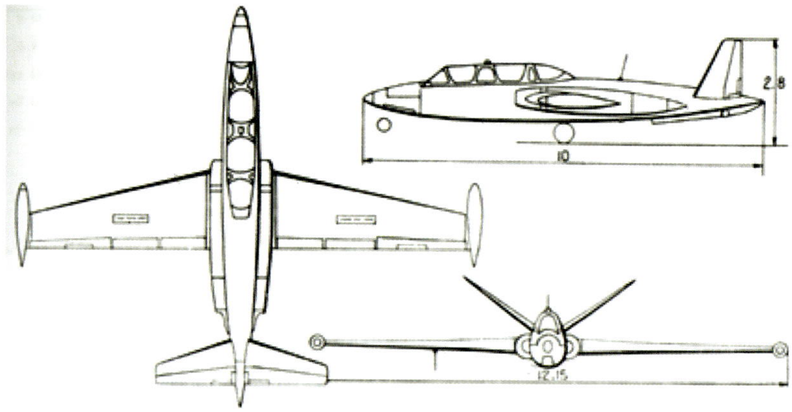

ABOVE **The Fouga CM170 was the base design for the Fouga Magister.** *Author's collection/Fouga document*

BELOW **The CM 174 was an unrealised attempt to design a Mach 1-capable Magister. Yet even in its refined version, the CM 195, problems with compressibility were revealed by wind tunnel testing and the aircraft was deemed unable to fly above Mach 0.85, so it was not built.** *Author's collection/Fouga document*

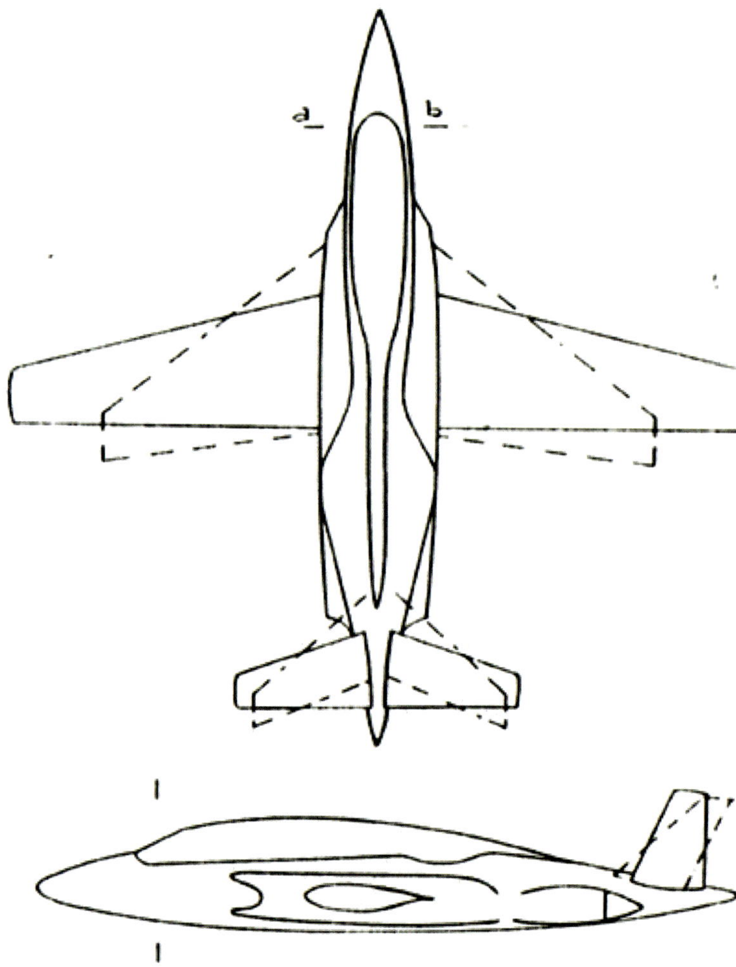

CM 171 Makalu

The name Makalu (a Tibetan mountain and the fifth highest point in the world), coupled with the revised and reinforced canopy of the CM 171, suggests that this was intended to be a high-altitude aircraft. A single prototype was flown on 5 November 1956 with two Turboméca Gabizo engines but was lost in an accident on 20 March 1957. It was not followed up with further airframes.

CM 173

See ECAT section.

CM 174

The CM 174 was begun as an improved CM 170 fitted with 1,410lb (6.3kN) Turboméca Gourdou III turbojets and with ejector seats installed in the cockpit. The estimated performance was improved somewhat over the standard Magister but the testing of a model in the St Cyr wind tunnel revealed compressibility problems at speeds above Mach 0.65. A much modified version introduced swept wings and a swept tail, plus enlarged engine fairings along the fuselage in accordance with Whitcomb area ruling. However, model testing showed that the compressibility problems could still not be overcome, but rather only delayed until Mach 0.85 was reached.

ABOVE Artist's view of the CM 175 ground attack project, which is not to be confused with the CM 175 naval version of the Magister. *Author's collection/Fouga document*

CM 175

As sometimes happens, there were in fact two versions designated CM 175. The CM 175 Zéphyr as built was the naval production version, of which thirty were manufactured for the *Marine Nationale*. The prototype first flew on 31 July 1956, by which time Fouga had been bought by Potez and the new management requested a change in designation to reflect the naval fittings. As such, the CM 170M became the CM 175.

Previously, in 1953, the designation CM 175 had been allocated to a single-seat, single-engine ground support aircraft. This would have featured wings with a slightly swept leading edge and was armed with two fuselage-mounted 20mm guns and sixteen rockets under the wings.

CM 180

A flying test bed for the Turboméca Ossau turbojet (mounted on the back of the fuselage) and flown in 1953.

CM 190

A 1953 designation for a two-seat trainer based on the Magister but with side-by-side seating. The landing gear would have been of the bicycle type and the wing would have been modified.

CM 191

Designed in 1955, this variant was proposed as a four-seat aircraft with optional roles of trainer and liaison, and it was hoped that it could be offered to the civilian market as well. The powerplant was to be twin Turboméca Marboré IVs. The original proposal fell through but it was launched a second time in 1961 under a combined Potez-Heinkel sponsorship. Since it was a co-operative Franco-German project, the first prototype was exhibited to the public for the first time in late April 1962 at that year's Hannover Show, following its maiden flight on 19 March

Fouga CM 191 (1955)	
Status	project
Span	-
Length	-
Gross wing area	-
Gross weight	9,083lb (4,120kg)
Powerplant	two Super Marboré 1,190lb (5.3kN)
Maximum speed/Height	485mph (780km/h) at 39,370ft (12,000m)
Armament	-

from Toulouse with Jacques Grangette and Pierre Caneil at the controls. Three prototypes were ordered by the German *Bundesluftwaffe* along with two airframes for static testing. At this point a contract for fifty CM 191A military high-speed communication and training aircraft was expected and a civilian version called the CM 191B was also planned, but in the end only two examples were built. One of them was apparently still flying in the twenty-first century!

CM 195

A two-seat trainer supposedly first proposed in 1955, but evidence suggests that this date actually relates to an earlier design, the CM 174. The CM 195 was definitely presented at the 1957 Paris Air Show and, like the CM 174, it was to have both its wings and V-tail swept to provide transonic performance (when fitted with two Turboméca Gabizo engines).

Fouga CM 195	
Status	project
Span	-
Length	-
Gross wing area	-
Gross weight	9,700lb (4,400kg)
Powerplant	two Gabizo 2,475lb (11.0kN)
Maximum speed/Height	597mph (960km/h) in level flight, Mach 1.1 in dive
Armament	-

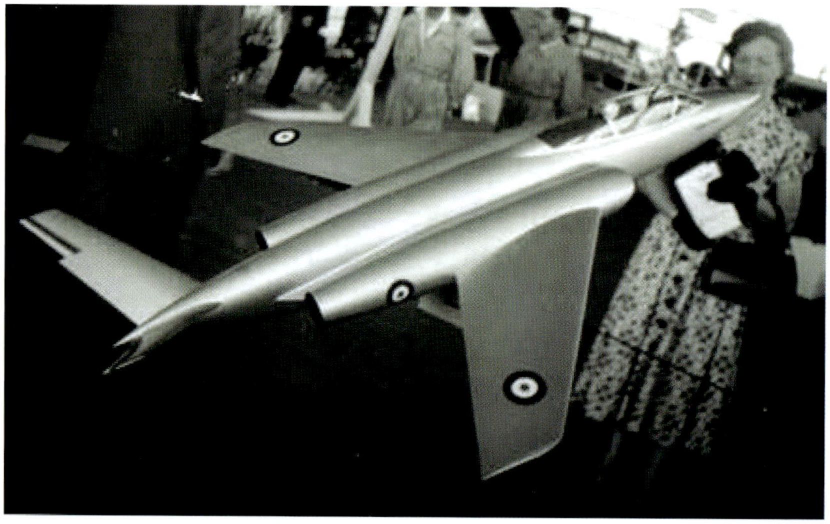

TOP & ABOVE The CM 195 model is seen on display at the June 1957 Paris Air Show. *Tony Buttler/ Author's collection*

RIGHT Artist's impression of the CM 195 in flight. *Author's collection/Fouga document*

CM 209

The CM 209 was a 1961 proposal for a re-engined Magister with two Marboré VI engines. It was in the end produced as the Super Magister CM 170-2.

Other Designs

Morane Saulnier MS 755 Fleuret

The MS 755 was designed to compete with the CM 170 but lost out to the Fouga proposal and never reached series production.

Payen PA 49B Katy

The very small PA 49B delta wing aircraft was, at the time of its first flight in 1955, the smallest delta aeroplane in the world. Although a single-seater, Roland Payen expected it to be able to fulfil a trainer role, in particular covering the transition from conventionally winged aircraft to delta wing fighters. However, for pilots the transition between these configurations proved to be easier than anticipated using standard aircraft types and so the Katy (named after Payen's daughter) did not progress beyond a single prototype. The B in the type number refers to the fact that there was also a PA 49A designed as a fighter, which was twice the size of the Katy.

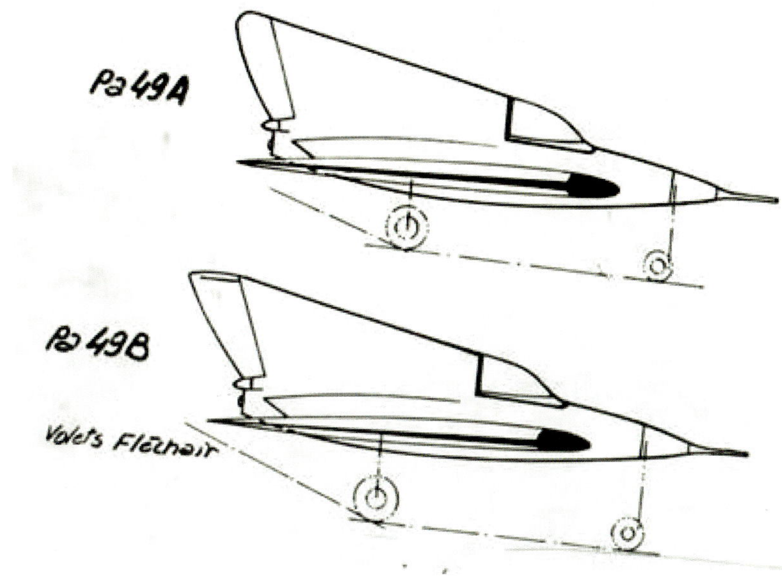

ABOVE **When first built the Pa 49 Katy had a bicycle ('monotrace') landing gear.** *Philippe Ricco*

ABOVE RIGHT **Later it received a more conventional landing gear.** *José Fernandez*

TOP **Roland Payen was eager to promote the *'volets Payen'* (the Payen flaps) and wanted to put them on the Katy.** *Author's collection*

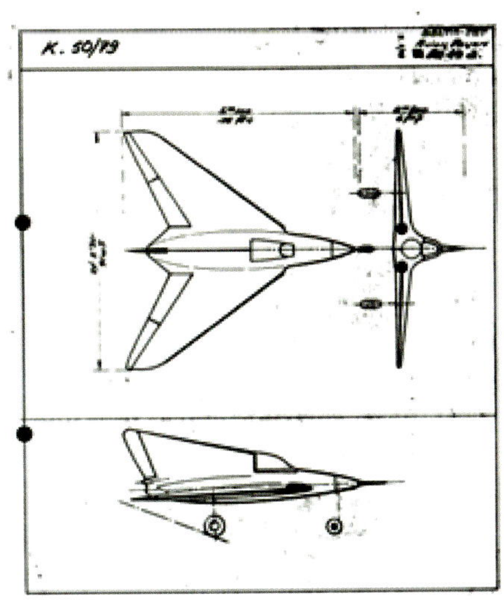

ABOVE **Official drawing of the Pa 49 Katy.** *Author's collection*

ABOVE **The Pa 49 Katy may be seen today in the Musée de l'Air et de l'Espace.** *J.C. Carbonel*

RIGHT **The Pa 57 Aton was a twin-jet trainer extrapolated from the Katy. This sketch and the two-view drawing show how the Payen flaps would have operated.** *Philippe Ricco*

MIDDLE RIGHT **Three-view drawing of the S-200.** *Author's collection*

MIDDLE LEFT **Drawings of the Pa 57 showing the *volets Payen* used as rudders on each fin. Note the perspective view with three fins.** *Author's collection/ Payen patent*

BELOW RIGHT **The SIPA S-200 first flew in 1952.** *José Fernandez*

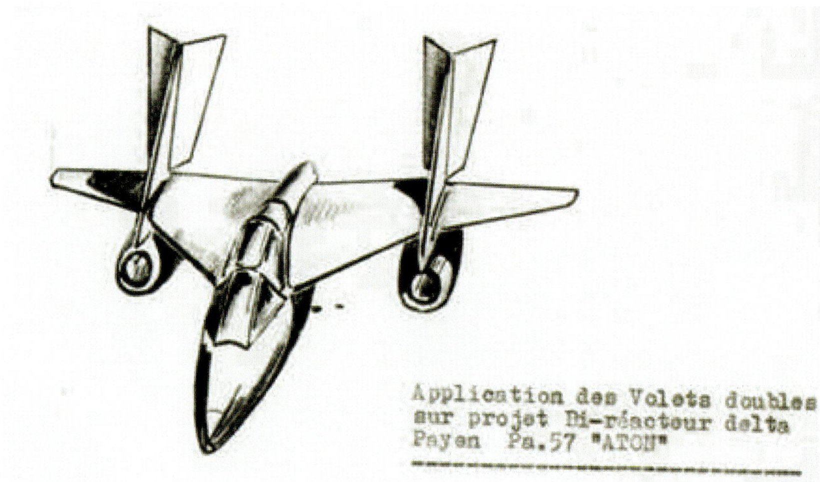

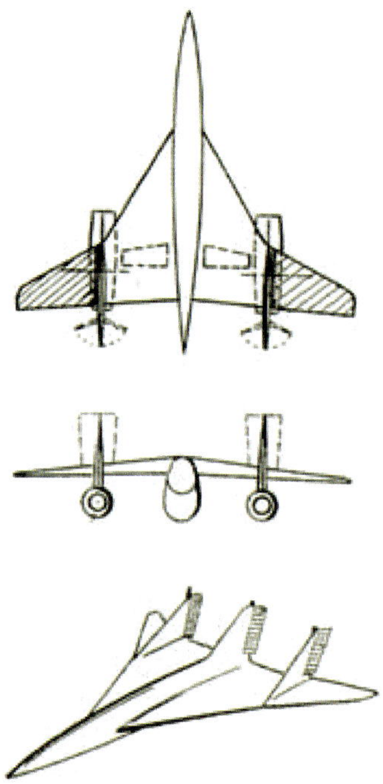

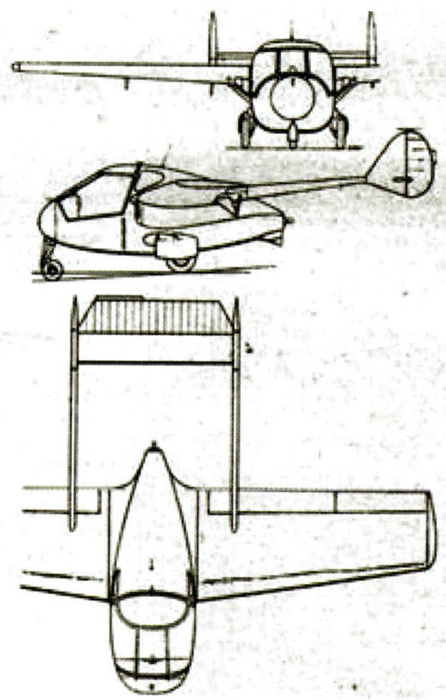

Payen PA 56 Jockey

This was an enlarged variant of the Katy, a two-seat trainer powered by either one Dassault Viper engine (built under licence) or two Turboméca Marboré II units. It was proposed in 1955.

Payen PA 57 Aton

Another trainer but this time with a 'double-delta' planform, the PA 57 would have been powered by two Turboméca Marborés. The student and the teacher would sit in tandem, the configuration favoured in France. Aton is the name of the Egyptian sun god, but anagrammatically it is also a form of NATO, suggesting Payen had his sights on the European market.

Payen Pa 57 Aton	
Status	project
Span	19ft 8in (6.00m)
Length	26ft 5.5in (8.06m)
Gross wing area	-
Gross weight	7,055lb (3,200kg)
Powerplant	two Marboré II, 900lb (4kN)
Maximum speed/Height	559mph (900km/h)
Armament	-

SIPA S-200

This aircraft was designed in 1951 by Yves Gardan with two goals: firstly to supply the *Armée de l'Air* with the smallest and cheapest jet trainer, and second to offer amateurs a high-speed sporty two-seater aircraft. Neither

objective was to be achieved and only seven prototypes were built. The first aircraft, exhibited at the 1951 Paris Air Show, never flew and was kept back for static load testing. The second prototype was the first of the bunch to fly, on 14 January 1952 with Roger Launay at the controls. Powered by a Turboméca Palas, it was able to reach 267mph (430km/h) and, having been designed purely to accustom pilots to jet flight, it was destined never to carry any weapons.

SIPA S-300

The prototype of this two-seat basic trainer was demonstrated for the first time on 22 July 1954 and later at the 1955 Paris Air Show. Student and teacher were seated in tandem and for this machine the accent was on simplicity and low cost (as with all Yves Gardan designs), with propulsion coming from a Turboméca Palas. The only example built was lost in a crash on 26 September 1955.

SIPA S-300	
Status	prototype
Span	26ft 4in (8.02m)
Length	22ft 0in (6.71m)
Gross wing area	105.4sq ft (9.80sq m)
Gross weight	1,940lb (880kg)
Powerplant	one Palas 340lb (1.5kN)
Maximum speed/Height	224mph (360km/h)
Armament	none

SIPA S-300M

The S-300M was an earlier trainer design that was propelled by a selection of piston engines.

SIPA S-300M	
Status	project
Span	33ft 5.5in (10.20m)
Length	26ft 3in (8.00m)
Gross wing area	179.6sq ft (16.70sq m)
Gross weight	2,789lb (1,265kg)
Powerplant	Various types 240hp (kW)
Maximum speed/Height	169mph (272km/h) at ground level
Armament	none

ABOVE The S-300 was the prototype for a basic trainer that flew in 1955. *José Fernandez*

ECAT Becomes a Feline, and Other Designs ...

The origin of ECAT goes back to a French ECAP requirement for a trainer with ground attack capability (ECAP for *Ecole/Appui*, School/Support). This was raised at the same time as a similar British RAF Air Staff Target AST.362 of 1963 for a trainer to replace both the Folland Gnat and the two-seat Hawker Hunter in 1974. In fact, AST.362 called for more than a mere trainer, it also required an aircraft with the ability to perform frontline strike operations. To undertake this role it was to be a twin-engine design to increase its survivability and to provide a maximum speed of up to Mach 1.7 (the British proposals to AST.362 are covered in *British Secret Projects Volume II: Jet Bombers since 1949*).

Meanwhile, in France the new requirement evolved further when the Air Ministry drew up an *Ecole de Combat et Appui Tactique* (ECAT) requirement for a light tactical trainer for service with the *Armée de l'Air* and the *Marine Nationale*. In January 1964 a call for proposals (*fiche programme*) was issued with the following requirements:

(i). Take-off (for the ground attack version) in less than 2,625ft (800m) from a rough track.
(ii). A speed of Mach 0.9 at ground level.
(iii). Excellent low altitude manoeuvrability.
(iv). Range 311 miles (500km) at 450 knots (834km/h).
(v). Rapid acceleration from 450 knots (834km/h) to Mach 0.9.
(vi). No aerodynamic disturbance at high speeds.
(vii). Excellent flight handling in rough weather.

At this time the British government, anxious to become a member of the European Economic Community (EEC), despite French opposition, sought to establish several joint aviation programmes with the French aircraft industry. The most remarkable of those programmes was to be Concorde, of course, but on the military side two planned projects showed promise due to their similarity in requirements: the AST trainer-cum-attacker and a variable geometry multi-role fighter. Then in March 1964 the French and British governments agreed on the two programmes:

1. A new trainer based on the ECAT requirement that would be led by French industry.
2. A larger multi-role fighter soon to be known as the Anglo-French Variable Geometry aircraft, or AFVG, with British leadership (see Volume I). However, according to

the aviation press at the time, in 1965 the RAF was still considering an advanced lightweight variable geometry aircraft.

Breguet Br 121

On 30 June 1964 Breguet offered as a candidate for ECAT its Br 121 project, which was a development of the earlier Br 1001 Taon (Volume I). Five versions were proposed: the Br 121A single-seater tactical ground attack aircraft, Br 121B two-seat tactical ground attack aircraft, Br

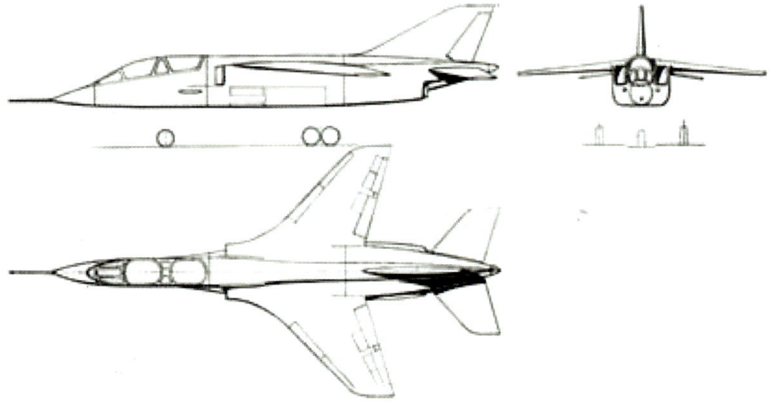

ABOVE RIGHT **Line drawing depicting the Breguet Br 121, which one day was to become the Jaguar.** *Philippe Ricco*

RIGHT **This three-view drawing of the Br 121 shows traces of the Breguet Taon, from which it had descended, and also the silhouette of the future Jaguar.** *Author's collection/Breguet document*

RIGHT **Artist's view of an Armée de l'Air Br 121 operating in the ground attack role.** *Author's collection/Breguet document*

BELOW **Three-view of the Br 121 made up from photographs of a project model of the aircraft, which appears to sport RAF roundels.** *Author's collection/Breguet document*

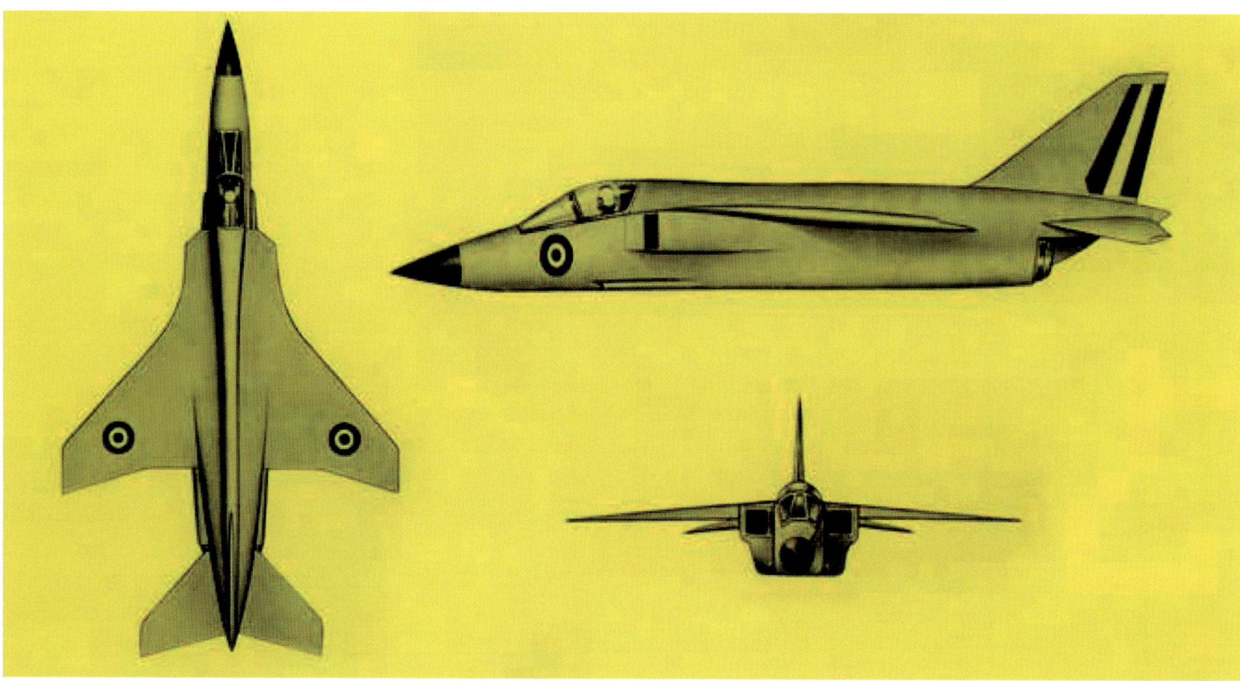

ABOVE A second artist's view of the Br 121, this time as an RAF machine. *Author's collection/Breguet document*

Br 121	
Status	project
Span	26ft 11in (8.20m)
Length	53ft 2in (16.20m)
Gross wing area	?
Gross weight	15,432lb (7,000kg)
Powerplant	two Tourmalet 4,500lb (20kN) without reheat
Maximum speed/Height	Mach 1.8
Armament	two 30mm cannon and bombs

121C interceptor (with supersonic capability and offered outside the *Armée de l'Air*'s requirements), the Br 121E trainer and Br 121P photographic reconnaissance aeroplane. The designation letters were the initials of the mission in French with A for *attaque* (attack), B *biplace* (two-seat), C *chasse* (fighter), E école (training) and P *photo*.

The manufacturer stressed the simplicity and ruggedness of the design, which made it easy to maintain, but also pointed out its versatility (i.e. the five different variants) while stressing especially the high speed of Mach 1.8 '*which would make an excellent interceptor*'. Another important element highlighted by the brochure was the aircraft's ability to take off in less than 1,970ft (600m) from an unprepared field. With a 1,328lb (600kg) load (underwing and fuselage ordnance) its range was 311 miles (500km), while on a ferry mission it could fly for up to 3,110 miles (5,000km). For propulsion Breguet had selected either two Rolls-Royce RB172-45s or two examples of the Turboméca Tourmalet, the latter giving about 6,750lb (30kN) of thrust each (as explained shortly, in 1965 the Ministry requested the merging of both the British and French engines into a single type). The fixed armament comprised two 30mm guns on the sides of the fuselage and three or five attachment points were available. The Breguet Br.121 was selected as the winner of ECAT in January 1965, although it did not completely fulfil the British requirements.

Dassault MD 911 Cavalier

The Cavalier project was launched by Dassault on 9 March 1964 with the intention of having the aircraft flying for the next year's Paris Air Show. Then, on 14 May, Dassault and Nord Aviation signed a co-operation agreement to respond to the ECAT programme. Each manufacturer would enter its own design to the competition but, if either the Dassault or Nord design was selected as the winner, then production will be shared between the two partners. Although a full-size mock-up was built, Dassault backed away from the competition after the Breguet proposal had been selected. The Cavalier would have been powered by two General Electric J85s, giving it a speed of Mach 1.5. During 1965, however, the design evolved somewhat further because, having begun as a low wing aircraft with a high T-tail, by the end of the first quarter of the year the wing had been moved to the shoulder position and now had a prominent leading edge root extension, or LERX, and the horizontal tail surfaces were attached to the lower part of the fuselage. It had been planned to produce the aircraft in two versions, a single-seater for the ground attack role and a two-seater for training. *RAF Flying Review* reported in March 1965, with a singular lack of prescience, that: '*If any trainer is ready to be for service in three years' time, then it will indubitably be the Dassault Cavalier which has gone ahead as a*

Dassault MD 911 Cavalier	
Status	mock-up
Span	28ft 2.5in (8.60m)
Length	45ft 3in (13.79m)
Gross wing area	-
Gross weight	13,646lb (6,190kg)
Powerplant	two GE J85 4,050lb (18kN)
Maximum speed/Height	Mach 1.5
Armament	two 30mm guns and bombs

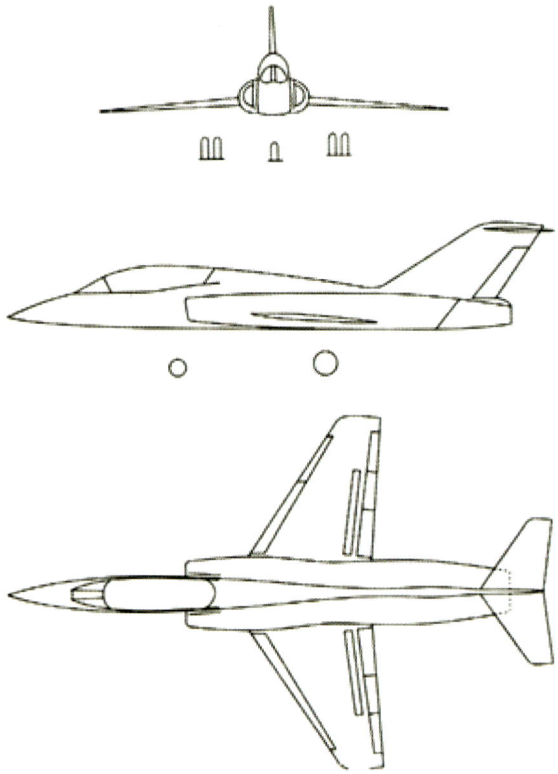

ABOVE The Dassault MD 911 Cavalier was the designer's main entry to the ECAT programme. *Author's collection/Breguet document*

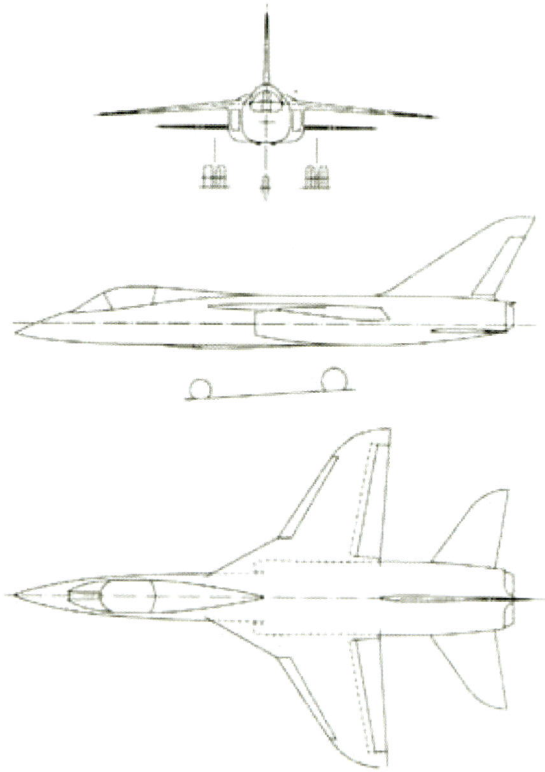

ABOVE The MD 912 Cavalier II was an evolution of the previous Dassault design. *Author's collection/Breguet document*

private venture and may be sufficiently advanced to make an appearance at the Paris Aero Show in June.' (the publication may have mistaken a photo of the Cavalier mock-up for one of a real prototype). It is interesting, however, that the magazine postulated how the J85 prototype would be followed by other machines powered by the SNECMA M-45 Mars turbojet ... something the Dassault archives do not support. Two months later, *RAF Flying Review* reported the abandonment of the Cavalier, although it still claimed that '*metal had been cut on the prototype*'.

MD 912 Cavalier II

This was a revised variant of the earlier Cavalier powered by two Rolls-Royce RB172-45 engines and with a shoulder-mounted wing and a marked LERX. Seven attachment points were specified for this version, which therefore meant it was geared more towards attack duties.

Dassault MD 912	
Status	project
Span	26ft 11in (8.20m)
Length	40ft 0in (12.20m)
Gross wing area	215.1sq ft (20sq m)
Gross weight	16,005lb (7,260kg)
Powerplant	two RB.172-45R 4,725lb (21kN) with reheat
Maximum speed/Height	Mach 1.6 at 36,090ft (11,000m)
Armament	one 30mm gun plus bombs

MD? Cavalier III

This showed a return to the lower position wing and with low rear surfaces. It would have used improved versions of the J85 but unfortunately the Cavalier III's performance was calculated to be lower than for previous projects, notably in its range, which fell to 197 miles (310km) instead of the 311 miles (500km) offered by the other Cavaliers.

MD 921

The MD 921 was Dassault's variable geometry entry to the ECAT requirements but it was not selected.

MD 922

This was a variant of the MD 921.

Nord Aviation

Nord 3600 Harpon (Harpoon)

The undated brochure for the Nord Aviation 3600 (which was the third aircraft designed at Nord to be named Harpon!) emphasised the fuselage concept, which used a modular arrangement. This would enable the same basic airframe to be configured easily as a single-seat ground attacker or two-seat trainer (the brochure referred specifically to the ECAT programme). The accessibility of the engines was also stressed (all the engine section panels were removable

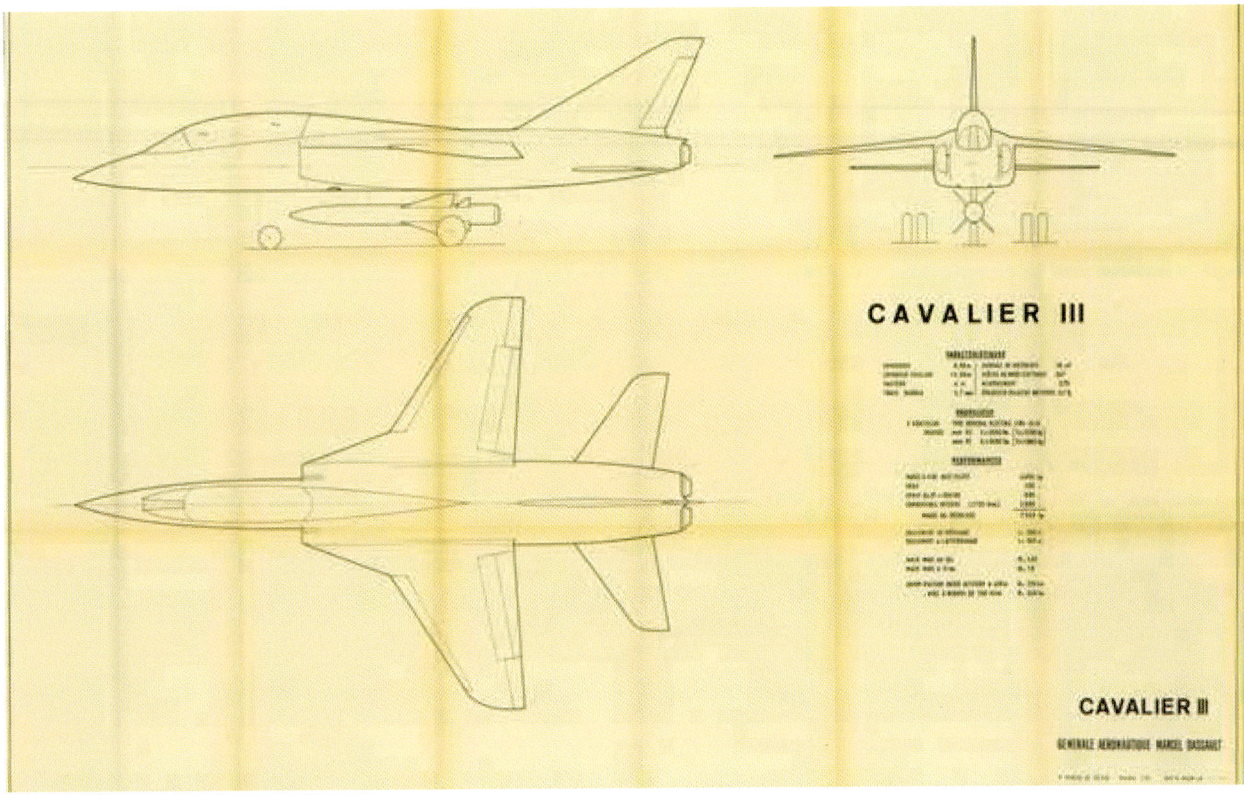

ABOVE The Cavalier III had disappointing calculated performance and was therefore abandoned. This drawing is dated 20 February 1965 and shows the aircraft with an AS37 Martel missile under its fuselage. *Dassault*

RIGHT Line drawing from the cover of the Nord 3600 Harpon brochure. *Tony Buttler*

Nord 3600	
Status	project
Span	-
Length	-
Gross wing area	290.3sq ft (27sq m) (344.1sq ft/32sq m for Turboméca & SNECMA versions)
Gross weight	22,487lb (10,200kg) Orpheus, 27,480lb (12,465kg) Tourmalet
Powerplant	two RB.172-45; Tourmalet, SNECMA M45, RB.172-49R or Orpheus 803
Maximum speed/Height	Mach 0.96 (Orpheus) to Mach 1.08 (M45) at 36,090ft (11,000m)
Armament	two guns (30mm?), one missile

and were set at a height for a man to carry out maintenance with ease while standing on the ground) along with the fact that it would be possible to introduce a different engine quite easily during the aircraft's development. A low 'between-mission' time of under fifteen minutes, and without the need of specific equipment or trained personnel, was also emphasised.

Consideration had been given to two configurations, the first having a swept wing of between 45° and 50° and the second a delta. In the end the Nord team selected a 'truncated' delta after tests in the Cannes wind tunnel revealed this to be the best option to fit the requirements of Mach 0.9 speed, a short take-off run and limited sensibility to rough weather. For armament it was planned to carry a missile on the belly attachment point and guns in the fuselage underside. The shape of the wing root leading edge extension, stretching well in front of the air intakes, was designed especially to avoid gun gas ingestion by the engines. The nose of the aircraft, with removable panels again set at 'a man's height', could receive cameras or antennas depending on the mission and the tricycle undercarriage would have low-pressure tyres.

While not required by the specifications, consideration was also given to the possibility of fitting engines with reheat. The Rolls-Royce RB.172-49R and the SNECMA M45B were suggested specifically, but with the observation that a smaller 4,500lb (20kN) thrust engine with reheat was financially a better prospect than a larger 6,750lb to 9,000lb (30kN to 40kN) unit because Nord thought that the smaller engine could get a share of the civilian market. In the meantime it was proposed to power the aircraft with a Rolls-Royce British Orpheus Mk.803, but in the end no fewer than five different engines were offered for the same airframe, the Rolls-Royce RB.172-45 or RB.172-49R, the Orpheus Mk.803, the Turboméca Tourmalet and the SNECMA M45.

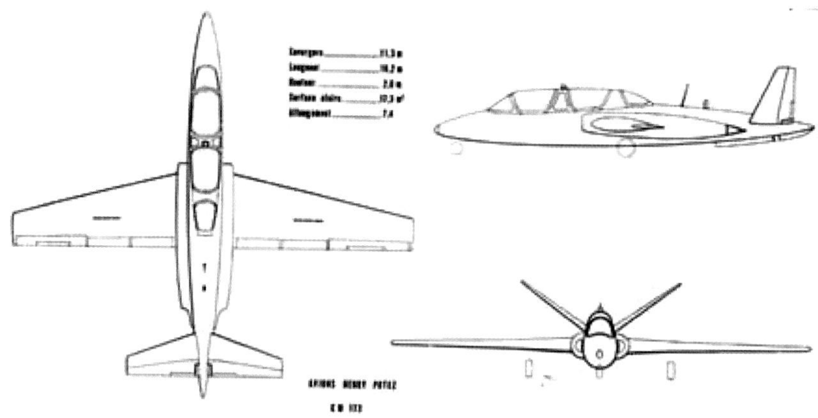

TOP The Potez CM173 Super Magister was an improved version of the original Magister, which first flew in 1964. *Author's collection/Fouga document*

ABOVE An artist's view of the CM 173 in flight. *Author's collection/Fouga document*

Potez CM 173 Super Magister

In 1963, with the Fouga Magister in service since 1956 in more than twenty countries, Potez, which had taken over Fouga in 1958, promoted an upgraded Super Magister fitted with Turboméca Marboré VIs giving 1,080lb (4.8kN) of thrust. Improvements were made to the airframe, which now featured structural fuel tanks and a reworked electrical power system. The radio and navigational equipment was also improved with new VHF and UHF transceivers, a radio magnetic indicator (RMI), gyromagnetic compass and gyro compass. The CM 173 first flew on 8 June 1964.

Potez CM 173	
Status	prototype
Span	37ft 1in (11.30m)
Length	33ft 5.5in (10.20m)
Gross wing area	186.0sq ft (17.3sq m)
Gross weight	7,451lb (3,380kg)
Powerplant	two Marboré VI 1,080lb (4.8kN)
Maximum speed/Height	Mach 0.82
Armament	two 12.7mm machine guns, bombs and rockets

Potez P.92

A very different design with no link to the Magister family, the Potez

Potez P.92	
Status	project
Span	?
Length	46ft 7in (14.20m)
Gross wing area	-
Gross weight	-
Powerplant	two Tourmalet, SNECMA M45 or RB.172-45
Maximum speed/Height	Mach 0.97 clean, Mach 0.92 to 0.95 with AS37
Armament	one AS37 missile

P.92 had its turbojets housed in pods positioned at the rear of the fuselage. This intriguing design, optimised for the ground attack role with no fewer than seven attachment points, failed to make an impression.

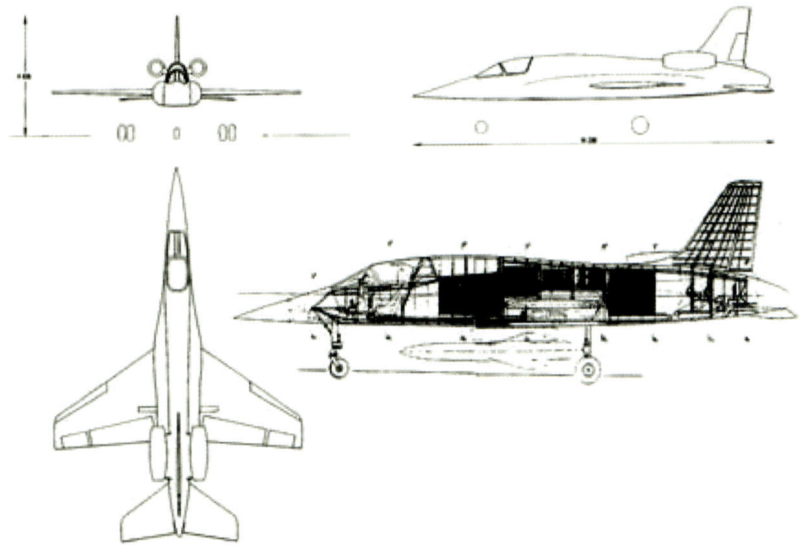

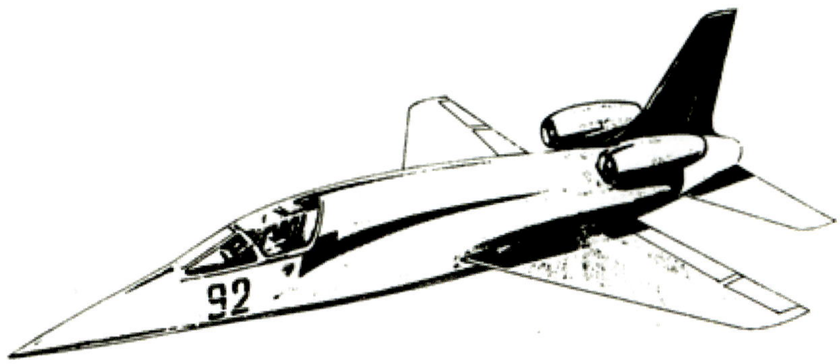

TOP **Three-view drawing of the little-known Potez P.92, which shows the aircraft carrying a large missile, possibly an AS37 Martel.** *Potez Document*

ABOVE **Perspective drawing of the Potez P.92.** *Michel Ledet*

Potez P.94

Another evolved version of the Magister airframe, this time using the Super Marboré VI now rated at 1,190lb (5.3kN). It was offered in 1965 and had no armament integrated into the airframe, but there was provision for gun pods under the reinforced wings as well as anti-tank missiles, rockets, bombs or other weapons. The longer stroke undercarriage of the naval Zéphyr variant was used and the CM 173 was considered to be the prototype for the P.94, being renamed P.94A in August 1965 and with the definitive aircraft becoming the P.94B. In 1966 there were talks about licence production of the P.94 in South Africa but this never materialised.

Sud Aviation

Sud Aviation SA 125

The SA-125 is a still a design about which nothing is known, although *RAF Flying Review* did say in its report that it would *'bear some resemblance to the Northrop F-5'*.

SEPECAT Jaguar

On 18 February 1965 the French Air Ministry announced that the RB.172/T.260 had been selected as the powerplant for ECAT. This married the British RB.172 and French Turboméca T.260 Tourmalet engines, the front coming from the T.260 while the middle and rear were taken from the RB.172-45R. Naturally this required the British-designed parts to be produced to metric drawings. In April 1965 the *Armée de l'Air* and the

RIGHT **The SEPECAT Jaguar, née Breguet Br 121. This view shows the Jaguar E trainer prototype E02.** *Author's collection/Breguet document*

SEPECAT Jaguar	
Status	production
Span	28ft 6in (8.69m)
Length	50ft 11in (15.52m)
Gross wing area	260.0sq ft (24.18sq m)
Gross weight	34,171lb (15,500kg)
Powerplant	two Adour 102, 7,200lb (32kN)
Maximum speed/Height	Mach 1.5 at 39,370ft (12,000m)
Armament	two DEFA 553 30mm and weapons on five attachment points

FIG. 6

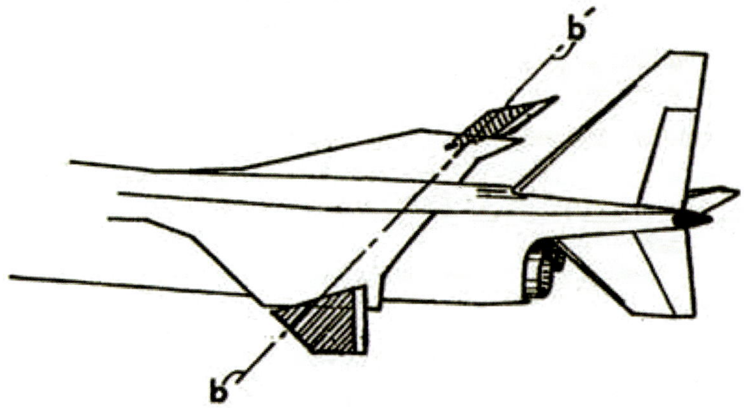

ABOVE Drawing of the ONERA proposal to fit the Jaguar with "improved" wingtip controls. *Author's collection*

Royal Air Force published a common requirement and on 17 May the British and French governments signed a Memorandum of Understanding on which the project was based. Breguet and the British Aircraft Corporation (BAC) were the two companies selected to lead the project on each side of the Channel and it was planned to build 300 machines; 150 trainers for the RAF and seventy-five trainers, and seventy-five strike aircraft for the *Armée de l'Air*. The name Jaguar was announced at the 1965 Paris Air Show, by which time the name of the engine (Adour) had already been released.

Work on the airframe design continued during 1965 and was finally frozen in November. In March 1966 a joint technical requirement was agreed and funding authorised for the development on the French side. In May 1966 a joint BAC/Breguet company called *Société Européenne de Production de l'Avion ECAT* (SEPECAT) was set up to build the airframe, while Rolls-Royce Turboméca Ltd was registered in London on 22 June to oversee the engine. It was only after the legal arrangements had been established that contracts could be issued. The work share meant that BAC would build the wing, tail surfaces and rear fuselage and assemble the British aircraft in its Warton factory, while Breguet would build the front and centre fuselage and assemble the French machines at Toulouse-Colomiers.

The following variants were detailed:

Jaguar A: single-seat trainer for the *Armée de l'Air*, 75 ordered.
Jaguar B: two-seat trainer for the RAF, 110 ordered.
Jaguar E: two-seat trainer for the *Armée de l'Air*, 85 ordered.
Jaguar M: single-seat carrier strike aircraft, 40 ordered.
Jaguar S: single-seat strike aircraft for the RAF, 90 ordered.
This was in addition to eight prototypes plus the static tests airframes.

BELOW the model seen previously on page 94 was also photographed in close-up. *Author's collection/Breguet document*

The full-size mock-up was reviewed in November 1966, and on 9 January 1968 a production agreement was signed by the respective French and British Defence Ministries for 200 aircraft to be produced for each country. The first Jaguar, airframe E01, made its maiden flight piloted by Bernard Witt on 8 September 1968, and on its third flight it achieved Mach 1. This aircraft was used for general aerodynamic flight testing until it crashed during the following year. E02, also a French two-seater, first flew on 11 February 1969 again with Witt at the controls and it was assigned to engine and flight performance, and was sent to Great Britain in 1971 to continue this role. A03, the first A-series machine, reached Mach 1 during its first flight on 29 March 1969 and was used for spin tests and for trials with the navigation and attack system

(*Systéme de Navigation et d'Attaque, or SNA*). A04 flew on 27 May and was to be the weapons testing aircraft, and Jaguar was to make its public debut at the 1969 Paris Air Show in late May/ early June. The first British prototype, S06 (XW560), first flew on 12 October 1969 and was followed by the first naval prototype, M05, on 14 November; S06 was also used for weapon testing. Another British example, S07 (XW563), made its maiden flight on 12 June 1970 and its role was to test the British navigation and attack system, while the next aircraft, B08 (XW566 flown 30 August 1971), was the UK's two-seat cockpit, navigation and attack systems test aircraft.

By 1970 the British order had been amended to 165 single-seat and thirty-five two-seat Jaguars. The first French production aircraft came off the assembly line at Toulouse-Colomiers on 4 May 1972 followed by the first British example from the Warton factory on 12 October 1972. Export orders were obtained from Ecuador (ten S and two B), India (thirty-five S and five B), the Sultanate of Oman (twenty S and four B) and Nigeria.

Of interest was a 1977 proposal by ONERA to fit a Jaguar with *'improved controls'*, described as control surfaces *'which could be disconnected from their command devices, enabling them to take their natural position in the airflow'*. These controls could then be operated either in 'piloted mode' or in 'floating mode' and in this second condition they became *'transparent'* (in other words the control surfaces would now move automatically with changes in flight condition, without input from the pilot).

The Alpha Jet Story

From the mid-1960s, both in Germany and in France, there was a need to replace the Fouga Magister and Lockheed T-33 trainers then in use. Later on a requirement evolved covering the need to replace the Fiat G-91 ground attack aircraft and this led to a common programme for a trainer with some ground attack

BELOW Along with the prototypes, the Jaguar was shown in model form at the 1969 Paris Air Show. *Author's collection*

capability, which, of course, was also the name of the game for the ECAT programme. However, once ECAT was up and running that aircraft soon grew larger and by the time it emerged as the Jaguar it was far too big for the requirements discussed here. Hence a new programme emerged.

Breguet Br 126/TA501

In 1968 Dassault (now merged with Breguet as Dassault-Breguet) reached an agreement with Dornier to build a new aircraft in this category. Then a Franco-German call for proposals was issued on 22 July 1969. Up to that point each of the two participants had had its own vision of what the aircraft should be. Breguet had produced its Breguet Br 126 design and tried to push it in France, while Dornier had a different vision that it called the P.375. There were major differences; for example the French aircraft had a low wing while the German project had a wing at shoulder level. No compromise appeared possible and Dassault could find no technical way to merge the two. In the end, Marcel Dassault met Claudius Dornier on 4 November 1969 and together they selected a baseline design around the Dornier project. While the Germans had originally required a 15,432lb (7,000kg) flying weight, in June 1970 they settled on a 13,007lb (5,900kg) machine but with more powerful engines, which then gave them the ability to boost their strike version up to 15,432lb (7,000kg) if desired, thereby paving the way for common ground between the two nations.

AMD-BA Br 126	
Status	project
Span	-
Length	-
Gross wing area	-
Gross weight	-
Powerplant	two Larzac 2,250lb (10kN)
Maximum speed/Height	Mach 0.8
Armament	-

AMD-BA Alpha Jet	
Status	production
Span	30ft 0.5in (9.16m)
Length	40ft 4in (12.29m)
Gross wing area	188.2sq ft (17.50m)
Gross weight	10,780lb (4,890kg) trainer, 15,430lb (7,000kg) strike
Powerplant	two Larzac 2,925lb (13kN)
Maximum speed/Height	Mach 0.85
Armament	three hard points for weapons (five on German version)

On 15 July 1970 *Armée de l'Air* General Gauthier and Luftwaffe General Steinhoff together approved an outline programme and reached a compromise between Germany's requirements for a light strike aircraft and the advanced trainer needed by France.

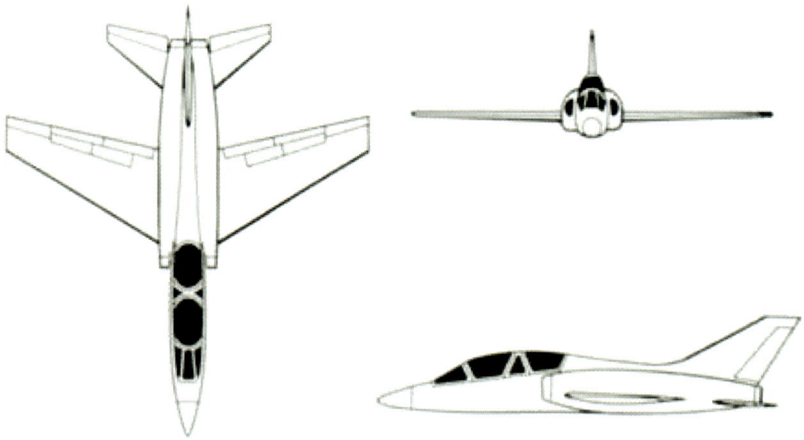

ABOVE LEFT An early (1969) three-view drawing of the Br 126, which was to evolve into the Alpha Jet. *Author's collection/Breguet document*

ABOVE A Br 126 artwork from 1969. Note how all of these illustrations do not detail the tail unit, which was probably not well defined at that time. *Author's collection/Breguet document*

LEFT In 1969 Paul Lengellé painted this action view of the Br 126. *Author's collection/Breguet document*

BELOW LEFT Another painting of the Br 126, again from 1969. Note that in this representation nothing is being carried under the wings. *Author's collection/Breguet document*

BELOW A fourth painting of the Br 126, again from 1969. Note that in this representation nothing is being carried under the wings. *Author's collection/Breguet document*

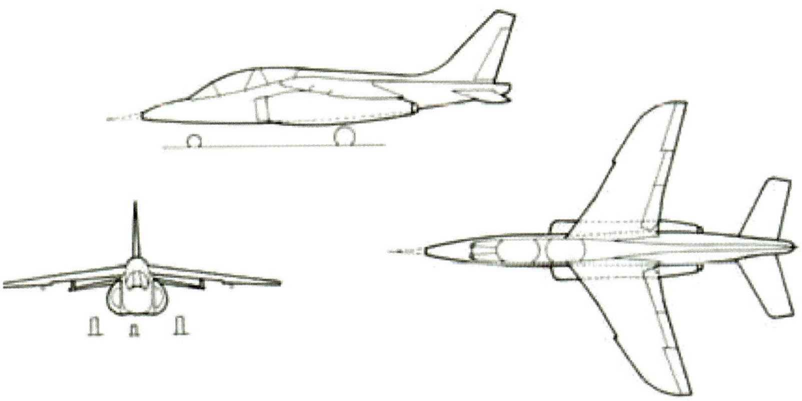

1 By 1970 the Br 126 had been renamed TA-501. *Author's collection/Breguet document*

2 During 1971 the project, now named Alpha Jet, was exhibited as a mock-up at air shows. *Author's collection/Breguet document*

3 In 1973 the Alpha Jet had reached its definitive shape, with the exception of the tall pointed fin, which was reduced in size for production. *Author's collection/Breguet document*

4 An artist's impression of the Alpha Jet in US Navy under the VTW competition. *Author's collection/Dassault document*

The TA501 Alpha Jet was then selected on 23 July 1970 for production by Mr Blancard, the French Ministry delegate for armament, and Mr Schiffers, his German counterpart. The competing VFW-Fokker VFT-291 and SNIAS-MBB E.650 Eurotrainer proposals were thus eliminated, much to the dismay of the SNIAS (Aérospatiale) chief Marcel Chassagny, who objected strongly to see his company being pushed out of the military combat aircraft market.

The TA501 designation came from Br 126 and Dornier P.375 added together (126 + 375 = 501). In March 1972 the design was revised slightly with a taller but less swept fin to improve the anti-spin characteristics, the rear fuselage was redesigned in accordance with the area rule, and the wing was modified to incorporate a small leading edge extension at the root. The first prototype flew on 26 October 1973 and production aircraft were rolled out in 1975. At that point the requirements were estimated to be 200 trainers for France and up to 250 strike aircraft for Germany. It seems that the French version had some nuclear ability.

Dassault VTX

On 14 July 1978 the Franco-German consortium contracted with Lockheed to promote a navalised Alpha Jet in an US Navy competition to select a new trainer. However, the Alpha Jet failed to win the order.

ABOVE The final version of the Alpha Jet would have been the Lancier, of which only one prototype was produced. Aimed at the export market, the aircraft is illustrated in this painting with fictitious foreign markings. *Author's collection/Dassault document*

Dassault Lancier (Lancer)

In 1985 Dassault proposed a new variant of the Alpha Jet trainer that was to be capable of operating at night and in bad weather through the introduction of improved avionics (an Agave radar, a forward-looking infrared FLIR system, and an improved CP2084 computer). The Lancier could be optimised either for air combat with Magic air-to-air missiles and 30mm gun pods, for ground attack with various iron or smart bombs, or for naval strike with an Exocet missile. Through its economical Larzac 04C20 engines the Lancier offered a good range and appreciable load-carrying capability, but it was not pursued.

BELOW The Sud E-650 Eurotrainer also reached the mock-up stage. *Author's collection*

SNIAS E-650 SNIAS Eurotrainer

A competing project for the competition won by the Alpha Jet was this joint proposal between Sud Aviation (later SNIAS Aerospatiale) and MBB. A mock-up (in French markings) was exhibited at the 1970 Hannover Air Show that, following the French trend exhibited by the original Br 126, had a low wing (and a T-tail) to provide a clearer rearwards view for both student and teacher.

ABOVE The competing project was the Sud Aviation Eurotrainer. *Philippe Ricco*

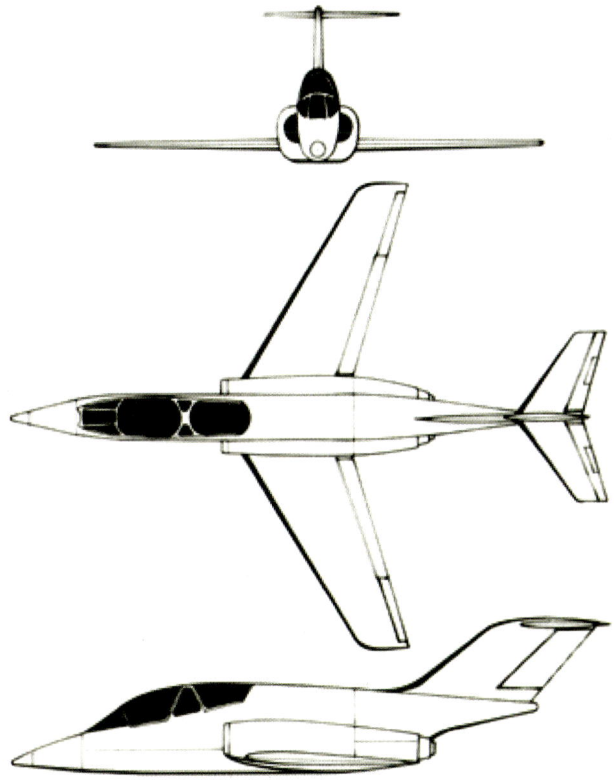

ABOVE The author has not been able to find an official plan of the E-650, but this three-view drawing by Jean Perard was published in Aviation Magazine in 1970. *Author's collection*

SNIAS E-650 Eurotrainer	
Status	mock-up
Span	31ft 6in (9.60m)
Length	44ft 3.5in (13.50m)
Gross wing area	193.5sq ft (8.00sq m)
Gross weight	-
Powerplant	two Larzac 2,250lb (10kN)
Maximum speed/Height	Mach 0.8 at 30,020ft (9,150m) ceiling 45,930ft (14,000m)
Armament	-

Two versions were proposed with different engines installed, either two SNECMA-Turboméca Larzacs for the E-650 or two General Electric J85s on the E-651.

Other Trainer Ventures and Small Jets

Fouga 90

This Aérospatiale design was intended as a follow-up to the Magister, the general shape of which it retained. It first flew on 28 August 1978 but did not met with success, although according to press sources Argentina was interested in buying a few examples.

Vitrotto RV-1

This is a bizarre story! Rémy Vitrotto, a young engineer of the *Ecole Spéciale d'Aviation* (Special School of Aviation) and of the *Conservatoire des Arts et Métiers* (Conservatory of Arts and Crafts), wanted to build a jet aircraft.

Vitrotto RV-1	
Status	project
Span	20ft 3.5in (6.18m)
Length	30ft 6in (9.30m)
Gross wing area	96.8sq ft (9.00sq m)
Gross weight	6,834lb (3,100kg)
Powerplant	one turbojet and rocket(s)
Maximum speed/Height	839mph (1,350km/h) at 45,930ft (14,000m)
Armament	none

He began collecting parts from the crashed aircraft that littered the country in the aftermath of the war, while in the meantime beginning the design of his machine. Helped by the director of the Eiffel wind tunnel, he built a test model, but by the time he told his story in the May 1952 issue of *Aero France* he had been sidetracked in his goal to build his own jet by the need to refurbish his house and to build a hangar. Although the use of a turbojet and rocket engines were specified, no engine types were ever indicated for the aircraft. If Mr Vitrotto had hoped to get state or private sponsoring for his project by this article then the idea certainly fell flat, for no one heard of the Vitrotto RV-1 again.

SNCASO Deltaviex

The small Deltaviex was built by SNCASO for ONERA in 1953 and made its maiden flight the following year. It was a purely research machine and was used to test 'blown' wings, in which the air blown on the upper surface generated lift at will and could therefore be used to replace conventional ailerons. The aircraft had a very sharp 70° sweep delta wing and was powered by a Turboméca Marboré II. It was, however, reputedly very difficult to fly and did not get airborne very much, but the Deltaviex remains as one of the very few pure 'X-planes' in this story.

SNCASO Deltaviex	
Status	prototype
Span	11ft 2in (3.40m)
Length	-
Gross wing area	53.8sq ft (approx 5sq m)
Gross weight	2,028lb (920kg)
Powerplant	one Marboré II of 900lb (4.0kN)
Maximum speed/Height	-
Armament	-

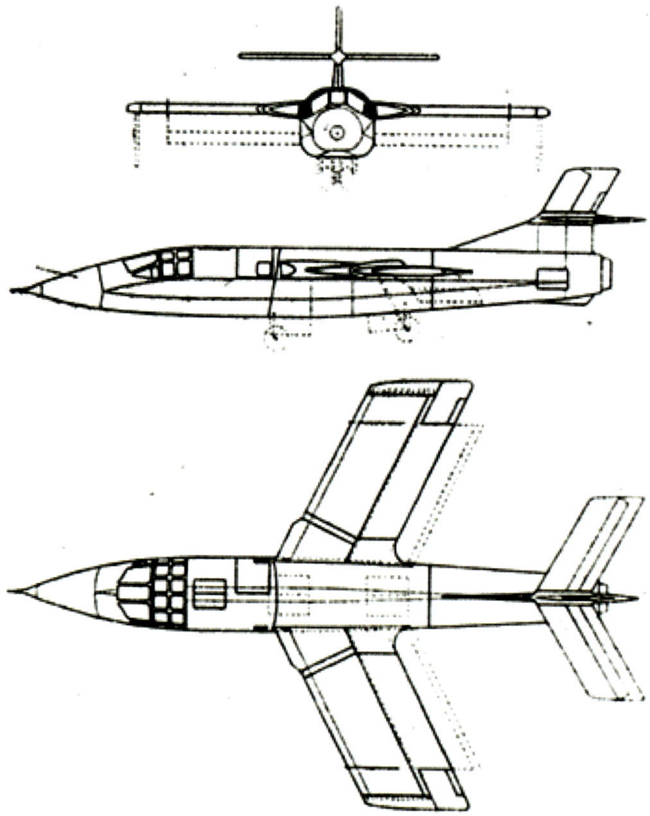

TOP RIGHT The Vittroto was an amateur design that was promoted by the Aero Club de France. It probably never went beyond this drawing. *Author's collection*

RIGHT One of the true pure experimental aircraft built in France was the ONERA Deltaviex. *Philippe Ricco*

BELOW RIGHT While the Deltaviex did not fly too much it was modified with different intakes, canopy, etc. *Philippe Ricco*

BELOW The Fouga 90 was the ultimate development of the Fouga family. *José Fernandez*

Chapter Six
In the Field (Baroudeur)

ABOVE Three Baroudeurs in the snow. An evocation of what an operational squadron of Baroudeurs would have looked like. *SNCASE*

During the 1950s research was undertaken by French manufacturers that looked into giving aircraft the ability to operate without needing long runways. One option was the seaplane fighter while another was to enable land-based aircraft to fly from unprepared terrain. In the end only one aircraft was proposed that could truly operate from grass and other surfaces, the SNCASE SE 5000 Baroudeur, although the conversion of existing aircraft to use 'unprepared' ground was also studied and realised with the so-called 'Barougan' derivative of the Dassault Ouragan. Ski-equipped aircraft were also assessed and various attempts were made to adapt existing fighters to ramp launching.

Ramp Launch

In 1955 the US Air Force succeeded in launching a manned Republic F-84G jet fighter from an adapted Martin Matador missile ramp. However, even before that, a catapult system had been designed in 1940 to launch the Lioré-et-Olivier LeO 45 twin-engine bomber, although this was not built. In the immediate post-war years and the 1950s the potential of launching aircraft from a ramp inspired French manufacturers to propose the following designs.

Breguet Br 1005 Taon

This was the definitive operational variant of the Br 1001 Taon (see Volume I) and it was proposed to launch it from a Matador ramp using a booster rocket.

BELOW Several aircraft were designed so they could be launched from a Matador missile ramp. Here we have the Breguet Br 1005 Taon. *Author from Breguet document*

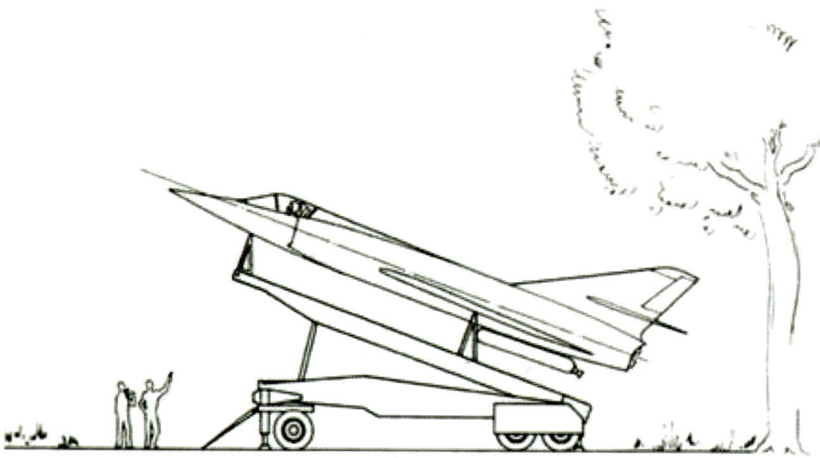

ABOVE **The Dassault Etendard IV could also have been launched from a Matador ramp.** *Dassault Aviation*

Dassault Etendard IVA

It was proposed to launch the land-based version of the naval Dassault Etendard from a ramp similar to the Matador launch ramp (but not identical as shown by the sketch). A solid rocket booster 9ft 0in × 1ft 3.5in (2.75m long × 0.40m) diameter, with a weight of 1,323lb (600kg) and providing a thrust of 32 tons, could be attached to the rear fuselage. The rocket would fire for 2.5 seconds and push the aircraft up to a speed of 200 knots (370km/h).

Dassault Mirage I

The Matador ramp was chosen again for this 1957 proposal to launch a Dassault Mirage, here with two solid propellant rocket boosters fixed under the wing in addition to the SEPR rocket engine integrated under the rear fuselage. This Mirage would have been able to reach 88,580ft (27,000m) with its rocket booster.

BELOW **This rather detailed drawing depicts an early Mirage on a Matador ramp with two underside-mounted rocket boosters.** *Dassault Aviation*

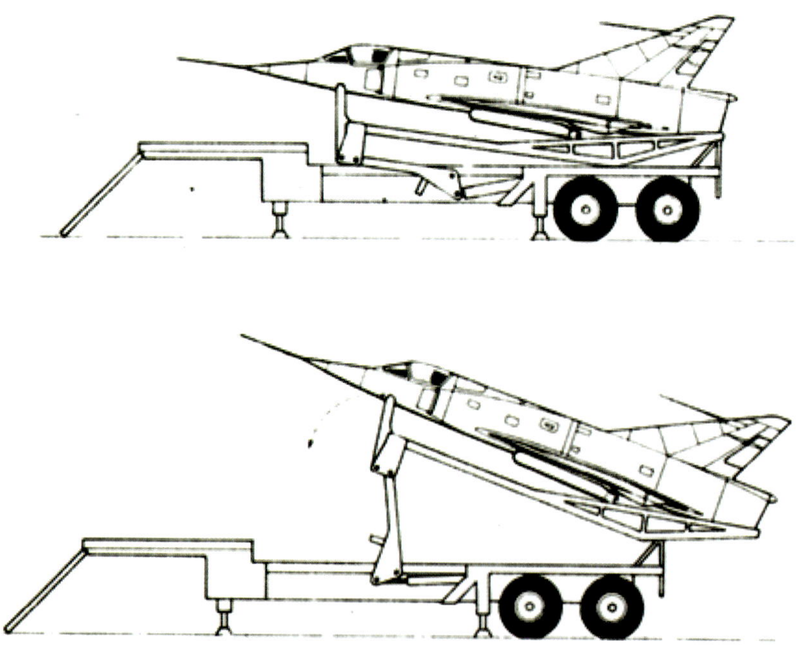

Latécoère Laté 768

M. Gaillard, of the Latécoère *bureau d'études* proposed, built and tested a mobile catapult that could be used to launch a group of fighters at the rate of five aircraft airborne in five minutes, and with forty minutes between each group. The resulting structure, named the Laté 768, was composed of 229ft 8in (70m) of ramp assembled from five sections each with a length of 45ft 11in (14m). The first four sections formed the launch ramp itself while the fifth would be used to brake the launch chariot. Propulsion of said chariot was obtained by using compressed air, 424cu ft (12cu m) being used for each launch and, because it was expected that tests on a reduced scale model would not be accurate enough, a full-scale catapult was built capable of launching an aircraft weighing 9,921lb (4,500kg). One hundred successful launches were achieved with this although, only the fuselage of a Morane-Saulnier Paris aircraft was used and no flight-capable aircraft ever took off using this system. Gaillard suggested that a '*fighter in the 8 to 9 ton range could be launched without any modification to the mechanism, just by reinforcing the frame of the catapult*'. He added: '*We have been asked whether a catapult to launch a 20 ton aircraft at 85m/sec or 300km/h* [280ft/sec or 186mph] *could be done. Indeed, it seems that the catapult launch of light bombers could be used to reduce their take-off run at full weight, the subsequent landing (with load and fuel exhausted) being seemingly easier, as a project for a 'shortened landing area' submitted at the same time as the catapult project was postponed.*' The 'shortened landing area' project involved placing two catapults in parallel with four landing cables stretched between them, the catapult being fitted with airbrakes. This idea was not pursued.

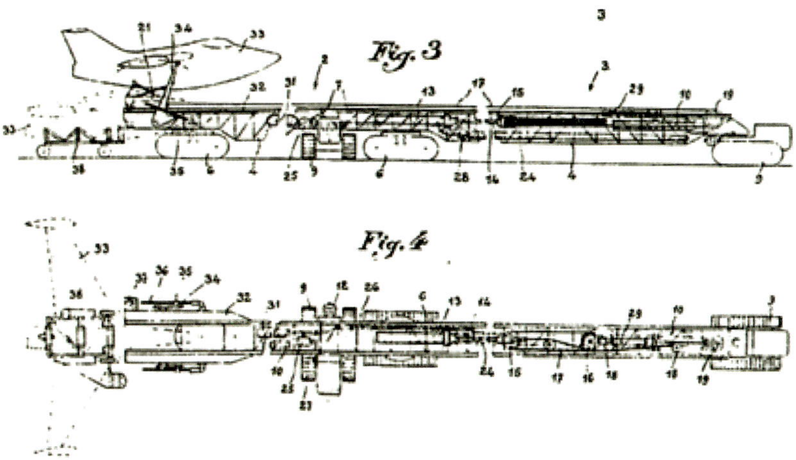

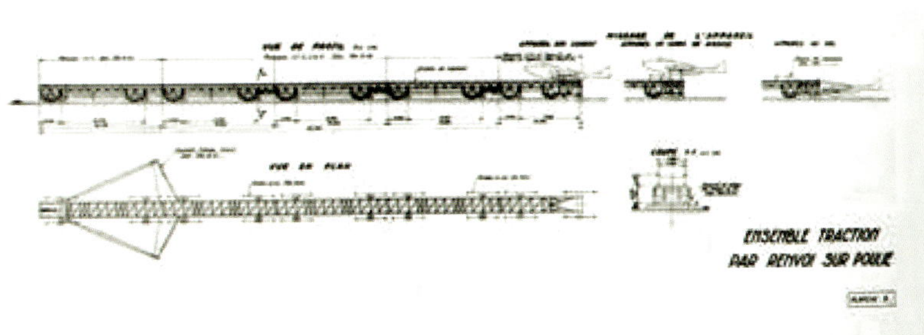

TOP Latécoère promoted the use of a modular ramp to launch small fighters quickly. Here we see two views of the ramp taken from the patent that covered the idea. *Latécoère patent*

ABOVE Seen on this second drawing of the Latécoère ramp is an SE 532 Mistral (a licence-built DH.100 Vampire FB.Mk.5) which, at 13,448lb (6,100kg) take-off weight as against 9,921lb (4,500kg) target weight, would have been slightly overweight for the quoted performance of the Laté catapult. *Latécoère*

BELOW Although actually built and tested, it does not seem that the Laté catapult was ever used to launch a manned aircraft. *Latécoère*

Matra

In 1945 the ever creative Roger Robert of Matra patented *'a track to allow take-off and landing from aerodynes, without the need for those aerodynes to include a special landing apparatus (or landing gear) and which* [would] *shorten the take-off and landing distance'.* His idea was to create a ramp launcher with small wheels or cylinders, and these *'rolling elements'* would be powered and so impose their own speed to the aircraft at take-off. To land the aircraft had to align itself with the ramp, the first *'rolling elements'* (those at the end of the ramp where the aircraft should touch down) having been put into rotation at a speed approximately the same as that of the aircraft. It should be noted that the ramp was made up of segments, each of which had *'rolling elements'* that ran at either an increasing speed for take-off or a decreasing speed for landing.

SNCASE SE 212C

This was SNCASE's entry to a planned lightweight fighter competition that eventually saw the selection of the SNCASO Trident (Volume I). It was powered by a SEPR 48 twin-chamber rocket motor, each chamber providing 3,375lb (15kN) of thrust. The 'C' in its designation stood for *chimique* (chemical), which seems to have implied in the mind of its designers that the propulsion system was based on a chemical reaction and not a mechanical engine. Five STRIM rockets giving 4,220lb (18.75kN) of thrust would have launched the aircraft along a 39ft 4in (12m) long ramp, which would have subjected the pilot to an acceleration of 3.7g. The aircraft would have used a Marbore II turbojet for its return to base and for the landing phase, and after landing on its belly skid the 212C would have been recovered using a chariot similar to the one designed for the Baroudeur. All in all it was felt that the recovery after landing was a more important aspect than the need to

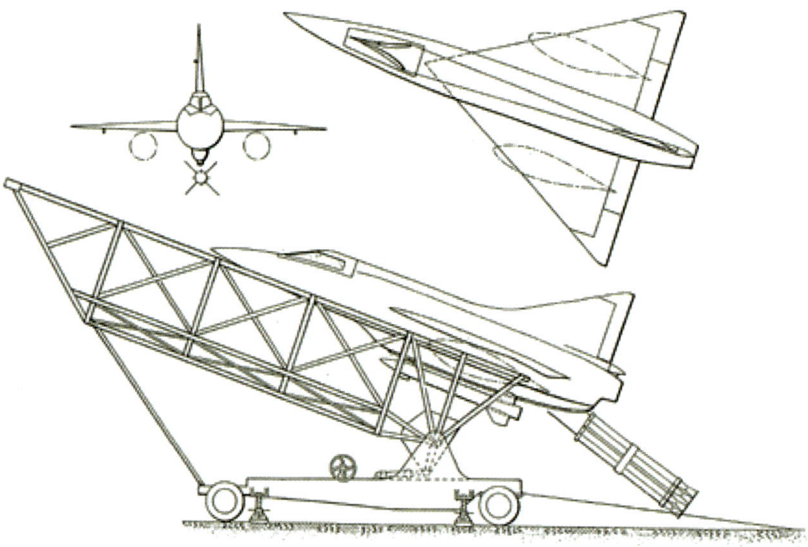

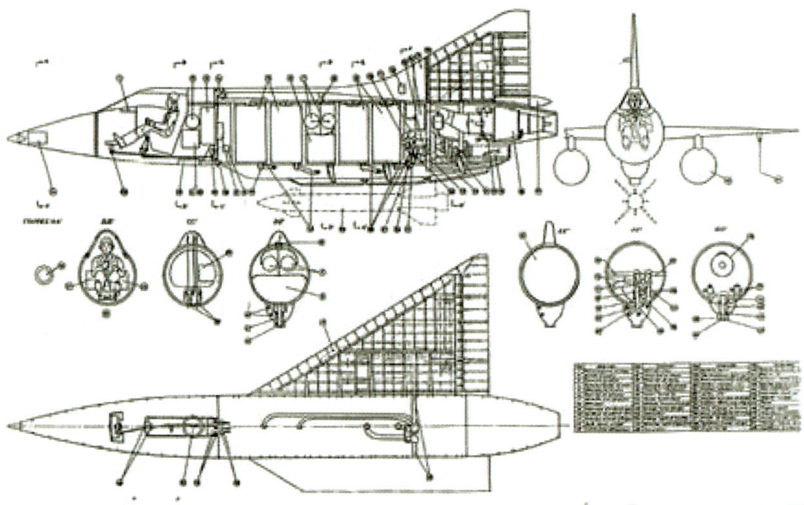

TOP **The SE 212C was designed from the outset to be ramp launched.** *SNCASE*

ABOVE **Detailed cutaway drawing of the SE 212C ramp-launched rocket fighter. An odd aspect of this design was the placement of the missile underneath the landing skid. Firing the missile was then compulsory to permit the aircraft to land!** *SNCASE*

SE 212C	
Status	project
Span	-
Length	30ft 11in (9.42m)
Gross wing area	-
Gross weight	-
Powerplant	SEPR 48 twin chamber rocket engine (two 3,375lb [15kN]) and Marboré II 900lb (4kN)
Maximum speed/Height	-
Armament	one missile AA20

use a runway. Another problem was that the SE 212C's Nord AA20 missile was attached under the fuselage and would therefore have to be fired before the aircraft could land.

Skid Take-Off

Company Société des Dispositifs Oléo-Pneumatiques (DOP), a subsidiary of Nord Aviation, suggested replacing an aircraft's conventional landing gear with retractable skids. In 1954 and through Nord, the second prototype Mistral (the French derivative of the de Havilland Vampire produced under licence by SNCASE) was acquired on loan for modification. The aircraft had its main wheels replaced by skids, initially 2ft 7.5in (0.80m) in length but later 3ft 7.5in (1.10m) long, the nose wheel was retained but with a low pressure tyre, and then after a few tests small 'rolling chariots' (*chaussons* or slippers) were added to ease moving the aircraft around on the ground. The rolling chariot would fit on to the skid and driving the aircraft into them before getting back on to the runway was found to be easy. Two more Mistrals, N° 61 and 127, were subsequently fitted with these skids and also participated in the trials, but in the end they proved inconclusive, the skids were never retracted and by 1957 the project had been abandoned.

BELOW **The DOP company, a specialist in landing gear, proposed to launch an aircraft using a rocket-propelled sled.** *DOP*

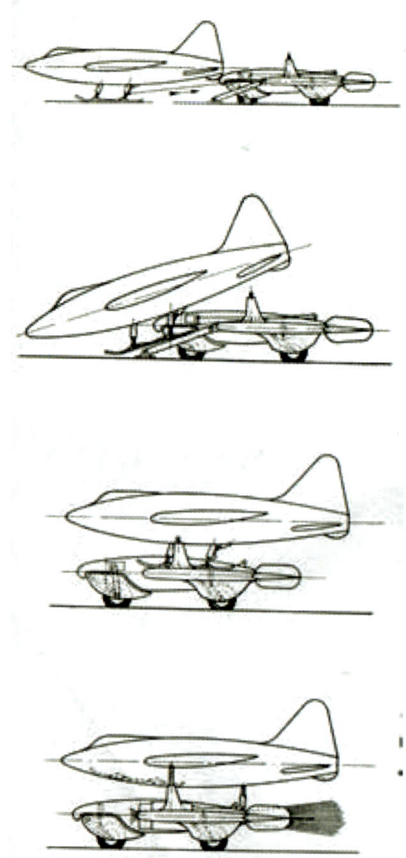

It should be noted that DOP also produced a larger version that encompassed both skid-landing in many variants and a rocket-sled take-off. The whole assisted take-off plus skid-landing concept was proposed by G. Renollaud, the head of DOP, and there were many variants. To begin with he explained that for carrier aircraft '*here we have catapults. So no hesitation, take-off will be by catapult. Skid landing will however require a slight modification of the landing deck*'. The solutions suggested for the latter were either a net made of fireproofed textile (of the kind used for camouflage), or a costlier but more durable covering of the deck with a plastic coating, or even tar macadam with a high friction coefficient.

For heavy load carriers (i.e. commercial airliners or strategic bombers) Renollaud suggested using a sled to remove the landed aircraft away from the field as quickly as possible. The sled could also be used to assist in its take-off since '*the additional thrust generating devices could be installed without any limitation on the sled, as the additional weight will not impact adversely the performance of the aircraft, the sled remaining on the ground during its whole operation*'. For tactical aviation with interceptor or infantry support types of aeroplane '*the problem is to be able to use airfields similar to those used in 1939. We can think of three solutions:*

> *(i) the catapult, which could be disassembled for transport (as suggested by M. Lecarme),*
> *(ii) the chariot propelled on a light railway track,*
> *(iii) the self-propelled chariot on low-pressure tyres*'.

Renollaud dismissed the first two solutions – the catapult being qualified by him as '*a complex solution, difficult to move, and requiring an important power source*', while the railway track was '*difficult to hide and cannot be turned into the wind*'. Consequently, he promoted the self-propelled chariot '*to carry the aircraft to its take-off position, to remove it from the airfield after landing and to move it from a secondary field to another secondary field*'. He concluded his presentation by saying that '*this formula* [the self-propelled chariot] *would give in all cases, a better take-off security, a*

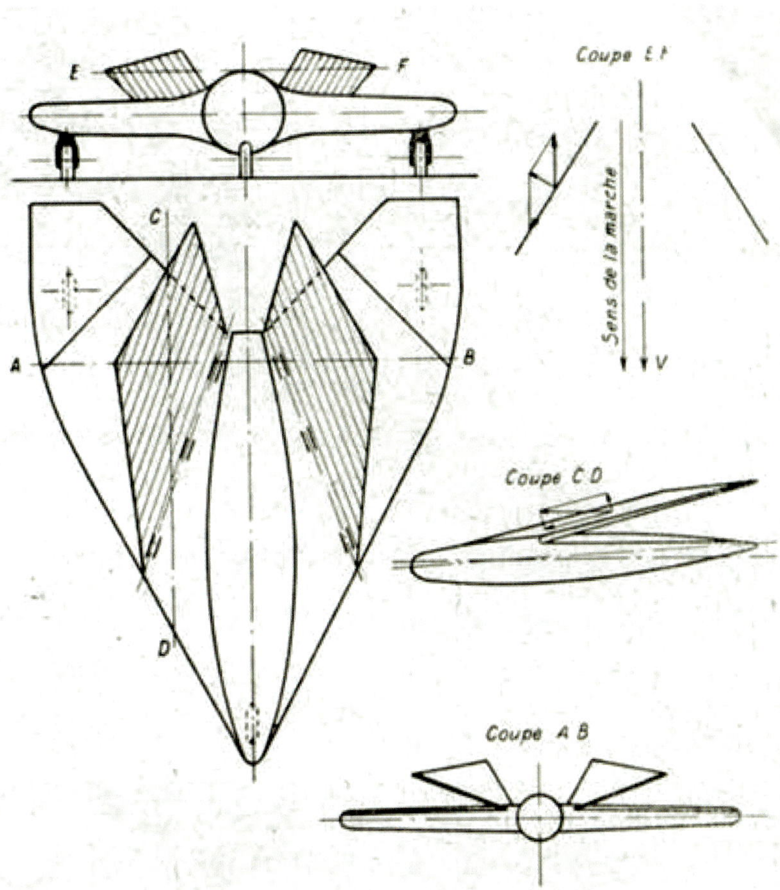

TOP **A more detailed view of the DOP-designed rocket sled.** *DOP*

ABOVE **The second prototype Mistral seen fitted with main undercarriage skis while in the hands of the DOP -** ***Dispositifs Oleo Pneumatiques*** **- at Les Mureaux.** *Nord via Delmas/Michel Cristescu*

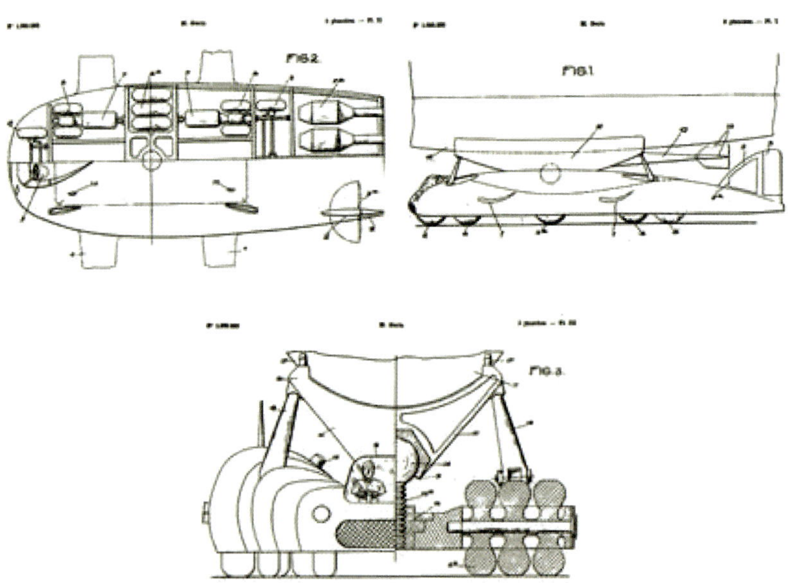

TOP **Jacques Gérin, who in the 1930s designed a biplane called the Varivol, proposed a powered sled to ease the take-off of large aircraft. The design could well have inspired *Thunderbirds* creator Gerry Anderson!** *Gérin patent*

ABOVE **The SE 1910 launch chariot seen here carrying a German Fieseler Fi 103 (V1) flying bomb. What looks like a gun turret at the front was actually a rocket brake device.** *Philippe Ricco*

seemingly complete landing security and an enormous gain in time and cost [because of the limited] *infrastructure required*'. And he referred to the past, quoting the Messerschmitt Me 163, the Arado [234] and the SO M2 and pointing out: '*What we propose today is nothing more than the adjunction of many existing solutions, but scattered over space and time*.'[1]

The temptation to use a motorised (powered) chariot to enable an aircraft to reach its take-off speed struck other designers and design teams – Leduc, SNCASE and Gérin. Leduc (see Volume 1) was conscious that the use of the Tuyère Thermo-Propulsive (his name for a ramjet) would require a certain speed to be reached before the ramjet could be activated. Therefore, he considered using a chariot propelled by powder rockets in order to get his Leduc 016 prototype airborne. It was planned to have the chariots running on a specially built railway track: '*We even thought of launching a complete squadron by having the chariots in file*,' wrote George Collet, a Leduc draughtsman, in Jean Lacroze and Philippe Ricco's book *René Leduc Pionnier de la Propulsion à Reaction*. Originally subcontracted to Aérocentre, the project faltered when this company failed. Leduc then turned to SNCASE, which actually built a rocket-propelled chariot as the SE 1910 and also a track for it at Istres, later at Cazaux. However, the SE 1910 never launched anything more than rebuilt Fieseler Fi 103 (V1) flying bombs.

Jacques Gérin, the designer of the Varivol variable geometry aircraft (see Volume 1), proposed a large piloted launch chariot that for propulsion would use various engines, including turbojets. While all the other designers had envisioned a chariot launch for small fighter-size aircraft, Gérin designed on a grand scale and his chariot could have tackled a bomber or an airliner ... but it was never built.

Dassault MD 550

This early delta design from Dassault was proposed in 1952 with a simplified landing gear consisting of a single skid. The idea was that by removing the landing gear and making the wing of '*integral structure*', it would be possible to house more fuel in the airframe. No indication was ever provided as to how the aircraft was supposed to take off (that is either on a skid, on a chariot Baroudeur-style or on a ramp).

1 These comments appeared in *Aero France* for October 1953, which also showed a Baroudeur taking off from its chariot on the cover!

Nord-Centre

A 1947 patent survives that depicts a propeller-driven (?) aircraft equipped with a folding wing and a skid landing gear. The main point of the patent itself was to link the lift devices (flaps) with the operation of the skid landing gear. The size of the aircraft appears to have been small and similar to a pre-war fighter.

Morane Saulnier MS 800

For ground attack and close support duties Georges Caillette's design office offered the MS 800, which in its first variant was a straight-winged aircraft. The baseline MS 800 had a single ATAR 101E2 engine but other versions would feature twin power units. The aircraft's nose contained the radio bay and then the cockpit, on the sides of which were located bays with a 20mm gun in each (or as an option a single 30mm just on the left side). The pilot had an ejection seat and was well protected behind titanium armour panels. A bay with a retractable rocket rack was also provided and a major feature of the design was its high T-tail. The MS 800 was offered in reply to the 10 August 1953 call for proposals and was submitted in 1954 (although Cuny claims the proposal was sent to the manufacturers only in December 1953).

BELOW The curious 1947 patent from SNCAC. The type number of the aircraft depicted (if any) is still unknown. *SNCAC patent*

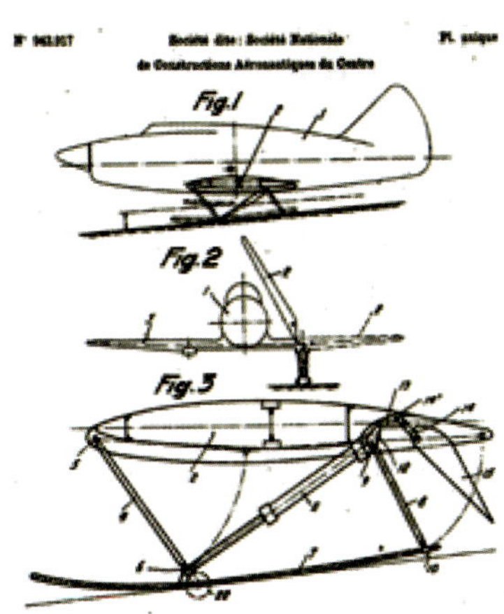

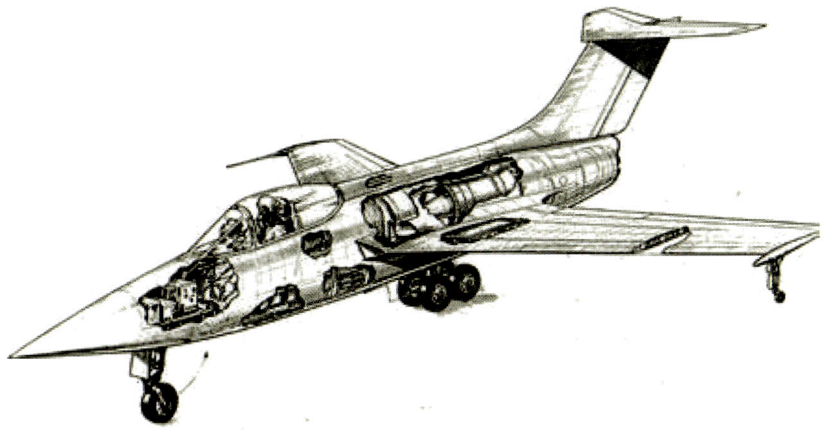

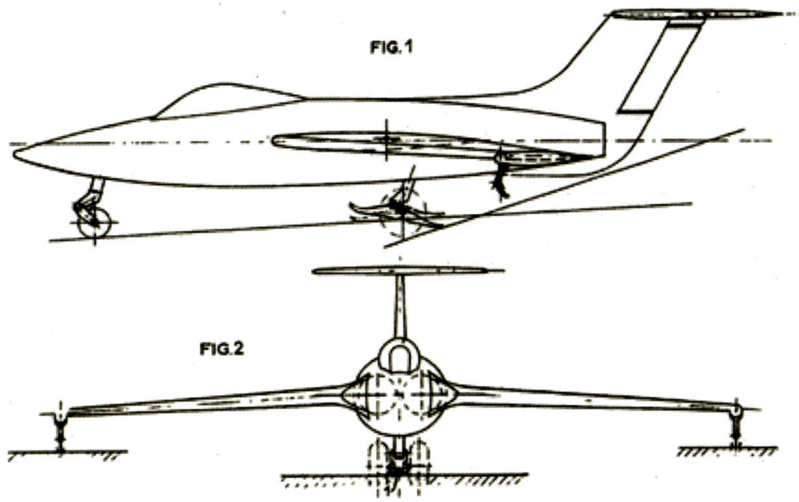

TOP Morane Saulnier proposed the wheel-cum-skid landing MS 800 ground attack fighter. This version has a swept wing. *Morane Saulnier*

ABOVE Cutaway drawing of the swept-wing MS 800. *Henri Lacaze*

The landing gear was also quite specific and warranted a patent. Morane-Saulnier pointed out that conventional skid landing gear aircraft had difficulty operating on the ground and that a take-off from a chariot (as promoted on the competing Baroudeur) was risky because it would induce oscillations due to its short wheelbase. Also, the chariot had to be quite large to carry a modern fighter and therefore was costly to move on its own. So the MS 800 design had a 'monotrace' (bicycle) landing gear with a front wheel to provide direction, a landing skid and balancines (outriggers) at the wingtips, all of which were, of course, retractable. The skid was attached to a small chariot consisting of an axle with two large wheels and in this configuration the balancines stabilised the aircraft and avoided any side oscillation. In the end, this project was not selected for the French programme, and it did not receive much further attention when it was proposed to the later NATO requirement. As with other MS fighter types of the period, a variant with 38° swept wings was also offered. The various MS 800 variants embraced the MS 800-1 (ATAR 101 E2), MS 800-2 (two 2,250lb [10kN] turbojets of an unspecified type), MS 800-3 (two

MS 800-1	
Status	project
Span	35ft 7in (10.85m)
Length	44ft 7.5in (13.6m)
Gross wing area	268.8sq ft (25sq m)
Gross weight	13,558lb (6,150kg)
Powerplant	one ATAR 101E 7,200lb (32kN)
Maximum speed/Height	Mach 1.08 at 32,810ft (10,000m)
Armament	two DEFA 20mm guns

MS 801	
Status	project
Span	35ft 7in (10.85m)
Length	44ft 7.5in (13.6m)
Gross wing area	268.8sq ft (25sq m)
Gross weight	13,131lb (5,956kg)
Powerplant	two SNECMA R105 2,475lb (11kN)
Maximum speed/Height	Mach 1.08 at 32,810ft (10,000lb)
Armament	two DEFA 20mm guns

MS 802	
Status	project
Span	35ft 7in (10.85m)
Length	44ft 7.5in (13.6m)
Gross wing area	268.8sq ft (25sq m)
Gross weight	13,131lb (5,956kg)
Powerplant	two Hispano R800 2,475lb (11kN)
Maximum speed/Height	Mach 1.08 at 32,810ft (10,000m)
Armament	two DEFA 20mm guns

1,690lb [7.5kN] Vipers), MS 801 (two SNECMA R105) and the MS 802 (two Hispano R800).

SE 5000 Baroudeur

The SE 5000 Baroudeur was a class of its own! Designed by John Wsiewolod Jakimiuk, this machine was optimised for close support and conceived from the beginning as an *'all terrain'* aircraft (*baroudeur* is a word relating to a soldier who likes close fighting, it comes from the Arabic word *baroud,* meaning fight). The Baroudeur was launched from a specially designed chariot that could

SE 5000	
Status	prototype
Span	32ft 10in (10.00m)
Length	44ft 10in (13.66m)
Gross wing area	272.0sq ft (25.3sq m)
Gross weight	-
Powerplant	ATAR 101D-1 5,850lb (26kN)
Maximum speed/Height	Mach 0.92
Armament	none

be accelerated at take-off using STRIM powder rockets, and after its release the chariot's wheels were be slowed down automatically and a parachute would deploy. Baroudeur would land on three retractable skids, two at the front and one at the rear, and control of the aircraft on the ground was achieved by braking hooks at the tip of the front skids. During the early stages it was the chariot itself that formed the secret part of the programme and an *Aviation Magazine* reporter ran into

ABOVE Ingénieur Jakimiuk in front of his creation. *Philippe Ricco*

trouble with the military police over this, his camera being confiscated because he had photographed the aircraft with its chariot. Such absurd secrecy (the aircraft and its chariot had previously been shown to various

BELOW The planned sequence of take-off and landing for a Baroudeur squadron.1. A Baroudeur climbs after separating from its trolley, 2. Trolley separation, 3. RATO rockets are fired, 4. The Baroudeur lights its turbojet and starts the take-off roll, 5. A jeep pushes a trolley for the recovery of a landed Baroudeur, 6. A landed Baroudeur skids along the ground, 7. Baroudeur about to land, 8. Baroudeur on approach and here it will land in the right-hand lane of the field. *SNCASE*

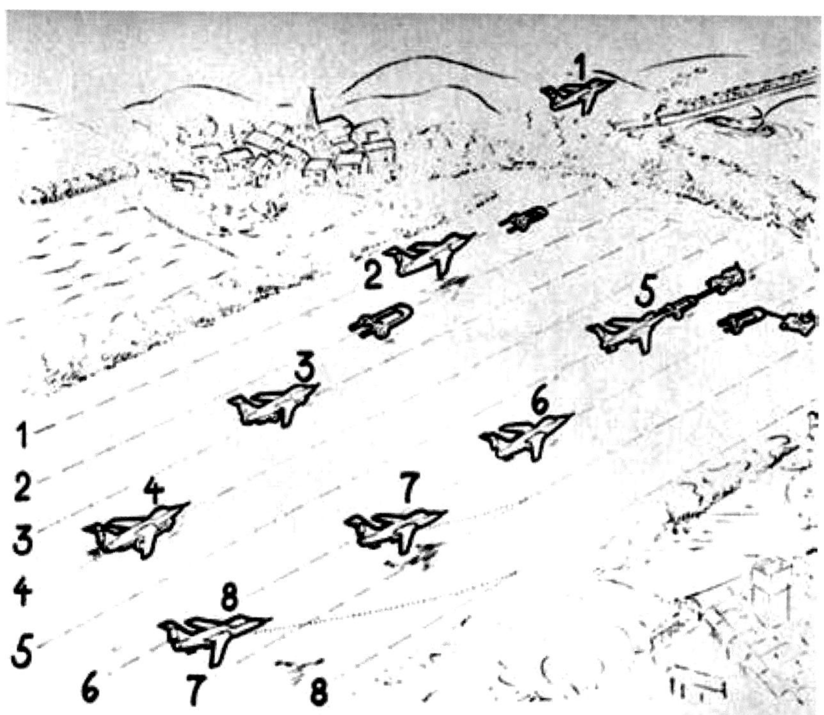

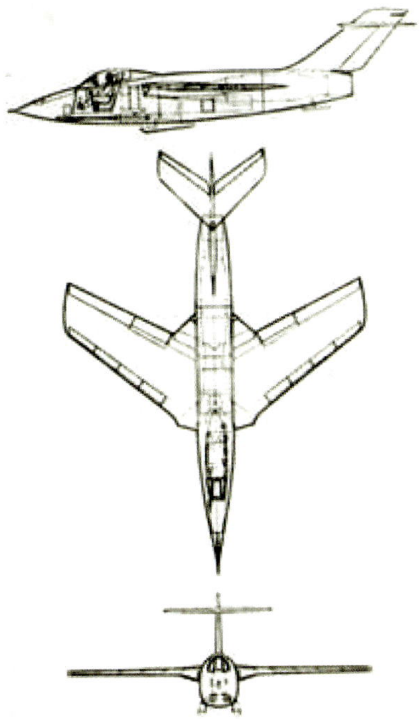

ABOVE Three-view drawing depicting the internal details of the SE 5000 Baroudeur. *SNCASE*

TOP A rare photograph of a test pilot in front of the full-scale model used to test the Baroudeur sled concept. *Philippe Ricco*

ABOVE The SE 5000 flew well but was seen as an oddball design, which in the end hampered its career and prevented it from being adopted by the French Air Force or NATO. *Philippe Ricco*

foreign officials and a model of the chariot was displayed at the 1951 Paris Air Show) prompted the columnist to denounces a '*sinister comedy*' played against France's aviation journalists. In response to criticism regarding the Baroudeur's lack of mobility after landing, something that had plagued previous chariot-launched, skid-landed aircraft (the wartime Me 163 and Ar 234) and which probably influenced the military's thinking when the Baroudeur was proposed, it was demonstrated that the aircraft could be recovered and put back on its launch chariot by a single winch-equipped jeep in less than forty seconds!

SE 5000-01

Two Baroudeur prototypes were built by SNCASE with private funding, number 01 making its maiden flight from Istres on 1 August 1953 piloted by Pierre Maulandi. SE 5000-01 had a 35° swept wing with leading edge slats and a whole assortment of flaps. Its pilot sat in a pressure cabin with armour plates around him and the planned weaponry included two 30mm or 37mm Hispano-Suiza HS606 cannon in the fuselage and four attachment points under the wings for bombs or rocket pods. The powerplant was an ATAR 101C turbojet installed in the rear fuselage. During 1953 prototype 01 was tested intensively, taking off and landing from various surfaces including grass at Toulouse and Melun Villaroche, rocky ground at La Crau flats near Istres, wet marshy ground at Tours, and even a sandy beach at La Baule (which was better known as a tourist spot!). Attempts were made to take off without the chariot (directly from the skids) and ferry flights were performed with the chariot still attached. All these tests met with great success and led in March 1954 to the *Armée de l'Air* buying prototype 01 retrospectively, along with the still incomplete prototype 02. In addition, an order was approved for three pre-series machines designated SE 5003. In the meantime, 01 was modified with an enlarged vertical tail, some anhedral was applied to the wings and boost

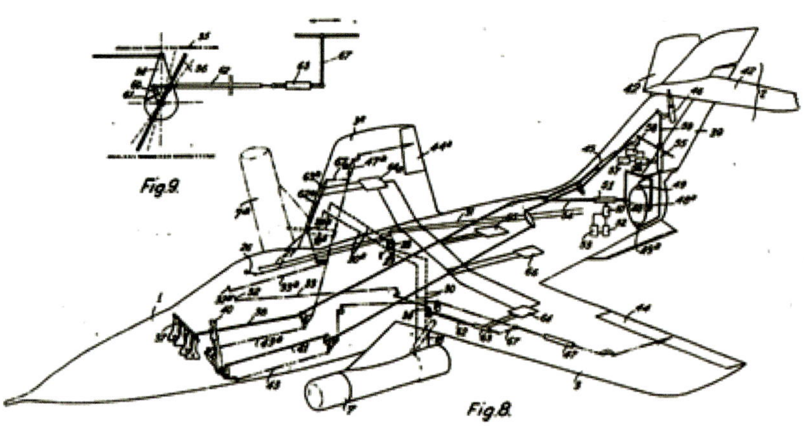

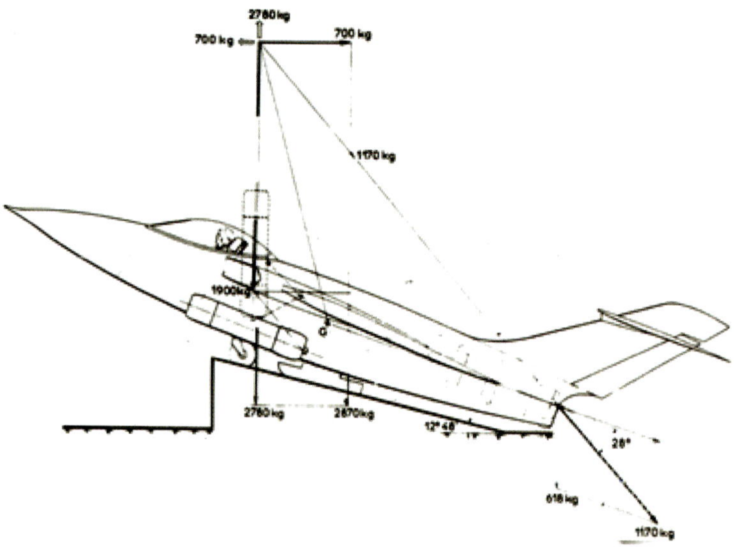

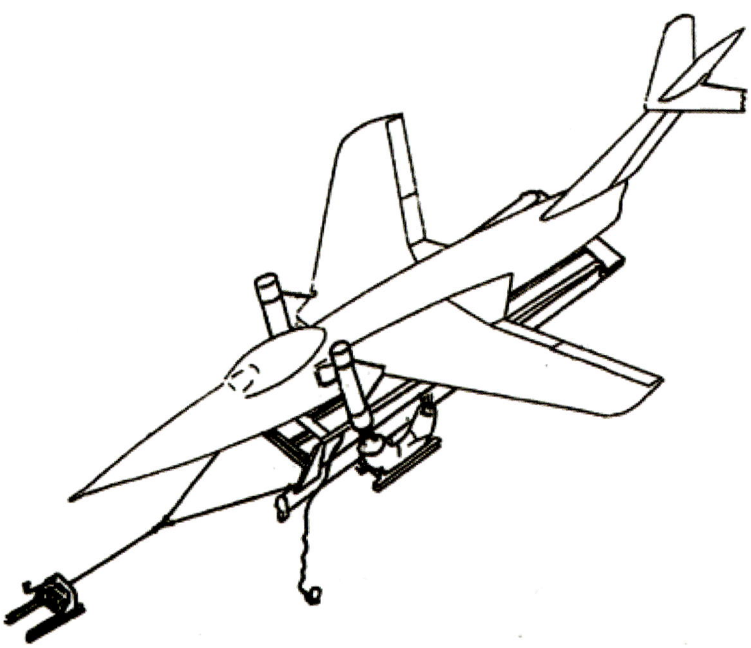

was added to its horizontal tail surface controls. Later the aircraft was used for trials with rocket-assisted take-offs and it was given a new controllable nose wheel to carry out direct take-offs, again without the chariot.

SE 5000-02

When completed, prototype 02 incorporated all the modifications retrofitted to 01 and it flew for the first time on 12 May 1954. With 01 having proved the type's main take-off and landing features and performance, 02 concentrated on exploring the Baroudeur's flight envelope and on 23 July 1954 it reached Mach 1 in a slight dive. The flight performance was deemed satisfactory when testing came to an end in 1955.

SE 5000 with Rolls-Royce Soar Booster Engines

Consideration was given to attaching small Rolls-Royce Soar engines to the front skids. Oriented downwards, the two additional engines would have reduced the take-off run on skids and on a hard rocky surface to 1,640ft (500m), and set at the optimal downward angle of 40° the take-off run would have been even less at just 920ft (280m). This idea reached the stage of wind tunnel testing, but its use limited the military load that the aircraft could carry.

TOP LEFT Another drawing illustrating how the Baroudeur fitted with additional tilting Soar engines would have been controlled. *SNCASE Patent*

ABOVE LEFT With rotating jet pods and a slightly angled ramp, it was hoped that the Baroudeur could take off near vertically. *SNCASE*

LEFT Perspective drawing of the SE 5000 fitted with tilting Soar jets for an ultra-short take-off. *Author from SNCASE Patent*

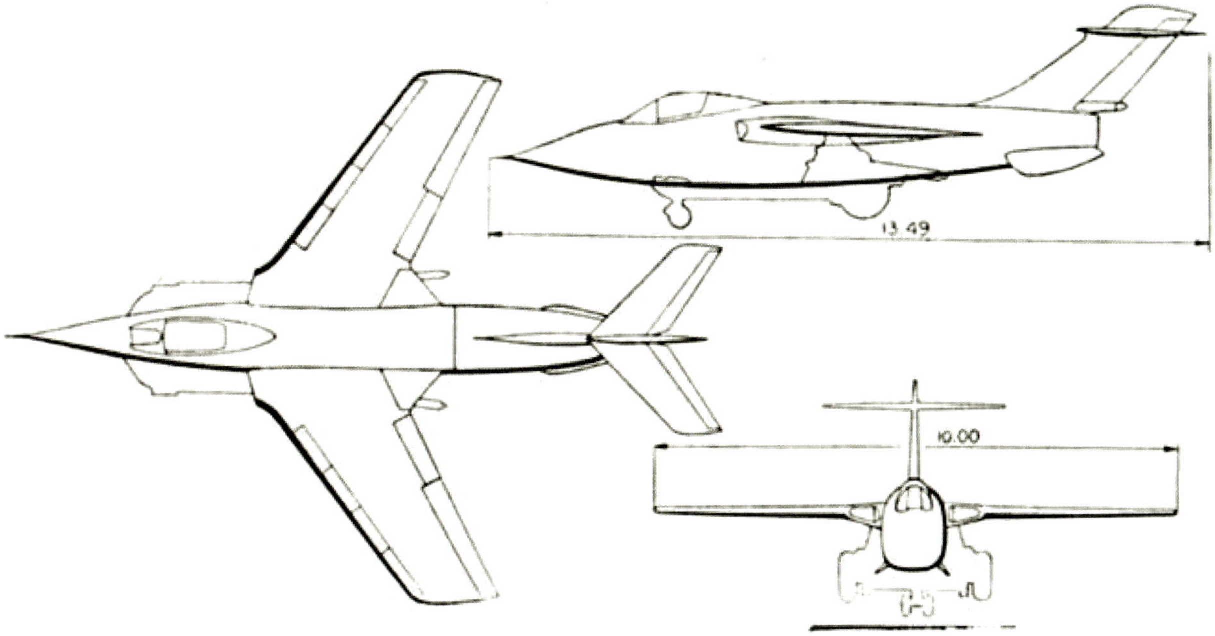

ABOVE Three-view drawing of the SE 5003 evolution of the Baroudeur. *SNCASE*

SE 5002A

NATO was quite interested in the Baroudeur and in 1955 proposals were made to develop a smaller version called the SE 5002A fitted with a Bristol Siddeley Orpheus II engine. This would have had a more sharply swept wing set at 42°, the two DEFA 30mm guns would have been moved to the nose cone while a 551lb or 1,102lb (250kg or 500kg) bomb could have been loaded between the front skids; it would also have received the steerable wheel trialled earlier. However, the 5002A design was not built and instead the SE 5003-01 was entered into the NATO competition of July 1957. It performed well, but it seems that in the end its 'unorthodox' landing and take-off arrangement puzzled the NATO officials when they saw it in operation. Also, the SE 5003 did not really fit in to the programme, which required a lighter machine.

SE 5002	
Status	project
Span	-
Length	-
Gross wing area	-
Gross weight	9,649lb (4,377kg)
Powerplant	Orpheus 11 4,950lb (22kN) + rocket engine 1,620lb (7.2kN)
Maximum speed/Height	Mach 1.75
Armament	two DEFA 30mm guns and 500kg (1,102lb) bomb

The 5002 was itself offered in various versions:

(i) with a rocket engine at the base of the tail and two air-to-air missiles to serve as a supersonic (Mach 1.82) interceptor,
(ii) with a standard wheeled undercarriage,
(iii) with Rolls-Royce Soar engines fitted as take-off boosters but here arranged differently to the similar SE 5000 format with only a 9° of downward angle.

SE 5003

The SE 5003 airframes were the pre-series version of the Baroudeur that incorporated all the military equipment and each aircraft used a different engine – 01 the ATAR 101E4 (8,160lb/36.3kN), 02 an ATAR 101D3 (6,280lb/27.9kN) and 03 an ATAR 101E3 (7,720lb/34.3kN). In addition, 01 had extra fuel tanks in the rear fuselage that actually improved its performance due to the Whitcomb area rule. The three machines were sent to *Centre d'Expériences Aériennes Militaires* (CEAM) at Mont de Marsan in late 1953, where the Establishment's military pilots greatly appreciated the aircraft (the first flight of first SE 5003 was in September 1953). They even announced that the take-off did not require the chariot and that the landing run could be shortened to a mere 1,215ft (370m) when using the skid hooks and brake chute. The machine proved quite manoeuvrable and during flight the pilot could spot his target, identify it and initiate his attack

SE 5003	
Status	pre-series
Span	32ft 10in (10.00m)
Length	44ft 10in (13.66m)
Gross wing area	272.0sq ft (25.3sq ft)
Gross weight	15,763lb (7,150kg)
Powerplant	various sub-types of ATAR 101
Maximum speed/Height	Mach 0.97
Armament	two DEFA 30mm guns and four attachment points

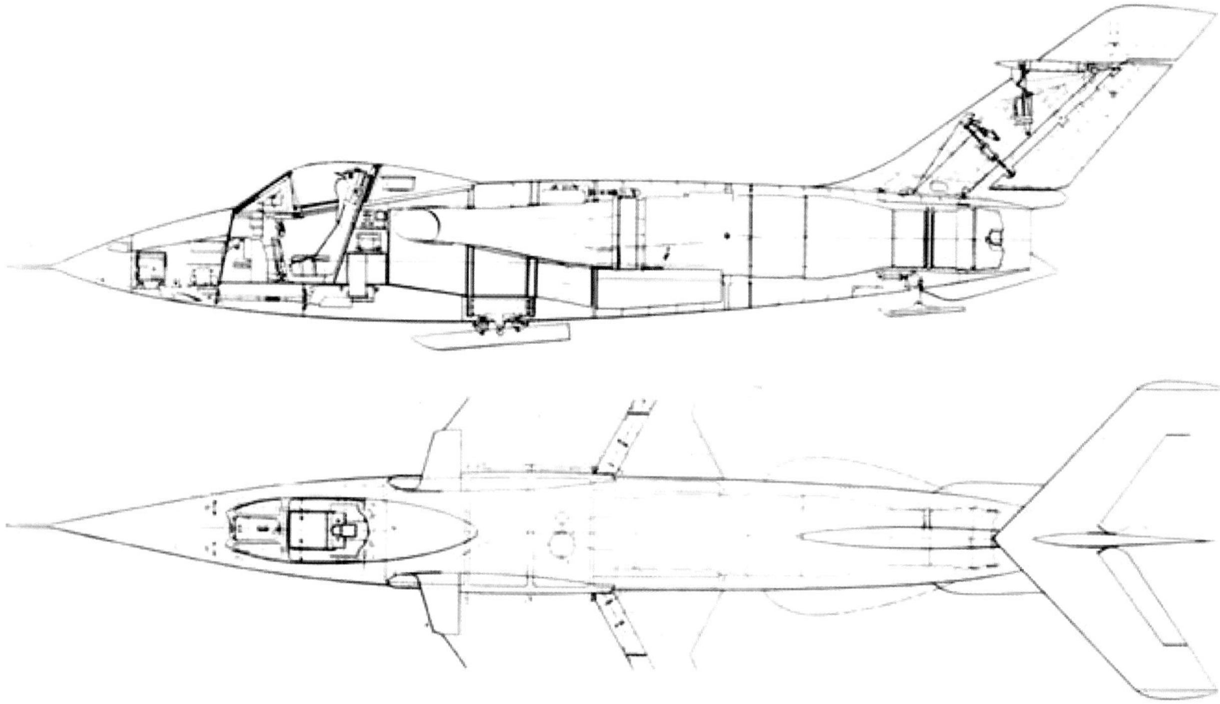

ABOVE **Cutaway of the SE 5004, a would-be production variant of the Barouduer.** *SNCASE*

in less than twenty seconds, '*less* [time] *than required to lay an AA gun towards it*'. However, by 1956 the *Armée de l'Air* had decided against the further use of the Baroudeur, claiming that the skid landing option had not been perfected completely and that the movement of the aircraft on the ground after landing had in particular been found difficult (low-pressure tyres were deemed to be a better solution). Also, although the flight performance was considered good (and comparable to the Dassault Mystère IVB), the Baroudeur was by this time being overtaken by the latest aircraft, an important point because the aircraft could not reach operational units until 1959. And there was the usual budgetary problems that did not allow for financing a dedicated '*all-terrain*' aircraft.

SE 5003 STOL

With a Bristol Siddeley BE45 engine this proposed STOL version of the Baroudeur would have been able to take-off on its skids in less than 656ft (200m) and clear the usual 50ft (15m) obstacle in 919ft (280m). A speed of Mach 1.05 at ground level was estimated for the design.

SE 5004

The SE 5004 was to have been the SE 5003 production version with an ATAR 101E4 engine giving a speed of Mach 0.98 at 36,090ft (11,000m). A reconnaissance version with cameras in the nose and in the wing roots was also planned.

SE 5008

Version fitted with a more powerful ATAR 8 turbojet and improved landing skids. This was a later project, drawn in around 1957-58.

SE 5008	
Status	project
Span	32ft 10in (10.00m)
Length	44ft 10in (13.66m)
Gross wing area	272.0sq ft (25.3sq m)
Gross weight	17,240lb (7,820kg)
Powerplant	ATAR 8 10,575lb (47kN)
Maximum speed/Height	Mach 1.06
Armament	two DEFA 30mm guns and four attachment points

SE 5010 Baroudeur L

This designation number was allocated to a lightened version requested in 1953 by STAé, with 'L' signifying *léger*, or lightened. Basically all the 'lightweight' versions of Baroudeur (of which none were built) shared the following features:

(i) a general lightening of the airframe,
(ii) simplified landing gear using fixed skids,
(ii) a revised bubbletop canopy, possibly made in one piece (in case of emergency the canopy could be ejected by a power-activated jack, which was studied during the spring of 1954),
(iv) new air intakes of more rounded design (these were studied in the Marignane wind tunnel during 1954 using half-scale models),
(v) conformal rear fuel tanks, which were preferred to wing-loaded tanks (in addition, these probably improved the fuselage aerodynamics, in accordance with the area rule).

All these improvements were calculated to reduce the aircraft's weight by 3,038lb (1,378kg) for a loaded aircraft.

SE 5012

A variant of the SE 5003 with the 8,325lb (37kN) Orpheus 12 with reheat.

SE 5012	
Status	project
Span	32ft 10in (10.00m)
Length	44ft 10in (13.66m)
Gross wing area	272.0sq ft (25.3sq m)
Gross weight	15,763lb (7,150kg)
Powerplant	Orpheus 12 6,750lb (30kN)
Maximum speed/Height	Mach 0.95
Armament	-

SE 5020 Baroudeur S

Another 1953 proposal for a simplified and lightened version of the SE 5000, this time equipped with an ATAR 101E and with the skids replaced by fixed spindle-shaped and non-retractable fairings in the form of a cigar. S probably refers to '*simplifié*' for simplified.

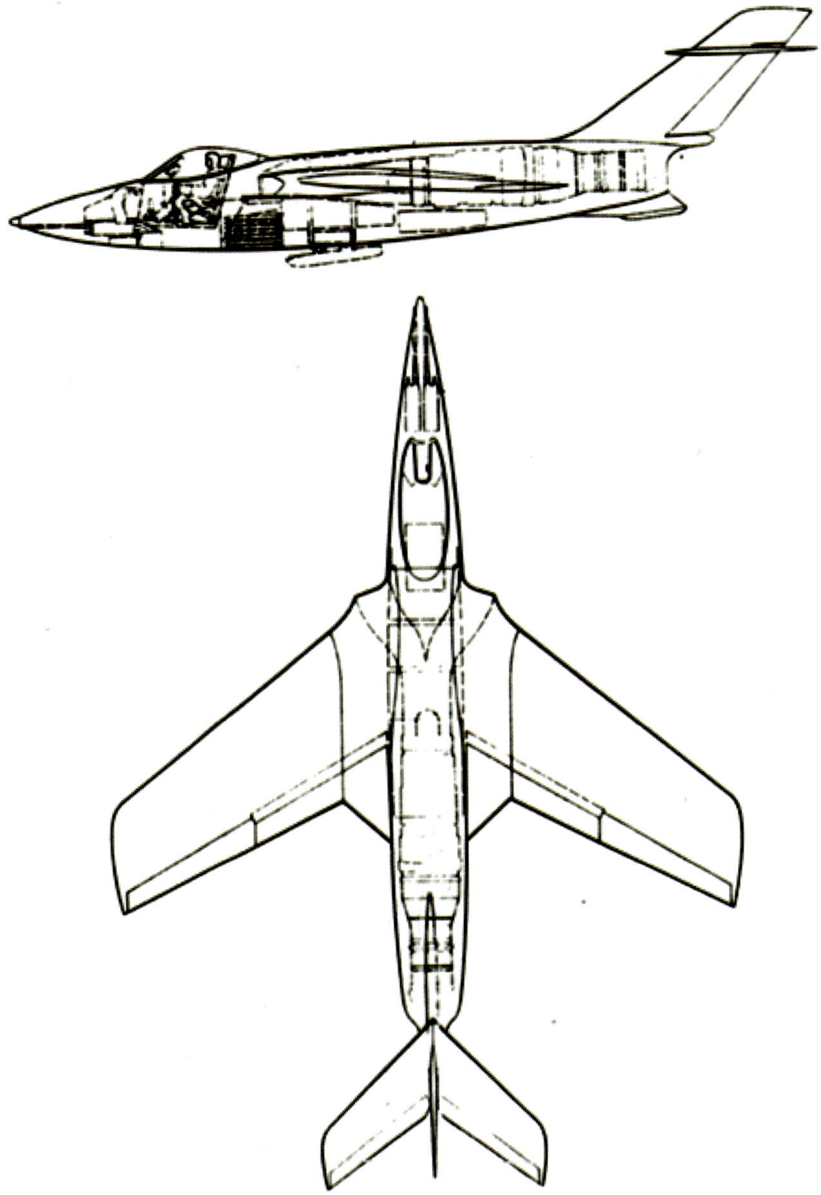

ABOVE RIGHT Two-view drawing of the SE 5020 Baroudeur S. *SNCASE*

BELOW Sectional view of the SE 5020 Baroudeur S, a simplified version of the aircraft. *SNCASE*

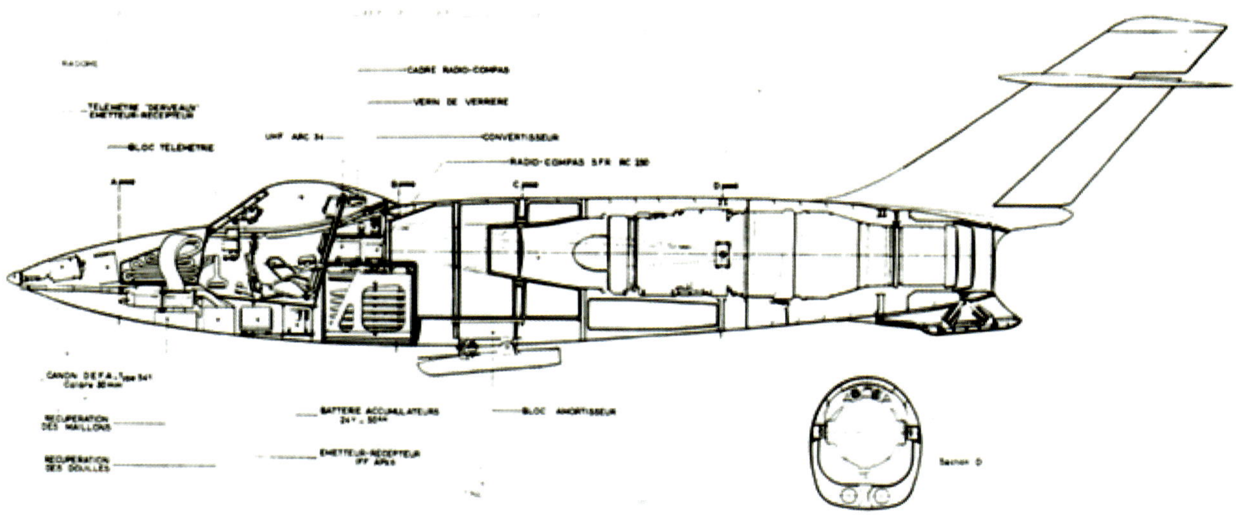

SE 5030 Baroudeur R

This was a derivative of the SE 5020 fitted with a 8,100lb (36kN) SNECMA M17 turbojet giving a speed of Mach 1.03 at 39,370ft (12,000m) altitude. Everything was sacrificed in favour of the weapon load with three attachment points per wing, two 30mm cannon or four 12.7mm machine guns in the nose, and a rocket rack in the bomb bay. R meant '*robuste*' (robust).

SE 5030	
Status	project
Span	32ft 10in (10.00m)
Length	44ft 10in (13.66m)
Gross wing area	272.0sq ft (25.3sq m)
Gross weight	13,228lb (6,000kg)
Powerplant	SNECMA M-17 8,100lb (36kN)
Maximum speed/Height	Mach 1.03
Armament	-

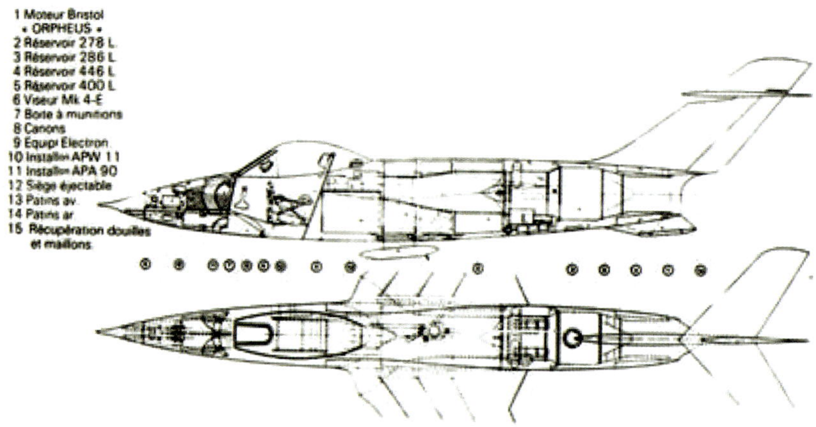

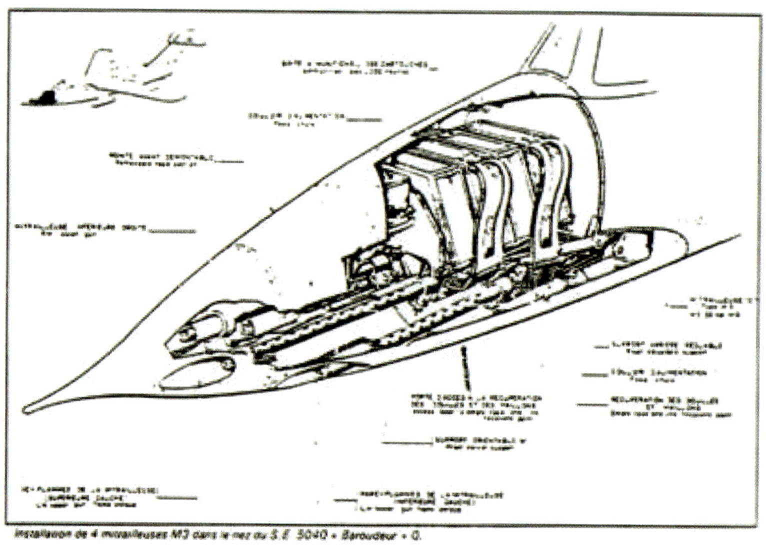

TOP Views of the SE 5030 Baroudeur R variant ('R' for robuste – heavy weapons). *SNCASE*

ABOVE The SE 5040 Baroudeur O (for Orpheus) would have been 80% the size of the SE 5000. *Philippe Ricco*

SE 5040 Baroudeur 0

By reducing all of the SE 5000's dimensions to 80% of the original it was hoped to reduce the weight by 4,409lb (2,000kg) while retaining the same armament. A significant departure on the SE 5040 from previous Baroudeur designs was the introduction of a wheeled undercarriage; actually a retractable wheel was fitted at the front while, as part of the weight reduction programme, the skids would have been replaced by the non-retractable fairings proposed for the SE 5020. Fitted with an Orpheus engine (O for Orpheus) this aircraft was expected to reach Mach 1.1 at 36,090ft (11,000m).

SE 5040	
Status	project
Span	26ft 3in (8.00m)
Length	36ft 11.5in (11.26m)
Gross wing area	174.2sqft (16.2sq m)
Gross weight	9,028lb (4,095kg)
Powerplant	Orpheus 12, 6,750lb (30kN)
Maximum speed/Height	Mach 1.01
Armament	-

SE 50xx Baroudeur A

An even smaller version of the Baroudeur, the 'A' was based on the Baroudeur O but it had a thinner wing (relative thickness 5%) with more sweep (45%) which resulted in a shorter span of 23ft 7.5in (7.20m). The Bristol Orpheus was still the main engine but two additional Rolls-Royce Soar engines could be added under the wings to boost the performance, and with these additional engines it was hoped to achieve a zero-length take-off from an inclined ramp. Base weapons were two 30mm guns in the nose plus up to 992lb (450kg) of ordnance in an internal bay (the wing attachment points were used by the Soars). It was also suggested (and patented) that the Soar boosters could tilt upward and this, coupled with a jet vectoring system in the Orpheus nozzle, meant that the aircraft could then have taken-off nearly vertically (or so Jakimiuk's team claimed) in a concept called the '*décollage ponctuel*' (the point take-off). These variants were all studied in 1954.

SE 50xx Baroudeur M

This was a February 1954 study for a navalised Baroudeur based on the

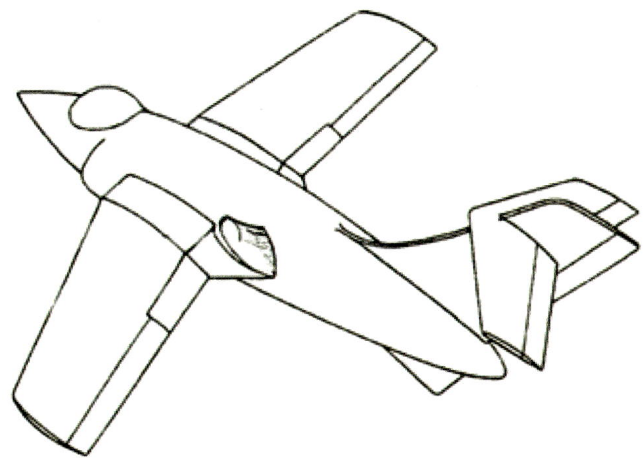

ABOVE **The blown wing SE 5050 appeared on the drawing board when SNCASE had already been amalgamated into Sud Aviation. Thus it became the SA 5050.** *Sud Aviation*

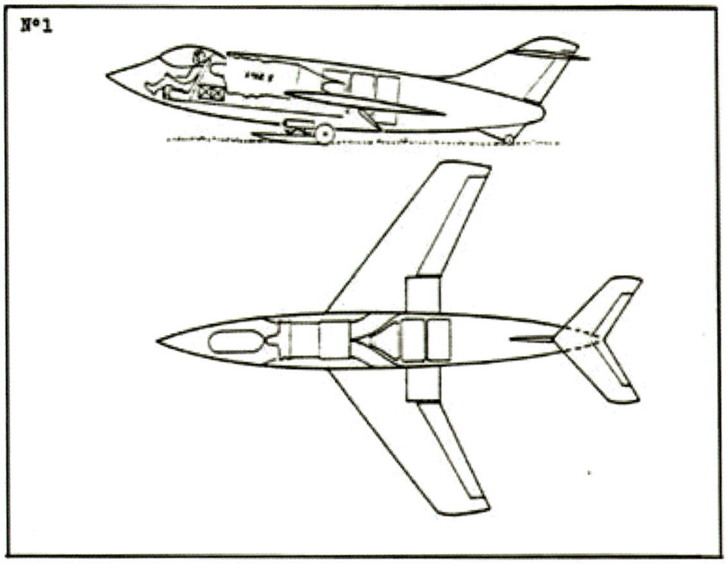

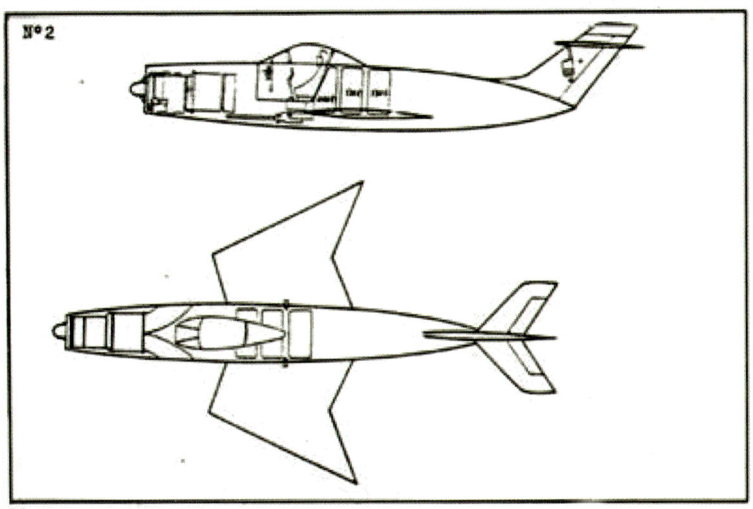

ABOVE **Various designs based on the Baroudeur were proposed fitted with blown wings. Here are two of them.** *Philippe Ricco*

original SE 5000. The project covered a full conversion of the aircraft to naval standards with folding wings and arrestor hook.

SE 5091

The SE 5091 was to have been a version of the 5012 with the wheeled undercarriage considered for the SE 5002. The jump in designation to 5091 came from the fact there was an agreement between SNCASE and Fiat (the manufacturer of the G.91) to produce this variant jointly if it had been accepted by NATO.

SE 5050 Baroudeur with Blown Wing

This was a derivative of the SE 5091 proposed made in 1958. Although it retained the Baroudeur's general architecture, the turbojet (an ATAR?) was positioned well in front of the wing so that its jet could be discharged through wing flaps. In this way '*the flow generated by the turbojet, used fully for propulsion during normal flight, was at low speed partially deflected downward while keeping in proximity with the upper surfaces of the lifting surfaces. This deflection could be improved by pointing the flaps downward, in which case it would impact the whole exhaust flow, contributing therefore both to propulsion and lift*'. It was also suggested that the exhaust nozzles should be shaped in the form of asymmetrical cones that could then be rotated to direct the flow either straight, to the rear of the aircraft or slightly downward, where the flow would impact the flaps in their downward position.

SE 5103

The SA 5013 was another blown wing design and based on the small Baroudeur O. Like the earlier version, its span was reduced (to 26ft 3in/8m) and it used a Bristol Orpheus as the main power unit. Fitted with the wheel-cum-fixed-skids undercarriage of the Baroudeur O, it weighed only 6,680lb (3,030kg) at take-off and had a minimal armament of just two 12.7mm machine-guns in the nose and two attachment points under the wings.

SA 5008 VS

One final blown wing variant was the SA 5008 VS (for '*voilure soufflée*' or blown wing), which was based on the SE 5008 and powered by an ATAR 8 turbojet. It should be noted that various blown wing designs were also studied that moved further away from the Baroudeur layout, although they still incorporated elements of the base design such as the skid landing gear or the tail unit.

Note that by this time SNCASO had recently merged (on 1 March 1957) with SNCASE to become Sud Aviation and consequently the project number prefix had been altered.

Dassault 'Barougan'

This was the nickname of a Dassault Ouragan variant adapted to operate from 'unprepared' terrain, the name Barougan having been coined by merging Baroudeur and Ouragan together. The first example, Ouragan number 140, was modified in having its main landing gear wheels doubled and a short skid inserted in between them and, because the wheels now bulged from their original bays, small fairings were also introduced to the underside of the fuselage to ensure they were enclosed. In all other respects the aircraft was identical to a production Ouragan and it first flew in this form on 24 February 1954. It was destroyed a few months later on 31 August, killing its pilot Lieutenant Tourangin. However, the experimental aircraft had performed sufficiently well to warrant the modification of three more machines, numbers 223, 225 and 336, and the last of these was even sent to North Africa for trials in a true operational environment (the war in Algeria was ongoing at that time). Although the conversion of fifty more aircraft was considered, due to the usual budgetary constraints this project was subsequently abandoned.

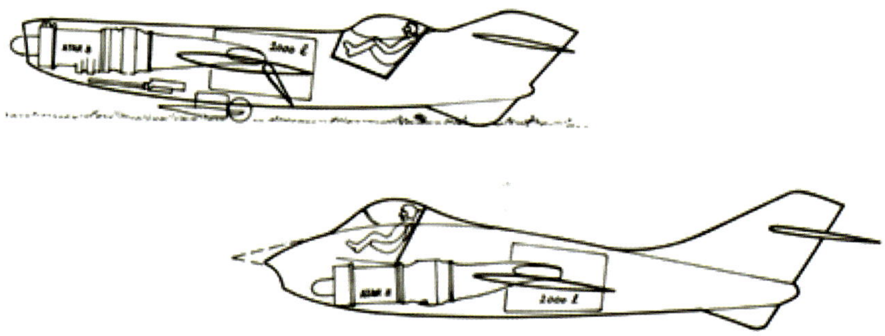

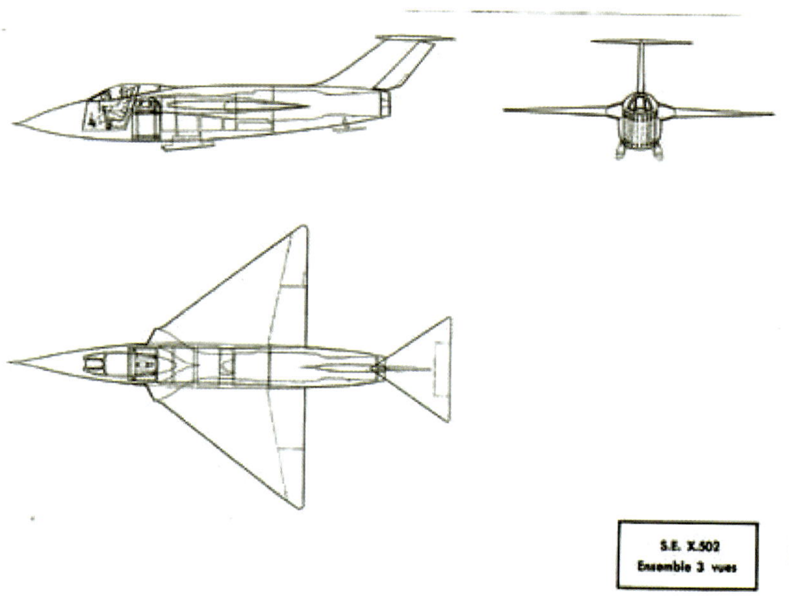

TOP **... and here are two more but moving further away from the original SE 5000 design.** *SNCASE*

ABOVE **Nothing is known about the Sud Est X-502 design but it clearly owed a lot to the Baroudeur.** *Philippe Ricco*

BELOW **Dassault Ouragan No. 336 is seen after being modified as the 'Barougan' with a beefed up landing gear. It was sent to Algeria for 'operational testing' in around 1957.** *Philippe Ricco*

Chapter Seven
COIN is Minted

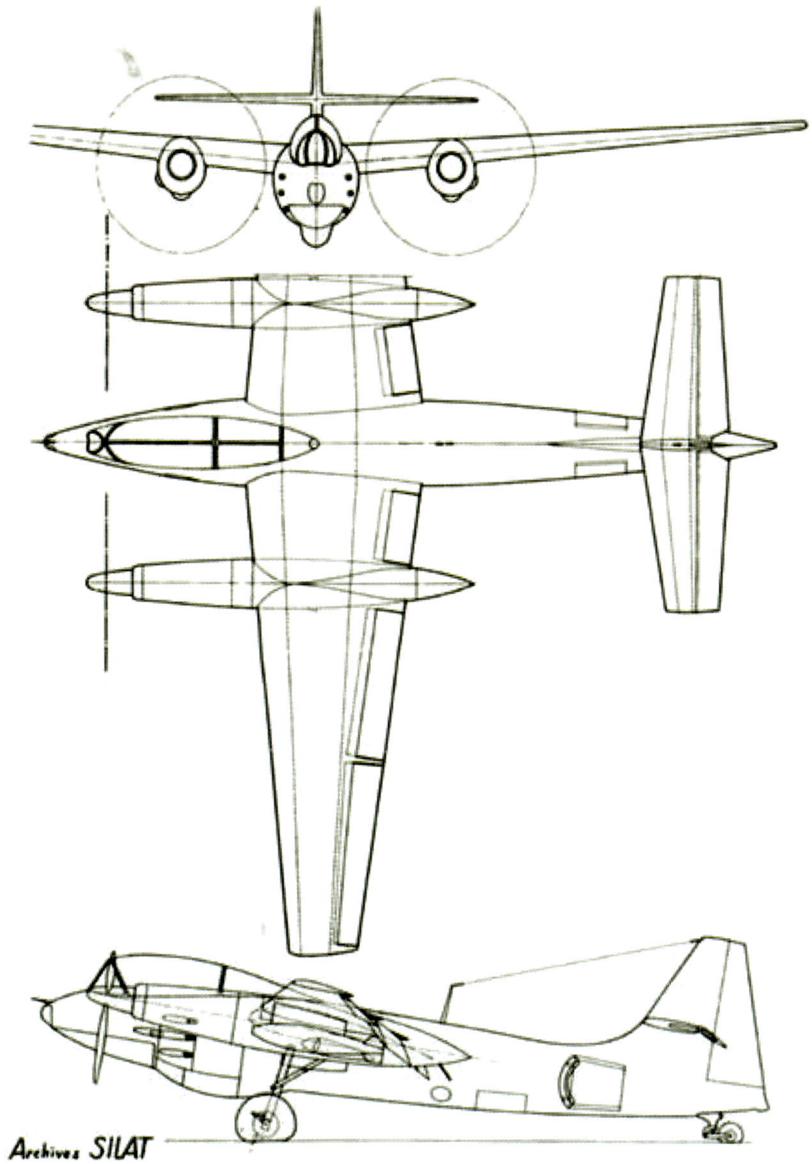

ABOVE The Laté 820 was Latécoère's entry to the *avions d'appui d'outremer* competition. *Latécoère*

The various 'decolonisation' wars, and in Europe the threat of a Soviet offensive backed by armoured formations, brought the need for France to develop specialised COIN (counter-insurgency) and ground attack aircraft. Up to now former Second World War aircraft, the Republic P-47D, Chance-Vought Corsair or North American T-6, had filled these roles in the various operations fought overseas, in North Africa or in Indochina, even when variants of the Coléoptère (see Chapter Eight) had been offered as replacements. In August 1955 the *Armée de l'Air* requested an '*avions d'appui d'outremer*' (ground support aircraft for overseas) and on 26 September a new programme was laid down. The aircraft was to be twin-engined, have a crew of two (or three if needed), a ferry range of 1,245 miles (2,000km) and the ability to loiter at low altitude for five hours for observation. The maximum speed requirement was only 255mph (410km/h) but the aircraft had to be able to operate from unprepared terrain. Armament was to be 30mm guns plus bombs or guided anti-tank missiles (the SS11) and a camera was to be carried for the reconnaissance role.

In parallel another requirement was raised for an '*avion de liaison et d'entrainement*' (training and liaison aircraft) that would retain some armament for a secondary ground attack role. Up to this point the NC 701 (née Siebel 204D), Dassault Flamant (Flamingo) and even the British Avro Anson had been used very well as liaison aircraft but with limited success in the ground support role. In due course the needs of the armed forces evolved further and, besides the armed support role, the updated programme required that the aircraft should be able to carry and then drop warloads, while combat experience had also demonstrated the need for side-mounted weapons. The submissions to the two new requirements are dealt with separately.

In the end nothing came from their proposals and American aircraft, the North American T-28 and Douglas AD-4 Skyraider, were acquired! Two reasons were offered for this fiasco:

first, politically, current national investment was to go to the *Force de Frappe*, which would mean that France was still a major player in the world affairs; second the Algerian War was at its peak when the need arose to replace the old T-6 and other types, and while French aircraft were favoured they would not be ready soon enough. Instead, American-procured machines bought off the shelf could reach operational units more quickly. These two factors removed any hopes of buying French-designed COIN aircraft in quantity, as good as they were. It must be noted here that while a specialised anti-tank aircraft (for use in the case of a European war with the Soviet forces) was never really considered by the *Armée de l'Air*, that did not deter manufacturers from offering one.

The Initial Approach: The Adaptation of Light Aircraft and Trainers

This route of using adapted light and trainer types of aircraft for COIN and ground attack was first used just after the Second World War had ended and the policy was continued well into the 1950s, until the ECAT programme took over (see Chapter Five). It was even resurrected in the late 1970s when manufacturers of light aircraft offered weapon-carrying versions of their designs.

Fouga Family

CM 82R

The Fouga designs all bear the type prefix CM in homage to their designers Robert Castello and Pierre Mauboussin. The CM 82R Lutin (Sprite) was the flying mock-up of a slightly larger aircraft, the CM 821, to be powered by two Marboré engines and armed with a 20mm HS404 gun and twelve 12cm rockets. The unusual aspect is that these aircraft were themselves derivatives of a performance glider! In fact, the mock-up displayed at the 1951 Paris Air Show had been concocted by a careful 'dressing up' of a CM 8-R13 Sylphe (Sylph), a jet-powered motor glider. The project disappeared after that, much to the chagrin of *Aviation Magazine*, which claimed that '*a thousand Lutin would do more damage* [to the enemy] *than fifty* [F-84] *Thunderjets, at an equal cost*'.

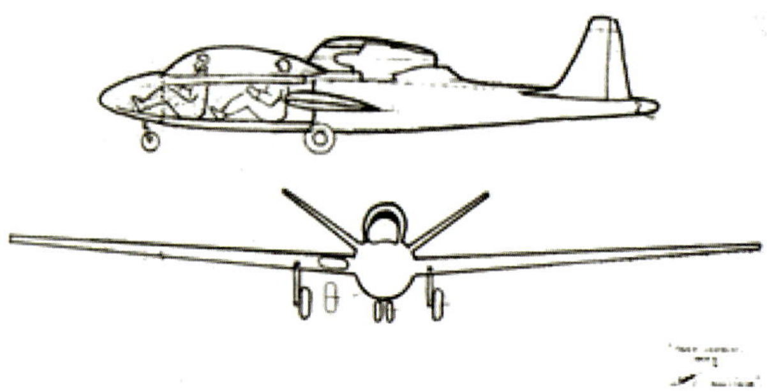

TOP The only surviving illustration of the Fouga CM82R Lutin is this artwork by journalist Robert J. Roux published in Aviation Magazine on 1 November 1951. *Author's collection*

ABOVE The Fouga Centaure was another experiment in designing a light aircraft from a glider airframe. *Author's collection/Fouga*

CM 82R	
Status	mock-up
Span	27ft 39in (8.85m)
Length	22ft 47in (6.85m)
Gross wing area	106.5sq ft (9.90 sq m)
Gross weight	2,167lb (983kg)
Powerplant	two Palas 340lb (1.5kN)
Maximum speed/Height	186mph (300km/h) at 16,405ft (5,000m)
Armament	twelve rockets

CM 821	
Status	project
Span	38ft 4.5in (11.70m)
Length	29ft 2in (8.90m)
Gross wing area	187.1sq ft (17.4sq m)
Gross weight	6,283lb (2,850kg)
Powerplant	two Marboré 790lb (3.5kN)
Maximum speed/Height	404mph (650km/h) at ground level
Armament	one HS404 20mm gun and twelve rockets

CM 170R

Single-seater derivative of the Fouga Magister (see Chapter Five).

CM 175 (1953)

The CM 175 was described as a variant of the Sylphe motor glider, which was basically a glider airframe with a Turbomeca Palas turbojet on its back, just behind the cockpit. Basically, the CM 175 would have been a Sylphe with armament pods or rockets under the wings (note: other descriptions have also suggested a Magister airframe with a single Ossau engine).

CM 178

In 1958 a major redesign of the basic Magister as a ground attack aircraft was proposed. The two Turbomeca Marboré turbojets were replaced by Turbomeca Astazou turboprops positioned in pods above the wings. This redesign saw new fairings in the positions previously occupied by the air intakes and in which various items of weaponry were to be installed, notably two DEFA 552 20mm guns. The two aforementioned guns would have been accompanied by two 12.7mm machine guns and up to 661lb (300kg) of ordnance (bombs or rockets). The crew was reduced to just the pilot and the V-tail was made 40% larger to enable the aircraft to be flown on one engine. However, by 1960 the project had lost its operational component and it was now proposed to operate the type simply as a test bed for the Astazou.

CM 178	
Status	project
Span	36ft 8in (11.17m)
Length	32ft 10in (10.00m)
Gross wing area	182.8sq ft (17.00sq m)
Gross weight	7,030lb (3,189kg)
Powerplant	two Astazou
Maximum speed/Height	298mph (480km/h) at ground level
Armament	two DEFA 552, two MAC 52 and 661lb (300kg) ordnance

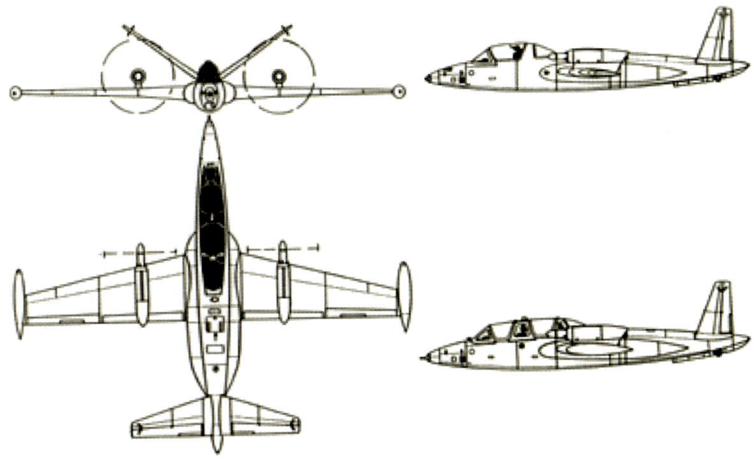

ABOVE **The Fouga CM 178 was a single-seat adaptation of the Fouga Magister airframe with turboprop propulsion for the ground attack role.** *Author's collection/Fouga*

Morane Saulnier

Morane Saulnier MS 733 Alcyon/MS 735

The MS 733 Alcyon was a trainer ordered after the war by the *Armée de l'Air*. Morane now offered a MS 735 fitted with a more powerful engine and four machine guns, and a prototype was produced by the conversion of MS 733 N° 76. This was sent to Algeria, where it performed successfully but no production orders followed.

MS 735	
Status	prototype
Span	37ft 0.5in (11.29m)
Length	30ft 7.5in (9.34m)
Gross wing area	235.5sq ft (21.90sq m)
Gross weight	3,748lb (1,700kg)
Powerplant	one Potez 6D 30 305hp (227kW)
Maximum speed/Height	177mph (285km/h) at 5,905ft (1,800m)
Armament	four 7.5mm machine guns

Morane Saulnier MS 750

This was a 1950 project for a tandem two-seater powered by two unspecified turbojets in pods suspended under the wing (it is known that the Aspin II and Marboré engines were investigated). The wing itself was quite wide with a swept leading edge and the fin, like many Morane projects of the period, supported high-mounted horizontal tail surfaces.

MS 750	
Status	project
Span	38ft 11in (1.60m)
Length	35ft 7in (10.85m)
Gross wing area	?
Gross weight	8,818lb (4,000kg)
Powerplant	two 1,350lb (6kN) turbojets
Maximum speed/Height	-
Armament	two guns in nose

Morane Saulnier MS 751

This type number may have been attributed to a 'reduced format' version of the MS 750 (which was quite a small aeroplane already).

Morane Saulnier MS 752

MS 752 two-seater	
Status	project
Span	32ft 10in (10.00m)
Length	33ft 1in (10.08m)
Gross wing area	215.1sq ft (20.00sq m)
Gross weight	6,664lb (3,023kg)
Powerplant	two Marboré 790lb (3.5kN)
Maximum speed/Height	398mph (640km/h) at sea level
Armament	one MATRA rocket tray

The MS 752 was the Morane project that lost out to the Fouga Magister. Intended as a primary trainer with trainee and teacher in a side-by-side cockpit, it would have been propelled by two Turbomeca Marboré engines and equipped with two 7.5mm machine guns. It was not produced.

Morane Saulnier MS 752 Single seater

From the aborted MS 752 trainer was developed a single-seat ground attack aircraft on which the armament was beefed up with a retractable rocket tray and wing attachment points for up to 2,205lb (1,000kg) of ordnance. A RATO rocket motor could be fitted into a recess in the rear fuselage, but this assault version was not built.

MS 752 single- seater	
Status	project
Span	30ft 4in (9.25m)
Length	33ft 1in (10.08m)
Gross wing area	204.3sq ft (19.00sq m)
Gross weight	8,708lb (3,950kg)
Powerplant	two Marboré 790lb (3.5kN)
Maximum speed/Height	398mph (640km/h) at sea level
Armament	up to 2,205lb (1,000kg) ordnance

Morane Saulnier MS 753

Morane Saulnier persevered with its opinion that side-by-side seating was the optimum position for a trainee and his teacher and proposed the MS 753 in this configuration. However, no more details are known.

Morane Saulnier MS 755

MS 755	
Status	prototype
Span	31ft 7.5in (9.64m)
Length	31ft 10in (9.7m)
Gross wing area	193.5sq ft (18.00sq m)
Gross weight	6,669lb (3,025kg)
Powerplant	two Marboré 790lb (3.5kN)
Maximum speed/Height	447mph (720km/h)
Armament	two guns in nose

ABOVE **The prototype of the MS 755 Fleuret, probably at an airshow.** *Author's collection*

Another unsuccessful attempt by Morane to compete with the Fouga Magister trainer, the MS 755 Fleuret (sword) did not go beyond the prototype stage.

Morane Saulnier MS 761

This type number was probably allocated to a version of the MS 760, a type that had been adopted by the *Armée de l'Air* with ninety-five units manufactured as liaison aircraft. The MS 761 had a modified fuselage and a bomb bay for 2,205lb (1,000kg) of stores.

Nord Aviation

Nord 1200 Norécrin

The Nord 1200 Norécrin (Nor from Nord plus écrin for jewel box) was first developed for a civilian competition organised by the French Ministry of Transport. It first flew on 15 December 1945 in the hands of Georges Detre, with the production version 1201 Norécrin I having three-seats. The variant of interest here was the 1203 Norécrin V, in which the number of seats was reduced to two (or even just the pilot), and for the COIN role all of the armament would be carried on two wing attachment points. The project was proposed in 1953 and a prototype was tested at the Cazaux range but again this variant was not produced, despite the fact that it was pointed out that sixty airframes were available for conversion and that it would have been easy to train pilots to use it because they were already familiar with the standard Norécrin.

Overseas Ground Support Aircraft

The corresponding 'ground support aircraft for overseas' resulted in the following designs and projects.

Breguet 1060

The Br 1060 would have been a ground-based variant of the Br 1050 Alizé (see

BELOW **The Breguet Br 1060 of 21 March 1957 was a ground attack version of the Alizé anti-submarine aircraft. It was not built.** *Philippe Ricco*

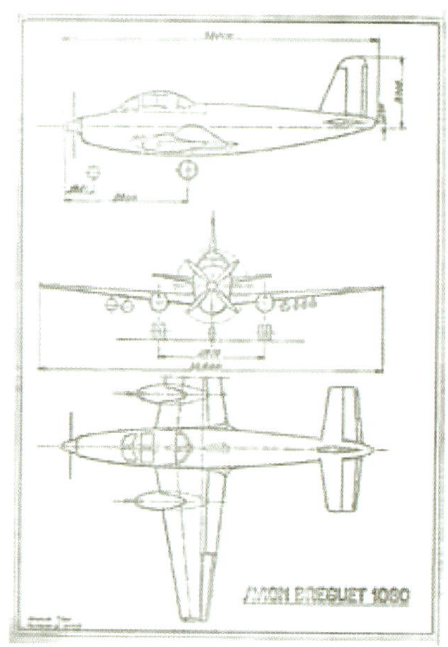

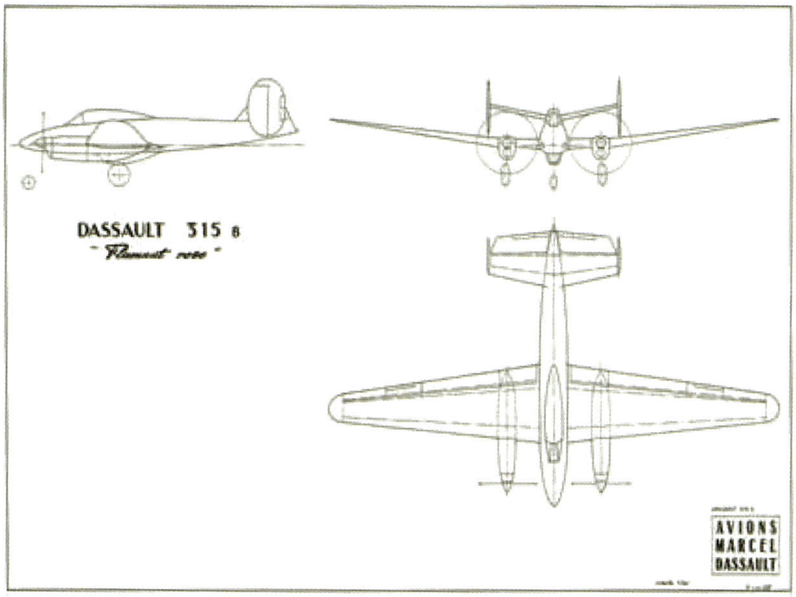

ABOVE Dassault's MD 315B Flamant Rose was a variant of the MD 315 fitted with a new fuselage. The drawing is dated 7 November 1955. *Dassault Aviation*

Chapter Eleven) optimised for the '*appui outremer*' role. All the naval equipment would have been removed and two 30mm guns would have been fitted in the wing, the wing fold facility also having been removed. Naturally, the electronic and radio equipment would have been to Army standards and not to the Navy's, but this proposal was rejected because it was feared that a single-engine aircraft would be more vulnerable to ground fire and that its low wing loading would not have allowed it to manoeuvre well enough.

Dassault MD 315B Flamant Rose (Pink Flamingo)

The MD 315B design of late 1954 to mid-1955 retained the wing (with engine pods) and tail units of the MD 315 (which itself was a derivative of the MD 311/312, the first French-designed military aircraft ordered into production after the war). However, mated to them now was a new fuselage with two crew under a bubble canopy at the front and the possibility of having a bombardier in a ventral gondola. The built-in armament would have been concentrated in the nose with either four heavy machine guns or two 30mm cannon (as was normal at the time, the armament was mounted on removable trays) and there would have been four load-carrying points under the wings for bombs or rockets. The crew would have been protected by armour plates and an armoured windshield. Consideration was given to building a prototype, which could have been followed by sixty-five production aircraft. Indeed some time before, in 1954 Dassault was ordered to produce sixty-six MD 316s (another variant of the basic Flamant) but due to an administrative glitch the manufacturer never officially received the contract, which was soon cancelled. However, SNCASE, to whom part of the Flamant production was subcontracted, had already produced sixty-six tail units! Thus it would have been beneficial for everyone to use these parts rather than to scrap them, but the Flamant Rose proposal was not taken up.

MD 315B	
Status	project
Span	64ft 3.5in (19.60m)
Length	39ft 8.5in (12.10m)
Gross wing area	486.0sq ft (45.20sq m)
Gross weight	13,205lb (5,990kg)
Powerplant	two SNECMA 12S 550hp (410kW)
Maximum speed/Height	224mph (360km/h) at 7,875ft (2,400m)
Armament	two DEFA 30mm guns and bombs and rockets

Latécoère Projects

Laté offered two designs, the 820 and 821, which differed in their powerplants. The 820 was to use two Turboméca Bastan turboprops while the 821 had the SNECMA 12 S-02. The basic aircraft was designed for easy maintenance with large access panels and the three crew members were housed under a large bubble canopy that was protected by armour plate and would have provided a good all-round view. Fixed armament would have comprised either four 20mm cannon or six 12.7mm machine guns in removable racks located on the sides of the cockpit and in an underfuselage bay. Two rearward firing machine guns would have been fitted in the rear of the engine nacelles (which seems an odd feature for a COIN aircraft) and two attachment points were located under each wing, outboard of the nacelles. Bombs, rocket launchers or

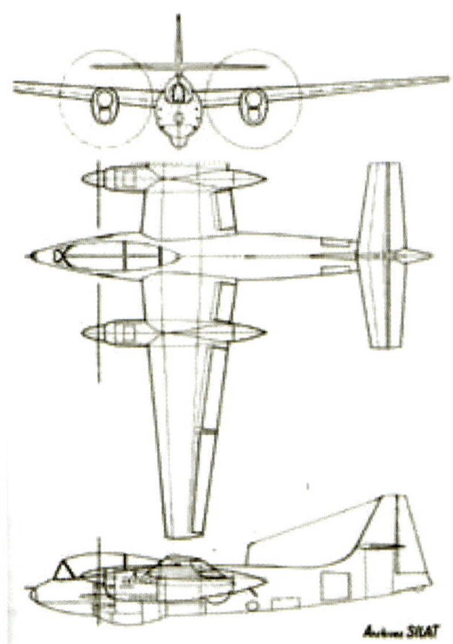

ABOVE The Laté 821 differed from the 820 in its powerplant (SNECMA 12S piston units instead of Turboméca Bastan turboprops). *Latécoère*

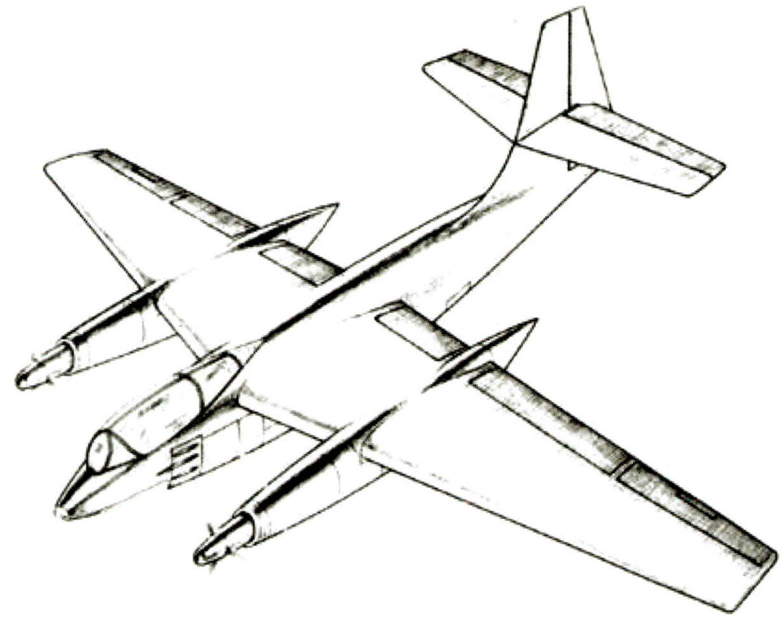

ABOVE Perspective illustration depicting the Laté 820 in fight. *Latécoère*

Laté 820	
Status	project
Span	52ft 6in (16.00m)
Length	39ft 4.5in (12.00m)
Gross wing area	354.8sq ft (33sq m)
Gross weight	up to 11,391lb (5,167kg)
Powerplant	two Bastan 650hp (485kW)
Maximum speed/Height	267mph (430km/h)
Armament	four HS 20mm or two DEFA 541/542 30mm or six 12.7mm mg, plus two machine guns in nacelles and 4,409lb (2,000kg) ordnance

Laté 821	
Status	project
Span	52ft 6in (16.00m)
Length	39ft 4.5in (12.00m)
Gross wing area	354.8sq ft (33sq m)
Gross weight	up to 12,044lb (5,463kg)
Powerplant	two SNECMA 12 S-02 600hp (447kW)
Maximum speed/Height	242mph (390km/h)
Armament	four HS 20mm or two DEFA 541/542 30mm or six 12.7mm machine guns, plus two machine guns in nacelles and 4,409lb (2,000kg) ordnance

even SS11/SS12 wire-guided anti-tank missiles could have been carried on these.

Morane Saulnier MS 775

The MS 775 was the early design from 1954-56 that evolved into the Epervier, or Sparrowhawk. It was to be powered by a Turbomeca Marcadau turboprop and above and slightly behind this came the pilot and the gunner in an extensively glazed canopy that offered excellent front and downward visibility. The design evolved slightly because, having originally been conceived with a T-tail, like many MS designs it was later redesigned with low horizontal surfaces. Originally it was intended to arm the MS 775 with missiles only (SS10/Entac) but later bombs and gun pods were also considered. Unusually for an aircraft intended to operate on land (but maybe influenced by the German Fieseler Storch that had been built by Morane during and after the war), the wings could fold alongside the fuselage.

MS 775	
Status	project
Span	45ft 3.5in (13.80m)
Length	30ft 2in (9.20m)
Gross wing area	258.1sq ft (24.00sq m)
Gross weight	5,214lb (2,365kg)
Powerplant	one Marcadau 360hp (270kW)
Maximum speed/Height	?
Armament	SS10 missile, gun pods, bombs, etc.

BELOW The Morane-Saulnier MS 775 was an early project that eventually evolved into the MS 1500 Epervier. *Henri Lacaze*

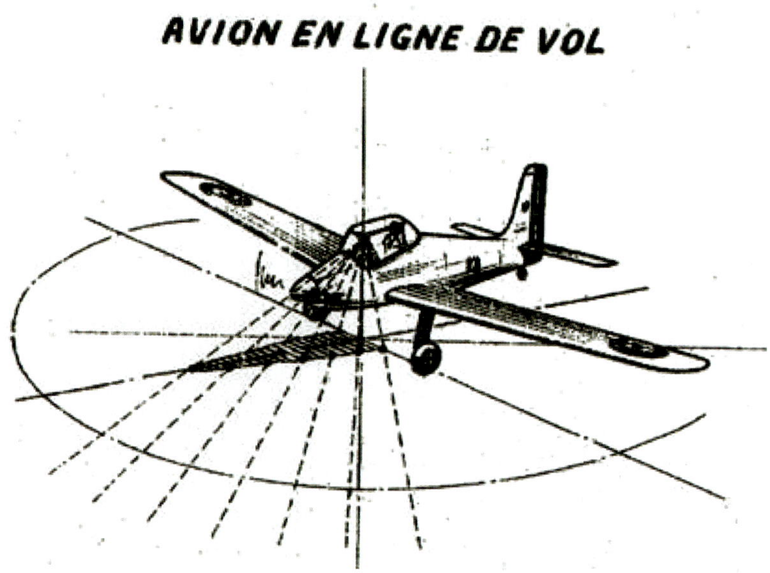

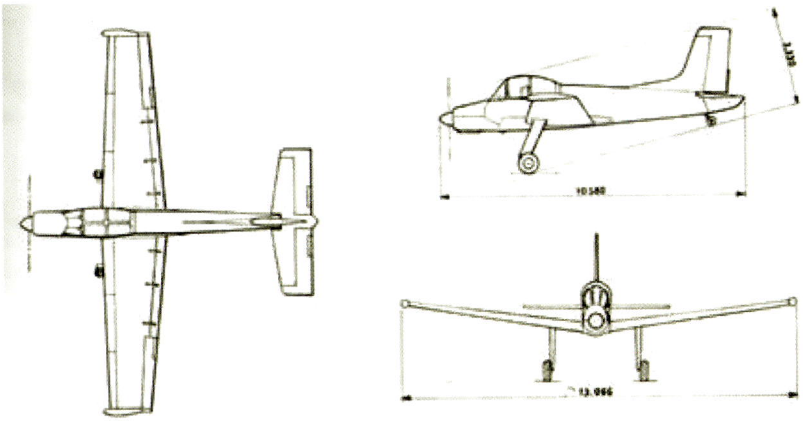

TOP This is a three-view drawing of the aircraft finally produced, the MS 1500 Epervier. *Author's collection/Morane Saulnier*

ABOVE While the MS 1500 was built this arrangement featuring underwing pods to carry commandos was not. *Henri Lacaze*

MS 1500	
Status	two prototypes
Span	42ft 10in (13.06m)
Length	34ft 8.5in (10.58m)
Gross wing area	261.3sq ft (24.30sq m)
Gross weight	6,063lb (2,750kg)
Powerplant	one Bastan III 870hp (649kW)
Maximum speed/Height	216mph (348km/h)
Armament	-

Morane Saulnier MS 1500 Epervier

The MS 1500 'Co-operation and Police Aircraft' made its maiden flight on 12 May 1958 after having been ordered under contract N° 3138/57 on 11 April 1957. The observer was seated in the forward seat just behind the Turbomeca Bastan engine, an excellent position for observation (note: the first forty-seven flights were made with a Marcadau engine from the same manufacturer). However, the aircraft had been criticised initially because, although the observer had a good 'perch', his pilot had a much less enviable position, yet the elongated nose gave both crew members good over-wing vision. The aircraft did not carry any internal weapons but could store gun pods, bombs, rockets and SS-11 anti-tank missiles under its wings. A second machine was flown on 25 February 1959 but no production ensued despite the contracted performance requirements being achieved and in a few cases bettered. Quite simply, the finance was just not available in the 1958-59 period to go ahead. Various attempts were made to save the project as the improved performance of the Bastan engine enabled the MS 1500 to be better protected (it was proposed to add 140kg/309lb of armour plate around the cockpit), to carry more ordnance and more fuel, etc. It was even suggested that faired wing containers should be used to carry three fully equipped soldiers each in a scheme reminiscent of an experiment carried out with the Junkers Ju 87 in the war.

Morane Saulnier MS 1510 Epervier II

This variant featured a retractable landing gear and an improved 940hp (700kW) Bastan IV turboprop.
(Info box on page 128.)

Morane Saulnier MS 1520

A twin-engine development of the basic Epervier design.

MS 1510	
Status	project
Span	42ft 10in (13.06m)
Length	34ft 8.5in (10.58m)
Gross wing area	261.3sq ft (24.30sq m)
Gross weight	6,063lb (2,750kg)
Powerplant	one Bastan IV 940hp (701kW)
Maximum speed/Height	216mph (348km/h)
Armament	-

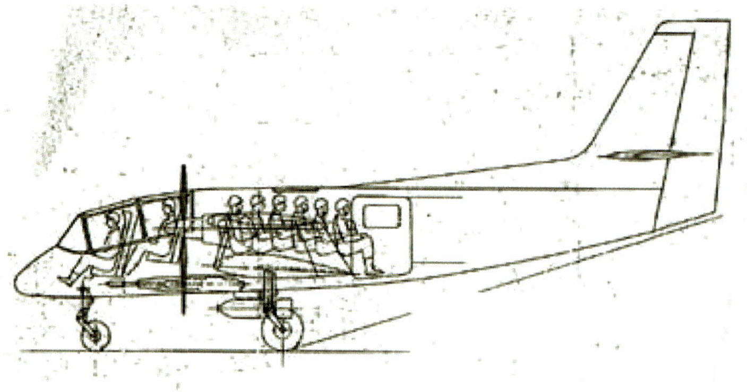

ABOVE **The MS 1530 was a twin-engine variant of the Epervier that also remained unbuilt.** *Henri Lacaze*

Morane Saulnier MS 1530

Another twin-engine development of the Epervier that had the original wing and tail surfaces mated to a new fuselage. The tricycle landing gear could be retracted and a powerplant of Turbomeca Astazou XIV engines in over-wing pods was selected. Along with its wing attachment points, the MS 1530 had two 30mm guns faired into the wing roots. The project was floated until the mid-1960s but without success.

MS 1530	
Status	project
Span	39ft 4.5in (12.00m)
Length	38ft 10.5in (11.85m)
Gross wing area	247.3sq ft (23.00sq m)
Gross weight	8,157lb (3,700kg)
Powerplant	two Astazou XIV 790hp (589kW)
Maximum speed/Height	?
Armament	two 30mm guns

Morane Saulnier MS 1550

The MS 1550 'Super Epervier' was to be powered by the Rolls-Royce Dart 6 turboprop, but it never left the drawing board!

MS 1550	
Status	project
Span	51ft 4in (15.65m)
Length	37ft 1in (11.30m)
Gross wing area	376.3sq ft (35.00sq m)
Gross weight	12,125lb (5,500kg)
Powerplant	one Dart Mk 510 1,670hp (1,245kW)
Maximum speed/Height	?
Armament	-

BELOW **The Morane MS 1600 was the final aircraft in the Epervier family.** *Henri Lacaze*

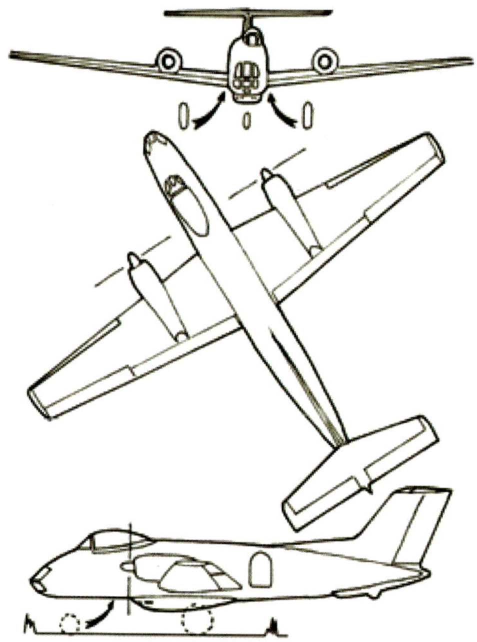

Morane-Saulnier MS 1600

This was a 1955 project incorporating some elements of the MS 1500 Epervier. The MS 1600 was to be a twin-turboprop, two-seat aircraft with a straight wing but a raked tail. The pilot sat in an off-centre armoured cockpit under a bubbletop canopy while the second crew member was located in the nose behind glazed panels. The turboprop powerplant here was the Armstrong-Siddeley Mamba and the armament was to be housed in a removable under-fuselage pod.

MS 1600	
Status	project
Span	?
Length	?
Gross wing area	?
Gross weight	up to 17,681lb (8,020kg)
Powerplant	two Mamba turboprops 1,000hp (746kW)
Maximum speed/Height	?
Armament	two 30mm guns or four 12.7mm machine guns

Nord 3300

This project was submitted in January 1956 but nothing else is known about it.

Fouga CM 220

The CM 220 was an old-fashioned looking design with fixed landing gear in large fairings (pantalons), a straight wing and a conventional (tailwheel) undercarriage. It had a crew of two with the pilot seated at the front and an observer at the rear with bulged side windows. The armament is unconfirmed but the illustration depicts the aircraft with side cannon bulges and four under wing attachment points for bombs and rocket clusters.

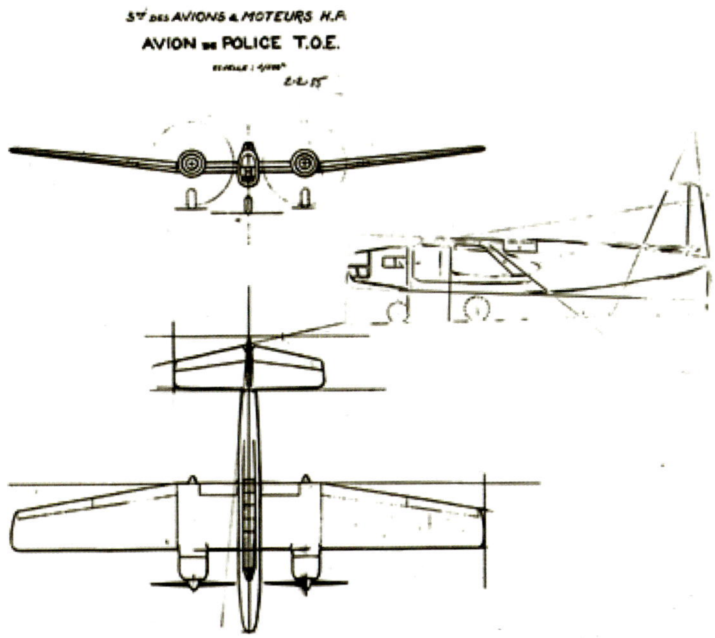

ABOVE LEFT The only thing known about the Fouga CM 220 is this illustration. *Author's collection/Fouga*

ABOVE The Potez TOE is another design of which only a drawing remains (it is dated 2 February 1955). *Potez*

Potez TOE

The Potez TOE design was never officially submitted. With a view of simplicity of production in mind it was designed with straight trapezoidal wings, a slab-sided fuselage and two piston engines in the 800hp to 1,000hp (600kW to 745kW) class. It would have been a three-seater with a long birdcage canopy for the nose bombardier position; in fact, it looked like an updated version of a bomber designed to the old 'B4' competition of the 1930s. With six heavy machine guns and up to 2,205lb (1,000kg) of ordnance, the TOE would have been one of the most heavily armed aircraft of the various contenders. However, it was also apparent that what it could gain in armament it would lose in size and manoeuvrability, which is probably why it was not entered in the competition.

Potez TOE	
Status	project
Span	70ft 6.5in (21.50m)
Length	33ft 3.5in (13.50m)
Gross wing area	?
Gross weight	?
Powerplant	two unnamed engines 800 to 1,000hp (597 to 746kW)
Maximum speed/Height	?
Armament	-

Potez 75

Special mention should be made of the Potez 75, which was perhaps the only French aircraft ever designed specifically to attack tanks. The Potez head of *bureau d'études*, M. Delaruelle, summarised his creation as follows: 'A *motorised ground combat weapon, but freed from the ground limits reducing the fighting power of purely terrestrial vehicles.*' Of course, this rather convoluted description could as well apply to the later Norapter (see Chapter Fourteen) but here it applied to a small, simple and heavily armoured aircraft. A prototype was built using Potez's private funds in the 75-1 configuration of two seats in tandem and carrying wire-guided anti-tank missiles. An unbuilt Potez 75-2 would have had a different crew arrangement with the pilot and gunner seated side-by-side while the 75-3 would have been a trainer version of the -2. Besides the SS-11 missiles, unguided rockets or cannon pods were also considered for the aircraft and the addition of a fixed 20mm gun in the nose was also studied.

Potez 75	
Status	prototype
Span	43ft 0in (13.10m)
Length	30ft 0.5in (9.16m), later version with fixed guns 30ft 4.5in (9.26m)
Gross wing area	247.3sq ft (23.00sq m)
Gross weight	5,291lb (2,400kg), later 5,842lb (2,650kg)
Powerplant	one Potez 8 D-32 500hp (373kW)
Maximum speed/Height	174mph (280km/h) at ground level
Armament	four SS11 AT guided missiles and later four 7.5 AS52 machine guns

ABOVE Views of the Potez 75 on public display in its original and later conditions and with different colour schemes. *Author's collection*

The single prototype made its maiden flight on 10 June 1953 with Georges Détré at the controls and was displayed at the Paris Air Show in the following days. Of note on this occasion were its mixed military-civilian markings with the civil registration F-WGVK combined with camouflage paint and a roundel on the fin (but not on the fuselage!). The aircraft was tested extensively and found to be easy to fly. It had the ability to take off from unprepared strips, it was a stable firing platform but was too weakly protected to be used in the European theatre of operations for which it had been designed. Yet it showed some potential for the 'overseas' role and so a contract was signed with Potez to modify the aircraft as a 'Police TOM' aircraft (TOM for *Territoires d'Outre-Mer* or Overseas Territories). The modifications saw the armour reduced, the canopies were fully enclosed and the gunner's canopy had side bulges added to improve his downward view, while the armament now included four fixed 7.5mm MAC 52 machine guns in the nose. The aircraft was displayed in this new configuration at the 1957 Paris Air Show and it proved very successful. In fact, in its revised configuration the seventy-five was perfectly suited for the conflict that was developing in Algeria and an order for fifteen pre-production machines was passed. A series run of 100 machines was expected but unfortunately this was not to be, budgetary reasons again cutting the wings of a promising machine whose role was finally taken over by helicopters. The prototype Potez 75 was destroyed in a crash in 1958.

BELOW While the prototype Potez 75 flew extensively for five years, this flying boat version did not leave the drawing board. *Potez*

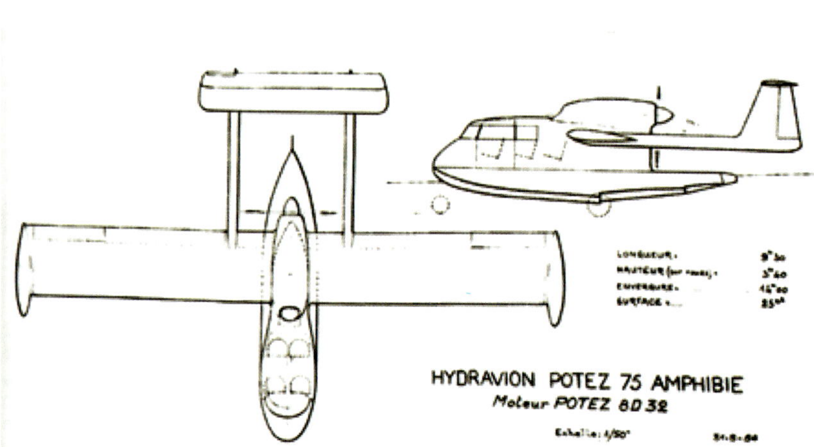

Potez 91

This re-engined variant of the Potez 75 was not produced.

SIPA 1100

The SIPA 1100 was to be the winner of the overseas ground support competition and an order for ten pre-series aircraft was placed in May 1956 under contracts 4136/56 and 4220/56. Unfortunately, by the time the prototype flew on 24 April 1958 the order had been reduced to just two aeroplanes! The original project showed a very simple aircraft with straight wings, twin turboprops and two seats and the landing gear was purposely kept old-style with a tail wheel. This design was, however, much modified subsequently and so the two prototypes differed somewhat from this original project. The turboprops

TOP & MIDDLE The SIPA 1100 was first exhibited as a model at the 1957 Paris Air Show. *Author's collection and Aeroplane magazine via Tony Buttler*

ABOVE Although an initial pre-series of tem SIPA 1100s was ordered, only the one prototype was completed and flown ... and it crashed. *Philippe Ricco*

had been dropped and replaced by Pratt & Whitney R-1340 Wasps (an engine already in widespread *Armée de l'Air* use on the North American T-6 serving as a ground attack aircraft in Algeria), but it was the cockpit that saw the most reworking and which gave the machine a remarkable appearance. At some point in the development process it had been requested that a third crew member should be introduced to operate a rearward-facing machine gun. This resulted in a bulged module composed mostly of flat glazed and armoured panels, which was nicknamed 'Viperhead'. To save time, the landing gear was taken from an NC 701 (Siebel 204D) and the weapons were to be either two 30mm DEFA 552 guns or four 12.7mm Browning machine guns, with three hard points positioned under each wing to carry up to 1,764lb (800kg) of bombs and rockets. The first prototype was flown extensively from May 1958 but unfortunately crashed on 2 July at Villacoublay during a low level display, and this led to the cancellation of the second prototype.

SIPA 1100	
Status	prototype
Span	48ft 6in (14.78m)
Length	37ft 0in (11.28m)
Gross wing area	452.5sq ft (42.08sq m)
Gross weight	11,243lb (5,100kg)
Powerplant	two R1340 Wasp 600hp (447kW)
Maximum speed/Height	218mph (350km/h)
Armament	two 30mm guns or four 12.7mm machine guns and 1,764lb (800kg) bombs or rockets

SIPA 1100B	
Status	project
Span	?
Length	?
Gross wing area	?
Gross weight	?
Powerplant	two R1340 Wasp 600hp (447kW)
Maximum speed/Height	?
Armament	none

SIPA 1120

This variant of the 1100 probably differed from the original through its powerplant (it may have referred to a SIPA 1100 fitted with Bastan turboprops but this is not confirmed).

SIPA 1130

The 1130 was another variant that used directly the wings and tail of the 1100 along with a new fuselage. It was an attempt to bring together both the ground attack mission (slimmer fuselage, bombardier nose and side-mounted weapons) with the capability to carry a few soldiers in its rear section.

SIPA 1130	
Status	project
Span	48ft 6in (14.78m)
Length	?
Gross wing area	452.5sq ft (42.08sq m)
Gross weight	?
Powerplant	two R1340 Wasp 600hp (447kW)
Maximum speed/Height	?
Armament	two 30mm guns or four 12.7mm machine guns

SNCASO SO 7100 Dogue (Mastiff)

In September 1953 SNCASO offered this *'avion de harcèlement de nuit'* (night harassment aircraft), which was supposed to be simple to build, strong and cheap. Its wing was rectangular with no dihedral and the fuselage was of monocoque construction with a large fin and rudder assembly. According to SNCASO, the Free French RAF Bomber Command pilot Philippe Level (who became Livry-Level after the war by prefixing his name with his nom-de-guerre Livry)[1] acted as a consultant for this project on the subject of night operations, but it seems that wartime Russian experience with the Ilyushin Il-2 Sturmovik and Polikarpov Po-2 was also taken into account. To keep the aeroplane cheap (because the operational life of a ground attack aircraft was expected to be quite short) three types of off-the-shelf engines could be used, the Alvis Leonides 502 radial piston type, the SNECMA 14X and the Pratt & Whitney R1340. All would deliver around 500hp (375kW), although the SNECMA 14X was favoured – causing some consternation when it was subsequently abandoned. Ultimately,

1 Capitaine Livry participated, among other missions, in Operation Jericho, the raid on the Amiens prison. Later he flew with 161 Squadron RAF, a unit specialising in agent and material delivery into Occupied France.

SNCASO SO 7100 (early)	
Status	project
Span	56ft 9in (17.30m)
Length	37ft 11.5in (11.57m)
Gross wing area	494.6sq ft (46.00sq m)
Gross weight	9,810lb (4,450kg)
Powerplant	two Alvis Leonides 502 570hp (425kW)
Maximum speed/Height	239mph (385km/h) at 8,200ft (2,500m)
Armament	two 30mm guns and sixteen 66lb (30kg) unguided rockets

SNCASO SO 7100 (late)	
Status	project
Span	56ft 9in (17.30m)
Length	37ft 11.5in (11.57m)
Gross wing area	494.6sq ft (46.00sq m)
Gross weight	9,810lb (4,450kg)
Powerplant	two Alvis Leonides 502 570hp (425kW)
Maximum speed/Height	249mph (400km/h) at 8,200ft (2,500m)
Armament	two HS 404 20mm guns and 992lb (450kg) bombs and eight rockets

therefore, the Alvis Leonides was selected.

The two crew were protected by 441lb (200kg) of armour plating and the armament would have been slightly below the requirements with two 20mm Hispano-Suiza HS 404 guns (although the specified DEFA 30mm could have been installed as well), four 112kg bombs (that is the British standard 250lb) and eight to sixteen unguided rockets under the wing (a desktop model of the Dogue shows eight rockets mounted four under each wing in a very Second World War-style arrangement). The landing gear was also 'old style' with a non-retractable tail wheel. According to SNCASO's presentation booklet, this design was full of virtues, as summarised here:

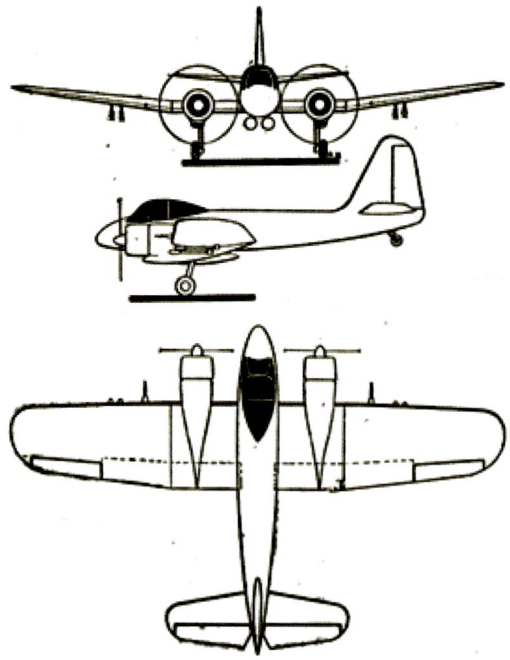

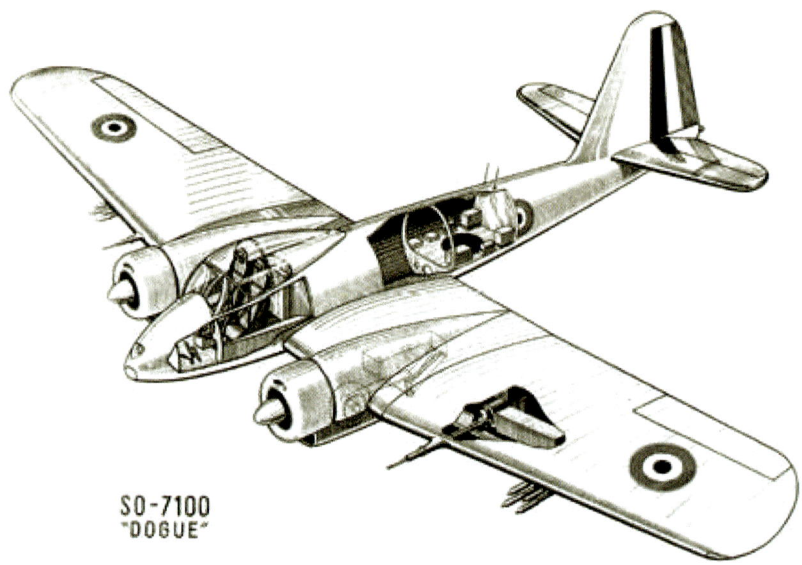

TOP **The SNCASO SO 7100 Dogue was a failed attempt to design a cheap and old-fashioned aircraft for the ground attack role. Having failed to make an impression through official channels, an attempt to save the project by 'leaking' its description in Les Ailes proved equally unsuccessful. This three-view drawing was the one revealed in that publication.** *Author's collection/les Ailes/SNCASO*

ABOVE **A cutaway view of the Dogue showing cockpit, radio equipment and armament.** *Philippe Ricco*

(i) the ability to use small fields near the frontline with a take-off run of 1,310ft (400m) on a grass or gravel track (which was why it had an old-fashioned landing gear and a 'generous' wing surface – the main wheels would have been taken from the de Havilland Vampire jet fighter),

(ii) a low minimum speed (about 75mph/120km/h with flaps and landing gear down and with a stall speed of about 62mph/100km/h) coupled with very good

manoeuvrability, even on a single engine;
(iii) heavy armament and good protection,
(iv) the ability to operate by day or night,
(v) and, as noted, the aircraft was cheap. In fact, it was purposely kept 'rustic' (that is Second World War-like) to ease front-line maintenance and to keep the costs down. A production Dogue was estimated to cost around twenty millions francs, which was claimed to be *'less than a quarter of the cost of a modern fighter'*.

However, the SO 7100 failed to impress and did not progress beyond the desk model stage, but it was still being discussed in the press in 1955.

Sud-Est SE 116

Work on the X-116 Fonceur (Charger) began in 1955 in the Marignane design office led by Jean Poitou. The brochure made a strong case that the drag curve was based on the data obtained during the flights of the earlier SE 1210, which was described as very similar to the X-116 and the first French aircraft with laminar wings. Quite a number of engines were considered for the SE 116 and rejected (between parenthesis are the opinions given in the brochure for each type):

1. Piston engines: SNECMA 12S ('*too weak and too long* [to fit]'), Pratt & Whitney R1340 ('*really too weak and too heavy*'), Wright R1300-1 ('*large diameter but short length, good flight duration, easy to procure*'), SNECMA 14X ('*too long, not produced in series*'), Alvis Leonides Major ('*really too long, production just beginning, procurement uncertain*') and Pratt & Whitney 1200 CV ('*too heavy*');
2. Turboprops: Turbomeca Artouste II ('*to list them all, too weak*'), Turbomeca Bastan ('*currently being developed, small diameter and very light*') and Lycoming (sub-type unspecified) ('*prototype*' status).

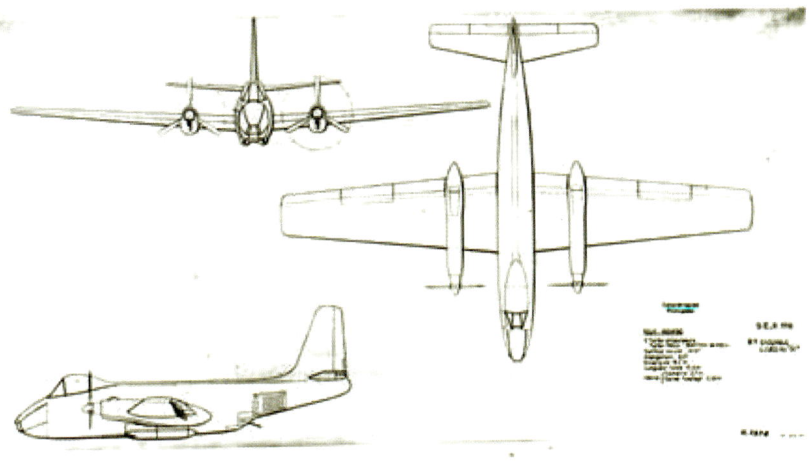

TOP Sud Est's proposal for this programme was the X-116, which was initially planned to be fitted with Turbomeca Bastan units but ended up being built with Wright Cyclone engines. A second SE 116 prototype fitted with Bastans disintegrated in mid-air and that effectively ended the project. *Author's collection/SNCASE*

ABOVE The prototype SNCASE SE 116 flew for the first time on 5 June 1958 with Roger Carpentier at the controls. *Author's collection/SNCASE*

SNCASE SE X-116B	
Status	project
Span	59ft 8.5in (18.20m)
Length	47ft 11in (14.60m)
Gross wing area	440.9sq ft (41sq m)
Gross weight	14,008lb (6,354kg)
Powerplant	two Wright R1300 Cyclone 7
Maximum speed/Height	231mph (371km/h)
Armament	-

SE 116	
Status	prototype
Span	58ft 11.5in (17.97m)
Length	40ft 1in (12.22m)
Gross wing area	443.0sq ft (41.20sq m)
Gross weight	12,537lb (5,687kg)
Powerplant	two Bastan 650hp (485kW)
Maximum speed/Height	277mph (445km/h)
Armament	-

The early version of this ground attack aircraft was to be fitted with the Bastan (the brochure declared: '*We will therefore present the X.116 aircraft fitted with two Bastan turboprops because of the very advantageous nature of this engine over piston engines*') but, as this engine was itself in development, the final proposal turned to the Wright Cyclone as the X-116B. On 11 June

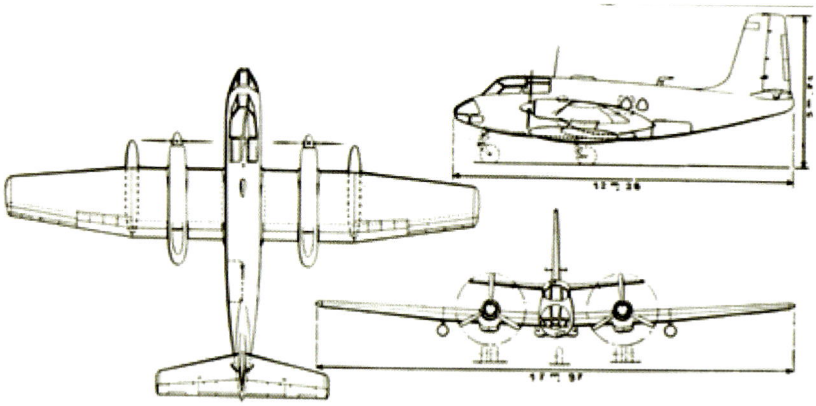

ABOVE Three-view drawing of the SNCASE SE 117 development of the SE 116. *SNCASE*

> 1956 two prototypes were ordered … fitted with turboprops, but then, after a change of mind in 1957, it was decided to complete one with Bastans and the other with Cyclones!

The original X-116 had its pilot under a bubbletop canopy, while the third crew member manned a rear gun position under the rear fuselage. The outline of the prototypes was more refined with the cockpit being faired into the fuselage and the step for the rear gun position being dispensed with. Curiously, it was initially considered that the pilot should have an ejector seat but this added weight ... and would have been of dubious benefit psychologically for the two other crew members! Armament consisted of two DEFA 552 30mm guns in an under-fuselage rack that could be replaced by another rack with cameras, and there were three attachment points under each wing to take bombs, rockets, napalm tanks or even anti-tank SS11/SS12 wire-guided missiles. A special variant was developed for what was called the 'Beyrouth' role – a night fighter adapted to deal with slow-moving targets, for example enemy aircraft parachuting equipment to guerrilla fighters, small nuisance bombers, etc. In this version the nose was modified to house a DRAC 25 radar set and anti-aircraft rockets were carried under the wings. The SE 116-01 Voltigeur (an old military term for scout troops operating on the side or front of the main army) flew for the first time on 5 June 1958 with Wright Cyclones. It was followed on 15 December by the Bastan-powered prototype, but this second machine disintegrated in mid-air on 9 January 1959, killing famous test pilot Roger Carpentier, who had earlier flown the SO 9050 and set the world altitude record aboard the rocket-powered interceptor on 2 May 1958 (Volume I).

Sud-Est SE 117

The third prototype flew on 21 January 1960 as the SE 117 and at that time it was planned to build 170 'frontline' aircraft plus eighty trainers. This machine was designed to be more flexible, being able to fly support, liaison or medevac (casualty evacuation) roles. It was intended to redesign the wing for the production version because it was thought that prototype 02 (above) had been destroyed by wing flutter. However, and while Morane-Saulnier and Hurel-Dubois were still retained as sub-contractors, the SE 116/117 programme was cancelled in the second half of 1960, the *Armée de l'Air* having once more changed its mind and stating that it now required an aircraft adapted first for the light transport role but retaining an attack capability. The SE 116/117 family, having been test flown at the height of the Algerian War, was the subject of much attention from politicians.

SE 117	
Status	prototype
Span	59ft 0.5in (18.00m)
Length	41ft 4.5in (12.61m)
Gross wing area	449.5sq ft (41.80sq m)
Gross weight	15,322lb (6,950kg)
Powerplant	two Bastan 750hp (559kW)
Maximum speed/Height	267mph (430km/h)
Armament	-

Initially pushed by the *Secrétaire d'Etat aux Forces Armées* in 1958, the project had been abandoned by 1960, much to the dismay of Members of Parliament, who wished to see new ground attack aircraft bought for the Algerian theatre of operations. MP Frédéric-Dupont stated in 1960: '*Is our army co-operation air force really sufficient in Algeria?* [and] *I see that the high command which had requested some examples of the Sud-Est 117 was not satisfied.*'[2]

Dassault Projects

In 1957 the *Armée de l'Air* requested a new aircraft for trainer and liaison roles to replace the by now somewhat outdated Flamant. This aircraft was also to retain some attack capability. Naturally, Dassault was the prime contender, and all the effort made by its competitors to 'evolve' a suitable aircraft from those designed for the '*appui outremer*' above would fail.

Dassault MD 415 Communauté

The MD 415 Communauté (for Communauty, probably in the sense of Commonwealth when used to describe Metropolitan France and French-speaking ex-colonies) was a private venture from Dassault that was designed to be able to fulfil any of the following roles – support, photo-reconnaissance, observation, navigation and bombing trainer, cargo and passenger aircraft. The resulting aeroplane looked like a small business aircraft with a bombardier nose and a

2 *Assemblée Nationale* archives. Second sitting of 18 October 1960.

MD 415	
Status	prototype
Span	53ft 10.5in (16.42m)
Length	41ft 0in (12.50m)
Gross wing area	387.1sq ft (36sq m)
Gross weight	13,007lb (5,900kg)
Powerplant	two Bastan 750hp (559kW)
Maximum speed/Height	?
Armament	two 30mm guns and six attachment points

sharply raked tailplane. The engines selected by Dassault for the prototype were Turbomeca Bastan turboprops driving Ratier-Figeac propellers 9ft 0.25in (2.75m) in diameter, and the planned weaponry comprised a ventral pack with two 30mm guns and wing attachment points for bombs, rockets and wire-guided SS11/SS12 missiles.

The first prototype flew on 10 May 1959 and demonstrated excellent flight characteristics. On 26 May, Dassault and Sud Aviation signed an agreement where, instead of working concurrently on two different proposals (the Voltigeur from Sud and Communauté/ Spirale (qv) from Dassault), the two manufacturers would unite their efforts. It was decided that whichever aircraft was selected then it would be developed and built jointly by the two partners. In the end, however the *Armée de l'Air* rejected them both. In 1961 the MD 415 was reworked as a business aircraft and civilian transport with an enlarged fuselage as the Communauté A1/A2. Sud Aviation would have carried out 80% of the work on it and Dassault 20% including the '*recette*' testing (the contractual time after the prototype is delivered to the customer who tests it to see if it meets all of the requirements], but unfortunately it did not attract any interest from civilian customers.

Dassault Super Communauté

This larger version of the MD 415 (enlarged by one third) was offered initially as a civilian airliner but could also have been developed into a military freighter capable of carrying a jeep in its 989cu ft (28cu m) cargo bay. It was also planned to fit remote-controlled turrets with 20mm guns to enable the aircraft to perform in the support role.

TOP **For the trainer/liaison/support programme of 1957 Dassault offered the MD 415 Communauté. Its very type number, 100 above the MD 315, showed that it was intended to supersede the Flamant.** *José Fernandez*

ABOVE **From the MD 415 evolved the MD 410 Spirale, optimised for ground attack and support.** *José Fernandez*

Dassault MD 410 Spirale (Spiral)

Yes, the MD 410 followed the MD 415! Basically this was a specialised version of the MD 415 that could be differentiated by its slimmer fuselage and canopies made from flat panels; nevertheless, it still shared a 90% commonality with the MD 415. The type first flew on 8 April 1960 and again

MD 410	
Status	prototype
Span	53ft 10in (16.40m)
Length	42ft 8in (13.00m)
Gross wing area	387.1sq ft (36sq m)
Gross weight	13,007lb (5,900kg)
Powerplant	two Bastan 750hp (559kW)
Maximum speed/Height	?
Armament	30mm guns and six attachment points

demonstrated excellent capabilities; for example it was appreciated that this was a very good firing platform. Although the MD 410 was designed especially for ground attack and support it could also be used in the logistic support role for the Mirage IIIV jet fighter. Yet, due to the rapidly changing military requirements, this was another type that in the end was not accepted.

Dassault MD 417

A turboprop version of the MD 430 below. Having started originally as the MD 430, the turboprop version was renamed MD 417 during 1958.

Dassault MD 430

Taking the wing and tail surfaces of the MD 415, the MD 430 had a revised fuselage that dispensed with the cabin completely and instead exhibited a bulged crew compartment in the extreme nose. The engines would have been Pratt & Whitney R1340s, the armament twin 30mm in side pods plus the usual six wing attachment points carried over from the earlier variants. The project was abandoned in 1958.

MD 430	
Status	project
Span	52ft 6in (16.00m)
Length	42ft 8in (13.00m)
Gross wing area	373.1sq ft (34.70sq m)
Gross weight	?
Powerplant	two R1340 600hp (447kW)
Maximum speed/Height	?
Armament	two 30mm guns and six attachment points

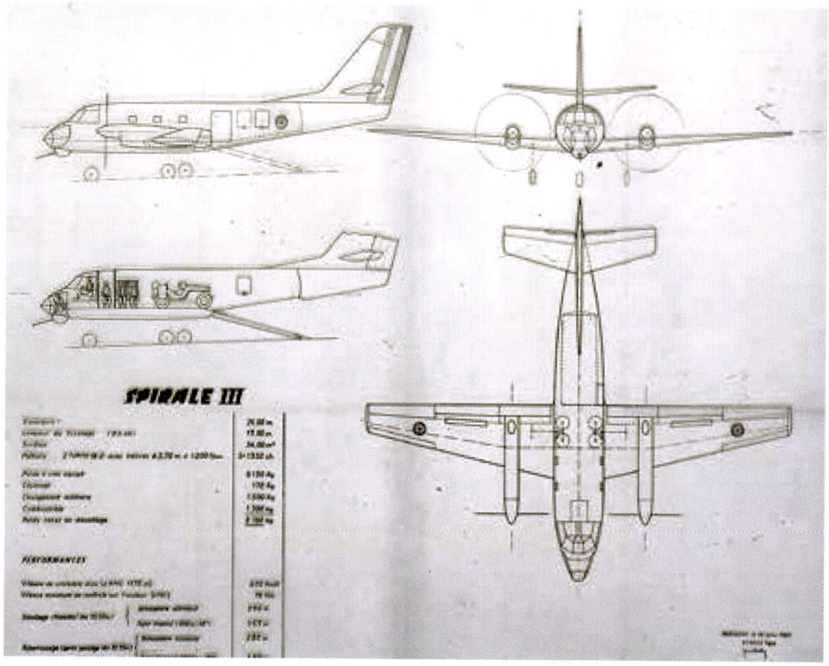

TOP The Spirale led to the Spirale III assault transport, shown in this drawing of 19 January 1961. This had the ability to disembark a jeep through a rear ramp while its nose turret could provide suppression fire. *Philippe Ricco*

ABOVE A nice display model of the Spirale III was produced by the manufacturer. *Dassault Aviation*

Dassault Spirale III

A variant of the MD 410 increased in size by 30% and powered by two Turbomeca Turmo III D turboprops, Dassault and Sud Aviation hoped to sell the Spirale III as a STOL freighter to both the *Armée de l'Air* and to local airlines (the fuselage had been designed so that it could be pressurised). In the military freighter role the aircraft featured a 1,236cu ft (35cu m) bay with a reinforced floor and a rear door doubling as a ramp for loading heavy items such as vehicles (two jeeps or even an Alouette II helicopter with its rotor disassembled could be taken on board). In addition, 20mm guns could be positioned at the port rear access door, which could be opened during flight for paradrops, while a large window to starboard was designed to be removed and serve as firing window for the support role. A third gun could fire from a position on the rear ramp, which again opened during firing and there was a gun turret under the nose. Dassault even thought of 'navalising' the Spirale III through the addition of an arrestor hook and folding wings. Noting that

ABOVE A full-size mock-up of the Spirale III fuselage was built and exhibited in various shows. It is seen here at the Paris Air Show of 1961. *José Fernandez*

the dimensions were similar to the Grumman Tracker, and taking the project beyond the replenishment mission, it was also proposed to fit the Spirale III with an early warning radar (clearly inspired by the Grumman design, one may wonder what kind of radar set was planned to go in this big radome). A mock-up was built to demonstrate the army freighter role but it is dubious that the naval version, and even more the AEW role, went beyond mere talks during Paris Salons. A contract for two prototypes was passed for the *Armée de l'Air* on 24 April 1962 with the production being turned over to Sud Aviation (because Dassault was too occupied with Mirage production). However, Dassault was not able to enjoy its victory over the rival Potez 840 and Hurel-Dubois HD 151 for very long as the contract was countermanded on 20 August of the same year.

Dassault Spirale IV

This was a variant of the MD 410 powered by four turboprops.

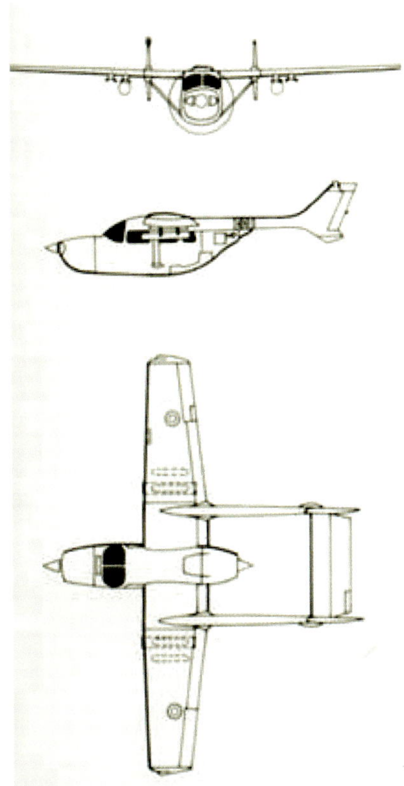

ABOVE In 1971 Reims Cessna produced a military variant of the Skymaster called the FTMA 337 Milirôle. *Author's collection/Reims Cessna*

Post-1970 Concepts

The very concept of the light army co-operation aircraft faded in France after the 1960s, possibly due to the fact that decolonisation was over, and the realisation that any combat

BELOW The prototype Reims Cessna Milirole. A production run of sixty aircraft followed. *José Fernandez*

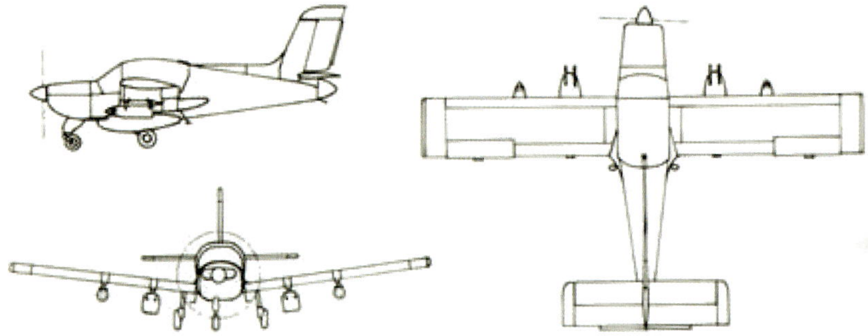

ABOVE SOCATA capitalised on the success of the MS 880 Rallye to offer a military version called the Guerrier. *Author's collection/SOCATA*

BELOW Not only was the Guerrier built but it achieved sales to various small air forces. *José Fernandez*

SOCATA 235 Guerrier

Status	production
Span	31ft 11.5in (9.74m)
Length	2ft3 10.5in (7.28m)
Gross wing area	137.3sq ft (12.77sq m)
Gross weight	?
Powerplant	one Lycoming O-540 230hp (172kW)
Maximum speed/Height	171mph (275km/h)
Armament	four attachment points for weapons

on the European battlefield would be an aircraft versus tank affair that would require reinforced armour and weapons. In addition, helicopters (see Chapter Nine) began to take over the role once devolved to the light COIN aircraft. However, during the 1970s a few attempts were made to develop a small COIN aeroplane.

First came Reims Aviation in 1971 with an adaptation of the Cessna Skymaster to the COIN role as the FTB337G Milirole (Reims Aviation was the Cessna agent in France and produced the Skymaster in France). Sixty-one of these machines were produced and one was evaluated by the *Armée de l'Air* in 1983.

In 1977 SOCATA (the heir to the Morane Saulnier tradition) produced a military version of its highly successful MS 880 Rallye. This was called the Guerrier (Warrior) and differed from the standard Rallye in that it had four attachment points for missiles, bombs and rocket clusters under the wings and a sight in the cockpit. The SOCATA 235 Guerrier did reach production and was sold to various small countries.

Chapter Eight
Low-Speed VTOL

The origins of VTOL aviation in France go back to before the First World War when Louis Blériot declared that the true flying machine will only come of age when it has dispensed with long take-off runs. Obviously a good response to this statement was the helicopter, and indeed Louis Breguet, Etienne Oehmichen and others pioneered helicopter development before the Second World War. By that time a few other engineers had also begun thinking about true VTOs. For example, in the late 1920s one M. de Chappedelaine proposed his Gyraptère, although it was more akin to a flying car. Yet Chappedelaine could be said to have planted the seeds that led to later concepts, something that appears to have been acknowledged by Michel Wibault who called his own design the *Gyroptère* (and that ultimately brought forth the Harrier)! A significant early design was the Guerre air-compressed flying machine, but it was only in the late 1950s that more serious studies looked into the subject, in particular the development of VTOL fighters and in parallel the necessary supporting logistics required to operate them.

Early 1950s Proposals

BTZ Coléoptères

The main idea suggested by Helmut von Zborowski of *Bureau Technique* Zborowski (BTZ) was to have the engine completely integrated within the airframe, the design's annular wing then doubling either as the shroud for a ducted fan or as the combustion chamber and nozzle for a ramjet (as seen in the most advanced of the SNECMA design studies). After the initial DERS design work (made before DERS became BTZ), SNECMA and BTZ then positioned themselves along two different lines of research or categories of aircraft: for SNECMA this arrangement could be used for armed aircraft, for BTZ on transport and co-operation machines. The SNECMA designs and their BTZ precursors are described in Volume

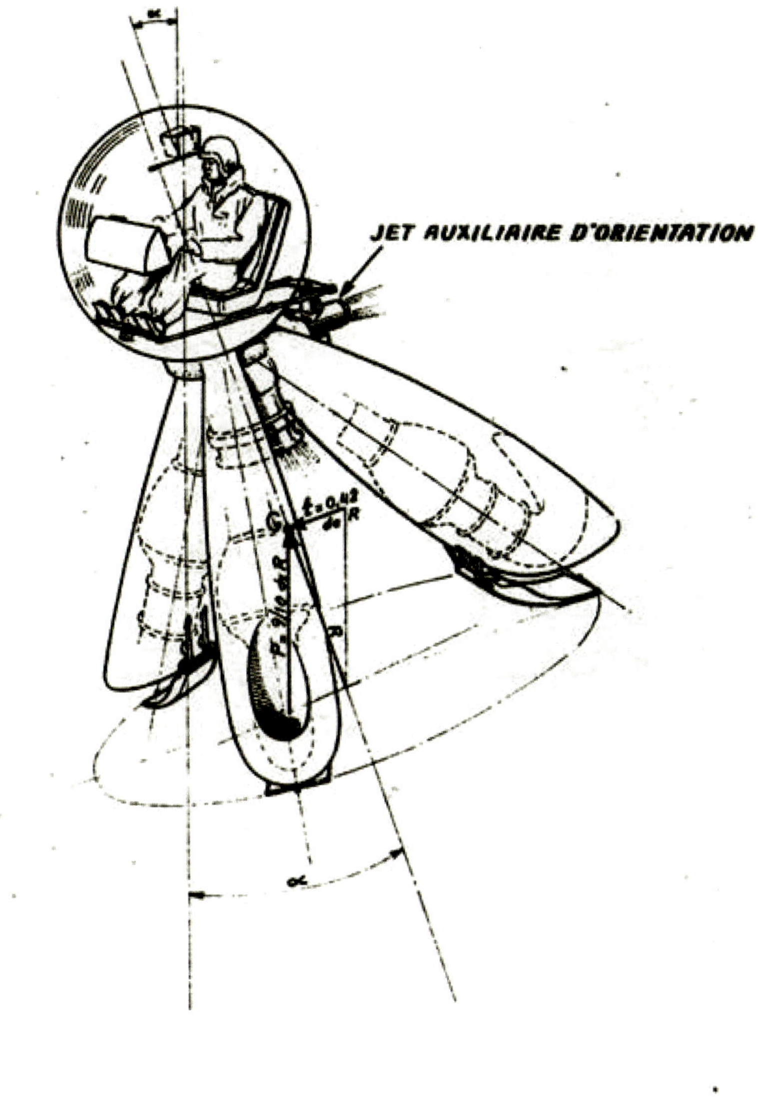

STATODYNE type E3 FIG. 3

ABOVE This perspective drawing depicts the Statodyne Type E3, certainly one of the more unconventional aircraft in this book. The turbojets may be Marborés but nothing else is known about the aircraft. *Morane-Saulnier*

I, so here we will focus mostly on the Hanneton and Polyvalent designs. BTZ was the commercial logo under which Zborowski and his team of designers operated, with the company incorporated as such only at the end of the 1950s (see Volume 1 for the interceptor designs based on the Coleoptère concept).

BTZ 324 Dragon

The 324 was a shrouded-propeller tethered radar platform, similar in concept to the Austro-Hungarian PKZ helicopter of First World War vintage. This project emerged in 1953 but went through considerable changes up until 1961. The similarity of the BTZ 324 to the Nord 501 (below) led Zborowski to want to take Nord to court, but this was not pursued.

BTZ 511 Hanneton (Cockchafer)

This designation covered a range of business aircraft, with three to six seats and various turbopropeller arrangements, and was the epitome of von Zborowski's dream of a Volkswagen Beetle-style of aircraft for wealthy families or businessmen. It was therefore one of the most detailed designs to emerge from BTZ, with a lot of work being put in to the aircraft's ergonomics (notably with integrated access stairs) and security (with the cockpit being designed as an escape capsule [and fitted with landing gear!] in case of engine failure). Strangely, it does not seem that the Cockchafer's

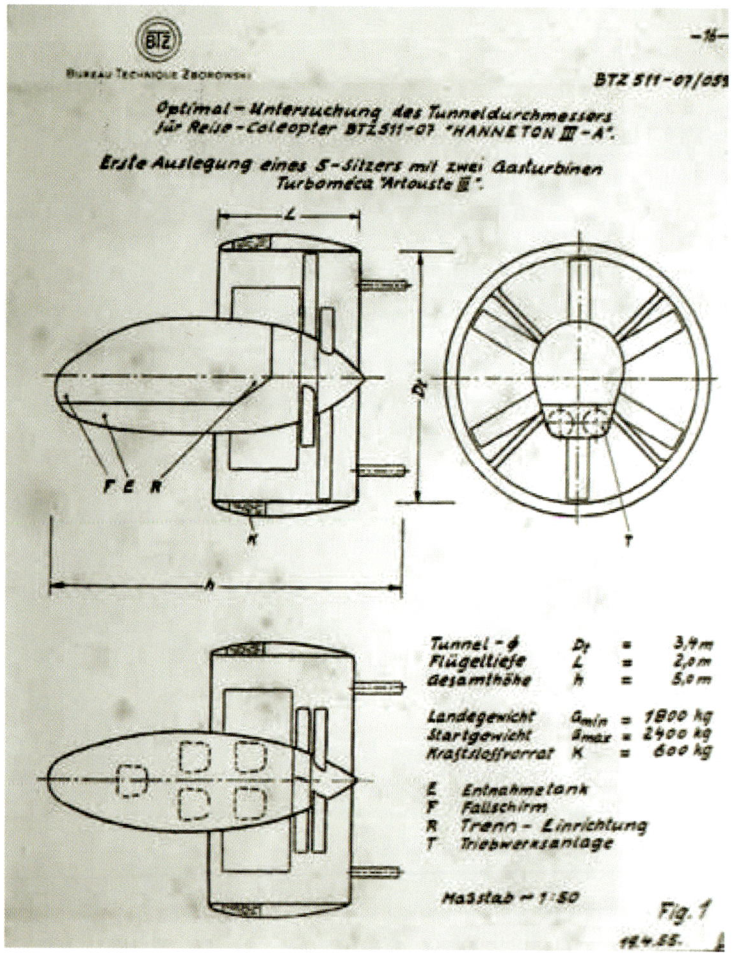

ABOVE RIGHT **A concept dear to Zborowski's heart was the Hanneton (cockshafer), a simple and cheap business aircraft able to carry you 'from your home to your factory'. The *Hanneton* concept was developed into various variants that differed in their numbers of passengers carried and their powerplants. This drawing depicts the IIIA.** *Famille Zborowski*

RIGHT **The *Hanneton* IV model was photographed by the author at the *Hubschraubermuseum* Bückeburg (Bückeburg Helicopter Museum) in Germany.** *J.C. Carbonel*

BTZ 511-07 Hanneton III A-1

Status	aircraft project
Span	13ft 5.5in (4.10m)
Length	16ft 5in (5.00m)
Gross wing area	?
Gross weight	6,173lb (2,800kg)
Powerplant	two Marcadau III
Maximum speed/Height	373mph (600km/h) at 16,405ft (5,000m)

BTZ 511-09 Hanneton 1S

Status	project
Span	9ft 10in (3.00m)
Length	19ft 8in (6.00m)
Gross wing area	?
Gross weight	4,409lb (2,000kg)
Powerplant	two Blackburn 600 (licence built by Turbomeca)
Maximum speed/Height	404mph (650km/h)

BTZ 511-13/1 Hanneton 20C

Status	project
Span	34ft 5.5in (10.50m)
Length	29ft 6.5in (9.00m)
Gross wing area	?
Gross weight	16,975lb (7,700kg)
Powerplant	four Gazelle or four GE T-58
Maximum speed/Height	342mph (550km/h) at 13,125ft (4,000m)

BTZ 511-17 Lucane

Status	project
Span	21ft 0in (6.40m) = outer diameter of annular wing
Length	26ft 3in (8.00m)
Gross wing area	?
Gross weight	16,093lb (7,300kg)
Powerplant	four Turmo III (1,000hp)
Maximum speed/Height	286mph (460km/h) at 13,125ft (4,000m)

rotating seats were subjected to any specific study. The question of pilot assistance for take-off and landing was rather overlooked, the general feeling throughout the Coléoptère programme being that a conventional autopilot was enough (but testing of the C.450 Coléoptère prototype would

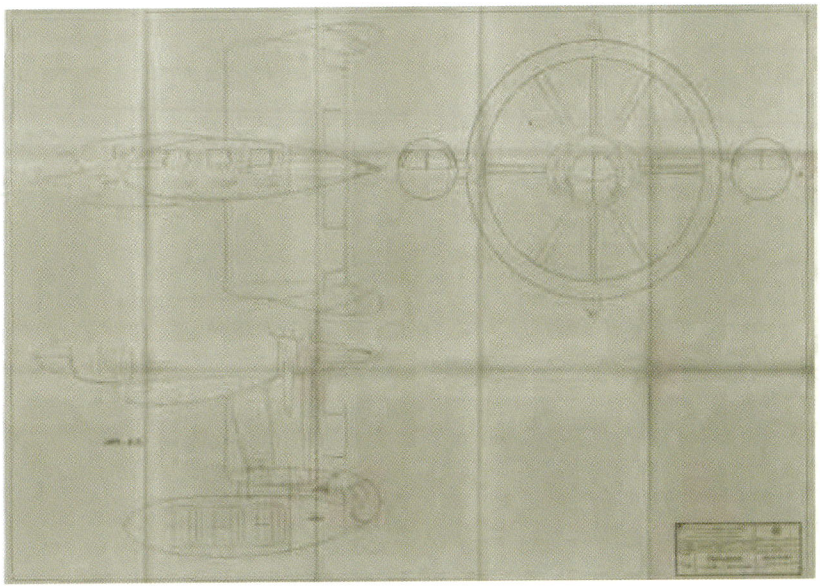

ABOVE **A drawing from 26 May 1957 showing a slightly different version, the BTZ 511-17. These larger types were promoted as commando-carrying aircraft for policing operations in Algeria.** *Archives Zborowski*

strongly disproved this). However, for the BTZ 511 the question should have been studied in depth because this would be crucial for an aircraft to be flown by non-professional pilots. However, completely automated aircraft such as the *Charançon* drone were also considered at the same time.

The 511 series also included a -1S single-seat sports aircraft and larger machines, including the -17. The 511-16 was named *Polyvälent* (a German name!) because it could be used as either a civilian feeder liner or in a military support role. This was a complex aircraft with the twin

BELOW **Ivan Labat was not only a designer, he was also a gifted artist and was able to draw his vision of the future Aéroblic in action. Here an Evasan (medical evacuation) is made in the jungle, shades of the then recently ended Indochina war.** *Famille Labat*

fuselages for passengers being rotated outside the ring wing during take-off and landing. The 511-17 Lucane (stag beetle) was a variant of the 511-16, and BTZ did a lot of lobbying towards French Ministries to get the 511-16 into production, pointing to its potential use in Algeria where helicopters were at that time pioneering air assault and air support duties.

ABOVE Possibly inspired by the explorer Paul-Emile Victor's voyage in Antarctica, Ivan Labat also draw the Aeroblic performing a polar supply mission. *Famille Labat*

Labat

Parisian engineer Ivan Labat worked at SNECMA and in 1956 he proposed and patented the Aéroblic. Labat's designs were quite similar to the BTZ studies but they placed the propeller inside the duct so that it benefited from the effects of a ducted fan, although this also added a complex system of flaps along the trailing edge of the duct. The Aéroblic name may have come from the view that the take-off and landing of this machine was not vertical but was angled (or oblique). In fact, Labat imagined that the Aéroblic would be able to hover, or more exactly '*to stay in the air with a nil translation speed*' as he phrased it. Various types of Aeroblics were proposed, including a small version for two crew members that could be used for '*colonial policing*', a small ground attack fighter (which reached the status of a presentation model being made), a light transport for rescue or polar missions, and an airliner. Ivan Labat was also a gifted artist and he drew several sketches showing his Aéroblic in operation, but no metal was ever cut on these intriguing designs.

Morane Statodyne Concepts

The statodyne (stato = static + dyne = mobile) concept was the brainchild of George Caillette, who was seemingly in charge of an 'advanced project group' that was independent from the *bureau d'études* proper (which at the time was headed by M. Le Guelinel). Caillette's idea was to have the thrust point above the centre of gravity of the aircraft, which would then help the control of the VTOL at low speeds or during the hover. To achieve this he proposed a number of solutions, most of them encompassing the use of multiple engines. Most of his designs came within a line of tail-sitter fighters and are, therefore, described in the first volume. However, among the various statodynes were a few in the E-series that were definitely intended for low-speed operations (although still jet-propelled).

Statodyne Type E1

This was a small, manned test bed ('E' possibly for experimental) in which the pilot sat in the front above a wheeled landing gear, the jet engine was at the rear but the exhaust nozzle was arranged just in the middle of

BELOW A curious design that may have been either a demonstrator or a test bed for a 'flying jeep'. It is identified as the Statodyne Type E1. *Morane-Saulnier*

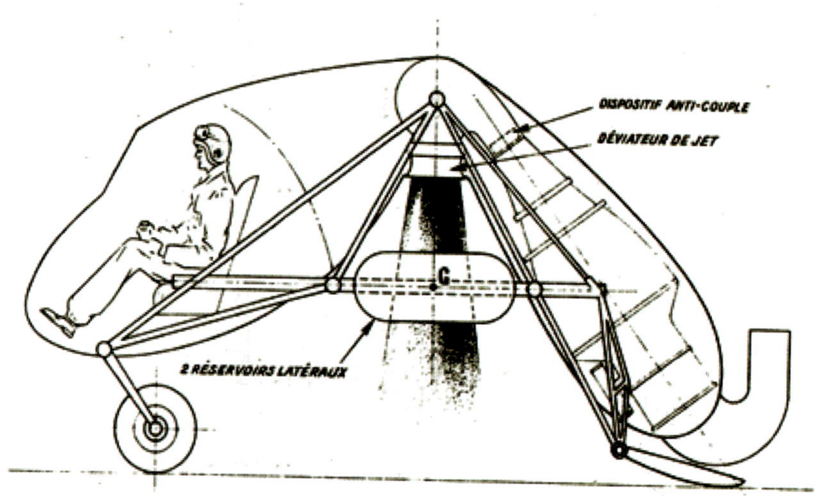

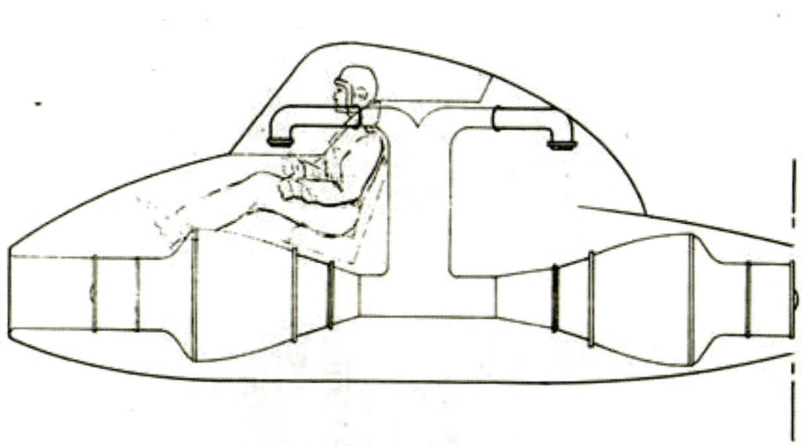

ABOVE The Statodyne Type E2 still appears to be a proof-of-concept machine along the lines of the E1. Unfortunately not much archive material survives to provide details for these designs. *Morane-Saulnier*

the machine with the jet going right through the aircraft's centre of gravity. No control thruster is shown on the drawing but they would certainly have been very necessary if someone had hoped to pilot this machine!

Statodyne Type E2

The E2 was a refinement of the previous design, with two engines installed back to back and exhausting through what seems to be (on the surviving drawing) four nozzles in an X arrangement. Again, this was a small machine probably only intended as a technology demonstrator, but it appears to be more 'flyable' than the E1. It was quite possibly linked to a still unknown MS 850 project.

Statodyne Type E3

Possibly one of the strangest flying machines ever designed, the E3 had a clear sphere housing a single pilot atop three fat legs, each of which housed a single jet engine, all three engines exhausting through a single nozzle just underneath the pilot and right above the aircraft's CofG. For orientation control a small gimballed nozzle, probably fed from the main nozzle, was operated through pedals, and shock-absorbing feet were provided underneath each leg. The intended use of this machine is unclear: for example why would three jet units would be necessary to lift just a single pilot in a design that was obviously not expected to reach high speeds? It has been suggested there was some connection with the Ludion, on which Caillette worked a few years later (see Chapter Fourteen).

Statodyne Type E4

The E4 was a small aircraft, actually more of the 'flying infantry' type vehicle that was realised in the USA during the 1970s with the 'Jet belt' or the 'STAMP'. Nothing more is known about it, not even which engines were to be used. Note however, that the same general arrangement would be

BELOW The Statodyne Type E4 was similar in appearance to later 'flying infantry' devices built in the USA during the 1960s. *Morane-Saulnier*

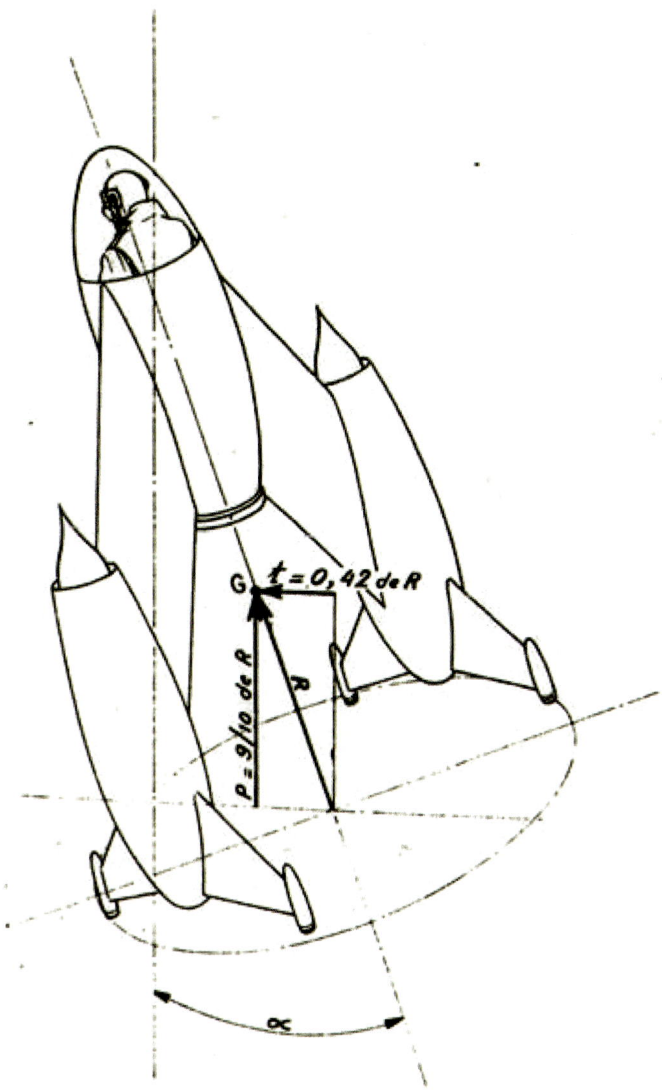

reused on the Statodyne Type F in Volume I.

Ducted Fans, Tilt-Rotors and Others

During the 1960s VTOL performance appeared to be just around the corner with the result that many people in the aeronautical field considered the design of VTOL transports. Such aircraft offered great commercial advantages in that, with minimum adaptation, they could be sold to both the services and to civilian customers. What would have been small or large assault transports to the military would have been business aircraft or feeder liners to the civil market.

Bertin HB 11

Before developing his '*trompes*' concept, Bertin had worked with Maurice-Louis Hurel and Breguet on the design of fan-in-wings aircraft. In 1956-60 the HB 11 design was considered by Bertin, working with both Louis Hurel and Marcel-Pierre Le Nabour. The project was based on the use of lift fans integrated inside the wing, and these fans were to be driven through the exhaust of a turbojet located in the nose of the aircraft. The gas expelled by the turbojet acted on an outer ring of blades, which put the fan into motion. Larger blades would act on the surrounding air to generate a downward thrust, thus providing lift to the aircraft in the 'hover' mode. In cruise mode Venetian blind-type flaps would close the duct into which rotated the fan, thereby restoring the continuity of the wing. In this

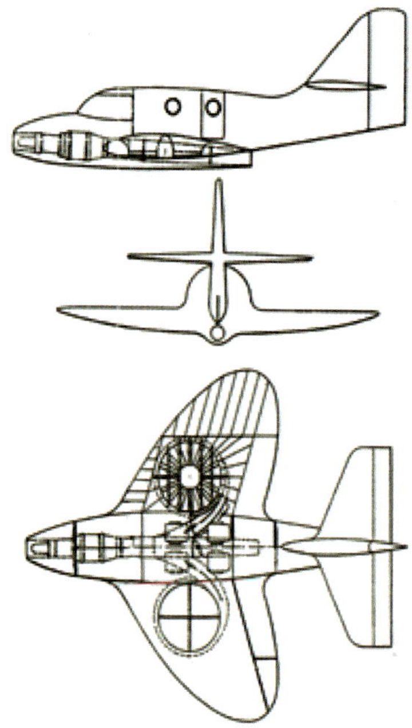

ABOVE **A three-view drawing of the HB 11 fan-in-wing aircraft designed by Jean Bertin and Maurice Hurel, with Breguet support.** *Author's collection*

condition the jet exhaust was also redirected away, through vanes, from the fans to a conventional nozzle to propel the aircraft.

The operation of the HB 11 was described as follows: '*For taking off, all the power (thrust) of the turbojet is directed to the lift fans and the aircraft begins to lift vertically. To put the aircraft in horizontal movement, the pilot turns the flap to maximum deflection, puts the nose down at 25°, then progressively deflects the upper flaps [of the fans] to the rear; the horizontal components of the lift thrust thus deflected by the lower flaps generates an acceleration sufficient for the aircraft to quickly acquire a forward movement. Then the pilot can pitch the fuselage upward, close the lift flaps, redirect all the thrust towards the propulsion nozzle and retract the flaps. For landing, the aircraft being in horizontal flight at high speed, the pilot cuts the thrust from the propulsion nozzle, progressively pitches up the nose of the machine, and then lowers the flaps until the horizontal speed is sufficiently reduced, he then redirects the turbojet thrust toward the fans, opens up the lift fans cover flaps, reduces the lift thrust once the horizontal speed is nullified, and reboosts the power of the lift fan when nearing the ground, so as to land with the minimal [vertical] speed.*'

As one can see from this description, piloting a VTOL aircraft as envisioned by Bertin would have been quite a job and would probably have required more than two hands! Wind tunnel tests proved the feasibility of the HB 11 design and in particular showed that it was extremely stable during all phases

HB 11	
Status	project
Span	28ft 10.5in (8.80m)
Length	34ft 5.5in (10.50m)
Gross wing area	-
Gross weight	8,157lb (3,700kg)
Powerplant	unspecified 2,925lb (13kN)
Maximum speed/Height	435mph (700km/h) at 29,530ft (9,000m)

BELOW **The HB 12 was an evolution of the HB 11 and was intended to be a light transport or liaison aircraft. The drawing is dated 17 July 1962.** *Philippe Ricco*

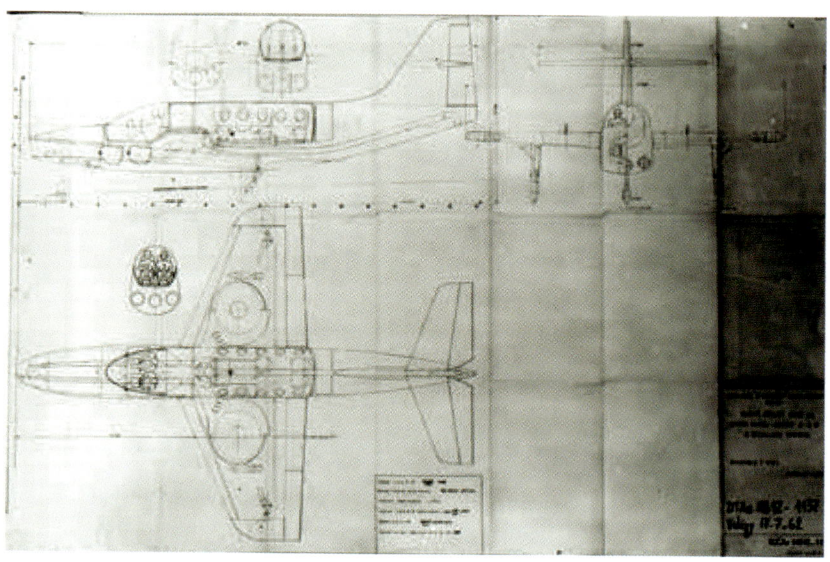

of the flight, including the transition from vertical to horizontal flight and back.

Bertin HB 12

The HB 12 was a variant of the same concept worked out with Breguet and was intended to be a small liaison/transport aircraft. It would have been built by Breguet if the decision had been made to take the prototype route. Three small (unspecified) turbojets were to be grouped in the front fuselage, either driving the two buried lift fans or supplying direct propulsion through nozzles exhausting under the mid fuselage. However, Bertin did not progress this design forward since he expected difficulties with the engineering: *'After a certain time, we did not push this solution strongly because of the rather difficult technological problem represented by the lift fans driven by a peripheral turbine.'*[1] Following this work Bertin moved on into ducted propellers/fans in association with M. Soulez-Larivière. The final outcome of this line of development was the Nord 500 and its associated projects (below).

HB 12	
Status	project
Span	38ft 11in (1.60m)
Length	54ft 8in (16.66m)
Gross wing area	-
Gross weight	?
Powerplant	-
Maximum speed/Height	-

Breguet Br 1030

This mid-1950s project used the lift-in-wing concept that appears to have been favoured by Louis Breguet. Unfortunately this design is only known through a conceptual layout used in a patent and no original blueprint of the aircraft itself is known to the author. With the death of Louis Breguet on 4 May 1955 this line of research and development was quickly abandoned.

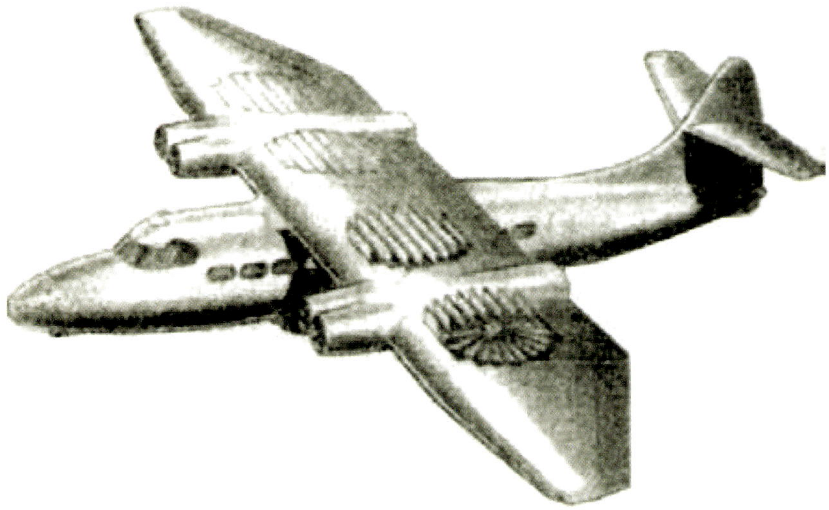

TOP **Poor quality drawing that is supposed to illustrate the final Breguet Br 1030 design.** *Author's collection*

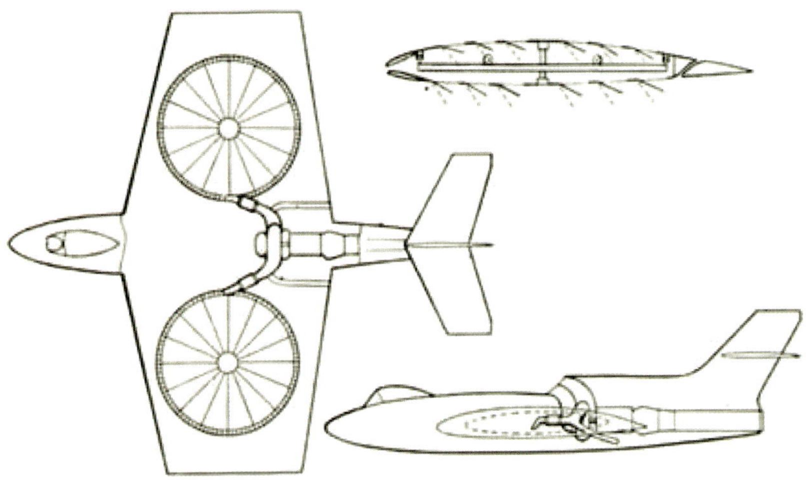

ABOVE **Two views of a more conceptual design investigated by Breguet during the work on the Br 1030.** *Author's collection/Breguet document*

Br 1030	
Status	project
Span	10ft 6in (3.20m) rotor diameter
Length	?
Gross wing area	-
Gross weight	13,228lb (6,000kg)
Powerplant	one TB 1000A 3,860hp (2,880kW)
Maximum speed/Height	497mph (800km/h) at 16,405ft (5,000m)

Nord Ducted Fan Projects

From 1958 onwards Nord Aviation developed a new line of research using ducted fans. To begin with the design team reviewed the worldwide 'state of the art' for this concept and came to the conclusion that it was not very advanced at all. Nord became wholeheartedly engaged in this work and, according to later Nord publications, the origin of this vein of study was the idea initiated by STAé of flying platforms and flying jeeps (see Chapter Fourteen). It is possible that Nord, having built the SNECMA

1 Recherches et développement sur le décollage court ou vertical. Le programme Aladin 2. Excerpt from *Aéronautique et Astronautique* N° 26.

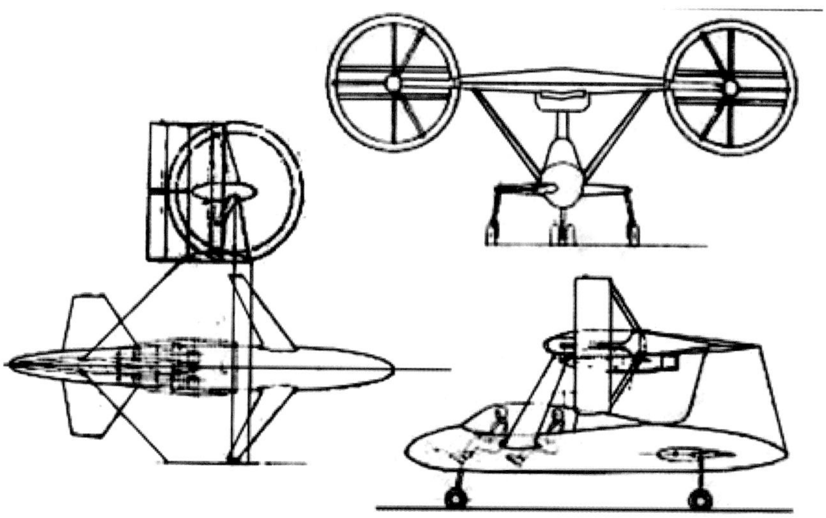

ABOVE A very early impression of the Nord 500. This arrangement with the ducted fans linked through a wing on stilt would later reappear on the Helcade and Rocade proposals. *Author's collection/Nord Aviation*

Coléoptère (Volume 1), favoured this orientation because ducted fans had previously been researched by SNECMA as part of the Coléoptère programme. Although SNECMA had originally been pushing the high-speed ramjet-powered interceptor, a new line of study, the Héli-Coléoptères or propeller-driven Coléoptères, had been started in the latter years before the final cancellation of the programme. It was this research that led to the consideration of ducted fans, and which in the end saw SNECMA working on flying saucers (see Chapter Thirteen).

From 1958 to 1962, and at the instigation of STAé, theoretical research was carried out that included a collaboration between Nord and Bertin; indeed from 1962 a *'likeable collaboration'* (as defined by Jean Soulez-Larivière in a paper written in 1966 and which summarised Nord's work on ducted fans) was set up between the two companies with the unwritten agreement that Bertin would do the advanced research work while Nord would turn this work into real aircraft. The Bertin influence is obvious in that some of the designs include complex duct intakes that could be compared to Bertin's early work on *'trompes'* (discussed in Volume I). The research moved on to comparing the advantages and disadvantages of tilt fans versus fans-in-the-wing, but no designs for the later configuration have surfaced. In 1965 this effort was brought together by the creation of a 'ducted fan vehicles' department at Nord led by Jean Soulez-Larivière. First revealed publicly in 1965 with the Nord 500 Cadet, the work also encompassed the Nord 510 tethered platforms, Helcade and Rocade medium-size transports, and the small Estocade attack aircraft. It is thought that in 1966 Nord received some co-operation on ducted fan projects from an (unnamed) British company. Unfortunately, the Nord 500 demonstrator never flew properly, and the whole research programme appears to have been terminated with the merger between Nord and Sud into SNIAS Aerospatiale.

BELOW A view of the first prototype Nord 500 being built in the Châtillon factory. *Author's collection/Nord Aviation*

Nord 500 Démonstrateur

Clearly meant to be a proof of concept machine leading to the Cadet, and actually presented as such as a full-size mock-up at the 1965 Paris Air Show, the Nord 500 *Démonstrateur* was quite a small craft with room for just a pilot, though it would grow in size slightly with its span increased from 18.7ft to 20.0ft (5.70m to 6.10m) but with the rotors reduced in diameter from 5.25ft to 5.17ft (1.60m to 1.575m).

It was described by Jean Soulez Larivière as *'more than a real aircraft, it is actually two ducted fans to which have been grafted the equipment required for flying – engines and drives, pilot and controls. This is a purely experimental programme which is guided by the wish to maintain it*

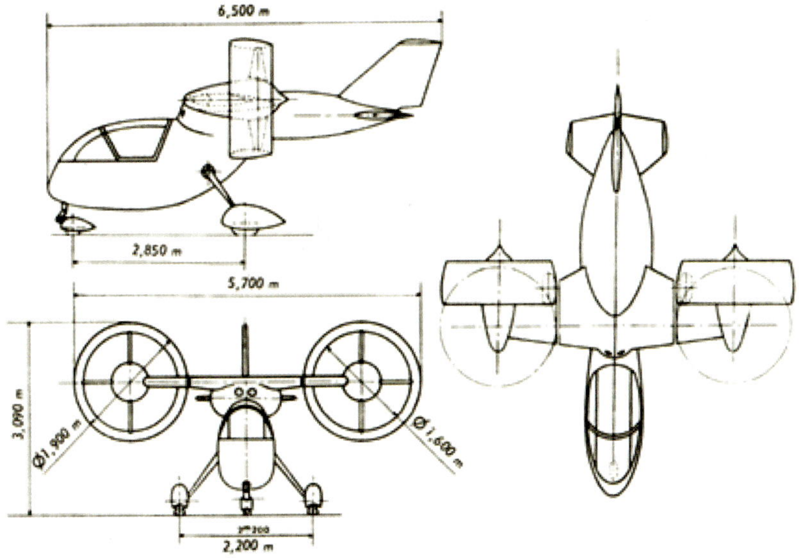

ABOVE **This later drawing illustrates the early appearance of the Nord 500, as displayed in mock-up form at the 1965 Paris Air Show.** *Author's collection/Nord Aviation*

Nord 500 (1965)	
Status	project
Span	18ft 8.5in (5.70m) over rotors
Length	21ft 4in (6.50m)
Gross wing area	-
Gross weight	2,315lb (1,050kg)
Powerplant	two Allison T63 250hp (186kW)
Maximum speed/Height	249mph (400km/h)
Remarks	one pilot

Nord 500 démonstratéur	
Status	prototype
Span	20ft 0in (6.10m) over rotors
Length	21ft 8in (6.60m)
Gross wing area	-
Gross weight	2,866lb (1,300kg)
Powerplant	two Allison 250-C18 315hp (236kW)
Maximum speed/Height	-
Remarks	1 pilot

within budgetary constraints. The result is a machine with a low engine output, and it is even less compact than the operational variants will be. Two main features of this design should be pointed out:

- *The ducted fans are doing all the work in all phases of the flight: lift at take-off, part of the lift and forward propulsion during cruise flight, and manoeuvring control in the three-axes during the whole flight.*
- *The second feature is the relative simplicity of the design compared to similar foreign designs which require four to five rotors.'*

At the 1967 Paris Show the real *Démonstrateur* was exhibited with a short tail but this was soon removed when it entered flight testing. In 1968 Jean Soulez Larivière could claim: '*In comparison with helicopters, one can keep the same engine output, the same lift/hover performance and nearly double the forward speed.* [...] *Other advantages that must be pointed out* [are] *the protection of ground personnel, the ability to fly in cluttered areas, the remarkable lack of noise, the minimal ground erosion and the low level of vibrations.*' The second prototype was shown in 1969 and had acquired a nose radome (but no radar). This machine reached the stage of tethered tests where it was piloted by Armand Jacquet but, while these were invariably described as '*successful*', in truth the aircraft proved very unstable and (reputedly) only its short tether prevented it from turning over on to its back! In those pre-computer days achieving stability for the aircraft just by manual control was impossible and the Nord 500 was abandoned.

Nord 500 Cadet

The Cadet was proposed in 1965 as a four-seat liaison aircraft with two swivelling ducted fans. By 1967 the name Cadet has been dropped ... but more realistically it was the whole project that had been abandoned, with the emphasis having moved on to the similar-size, similar-engined but single-seat demonstrator above.

Nord 500 Cadet	
Status	project
Span	18ft 8.5in (5.70m) over rotors
Length	23ft 3.5in (7.10m)
Gross wing area	-
Gross weight	4,078lb (1,850kg)
Powerplant	two Oredon 111 350hp (260kW)
Maximum speed/Height	218mph (350km/h)
Remarks	four people

Nord 500 Militaire

BELOW **A model of the Nord 500 Militaire seen in a Nord advertising film.** *AIRITAGE*

ABOVE A large wind tunnel model of the Nord 500. *J.C. Carbonel*

ABOVE RIGHT The second prototype Nord 500 during tethered tests. *Author's collection/Nord Aviation*

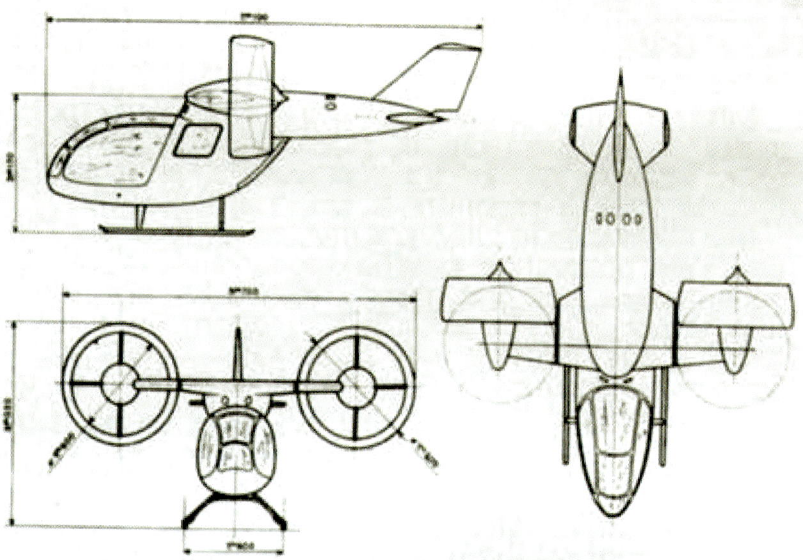

RIGHT An impression of the Nord 500 Cadet with a front fuselage that appears inspired by the cockpit of the Alouette helicopters. *Author's collection/Nord Aviation*

BELOW Two pictures taken from a Nord Aviation demonstration film showing a Nord 500 model and how control would be obtained along the longitudinal and side axes. *AIRITAGE*

Like the other military design from this series, the Estocade, the Nord 500 Militaire is still a quite mysterious machine about which only visual documents survive, including a short colour film depicting the model, painted blue and sporting the anchor emblem on its cockades (thus pointing to the Marine Nationale" as the intended customer).

Nord 501

The Nord 501 was a larger aircraft than the 500 and was intended to be a utility machine for several passengers. It was proposed in 1967, but what appears like an earlier version of this design fitted with short vestigial wings and normal tail surfaces was in fact shown in a 1964 patent. Designated Nord 501, a beautiful 1/20th scale model of this machine survives and is currently exhibited at the *Musée de l'Air et de l'Espace*. Using the same logic, the demonstrator Nord 500 was called Helcade B.

Nord 510

The 510 was a tethered platform for use in battlefield observation with radar or cameras. This project proved to be the source of conflict between von Zborowski and Nord Aviation. Zborowski had during the 1950s proposed and patented a similar machine under the name Dragon (above), and on seeing this Nord

TOP **A 1968 illustration showing the Nord 500 Militaire in action.** *Nord Aviation*

ABOVE **A perspective illustration of the Nord 500 Militaire by Paul Lengellé for the 1967 book Industries *Aéronautiques et Spatiales Françaises.*** *GIFAS*

BELOW **A simple line drawing illustrating the Nord 501 utility and liaison aircraft.** *Author's collection/Lazareff patent*

BELOW LEFT **The Nord 501 '8 Passengers Aircraft' painted by Paul Lengellé in 1967.** *GIFAS*

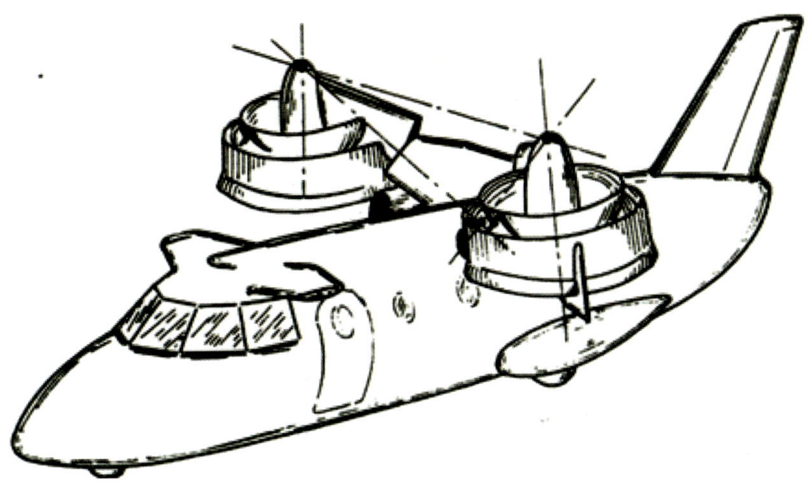

ABOVE **A beautiful large display model of the Nord 501 is on view at the *Musée de l'Air et de l'Espace*.** *J.C. Carbonel*

project at the 1963 Paris Air Show Zborowski claimed: '*They* [Nord] *have stolen my baby!*' However, Zborowski's premature death in 1964 prevented him from taking to trial what he saw as an infringement on industrial property.

Ingénieur Soulez-Larivière described the concept in 1966, saying: '*It is an uninhabited vehicle, which components can be arranged at will. It can be said that the fuselage holding equipment bays and fuel tanks have been wrapped around the propeller, giving for free the advantages of a ducted fan. The whole architecture of the aircraft is therefore kept extremely simple.*' A flying model was tested from 1964 and the full-size Nord 510 began flying in April 1966 after being exhibited statically at the 1965 Paris Air Show. Nord claimed that three prototypes were built, but by 1968 the limitations of the concept when carrying the Orphée (Orpheus) battlefield surveillance radar caused it to be cancelled, although a free-flying wire controlled version was

BELOW **The Nord 510 on its trailer.** *Author's collection/Nord Aviation*

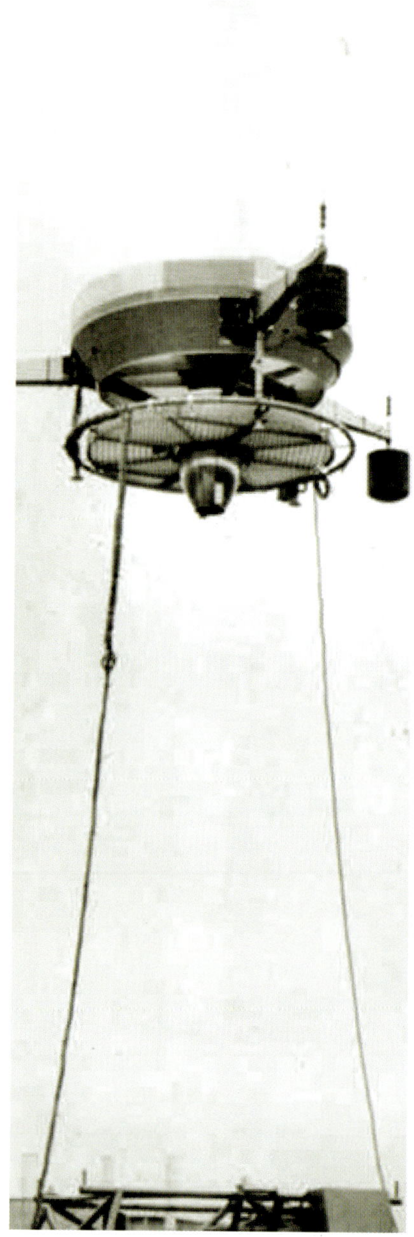

ABOVE **The Nord 510 prototype flew in 1966.** *Author's collection/Nord Aviation*

Nord 510

Status	prototype
Span	5ft 11in (1.80m) rotor diameter
Length	-
Gross wing area	-
Gross weight	-
Powerplant	-
Maximum speed/Height	0 at 985ft (300m) - aircraft is tethered so horizontal speed is nil

Nord 511

Status	project
Span	5ft 11in (1.80m) rotor diameter
Length	-
Gross wing area	-
Gross weight	1,874lb (850kg)
Powerplant	United Aircraft of Canada PT6 B16 615hp (460kW)
Maximum speed/Height	-

toyed with briefly as the Nord 511 (it is understood that the name Orphée was given to both the radar hardware *and* the airborne radar programme or idea).

This design was self-contained and, like most modern drones, was carried aboard and deployed from a specially equipped truck (a Berliet GBC 8KT). The Orphée was to have been superseded by a helicopter-borne radar, but it was to be twenty years before the SA 330 B Orchidée (Orchid) flew … and that remained a prototype!

Nord Helcade

A mid-size sixteen-passenger four-engine transport, the Helcade remained on the drawing board and the name itself was never completely explained, but it was possibly linked to *HELice CArénée Development* (Development of a Ducted Propeller aircraft). Based on the experience of the Nord 500, the Helcade had a very high position wing supporting two swivelling ducted rotors. These were placed high to limit ground effect since it had been guessed that this phenomenon had been a major source of instability in the Nord 500. The design was rather well detailed, including the interior arrangement, although the brochure itself concentrated mostly on the theoretical aspects of the flight.

A smaller five-passenger Helcade was also designed using two shoulder-mounted tilting fans with a complex arrangement of curved ducts inside the mouth of the main fairing. These

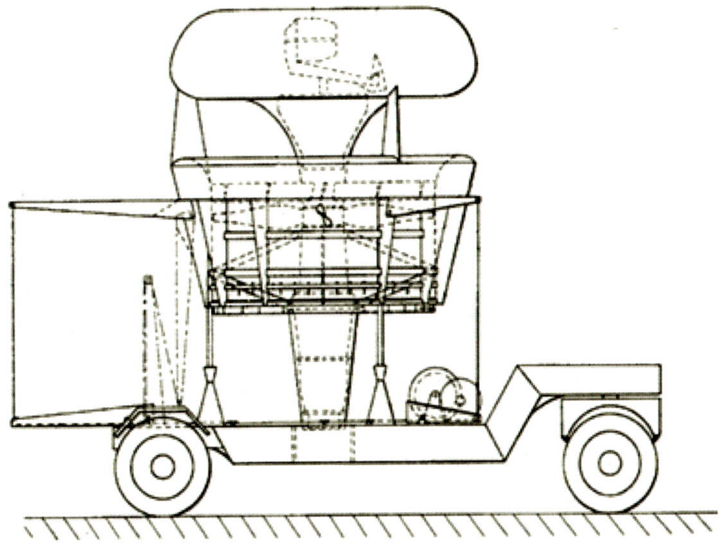

ABOVE A side view of the Nord 510 platform on its transport trailer. *Author's collection/Nord Aviation*

BELOW An improved 'free flying' version would have been called the Nord 511. *Author's collection/Nord Aviation*

BOTTOM The Nord 511 mounted on the platform of a Berliet truck. *Author's collection/Nord Aviation*

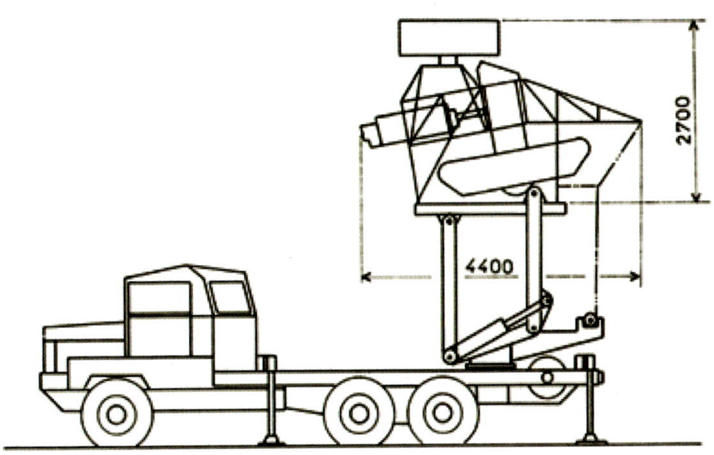

are oddly reminiscent to some earlier Bertin patents, which suggest an influence here.

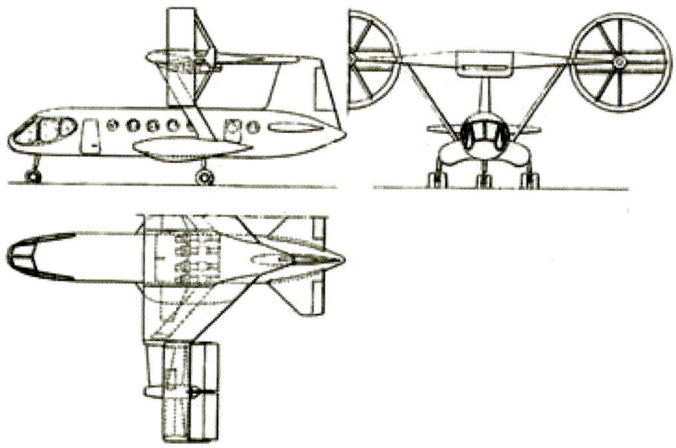

ABOVE **Three-view drawing of the Helcade transport.** *Author's collection/Nord Aviation*

BELOW **The Rocade transport project was a variation of the Helcade design.** *Author's collection/Nord Aviation*

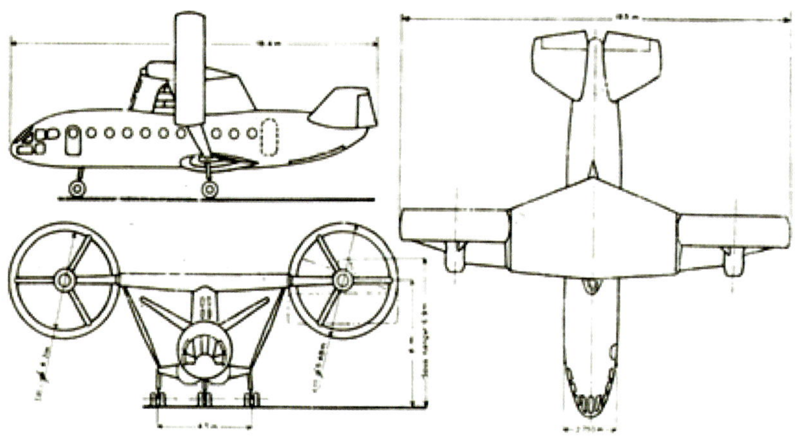

Nord Rocade

The Rocade was a larger variant of the Helcade, similar in architecture but with a much reduced wing and a somewhat simplified rotor-carrying frame. It was intended to carry forty passengers and Soulez-Larivière wrote: '*Within 10 years this kind of aircraft will solve the problem of aeromobility for the Army, which are consequences of the availability of tactical nuclear weapons, and those of short-range civilian transports with door-to-door speeds unreachable with current means of transportation.*' The name Rocade was never explained.

Nord Rocade	
Status	project
Span	63ft 11.5in (19.50m) over rotors
Length	60ft 4.5in (18.40m)
Gross wing area	-
Gross weight	34,612lb (15,700kg)
Powerplant	four Turmo III C3 1,475hp (1,100kW)
Maximum speed/Height	336mph (540km/h)
Remarks	forty passengers

Nord Estocade

This is another military project of which very little is known apart from a series of photos of a model. In recent years a three-view drawing has been circulated on the web, but as yet no original document (drawing or brochure) has surfaced. This design would have been armed with air-to-ground missiles. The name Estocade refers to a technique in sword fighting where a single point blow is used to kill an opponent.

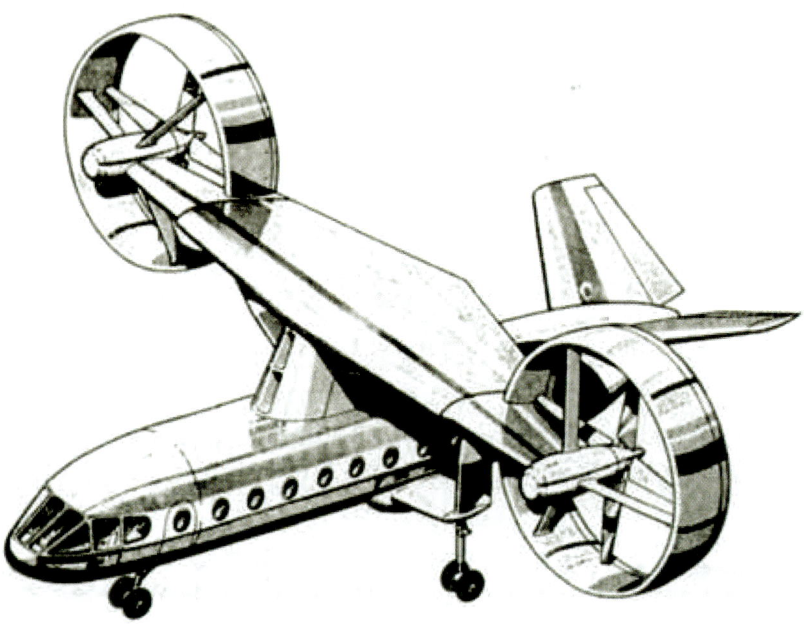

LEFT **Perspective illustration of the Nord Rocade.** *Author's collection/Nord Aviation*

ABOVE Three views of a display model of the Nord Estocade. *Author's collection/ Nord Aviation*

Richard Hélicoplane

In the mid-1930s Gilbert Camille Richard, an engineer with the *Société Nationale de Constructions Aéronautiques du Centre* (SNCAC), began designing VTOL rotary wing aircraft. In 1944 he patented the basis for his Hélicoplane, which he then developed after the war. A complete rotor pod was tested successfully in the Chalais-Meudon wind tunnel in about 1951, and by 1954 Richard could propose various types of

Richard Hélicoplane (base design)	
Status	project
Span	29ft 6.5in (9.00m) over rotors
Length	21ft 4in (6.50m)
Gross wing area	-
Gross weight	1,157lb (525kg)
Powerplant	one Continental C90 83hp (62kW)
Maximum speed/Height	112mph (180km/h)
Remarks	no armament

Richard Hélicoplane (pancake design)	
Status	project
Span	19ft 8in (6.00m) not including rotors
Length	15ft 5in (4.70m)
Gross wing area	-
Gross weight	258.1lb (24kg)
Powerplant	one 434hp (324kW) engine
Maximum speed/Height	-
Remarks	no armament

Richard Hélicoplane (twin-fuselage design)	
Status	project
Span	not specified; 13ft 1.5in (4.0m) diameter rotors
Length	-
Gross wing area	-
Gross weight	1,157lb (525kg)
Powerplant	one Continental C90 83hp (62kW)
Maximum speed/Height	-
Remarks	no armament

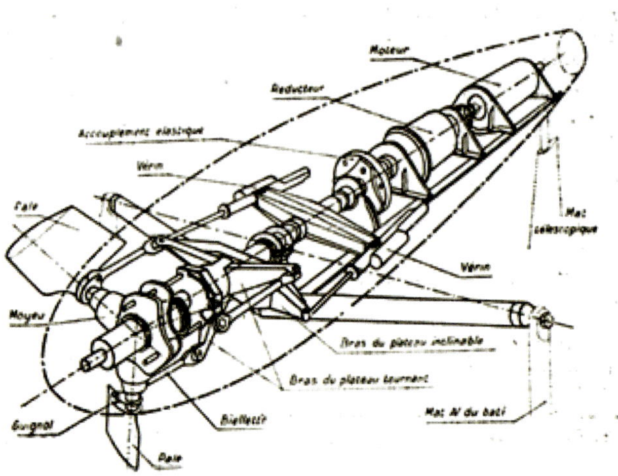

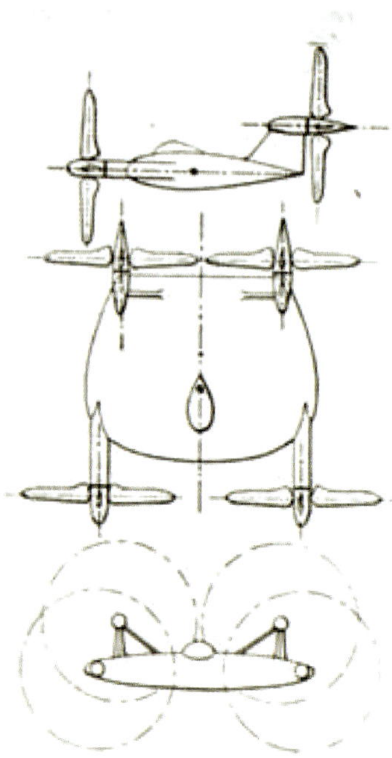

Une « crêpe volante »

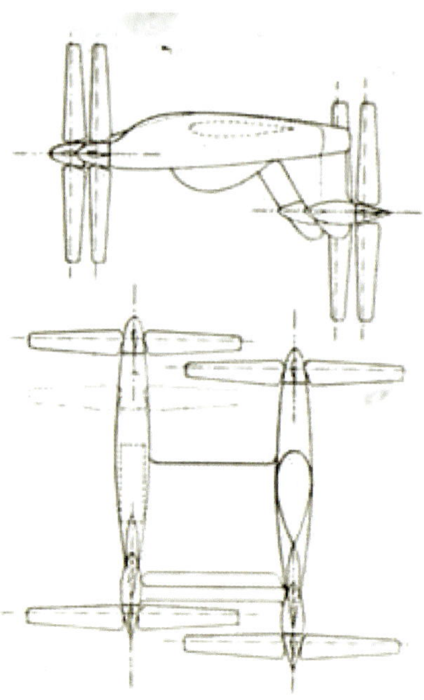

Un bifuselage

LEFT **A full-size rotor pod for the Hélicoplane was tested in the Meudon wind tunnel.** *Author's collection*

BELOW LEFT **Cutaway view of the rotor pod as tested in the wind tunnel, with an electric motor powering it.** *Author's collection*

BOTTOM LEFT **Two planned variants of the Hélicoplane were the 'flying pancake' type and the asymmetric variant.** *Author's collection*

hélicoplanes. A base project was fitted with four four-bladed rotors of 13.12ft (4m) diameter, and no, Richard was not obsessed with the number four because the experimental rotor tested at Chalais-Meudon was three-bladed, but he did think that it would be useful to increase the load-carrying capacity of each rotor by increasing the number of blades. Direction was achieved either by normal tail controls or by playing on the rotors' thrust. The hélicoplane was not a true VTOL aircraft but rather a STOL type because only two-thirds of the lift came from the rotors (although Richard assumed a '*very short take-off run*'). The take-off was achieved at a speed of 34mph (54km/h) but he did not say exactly how much of a run was required to reach this speed. For landing, Richard claimed that a '*parachute descent*' (which the author understands as meaning a point landing) could be attempted. The performance of Richard's design was to be equalled by the American Custer Channel wing aircraft tested in the 1940s and 1950s and the unflown Vought XF5U piston fighter, but Richard estimated that he could obtain their performances with half the amount of power!

Three hélicoplanes were designed with all of them using the same four-rotor arrangement. There was the base-design itself, a 'pancake' design as inspired by the Vought XF5U (but modified with two rotors replacing the rear winglets) and a twin-fuselage somewhat asymmetric aircraft with the pilot in the right-hand side of the fuselage and the propulsion unit in

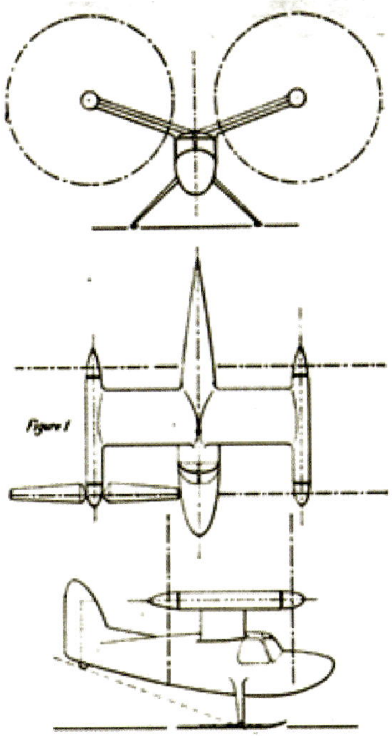

ABOVE A drawing of the Richard Hélicoplane. *Author's collection*

the left. No landing gear was designed for the second and third types, but for the twin-fuselage variant Richard envisioned a retractable skid under each fuselage. Although Gilbert Camille Richard went on to refine his conceptions at ONERA, none of his hélicoplane designs would ever be built.

Aérospatiale Tilt-Rotor Research

From 1972, Aérospatiale, following-up the work previously done at Sud Aviation on advanced rotary-wing machines, begun studying the feasibility of a tilt-rotor aircraft in co-operation with ONERA. The first concept to emerge from this reflection was the X-910, a small machine that was compared in the contemporary press to the XV-15 research aircraft then flying in the USA.

Aérospatiale X-910

This small and compact (22ft [6.70m] long) tilt-rotor aircraft was promoted officially for commuting services between the coast and oil rigs, but it seems likely that coastal patrol and

Aérospatiale X-910	
Status	project
Span	22ft 11.5in (7.00m) without rotors
Length	22ft 0in (6.70m)
Gross wing area	?
Gross weight	5,412lb (2,455kg) prototype, 5,644 (2,560kg) series
Powerplant	Arriel I Turbomachine 650hp (485kW)
Maximum speed/Height	321mph (517km/h)

other military duties could have been performed by this machine as well. Its development began with wind tunnel tests at Marignane in 1974 using a 1/5-scale model, and was then continued with the testing of a full-scale tilt-rotor system at the *Office National d'Études et de Recherches Aérospatiales* (ONERA) S1 subsonic wind tunnel in Modane-Avrieux during June and July 1975, and again in June and July 1976; the conversion between hover and forward flight was the primary focus of these tests. The design was promoted in the press from 1975 to 1977 with the possibility of having a prototype ready to fly in 1981. However, the project did not live past 1977, possibly due to the fact that a VTOL performance was only possible at a weight of 3,616lb (1,640kg) when the maximum flying weight was 5,644lb (2,560kg), suggesting that the load-carrying ability (four to six passengers) was actually very limited if VTOL was to be achieved. This research was continued later as the EUROFAR.

EUROFAR (European Future Advance Rotorcraft)

During the 1980s a new VTOL concept emerged as part of the European programme EUROFAR, and it involved the Aérospatiale, Agusta, Casa, MBB and Westland companies. This project was remarkable in that it was the only tilt-rotor concept ever studied in France. Contrary to most tilt-rotor projects designed elsewhere, the engines did not tilt with the rotor but instead remained fixed in their nacelles, a gearbox allowing the rotor axle to tilt with the front of the nacelle. The design was finalised in 1991 and that led to a second phase financed as part of the Eurekâ European research programme. This second phase, to last eighteen months, studied both

BELOW An illustration depicting the EUROFAR in flight. *Author's collection/ Eurocopter*

EUROFAR series

Status	project
Span	36ft 9in (11.20m) rotor diameter
Length	65ft 7.5in (20.00m)
Gross wing area	?
Gross weight	33,069lb (15,000lb)
Powerplant	-
Maximum speed/Height	385mph (620km/h) with range of 622 miles (1,000km)

EUROFAR demonstrator

Status	project
Span	?
Length	?
Gross wing area	?
Gross weight	13,228lb (6,000kg)
Powerplant	two RTM 322
Maximum speed/Height	-

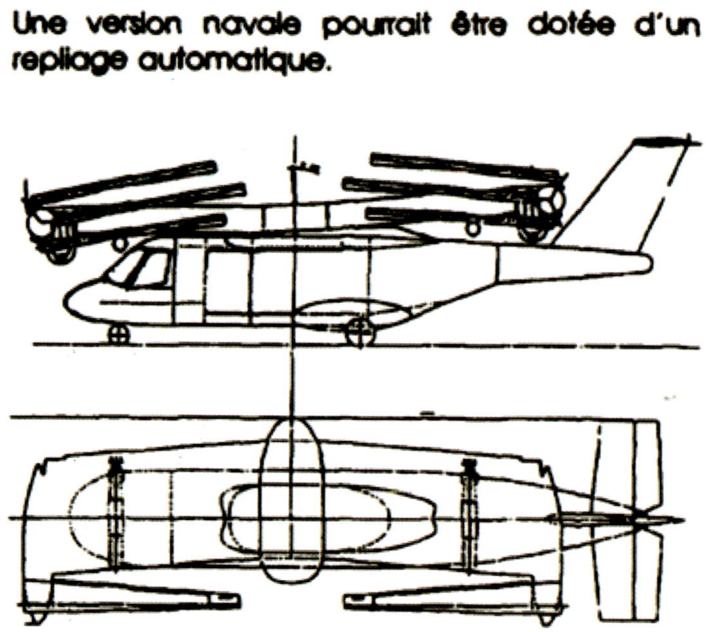

ABOVE **The naval version of the EUROFAR showing the folded configuration.** *Author's collection/Eurocopter*

the civilian and military markets for this machine and defined its potential roles. At that time it was also planned to begin the design of a smaller proof of concept aircraft, which was to be built from 1995 to fly *'before the end of the century'*. Only the results for the civilian market study have been made public and they showed that the basic demands were for a machine able to carry thirty passengers and three crew, to fly at 300 knots (550km/h) and 24,600ft (7,500m) for 600 nautical miles (1,100km), and to have the ability to continue flying with one engine off. From this data military versions were extrapolated covering an assault transport with seating for thirty commandos and with a 20mm gun turret under the nose, an assault cargo aircraft, and medevac duties. It was also planned, possibly under the influence of the American V-22 Osprey, to have a naval version with a folding wing and folding rotors.

By 1993 the project was well advanced and Eurocopter France had become the programme leader. A scale model of one of the rotors with a diameter of 13.12ft (4m) had

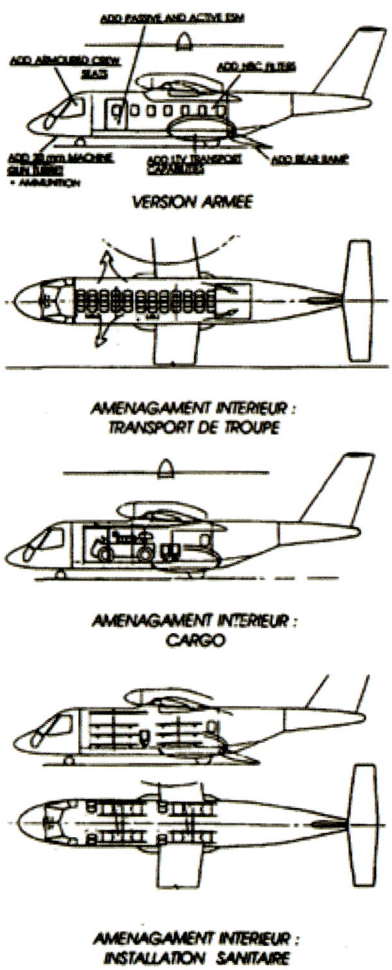

LEFT **Four planned variants of the Eurofar. From top to bottom: a side view of the armed military assault variant (note the arrow pointing to an invisible nose turret); a plan view of a troop transport variant; a side view of a cargo transport variant; and a side and plan view of an Evasan variant.** *Author's collection/Eurocopter*

BELOW **An unnamed Eurocopter tilt-fan VTOL concept.** *Author's collection/Eurocopter*

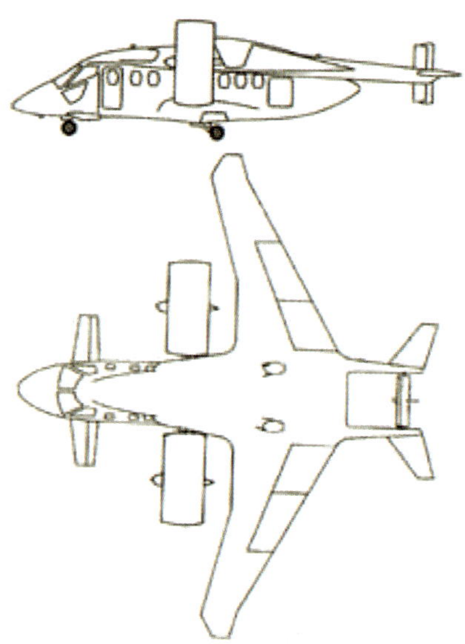

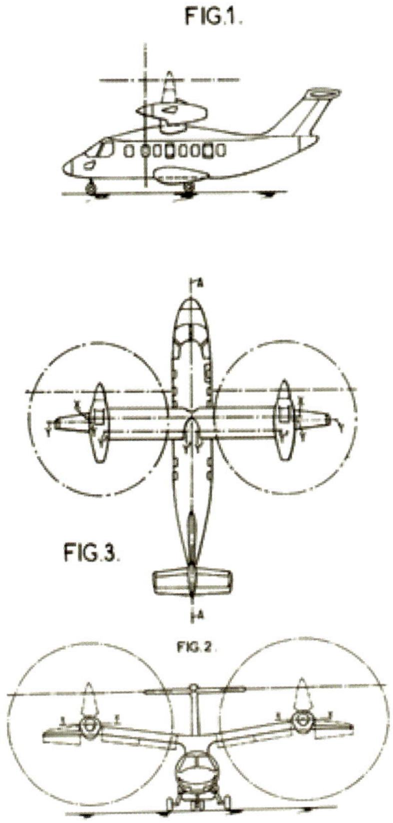

ABOVE **Unnamed Eurocopter tilt-rotor VTOL concept.** *Author's collection/Eurocopter*

been successfully tested in the S1 wind tunnel at Modane, a full-scale section of the fuselage was built for pressurisation tests and the cockpit design and man-machine interfaces were nearly complete. Aérospatiale had undertaken a market study that pointed out two main roles, offshore oil rig replenishment and a feeder liner for international airports. However, by 1999 the project had been cut back considerably and it was transferred to another European partner. It should be noted that a ducted fan design was also examined.

René Dorand's Thrust Wing Concept

René Dorand, besides working on rotary wing design in the *Société du Gyroplane*, also became interested in '*ailes propulsives*' (thrusting wings). His idea was to design a small aircraft with a power output of 740hp (550kW), a rather low maximum speed (218mph/350km/h) but capable of staying in the air at very low speeds of the order of 31mph (50km/h), and of taking off from small unprepared airfields. He thought of four possible applications for this idea – a military observation aircraft, an agricultural aircraft, a passenger aircraft and a freight carrier (the latter possibly for the post office). Dorand thought that his thrust wing would provide the following improvements in performance – at equal performance, the take-off run would be reduced by a factor of four and the horizontal speed would be improved by 30%. In 1956 he proposed to fit a Fouga Magister with his thrust wing to give the following estimated improvements: a speed of 435mph (700km/h) (similar to the

Fouga Magister (thrust wing version)	
Status	project
Span	?
Length	?
Gross wing area	186.0sq ft (17.30sq m)
Gross weight	5,952lb (2,700kg)
Powerplant	Turbine similar to the two Marboré
Maximum speed/Height	435mph (700km/h

Dorand DA-08-A observation	
Status	project
Span	?
Length	?
Gross wing area	?
Gross weight	3,197lb (1,450kg)
Powerplant	?
Maximum speed/Height	242mph (390km/h)
Remarks	one observer

Dorand DA-08-D freighter	
Status	project
Span	?
Length	?
Gross wing area	?
Gross weight	6,063lb (2,750kg)
Powerplant	?
Maximum speed/Height	162mph (260km/h)
Remarks	2,205lb (1,000kg) of cargo

BELOW **Variant of the Eurocopter tilt-rotor concept.** *Author's collection/Eurocopter*

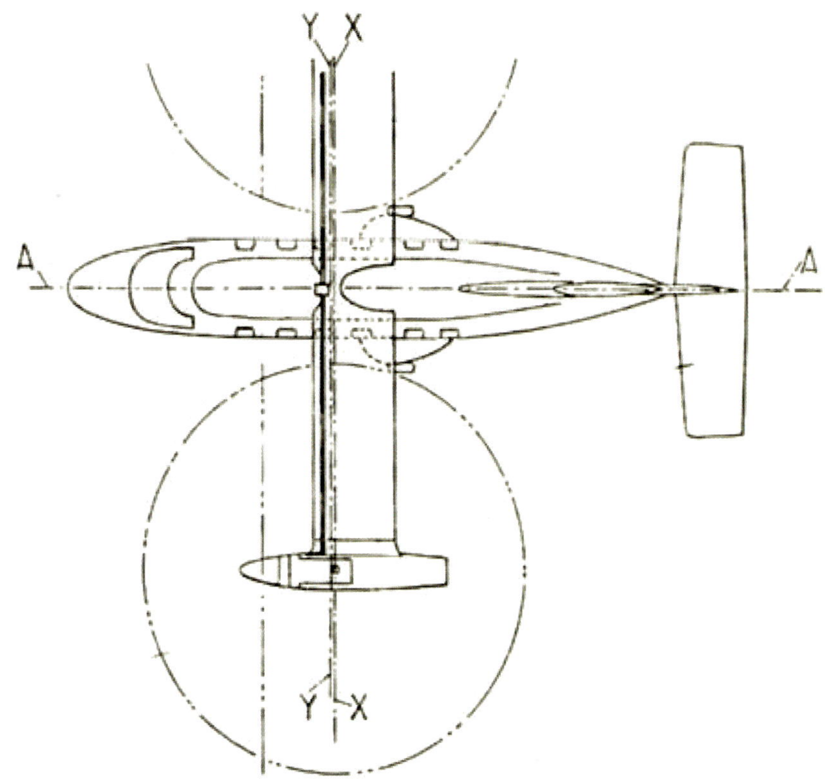

standard aircraft), a minimum speed (stall speed) of 56mph (90km/h) (as against 112mph [180km/h] for the standard Magister), and clearance over a 50ft (15m) high obstacle in just 785ft (240m) from brakes release (when the normal was 1,900ft [580m]). He designed a small proof of concept aircraft, the Dorand DH G4, but this was not built. Neither was the DA-08A observation machine, nor the DA-08-D freighter.

A Side Approach: Morane Saulnier

By 1960 Morane Saulnier had dropped its Statodyne concept (although Caillette himself had not and was involved in the Sud Ludion project, see Chapter Fourteen) and instead had begun working on lift fans. Since the company had been more active in the light transport and in the COIN categories, it decided to develop a VTOL ground attack aircraft using the lift fan concept.

Morane Saulnier MS 2000

The MS 2000 was a small side-by-side ground attack machine and although its architecture was rather classical its propulsion system was not. A single Marboré VI turbojet was positioned under the fuselage near the centre of gravity, it was fed by a nose intake and exhausted under the rear fuselage just behind the trailing edge of the straight wing. For take-off the exhaust was redirected toward a turbine moving a lift fan. The intake for this fan opened on the top of the fuselage, air came in through two doors (which were closed in forward flight) and the exhaust exited under the fuselage using nozzles positioned on each side of the turbojet. Four attachment points were located under the wings for weapons, but this 1961 project did not go beyond the drawing board.

MS 2000	
Status	project
Span	31ft 10in (9.70m)
Length	29ft 10in (9.10m)
Gross wing area	139.8sq ft (13.00sq m)
Gross weight	5,273lb (2,392kg)
Powerplant	one Marboré VI 1,125lb (5kN)
Maximum speed/Height	360mph (580km/h)
Armament	four attachment points

MS 2010

This was an evolution of the MS 2000 with a slightly bigger fuselage, the engine had been moved forward under the side-by-side cockpit and the wings were swept at an angle of 26°. A more powerful engine than the Marboré was selected in the form of a General Electric CJ 160.1, which gave 2,860lb (12.7kN) of thrust in direct thrust mode and 7,200lb (32kN) in lift fan mode. Only 551lb (250kg) of warload could be carried.

MS 2010	
Status	project
Span	33ft 9.5in (10.30m)
Length	30ft 2in (9.20m)
Gross wing area	193.5sq ft (18.00sq m)
Gross weight	7,341lb (3,330kg)
Powerplant	one CJ 160.1
Maximum speed/Height	516mph (830km/h)
Armament	four attachment points

MS 2015

Evolved from the MS 2010 and using the same engine, the ultimate MS 2015 development was a larger aircraft that could be used in three different roles – ground support (using the four weapon attachment points under the wings), reconnaissance with a side-looking radar pod under the fuselage (how this would be fitted around the nozzles for the lift fan is unknown) and photo reconnaissance. This design was no more successful than the earlier pair of projects.

MS 2015	
Status	project
Span	34ft 1.5in (10.40m)
Length	37ft 0in (11.28m)
Gross wing area	209.7sq ft (19.5sq m)
Gross weight	up to 9,921lb (4,500kg)
Powerplant	one CJ 160.1
Maximum speed/Height	466mph (750km/h)
Armament	four attachment points

BELOW Three-view drawing of the proposed Dorand thrust-wing demonstrator. *Authors' Collection/Dorand*

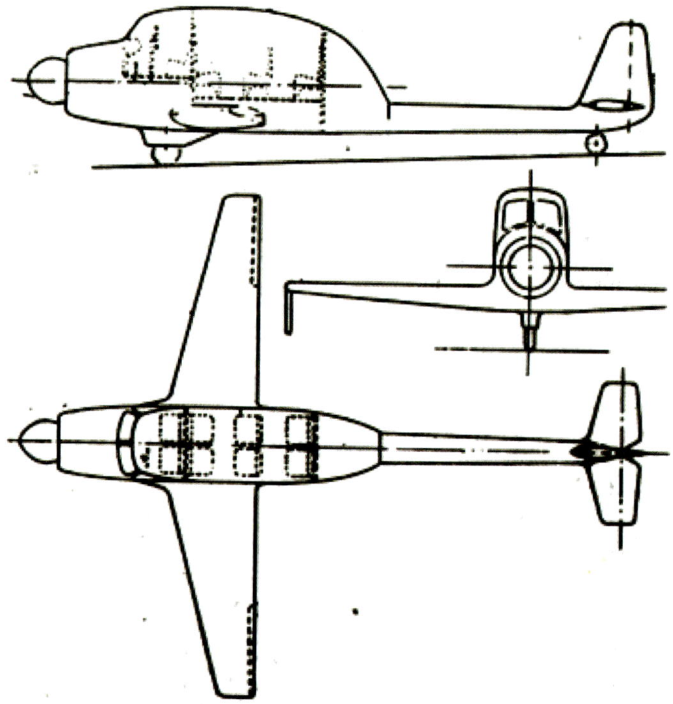

Chapter Nine
Helicopters

ABOVE Model of the Breguet (Dorand/Chartier) Gyroplane G.161.1 *Anti-feu* (fire-fighter) *type porteur* (load-carrier) model P.B.C. 6.2, which today is preserved at the Musée de l'Air et de l'Espace. *J.C. Carbonel*

France has a long tradition with helicopters and the first section of this chapter looks at the roots of the nation's success developing this category of aircraft.

Cornu entered the history books with the first man-carrying helicopter to achieve a take-off, Papin and Rouilly designed and tested the first jet helicopter during the First World War (unfortunately unsuccessfully), and during the 1930s Breguet vied with Focke for the first really operable helicopter. Dorand and the *Compagnie du Gyravion* were even building the first anti-shipping, torpedo-armed helicopter (the Gyroplane G20) when the Wehrmacht overran France in 1940. And during the Occupation SNCASE designed and built a small autogiro, the SE 700, which after the Liberation was earmarked for coast guard duties.

Directly after the war, and while it was experimenting with a copy of the wartime Focke-Achgelis Fa 223 named the SE 3000, the SNCASE design office produced a fully French design, the SE 3100. This was a large for the period (twelve-passenger) mono-

ABOVE A well-known picture of the Papin-Rouilly jet helicopter taken in 1915 during testing. The aircraft never reached the number of revolutions per minute needed to actually perform a take-off, although according to official reports some lift was generated. *Famille Rouilly.*

BELOW This rather ungainly machine, the SE 3120 Alouette, sired a successful line of helicopters with the Alouette II, Alouette III and Lama, etc. *Philippe Boulay*

rotor helicopter with a twin tail rotor. The SE 3100 remained a project but the small demonstrator SE 3101 built for it did fly, on 15 June 1948, having been developed by Heinrich Focke. Although seriously underpowered, the SE 3101 proved stable and manoeuvrable and Jean Boulet got the job of test flying it because he was the smallest man in the team. A two-seat development, the SE 3110 made its maiden flight on 10 June 1950 and, with its egg-shaped fuselage extended by a long boom, it was the anticipation of things to come, but it did not reach production. The design that followed was the SE 3120, the first to be given a name (Alouette – Lark), and this was expected to fulfil four roles: passenger transport with two seats as well as the pilot (it was thought this could be used for observation, liaison, civilian forest fire surveillance, and the inspection of pipelines or acrial power lines), medevac duties (with two stretchers, one on each side), crop-spraying, or freight transport. It was still a very basic design with an open-truss fuselage and it was not until the third iteration of the style arrived with the Alouette III that the type presented a more enclosed and solid appearance. Both the Alouettes achieved success with production in large numbers.

At Aérocentre René Dorand promoted the NC 2001 Abeille (Bee), which used the overlapping style of rotors originally designed before the war by Flettner. After being displayed at the 1948 Paris Air Show (as a static exhibit under the *Grand Palais* glass roof) it flew in 1949 … and crashed. Although considered to be too complex, a pre-series was proposed at the time and a NC 2002 Libellule (Dragonfly) prototype was built, but the company folded before this second machine could be flown.

During the same time period, René Dorand, together with Marcel Vuillerme, Paul Gabet, René Leduc

ABOVE Although it looked good, the NC 2001 was not a successful design. *Philippe Ricco*

ABOVE The NC 2002 was an evolution of the Abeille but it never flew. *Philippe Ricco*

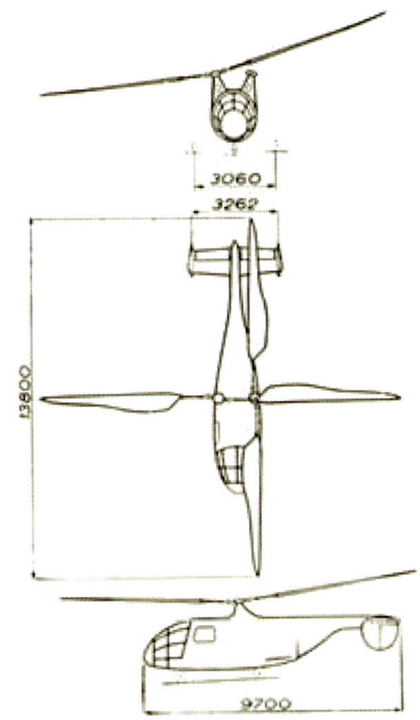

ABOVE Contemporary three-view-drawing of the NC 2001. *Revue Aéronautique/Author's collection*

and Maurice Chartier, worked on some jet-propelled helicopter designs called 'Gyroplanes'. Dorand defined the Gyroplane as twin co-axial rigid-blade rotor helicopter and rotation was initiated by the use of 'mini-jets', which had nozzles near the tip of the blades (the author speculates that René Leduc's involvement with the project came with those nozzles). Two Gyroplane designs are known through some models that survive in the *Musée de l'Air* – the transport G.130.4 Gyrobus capable of carrying forty passengers and the G.161.1 '*Anti-feu*' fire-fighting machine. Curiously the models, which are dated 1945-47, are labelled Breguet and yet the Dorand-Gabet patents of 1946-47 covering jet propulsion were credited to SCAC (Aérocentre)!

Jean Cantinieau was another innovative designer who was at first backed by Matra in building two examples of the lightweight two-seat MC 101, but with finance lacking he went on to work in Spain with Aerotecnica and there designed the AC 11 to AC 21 series of light helicopters.

Nord Aviation, under the leadership of André Bruel (who had already patented a helicopter during the war), built the Nord 1700 Norélic [Nor for Nord + élic for *hélice* or propeller] but this was unsuccessful. The main feature of this machine was the use of a faired propeller thrusting against a vertical surface to serve as counter-torque device. Bruel thought this would make the machine more manoeuvrable but in fact it proved difficult to control and was damaged twice. The smaller Nord 1710 was equally unsuccessful, while the Nord 1750 Norelfe [Nor for Nord + Elfe for Elf] was a derivative of the Aerotecnica AC 12 fitted with an early form of NOTAR (no tail rotor). Tested at Villaroche, this helicopter did not seem to have made any impact, but the Spanish government was interested in the design and it became the AC 13 there.

BELOW Model of the Breguet (Dorand/Chartier) Gyroplane G.130.4 Gyrobus type traffic model E.A.31, which is also preserved at the *Musée de l'Air et de l'Espace*. *J.C. Carbonel*

ABOVE **A special 'VIP' version of the Alouette III was designed under the name Gouverneur (Governor). The outer fuselage was redesigned slightly to improve the aerodynamics.** *Philippe Boulay*

After the war the Alouette, Gazelle, Puma, Ecureuil (A-Star), Super Frelon and Dauphin all proved a success in the export market and today Airbus Helicopters is a major player in the global aviation scene, but numerous intriguing rotary-wing designs were less lucky and were passed by without siring any useful descendants at all. The helicopters produced in France from this point can be grouped as follows.

Assault Helicopters

Aérospatiale SA X-326A Hélicoptère de Manoeuvre

Aérospatiale's X-326A was the original project number for what was to become the SA 330. The '*hélicoptère de manoeuvre*' title was not in reference to its manoeuvring capability but rather it indicated that it was to be used in close collaboration with the ground forces during operations and combat.

SA X-326B

This was an alternate version with a ducted fan as a counter-torque system. The centre fuselage was similar to the SA 330 but had a revised glass nose seemingly inspired by the Frelon (Hornet). Contrary to the SA 331 below that had a plain shrouded propeller as its anti-torque device, the X-326B had a dorsal intake with air ducted through the rear boom and then ejected through a nozzle with multiple flaps to deflect the jet. No fixed armament was planned for this variant.

Sud X-326B	
Status	project
Rotor diameter	51ft 2in (15.60m)
Length	59ft 6.5in (18.15m)
Rotor disc area	-
Gross weight	13,889lb (6,300kg)
Powerplant	two Bastan III 1,200hp (895kW)
Maximum speed/Height	?
Armament/load	twelve fully equipped soldiers/one jeep

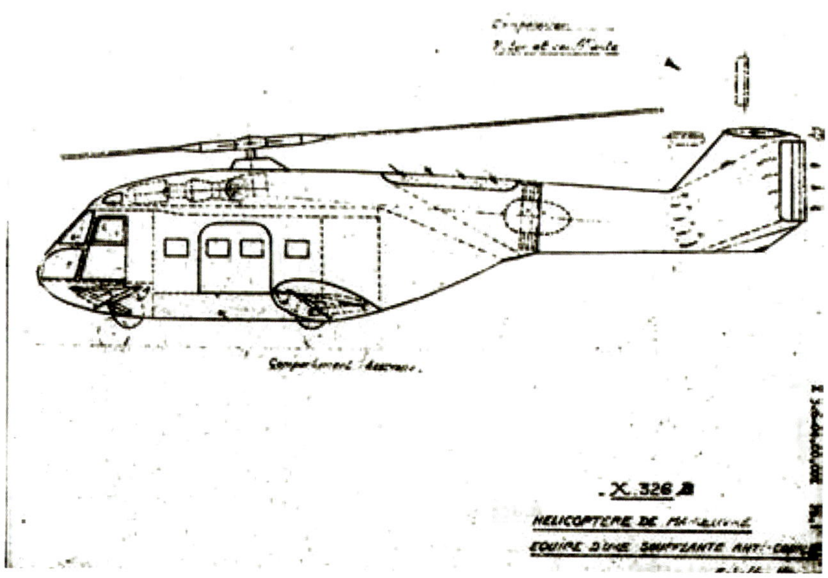

RIGHT **The alternative X-326B design with a shrouded fan system acting as an anti-torque device. This would have resulted in a very thick tail section.** *Sud Aviation*

SA 330 Puma

The original project leading to the Puma emerged in 1963 as the Alouette IV. The base requirement issued by the *Armée de Terre* in 1962 covered the carriage of a 2,866lb (1,300kg) load or twelve commandos to the battlefield. For this it featured a large cargo bay 293.1cu ft (8.30cu m) in size that could be accessed through two large side sliding doors. A lot of research and testing went into the design of the mechanical components to be used in this aircraft; for example in 1964 endurance and fatigue testing was carried out on the engines, gearbox and rotor. The machine was particularly powerful through its twin 1,300hp (969kW) Turbomeca Bastan III engines and an order for two prototypes and five pre-production

BELOW **Artist's view of the earliest version of what was to become the well-known SA 330 Puma, produced jointly by France and the UK. It was called the X-326A.** *Sud Aviation*

aircraft was placed by the STAé on 20 August 1964. Most unusually, the first prototype flew three months ahead of schedule on 15 April 1965 and two more became airborne that year. (Note: Sud Aviation had been experimenting with two Sikorsky H-34 helicopters produced under licence that were fitted with two Bastan IV engines coupled together to provide 1,900hp/1,420kW of power instead of the original piston engine's 1,525hp/1,140kW. However, this idea was quickly abandoned.)

The early examples were used for the following trials work:

SA 330-01: general flight testing.
SA 330-02: auto-pilot testing.
SA 330-03: avionics testing.
SA 330-04: fitted with the new Turmo III C4 engine with improved performance which became the production powerplant.
SA 330-05: general flight testing.
SA 330-06: operational flight testing including the special ability to move around on its landing gear after landing in order to reach a camouflaged area, and while folding the rotor at the same time. The design of this 'powered landing gear' was undertaken by the DOP company that had proposed other exotic means of take-off during the 1950s (see Chapter Six).
SA 330-07: demonstration aircraft.

SA 330C

In 1966 a programme of co-operation was arranged with the British and it was intended that this should remain active until 1975. It covered the SA 330 Puma (which was ordered by the RAF) and the Super Frelon (which was not).

Sud SA 330 project 1961	
Status	project
Rotor diameter	49ft 2.5in (15.00m)
Length	59ft 8.5in (18.20m)
Rotor disc area	-
Gross weight	13,668lb (6,200kg)
Powerplant	two Bastan VII 1,300hp (969kW)
Maximum speed/Height	180mph (290km/h) at sea level
Armament/load	two gun positions under cockpit (for machine guns or 20mm guns?)

Sud SA 330 project 63	
Status	project
Rotor diameter	49ft 2.5in (15.00m)
Length	47ft 11in (14.60m)
Rotor disc area	-
Gross weight	13,668lb (6,200kg)
Powerplant	two Bastan III
Maximum speed/Height	180mph (290km/h) at sea level
Armament/load	-

Sud SA 330	
Status	production
Rotor diameter	49ft 2.5in (15.00m)
Length	48ft 7in (14.80m)
Rotor disc area	1,903.2sq ft (177sq m) rotor disc
Gross weight	14,109lb (6,400kg)
Powerplant	two Turmo III C4 1,300hp (969kW)
Maximum speed/Height	174mph (280km/h) at sea level
Armament/load	-

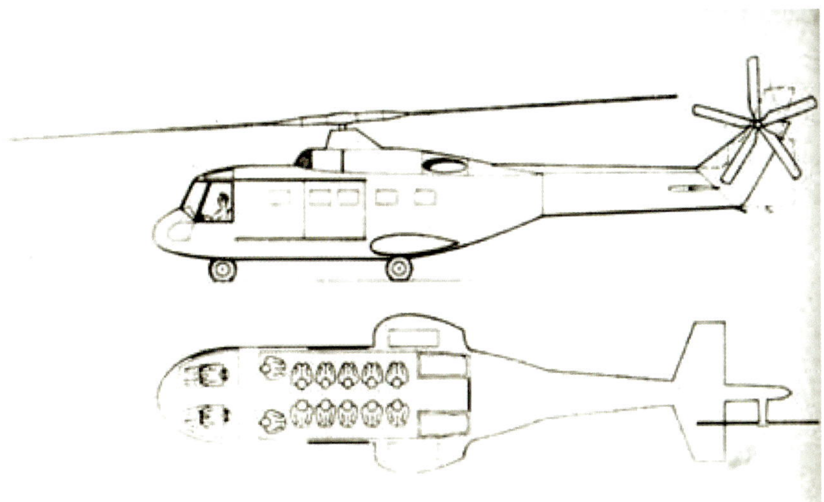

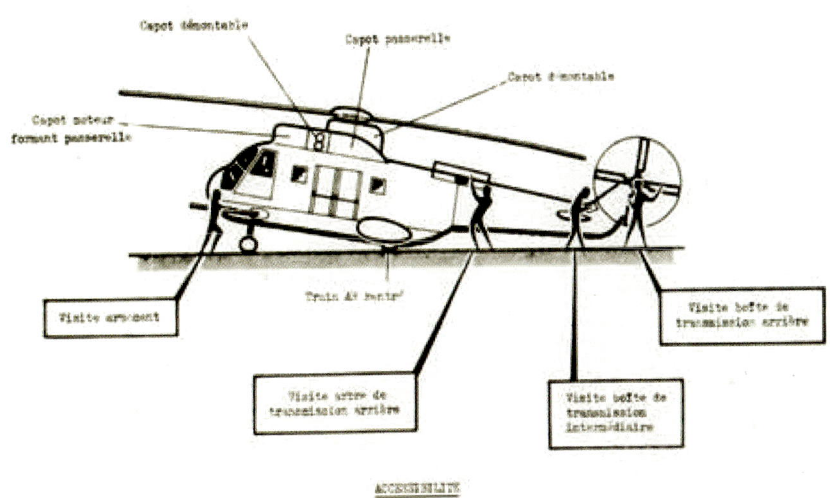

ABOVE RIGHT By the time this plan was issued in 1963 the SA 330 had begun to take final shape. *Sud Aviation*

RIGHT In this document vaunting the accessibility of the future SA 330, the four mechanics are shown carrying out maintenance on (left to right): the guns, rear drive axle, intermediate transmission box and rear transmission box. The sketch shows that at this time the SA 330 had built-in armament. *Sud Aviation*

Sud SA 330C	
Status	project
Rotor diameter	?
Length	?
Rotor disc area	-
Gross weight	?
Powerplant	two Turmo III C4 1,300hp (969kW)
Maximum speed/Height	
Armament/load	

RIGHT The SA 330 prototype. *José Fernandez*

This version of the Puma appeared in 1965 and may have been inspired by the American AH-56 Cheyenne. Differences from the standard Puma included the addition of short wings, the integration of the rear rotor into a fenestron (protected tail rotor) and the addition of a pusher propeller.

SA 330Z

This was the fifth prototype SA 330-05 fitted with a large fenestron tail rotor. This configuration proved disappointing and was not pursued.

SA 330 with Propulsive Rear Rotor

In 1965 a study was made into the possibility of making the tail rotor swivel, so that during high-speed flight it would add a component to the forward thrust.

SA 330 with Air Cushion Landing Gear

This was proposed in December 1964 by Société Bertin & Cie, although the study was funded privately by Bertin and Sud Aviation. The system used eight tubular skirts and three motorised wheels (the normal landing gear for the SA 330), the air for the cushion having been bled from the

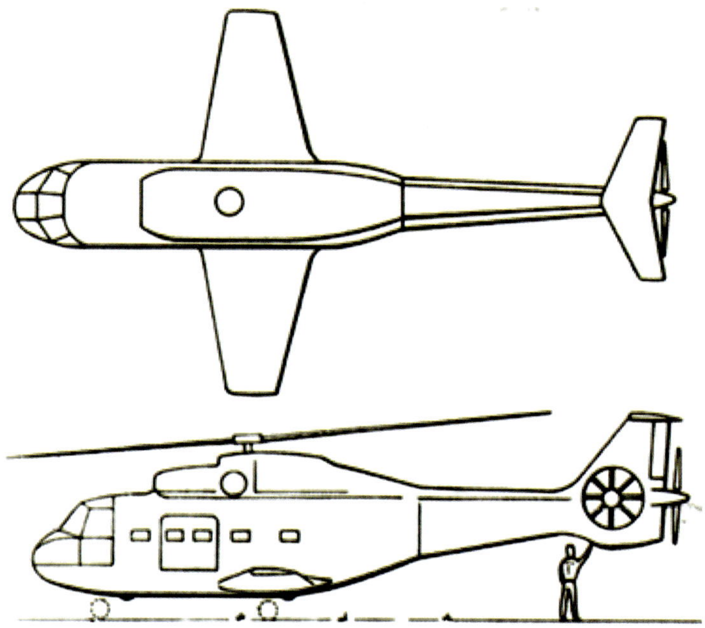

ABOVE RIGHT The SA 330C was a 1965 proposal for a high-speed assault version fitted with wings and pusher tail rotor. *Sud Aviation*

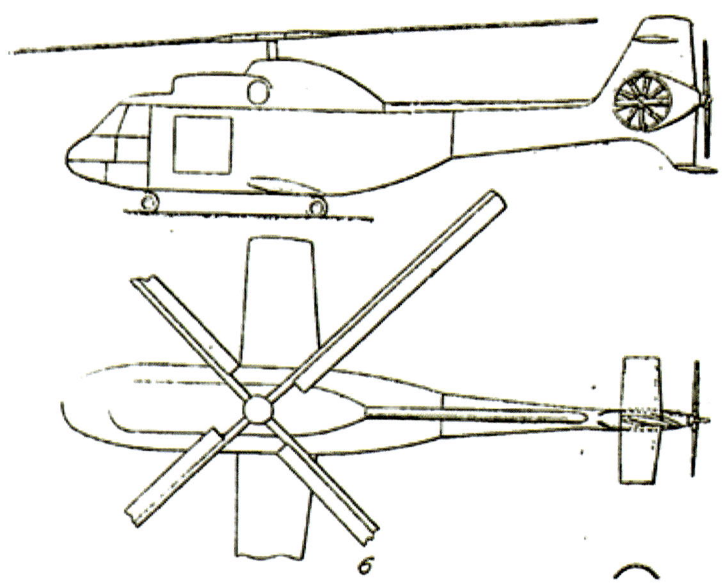

RIGHT A variant investigated the use of a fenestron (a protected tail rotor) but this proved inadequate for large helicopters. *Sud Aviation*

RIGHT **Bertin briefly investigated the possibility of installing an air cushion landing gear on the SA 330.** *Bertin*

BELOW RIGHT **A more recent (1986-91) project was the experimental installation of the Orchidée (Orchid) battlefield surveillance radar. The single prototype was used during the first Gulf War.** *José Fernandez*

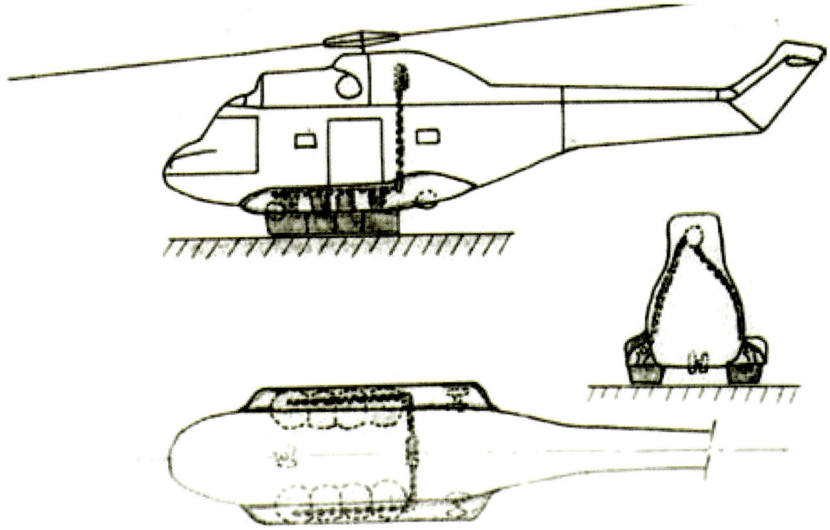

turbojets. A full-size skirt was built but funding dried up before it could be tested. Bertin also proposed an 'air cushion track' that would fully replace each landing gear unit, but as far as is known this was not developed further.

SA 331

This type number was allocated to a variant of the SA 330 in which the rear tail rotor was to be replaced by a ducted propeller and a V-tail. The technical data was identical to the early SA 330 but the project had already been abandoned when the prototypes flew. The number was reused in 1977 for a Super Puma featuring the new Starflex rotor (a radically simplified rotor-head system).

Sud SA 331	
Status	project
Rotor diameter	49ft 2.5in (15.00m)
Length	46ft 3in (14.10m)
Rotor disc area	-
Gross weight	?
Powerplant	two Bastan VII 1,300hp (969kW)
Maximum speed/Height	-
Armament/load	-

BELOW RIGHT **An early design in which the anti-torque device was a large ducted fan. This SA 331 variant was quickly abandoned.** *Sud Aviation*

BELOW LEFT **An artist's impression of the early SA 331.** *Sud Aviation*

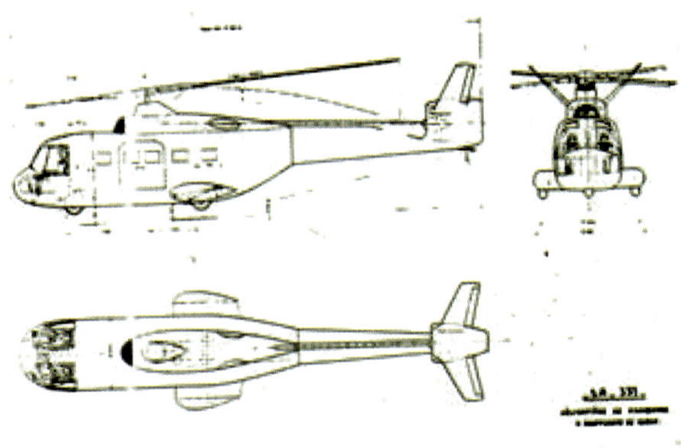

Naval Patrol Helicopters

SE 3160 Alouette III Navale

This naval version of the Alouette III, proposed in 1968, was to be fitted with Nord AS 12 missiles controlled by an APX Bezu 260 gyro sight. A search radar of an unspecified type would have been fitted in a nose radome, while an alternative version of the aircraft was to carry a conventional torpedo on the right side and a MAD fish on the left side (a small magnetic anomaly detector that was streamed behind the helicopter on a cable to move the sensor away from the helicopter's magnetic field).

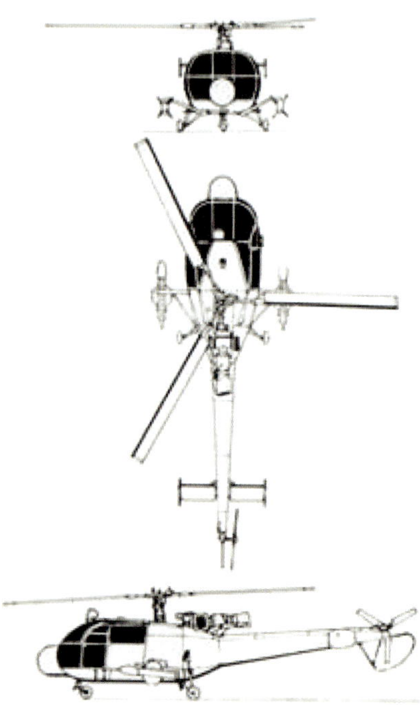

BELOW **This three-view drawing depicts the proposed naval (anti-shipping) version of the Alouette III.** *Sud Aviation*

SE 3200 Frelon

From 1955 SNCASE studied a heavy helicopter capable of lifting a 13,228lb (6,000kg) load under the project designation X-316. Two prototypes were ordered in 1956 as the SE 3200 and the type first flew on 10 June 1959. It was a compact design aimed at the needs of the *Marine Nationale*, with the short airframe easing the problem of storage aboard ships. However, the SE 3200 proved to be overweight and was cancelled in 1961, a decision that led to the Super Frelon being developed.

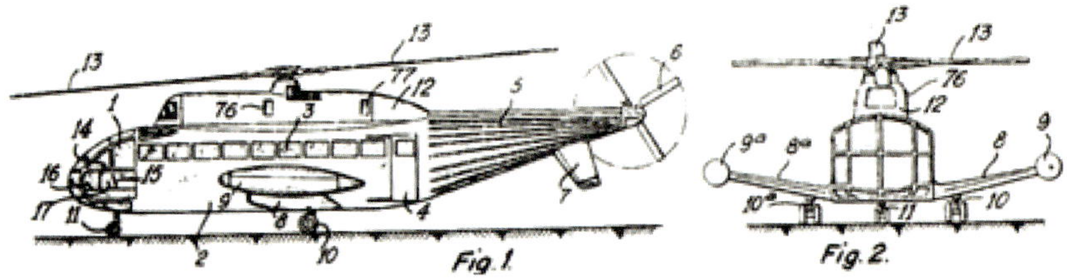

TOP **This early version of the Frelon anti-shipping helicopter is shown with additional wings and wingtip tanks.** *Sud Aviation*

ABOVE **One of the two SE 3200 Frelon prototypes in flight.** *Sud Aviation via José Fernandez*

SA 321 Super Frelon

The Super Frelon first flew on 28 May 1963. In 1962 the *Bundeswehr* announced its intention to order three pre-production machines when the French Air Force had ordered only two prototypes. A Franco-German committee established previously for sharing orders for the Frelon was reactivated and the Germans appeared interested in the type. However, after evaluating prototype SA 3210-03, and then prototypes -04 and -05, they looked at the American Boeing CH-47 Chinook, and then finally purchased the Sikorsky CH-53 Sea Stallion! So in the end no Super Frelon was ever acquired by Germany.

From 1973 experiments were made to carry the Exocet missile on the Super Frelon. In all, the following Super Frelon variants were designed:

SA 321A: ground-based production version (without side floats). Not produced as such.
SA 321B: transport variant for the *Armée de l'Air* (without side floats). Not produced.
SA 321C: civilian variant for twenty-four passengers (without side floats). Not produced.
SA 321D: original base design optimised for anti-submarine (??) duties (with side floats). Not produced.
SA 321E: transport variant for the *Marine Nationale* (with side floats). Not produced.
SA 321F: civilian variant for thirty-four to thirty-seven passengers

(without side floats). One unit produced for Olympic Airways in 1968 (airframe N° 116). Later used briefly by the GLAM (a government squadron).

SA 321G: the variant produced in quantity for the *Marine Nationale*, Libya and Iraq.

SA 321H: military export version without side floats.

SA 321I: not built.

SA 321J: civilian freighter version. One example for Bergen Air Transport (N° 113).

SA 321Ja: civilian freighter version with improved cargo capacity (28,660lb/13,000kg instead of 26,455lb/12,000kg): one unit sold to Zaïre, thirteen sold to China.

SA 321K: similar to the H variant, twelve units sold to Israel.

SA 321L: similar to the H variant, seventeen units sold to South Africa.

SA 321M: similar to the H variant, eight units sold to Libya.

SA 330

The Puma was also assessed as a naval helicopter.

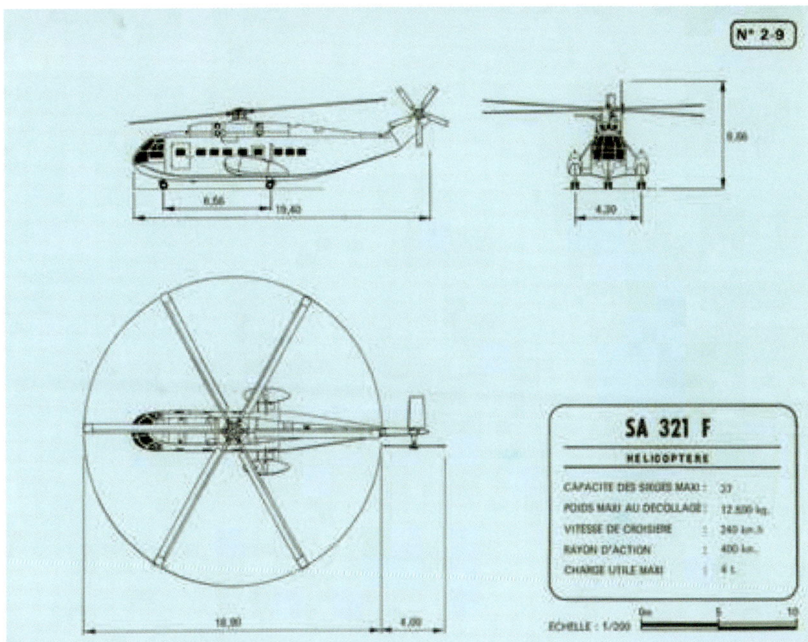

TOP RIGHT The sole SA 321F, still in its Olympic Airways livery and now preserved at the Helicopter Museum, Weston-super-Mare in the UK. *J.C. Carbonel*

ABOVE RIGHT Three-view drawing of the Super Frelon, which went into production mostly for the French Navy and the Israeli, South African and Libyan armies. *Author's collection*

RIGHT The Super Puma derivative of the Puma was offered as an anti-shipping aircraft armed with Exocet missiles. *José Fernandez*

ABOVE The Dauphin was also loaded up with missiles and radar appendages, as illustrated in this 1981 Lengellé artwork. *GIFAS*

Sud/Westland WG.13	
Status	project
Rotor diameter	42ft 0in (12.80m)
Length	49ft 10.5in (15.20m)
Rotor disc area	-
Gross weight	7,937lb (3,600kg)
Powerplant	two Rolls-Royce 360-07 900hp (671kW)
Maximum speed/Height	218mph (350km/h)
Armament/load	one 20mm gun, six SS 11 missiles

SA 365

Among various militarised variants of the Dauphin was the SA 365 designed for the anti-shipping role.

Anti-Tank and Battlefield Helicopter

Westland WG.13

The Westland WG.13, which was to become the Lynx, formed part of the 1966-67 Franco-British agreement which, beside the Jaguar, included three different helicopters: the SA 330 Puma, the SA 340 Gazelle and the WG.13. The last of these was designed originally in four forms: a 'utility' version for the British Army, an armed version for the Royal Navy and the *Marine Nationale*, a civilian version and an armed reconnaissance version for the French ALAT (*Aviation Légère de l'Armée de Terre* – i.e. aircraft belonging to the ground forces). As part of the co-operation with Westland, Sud Aviation built a mock-up of the WG.13 armed reconnaissance type, which was a high-speed three-seater machine armed with guns and missiles. It was intended to fly at 218mph (350km/h), it had an aircraft-style fuselage with a cockpit to accommodate three (pilot, co-pilot and gunner), a fully retracting undercarriage and winglets. The armed version fitted with a 20mm ventral turret, which was sometimes described in the press as the '*Cheyenne à la Française*', was apparently a purely French development. This project appeared in the press in around 1968

ABOVE This 1968 vintage art by an unidentified artist illustrates how the military WG.13 should have looked. *Sud Aviation*

but the cockpit mock-up was probably built earlier than that. It was to fly reconnaissance missions, anti-tank missions (with the 20mm turret + three SS11 missiles under each wing) or even attack enemy helicopters, but nothing materialised from these studies. By 1971 this design had been abandoned, and the heavily armed Super Alouette was being considered instead (see SA 360).

SNCASE Designs

SE X-310

Using this cover designation SNCASE, under Pierre Renoux, established the concept for a light turbine-powered helicopter using Turbomeca powerplants. The different designs were identified through letters ranging from A to G, and ultimately the G variant was developed into the SE 3130, later the successful SA 313 Alouette II.

SE X-315

This design, developed during the 1950s, was a turbine-powered single-rotor helicopter with a large cabin that could take up to seven passengers. It was intended to be a utility helicopter and surviving art renderings depict

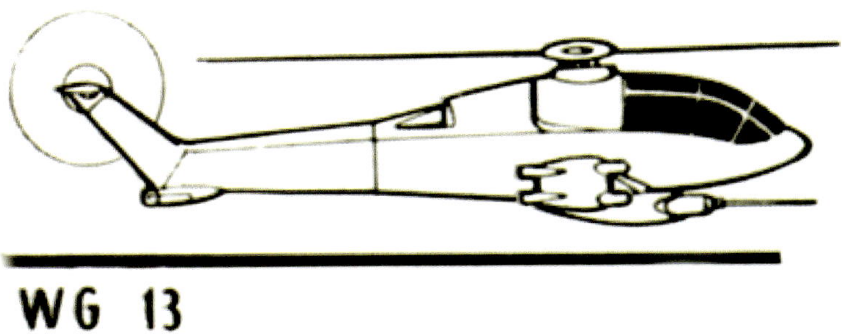

TOP A mock-up of this WG.13 was built but the design never progressed to the flight stage. *Philippe Boulay*

ABOVE This small drawing is a rendition by Aviation Magazine's Jean Pérard of the side profile of the WG.13 as the design appeared in 1969. *Aviation Magazine*

BELOW However, another version named 'WG.13Q' has also emerged in publications. Was it a follow-up to the earlier Army WG.13, or a misrepresentation of the same aircraft? *Aviation Magazine/Author's collection*

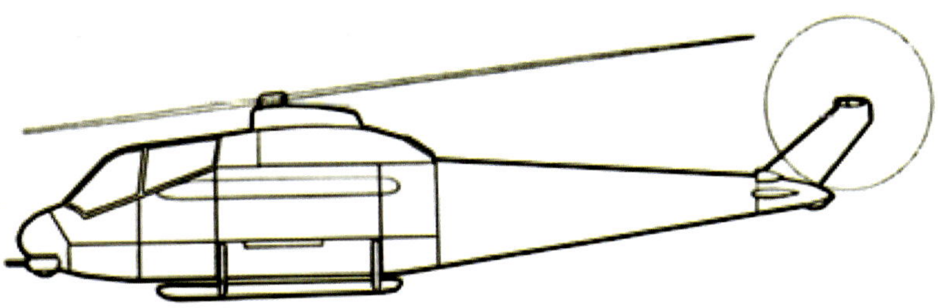

BELOW LEFT A rare colour photograph of the prototype Alouette II. This single aircraft can be said to have been the father of the whole French helicopter industry. *Philippe Ricco*

BELOW RIGHT Head-on view of an Alouette II fitted with four SS 10 Anti-tank missiles. At the time, no one knew it but this was a vision of the future. *Philippe Ricco*

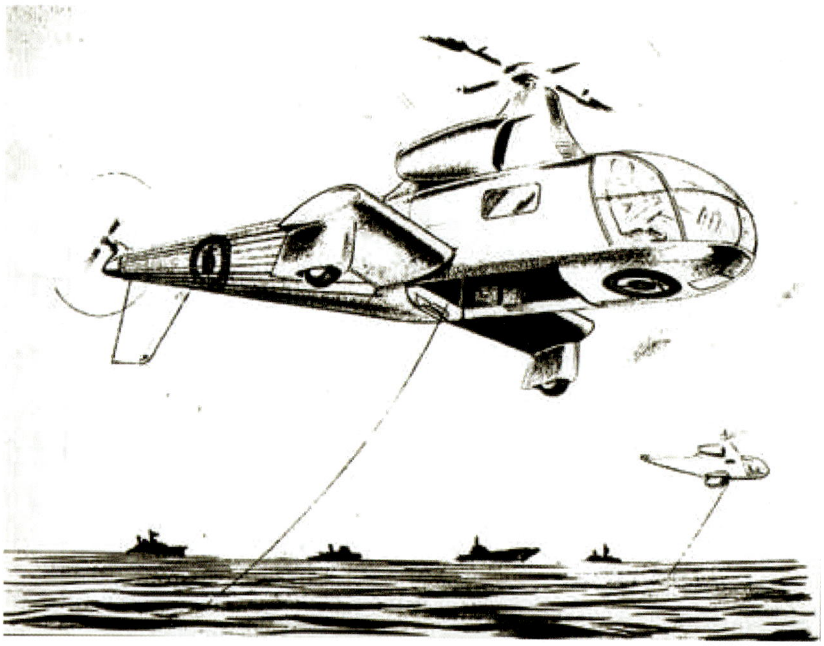

ABOVE The SE X315 was seen as a successor to the Alouette. Among the various roles considered for it was this naval operation. *Philippe Ricco*

it being used in a mountainous environment, as a flying crane on a civil engineering project and laying a sonar for Navy use. One of Jean Perard's sketches depicted twin nozzles at the rear of the engine deck, strongly suggesting that two turbines would have been used.

SE 3160 Alouette III

A version was proposed in 1968 armed with a 20mm gun in a turret attached on its starboard side on a shock-absorbing mount. The gun could fire 600 rounds per minute and the weapon and its mount and ammunition weighed 611lb (277kg). The endurance time for the Alouette thus equipped was two hours and twenty minutes. An alternative version carried four Nord AS 11 missiles for the tank hunter role and this was ordered, although Matra rocket launchers for thirty-six or seventy-two rockets could also be installed on the 'horned beasts' (the masts on which the weapons were attached to the aircraft).

SE 3164 Armed Alouette

This variant was based on the earlier experiments that looked at arming the Alouette but it featured a somewhat redesigned canopy with an opaque nose and a stepped windshield. A 20mm MG 151/20 cannon was installed in the nose and an SS 12 anti-tank missile (guided via a sighting periscope on top of the canopy) or Matra rocket pods could be loaded on side mounts. This version flew for the first time on 24 June 1965.

SE X-300

The X-300 was designed as a light observation helicopter, but its role was later expanded to include light transport, medevac and utility helicopter duties. It had an Astazou turbine driving an improved gearbox and rotors designed for an 'Alouette II revalorisée' (a proposed improved Alouette II studied during, it is thought, the 1963-65 period). Its

BELOW A design fitted with a NOTAR system was investigated during the 1960s. *Sud Aviation*

BOTTOM A mid-1960s idea was to turn this successful helicopter into a gun platform. *Philippe Ricco*

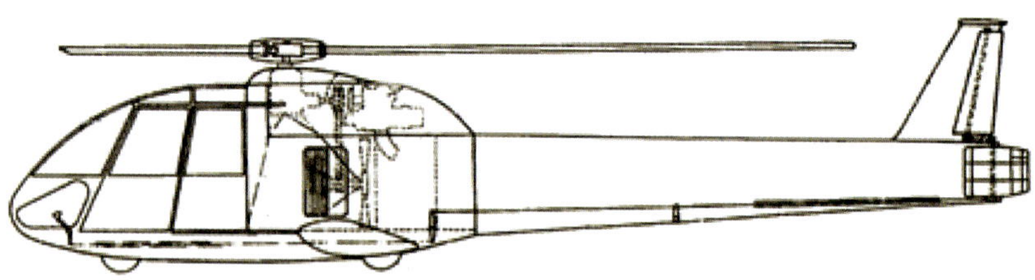

Sud X-300	
Status	project
Rotor diameter	30ft 2in (9.20m)
Length	27ft 7in (8.40m)
Rotor disc area	-
Gross weight	?
Powerplant	one Astazou II
Maximum speed/Height	155mph (250km/h)
Armament/load	-

refined aerodynamic shape marked the introduction of the fenestron concept in the Sud design philosophy, although at the time it was described as a *'fully faired rear rotor'*. X-300's range was expected to be 485 miles (780km) and its maximum speed 155mph (250km/h). The design ultimately led to the SA 340 prototype and later to the successful SA 341 Gazelle.

SA 330C

This SA 330C project appeared in *Aviation Magazine* during the 1960s but it bore no relation to the SA 330C seen above. It may have been a misrepresentation of the high-speed Puma, but it might also be the only remaining trace of an attempt by Sud Aviation to create a heavy combat/battlefield helicopter/gunship.

SA 340

The first prototype of the SA 340, which made its maiden flight on 7 April 1967, had a traditional tail rotor. The second example received the new fenestron but with a T-tail following on from the original X-300 design. It was also equipped with a new semi-rigid rotor with composite blades developed in a co-operative effort with the German company Bolköw.

SA 341 Gazelle

The SA 341 Gazelle was co-produced with Westland in the UK. A fenestron was introduced on the second

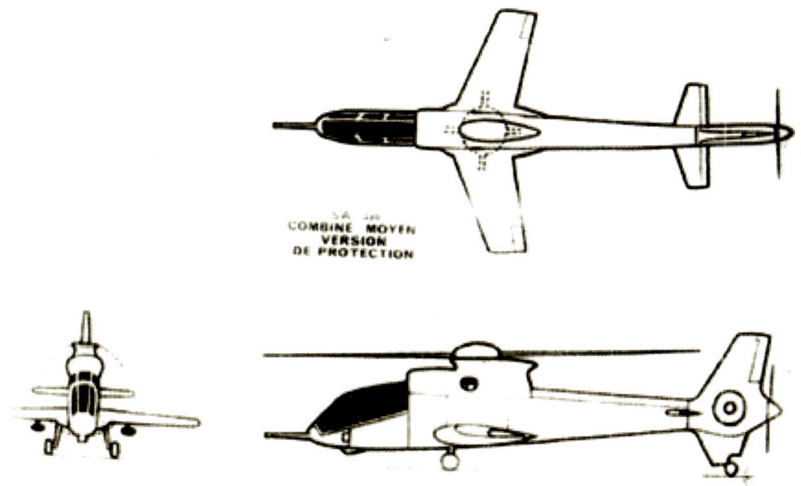

TOP Besides being used for a winged derivative of the Puma, it seems the designation SA 330C was also applied briefly to an armed *'hélicoptère de protection'*, as shown by this Jean Pérard drawing published during the 1960s. *Sud Aviation*

ABOVE The early prototypes of the Anglo-French SA 341 Gazelle had an appearance similar to this 1967 art with a high T-tail. *Sud Aviation*

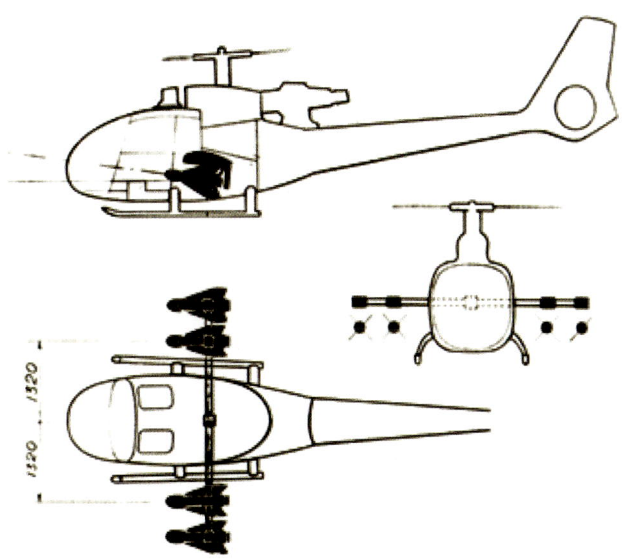

RIGHT The missile-armed version has been widely used by armed forces around the world. However, by the time SA 341 production was in full swing the SS 11 missiles shown here were becoming obsolete. *Sud Aviation*

ABOVE An experimental Gazelle fitted with wings was tested briefly during the 1970s. *Eurocopter via Philippe Boulay*

prototype but the final production variant lost the T-tail in favour of a horizontal plane attached directly to the tail boom. For the anti-tank role the early designs were shown fitted with SS 11 missiles but in the end the newer HOT missile (*Haut subsonique Optiquement Téléguidé Tiré d'un Tube*, High subsonic Optical remote-guided, Tube-launched) was used operationally.

SA 349

This was an experimental winged version of the Gazelle that in December 1972 was fitted with a Turbomeca Astazou XIV. It was hoped to reach a speed in excess of 186mph (300km/h) with this modified machine as part of a study into 'compound' helicopters, but it was not pursued.

SA 350 Rotojet

This compound aircraft, in which the rotor was moved by a jet of air bled from the turbojet and ejected at mid-blade, was designed in 1966 as the possible successor to the Gazelle (which itself had then still to begin its flight testing). The early design used an Alouette cockpit but extended into a fully faired fuselage and ended in a conventional tail. It had wings and the rotor could rotate freely during forward flight when the turbojet was devoted fully to propulsion. An unspecified turbojet was housed in a pod on top of the fuselage and exhausted through either the rotor nozzles or through a conventional rear nozzle, and the shoulder-mounted wings could serve both as a lift device to alleviate the rotor's load when in autogiro mode (at speed) and as a support for the weapon attachment points. The conventional undercarriage retracted into the fuselage and it was hoped to reach a speed of 249mph (400km/h) with this machine.

A year later the design had been developed further – the turbojet was now installed inside the fuselage and exhausted through twin side nozzles and the wings had been moved to a low position, while the estimated speed had been brought down to a more realistic 218mph (350km/h). A maximum load of 1,102lb (500kg) could be carried internally or 441lb (200kg) under a sling and the various roles envisioned for this machine at the time covered military reconnaissance, anti-tank with missiles, search and rescue or mountain rescue, VIP transport and crop spraying. In the late 1960s there was considerable

Sud SA 350 Rotojet (1968)	
Status	project
Rotor diameter	11ft 6in (3.50m) approx
span	
Length	22ft 0in (6.70m) approx
Rotor disc area	-
Gross weight	3,307lb (1,500kg)
Powerplant	one Astazou XIV
Maximum speed/Height	218mph (350km/h)
Armament/load	-

BELOW In 1967-69 Sud Aviation put a lot of effort into the design of a high-speed helicopter designated the SA 350. *Sud Aviation*

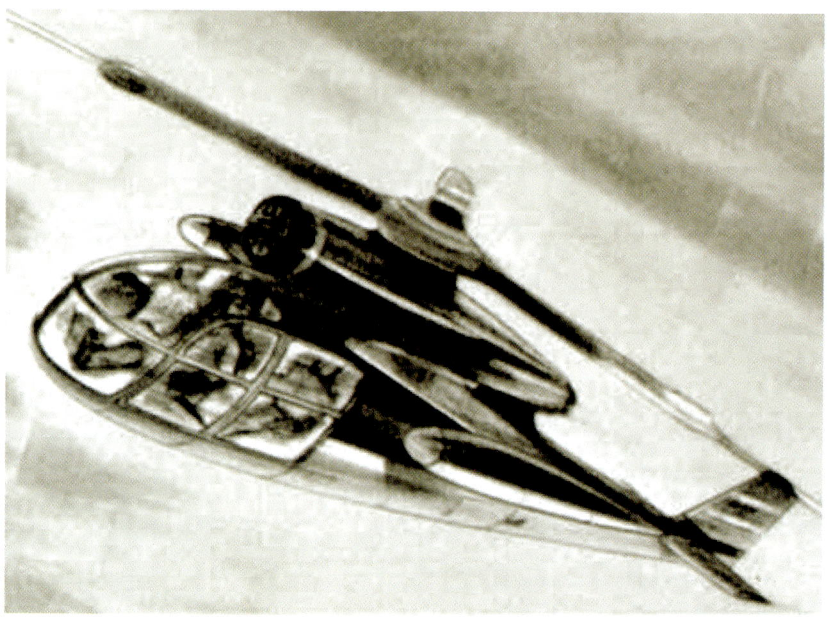

optimism that this design would be successful but it was not to be, the Gazelle and Ecureuil (Squirrel) light helicopters winning through, and the project was abandoned circa 1969.

SA 360

From the early design work carried out in around 1968 the SA 360 was seen as the replacement for the Alouette III, so therefore it was named originally the Super Alouette (because, of course, earlier there had been a Super Frelon). In 1971 a heavily armed version with six to eight HOT missiles and a 7.62mm gun belly turret was rumoured following the presentation of a Gazelle mock-up in this form at that year's Satory Armaments Show. While the cockpit section was obviously inspired by the Alouette, the drive was extrapolated from the Gazelle with its 'semi-rigide' rotor (but with four blades instead of three) and most visibly with its fenestron. The SA 360-001 made its maiden flight on 2 June 1972 powered by an Astazou XVI giving 980hp (1,315kW), but it was subsequently re-engined with a more powerful 1,045hp (1,400kW) Astazou XVIII and flew for the first time with this powerplant on 4 May 1973. The name Cigalon (young cicada) was also suggested, but Dauphin (Dolphin) was finally selected.

SA 360C

In 1977 a production Dauphin was taken out of the series (airframe N° 1011) and fitted with a skid landing gear, and from then on this was to become the standard.

SA 365

A Dauphin variant originally proposed with two Turbomeca Ariel power units. The landing gear was to be retractable.

SA 365M

Military variant offered in 1985 powered by two Turbomeca TM 333 1M engines that could carry 20mm guns in pods or up to eight HOT anti-tank missiles. (Note: it is uncertain if

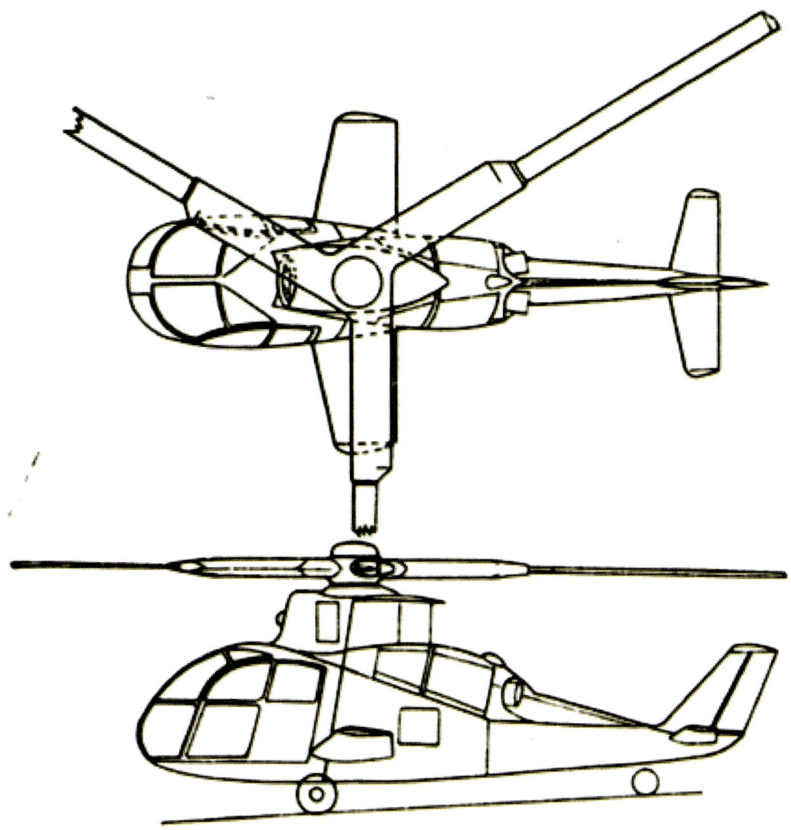

TOP Although only civilian scenes were depicted in the promotional art created for the SA 350, military versions would no doubt have been produced as well. *Sud Aviation*

ABOVE This two-view drawing depicting the general appearance of the new SA 350 design. *Sud Aviation*

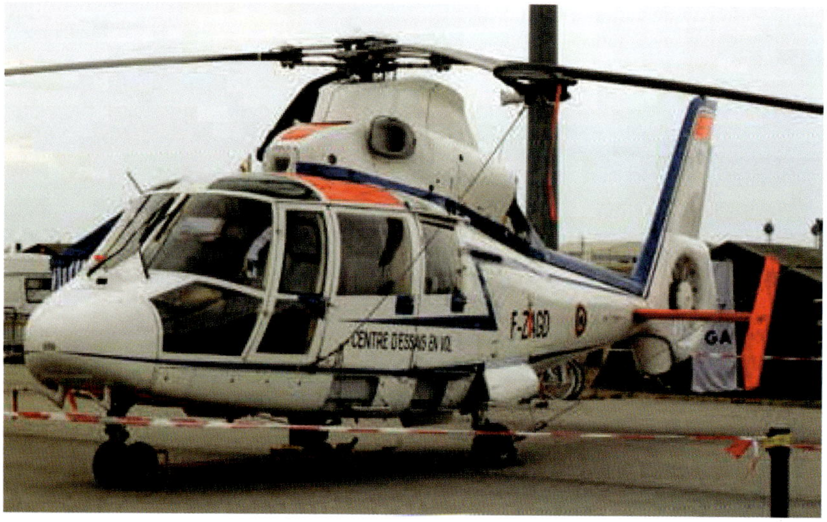

ABOVE **A Dauphin AS 365N of the Centre d'Essais en Vol (Flight Test Centre) photographed at Istres in 2010.** *Franck Journet*

the TM 333 1 was produced. There are references to a TM 333 2 but the Dauphin I is mentioned as being fitted with the Astazou XVIII. A 'TM 333' does not feature in a list of Turbomeca products of this period and it is possible that TM 333 could be a technical name – 'Turbo Motor 333' – with Astazou XVIII being the commercial title.)

AS 350 Ecureull

The military version, the AS 350L1, appeared in 1985 fitted with a new rotor and a more powerful 693hp (930kW) Turbomeca Ariel 1D. Series production began in 1986. From 1990 the AS 350L1 was relabelled AS 550 (from 1 January 1990 military variant designations started with the digit '5'), and in America the Ecureuil was named AStar (variants AS 350C and AS 350D).

Unnamed Eurocopter Design

During the 1990s Eurocopter produced a design for an attack helicopter, which was duly patented (although no weapon is apparent on the drawings, the tandem configuration of the crew position is a sure clue of the intended gunship role). This design is far removed from the Tiger helicopter but has a few features that evoke early

BELOW LEFT **A perspective view of the Eurocopter attack helicopter design.** *Eurocopter*

BOTTOM LEFT **An Ecureuil AS 550 Ecureuil of the Armée de l'Air seen at Istres in 2010 with air commandos on board.** *Franck Journet*

BELOW **In recent years Eurocopter has designed the still-classified Tiger helicopter, but it has also proposed other designs in the attack helicopter category, such as this machine patented during the 1980s.** *Eurocopter*

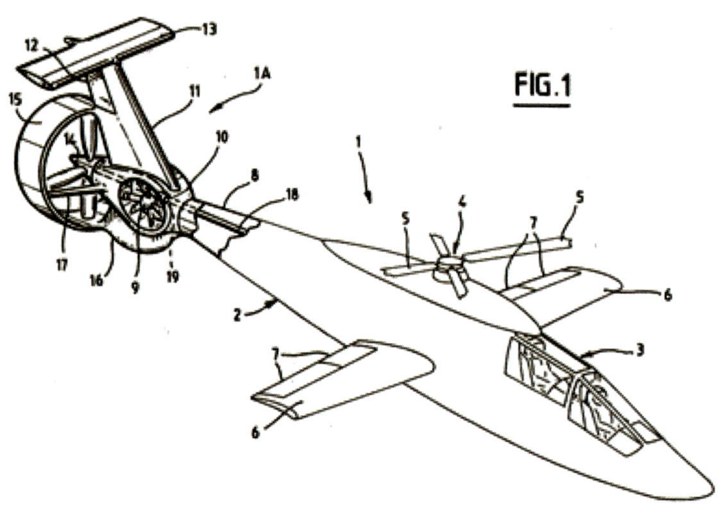

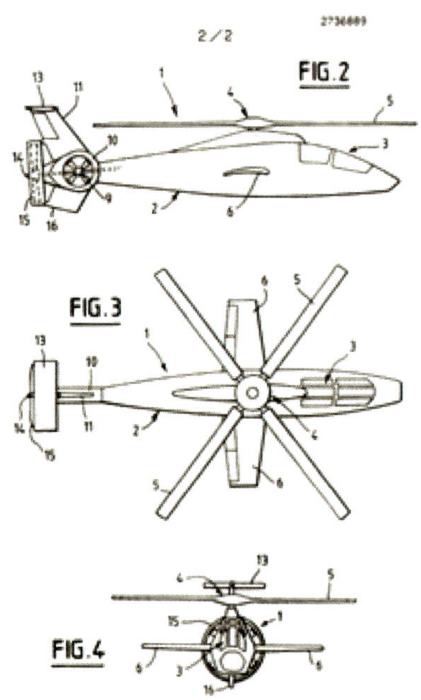

Puma studies of thirty years before, such as the faired rear propulsion propeller, fenestron, and wings with control surfaces.

SNCASO SO 1100 Ariel

This design was laid down in the months immediately following the Liberation. It was intended to be a cheap, compact machine for the suburban feeder liner and aero taxi roles but the type was only built as a demonstrator with room for a pilot and a passenger. The aircraft was powered by a 170hp (127kW) Mathis and it was designed to be used in helicopter mode only for take-off and landing. In this phase the rotor was driven by ramjet nozzles at the tip of the rotor blades, compressed air being fed through the Mathis engine. Once in flight, however, the rotor would be disengaged and put into autogiro mode while the power of the engine would be directed to the pusher propeller. This propeller was encased in a circular

TOP The first helicopter design by SNCASO after the war was the SO 1100, which at the time was conceived as a compact design for use in an urban/suburban environment. *Revue Aéronautique*

ABOVE An early wind tunnel model of the Ariel I. *José Fernandez*

BELOW LEFT However, the egg-shaped Ariel I proved unsuccessful and grew a tail. *José Fernandez*

BELOW RIGHT ... and a more powerful engine as the Ariel II, which is now preserved at the ***Musée de l'Air et de l'Espace***. *J.C. Carbonel* (Information on next page)

SNCASO SO 1100 Ariel	
Status	prototype
Rotor diameter	32ft 10in (10.00m)
Length	13ft 9.5in (4.20m)
Rotor disc area	845sq ft (78.50sq m)
Gross weight	1,698lb (770kg)
Powerplant	one Mathis G-7 170hp (127kW)
Maximum speed/Height	93mph (150km/h)
Armament/load	none

ring that served three functions – as a shroud, it provided support for the triple rudder, and it gave protection to the ground crew. The rotor could be folded for storage. The SO 1100 Ariel flew for the first time on 13 May 1947, though still tethered to the ground. It flew again on 15 October 1947 with the propeller shroud removed, but the idea of converting from helicopter mode to autogiro mode in flight was eventually dropped.

SO 1100 Ariel II

This was an SO 1100 modified by the addition of a longer tail and it first flew on 7 March 1949. Two more prototypes were built along these lines, the first making its maiden flight on 21 April 1950.

SO 1120 Ariel III

This design introduced the use of a Turbomeca Artouste turbine instead of the Mathis piston engine used on the previous designs. Test flights were carried out by pilot Claude Dellys and an engineer called Provensal from 18 April 1951 and, because the machine's centre of gravity was different depending on whether it flew with a single pilot or with two passengers, there were two positions for the batteries.

BELOW **Finally, it used a turboshaft engine as the Ariel III. This is a contemporary drawing of the SO 1120 Ariel III.** *via J.C. Carbonel*

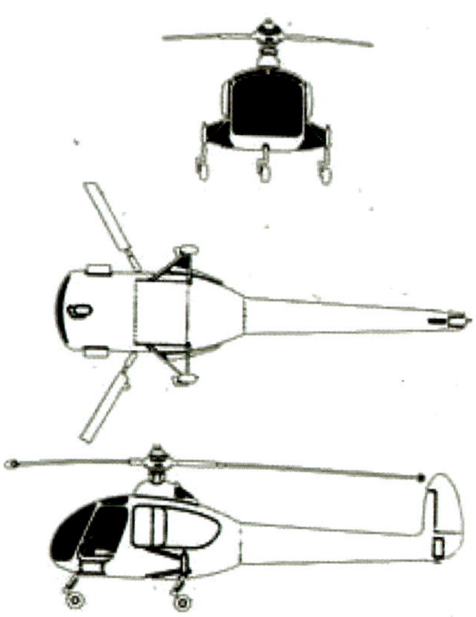

TOP **A later effort with the jet-copter concept, the SO 1221 Djinn at last proved to be successful.** *José Fernandez*

ABOVE **In this very bucolic setting we see the prototype SO 1220, a single-seater.** *SNCASO*

SNCASO SO 1120 Ariel III	
Status	prototype
Rotor diameter	35ft 5in (10.80m)
Length	27ft 2in (8.28m)
Rotor disc area	986sq ft (91.60sq m)
Gross weight	2,646lb (1,200kg)
Powerplant	one Artouste 220hp (164kW)
Maximum speed/Height	112mph (180km/h)
Armament/load	none

SO 1221 Djinn

The Djinn (wind spirit of the Arabian desert) was a compressed air-powered helicopter that first appeared in 1952. The air was compressed by a Turboméca Artouste engine and ejected through nozzles integrated within the blades. This simplified the propulsion/lift system considerably, it reduced noise and made the aircraft cheaper all round. The Djinn was

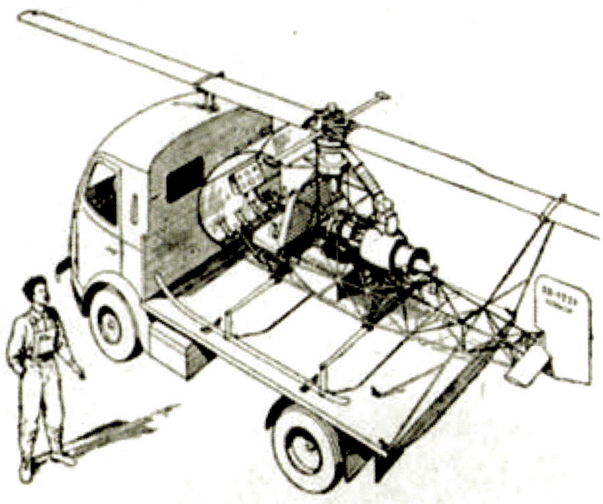

ABOVE LEFT The Djinn was much touted for its ability to operate from a flatbed truck. *SNCASO*

ABOVE RIGHT A Djinn is now preserved at the *Musée de l'Air et de l'Espace*. *J.C. Carbonel*

BELOW This SNCASO advertisement depicts the Djinn as 'a true air-motorcycle'. Note that it is shown taking off from a truck. *SNCASO*

inspired by the wartime work of Friedrich Doblhoff and Theodor Laufer with a design called the WNF 342, and after the war Laufer went on to work in France for SNCASO. The SO 1220 single-seater, which had a simple uncovered airframe with an exposed pilot's seat and was used to test the powerplant, was then developed into the SO 1221 two-seat version together with an interesting new concept – a helicopter carried, ready-to-fly, on a truck. The first prototype, the SO 1220-01, first flew on 2 January 1953 with an 28.22ft (8.60m) diameter rotor, and was followed by 1220-02 which made its maiden flight on 26 June that year fitted with a larger 32.81ft (10.00m) diameter rotor. The SO 1221

SO 1221 Djinn

Status	production
Rotor diameter	36ft 1in (11.00m)
Length	17ft 4.5in (5.30m)
Rotor disc area	-
Gross weight	1,764lb (800kg)
Powerplant	one Palouste 240hp (179kW)
Maximum speed/Height	81mph (130km/h)
Armament/load	-

ABOVE Close-up of the jet exhaust nozzle of another preserved Djinn, this one at the Helicopter Museum, Weston-super-Mare. *J.C. Carbonel*

first flew on 16 December 1953 and in all 178 examples were subsequently produced, some being used by the German Luftwaffe and the US Army.

SO 1300 Farfadet (Leprechaun)

This was a convertible helicopter design first flown in 1953. The rotor was powered by a 360hp (268kW) Turbomeca Arrius turboprop while the two-bladed propeller was driven by an Artouste II, also giving 360hp (268kW) of power! The prototype was designated SO 1310 and could carry two passengers (in addition to the pilot) or two litters (a litter is a rigid stretcher used for casualty evacuation). The aircraft would take off as a helicopter, but during forward flight its lift was provided by the wings and by the auto-rotating rotor, the engine driving the rotor having been shut down. Of the two 1300 Farfadet prototypes built only the first ever flew, taking to the air for the first time on 1 July 1953, and for this flight a Turbomeca Marcadau was installed due to the unavailability of the Artouste engine. An enlarged version able to twenty passengers on a 250 miles (400km) flight was also designed called the SO 1340, while a final variant, the SO 1350, was intended to be a freight machine or a flying crane and for this reason it reverted to being a pure helicopter.

BELOW The SO 1310 Farfadet was a trials helicopter built along the lines of the experiments made in UK by Fairey Aviation. During flight the main rotor was disconnected from the turboprop and left to rotate freely. *José Fernandez*

SO 1310	
Status	prototype
Rotor diameter	36ft 9in (11.20m), wing span 20ft 8in (6.30m)
Length	?
Rotor disc area	-
Gross weight	?
Powerplant	one Arrius and one Artouste II 360hp (268kW) each
Maximum speed/Height	211mph (340km/h)
Armament/load	two passengers

SO 1340	
Status	project
Rotor diameter	78ft 9in (24.00m)
Length	42ft 8.5in (13.02m)
Rotor disc area	-
Gross weight	14,000lb (6,350kg)
Powerplant	four Artouste III 600hp (447kW)
Maximum speed/Height	106mph (170km/h)
Armament/load	twenty passengers

SO 1350	
Status	project
Rotor diameter	78ft 9in (24.00m)
Length	?
Rotor disc area	-
Gross weight	14,770lb (6,700kg)
Powerplant	three Artouste III of 600hp (447kW) each
Maximum speed/Height	99mph (160km/h)
Armament/load	-

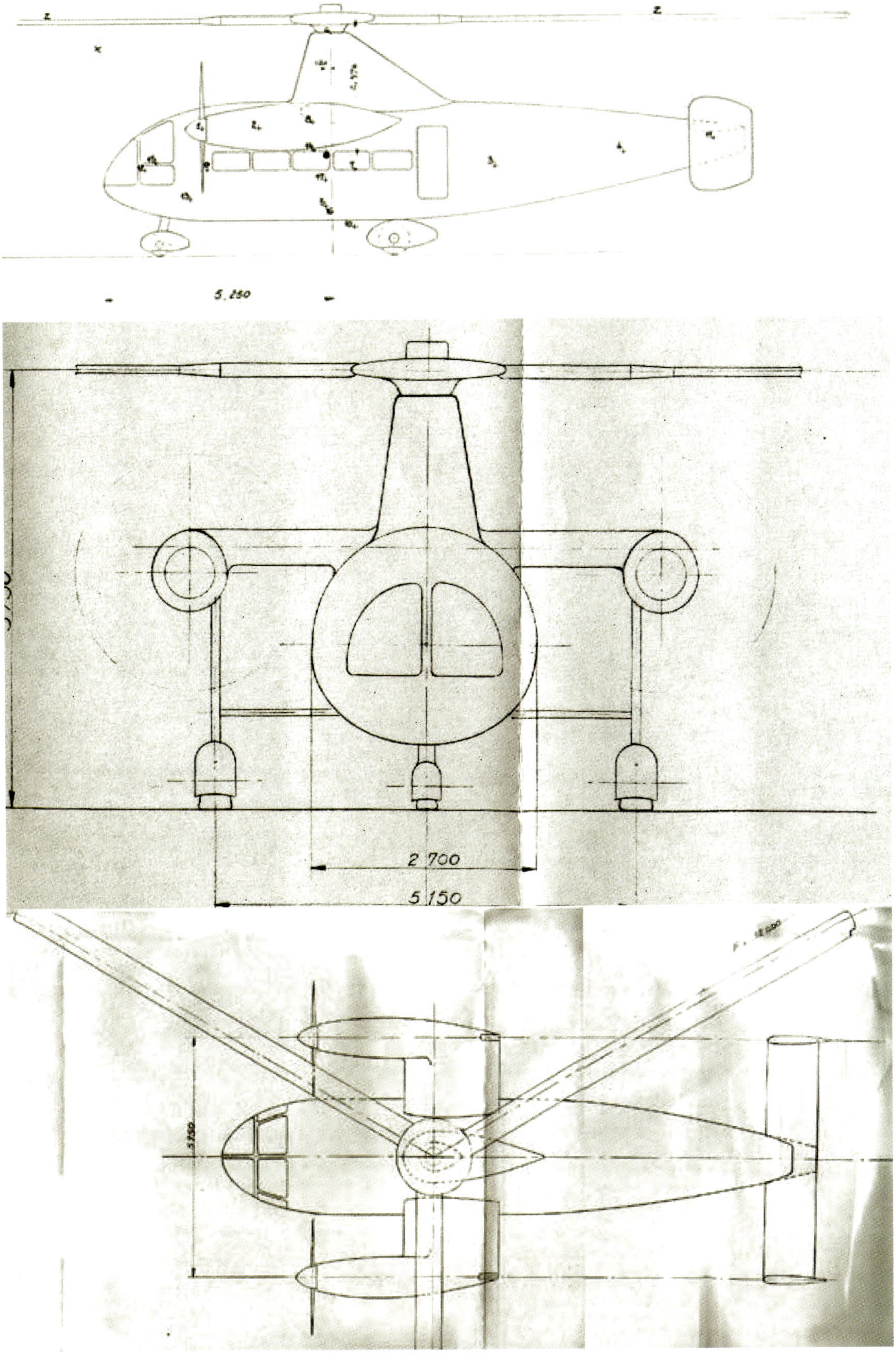

ABOVE Three-view drawing of the SO 1340, a small convertible helicopter. *Philippe Ricco*

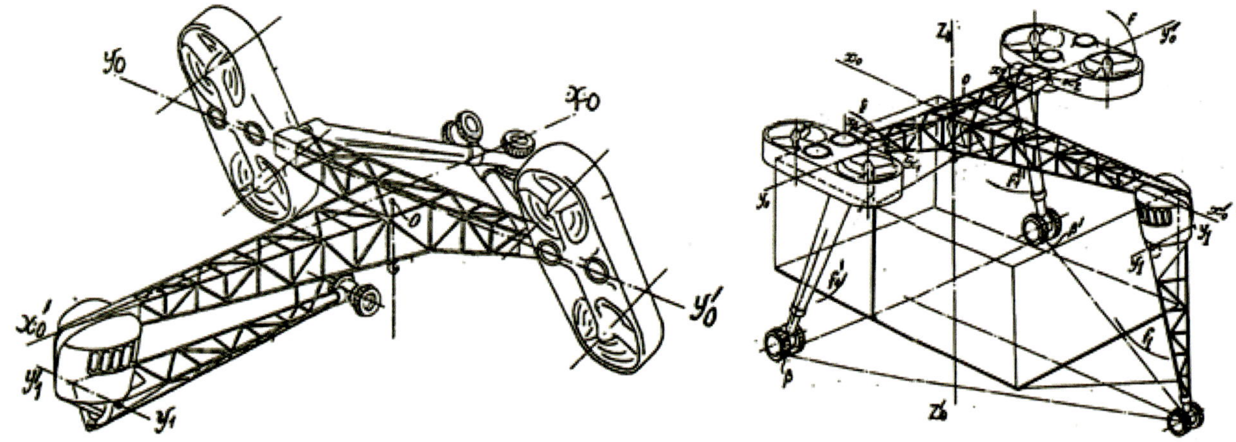

ABOVE These two drawings depict a flying crane developed by Nord Aviation as part of its research on faired propellers. The left view shows the machine in flight without any load and with its spidery legs folded over, the right view sees it with the legs extended and a large load attached. *Author from a Nord patent*

Flying Crane Helicopter

Nord Aviation VTOL Crane

As part of the research on ducted fans (see Chapter Eight), in 1968 Jean Soulez-Larivière, the chief engineer of the ducted fan department at Nord Aviation, designed what was called a 'Vertical Take-Off and Landing Crane Aircraft'. This design appeared to be an update of the wartime Focke-Achgelis Fa 284 Fliegende Kran aircraft with its simple truss structure. Here, however, in lieu of rotors, two power packs with two turbine-driven ducted fans each were mounted laterally and these were able to tilt to provide lift or forward flight. In an unusual, but probably not very efficient way (because the added complexity of the system more than compensated for the reduction in drag), the two front landing gear legs folded forward while the rear leg would fold underneath the backbone truss (this could be done only in ferry mode, without any load being carried). Again similar to the wartime Fa 284, the cockpit was placed at the extreme rear to enable the crew to view their load during the complete flight. No technical data is available for this aircraft.

BELOW The only flying crane actually put into production was the small SA 315B Lama, but in fact this achieved fame serving with the Indian Armed Forces more as a high-altitude helicopter. *Aerospatiale*

Sud-Aviation

Nord Aviation SA 315 B Lama

First flown in March 1969, this little machine was a success on the civil market but not with the military.

SA 321 Super Frelon

A flying crane derivative was reported as being studied in 1965.

Sud 'Hélicoptère Grue'

In 1962 Charles Marchetti, who had not yet left Sud Aviation to establish his own company (see Volume I), designed a flying crane helicopter that was intended to 'straddle' its load. Twin girder-type fuselages housed the pilot and co-pilot on the left in a widely glazed cockpit, which also incorporated seats for three passengers. Two five-bladed rotors were driven by turbines of an unspecified type and these were linked via a common axle so that, in the event of the failure of one engine, power from the remaining one could be distributed equally to the two rotors. Although the drawing shows the machine straddling a container, the latter's dimensions do not appear to be specified, so it is impossible to deduce the overall dimensions of the helicopter from the container.

SNIAS Aerospatiale 'Jumbo Hélicoptère'

In 1970 *Aviation Magazine* reported that SNIAS was working 'officially' on a jumbo-size helicopter having an in-flight weight of 'many hundreds of tons'. The magazine speculated that this machine would use the 'rotojet' concept with a six-bladed rotor driven by the thrust of nozzles mounted on independent arms.

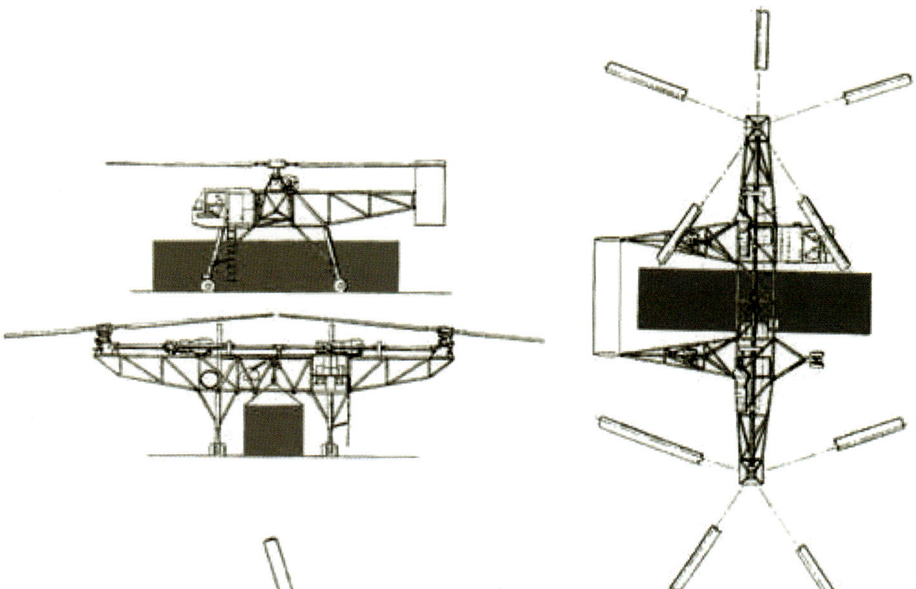

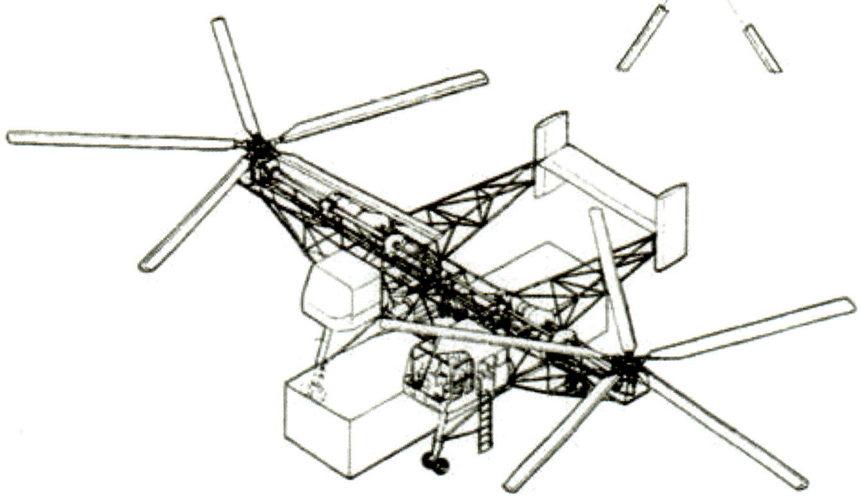

ABOVE **This three-view represents Sud Aviation's vision of a large flying crane. A standard commercial container is shown in grey as a potential load.** *Author from a Sud patent*

BELOW **A perspective view of Sud's flying crane.** *Author from a Sud patent*

Chapter Ten
Assault Transports

ABOVE The Breguet Br 941S began its American tour in Eastern Airlines livery. *Breguet document/Author's collection*

Since the end of the Second World War the French Army has been very sensitive to the issue of assault transport aircraft. This all began with General Demetz, who in 1945 was put in charge of rebuilding the French paratroop forces. The fiasco at Arnhem when British paratroops were overwhelmed by German Panzer units had left an impression on him, and so he asked for the creation of two paratroop divisions under the control of the *Armée de Terre* (the land Army) when, up until this time, the paratroop units had been subordinated to the *Armée de l'Air*. These two divisions were to be equipped with tanks and artillery, like a ground division, and the idea was to give the paratroopers the ability to tackle opposing regular forces on equal terms and not to restrict them to commando-style operations or short-range bridgehead actions. However, this charter required that the new division be equipped with armoured vehicles and other heavy hardware, and it also implied that the Air Force should receive the appropriate transport aircraft. This early idea was quickly rescinded but the thought of having medium-sized transports able to carry bulky loads including light combat vehicles and land in the combat zone would permeate the *Armée de l'Air*'s opinions towards transport aircraft well into the 1960s.

The First Generation

The NC 211 Cormoran was designed immediately after the war and the Breguet 'Deux-Ponts' was adapted for military use soon afterwards. The Cormoran was a failure and the Deux-Ponts was not produced in any quantity, but the next project, the Nord Noratlas, would prove a success. In the meantime, just about every manufacturer with a transport or airliner project in its catalogue tried to sell it to the military services. The very innovative Hurel-Dubois company is a special case, its high aspect ratio aircraft concept being used for everything from airliners to dedicated cattle transport aircraft to special agent insertion aircraft (the latter something like an overgrown Westland Lysander!). Even the highly successful Caravelle was offered as a military transport during the 1950s.

Breguet Deux-Ponts Family

This aircraft began life as a land variant of the Br 730 flying boat built before the war, but it was redesigned immediately after the conflict had ended, renamed Br 761 Deux-Ponts (two deck or double deck) and first flew on 15 February 1949. The Br 761 was produced in limited quantities (just twenty aircraft in all and in different versions), but its unmistakable size and shape made it a well-known type during the 1950s.

Br 760

This designation was attributed to a wartime study, extrapolated from the Br 730, for a double-deck transport

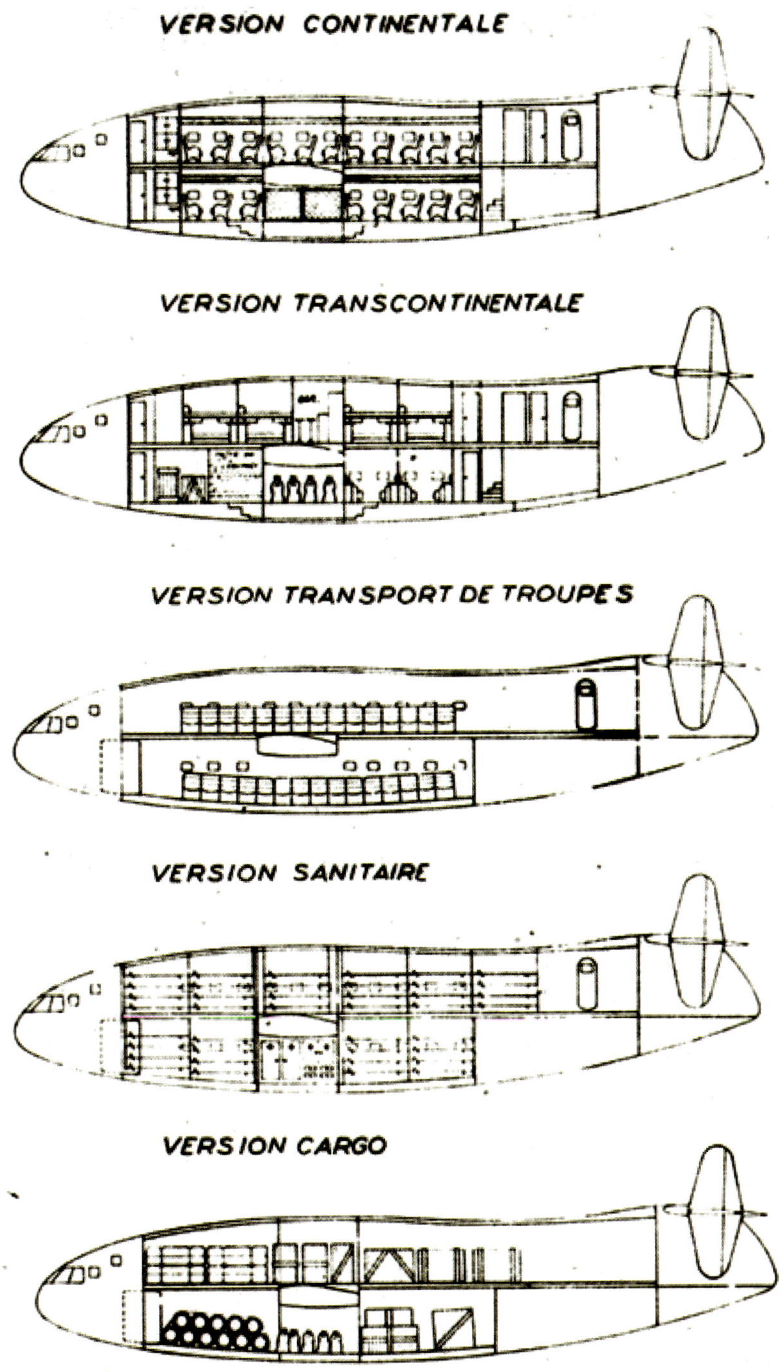

ABOVE **Variants of the Br 760 from top to bottom: *Continentale* (medium range), *Transcontinentale* (long range with special accommodation for passengers), troop transport, *Sanitaire* (air ambulance), and cargo freighter.** *Author's collection/ Breguet document*

aircraft. It had a fixed landing gear but with retractable wheel covers for the main undercarriage. This configuration was soon dropped and by August 1944 a tricycle undercarriage had been adopted.

Br 761

This is the designation of the first prototype fitted with 1,450hp (1,081kW) SNECMA/Gnome et Rhône 14R engines, which in fact were found to be underpowered after its first flight on 15 February 1949. Consequently the three subsequent production aircraft were fitted with 2,100hp (1,566kW) Pratt & Whitney R-2800-B31s as the Br 761S (Breguet had anticipated an order and put its factory into production very quickly, and possibly too quickly, with the original choice of engine). The Br 761Ss built were used by various operators, including Air Algerie, Silver City and ultimately the *Armée de l'Air*, from 1953. As military freighters they were employed on assessing the transportation of bulky loads such as light tanks (the AMX 13/75 tank or the EBR eight-wheel scout cars).

Br 762

This variant would have been fitted with a Bristol Hercules 630 powerplant with the intention of exporting the aircraft to the British market.

Br 763 Provence

The production version fitted with more powerful 2,400hp (1,790kW) Pratt & Whitney R-2800-CB 16s, portholes on the lower deck and a revised tail. Originally used by Air France, these aircraft were transferred to the *Armée de l'Air* in 1964.

Br 764

This designation number was assigned to the unbuilt ASW variant (see Chapter Eleven).

Br 765

Originally this designation was applied in 1952 to a larger version with a

Breguet Deux-Ponts Br 765

Status	production
Span	141ft 1in (43.00m)
Length	95ft 0in (28.95m)
Gross wing area	?
Gross weight	119,511lb (54,210kg)
Powerplant	four R2800-CA16 2,400hp (1,790kW)
Maximum speed/Height	277mph (445km/h)
Equipment	130 soldiers with kit or 37,478lb (17,000kg) of freight

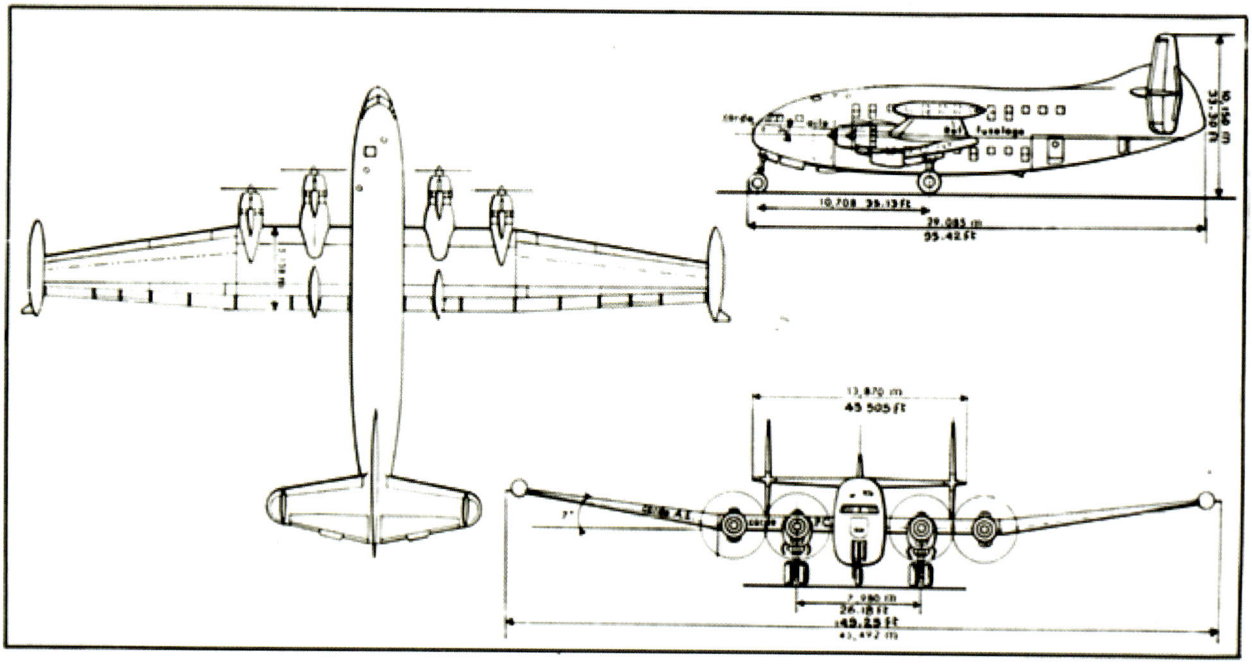

ABOVE The Breguet Br 760 Deux-Ponts family was considered successful, although few aircraft were actually produced. This is a three-view drawing of the Br 765 Sahara military transport with redesigned rear doors. *Author's collection*

bilobed (split deck) fuselage stretched by 9ft 10in (3m) (bilobed referred to a section of fuselage formed in the shape of a figure eight to allow both decks to be pressurised independently if required). The design was intended to be a competitor to the Lockheed Super Constellation on the North and South Atlantic routes and would have been fitted with four 3,750hp (2,796kW) Wright Cyclone 18 engines.

Br 765 Sahara

This real Br 765 was a variant specifically adapted to military needs with extra fuel and redesigned rear-loading doors. Four examples were produced.

Br 766

The Br 766 was to have been a variant fitted with a pressurised fuselage to carry 150 passengers and three tons of freight. The powerplant would have consisted of four Rolls-Royce Tyne turboprops.

Br 767

A variant of the Br 766 with either Bristol BE.25 turboprops or even Rolls-Royce Conway turbojets.

Un-designated Hurel Breguet Project

In 1953 Maurice Hurel studied the use of the ultra-high aspect ratio wing with reinforcing struts specifically to go on the Breguet Deux-Ponts. This would have taken the aircraft's total take-off weight up to 132,275lb (60,000kg) and, as reported by *Aviation Magazine*, '*The new machine constitutes a satisfactory reply to the hopes of the users regarding a transatlantic freighter aircraft.*'

Breguet Br 891

This was Breguet's reply to the call for proposals ultimately won by the Noratlas (below). It was a derivative of the Br 890 Mercure (Mercury) civilian airliner, of which only one unit was built. The Br 891 was also built as a single prototype, Breguet selecting a

BELOW Illustration showing the Br 765 Sahara in long-range '4,000km' (2,485 miles) configuration with wingtip fuel tanks. *Author's collection/Breguet document*

ABOVE **Advertising for the Breguet Br 89 Mars medium military transport. One prototype was built.** *Author's collection/Breguet document*

side-hinged rear fuselage instead of the podded fuselage used on the Fairchild Packet (and on the Noratlas), and a specific feature of this project was a 'toboggan' door in the floor to air drop jeeps! This latter device was patented in 1951. (Note: in all three aircraft of the Breguet type Br 890 series were built – one prototype Br 890 with two Hercules engines, one Br 891 with two Gnome Rhone 14R Mars engines and one Br 892 with four Renault 12S engines).

Breguet Br 891	
Status	prototype
Span	100ft 5.5in (30.62m)
Length	70ft 10.5in (21.60m)
Gross wing area	1,086.0sq ft (101.00sq m)
Gross weight	37,147lb (16,850kg)
Powerplant	two SNECMA 14R 1,600hp (1,193kW)
Maximum speed/Height	261mph (420km/h) at 19,160ft (5,840m)
Equipment	Max load five × 772lb (350kg) = three jeeps

Fouga
Fouga CM 101 R

Fouga CM 101R	
Status	prototype
Span	87ft 7in (26.70m)
Length	58ft 8.5in (17.90m)
Gross wing area	773.1sq ft (71.90sq m)
Gross weight	19,012lb (8,624kg)
Powerplant	two SNECMA Argus 12S 580hp (433kW) and two Piméné 248lb (1.1kN)
Maximum speed/Height	174mph (280km/h)
Equipment	fourteen passengers

BELOW **Period three-view drawing of the CM 100 transport.** *Author's collection/Fouga document*

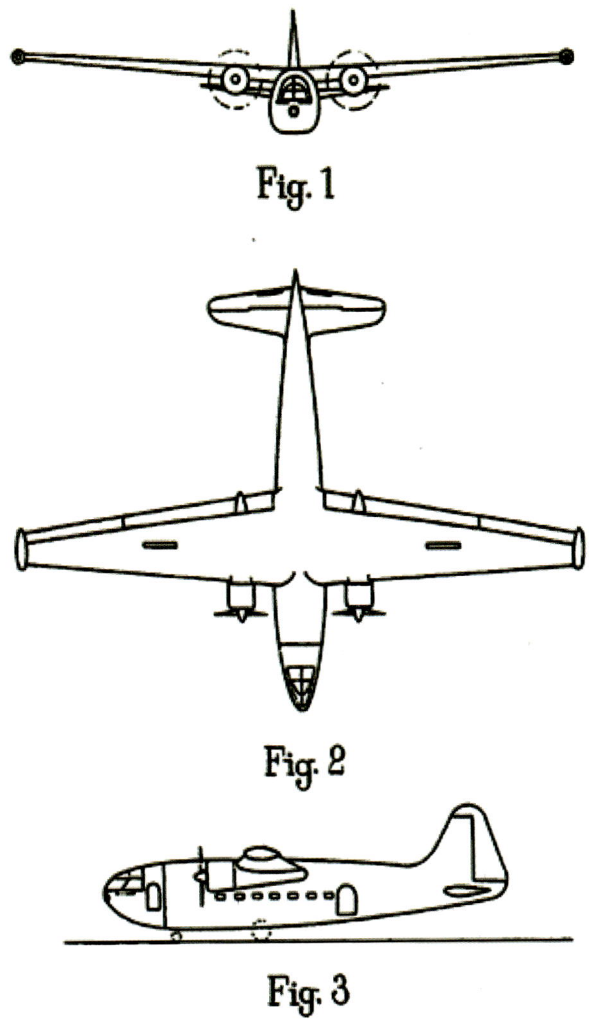

ABOVE The prototype of the Fouga CM 100 light transport was developed from the CM 10 assault glider. *José Fernandez*

Working forward from the CM 10 assault glider, Fouga offered a small transport called the CM 100 powered by two SNECMA Argus 12S engines. The CM 101R was a modification of the original prototype with a pair of Turbomeca Piméné turbojets added to provide a boost in power at take-off. While designed to a civilian requirement, due to its STOL capabilities the CM 101R was also looked upon as an assault transport.

Fouga CM 103 R

Projected variant of the CM 101R with the Piménés replaced by more powerful Marboré II jets.

Hurel-Dubois

The Société de Construction des Avions Hurel-Dubois was incorporated in 1947, was, as of January 1st 1955, split, into two independent entities, the *Société de Construction* in charge of building aircraft and the *Société de Brevets HD* to manage the patents and the know-how pertaining to *Commandant* Maurice Hurel's inventions (Dubois was the financial side of the founding members).

BELOW The Hurel-Dubois HD 10 proof of concept aircraft is now preserved in the *Musée de l'Air et de l'Espace*. *J.C. Carbonel*

HD 10

The HD 10 was a technology demonstrator and was first revealed at the 1949 Paris Air Show. Originally fitted with a Mathis 40hp (30kW) engine, it first flew on 25 August 1948 piloted by Hurel himself. This first flight was difficult, the machine undeniably being underpowered, so it was later refitted with a 75hp (56kW) Praga engine that gave it a maximum speed of 165mph (265km/h).

HD 10	
Status	prototype
Span	39ft 4.5in (12.00m)
Length	18ft 0.5in (5.50m)
Gross wing area	48.0sq ft (4.46sq m)
Gross weight	1,151lb (522kg)
Powerplant	one Mathis 40hp (30kW); replaced by one Praga 75hp (56kW)
Maximum speed/Height	158mph (255km/h) at ground level
Equipment	none

HD 31

This design was proposed by Ingénieur Hurel in 1951. One prototype was built and this first flew on 27 January 1953. While being evaluated by the *Centre d'Essais en Vol* at Marignane

HD 31	
Status	prototype
Span	147ft 7.5in (45.00m)
Length	72ft 2in (22.00m)
Gross wing area	1,075.2sq ft (100sq m)
Gross weight	29,762lb (13,500kg)
Powerplant	two SNECMA 14X 700hp (522kW)
Maximum speed/Height	174mph (280km/h) at 9.840ft (3,000m)
Equipment	up to 8,818lb (4,000kg) load

LEFT Viewed from above the HD 31 illustrates perfectly the long, thin, strut-supported wing that was the feature of all Hurel aircraft. *José Fernandez*

it received a few modifications, the most remarkable being that the wings (originally perfectly horizontal) were given a few degrees of dihedral to the outer portion outside the engine nacelles. While originally planned to be used as test bed for various items of equipment intended for the jet-propelled HD 45, it did see active service with the *Marine Nationale* with Escadrille 10S. In early 1955 it was sent to Africa for hot climate trials.

HD 32

Designed as a transport aircraft, the HD 32 was assessed with various internal arrangements, including fittings for the transportation of livestock, either ten cattle or eighty-five sheep. However, the version that saw two examples built was an assault transport for the *Armée de l'Air* and these were used mostly to resupply outposts during the war in Algeria. The two examples differed in their powerplant, with one having the 1,200hp (895kW) Pratt & Whitney R-1830-92 and the other 790hp (588kW) Wright R-1820 Cyclones. The second airframe had Pratt & Whitney engines fitted to enable a direct comparison to be made with the Douglas DC-3, because Hurel took this classic aircraft as a reference when designing (and promoting) his aeroplanes. This also had a single tail fin when the other prototype had twin fins, and it first flew on 11 February 1955. The Wright Cyclone was favoured by would-be customer Air France, which at the time was rumoured to have ordered twenty-four machines. The Cyclone prototype had flown little more than a year earlier, on

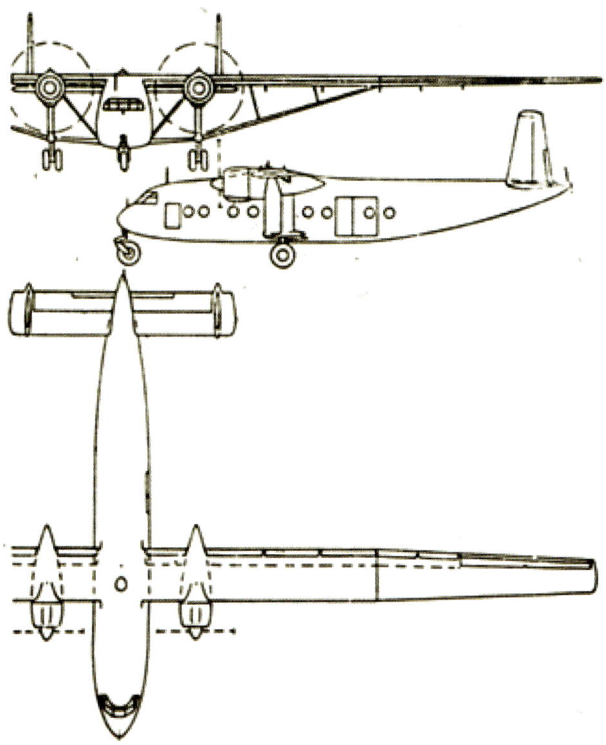

MIDDLE LEFT Three-view drawing of the HD 31. *Author's collection/Hurel-Dubois*

LEFT The first full-size aircraft produced under the Hurel-Dubois designation was the HD 31 seen here in 1953. The machine was to serve with Escadrille 10S of the Marine Nationale. *José Fernandez*

TOP **Two HD 32s were built and they lived a cloak and dagger life with the French intelligence service, the SDECE.** *José Fernandez*

ABOVE **The prototype HD 32 No. 01 seen on 13 June 1957 during the Paris Air Show.** *Author's collection*

29 December 1953. Another difference between the two was that prototype 01 had round portholes while 02 had square.

The HD 32 was demonstrated to British European Airways (BEA) in 1954 and that included the display of the Cyclone prototype at the British National Air Races at Coventry in June of that year. However, no orders were forthcoming from the UK, although British pilots from BEA and Miles Aircraft later visited France to test fly the aircraft. Consideration was even given in 1955 to the setting up of a British Hurel-Dubois company to promote the ultra-high aspect ratio wings in the UK. Air France had also displayed some interest in using the HD 32 overseas. If the HD 32 had reached production, an agreement had been reached between SNCASE and Hurel-Dubois whereby the assembly of series aircraft would have been undertaken in SNCASE factories.

HD 32/HD 321	
Status	prototypes
Span	147ft 7.5in (45.00m)
Length	72ft 2in (22.00m)
Gross wing area	1,075.2sq ft (100sq m)
Gross weight	44,092lb (20,000kg)
Powerplant	two Wright Cyclone 982C9HE2 1,500hp (1,119kW)
Maximum speed/Height	180mph (290km/h)
Equipment	up to 13,228lb (6,000kg) load

In the second half of 1956 HD 32-02 was modified by having its fuselage stretched and by the replacement of its Pratt & Whitney engines with more powerful Wright 982-C9H1 units of 1,500hp (1,122kW). After being re-engined and stretched the machine became the HD 321 but retained its construction number and so was known as the HD 321-02.

The HD 321-02 was sent to Brazil in late 1956 but then crashed during a test flight on 30 October. While the 321 was flying on its starboard engine only the pilot tried some low speed manoeuvres, but unfortunately the sea was screened by fog and he could only tell how low he was flying from his instruments. He tried to restart the other engine to climb higher but it did not work as intended and the aircraft hit the water.

Prototype 01 began as an HD 31 and was then re-engined as an HD 321 with an elongated fuselage and small vertical fins added to the rear horizontal surfaces. During its life 01 was used at various times by the SDECE and, according to Constantin Melnik (who worked with French Premier Michel Debré from 1958 to 1962 during the War in Algeria), it was bought outright by the French Intelligence Service for covert operations somewhere around 1960-62.

On 5 November 1956, during Operation Mousquetaire (the Anglo-French attack on the Suez Canal), the HD 32 was used as part of Operation Amilcar, an effort to take commando troops behind the Egyptian lines. However, the aircraft never went beyond Cyprus, which was the Anglo-French rear base of operation. Later, the head of Service 7 of the SDECE (in charge of obtaining secret documents), Colonel Marcel Le Roy-Finville, learned that due to a shortage in supplies in East Germany, the duplicates of reports and official documents produced by the East German administrations and ministries were recycled as … toilet paper! On learning where the sewers led, French secret agents began recovering the said refuse and put it in special bags to pass it quickly to the West. The Hurel-Dubois would then land stealthily in a discreet field, be loaded with the bags and fly back to France, where the paper revealed its secrets. However, these nocturnal flights begun to attract attention and the operation was halted.

Another Bondian caper involving the Hurel-Dubois revolved around the Soviet diplomatic pouch, which left France aboard the famous Orient-Express and visited Varna, in Bulgaria, and then Moscow. The idea was to introduce sleep-inducing gas in the train compartment booked by the Soviet couriers and once they were asleep, get into the compartment and microfilm the secret documents. A quite scabrous plan indeed, but at first it did not appear to require an aircraft. However, if the French secret agents did not have enough time to photograph all the documents then they were to throw the diplomatic bags overboard. The Innsbruck-based Hurel-Dubois, which would by that time be flying over the train, would then drop down and pick up the bags without landing (presumably they would have been attached to some devices such as self-inflating balloons, which could then be snatched in flight by the HD 32 and hauled aboard). However, an experiment carried out in France with this idea in mind was not a success and this rather wild scheme was abandoned. It should be noted that the HD 32/321-01 was damaged twice on French airfields, on both occasions while being operated by *Groupement Aérien Mixte* GAM 56 Vaucluse, the French Intelligence Service Squadron!

TOP **Production of the HD 34 reached eight machines and all of them were used by the *Institut Géographique National* (IGN), the agency in charge of mapping France.** *José Fernandez*

ABOVE **One of the ex-IGN HD 34s has been kept in the *Musée de l'Air et de l'Espace*.** *J.C. Carbonel*

HD 321

Originally the HD 321 was to have been a specialised assault transport version.

HD 33

Designation for a military transport version studied in 1953. Its major feature was a reinforced floor and a rear door, which also acted as a ramp to allow vehicles to board and disembark.

HD 331

In 1957 this military transport with a rear ramp was offered in the following sub-variants:

Mission I – assault transport able to carry sixty fully equipped soldiers over a distance of 435 miles (700km).

Mission II – ground surveillance and police, able to loiter for twenty-seven hours with a crew of six including three gunners.

Mission III – rescue aircraft able to carry thirty-two stretchers.

Mission IV – transport able to carry three light trucks.

HD 34

This was the major production version with eight machines being produced for the *Institut Géographique National.* The initial order for four machines was issued on 5 August 1955 and (based on the HD 32) this variant had a new glass nose, a new cockpit and

HD 34	
Status	production
Span	148ft 2in (45.16m)
Length	77ft 5.5in (23.61m)
Gross wing area	1,075.2sq ft (100sq m)
Gross weight	41,005lb (18,600kg)
Powerplant	two Wright Cyclone 982C9HE2 1,500hp (1,119kW)
Maximum speed/Height	174mph 280km/h)
Equipment	-

larger fuel tanks (the fuel capacity was nearly doubled from 792 to 1,320gal [3,600 to 6,000 litres]). The HD 34 made its maiden flight on 26 February 1957 and the examples built were used widely for aerial mapping in either of three configurations:

1. with 5,732lb (2,600kg) of photo equipment on a 746 miles (1,200km) route flying at 124mph (200km/h) and 9,845ft (3,000m).
2. with 5,732lb (2,600kg) of photo equipment on a 994 miles (1,600km) route flying at 174mph (280km/h) and 16,405ft (5,000m).
3. with 1,874lb (850kg) of photo equipment on a 994 miles (1,600km) route flying at 155mph (250km/h) and 22,965ft (7,000m).

HD 35

The HD 35 project was initially a variant of the HD 321 assault transport fitted with a rear ramp. By the end of 1953, however, the HD 35 had been 'demilitarised' and now offered as a 'flying ferry' (that is with a car deck and passenger deck) to the British company Silver City, which showed some interest in the design. At the time it was hoped to have a prototype flying by mid-1954. In the end, however, the HD 35 designation was reassigned to a military proposal for the medium anti-submarine patrol aircraft competition of 1954 (see Chapter Eleven).

HD 36

Proposed in 1955, this was to be a 'flying classroom' variant for the French Navy to be used for training navigators and radar operators. It was not built.

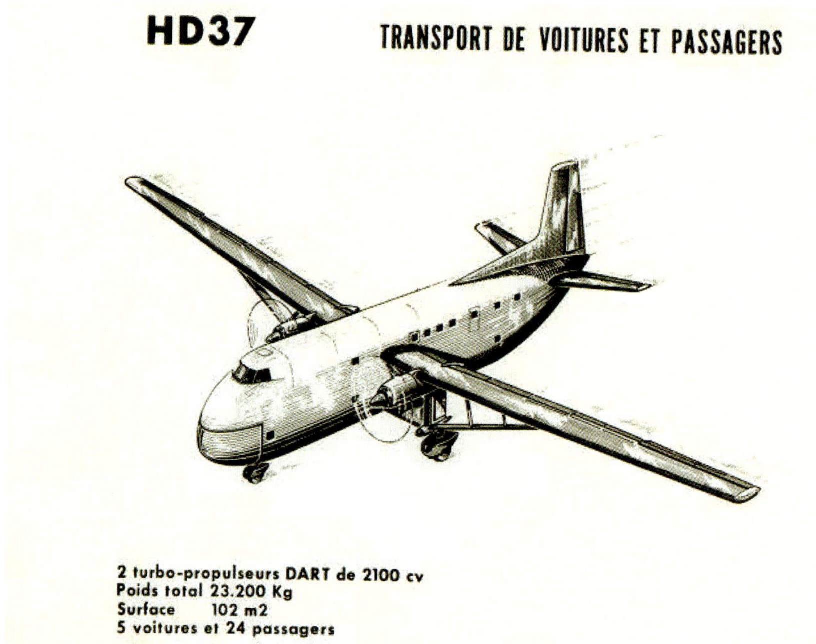

ABOVE The HD 37 was a 'car ferry' design. Author's collection/Hurel-Dubois

HD 37

A project aircraft of the late 1950s intended for the car ferry role. It appears to have been a double decker with the passengers in the rear upper deck and the cars in the front upper deck and the lower deck. Displayed as a cutaway model at the 1959 Paris Air Show, it was quickly forgotten.

HD 37	
Status	project
Span	?
Length	?
Gross wing area	1,096.8sq ft (102sq m)
Gross weight	51,146lb (23,200kg)
Powerplant	two Dart 2,100hp (1,566kW)
Maximum speed/Height	-
Equipment	five cars and twenty-four passengers

HD 40

In 1952 the HD 40 designation was applied to an aircraft that was a sort of sesquiplane (a biplane where usually the lower wing has less than half the surface area of the other wing). Here the lower (stub) wings carried the retractable undercarriage and two turbojets.

HD 40	
Status	project
Span	?
Length	?
Gross wing area	?
Gross weight	?
Powerplant	two turbojets
Maximum speed/Height	-
Equipment	

HD 41

This was a variant of the HD 40 with four turbojets, two being mounted on the lower stub wings and two suspended on the upper wing, where the support mast would join it.

The HD 45 was originally announced

HD 41	
Status	project
Span	?
Length	?
Gross wing area	?
Gross weight	?
Powerplant	four turbojets
Maximum speed/Height	-
Equipment	-

ABOVE Artist's impression of the jet-propelled HD 45 airliner, which was turned down in favour of the Sud Est SE 210 Caravelle. *Author's collection/Hurel-Dubois*

HD 45

in 1952 as a jet version of the HD 32 with two Rolls-Royce Avon RA16s, the statement adding that a contract had been obtained in October; however, in the following month it was revealed that the commission in charge of civilian transports had selected the Sud Est SE 210 (the future Caravelle). The HD 45's landing gear was fully retractable with double bogies for the main gear, which when retracted were housed in the fuselage at the roots of the stub wings. The aircraft was expected to be able to carry eighty passengers for 1,555 miles (2,500km) at 454mph (730km/h). A military version (probably with a rear ramp) was studied in 1953. A year later, the aircraft was supposed to be under construction at the Vélizy factory, by which time the design had been modified through the introduction of large fairings at the junction between the wing and the fuselage and a T-tail. However, by December 1954, the assembly of this aircraft had been cancelled.

HD 45 (early)	
Status	project
Span	147ft 7.5in (45.00m)
Length	(82ft 0in (25.00m), other sources 98ft 5in (30.00m)
Gross wing area	1,182.8sq ft (110sq m)
Gross weight	90,388lb (41,000kg)
Powerplant	two Avon 9,225lb (41kN)
Maximum speed/Height	466mph (750km/h) at 32,810ft (10,000m)
Equipment	17,637lb (8,000kg) freight or eighty passengers

HD 45 (late)	
Status	prototype?
Span	149ft 11in (45.70m)
Length	96ft 5.5in (29.40m)
Gross wing area	?
Gross weight	90,388lb (41,000kg)
Powerplant	two Avon 9,225lb (41kN)
Maximum speed/Height	435mph (700km/h) at 32,810ft (10,000m)
Equipment	17,637lb (8,000kg) freight or eighty passengers

HD 70

This was a short-range transport aircraft aimed at the market filled by the Fokker F-27 Friendship. Using the same configuration as the other Hurel-Dubois projects, especially the HD 45, the HD 70 was to be powered by two Rolls-Royce Dart turboprops and its new fuselage was perfectly circular in section for pressurisation. It was designed for thirty-six passengers in nine rows of four seats but other configurations were possible and the service ceiling was 27,890ft (8,500m).

HD 70	
Status	prototype?
Span	105ft 0in (32.00m)
Length	72ft 2in (22.00m)
Gross wing area	559.1sq ft (52.00sq m)
Gross weight	36,376lb (16,500kg)
Powerplant	two Avon 9,225lb (41kN)
Maximum speed/Height	311mph (500km/h) at 19,685ft (6,000m)
Equipment	11,464lb (5,200kg) freight or thirty-six passengers

The HD 70 was presented to the *Comité du Matériel Aérien* in November 1954, but it was not ordered.

HD 109A and HD 130

In 1961 Hurel offered two light transport aircraft powered by two Astazou turboprops called the HD 109A and HD 130. These shared the same fuselage and tail unit but one had low-mounted wings, the other had (braced) shoulder wings. The 109A was to be able to carry a 2,381lb (1,080kg) load over a distance of 622 miles (1,000km), or 2,822lb (1,280kg) for 311 miles (500km), its take-off run would have been under 1,844ft (562m) and the landing distance was 2,096ft (639m). The 130 would have had the same load-carrying abilities but would have taken off in just 1,562ft (476m) and landed in 1,962ft (598m). The latter aircraft was designed to operate in both temperate and tropical countries, in high-altitude conditions and with poor infrastructure on the ground, and for this latter reason it was to be fitted with a rugged, short undercarriage able to cope with any terrain. The landing gear would have been retractable for the civilian (passenger) version but fixed for the military (freighter) version. In its freight configuration a rear ramp-type door would allow the loading of a 'mid-size car' and a 3,307lb (1,500kg) payload was presented as standard (a jeep weighed 2,205lb [1,000kg] plus its own equipment and for the civilians the reference load was a Peugeot 403 saloon car). The passenger version

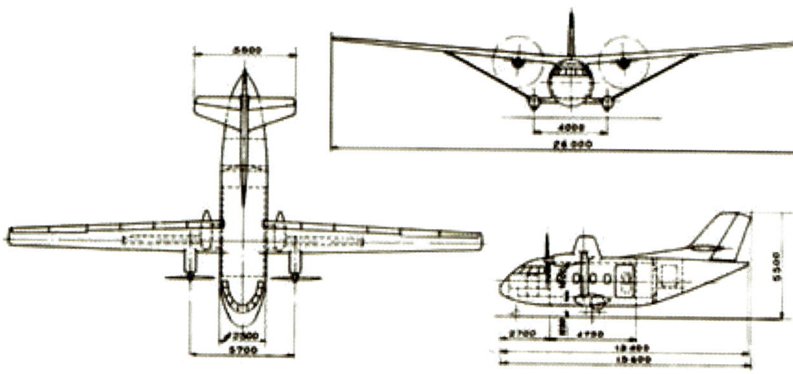

TOP **Artist's view of the HD 130 light transport aircraft.** *Author's collection/Hurel-Dubois*

ABOVE **Three-view drawing of the HD 130, which could carry a jeep in its cargo bay.** *Author's collection/Hurel-Dubois*

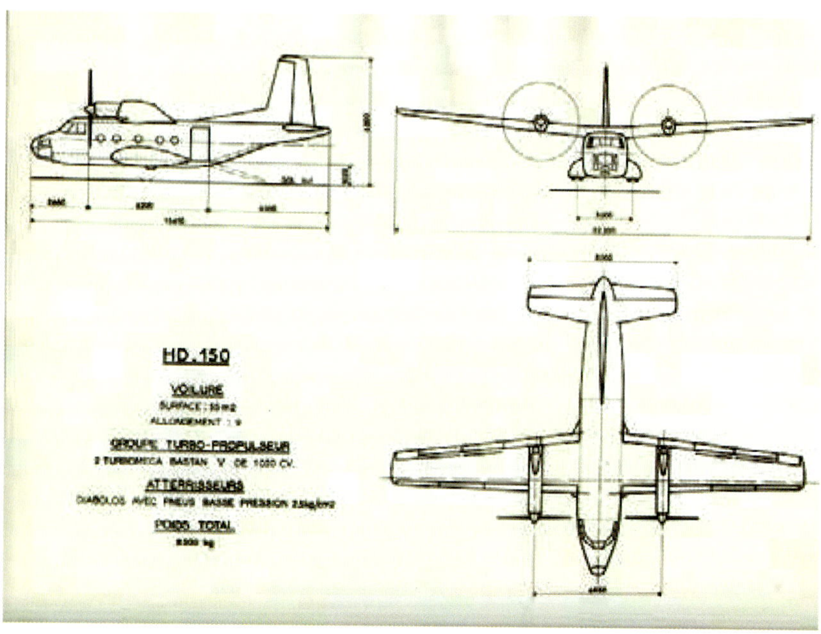

Hurel HD 109A

Status	project
Span	61ft 8in (18.80m)
Length	43ft 11.5in (13.40m)
Gross wing area	376.3sq ft (35sq m)
Gross weight	11,199lb (5,080kg)
Powerplant	two Astazou 11 530hp (395kW)
Maximum speed/Height	229mph (368km/h) at 19,685ft (6,000m)
Equipment	-

Hurel HD 130

Status	project
Span	85ft 3.5in (26.00m)
Length	43ft 11.5in (13.40m)
Gross wing area	376.3sq ft (35sq m)
Gross weight	11,464lb (5,200kg)
Powerplant	two Astazou 11 530hp (395kW)
Maximum speed/Height	221mph (355km/h) at 19,685ft (6,000m)
Equipment	3,307lb (1,500kg) or seventeen passengers

would have been pressurised, the freighter version would not have been pressurised but would have a swing-tail to ease loading. To help the sales campaign the manufacturer stressed the simplicity and the sturdiness of the design, pointing out that it was only a base airframe that *'could be adapted to highly diverse special uses, both civil and military'.*

Since both the HD 109 and HD 130 would have been nearly identical, save the wing, which appeared to be conventional on the 109A, and to conform to Hurel design philosophy on the 130, one is led to think that the real project was the 130, the 109A being just a foil. This is further backed up by the fact that only the 130 was publicised at the Paris Air Show.

HD 150

This was the military version of the HD 130 with a swing tail to ease the loading of vehicles.

LEFT **The HD 150 was a development of the HD 130 and, with its rear loading ramp, was aimed at military customers.** *Author's collection/Hurel-Dubois*

Hurel HD 150	
Status	project
Span	85ft 3.5in (26.00m)
Length	43ft 11.5in (13.40m)
Gross wing area	376.3sq ft (35sq m)
Gross weight	11,464lb (5,200kg)
Powerplant	two Astazou 11 530hp (395kW)
Maximum speed/Height	221mph (355km/h) at 19,685ft (6,000m)
Equipment	jeep with equipment in cargo bay

HD 151

The HD 151 project was unveiled in 1962 as a STOL utility transport and army co-operation aircraft powered by two 930hp (694kW) Turbomeca Bastan IV engines and with two Turbomeca Autan III air generators mounted at the wingtips to blow air under pressure over the flaps and ailerons. This technology provided the same low-speed performance as the Breguet Br 940 series (i.e. it could approach at very low speed and still remain airborne) but using a different solution that allowed Hurel to shorten the span of this machine somewhat. The aircraft was derived from the HD 130 and a rear-loading ramp would enable it to carry a 4,409lb (2,000kg) load over 1,550 miles (2,500km).

Hurel HD 151	
Status	project
Span	?
Length	?
Gross wing area	?
Gross weight	?
Powerplant	two Astazou 11 530hp (395kW) and two Autan III
Maximum speed/Height	?
Equipment	Machine guns etc, up to 4,409lb (2,000kg) military equipment for 1,554 miles (2,500km) flight

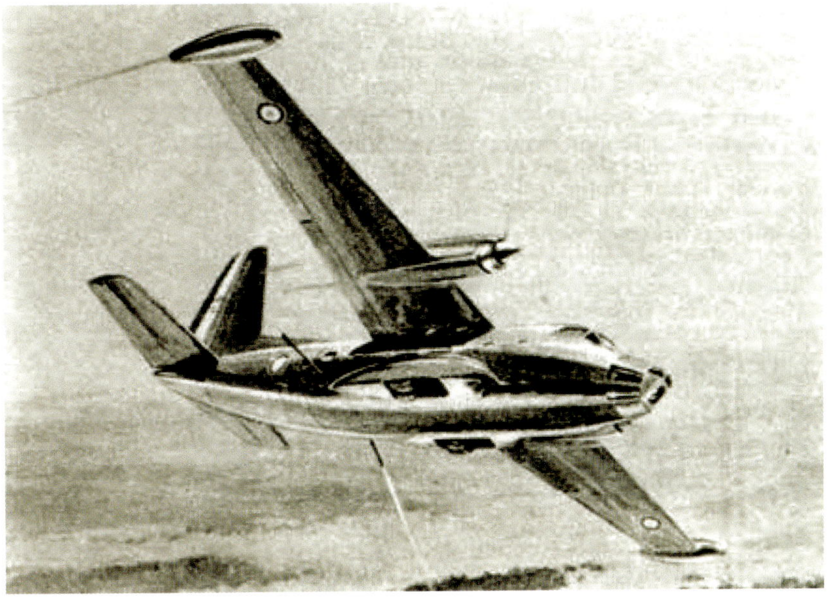

ABOVE Artist's view of the HD 151 operating in a ground support role. *Author's collection/Hurel-Dubois*

Hurel-Dubois/Jacques Gérin Assault Transport Project

Jacques Gérin teamed up with *Commandant* Hurel to design a small aircraft for commando insertion. This project is unfortunately known only through an artist's impression.

Other Manufacturers

Latécoère 853

In 1961 Latécoère entered the fray with the Laté 853 STOL light transport and, like many of its competitors, this was to be powered by two Turbomeca Astazou turboprops (this design was not submitted to a specific competition). A specific feature of

Laté 853	
Status	project
Span	63ft 2in (19.25m)
Length	38ft 10.5in (11.85m)
Gross wing area	397.8sq ft (37sq m)
Gross weight	10,891lb (4,940kg)
Powerplant	two Astazou 11 530hp (395kW)
Maximum speed/Height	227mph (365km/h) at 19,685ft (6,000m)
Equipment	jeep with equipment in cargo bay

ABOVE Aircraft designer Jacques Gérin worked together with Hurel to design a small aircraft for commando assault. The type identity of this design is unknown. *Author's collection/Gérin patent*

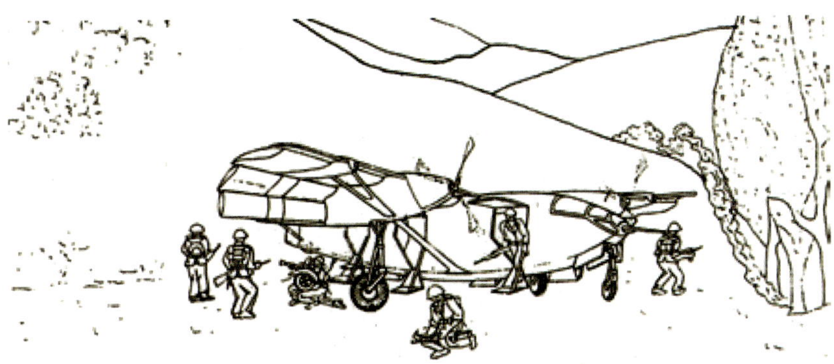

this aircraft was that the whole rear fuselage could swing to the right to give access to the pressurised cargo bay, which was capable of holding up to 2,756lb (1,250kg) of load; for example, a jeep (a passenger version could take fourteen people). The design's twin fin and rudder assembly was supported by a fixed boom above the swinging rear hull.

SNCAC Aerocentre NC 211 Cormoran

The NC 211 Cormoran (Cormorant) was a direct reply to General Demetz's request for an aircraft able to carry a light tank, although SNCAC also had hopes of selling it on the civilian market. The uncompleted airframe was exhibited at the 1946 Paris Air Show as a static display under the Grand Palais (near the Champs Élysées in Paris) and it made its maiden flight on 20 July 1948. Unfortunately this flight ended in a crash that killed the entire crew of five. The second prototype only flew the following year on 9 April 1949, but series production had been approved before then and four more aircraft were built, although they never flew. The aircraft was just too big for civilian use in cash-strapped France, which was still being rebuilt after the war, while the military would have liked an aircraft able to paradrop its cargo (which would have required a complete redesign of the fuselage). So this large machine's career ended as something of a fiasco.

Nord Centre NC 211 Cormoran	
Status	prototype
Span	144ft 4.5in (44.00m)
Length	100ft 0.5in (30.50m)
Gross wing area	2,150.5sq ft (200.00sq m)
Gross weight	92,593lb (42,000kg)
Powerplant	four SNECMA 14R 1,200hp (895kW)
Maximum speed/Height	255mph (410km/h)
Equipment	34,171lb (15,500kg) freight

TOP At the 1946 Paris Air Show, held indoors at the Grand Palais at the lower end of the Champs Elysées, the NC 211 Cormoran was displayed in model form and in a huge mock-up of the fuselage. *José Fernandez*

ABOVE The NC 211 making a rotation just before taking off for its only flight. *Aeroplane*

BELOW The NC 211 Cormoran was designed just after the war to carry elements of a paratroop division including armoured vehicles. *José Fernandez*

Nord 2100 Norazur

This was a light transport aircraft first flown on 30 April 1947 with test pilot Georges Détré at the controls. Designed to carry a dozen passengers, it had the curious feature of having its two Potez 8D-03 engines driving pusher propellers. A second prototype, designated N 2101, was powered by Renault Béarn 6D-07 engines, and a third version (the N 2102) would have received SNECMA 12S engines with conventional tractor propellers but it was not built. Beside its role as a light transport, it was also hoped to use the Norazur in the 'flying classroom' training role, but in the end the type remained a curiosity in the history of French aircraft and was not developed further. The name came from Nord and azure, the colour of the sky.

Nord 2100 Norazur	
Status	prototype
Span	59ft 0.5in (18.00m)
Length	44ft 3.5in (13.50m)
Gross wing area	408.6sq ft (38.00sq m)
Gross weight	10,207lb (4,630kg)
Powerplant	two Potez 8D03 420hp (313kW)
Maximum speed/Height	208mph (335km/h) at 6,560ft (2,000m)
Equipment	ten passengers

Nord Noratlas Family

This aircraft was designed by Jean Calvy in reply to a call for proposals issued by the *Direction Technique et Industrielle* (Air Ministry) in 1947. The other contestants were the Sud Ouest SO 30C (a derivative of the SO 30 airliner) and the Breguet Br 891R Mars.

Nord 2500

Having been ordered on 27 April 1948, the original Nord 2500 prototype, powered by 1,600hp (1,193kW) SNECMA 14R engines, was first flown on 10 September 1949 crewed by Claude Chautemps and Georges Détré.

ABOVE The mainstay of French military transport until 1989 was the Nord 2501 Noratlas. This is the last flying example, seen in 2012 at Salon de Provence. *Franck Journet*

Nord 2501 Noratlas

The second prototype was fitted with two 2,000hp (1,491kW) Bristol Hercules 739s. Although this prototype crashed on 6 July 1952 killing the famous aviatrix Maryse Bastié, it was this version that had been selected for production on 10 July 1951. It became the French military's basic transport aircraft and a total of 208 machines were produced for the *Armée de l'Air* following three pre-production aircraft. The name Noratlas came from Nord and Atlas, the Greek god who carried the world on his shoulders, a most apt name for a freighter aircraft.

Nord 2501	
Status	production
Span	106ft 7.5in (32.50m)
Length	72ft 0.5in (21.96m)
Gross wing area	1,088.2sq ft (101.2sq m)
Gross weight	48,501lb (22,000kg)
Powerplant	two (licence-produced SNECMA) Hercules 2,068hp (1,540kW)
Maximum speed/Height	252mph (406km/h)
Equipment	-

Nord 2501A

Two examples of a civilian version produced for the UAT (*Union Aéromaritime de Transport*, an old French Airline). They later were renamed N 2502.

Nord 2501 Water Bomber

Originally this was a 1965 proposal by the famous designer Roland Payen to convert the Noratlas into a water bomber by installing a water tank in the cargo bay and a foldable scoop mounted on a mast articulated just behind the nose undercarriage bay. In Payen's nomenclature this was known as project K.108. The idea was revived in 1982 by a company named SECA but it did not produce any prototype.

Nord 2501 with Turboprop

In 1956 the Nord Aviation *bureau d'etudes* studied the possibility of fitting Rolls-Royce Dart turboprops to the Noratlas. Many airlines favoured this form of propulsion rather than the by now old fashioned-looking piston engines. However, the performance improvement would have been limited so this project was dropped.

Nord 2501 Calibration

Three aircraft produced for the *Armée de l'Air* for radar calibration.

Nord 2501D

Variant produced to the German standards for the *Bundesluftwaffe* (186 units).

Nord 2501 Gabriel

Eight aircraft produced for the *Armée de l'Air* as electronic reconnaissance aircraft. The nickname Gabriel was given to these machines because Gabriel is the patron saint of messengers, including the Army's radio operators. The name was later carried over to the Transall.

Nord 2501IS

Variant exported to Israel (six aircraft).

Nord 2501PC

Not a variant per se, but various examples were fitted as 'flying command posts' for the *Armée de l'Air* (PC = *Poste de Commandement*, or Command Post).

ABOVE One of the few Nord 2502 civilian transports produced. *Author's collection/ Nord Aviation*

Nord 2501 RNR (Radio Navigation Radar)

Six aircraft produced for the *Armée de l'Air* as trainers for radar operators.

Nord 2501 SNB

Five aircraft produced for the *Armée de l'Air* as navigation and bombing trainers. (SNB = *Système de Navigation et de Bombardement*, or Bombing and Navigation Systems, the dedicated navigational and aiming avionics aboard types such as the Vautour and Mirage IV.).

Nord 2501 VIP

Five aircraft produced for the *Armée de l'Air* as VIP transports.

Nord 2502

This is the civilian transport version, recognisable by the wingtip Turbomeca Marboré II booster turbojet and produced in limited quantities for UAT (Nord 2502A: seven), Air Algérie (Nord 2502B, three), *Centre d'Essais en Vol* (a single aircraft originally intended for an Indian airline), and Força Aérea Portuguesa (Nord 2502F: six machines).

Nord 2502 VTOL

A 1961 project to fit the Noratlas with Rolls-Royce lift engines in underwing nacelles. In December 1961 a British group from the Armstrong Whitworth company came to France to meet the Nord Aviation *bureau d'études* at Châtillon to discuss the feasibility of converting the Noratlas to take this powerplant. In January 1962 the British Ministry of Aviation gave its agreement to the whole scheme and AW sent an official request to Nord Aviation for a quotation for two airframes but without equipment. The project was known by the British manufacturer as the AW.690 and a pod with nine Rolls-Royce RB161-1 units was to be installed under each wing just outside the propeller disc (the standard Bristol Hercules engines and the wingtip Turbomeca Marboré were retained in this design). An agreement between the two companies must have been reached because in May 1962 a proposal was made to the RAF to have two prototype AW.690s flying by 1965. However, it seems that nothing came out of this proposal.

Nord 2503

Variant powered by Pratt & Whitney engines. A single prototype was built but this development was not pursued and the aircraft later became the Nord 2508.

Nord 2504

One unit procured by the *Marine Nationale*, ostensibly as a trainer for ASW operators (see next chapter).

Nord 2505

Unbuilt dedicated ASW variant (next chapter).

Nord 2506

Based on the Nord 2502 (and thus having Marboré boosters) this single prototype was equipped with 'kneeling' landing gear to bring the rear fuselage down to ground level and ease the problems of loading.

Nord 2507

A dedicated SAR variant with improved range. Not built.

Nord 2508

This was similar to the 2503 but it had the Marboré wingtip turbojets of the 2502. The prototype 2503 was converted to this standard and was joined by another converted aircraft. Promoting the 2508 as the 'flying container', Nord Aviation associated itself with a demonstration of the NATO light ground attack aircraft (see Volume I) held at Rivolto airfield in Italy in early July 1959, in doing so illustrating how a Fiat G.91 could be carried inside the 2508's cargo bay. This development was not pursued and the two aircraft were returned to 2501 standard.

Nord 2520

This was a civilian variant with a stretched fuselage for sixty passengers. Not produced.

Nord 2600

The 2600 was a short-lived variant studied in 1954 that would have used Rolls-Royce Dart turboprops. However, the radical development that would have set this design apart from the rest of the Noratlas family was the abandonment of the twin-boom formula and its replacement by a standard fuselage with a high tail and a rear-loading ramp.

Nord 3100

This 1952 project was described as a derivative of the Nord 2501 fitted with Bristol Proteus 705 turbojets along with Turboméca turbojets (Marborés?) to serve as boosters. It was stated as being able to carry a 28,660lb (13,000kg) load at a speed of 373mph (600km/h) over a distance of 932 miles (1,500km). The aircraft's STOL performance was highlighted, but no specific data was supplied.

Sud Aviation (SNCASE) SE 210

It should come as no surprise that, when just about every manufacturer of transport aircraft was trying to sell its products to both the military and the airlines, in November 1959 Sud Aviation should offer a version of its successful SE 210 as a 'cargo militaire' or military freighter. The design was based on the Rolls-Royce RB.141-powered Caravelle VIII and could be used for the following missions (with conversion equipment carried in a forward bay):

1. Parachute dropping of loads through the rear door. The standard load would be five jeeps or VLR Delahaye, or various guns, howitzers and mortars, or an *Antenne Chirurgicale Aéroportée 58* (a military surgical unit packed into five paradropable containers).
2. Parachute dropping of sixty-nine fully equipped paratroops.

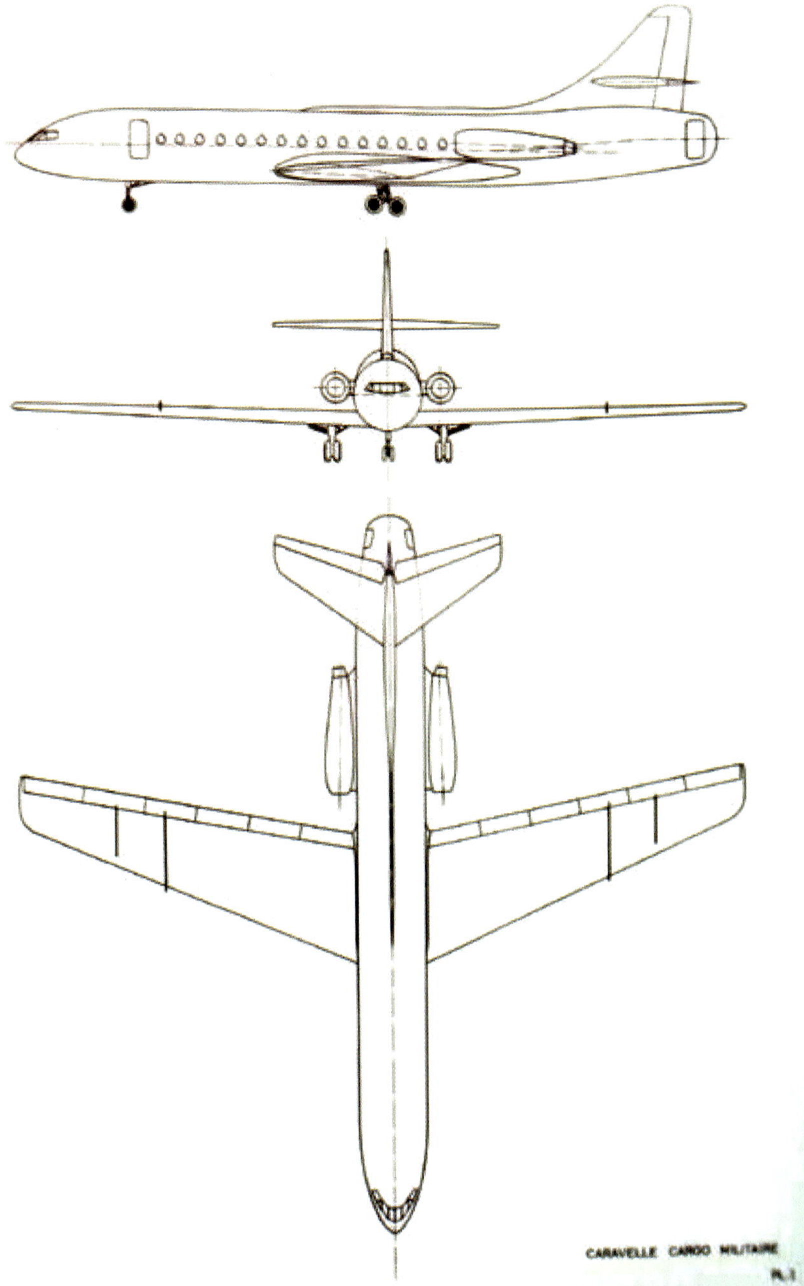

ABOVE The Caravelle was proposed as a military transport with a revised rear fuselage to permit the air dropping of large loads. *SNCASE/Author's collection*

Sud Aviation SE 210 Cargo Militaire

Status	project
Span	?
Length	?
Gross wing area	?
Gross weight	110,230lb (50,000kg)
Powerplant	two RB.141 11,800lb (52.4kN)
Maximum speed/Height	344mph (553km/h), reduced to 93mph (150km/h) during airdrop operations
Equipment	5 jeeps or 18,740lb (8,500kg) load

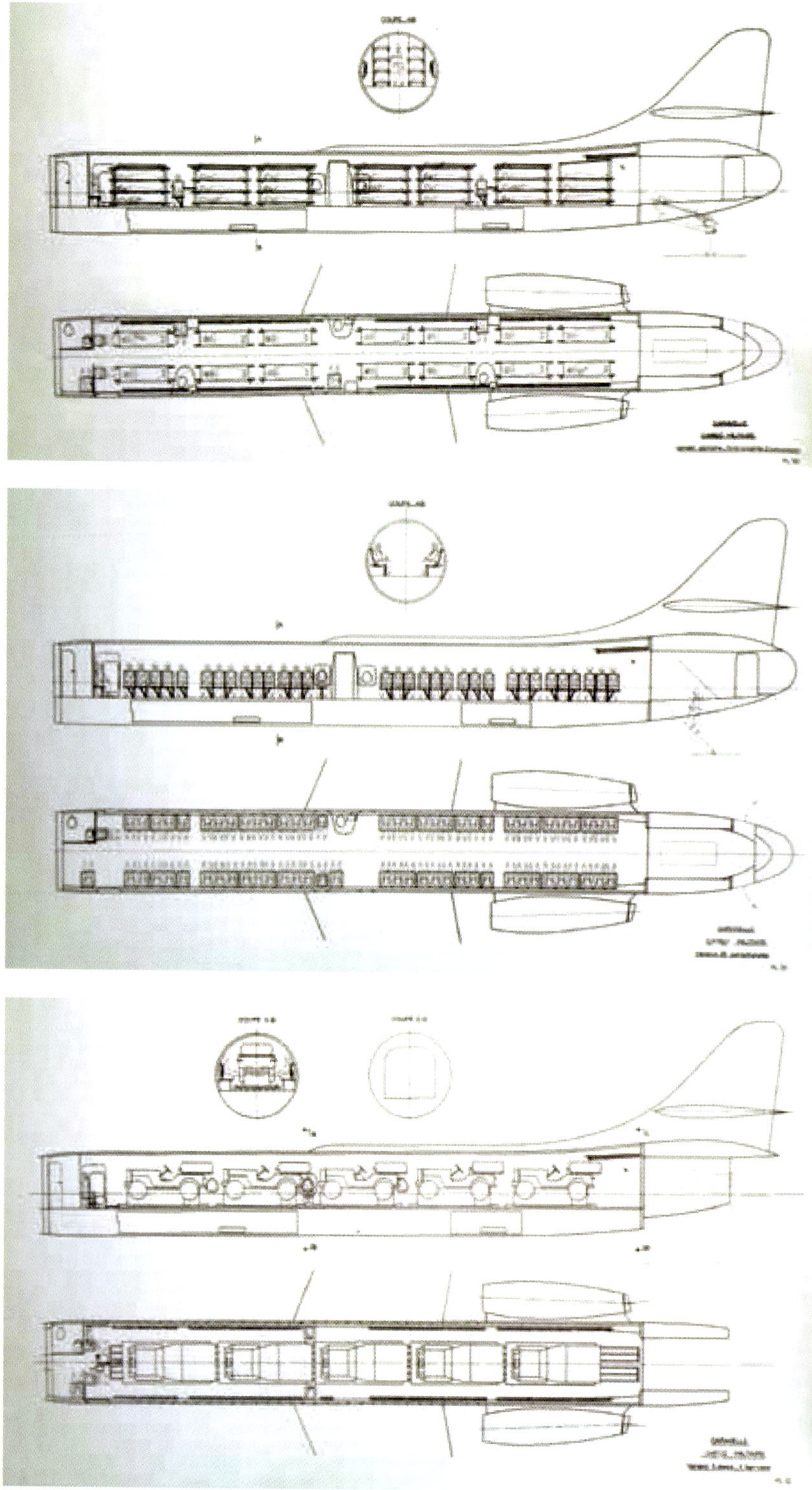

ABOVE **Drawings illustrating the various internal configurations planned for the Caravelle Military Transport – air ambulance, paratroop transport and paraload transport (here with five jeeps).** *SNCASE/Author's collection*

3. An air ambulance capable of taking fifty-four wounded soldiers on stretchers with six orderlies.

This project, like many other unsolicited proposals, remained on the drawing board.

SNCASO SO 30C

This was a variant of the SO 30N, a twin piston-engine airliner first flown as a prototype on 26 February 1945. The definitive SO 30P Bretagne variant first flew on 11 December 1947 (the original SO 30N had proved under-powered) and was a limited commercial success with forty-five units sold to Air Algérie, Air Maroc, Aigle Azur, Air Laos, and la STAEO (*Société Transatlantique Aérienne d'Extrême-Orient* a subsidiary of COSARA (*Comptoirs Saigonnais de Ravitaillements*). It was also used by the Government's GLAM squadron (*Groupement de Liaisons Aériennes Ministérielles*) and the CEV (the *Centre d'Essais en Vol* flight test centre), and briefly by the *Marine Nationale*. The SO 30C was a freighter version of the basic aircraft with a reinforced floor and a single prototype was built. It is certain that its fuselage, positioned high off the ground and therefore requiring special equipment to gain access, was a handicap when the design was compared with its two competitors.

SNCASO SO 30C	
Status	prototype
Span	88ft 3in (26.90m)
Length	62ft 2in (18.95m)
Gross wing area	924.7sq ft (86.00sq m)
Gross weight	44,643lb (20,250kg)
Powerplant	two SNECMA 14R 1,825hp (1,360kW)
Maximum speed/Height	273mph (440km/h)
Equipment	-

The Second Generation

At the end of the 1950s the question arose regarding the replacement of the Noratlas, and two major competing designs would result:

1. The Breguet Br 940 series – a dedicated STOL machine with a wing especially adapted for STOL operations.
2. The C 160 Transport Alliance (Transall) – a joint design by Nord Aviation and the German companies Weser Flugzeugbau and Hamburger Flugzeugbau.

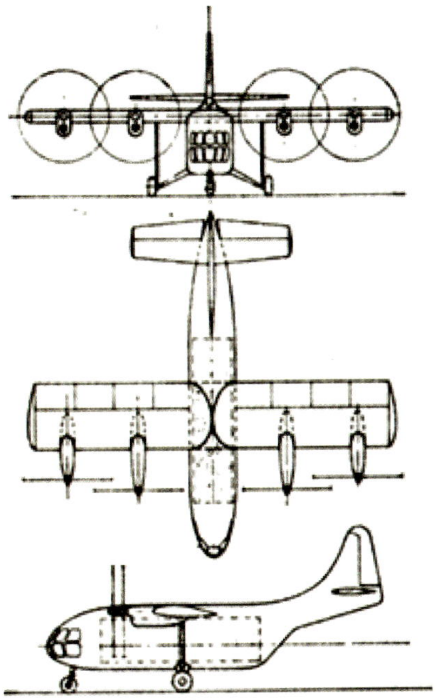

ABOVE **Three-view drawing of the Breguet Br 941 STOL assault transport as envisioned in 1956.** *Author's collection/ Breguet document*

Hurel-Dubois had also hoped to position itself on this market but without success. Later efforts involved the Potez P.880 and then more recently military versions of the successful ATR 42 regional airliner.

Breguet 940 Series

Although Breguet had initially favoured the fan-in-wing approach (see Chapter Eight), after the death of Louis Breguet the firm's efforts were reoriented toward lift augmentation devices. These were adapted to a series of assault transport aircraft.

Breguet Br 940 (Early)

In 1954 two projects were proposed – the Br 940-01, which was to be a 5,511lb (2,500kg) twin-engine technology demonstrator, and also a four-engined machine having a take-off weight of 14,330lb (6,500kg) and which could be seen as a prototype for the production aircraft. Hopes were high at the time and the Br 940-01 was described as having a minimal forward translation speed of 0mph, which meant it was very near to being a true VTOL aircraft but without the ability to hover. At that time it was intended to fit a Turbomeca Marboré turbojet inside the tail of the aircraft for propulsion and jet control (in Br 940 prototype 03). Then, in 1955, an enlarged version powered by four SNECMA TB-1000 turboprops was proposed where the turboprops were to be paired in two pods fixed to the wing, the propellers being driven

Br 940-01 (project)	
Status	project
Span	40ft 4.5in (12.30m)
Length	33ft 7.5in (10.25m)
Gross wing area	?
Gross weight	5,511lb (2,500kg)
Powerplant	two Turmo II 400hp (298kW) and one Marboré
Maximum speed/Height	218mph (350km/h)
Equipment	-

Br 940-03	
Status	project
Span	56ft 5in (17.20m)
Length	40ft 4in (12.30m)
Gross wing area	498.9sq ft (46.40sq m)
Gross weight	14,330lb (6,500kg)
Powerplant	two Turmo II 400hp (298kW)
Maximum speed/Height	233mph (375km/h)
Equipment	-

BELOW **At the 1955 Paris Show a model of the Breguet Br 941 was shown to President Coty. Note in this early version the main gear is fitted with skids, and that the design has only one propeller on each wing.** *Author's collection/Breguet document*

BOTTOM **The first step before committing to building a Br 941 prototype was to investigate the design using free-flight models.** *Philippe Ricco*

ABOVE **The first prototype Breguet Br 940 flew in 1958.** *Philippe Ricco*

through side extension shafts. Finally, the simpler solution of having the engines behind each propeller was retained. Yet a single shaft would link all four engines together so that, in the event that one should break down, all four propellers could be driven by the three remaining engines (this concept was tested successfully as a free-flight scale model). A desk model of the Br 940 in this configuration was shown to Président de la République Monsieur René Coty at the 1955 Paris Air Show, and the assault transport to be produced from the Br 940 demonstrator was named Br 941 as early as 1955. By 1956 the project had been revised with the engines now separate, *Aviation Magazine* describing a twin tail '*similar to the one used on the* [wartime] *Br 690*' and a retractable landing gear in side pontoons '*like that used on the Lockheed C-130 Hercules*'.

BELOW **After the proof of concept Br 940, the Br 941 was the prototype of a fully operational machine. It is seen here flying above the Alps in 1962.** *Philippe Ricco*

BOTTOM **Three-view drawing of the prototype Br 941.** *Author's collection/Breguet document*

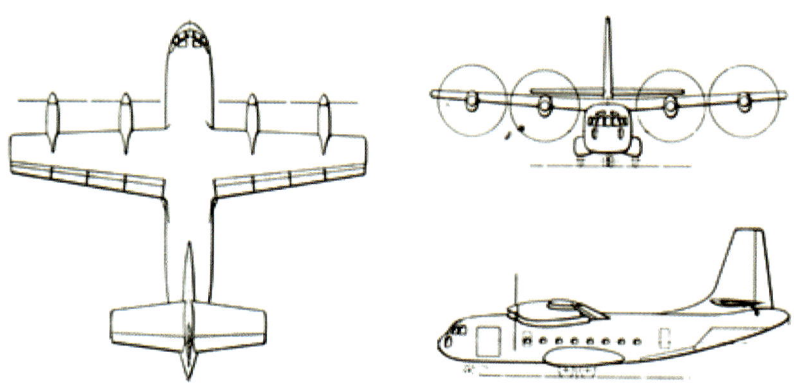

Breguet Br 940

The prototype Br 940 made its maiden flight on 21 May 1958 with Bernard Witt at the controls. Over the following years this machine was to complete more than 300 successful flights, including regular displays at Paris Air Shows from 1959.

Br 940 Prototype	
Status	prototype
Span	58ft 10in (17.93m)
Length	49ft 6.5in (15.10m)
Gross wing area	?
Gross weight	16,446lb (7,460kg)
Powerplant	four Turmo IID 400hp (298kW)
Maximum speed/Height	?
Equipment	-

Breguet Br 941

The Br 940 was more of a technology demonstrator but a prototype for an operational version, the Br 941, was built in 1958-60 and first flown on 1 June 1961. This machine was also exhibited at several Paris Air Shows

Br 941 Prototype	
Status	prototype
Span	76ft 1in (23.20m)
Length	68ft 10.5in (21.00m)
Gross wing area	?
Gross weight	23,104lb (10,480kg)
Powerplant	four Turmo IIID 1,235hp (920kW)
Maximum speed/Height	249mph (400km/h)
Equipment	-

and a model of the 941 was exhibited at the 1961 New Delhi Air Show. The type made its 1,000th flight on 4 November 1965.

Breguet Br 941AR

This aircraft was similar to the Br 947.

Breguet Br 941B

A variant briefly announced in 1967 that was aimed at both the civilian and military markets.

Breguet Br 941C

This was a civilian variant designed in 1960 with side passenger doors and a 'Caravelle airliner-style' rear door with integrated stairs. A mock-up was exhibited at the 1961 Paris Air Show.

Breguet Br 941M

The military version designed in 1960 with a rear ramp and large cargo doors. It was intended to be used for various roles including the replenishment and support of front-line units, commando landings, etc. (a Breguet brochure showed that NATO's main tactical and ground-to-air missiles could be carried in the cargo bay).

Breguet Br 941S

For the 1965 fiscal year a budget was allocated to the acquisition of five production machines, designated Breguet 941S, of which four were actually built. The first production aircraft was first flown on 19 April 1967 with test pilot Witt at the controls. In a November 1968 press conference, Marcel Dassault (then negotiating for a merger between his company and Breguet) announced that talks were ongoing with the *Armée de l'Air* for a series of thirty to forty aircraft. This declaration was met with scepticism by reporters and *Aviation Magazine* commented: '*To obtain an order for the Br 941 from the Armée de l'Air is a*

Br 941S	
Status	series
Span	76ft 9in (23.40m)
Length	79ft 10.5in (24.35m)
Gross wing area	?
Gross weight	58,422lb (26,500kg)
Powerplant	Turmo IIID3 1,500hp (1,119kW)
Maximum speed/Height	323mph (520km/h)
Equipment	-

ABOVE The production version was called the Breguet Br 941S. *Author's collection/ Breguet document*

LEFT Although only four Br 941s were produced they sported different markings: in this case military camouflage ...

BELOW LEFT ... or here bare metal with a white upper fuselage. *José Fernandez*

budgetary utopia. However, by placing this programme in another budgetary category, military or civilian, there could still be hope.' The next month, an agreement was reached between Breguet and Sud Aviation where Sud would have priority for the industrial production of the Br 941.

McDonnell-Douglas MD 188

At the same time, the second Br 941S had been repainted as the MD 188S for demonstration purposes in the United States. At some point in 1965 it was even thought (feared?) that the French design, due to a lack of home orders, would be produced and sold in the USA as the MD 188. The military variant for the US Army would have been the MD 941.

Breguet Br 941Z

A maritime patrol variant about which little is known.

Br 941Z

Status	project
Span	76ft 9in (23.40m)
Length	79ft 10.5in (24.35m)
Gross wing area	?
Gross weight	57,319lb (26,000kg)
Powerplant	-
Maximum speed/Height	Cruise 286mph (460km/h)
Equipment	-

ABOVE LEFT One of the Breguet Br 941S versions survives to this day in the Musée de l'Air et de l'Espace. *J.C. Carbonel*

LEFT The Breguet Br 941S flew under American Airlines colours during its demonstration flights in the United States. *Breguet document/Author's collection*

Breguet Br 942

The Br 942 was a civilian 'airbus' proposed in the 1960-63 period that used the Br 941's wing.

Br 942	
Status	project
Span	76ft 1in (23.20m)
Length	78ft 1in (23.80m)
Gross wing area	?
Gross weight	44,092lb (20,000kg)
Powerplant	four Turmo IIID 1,170hp (872kW)
Maximum speed/Height	Cruise 249mph (400km/h)
Equipment	-

Breguet Br 943

The Breguet Br 943 was a variant of the Br 945 proposed in 1962. Its main modification saw the enlargement of the landing gear fairings to house Rolls-Royce RB.162 lift jets and this design was to be Breguet's entry in the NATO NMBR.4 transport competition (NATO Basic Military Requirement NMBR.4 was issued in 1960 to supply support transport aircraft to accompany the VTOL ground attack aircraft designs produced against NMBR.3. Other known competitors are the British English Electric P.36 and the AERFER-BAC Type 224). The cargo bay had a volume of 1,942cu ft (55cu m) and a floor surface area of 263.4sq ft (24.50sq m), but this could be extended to 344.1sq ft (32.00sq m) if the rear ramp was used. Strangely, all press reports from the time mention larger wings that do not fit the dimensions found in the Breguet brochure material.

Br 943R	
Status	project
Span	87ft 1in (26.54m)
Length	72ft 11in (22.23m)
Gross wing area	1,075.3sq ft (100.00sq m)
Gross weight	57,540lb (26,100kg)
Powerplant	four Turmo VI 1,800hp (1,342kW) and four RB162 4,725lb (21kN)
Maximum speed/Height	-
Equipment	-

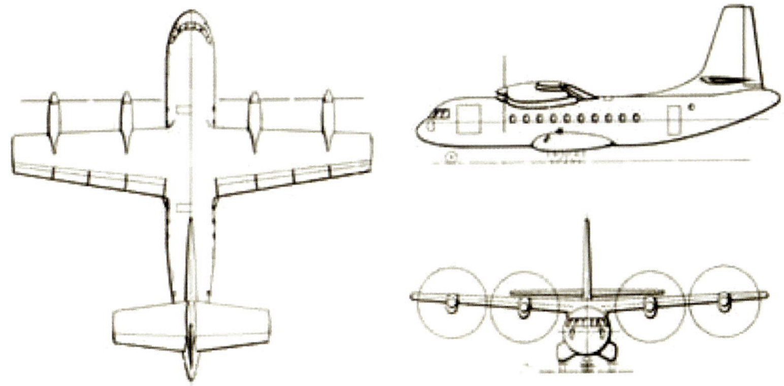

TOP **The Breguet Br 942 passenger transport was a direct extrapolation of the Br 941.** *Author's collection/Breguet*

ABOVE **A model of the Breguet Br 942 in generic airline livery.** *Author's collection/Breguet document*

Breguet Br 944

BELOW **The Br 944 was a passenger transport with a pressurised fuselage.** *Author's collection/Breguet document*

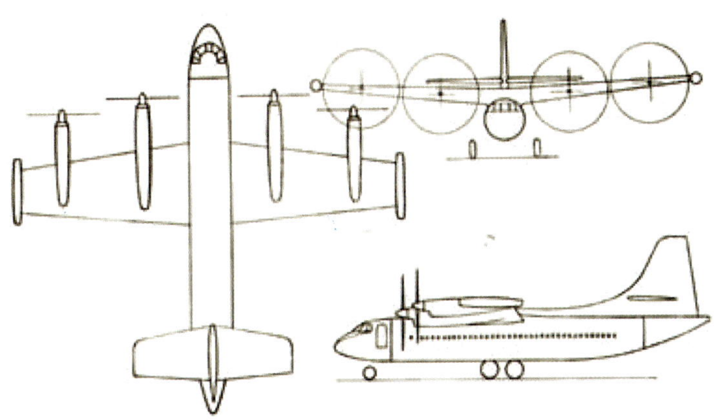

ABOVE **An artist's impression of the Br 944 in flight. The large tricolour rudder shows that the intended customers were not only in the civilian market.** *Author's collection/ Breguet document*

A large aircraft that mated the bilobed fuselage of the Breguet Br 124 'Airbus' with wings developed from those used on the Br 941.

Br 944	
Status	project
Span	118ft 1.5in (36.00m)
Length	114ft 10in (35.00m)
Gross wing area	?
Gross weight	?
Powerplant	four Tyne
Maximum speed/Height	373mph (600km/h)
Equipment	120 to 150 passengers

Breguet Br 945

The smaller Br 945 was designed as a reduced-size Br 941 propelled by two Turbomeca Turmo IIID units. This aircraft was specially designed for operations in tropical areas and was intended for delivery in 1964. As the Br 945 had a turn radius of only 196ft 10in (60m) when flying at 78mph (125km/h), it was intended to install a side-firing 20mm gun in a similar way to the Sikorsky S-58 'pirate' helicopters used during the fighting in Algeria. Other weapons under consideration were wire-guided SS 11 missiles and rocket pods, while variants of the Br 945 were studied

Br 945	
Status	project
Span	66ft 9in (20.35m)
Length	54ft 5.5in (16.60m)
Gross wing area	?
Gross weight	24,250lb (11,000kg)
Powerplant	two Turmo IIID
Maximum speed/Height	249mph (400km/h)
Equipment	four SS 11, 20mm gun

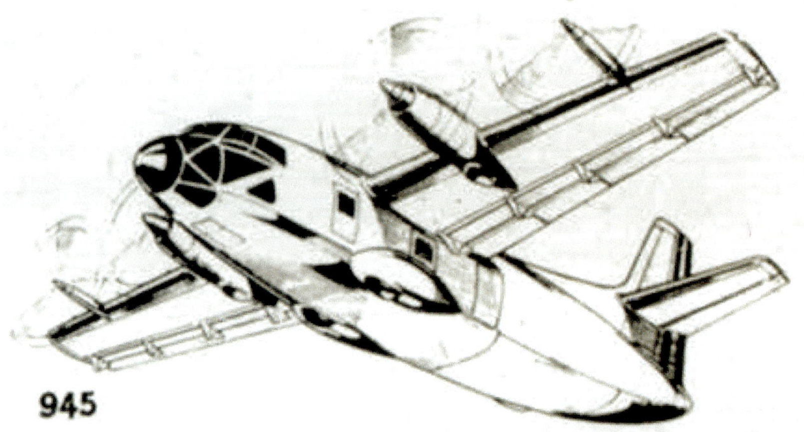

BELOW **The smallest machine of the family was the Br 945 intended for army co-operation duties. It could carry troops or receive weapons either in the fuselage or under the wings.** *Author's collection/Breguet document*

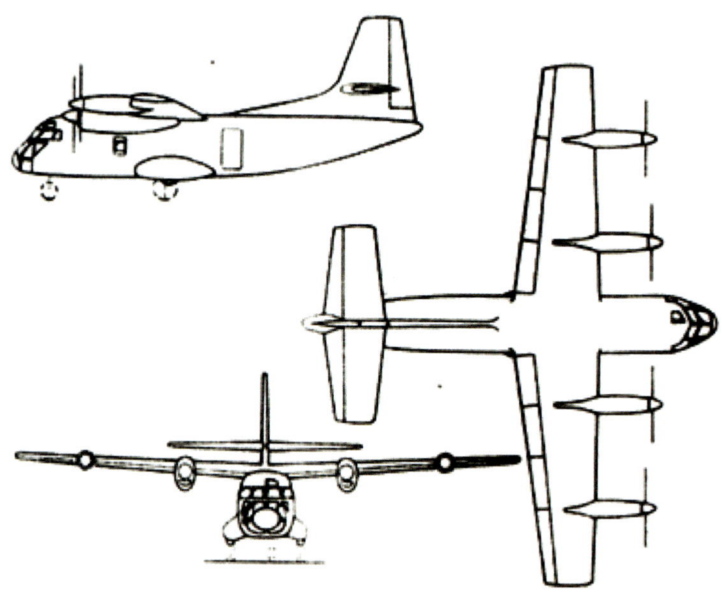

BOTTOM **Three-view drawing of the Br 945.** *Author's collection/Breguet document*

with four propellers 'flowing' over the whole span or, in the case of the Br 945A, only two propellers 'flowing' over a portion of the span. However, this was found to be too complex for overseas operations because the whole point of the programme was to have a rugged aircraft that was easy to operate and maintain in remote locations, for example deep in Africa. Breguet, with its Br 945, had produced a machine that satisfied the technical specification of the requirement but not its spirit ('keep it simple and rugged'), so it was not produced.

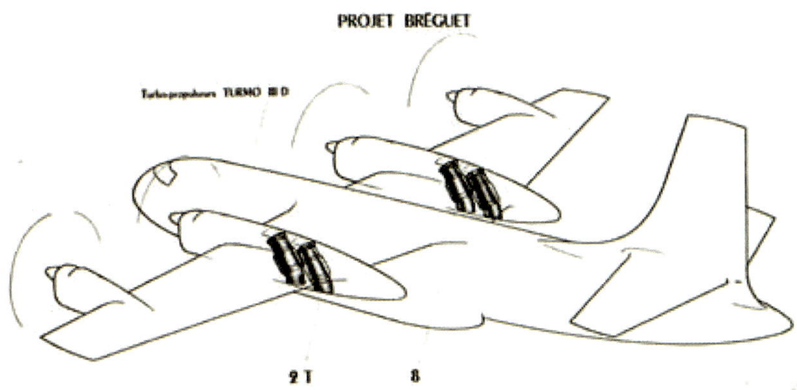

TOP SNECMA identified this drawing as Breguet's entry to the NATO NBMR.4 competition (therefore depicting the Br 943, which was a Br 945 with four lift engines added to shorten the take-off run even further). However, to the author this seems to depict the Br 947. *Author's collection/SNECMA Document*

ABOVE A late derivative of the Br 941 was the AMD 188 (AMD for Avions Marcel Dassault after the Breguet company had been bought by Avions Marcel Dassault), which is seen here in model form preserved at the *Musée de l'Air et de l'Espace* in Le Bourget. *Author's collection*

Breguet Br 946

The Br 946 design number was originally attributed in 1961 to a 'mini Br 942' feeder liner. By 1967 it had became a 'Super 942' of 90 tons flying weight and able to carry 250 passengers.

Br 946	
Status	project
Span	?
Length	?
Gross wing area	?
Gross weight	198,413lb (90,000kg)
Powerplant	four Tyne
Maximum speed/Height	311 to 373mph (500 to 600km/h)
Equipment	250 passengers

Breguet Br 947

This was a variant of the Br 941 fitted with additional Rolls-Royce RB.162 lift jets in enlarged landing gear fairings. The idea was not to turn the aircraft into true VTOL type, but rather just to shorten its take-off run even more.

AMD 188

The final development of the Breguet 940 series was the AMD 188, which was designed after the merger of Breguet with Dassault, hence the new design suffix. Its pressurised fuselage was entirely new and obviously aimed at the civilian market. An oddity in this design was the fixed undercarriage.
<table 216>

Potez P.870

This design came about in reply to an 'Avion de Co-operation' programme and was offered in both twin and four-engined versions using the Turbomeca Bastan V. A programme for an overseas co-operation aircraft had been opened on 13 September 1960 to which Breguet, Hurel-Dubois, Dassault and Nord Aviation replied initially, with Potez joining the fray later on. Neither the Nord N 262 nor the Dassault Communauté (see Chapter Seven) were especially good proposals but both had supporters in the French government. Also, an unnamed civil servant who probably knew more about accounting than about aviation suggested a Frankenstein-like mating of a Dassault wing with a Nord fuselage! With the end of the war in Algeria the military lost interest in

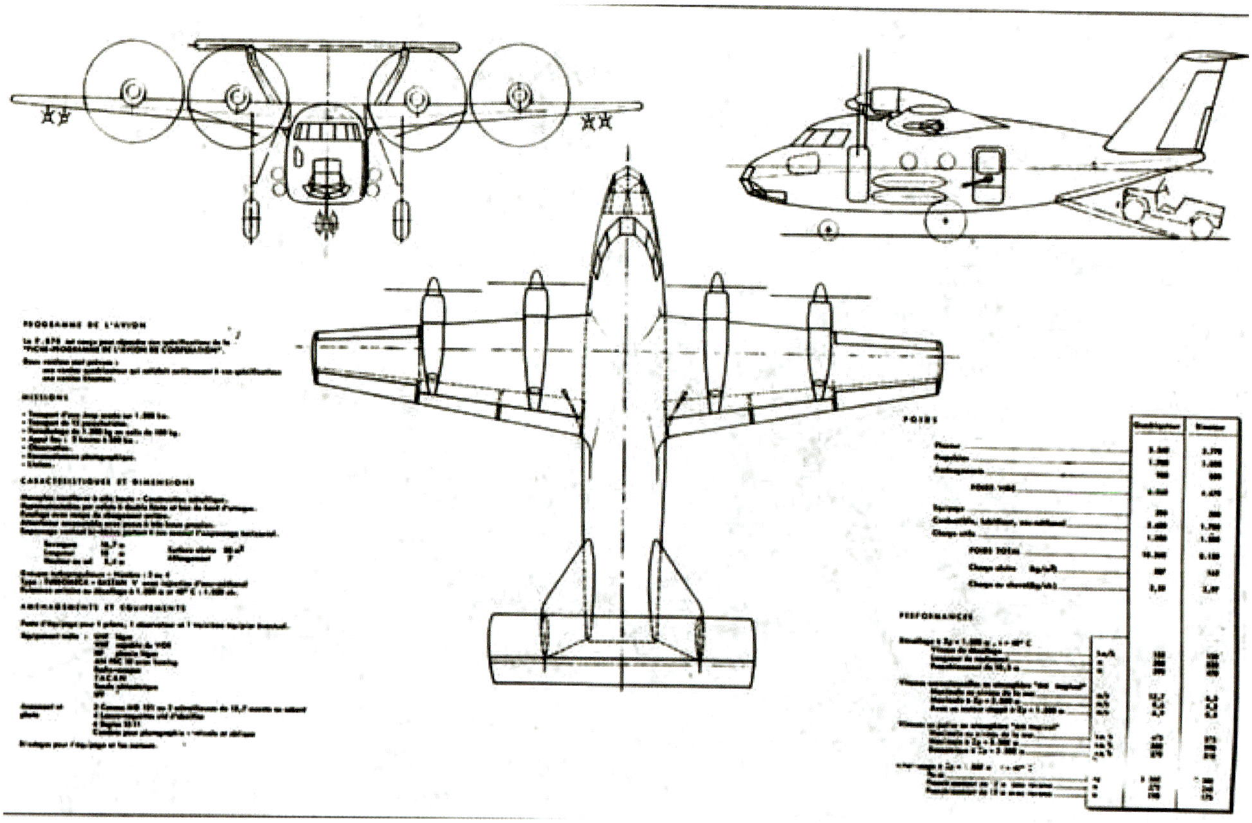

ABOVE The Potez 870 was a small freighter aircraft that could also carry weapons in its fuselage and under the wings, rather like the Br 945. It was not built. *Author's collection/Potez*

this programme while the civilian sector found that these machines were too costly for their intended use in soon-to-be independent territories. By 1963 this was all old history and no series production ever came out of these studies.

The P.870 was aimed more directly at the military side and could transport either a jeep with a weapon (usually a 12.7mm/.303 machine gun), fifteen paratroopers with their full equipment, or 3,310lb (1,500kg) of load which could be air-dropped using 220lb (100kg) containers. It could also be used for Army co-operation duties carrying either two 20mm guns in side mountings, four SS-11 anti-tank missiles or four unguided rocket packs, and for Army observation, photographic recognition or in the ferry role. Armour was provided for both crew and passengers and the design was eventually stabilised in its four-engined format, before it evolved into the P.880.

Potez P.870	
Status	project
Span	61ft 4in (18.70m)
Length	49ft 2.5in (15.00m)
Gross wing area	537.6sq ft (50sq m)
Gross weight	twin engine 17,901lb (8,120kg), four engine 22,840lb (10,360kg)
Powerplant	two or four Bastan V 1,005hp (750kW)
Maximum speed/Height	two engines 242mph (390km/h); four engines 311mph (500km/h) at 11,480ft (3,500m)
Equipment	various, see text

Potez P.880

In 1962 Potez designed the P.880 to fit the requirement of STOL co-operation (read army co-operation – i.e. the resupply of forward troops). Fitted with four Bastan turboprops it was expected to be able to carry 3,307lb (1,500kg) over 932 miles (1,500km) after taking off from an unprepared field of less than 984ft (300m) in length and situated at up to 3,280ft (1,000m) above sea level. In a pure transport role the load could be increased to 7,055lb (3,200kg) and both configurations had a pressurised cargo bay of 883cu ft (25cu m) capacity with a platform 27ft 10.5in (8.50m) in length, enabling it to carry two jeeps, thirty-two soldiers or twenty-five paratroopers. A rear-loading ramp and a side door adapted for paratroopers were included in the layout and the machine was designed especially to operate from grass or sand surfaces and in tropical climates. The P.880 was entered into the STOL Army co-operation aircraft competition (the *Avion de Co-operation programme*) against the Breguet Br 945 and a version of the Dassault Spirale (see Chapter Seven) but lost out to the Dassault entry. Neither the military P.880 nor a civilian P.881 (forty passengers) version were built, although the P.881

Potez P.880	
Status	project
Span	68ft 10.5in (21.00m)
Length	60ft 4.5in (18.40m)
Gross wing area	677.4sq ft (63sq m)
Gross weight	transport version 29,894lb (13,560kg), co-operation version 25,705lb (11,660kg)
Powerplant	Bastan IV 930hp (694kW)
Maximum speed/Height	?
Equipment	-

apparently shared a lot of similarities (except the engines) with the P.840 passenger airliner, which did fly in 1961 but failed to find a market.

Nord C-160

Starting in 1960, three companies, Nord Aviation in France and VFW (*Vereinigte Flugtechnische Werke*) and HFB (*Hamburger Flugzeugbau*) in Germany, established a consortium to design and build a STOL transport adapted to the needs of their two countries. That aircraft became known as the C-160 Transall (as in *TRANSport ALLianz*). Originally four companies had bid for participation – Nord-Aviation, Hurel-Dubois, Weser Flugzeugbau and HFB, but for unknown reasons Hurel was left on the side when the consortium was created. Originally a four-engined aircraft was contemplated that was to be powered by Rolls-Royce Dart turboprops, but in the end a twin-engined type was selected powered by Rolls-Royce Tynes.

C-160-01

The first prototype flew on 25 February 1963 at Melun Villaroche. It was used to define the aircraft's flight envelope and in February and March 1966 participated in cold weather tests in Sweden.

C-160-02

Prototype 02 followed the first aircraft into the air on 25 May of the same year in Bremen. It was used to test the avionics and did a programme of tropical testing in Addis Abeba.

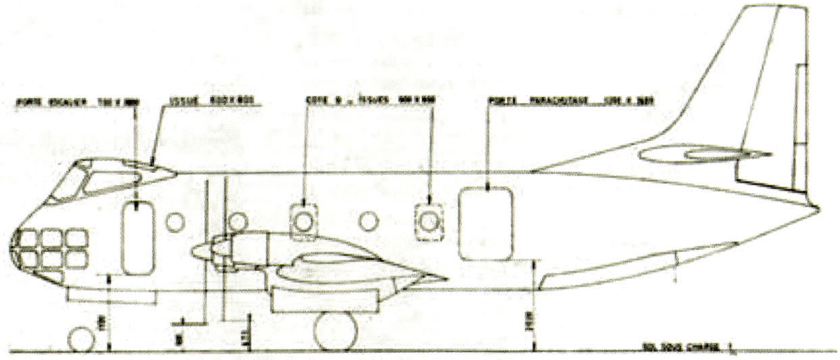

TOP **An artist's view showing the Potez 880 being unloaded.** *Author's collection/Potez*

ABOVE **The Potez 880 was a larger design intended for paratroop operations.** *Author's collection/Potez*

C-160-03

The third machine made its maiden flight on 19 February 1964 in Hamburg. Later it was transferred to Toulouse for paradrop testing. In 1966 the following improvements were discussed:

(i). Range increased by 622 miles (1,000km) through the fitting of auxiliary tanks.

(ii). Improved avionics, notably with the possibility of installing an automatic landing system.

BELOW **The C-160 Transall, a medium-size military freighter for the** ***Armée de l'Air*** **and German Luftwaffe, first flew in 1963.** *Author's collection/Nord Aviation*

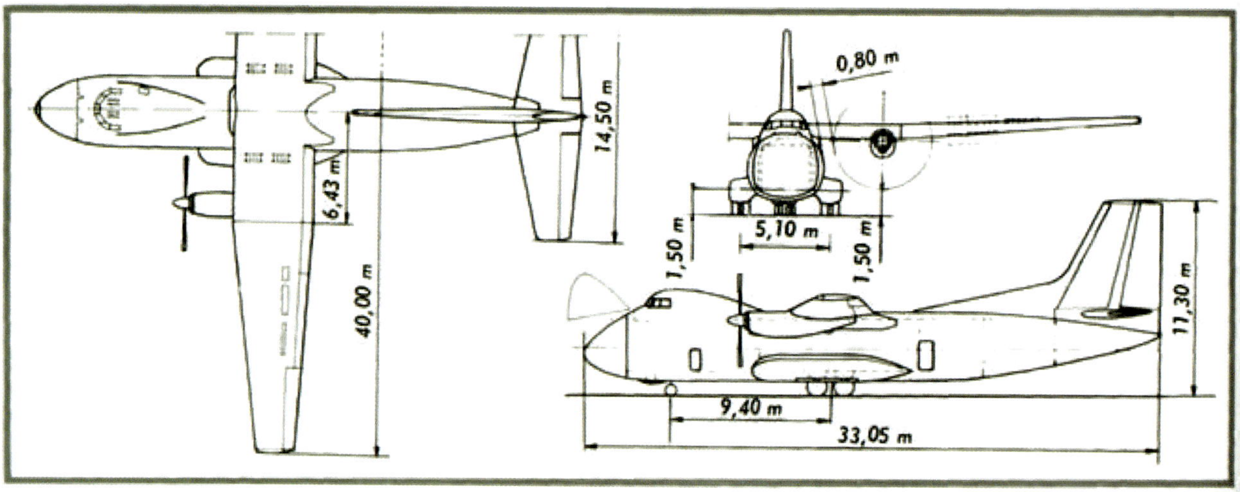

ABOVE Three-view drawing of an aborted civilian version of the C-160 Transall. *Author's collection/Nord Aviation*

(iii). The fitting of an automatic drop system (thought to mean that no operator was needed to throw the parachute charge overboard).

(iv). Shortening of the take-off run by changing to more powerful engines, along with new scimitar-bladed propellers of 17ft 11.5in (5.48m) diameter and the addition of lift-generating devices to the wing.

C-160 AAA

A variant fitted for the early warning and surveillance role. Not built.

C-160 ASF

This version would have carried Exocet missiles under the wings in its role of anti-shipping patrol aircraft.

C-160C

This designation referred to a civilian freighter designed in around 1966 and to be operated by three crewmen. It would have had a range of 572 miles (920km) while carrying 38,580lb (17,500kg) of payload. Earlier, at the Paris Air Show in 1963, Nord Aviation had exhibited a model of an airliner for 130 passengers in a slightly elongated fuselage.

C-160D

The 113 production aircraft delivered to the Luftwaffe (D = Deutschland).

C-160F

The fifty-three production aircraft delivered to the *Armée de l'Air* (F = France).

C-160H Astarté

The C-160H's Astarté name stood for *Avion STAtion Relais de Transmissions Exceptionnelles* (or Aircraft for Relaying Transmissions on an Exceptional use). A short batch of four aircraft in the NG series was used by the *Armée de l'Air* as communication relay aeroplanes and fitted with advanced radio equipment. These were to relay the presidential order '*to fire missiles*' to the *Marine Nationale*'s ballistic missile-launching nuclear submarines on patrol should the situation have arisen that other forms of transmission had been made inoperative by the enemy. A long wire antenna was deployed behind and underneath the aircraft from a spool

BELOW Artist's view of the civilian C-160 in operation. *Author's collection/Nord Aviation*

ABOVE **The Transall C-160H Astartée was among the most secret aircraft to have been flown operationally by the *Armée de l'Air*, being used to communicate with nuclear submarines.** *Philippe Ricco*

in the former cargo bay (the rear ramp was welded shut). Today these aircraft have been superseded by satellites and are now in storage.

C-160G Gabriel

Two machines in the NG series equipped for electronic intelligence. They were easily identified by their numerous antennas on top of the fuselage.

C-160NG

The Transall is among the few aircraft types for which production has been restarted after a period of inactivity. In the late 1970s Aérospatiale (taking over from Nord Aviation), Messerschmitt-Bölkow-Blohm (taking over from Hamburger Flugzeugbau) and Vereinigte Flugtechnische Werk built twenty-nine aircraft with improved avionics, additional fuel tanks and the ability to refuel in flight. This new version first flew on 9 April 1981.

C-160P

From 1973 to the late 1990s four C-160Fs were loaned to the French Post Office for night mail operations and they were then returned to the *Armée de l'Air*.

C-160R

Between 1994 and 1999 all French Transalls were upgraded to the R standard (*Rénové* = refurbished) with improved avionics and decoy dispensers.

C-160T

Twenty of the aircraft originally bought by Germany were later sold to Turkey (T = Turkey).

C-160Z

Nine aircraft were produced for the South African Air Force (Z = Zulu).

C-160S

Another avionics-heavy variant optimised for maritime patrol, but not produced.

C-160SE

This was an electronic warfare variant that was not ordered.

C-161J

In 1968 consideration was given to a jet-powered version of the Transall. This cargo aircraft would have had a repositioned cockpit to increase the loading bay volume to 6,674cu ft (189cu m) and a nose door to provide the capability of taking vehicles, or more usually nine 5,511lb (2,500kg) pallets. This was seen as an advantage over the original C-160's tail ramp configuration because it allowed for an improvement to be made to the aerodynamics of the rear fuselage. The biggest change, however, would have been the replacement of the Rolls-Royce Tyne turboprops by Pratt & Whitney J4D or JT3D-3B turbojets. This move was intended not only to increase the speed and load but also to help the integration of the type into

BELOW **The nickname associated with this version of the Transall comes from Gabriel being the patron paint of messengers, including the Army's radio operators.** *Philippe Ricco*

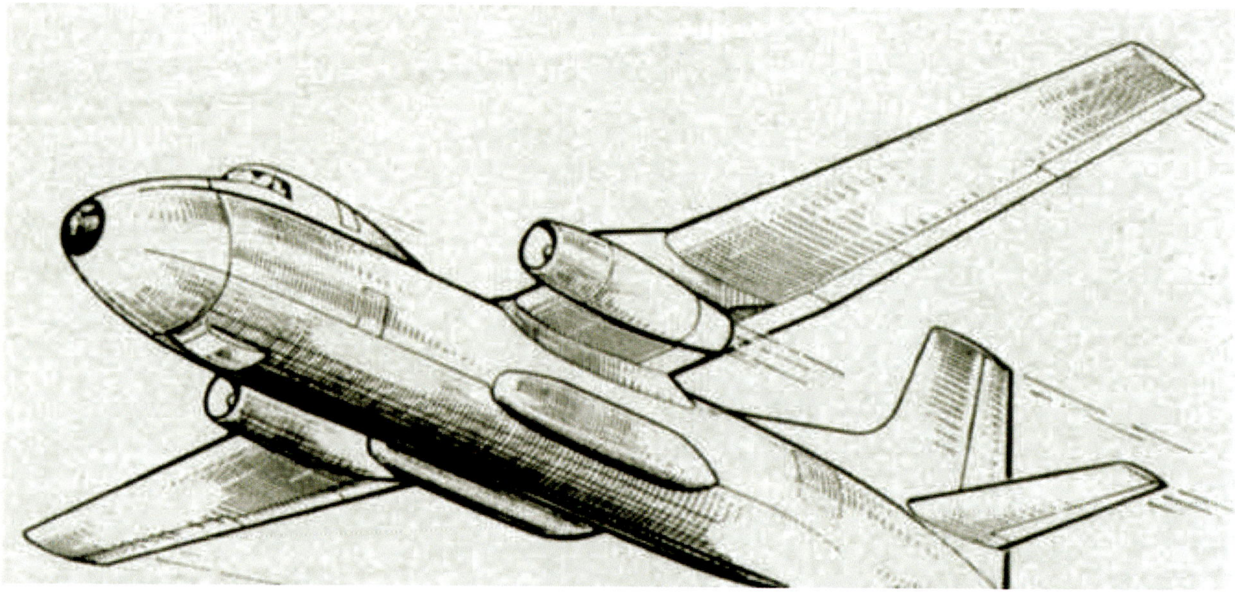

ABOVE **A jet-propelled version of the C-160 was also proposed as the C-161J.** *Author's collection/Nord Aviation*

civilian air fleets. The cockpit would have been reconfigured for operation by just two crew members and a Garrett TPE-331 auxiliary power unit was integrated in the port sponson, in front of the landing gear bay.

Transall C-161J	
Status	Project
Span	131ft 3in (40.00m)
Length	114ft 10in (35.00m)
Gross wing area	1,720.4sq ft (160sq m)
Gross weight	141,755lb (64,300kg)
Powerplant	two JT3D-3B 18,000lb (80kN)
Maximum speed/Height	435mph (700km/h) at 24,935ft (7,600m)
Equipment	52,910lb (24,000kg) payload

ATR 42

After the introduction of the Franco-Italian ATR 42 as a civilian regional airliner in the early 1980s, built by a combined company called ATR (*Aerei da Trasporto Regionale*, or *Avions de Transport Régional*), military versions were also projected. In 1985 the following were announced:

ATR 42F

F for *Fret* (Freight). This variant was to be fitted with a reinforced load-carrying floor to enable it to carry up to 8,377lb over 1,429 miles (3,800kg over 2,300km). The left rear door could be opened during flight to drop paratroops.

ATR 42R

R stood possibly for *Rampe* (Ramp) since it was fitted with a rear-loading ramp. The freight capacity was increased to 11,023lb (5,000kg).

ATR 42S

'S' possibly stood for 'Sea' because this variant was designed for naval patrol (see next chapter). A new set of communication, detection and observation equipment was planned and even the installation of offensive weapons (of unspecified type) was considered. The aircraft's patrol time would have been three hours and thirty minutes, reaching a distance of 684 miles (1,100km) from its base.

SAR 42

This was the search and rescue variant with a patrol time of up to four hours at 684 miles (1,100km) from base.

BELOW **A model of the ATM 42R, a military version of the ATR 42.** *Author's collection/ Potez*

Chapter Eleven
Maritime Patrol and Anti-Submarine

ABOVE **A nice model of the Avion d'Exploration Marine Arsenal.** *José Fernandez*

Once again this category of aircraft was born out of the Second World War. On one side land-based, long-range converted bombers (the Focke-Wulf Fw 200 Condor, Consolidated B-24, Boeing B-17 and Vickers Wellington) had hunted submarines and convoys across the oceans, while on the other side smaller machines, often carrier-based, had performed the same role in shorter-range engagements (the Grumman TBM Avenger, Yokosuka 'Judy' and Fairey Swordfish). In 1945 some people in France still advocated the flying boat for the long-range anti-submarine warfare (ASW) task, in view of the roles played by the Short Sunderland, Kawasaki H6N Emily, Consolidated PBY Catalina or the Blohm & Voss Bv 138. To support their vision, some manufacturers who had built large flying boats before the war were consulted about what to do next. However, it soon became apparent that the future lay in ground-based aircraft.

The Long-Range Maritime Patrol Aircraft

Early Proposals

Arsenal Avion d'Exploration Marine (Maritime Reconnaissance Aircraft)

This design from Arsenal was put forward very quickly after the Liberation in mid-1944. In common with most Arsenal projects of the time, it featured engines mounted in tandem that gave it the outward appearance of a twin-engined machine, when actually it was a four-engined aircraft. Experience would prove that this

Arsenal 1944	
Status	project
Span	139ft 5in (42.50m)
Length	(95ft 11.5in (29.25m)
Gross wing area	?
Gross weight	88,183lb (40,000kg)
Powerplant	four Hispano Suiza 12Z 1,580hp (1,178kW) + turbojets (undefined)
Maximum speed/Height	-
Armament	-

Arsenal 1946	
Status	project
Span	124ft 8in (38.00m)
Length	107ft 3.5in (32.70m)
Gross wing area	1,720.4sq ft (160sq m)
Gross weight	110,229lb (50,000kg)
Powerplant	four Arsenal 24 H 3,550hp (2,647kW) and two Nene
Maximum speed/Height	Over 466mph (750km/h)
Armament	four 15mm turret, X-4 defensive missiles, undefined 11,023lb (5,000kg) missile

was not that good an idea and it was proposed to add turbojet engines to increase the speed during combat. Although soon forgotten, the project was still being promoted by Arsenal in the late 1940s.

Bloch 161 Explorateur (Explorer)

This was a militarised version of the MB 161 transport aircraft then in production and was known as the MB 161E (or MB 164). It was planned to equip it with two twin-13mm turrets with another pair of 13mm guns firing through a lower hatch. The crew of ten would have been protected by armour plates and the offensive load was to have totalled 2,205lb (1,000kg). A range of 1,243 miles (2,000km) at a cruise speed of 186mph (300km/h) was required by the *Marine Nationale*. A mock-up was prepared in September 1945 and at that time it was expected that up to eighty aircraft would be ordered but by 1946, in order to reduce costs, the *Marine Nationale* had sacrificed this national product and decided to buy second-hand British Wellingtons and Lancasters!

Breguet Br 1011 Capricorne (Capricorn)

In 1945, in an effort to revive the project, Breguet proposed to convert its pre-war Br 1011 transatlantic airliner to the anti-submarine role. A bomber version had been studied during the Vichy years as the Br 1012,

ABOVE **Full-size interior mock-up of the Avion d'Exploration Marine Arsenal.** *José Fernandez*

BELOW **The SNCASE SE 1020 project was quite pre-war in its appearance.** *Author's from Cuny*

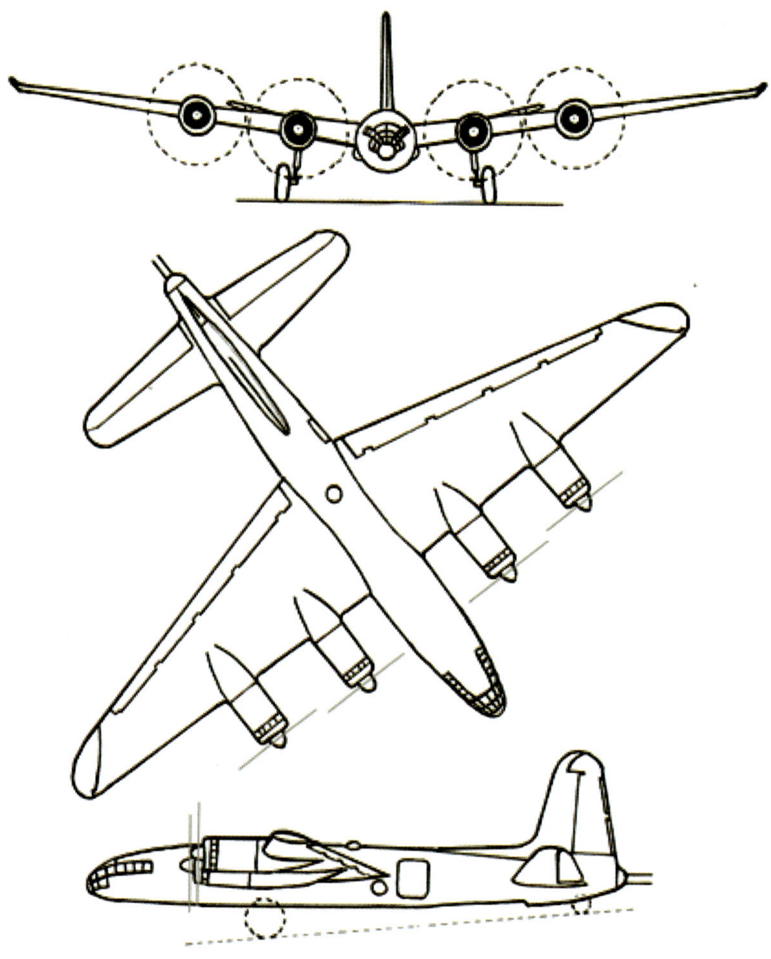

but by 1944-45 both the passenger airliner and bomber were now hopelessly outdated. The ASW idea remained wishful thinking and did not even receive a project number.

SNCASE SE 1020

This was another case of a manufacturer producing an ASW patrol aircraft swiftly from a former long-range 'transatlantic' transport, the SE 1010. Naturally the conversion to military use would have required the introduction in the base design of a bomb bay and defensive turrets. Although estimated to have a valuable capability in range (more than 1,555 miles/2,500km because the transport could fly 3,110 miles/5,000km across the Atlantic) when flying at 373mph (600km/h), this project was turned down by the *Marine Nationale*, which was not satisfied by this performance.

SNCASO SO 4000 ASW

Sud Ouest suggested grafting a Rolls-Royce Tyne turboprop on to its SO 4000 bomber (see Chapter One) to enable it to stay aloft during the duration required for an ASW patrol. This 1946 idea was quickly forgotten.

The 1946 'Avion de Haute Mer' Programme (Aircraft for Open Seas)

All of these unsuccessful projects paved the way for a call for proposals issued on 8 June 1946 that put forward some stringent requirements:

1. A range of 932 miles (1,500km) at 249mph (400km/h) at a height of 19,685ft (6,000m) and with the capacity, once the patrol area had been reached, to loiter for ten hours at 218mph (350km/h) at 3,280ft (1,000m).
2. A dash capability if necessary of 435mph (700km/h) for thirty minutes at 19,685ft (6,000m), or 466mph (750km/h) for five minutes.
3. Take-off run in less than 3,940ft (1,200m).
4. Fixed armament of two 30mm guns and two turrets.
5. Offensive armament of 2,205lb (1,000kg) of stores with the added possibility of replacing part of the fuel reserve by another 11,023lb (5,000kg) of ordnance.

Arsenal 'Avion de Haute Mer'

This was a rework of the earlier 1944 project (above) now adapted to the new requirements. The tandem engines were still there but as an alternative Arsenal 24H engines were also offered to make this a true twin-engined machine. However, it was also planned to give it a dash capability by installing two Rolls-Royce Nene turbojets at the rear of the engine nacelles. These mixed propulsion arrangements were much favoured at the time because the turbojets did not have enough endurance for the patrol requirement while the piston engines were clearly outdated in terms of their pure speed performance. The defensive armament was limited to a rear turret but an offensive load of up to 16,534lb (7,500kg) could be carried in a long (47ft 11in/14.60m) bay. It seems that Arsenal, which was in charge of translating captured German documentation and for carrying out some experiments with captured missiles, already envisioned the use a large missile weighing about 11,023lb (5,000kg) as an attack weapon. Even more innovative smaller missiles, derivatives of the German wartime X-4, were considered as defensive weapons.

Breguet Br 764

While most of the projects discussed here were prepared during the 1946-47 period in direct response to the call for proposals, the Breguet Company at first offered just flying boat designs and then only moved on to investigating a land-based aircraft in around 1949. However, while this was an adaptation of an already existing machine, the Br 761, thanks to this factor the project was able to take a step further than most of the others, with a 'flying mock-up' of the Br 764 becoming airborne in 1951. By that time the *Marine Nationale* policymakers had reasoned that encounters between patrol aircraft of opposite forces turning into a dogfight, as had happened a few times during the Second World War, were unlikely to happen again and so the requirements for combat were softened, notably in term of speed. However, the flight time and offensive armament load requirements were not reduced.

Breguet Br 764 ASW	
Status	flying mock-up
Span	141ft 0.5in (42.99m)
Length	112ft 6.5in (34.30m)
Gross wing area	?
Gross weight	97,002lb (44,000kg)
Powerplant	four R-2800 CA-18 2,365hp (1,764kW)
Maximum speed/Height	Cruise speed 149mph (240km/h) at 3,280ft (1,000m) for fifteen hours
Armament	twelve depth charges, fifty sonobuoys, twenty markers and eight 20mm guns

The long-range Breguet Provence transport or its Sahara military transport version, better known by its nickname Deux-Ponts (two-decks) (see Chapter Ten), appeared a perfect base on which to design a large ASW aircraft. The lower deck could be devoted to weapon bays (twelve depth charges, fifty sonobuoys, twenty markers, or alternatively torpedoes could replace the depth charges), a retractable radome for a Thomson 'radioscope marine' radar, a magnetic anomaly detector (MAD) and even a passive scanner to detect incoming radar detection (an ex-German Naxos). An additional navigation radar was also planned and other offensive armament under consideration included rockets to be fired from underwing racks. Retractable panniers were also assessed, which may seem a little strange, but in fact retractable rocket racks were at that time all the rage for fighters and it seemed only

TOP **A Breguet 'Deux-Ponts' was modified into a 'flying mock-up' of the specialised Br 764 naval patrol variant.** *Philippe Ricco*

ABOVE **A detailed model showing the structural arrangement for the Br 764.** *Philippe Ricco*

logical that they should be studied here. Curiously however, the defensive armament was maintained at a high level with three SAMM (*Societe d'Application des Machines Motrices*) turrets – two twin 20mm with German MG 151/20 guns above the fuselage and a four 20mm installation under the tail. The flying mock-up, however, had only a single gun turret at the rear, and it should be noted that the *Marine Nationale* had only requested two turrets. The engines would have been Pratt & Whitney R-2800s already in use on the production transports and the aircraft was to be able to stay aloft for twenty-four hours at a time.

By mid-1950 it was planned to order either sixteen or thirty-two examples of this interesting machine but the contract was never issued. Technical issues have been put forward as to why the programme was stopped (delays in the production of 'national' avionics was given as one reason, and the necessity to strengthen the airframe to enable it to carry out sharp manoeuvres at low altitude was another), but again it is quite likely that funding was the real obstacle. Buying readily available and well-equipped Lockheed Neptunes was a more convenient solution!

Breguet 895 ASW

While this project retained the type number of an earlier transport (the Breguet Br 89 series – see chapter Ten), in fact it had nothing in common with it except a slight similarity in the wing design. Yet even in the wing the similarity stopped short, the ASW design having less wing area (1,290.3sq ft/120sq m) as against 1,559.1sq ft/145sq m), while its four engine nacelles were positioned slightly over the wing surface when the transport's two wing nacelles were underslung. This project is notable also for its total lack of defensive armament, in contrast to the wartime Short Sunderland patrol flying boat – which was given the nickname 'hedgehog' because of its large number of guns – as this design feature had been carried over to all the other projects studied so far. The airframe structure continued the experiments started with the Br 764, notably in its two-deck fuselage with a lower deck occupied by a 39ft 4in (12m) long bomb bay to take 13,228lb (6,000kg) of ordnance including depth charges, torpedoes, and sonobuoys, and the avionics including a large radome fitted underneath the fuselage. The upper deck was home to the fifteen crew members, while fuel for the four Bristol piston engines was located in tanks in the wing or in wingtip nacelles. Large lift-improving flaps were also introduced to facilitate low-speed manoeuvring and these flaps were to become a Breguet trademark, hypersustentation (the terminology used by Breguet to describe the sometimes complex flap system used to improve lift, usually to shorten take-off and landing runs) becoming a constant preoccupation of the manufacturer's designers from this point onwards. (Note: Breguet aircraft had complex flaps, not just one articulated panel but a mechanically complex system in which one flap panel would be formed from joints or jointed segments articulating from another flap panel. An extreme was reached with the Br 941 STOL in Chapter Ten, where the outer [chord-wise!] flap could articulate backwards – i.e. more than 90° downward.)

Latécoère 22

This manufacturer, while still supporting the flying boats that were its pre-war *chef d'oeuvre*, also offered land-based designs of the same configuration favoured by the other competitors – high aspect ratio wings, mixed propulsion with buried turbojets for dash speeds, plus a limited defensive armament (although Latécoère, like Arsenal, promoted missiles of its own design for offence and defence). Only the tail unit revealed the Latécoère legacy in these designs which differed mostly in their powerplant:

Laté 221: Four SNECMA 14R piston engines plus a Rolls-Royce Nene buried in the rear fuselage.
Laté 222: Piston engines reduced to two Pratt & Whitney R-4360 but two Nenes were integrated into the rear of the engine nacelles.
Laté 223: The original piston engines were replaced by two Bristol Centaurus units.
Laté 224: Four Bristol Hercules, SNECMA 14U or Arsenal 12H (formerly the German Jumo 213) were all considered for this type, coupled with the Nene, of course.
Laté 225: The two piston engines were again Bristol Centaurus, the major modification here being the replacement of the bicycle landing gear envisioned for the previous designs by a conventional tricycle undercarriage.
Laté 226: A return to the 224 configuration (landing gear and engines) but with the defensive armament moved from a rear turret

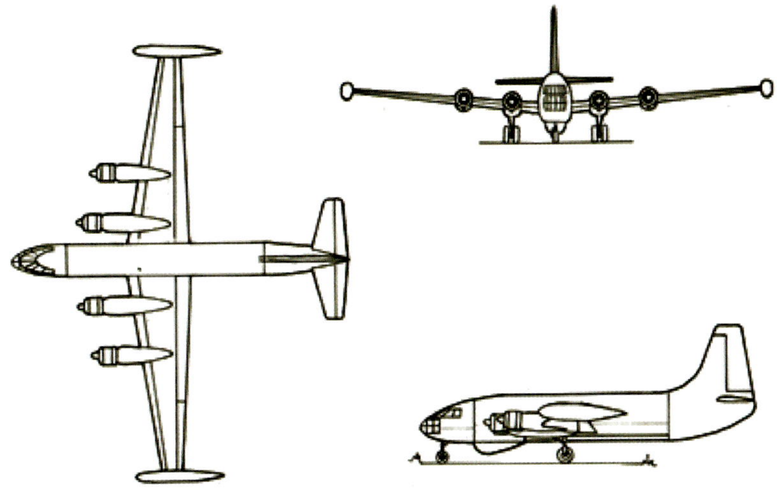

ABOVE The Br 895 ASW project from the early 1950s took its base-type number from the earlier Breguet 89 transport, but it was a new design that introduced modern equipment such as a MAD device in the rear fuselage. *Author's from Cuny*

BELOW The Laté 228 used a version of the Laté 631 flying boat wing mated with a new fuselage. *Latécoère*

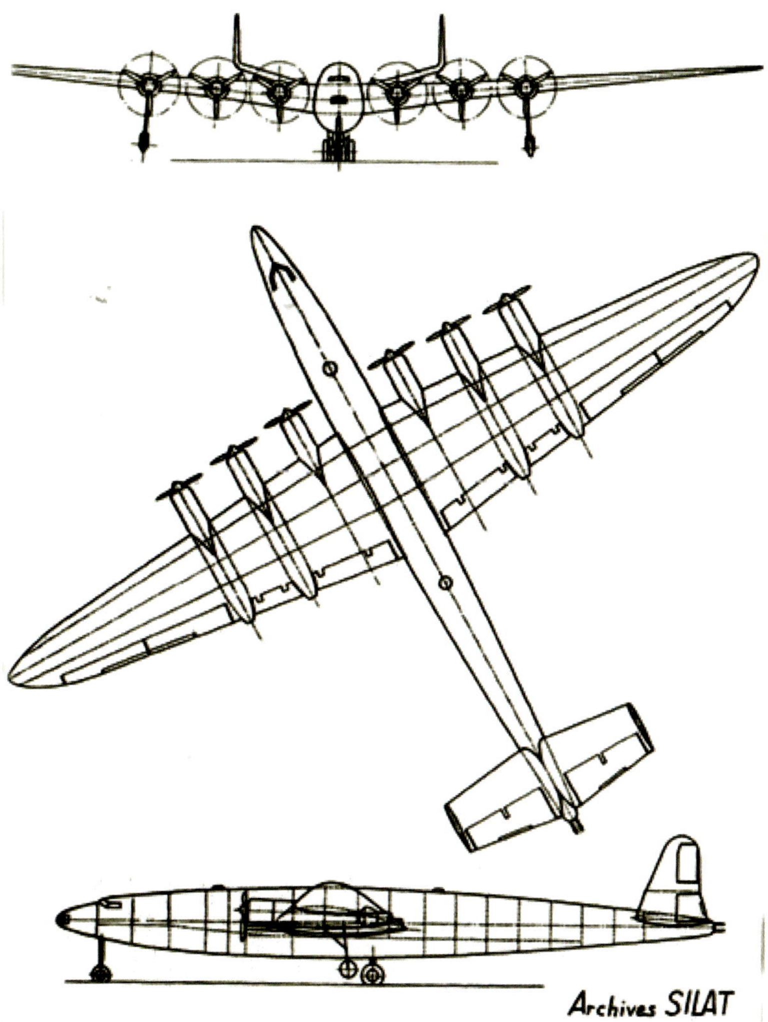

Laté 224	
Status	*project*
Span	*122ft 8.5in (37.40m)*
Length	*83ft 10in (25.56m)*
Gross wing area	*1,290.3sq ft (120sq m)*
Gross weight	*88,183lb (40,000kg) approx*
Powerplant	*various combinations*
Maximum speed/Height	*249mph (400km/h) piston only, 497mph (800km/h) with turbojets*
Armament	*20mm guns in rear turret. Missile in bay*

Laté 228	
Status	project
Span	187ft 8.5in (57.21m)
Length	144ft 4in (44.00m)
Gross wing area	3,763.4sq ft (350sq m)
Gross weight	155,298lb (70,443kg)
Powerplant	six R-2600 and four Nene
Maximum speed/Height	-
Armament	-

(now taken out) to the rear of the engine nacelles.

Laté 227: Return to the 225 engine configuration but with a bicycle landing gear and only one Nene buried in the fuselage.

Laté 228: This variant used the wing from the Laté 631 flying boat married to the new landplane fuselage with the bicycle landing gear et al. Propulsion was provided by six Wright R-2600 engines with four Nene turbojets added to provide boost speed.

Nord 2700

Nord's entry in this competition again followed the same arrangement as its competitors – long wings, four reciprocating engines and two turbojets. This project went far enough for a prototype to be ordered under contract 4032/49 dated 19 May 1949, only for it to be cancelled for the usual budgetary reasons at the end of the year.

SNCASE SE 1020

This was a refurbishment of the earlier project mentioned above but adapted slightly to fit the new requirements. The engines were now four Arsenal 12H and a rear turret with a quadruple 15mm installation had been added.

SNCASE SE 1010 ASW	
Status	project
Span	101ft 8.5in (31.00m)
Length	72ft 2in (22.00m)
Gross wing area	1,250.5sq ft (116.30sq m)
Gross weight	-
Powerplant	four Gnôme Rhône 14R-4/5 1,580hp (1,178kW)
Maximum speed/Height	Over 373mph (600km/h)
Armament	two 30mm fixed guns, two 30mm (rear turret) and ordnance

SNCASE SE 1020	
Status	project
Span	101ft 8.5in (31.00m)
Length	72ft 2in (22.00m)
Gross wing area	1,250.5sq ft (116.30sq m)
Gross weight	-
Powerplant	Arsenal Ars 12 H 1,970hp (1,469kW)
Maximum speed/Height	-
Armament	four 15mm (rear turret) + ordnance

SNCASE SE X-108

A Boeing B-29-style design with a glass nose and fitted with a choice of Bristol, Arsenal or SNECMA piston engines, to which were added the ubiquitous Nene, or more presciently the ATAR 101; even more interestingly the jets were positioned at the tip of the wings, thereby improving their aerodynamic performance. Just like the B-29, the crew was housed in two distinct sections with a nose compartment for the pilots, navigator and bomber and a rear compartment from which the tail turret was controlled remotely. The defensive armament consisted of two fixed 30mm HS 602 guns under the cockpit and a quartet of 20mm in the rear turret (or alternatively at the back of the engine nacelles), while for attack

BELOW The SNCASE X-108 was another project turned down for financial reasons. *Author's from Cuny*

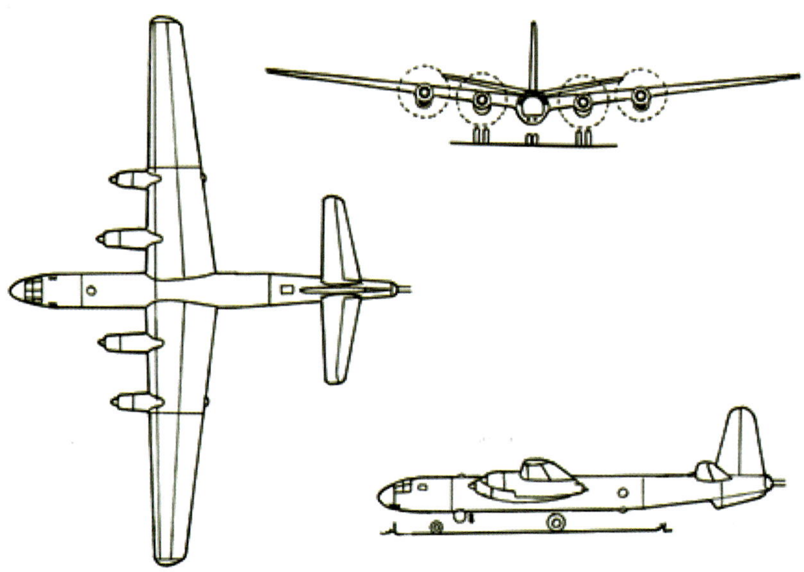

SE X-108J

Status	project
Span	121ft 4.5in (37.00m) ATAR version, 131ft 3in (40.00m) Nene version
Length	92ft 10in (28.30m)
Gross wing area	1,828.0sq ft (170sq m) ATAR, 1,720.4sq ft (160sq m) Nene
Gross weight	103,616lb (47,000kg) Nene
Powerplant	four Jumo 213 1,970hp (1,469kW) and two ATAR 101 4,725lb (21kN) or two Nene 4,725lb (21kN)
Maximum speed/Height	477mph (767km/h) (Nene)
Armament	-

a SE 1520 missile was considered, or bombs, depth charges and even a retractable rocket rack. This project was well received and studied in depth during the whole of 1948, and by the end of the year it was possible for SNCASE to offer the construction of a prototype to the *Marine Nationale*. Unfortunately, for financial reasons this was once more turned down.

Mid-Size ASW Aircraft

On 9 April 1954 a call for proposals was issued for middle-size land-based ASW aircraft. The requirements expressed were as follows:

1. A total of eight hours of patrol flying at 140 knots (approx 260km/h) at 300 nautical miles (approx 550km) from base.
2. A load of 9,480lb (4,300kg) of military equipment and ordnance.
3. A crew of eleven.

An order for about 100 machines was expected, with seventy-two going to operational units and the remainder used for training, and two manufacturers responded – Hurel-Dubois and Nord Aviation.

Hurel-Dubois HD 35

This latter ASW proposal was in 1955 preferred to the Nord Aviation 2505 because it offered more endurance and could take off from smaller fields. The modifications to the base aircraft would have involved the installation of a bomb bay under most of the fuselage length, of a downward-looking radome for an APS 33 radar (which it was hoped would be replaced by French Thomson CSF equipment for the production version), reworking of the front fuselage to include a glass nose for observation, and the introduction of a retractable nose gear to clear the field for the search radar (the HD 321 had a fixed landing gear). A short magnetic anomaly detector (MAD) boom was integrated into the rear fuselage and ECM equipment would have been fitted atop the fuselage under a fairing. The *Marine Nationale* was expected to order about 100 HD 35s for ASW and coastal patrol duties and a model of the HD 35 was displayed at the 1955 Paris Air Show, but by that time only two prototypes were planned for the financial year 1955-56. However, test flights with the HD 321 revealed that the performance expected of the HD 35 would not be achieved because of its Wright engines and so the anti-submarine HD 35 remained a paper plane. (See Chapter Ten.)

HD 355

This was a development of the HD 35 brought about by the need to increase the available power due to the gain in weight through having all of the military equipment needed for ASW operations. The transport version's Wright R-1820 engines were unsuitable for a military aircraft – they were not powerful enough and they were costly in dollars. For these two reasons they were to be replaced by licence-produced Bristol Hercules units, and then Turbomeca Marboré turbojets were also added. A prototype was ordered to be delivered by 1 April 1957 and two more pre-production aircraft would have followed before series production was launched. However, due to the lacklustre performance of the HD 321, interest in the HD 35 waned. The contract for the first prototype was cancelled and the order for the two pre-production aircraft was never issued. Yet the Hurel-Dubois proposal would later, through the HD 35 mock-up, provide the inspiration for the interior equipment of the Breguet Atlantic.

HD 355

Status	uncompleted prototype
Span	148ft 2in (45.16m)
Length	77ft 5.5in (23.61m)
Gross wing area	1,075.2sq ft (100sq m)
Gross weight	58,311lb (26,450kg)
Powerplant	two Hercules
Maximum speed/Height	226mph (364km/h), cruise 115mph (185km/h), endurance over thirteen hours
Equipment	four torpedoes

Nord 2501 ASW

The first Nord 2501 ASW was proposed in 1950, in direct opposition to the Br 764, and it was turned down immediately because the Breguet proposal seemed much more likely to fill the requirements. The Nord 2504 '*Appareil École Anti-Sous-Marine*' actually came after the Nord 2505 (qv), it was a standard 2501 airframe fitted with ASW avionics and had a small radome installed under the fuselage. First flown in 1956, according to Jean Cuny in *Les Avions de Combat Français* Volume 2: '*This aircraft played for a long time an obscure but important role*,' which may mean that it was more than just a training aircraft! (See Chapter Ten.)

Nord 2505 ASW

Status	project
Span	108ft 7in (33.10m)
Length	72ft 0in (21.95m)
Gross wing area	1,075.3sq ft (100sq m)
Gross weight	up to 52,910lb (24,000kg)
Powerplant	two Hercules 1,970hp (1,469kW)
Maximum speed/Height	255mph (410km/h), patrol: cruise 138mph (222km/h)
Armament	two torpedoes, four depth charges

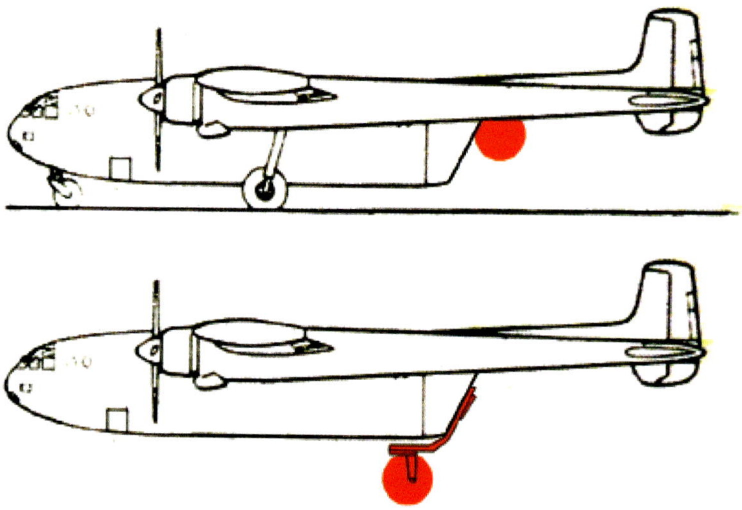

ABOVE Reconstruction by the author of the Nord 2501 AEW. The retractable sphere would have contained a radar of unspecified type. *Author's drawing*

In 1954 Nord Aviation offered the Nord 2505 to the 'mid-size' requirements with an airframe that had been reworked entirely for the ASW role. It featured a redesigned fuselage, an observer's nose, a bomb bay, and a retractable radome (the low position of the fuselage, an asset for loading a freighter, was a handicap for an ASW aeroplane requiring downward-facing detection equipment). The transport version's two Bristol Hercules and two wingtip-mounted Turbomeca Marboré auxiliary turbojets were retained, which meant that a 63% commonality with the military transport already in operation was expected. The final evolution, designed in 1957, featured a large radar of unspecified type with the array enclosed in a large sphere mounted on a movable arm that could be retracted into the rear fuselage. However, the *Marine Nationale* selected the Hurel Dubois HD 35, and then in the end bought neither!

The NATO Programme

In 1958 NATO, seeing the growing trend by the Soviet Navy towards the extensive use of submarines, issued a call for proposals for a new ASW patrol aircraft to replace the Lockheed Neptune, and this was expected to fulfil the needs of the European members and to be built in co-operation. The requirements focused on speed (300 knots, approx 550km/h), endurance (up to eighteen hours of patrol at low altitude, even on a single engine), avionics and ordnance (which had to be of the latest standard) and ergonomics (the fuselage had to be a comfortable place for up to thirteen crew). The submissions had to be received before 21 June 1958, and after their assessment by the evaluation team only three designs were selected for further evaluation: Breguet's Br 1150 was the top scorer, followed by the British Avro 745 and then a Nord Aviation project. On 21 October 1958, the Breguet design was declared the winner.

Breguet Br 1150 Atlantic

The Br 1150 design was the logical evolution of the previous Breguet studies on the subject. It featured a two-deck airframe in which the crew was housed in a rather spacious cabin in the upper deck, while the lower deck (neatly visible from the outside due to the bilabial structure with its figure of eight section) was devoted entirely to accommodating the armament (by now reduced to torpedoes and depth charges, although underwing rockets were considered) and avionics (two radomes). A long MAD boom also featured and the large aspect ratio wings had wide slotted flaps for low-speed operation. The engines were Rolls-Royce Tyne turboprops.

The prototype Br 1150-01 made its maiden flight on 21 October 1959 flown by Bernard Witt. It was distinguished from the examples that followed in having a shorter fuselage, no MAD boom and no tail radome, but it did have wingtip nacelles and the aircraft was used mostly for aerodynamic testing. Subsequent to the launch of the Atlantic there was some soul-searching in the UK regarding the lack of participation of Great Britain in this programme. In the May 1960 issue of *RAF Flying Review* the technical editor wrote: '*The Atlantic will constitute one of the key anti-submarine defence weapons of the NATO countries in the years ahead and a very effective weapon it promises to be. The British government may yet take another look at the possibility of acquiring this aircraft for RAF Coastal Command. National pride should not be allowed to affect the future efficiency of one of our most operational commands.*' In 1961 the sale of the Atlantic to RAF Coastal Command as a replacement for the Avro Shackleton was still rumoured, including suggestions for a turbojet to be installed in the tail to provide a boost in speed.

The second Atlantic, Br 1150-02, first flew on 23 February 1962 but crashed a few weeks later on 19 April, killing its crew. Br 1150-03 made its first flight nearly a year later, on

Breguet Br 1150 Atlantic	
Status	production
Span	120ft 13in (6.60m)
Length	104ft 2in (31.75m)
Gross wing area	1,294.0sq ft (120.34sq m)
Gross weight	95,899lb (43,500kg)
Powerplant	two Tyne 20 5,670hp (4,230kW)
Maximum speed/Height	404mph (650km/h)
Armament	torpedoes and depth charges

25 February 1963. It had a fuselage stretched by 3ft 3.5in (1m) and the full complement of avionics, so this aircraft was used to test the type's equipment and armament. The final prototype was Br 1150-04; it was quite similar to the eighty-seven production machines that followed and first flew on 10 September 1964. The production run of eighty-seven lasted until 1974 and examples were delivered to the French, German, Italian, Netherlands and Pakistan navies (the last named using ex-French aircraft). Five of the German machines later received new avionics as electronic intelligence aircraft. One curious variant of the Atlantic came in an effort to turn the aircraft into a flying boat.

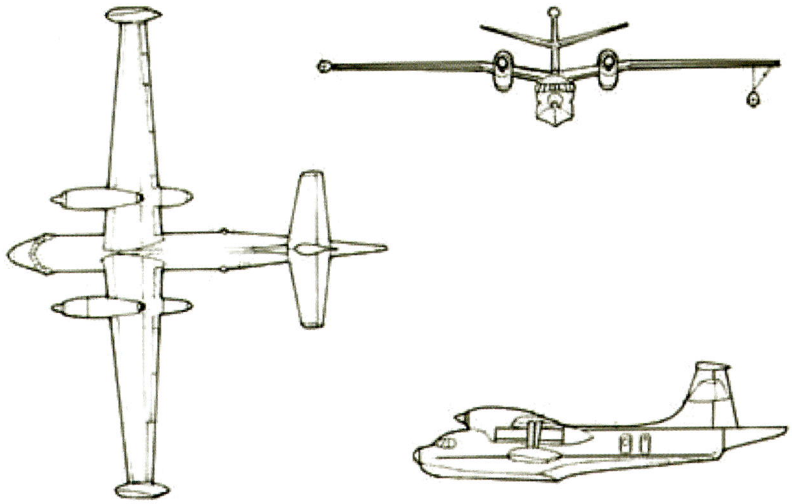

ABOVE **A most curious variant of the Atlantic was the Breguet Br 1250, an adaptation of the airframe into a flying boat with the lower fuselage modified into a boat hull.** *Author's from Cuny*

Breguet Atlantic Mk.II

A version called 'Atlantic Mk.II' was proposed by Avro, the British partner in the NATO programme, in 1960. This was heavier but benefited from two additional turbojets under the wing. Although this project was abandoned with the selection by the RAF of the Nimrod for its new ASW aircraft, the project was resurrected in the early 1970s as the 'Atlantic Mk.II' and fitted with state of the art avionics and turbojet 'boosters'. The latter was no longer a Breguet Atlantic of course, but rather an AMD-BA Atlantic, since by that time Dassault and Breguet had merged.

Breguet Atlantic AWACS

This variant, which was based on the Br 1191, one of the Breguet MINERVE proposals (see Chapter Four), was fitted with a rotating saucer-type antenna above the fuselage. An alternative version was fitted with a large nose radome in the style used on the cancelled BAe Nimrod AEW.Mk.3.

Breguet Br 1160

This was a development that saw the mating of a new freighter fuselage with the wings and tail of the standard

Breguet Br 1190

Status	project
Span	119ft 1in (36.30m)
Length	92ft 11.5in (28.33m)
Gross wing area	1,290.3sq ft (120sq m)
Gross weight	99,206lb (45,000kg)
Powerplant	two Tyne 20 6,015hp (4,485kW)
Maximum speed/Height	404mph (650km/h)
Armament	Matra 600 missile

Breguet Br 1191

Status	project
Span	119ft 1in (36.30m)
Length	98ft 5in (30.00m)
Gross wing area	1,290.3sq ft (120sq m)
Gross weight	99,206lb (45,000kg)
Powerplant	two Tyne 20 6,015hp (4,485kW)
Maximum speed/Height	404mph (650km/h)
Armament	Sud Aviation Minerve missile

BELOW **Interior arrangement of the 'veille basse altitude' aircraft proposal.** *Dassault Aviation*

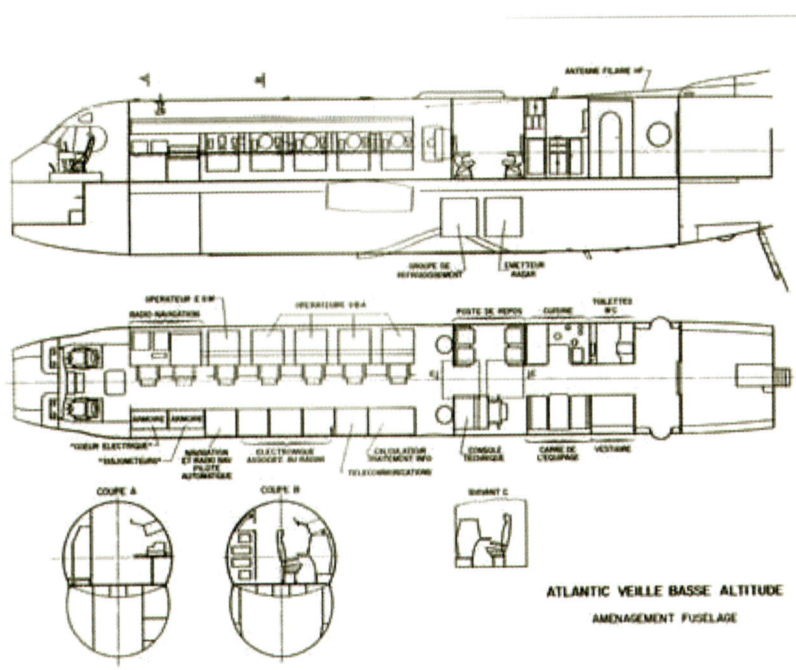

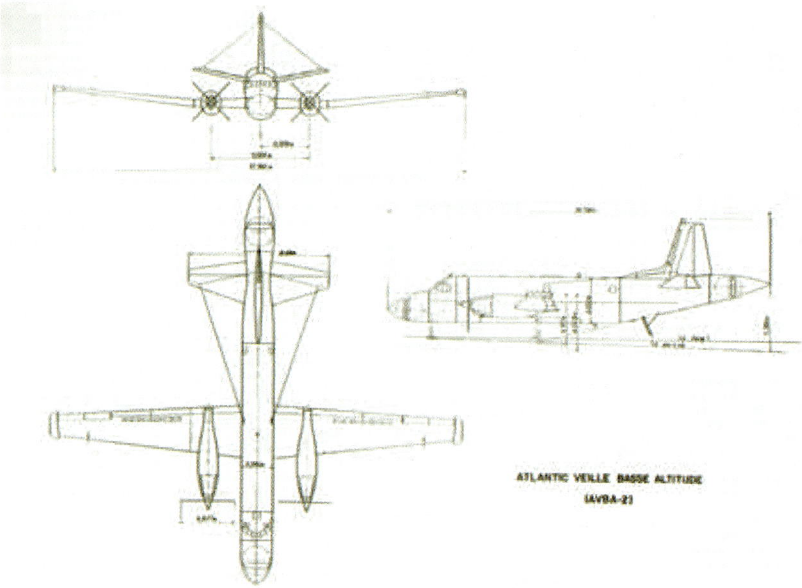

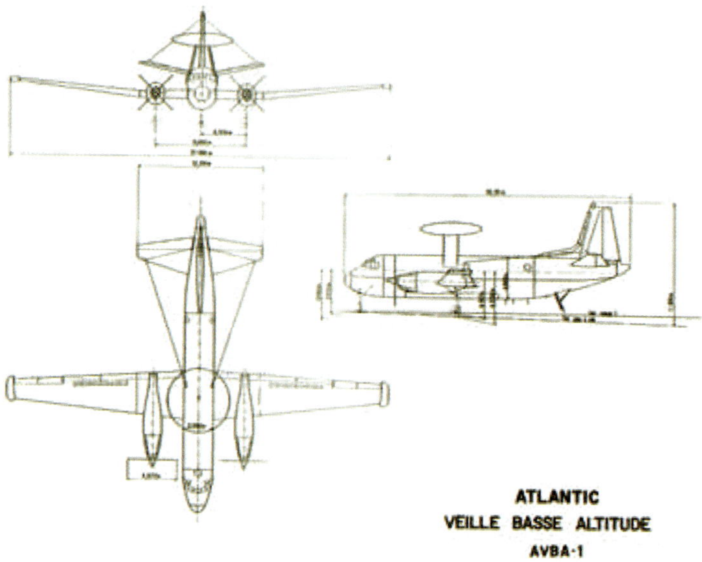

TOP **The Breguet Atlantic was developed into AWACS-type versions (*'veille basse altitude'* or low altitude patrol). This one was intended to have large radomes at both ends of the fuselage, rather like the British Aerospace Nimrod AEW3.** *Dassault Aviation*

ABOVE **The same brochure also offered a variant with a large rotodome above the fuselage.** *Dassault Aviation*

Atlantic. The project arrived at a time when Breguet already had its assault transport Br 940 (Br 941) flying and Nord Aviation was engaged in the Transall programme. So it was soon forgotten, the emphasis being placed on the more innovative Br 940 series (See Chapter Ten).

AMD-BA Atlantic ANG

From the early 1980s a new and improved version of the Atlantic was designed called the ANG for 'Atlantic New Generation'. At that time it was planned to begin deliveries in 1986 with production by the same international consortium that had built the first version. The ANG benefited from new powerplants (improved 6,000hp [4,475kW] Rolls-Royce Tyne Mk.21s), improved avionics and the possibility of carrying anti-shipping missiles under the wings. Curiously, while models and mock-ups were shown with four missiles of an unnamed type under the wing, the brochure in its description of the missile-armed missions only mentioned two; anti-surface patrol missions would have two missiles while operations at extreme long range would see the aircraft carry just a single missile (this description reminds the author of the Minerve mission of fifteen years before – Chapter Four!). One aircraft flew as the Atlantic ANG 'demonstrator' at the 1979 Paris Air Show.

AMD-BA Atlantic ATL2

By 1984 the developed Atlantic had been rebranded the ATL 2 and without any obvious changes to the airframe, although various bulges and pods signalled that new scanners and detection systems had gone into it. A new brochure put the emphasis on the ATL 2 combined with an AM 39 Exocet missile – '*launched against a target at a distance of several tens of nautical miles, and quickly homing at nearly sonic speed and at wave crest height, the AM 39 is almost inescapable. This particular weapon provides the ATL2 with an impressive firepower*'. Installation of the Exocet had been planned since

AMD-BA ATL2	
Status	production
Span	122ft 7in (37.36m)
Length	107ft 0in (32.62m)
Gross wing area	?
Gross weight	101,852lb (46,200kg)
Powerplant	two Tyne 6,100hp (4,550kW)
Maximum speed/Height	403mph (648km/h)
Armament	torpedoes, missiles and depth charges

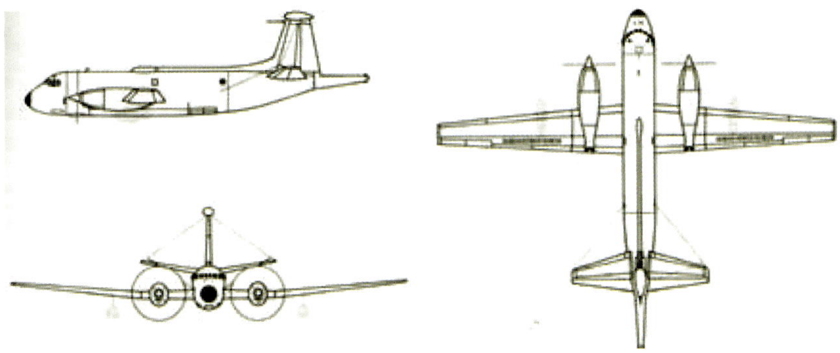

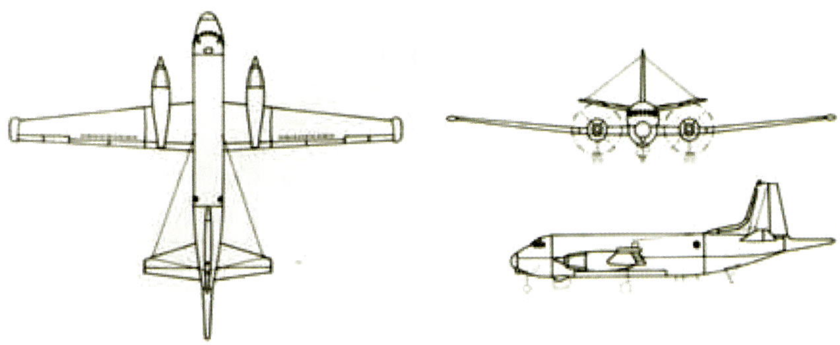

TOP Another development of the Atlantic was the M4B of 1977, which differed little from the original configuration. *Author's collection/Breguet*

ABOVE Two years later the configuration had evolved into the Atlantic Nouvelle Génération or ANG. Again, from the outside the configuration was little modified, but inside the avionics had changed considerably. *Author's collection/Breguet*

BELOW The Atlantic Nouvelle Génération did fly. Note the four missiles – the brochure showed only two for the anti-shipping configuration. *Author's collection/Breguet*

1973, with the missiles being carried in the armament bay. Explosive bolts would release an Exocet from its rack and its motor would be fired when the weapon had fallen to 10 to 13ft (3 to 4m) beneath the aircraft. The missile's range was dependent on the altitude at launch, starting at about 31 miles (50km) if the launch was made at 985ft (300m) height, going up to 35 miles (55.5km) when it was released at 16,405ft (5,000m). A prototype first flew in May 1981, other examples were used for weapon system development during the 1980s, and twenty-eight units were delivered to the *Marine Nationale* from 1989.

AMD-BA Atlantic ATL3

This further development was announced by AMD-BA at the 1995 Paris Air Show. It naturally included renewed avionics and armament, but also in-flight refuelling capability and a new cockpit enabling just two crew to fly the aircraft. The powerplant would also have been upgraded and the intended customer was the RAF, but the aircraft could not meet that service's specification.

Breguet Br 123

The Br 123 type number covers a range of rather dissimilar aircraft (in two groups) studied in 1965 at the request of the *Marine Nationale* for the Anglo-French Early Warning Aircraft programme. Since Breguet had already embarked on various co-operation projects with British partners, it seemed logical to call upon the firm for this new type. Breguet consulted with various avionics specialists (CSF, CFTH, Elliott, and Marconi) and engine suppliers (Bristol, Rolls-Royce, SNECMA) and it was noted that the different types of antennas seemed to be better adapted to different avionics. For example: '*The rotodome has serious difficulties for using certain wave ranges: it is perfectly adapted for UHF bands, but not applicable to S-band.*'

The idea here appears to have been to develop an aircraft along the lines of the American Grumman Hawkeye (which, ironically, the *Marine Nationale* finally ordered three decades later!).

Br 123A

The versions designed under the Br 123A reference were quite strange-looking machines in that the whole fuselage looked like a massive radome! Actually the centre fuselage housed the crew cabin and cockpit, the landing gear and the fuel tanks, but the two extremities were indeed large radomes of more than 8ft 2.5in (2.50m) diameter. To avoid interference between the airframe and the radar, notably for the rearward installation, a twin-boom layout was selected with the horizontal tail surface barely extending beyond the radome. Bristol/General Electric T64 turboprops were selected to provide the propulsion, although more advanced SNECMA M46 turbofans were also offered. At this time ducted fans were seen as one of the powerplants of the future and may have been investigated for this design.

Breguet Br 123A	
Status	project
Span	60ft 0.5in (18.30m), approx 25ft 3in (7.70m) folded
Length	52ft 0in (15.85m)
Gross wing area	591.4sq ft (55sq m)
Gross weight	39,683lb (18,000kg) approx
Powerplant	two Bristol (GE) T64 4,000hp (2,985kW)
Maximum speed/Height	-
Armament	none

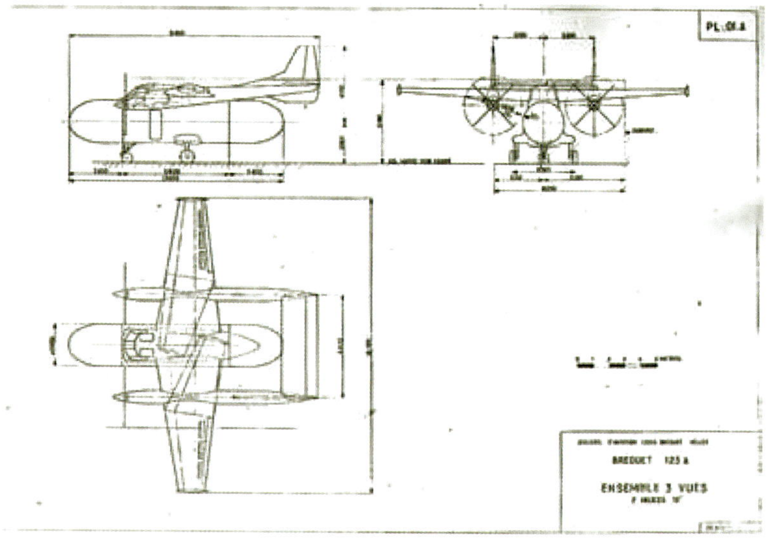

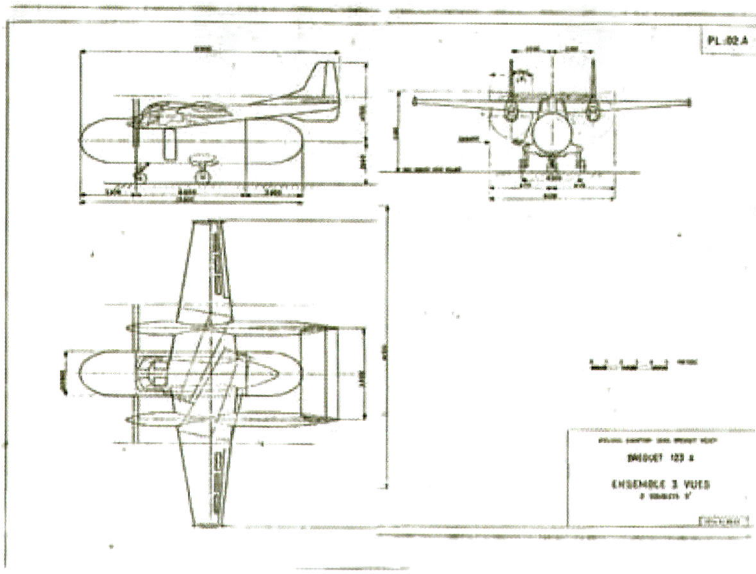

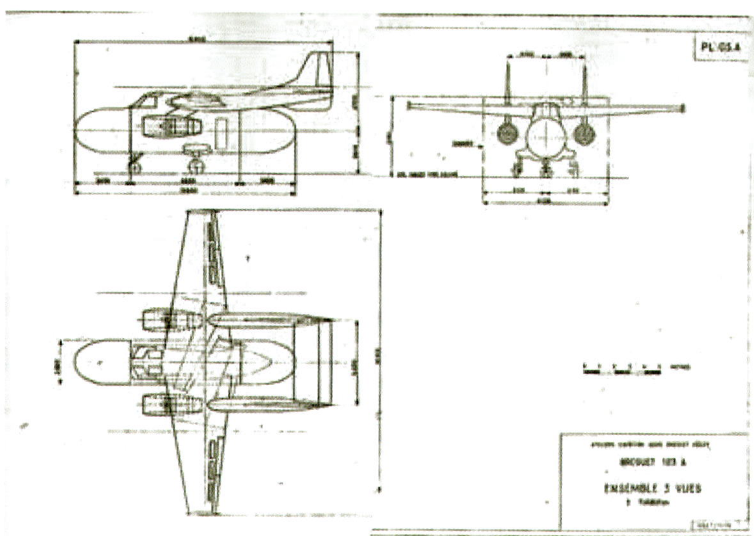

This and the next page The Breguet Br 123 was turned into six variants, which were distinguished by their propulsion system and their radar/radome fittings. *Philippe Ricco*

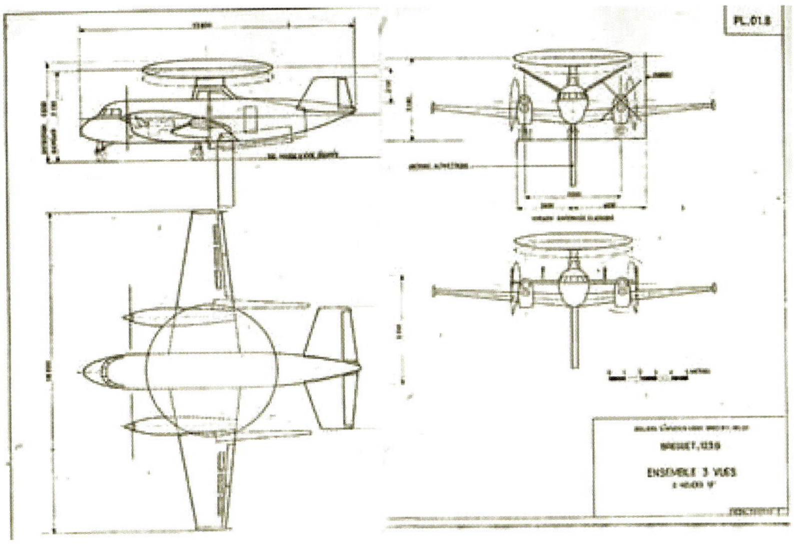

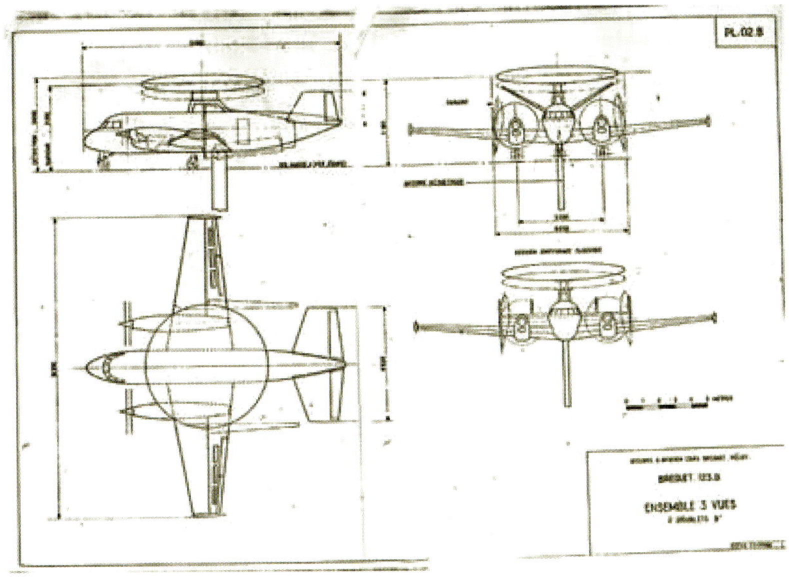

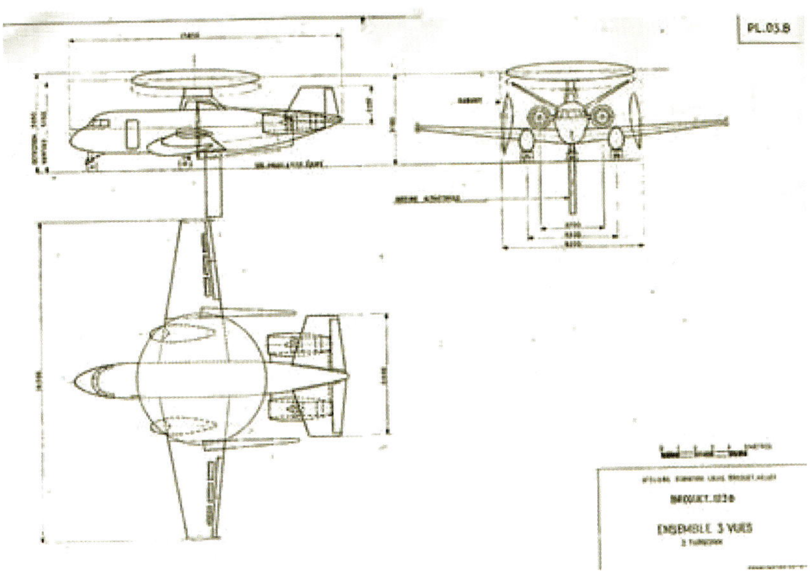

Breguet Br 123B	
Status	project
Span	60ft 0.5in (18.30m)
Length	52ft 6in (16.00m) approx
Gross wing area	591.4sq ft (55sq m)
Gross weight	39,683lb (18,000kg) approx
Powerplant	two Bristol (GE) T64 4,000hp (2,985kW)
Maximum speed/Height	-
Armament	none

Br 123B

The versions suggested under the second basic design, the Br 123B, were more classical in appearance; in fact, the layout could be likened to a 'mini-Atlantic' with a 'saucer'-type radome above its fuselage of approximate 24ft 11in (7.6m) diameter. The only unusual aspect here was the flattened butterfly-type tail surfaces. A foldable altimetry radar antenna was carried under the fuselage and the same powerplant options were available as for the Br 123A types.

Nord 'Patrouilleur NATO'

The Nord Aviation entry was classed third in the initial evaluation. It had a similar airframe layout to the winning Breguet Atlantic design with a bilobed fuselage, the crew in the upper deck and the bomb bay and avionics underneath them (two radomes were prominent in the front fuselage), long thin wings and the selection of Tyne turboprops for propulsion. However, the design had a more pointed nose and no apparent MAD boom (which may have been added later).

Petrel

In 1985, Dassault, in association with Aérospatiale, offered a dedicated naval patrol version of the ATR 42 transport called the Petrel. This was to be able to carry key items of detection equipment and four missiles.

AMD-BA/Aérospatiale Petrel	
Status	project
Span	74ft 4.5in (22.67m)
Length	80ft 7.5in (24.57m)
Gross wing area	586.0sq ft (54.50sq m)
Gross weight	-
Powerplant	two P&W Canada PW100-series
Maximum speed/Height	-
Armament	four Aérospatiale missiles

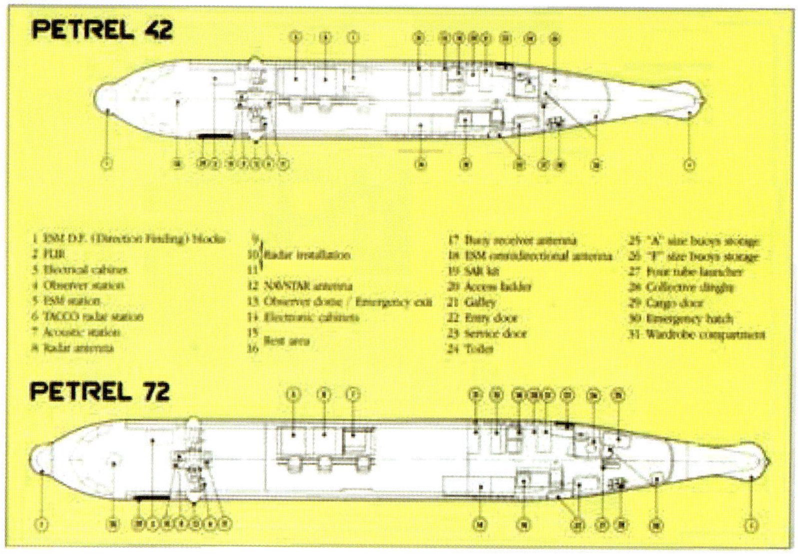

TOP Taken from a Dassault brochure, this illustration depicts a Dassault Petrel, an ASW adaptation of the ATR 42 airliner. *Dassault Aviation*

ABOVE From the same brochure, this drawing shows some of the interior equipment proposed for the Petrel. *Dassault Aviation*

The Smaller ASW Aircraft

The types that follow are the direct descendants of the Avengers of Midway or the Swordfish of Taranto … or of the Laté 293 of the 1930s. Although a few Laté 293s did survive the war, they were no longer up to date, so it came as no surprise that the Latécoère *bureau d'études* tried, as soon as the war had ended, to find a worthy successor for the type. This was to be the Latécoère Laté 200 of 1947. Nord Aviation is also supposed to have had a torpedo bomber project under way at the same time but nothing is known about it.

Latécoère Laté 200

This was an unusual design with a large tubular fuselage housing two Rolls-Royce Nene turbojets placed side-by-side. The most unusual part was that the two engines were fed by a single annular intake and exhausted by a single circular outlet just behind the tailplane, which was of typical Latécoère design. The two crew were seated side-by-side too in the front fuselage and a long two-door bay underneath the fuselage could house a single torpedo. The tricycle landing gear was another sign of modernity and this machine was carrier-based as it featured an arrestor hook. This project was published in February 1947 and it well reflects the uncertainties of the time when modern advances (jet power, tricycle landing gear, cigar-shaped fuselage with faired-in canopy) were mixed seemingly haphazardly with pre-war elements (Latécoère twin-tail, single torpedo armament). The Laté 200 was not built.

On 28 March 1947 the *Marine Nationale* had elicited interest in the idea of a modern torpedo bomber, indicating that this would need to be powered by a turboprop engine to have enough endurance and range for its mission. The need was precised by the issuing on 12 November of a call for proposals asking for an aircraft to fulfil the roles of anti-shipping operations using rockets or missiles and rockets, or anti-submarine operations with depth charges and rockets.

The information obtained through the reverse engineering of captured German hardware such as the Ruhrstahl 8-344 (X-4) and Henschel Hs 293 missiles probably explains the interest in missiles for the anti-shipping operation. This call for proposals was amended in July 1948 with these additional requirements:

(i). The possibility of using JATO rocket bottles for take-off.
(ii). An endurance of four hours at sea level.
(iii). Speeds ranging between 186mph and 435mph (300km/h and 700km/h).
(iv). A landing speed of less than 96mph (155km/h).
(v). The installation of armour for the crew.

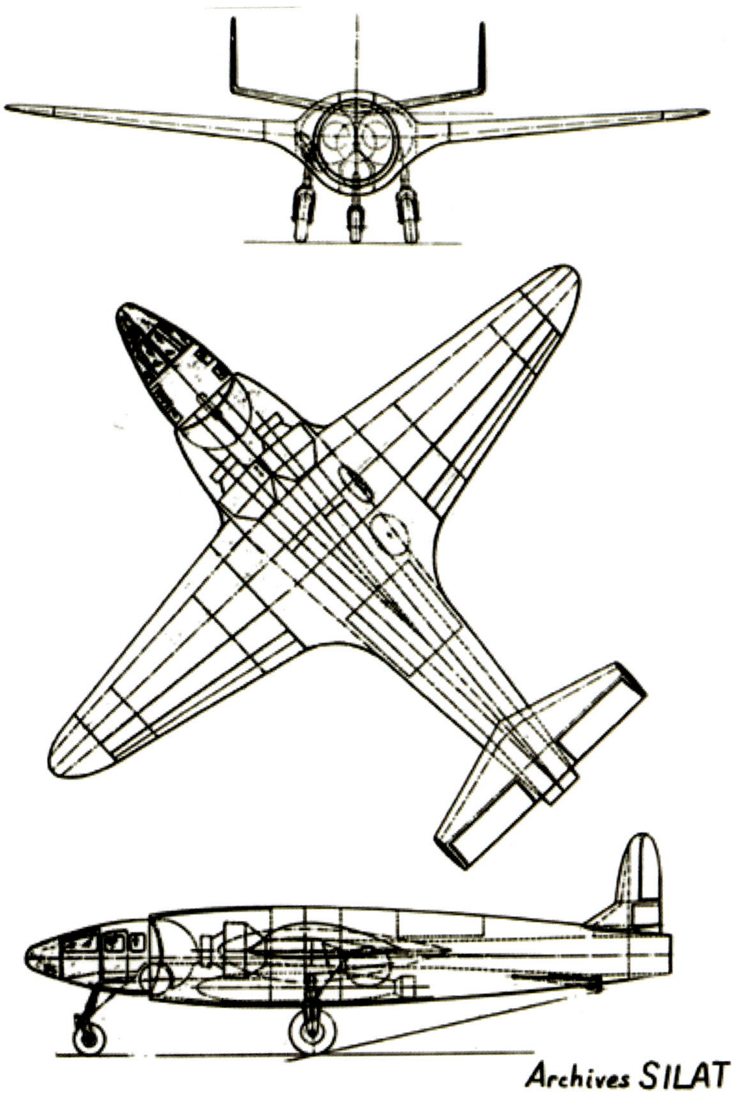

ABOVE An unusual twin-turbojet project from Latécoère was the Laté 200. The tail is a typical Latécoère design. *Latécoère*

BELOW The predecessor to the Alizé was the Breguet Br 960 Vultur, the first prototype of which made its maiden flight on 4 August 1951. Here the two prototypes appear side-by-side. *Philippe Ricco*

Path to the Alizé: The Breguet Br 960 Vultur and Family

The Breguet design team responded with the Br 960 Vultur (Vulture) and the design exhibited the following features:

1. The aircraft had a mixed powerplant: a turboprop (an Armstrong Siddeley Mamba I) ensured endurance while a turbojet (Rolls-Royce Nene) provided the requested higher speeds (in fact, comparable to the speeds of jet fighters then flying).
2. The need to carry and launch anti-ship missiles (Henschel Hs 293 or Ruhrstahl Fritz-X glide bomb) had an impact on the design of the landing gear, with the main legs set wide apart to give enough ground clearance to carry the missile underneath the fuselage. Since the missile would be guided visually by the bomber, the cockpit had to offer a good all-round vision and so for this reason side-by-side seating for the pilot and the bomber was preferred.
3. The wings could fold automatically (the aircraft was expected to operate from a carrier).
4. One wingtip nacelle contained a fuel tank and the other a search radar.

As first designed the aircraft had a twin fin and rudder assembly, possibly with a view to installing a defensive weapon in the cockpit. However, when built it had shed this outdated vision of ASW operations and was fitted with a single large fin and rudder.

Br 960-01

This first prototype made its maiden flight on 4 August 1951 at Toulouse with Yves Brunaud at the controls. It was somewhat underpowered and could not fly at full load without having the turbojet running. After its 1952-53 trials programme the first 960 was used as a test bed for lift-improving devices under the designation Br 963.

Breguet Br 960 Vultur 01	
Status	prototype
Span	52ft 0in (15.85m)
Length	43ft 9.5in (13.35m)
Gross wing area	390.3sq ft (36.30sq m)
Gross weight	up to 21,605lb (9,800kg)
Powerplant	one Mamba I 966hp (720kW) and one Nene 101 24,725lb (1kN)
Maximum speed/Height	559mph (900km/h)
Armament	Fritz X, Hs 293 (never installed)

Br 960-02

Yves Brunaud also performed the first flight of the second machine, on 15 September 1952. It differed from the first in the fitting of the more powerful Mamba III and Nene 104 engines. Its 1952-53 trials included carrier landing tests carried out at Farnborough in the UK and these showed that the type completely fulfilled the requirements. This aircraft was later heavily modified as the Br 965 to become the first prototype of the Alizé.

Breguet Br 960 Vultur 02	
Status	prototype
Span	54ft 9.5in (16.70m) with wingtip tanks
Length	43ft 9.5in (13.35m)
Gross wing area	390.3sq ft (36.30sq m)
Gross weight	up to 21,605lb (9,800kg)
Powerplant	one Mamba III 1,250hp (932kW) and one Nene 104 4,725lb (21kN)
Maximum speed/Height	559mph (900km/h)
Armament	various

Breguet Br 960F1

Variants were offered to the French Navy for the hunter/killer role under the 'F' series. The killer version was quite similar to the standard Vultur but had a revised bomb bay with bulged doors, while the hunter was fitted with a large radome to house a search radar underneath the fuselage. These F1 aircraft had an old-style landing gear with tail wheels, probably in the hope of saving weight, and the rear turbojet was also left out for the same reason; the front power unit was now a Mamba VI. These two types were intended to

BELOW **The Vultur was turned into the Breguet Br 961 hunter/killer aircraft in which one version would be carrying weapons and the second a search radar. The landing gear reverted to the old-fashioned tail wheel configuration to save weight.** *Author's from Cuny*

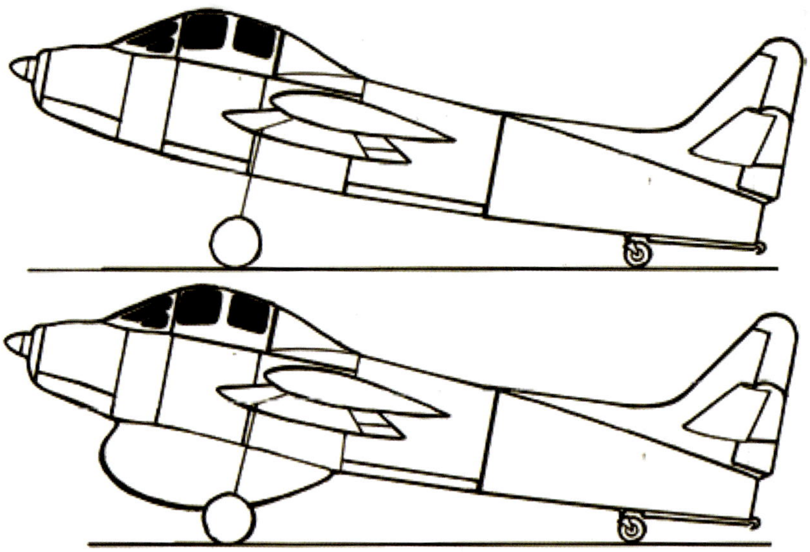

BOTTOM **This further version of the Br 961 hunter/killer concept had the tricycle undercarriage used by the Vultur prototypes.** *Author's from Cuny*

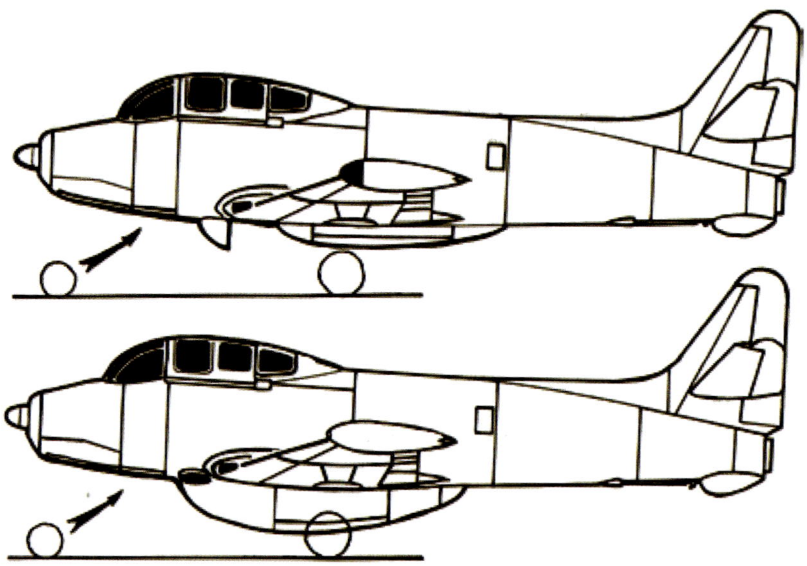

Breguet Br 960F	
Status	project
Span	54ft 9.5in (16.70m) with wingtip tanks
Length	43ft 9.5in (13.35m)
Gross wing area	390.3sq ft (36.30sq m)
Gross weight	up to 17,857lb (8,100kg)
Powerplant	one Mamba VI 1,625hp (1,212kW)
Maximum speed/Height	277mph (445km/h) at sea level
Armament	various

operate together (along the lines of the American Grumman AF Guardian) and were designed in late 1953.

Breguet Br 960F2

The F2 variant retained the tricycle undercarriage of the Vultur but was otherwise similar to the F1.

Breguet Br 961

A ground attack version for the *Armée de l'Air* with naval fittings removed, single seat and with one 30mm gun in each wing. An improved version with a slightly swept wing (30° at the leading edge) and more powerful engines would have been designated Br 962.

Status	**project**
Span	54ft 9.5in (16.70m)
Length	43ft 9.5in (13.35m)
Gross wing area	390.3sq ft (36.30sq m)
Gross weight	up to 24,250lb (11,000kg)
Powerplant	one Mamba III 1,575hp (1,175kW) and one Avon 6,075lb (27kN) or ATAR 101 6,075lb (27kN)
Maximum speed/Height	590mph (950km/h)
Armament	two HS 411 30mm guns and bombs, rockets

ABOVE Artist's view of how an operational Br 961 would have appeared, which was reproduced on the cover of Sciences & Vie magazine for January 1951. *Author's collection*

BELOW Another version of the Br 961 was this ground attack aircraft intended for the *Armée de l'Air.* *Author's from Cuny*

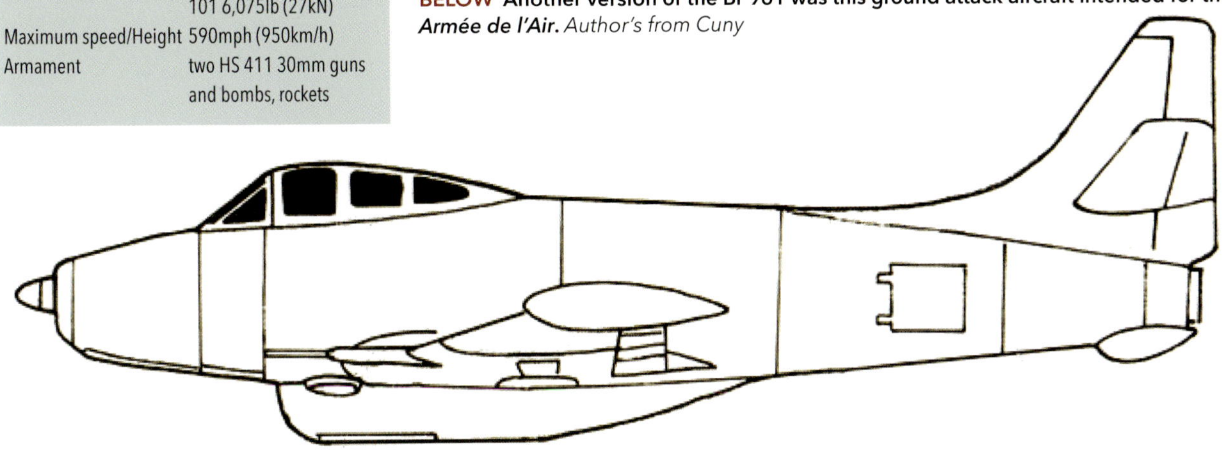

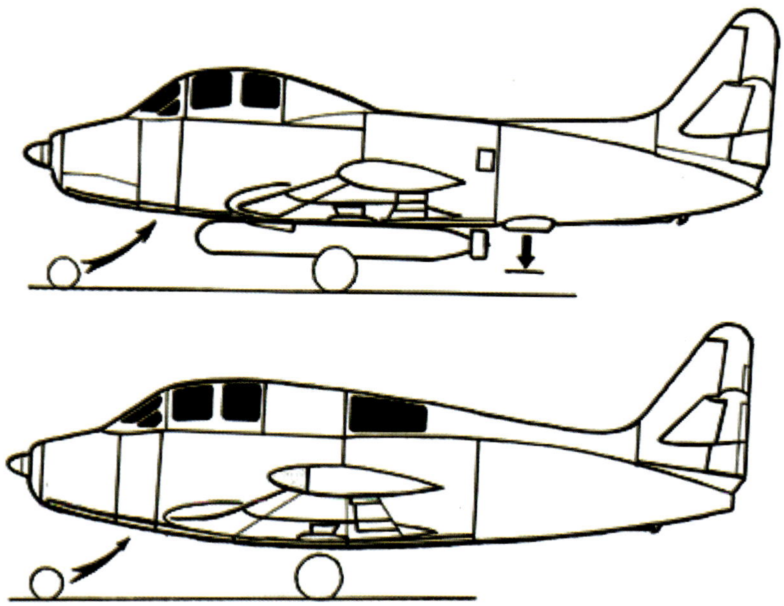

ABOVE These early 961 variants were also intended for the hunter/killer role. One version had an enlarged bomb bay and the other carried a third crew member in an extended fuselage to operate the avionics. *Author's from Cuny*

Breguet Br 962 ASW

An early 1953 design with an elongated cabin stretched along the whole fuselage spine, a single Mamba VI and an AS 33B radar located in the left wingtip nacelle.

Breguet Br 963

The Br 963 was the Breguet Br 960-01, but now on the civil register as F-WEVU and reconfigured as a test bed for lift-improving 'hypercirculation' trials (that is by bleeding air from the Nene turbojet and directing it through slots in the wing upper surfaces). The initial 1964 trials were successful but a second test programme was cut short by a lack of funds.

Breguet Br 965

This was the second Vultur modified to approach the configuration of the planned production ASW aircraft (the soon-to-follow Alizé). The cockpit was enlarged to house a third crew member, a radar operator who would work an APS 15A search set fitted in a retractable radome under the rear fuselage. The Nene was removed to make room for the radar while at the same time the Mamba III turboprop was replaced by a more powerful Mamba VI. Testing was ongoing until the aircraft was damaged on 2 May 1956, by which time the trials had been sufficiently successful to validate the concept and pave the way for the Alizé.

Breguet Br 965	
Status	prototype
Span	52ft 0in (15.85m)
Length	43ft 9.5in (13.35m)
Gross wing area	(390.3sq ft (36.30sq m)
Gross weight	up to 21,605lb (9,800kg)
Powerplant	one Mamba VI 1,625hp (1,212kW)
Maximum speed/Height	277mph (445km/h) at sea level
Armament	-

Breguet Br 966

Early type number for the future Alizé.

Breguet Br 1050 Alizé (Tradewind)

The Br 1050 Alizé was the refined and definitive version of the Breguet turboprop ASW aircraft, for which the general concept had been tested with the Br 965. The main differences between this aircraft and the Br 695 were the engine, a Rolls-Royce Dart (more powerful than the Br 695's Mamba VI), the landing gear now retracted into wing nacelles, which made room for fuel tanks, and the shape of the canopy. As many elements of the design had already been tested, there was no prototype, but there were four pre-production machines, the first of which flew on 5 October 1956.

BELOW The Breguet Br 965 was the final evolution of the Vultur and the second aircraft was reworked into a proof of concept prototype for the Alizé. *Philippe Ricco*

The first production Alizé flew in 1959 and seventy-five examples were produced for the *Marine Nationale*, with twelve more for the Indian Navy. Negotiations with Brazil (Commander Leoncio Martins from the carrier *Mineas Gerais* came to France in 1960 to assess the Alizé) and Indonesia did not generate any orders.

Breguet Br 1050 Alizé	
Status	production
Span	51ft 2in (15.60m)
Length	45ft 5in (13.85m)
Gross wing area	376.3sq ft (35.00sq m)
Gross weight	18,078lb (8,200kg)
Powerplant	one Dart 21 1,920hp (1,432kW)
Maximum speed/Height	270mph (435km/h) at sea level
Armament	five depth charges and six points under wings for AS 12 missiles, gun pods, etc.

ABOVE The Breguet Br 1050 Alizé was the success story of the Vultur-Alizé family, even gaining an export success with an order from India. *Philippe Ricco*

Breguet Alizé AEW

An early warning version of the Alizé was designed during 1957-59 with a radome installed either ventrally or dorsally. The best option would have been the dorsal installation because this did not need any reworking of the landing gear, the wing folding mechanism or the catapult hooks. However, a two-fin tail would have been needed otherwise the flying controls would have been masked by the large radome. The design appeared sufficiently interesting for testing to be performed on the Br 965 but, as usual, financial restraints led to its curtailment. During 1962-63 the idea of fitting a rotodome similar to the one installed on the Grumman Hawkeye was revived on a variant of the Br 1191 (see Chapter Four), a derivative of the Atlantic.

Breguet Br 1060

A de-navalised variant of the Alizé without folding wings or arrestor hook, and with all the ASW avionics removed, was called the Br 1160. Instead, a 30mm DEFA gun was mounted in each wing nacelle, the

Breguet Br 1060	
Status	project
Span	51ft 2in (15.60m)
Length	45ft 5in (13.85m)
Gross wing area	376.3sq ft (35.00sq m)
Gross weight	18,078lb (8,200kg)
Powerplant	one Dart 21 1,920hp (1,432kW)
Maximum speed/Height	290mph (466km/h) at 3,280ft (1,000m) with underwing loads
Armament	up to 2,205lb (1,000kg) ordnance

BELOW An early warning version of the Alizé was designed in 1958-59 with a large radome fitted either dorsally or ventrally. *Author's from Cuny*

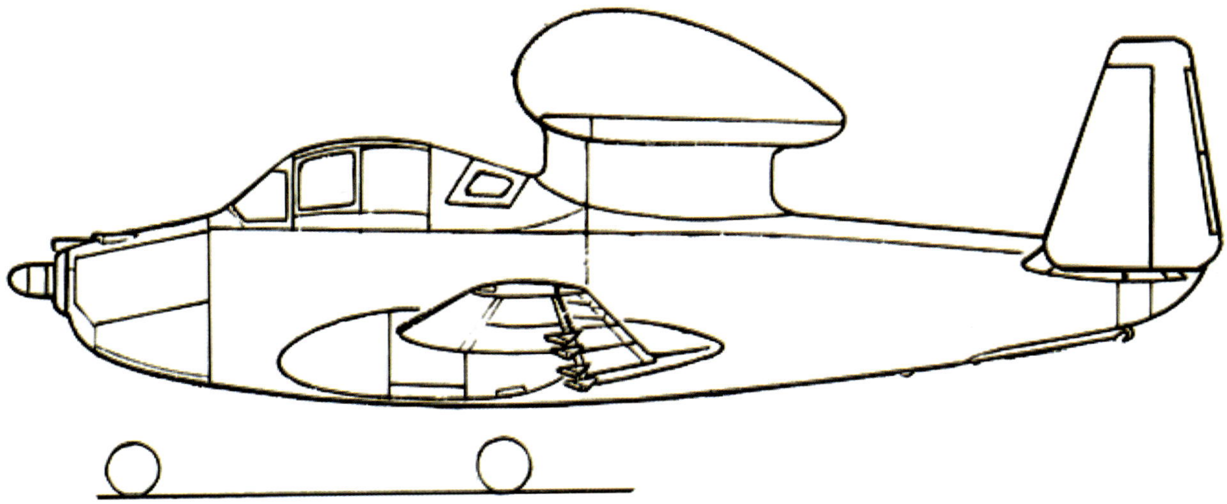

crew was protected by 772lb (350kg) of armour plating and a large choice of armament could be installed inside the bomb bay or under the wing attachment points. This design was proposed in 1957 when the war in Algeria was escalating and after the need for specific ground attack aircraft had become apparent.

Light Twin-Engine ASW Aircraft

Like all navies, the *Marine Nationale* had long cast a favourable eye towards twin-engine aircraft, which were seen as being more resilient and able to bring back their crew even in the advent of trouble with one engine. Therefore, in 1954 the *Marine Nationale* asked the French aircraft manufacturers if they could come up with a twin-engine aircraft for ASW duties. Naturally these would be competitors to the Alizé then under evaluation, which may explain why only two manufacturers responded. One was Breguet, competing against itself, probably with the idea of getting the best of both worlds, and the other was Dassault, which recycled its well-known and most successful Flamant light transport in the role. However, in the end, it was thought that selecting an all new design over the proven Vultur (future Alizé) would delay the aircraft's delivery to operational units by two years. These considerations effectively stopped the idea of ordering light twin-engine ASW aircraft.

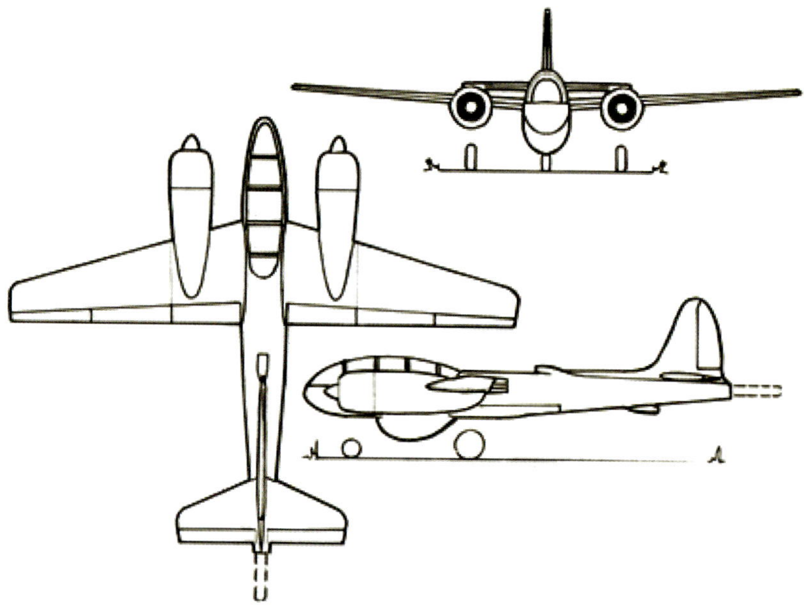

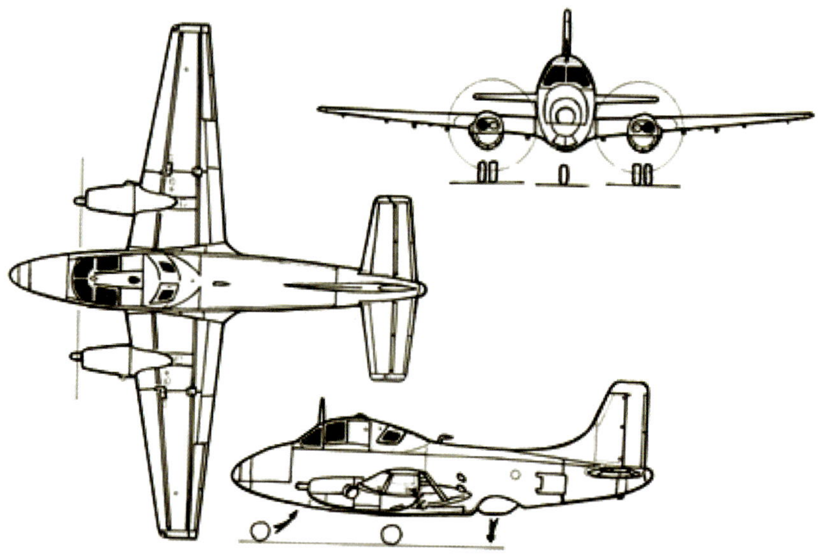

TOP **This unnamed Breguet project from 1954 was designed as a light anti-submarine aircraft.** *Author's from Cuny*

ABOVE **An unusual projected variant of the Alizé was this twin-engined version.** *Author's from Cuny*

Breguet Twin-Engine ASW

Breguet's first design was offered in early 1954 but it was too big and too heavy at more than 22,046lb (10,000kg) weight, nearly 20% above the maximum for an Alizé; it was also too powerful, having two 2,465hp (1,840kW) Mambas, and so was consequently rejected. Breguet reviewed its design and a revised version was proposed in April 1954. For propulsion two 790hp (589kW) Wright R-1300s were now specified with a Turbomeca Aspin II turbojet in the tail to boost the speed when required. This revision did look good but an economic study revealed that the twin-engine aircraft would cost 35% more to operate than a single-engine type.

Breguet Alizé Twin

This was a 1956 design in which the two wing nacelles were extended forwards to receive General Electric T-58 turboprops, the nose consequently being more rounded following the removal of the Rolls-Royce Dart. This design was not offered in response to the *Marine Nationale* request for a twin-engine aircraft, but may have been inspired by the same idea and it could have been offered as an alternative to (foreign) customers who were interested in the

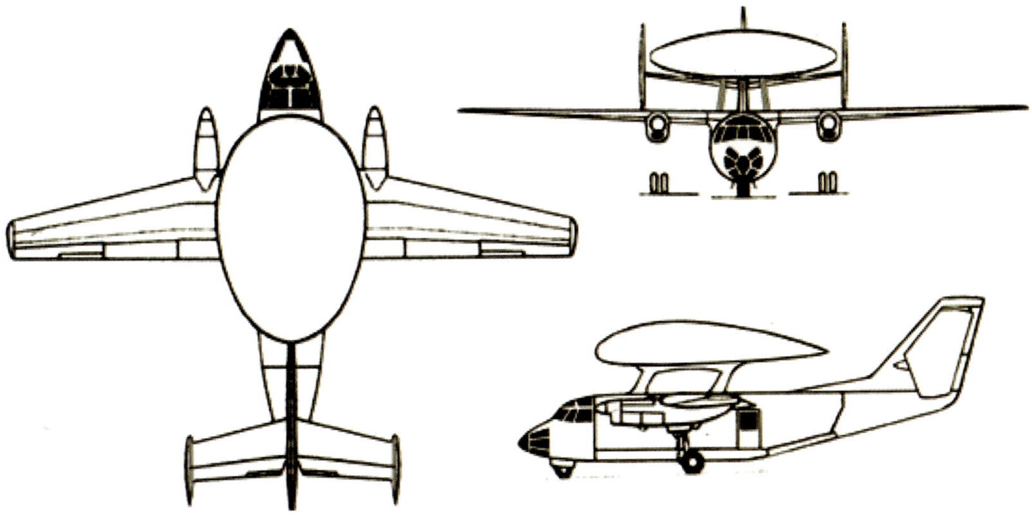

ABOVE Dassault also offered a variant of the Spirale III with a large radome for the early warning role. Author's from *Aviation Magazine*

potential of the Alizé, but who might have reservations about using a single-engine aircraft over the sea.

Dassault MD316T ASW

This project was a straight adaptation of the Flamant for the ASW role with a minimum of modifications. It was criticised heavily by the *Marine Nationale*, which thought the aircraft would be unable to fulfil its intended role.

Dassault MD 410 Spirale Early Warning

Before the Spirale programme was abandoned (see Chapter Seven) Dassault proposed a number of variants of its base design, including an early warning version conceived in around 1960.

Small Jet Patrol Aircraft

SN 600 Diplomate

This multi-role twin-jet 'executive' type aircraft was designed jointly by Nord and Sud Aviation, just before their merger into SNIAS Aerospatiale. It was basically designed to carry eight passengers at a speed of 466mph (750km/h) but the description of the machine as 'multi-role' suggested more variants could be in the offing than just a mere biz-jet. Some illustrations also depicted the machine sporting roundels, another pointer that military versions were anticipated.

Dassault Guardian/HU-25 Guardian

In 1979 forty-one Dassault Falcon 20 business jets were fitted with maritime patrol equipment and delivered to the US Coast Guard as the HU-25A Guardian. A later variant, the HU-25B, was optimised for anti-drug operations. New sensors were added including side-looking airborne radar, an APG-66 multi-mode pulse-Doppler radar and upgrades to the FLIR (forward looking infrared) turret, before finally a 360° scan AN/APS-143BV3 inverse synthetic aperture radar (ISAR) appeared in the ultimate HU-25D version. The Guardians were retired in 2014. In 1977 the *Marine Nationale* ordered five naval patrol Falcons as the Falcon 20H, and later seven examples of the Falcon 10MER for training purposes.

Nord/Sud SN 600 Diplomate	
Status	project
Span	42ft 0in (12.80m)
Length	40ft 10in (12.45m)
Gross wing area	?
Gross weight	under 12,566lb (5,700kg)
Powerplant	two M49 Larzac 2,250lb (10kN)
Maximum speed/Height	497mph (800km/h)
Armament	none

BELOW Artwork for Dassault by Paul Lengellé promoting the future Guardian. *Dassault Aviation*

Chapter Twelve
Atomic Power

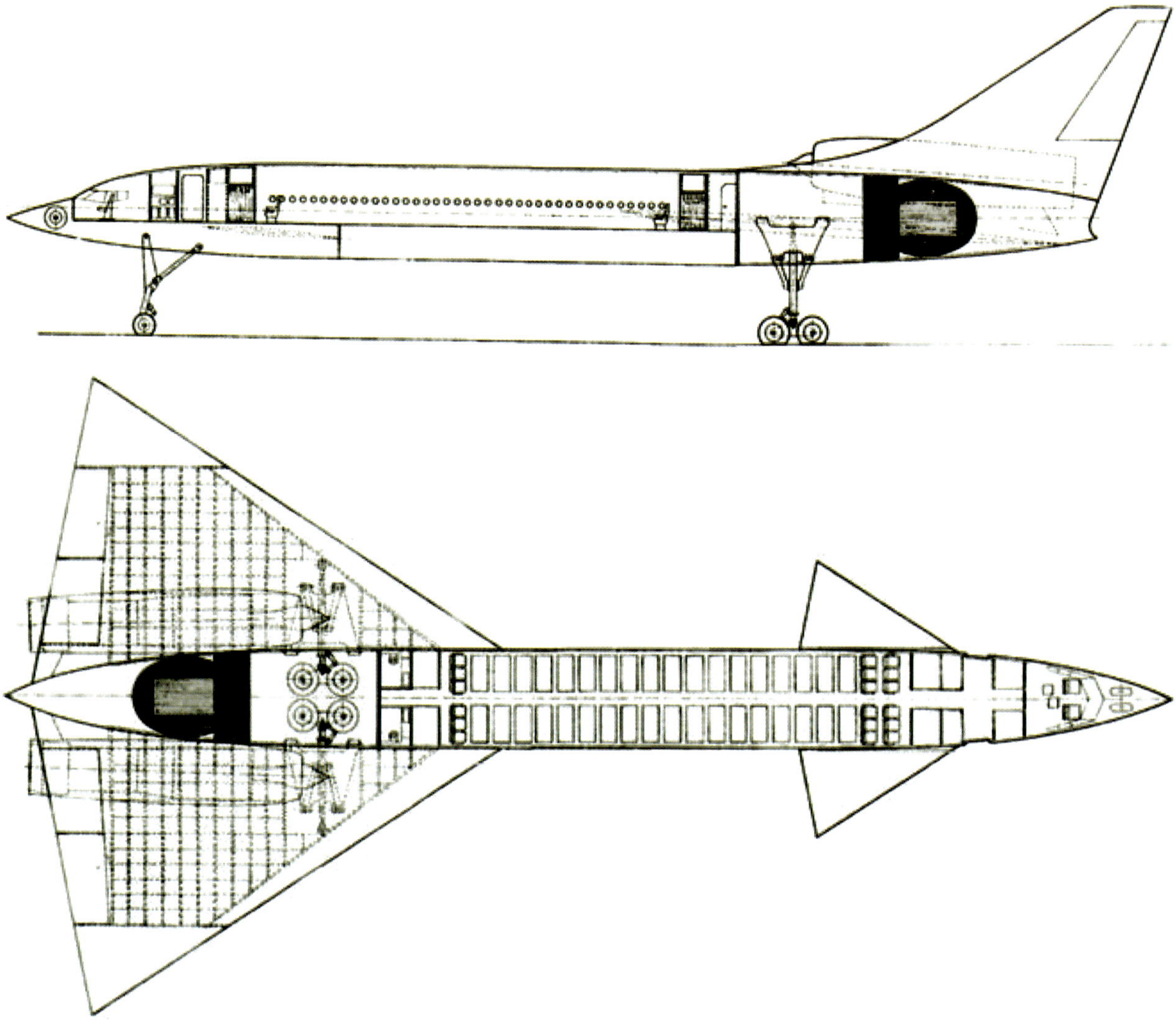

ABOVE **Two views depicting the SNCASE nuclear-powered aircraft.** *SNCASE*

Chronologically, the first consideration towards nuclear-powered aircraft to be made in France was a patent by Helmutt von Zborowski, who in 1953 put forward the basic outlines of what a nuclear-powered Coleoptère could look like. In terms of the technology involved this patent revealed nothing really new, and was more of the order of taking precedence than of revealing a new invention. Then, in January 1956, SNECMA established a 'Nuclear Division' under Raymond Marchal, its scientific director. Previous to that appointment, Marchal had spent two years with the *Commissariat à l'Energie Atomique* (CEA, the Nuclear Energy Agency) to learn the subject. Although it occupied up to 200 with a *bureau d'études* led by Louis Meulien, the new division really only became active in 1958 and, retrospectively, it appears that it never made much progress towards its declared goal of building a flight-rated nuclear engine.

In 1959 some of the budget of the *Commissariat à l'Energie Atomique* was allocated to financing SNECMA's research on using nuclear energy for aircraft propulsion. This work was done as part of the *Compagnie d'Application et de Recherches Atomiques*, whose

CEO was M. Ziegler, and Hispano-Suiza, Turboméca, Breguet and Matra participated in the effort. At the same time, the head of SEPR was also the chief of the France-Atome Association. The output from this appears to have been the 'Pile Brenda' programme (Brenda meaning *Bi-Reacteur, Energie Nucléaire, Détente Adiabatique* for twin-reactor, nuclear energy, without losing heat to the environment), work on which had begun in early 1959 and which was to be constructed at the experimental nuclear station at Cadarache. Designed by CEA, this enriched uranium oxide reactor was operated by SNECMA with the stated intention of turning it into an aircraft powerplant. Moderated by beryllium oxide bars (graphite and water moderation was also investigated), this air-cooled reactor was clad in ceramics. The Brenda reactor was intended to replace the combustion chamber of a conventional turbojet, but it was stopped in 1963 and SNECMA's nuclear research was then transferred to Hispano-Suiza's nuclear branch. A patent for this reactor design was eventually filed by Claude Fourré, department director for SNECMA's Atomic Division, and his co-worker Claude Moussez. Moussez later bought a 20ft (6m) long boat that he named Brenda after this experience; he still owned it a few years ago and this is most probably the only vehicle ever associated with the Brenda programme.

By 1965 all work related to atomic propulsion systems in France had been halted and from now on the 'atomic activities of SNECMA' were mostly concerned with helping the *Electricité de France* (EdF) build reliable and efficient nuclear powerplants.

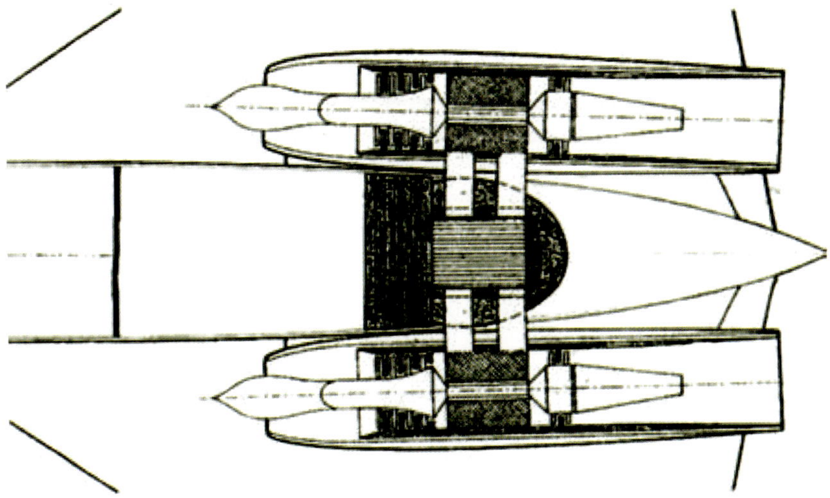

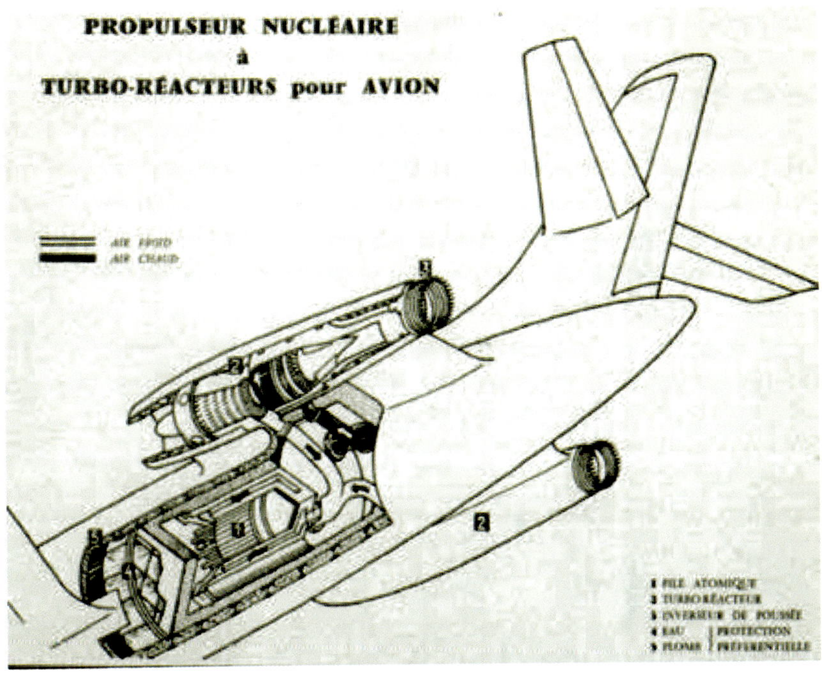

TOP **So far only one French project to develop a nuclear-powered aircraft (an airliner) has surfaced in the archives. This is a schematic drawing showing how the turbojets for this aircraft would have been heated by the reactor in a closed-circuit system.** *SNCASE*

ABOVE **This cutaway view depicts the installation of a nuclear reactor in a SE 210 Caravelle-type airframe.** *Safran, GDA - Espace Patrimoine, Fonds SNECMA*

Identified Sud Projects

Super Caravelle Nucléaire

Sud Aviation had planned to design a nuclear-powered aircraft and this project would only be revealed to the public fifty years later as a variant of the Super Caravelle supersonic airliner. Although it retained the basic fuselage shape of the SE 210, the layout now showed a canard with a large delta wing and only the rear tail unit remained as a 'souvenir' of the original Caravelle. The aircraft had two podded engines fixed to the sides of the rear fuselage and the nuclear reactor was positioned in between these. It should be noted that in the process of installing this 'powerplant', the fuselage diameter had been increased from 10ft 6in to 12ft 5.5in (3.20m to 3.80m). The nuclear-powered turbojets were of the closed-circuit arrangement in which the heat exchange fluid was liquid bismuth, while the fuselage layout reflected the 'nuclearisation' of the aircraft with the passenger section separated from the powerplant by two armoured partitions with a layer of air between them. Gone was the Caravelle's famous rear access door with its integrated steps and in this development all the doors (for passenger and crew) were positioned in the forward section of the fuselage.

Project Attila

Another nuclear 'reflection' made by Sud Aviation centred on an ultra-long-range cruise missile named 'Project Attila'. The Attila name may have come from the propulsion system to be used, a nuclear (direct cycle) ramjet, which was a concept also studied in the USA as 'Pluto'. In the direct-cycle or open-circuit system thrust was gained from air heated directly from contact with the core reactor; thus the jet of air emanating from the engine nozzle was very radioactive. This was in opposition to the closed-circuit system in which the heat exchange between the core reactor and the 'jet engine' per se was made through a flux of liquid material (liquid metal – sodium was a good candidate – or pressurised water), so that the jet efflux exhausting from the engine had no direct contact with the radioactive elements. A system with two heat-exchange circuits, one going through the core and another that never approached the radioactive area, was also proposed by scientists.

The SNECMA-designed ramjet would have ejected a highly radioactive efflux, and hence, like Attila, '*the grass would not grow again where it passed*'. Also, because it was intended to fly 'nap of the Earth' missions (at less than 100m/330ft altitude), the cruise missile's shockwave blast would have added to the radioactive jet and so would considerably increase the level of destruction left in the weapon's path. It was also thought that at the intended flight speed, Mach 3.5, the cylindrical fuselage would have provided enough lift on its own and so the missile was not given a wing. The structure would have been built entirely in steel or, even better, in an advanced nickel-chromium-based alloy such as Inconel, but the latter might have been difficult to obtain in sufficient quantity in France. The missile launch would have been made using a solid fuel (powder) booster, but a difficult aspect to overcome would have been its guidance. It was hoped to use an inertial guidance system but it was expected that checking this against ground locations would have been difficult above the featureless plains of central Europe (yet interestingly, for the cruise missiles designed by Sud Aviation for the Minerve programme in Chapter Four, it was claimed that navigation over central Europe would have been helped by maps drawn by the German Wehrmacht during the invasion of Russia and which had since been acquired by the French Army). It is understood that no hardware was ever produced for Attila.

Attila	
Status	project
Span	5ft 11in (1.8m) = diameter of fuselage
Length	55ft 9in (17.00m) approx
Gross weight	27,557lb (12,500kg), or 77,160lb (35,000kg) with booster
Powerplant	1,000 MW reactor powering a direct-cycle ramjet
Maximum speed/Height	Mach 3.5
Armament	2,205lb (1,000kg) nuclear bomb

BELOW Sud Aviation also designed a nuclear-powered missile with an open-circuit system, which was codenamed Attila. *P. Lacaze*

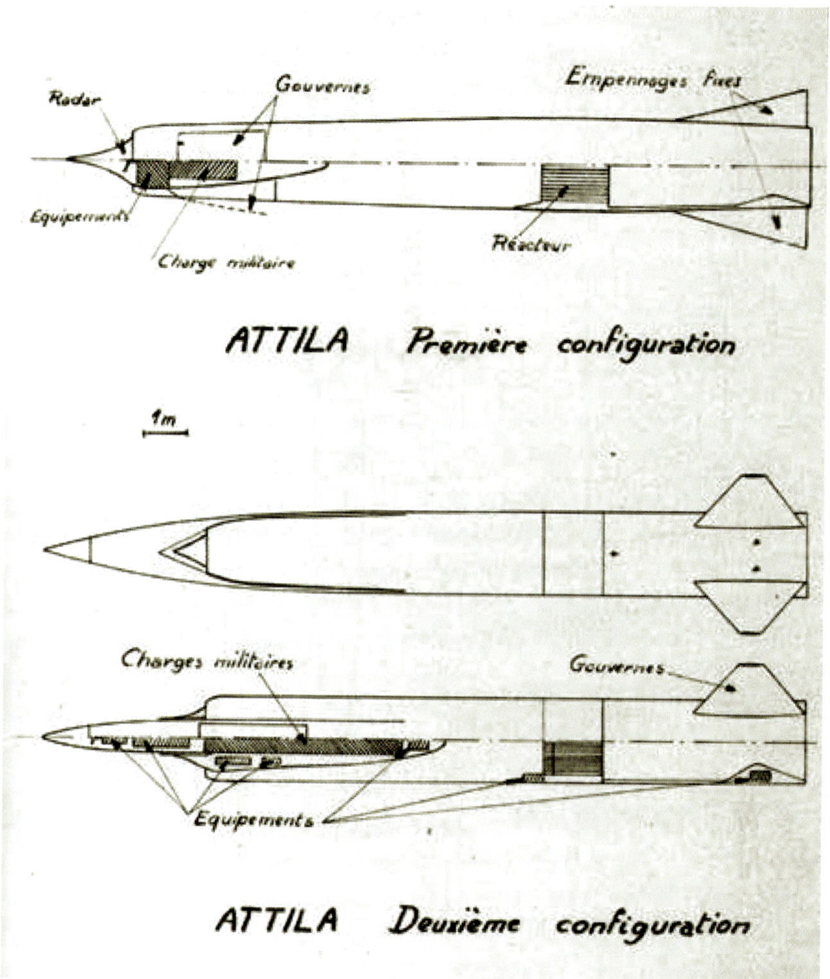

Chapter Thirteen
I Dreamt of Saucers

ABOVE The RC-360 mock-up with its 'wings' in rotation. *Author's collection*

During the 1950s, following the many sightings of 'flying saucers', there was a strong interest around the world in disc-shaped aircraft (see the book *Flying Saucer Aircraft* by Bill Rose, Midland Publishing 2006, for more background). And this was in spite of the fact that the idea that declared 'flying saucers were always disc-shaped' was now looked upon as journalistic fabrication, because the aircraft described by Kenneth Arnold in his famous original sighting were more like crescent-shaped flying wings. Besides its own specific lines of development, for example ramjets, the annular wing or delta-winged aircraft (all specialities of France's aircraft industry with Dassault in particular convincing everyone about the latter), France had always been very open to ideas emerging elsewhere. This is very obvious, for example, when it comes to 'flying jeeps' (see Chapter Fourteen), but it must have been the case too with disc-shaped aircraft because before the Second World War they had not featured very much in the minds of French designers. However, during the 1950s no fewer than four well-known designers or manufacturers offered disc-shaped aircraft: Henri Coanda, René Couzinet, Roland Payen, and SNECMA. And an engineer associated with Breguet, Robert Leloup, also patented a saucer design under his own name.

Coanda

Henri Coanda is well known as the designer and builder of the first jet aircraft in history, which took-off in 1910 (and crashed in seconds). In 1938 he also patented a mushroom-shaped 'propelling device' that has been viewed by many authors as a disc-shaped aircraft to be (actually one should really see this as a form of engine). During the war Coanda claimed to have been invited by Willy Messerschmitt to watch the Me 262 jet fighter in flight and indeed, after the Liberation of Paris, he was sentenced by the French authorities for collaborating with the Germans and was jailed for a few weeks. An Allied investigation team that was given access to his Parisian laboratory while he was in jail found nothing of interest there, but the aggregation of all these different facts means that modern alternative history theorists still claim that he built a working flying saucer for the Nazis!

However, during the second part of the 1950s Coanda did design a 'lenticular aerodyne'. This project was probably never worked out in detail but its theoretical elements were patented. This document described (in July 1956) '*an aircraft* [in the form of a lens] *that aspires* (breathes) *air from its upper side to thrust it downwards through orifices or nozzles to generate lift for a vertical ascent. The aspired air is also fed, in a lesser way, to other nozzles situated at the periphery of the aircraft, which generate directional thrust* (and control). *The blowing devices used for feeding the lift and the directional nozzles use the physical effect called the Coanda effect*'. The said machine was patented in the USA in 1957 as the 'Jet Sustained Aircraft'.

In September 1956 Coanda also patented '*a device for the simultaneous control of lift and directional thrust elements*' (Patent FR 1 158.539), which was to be a piece of mechanical equipment for gimballing (pivoting) eight nozzles using a single control stick (or, as the patent described it, '*from a gyroscopic autopilot*'). One can think that this second patent, in fact, referred to the control system required for the aircraft described in general in the first patent. In September 1956 *RAF Flying Review* reported that Coanda was '*working on a new personal aircraft design which will be of true disc shape. A four place aircraft with an empty weight of less than 900lb (408kg), Coanda's latest invention will have an engine with no moving parts. It will cruise at 300mph (483km/h), have a range of 1,000 miles (1,610km) and be capable of hovering and of vertical ascent and descent. He reckons it will sell at about the same price as a medium-priced car. It will do anything a helicopter can do, but will do it better.*' Coanda added to the *Flying Review* report by saying: '*We need a machine that can hover and the flying saucer is the answer.*' Over in America, Coanda tried to gain publicity by claiming: '*I have designed a Flying Saucer*,' but in the end nothing came of this project. Apparently, all the claims made above were really examples of marketing hype rather than technological facts!

In recent years a few authors have also tried to link Coanda with the Avro Avrocar and John Frost's work in Canada. However, the proof given for this is tenuous to say the least and it seems unlikely that Frost did anything more than take a look at Coanda's patents.

Couzinet

René Couzinet's effort is the most well known of the 'saucers' designed in France because a flying mock-up was actually built and photographed many times. Also, the machine was shrouded in controversy because Couzinet took his own life on 16 December 1956 before it could be flown. The basic idea

ABOVE Although Henri Coanda made a lot of fuss in the media during the 1950s and early 1960s claiming to have invented the flying saucer, very little remains to back this up. This drawing is the best that the author has found depicting his alleged saucer. *Philippe Ricco*

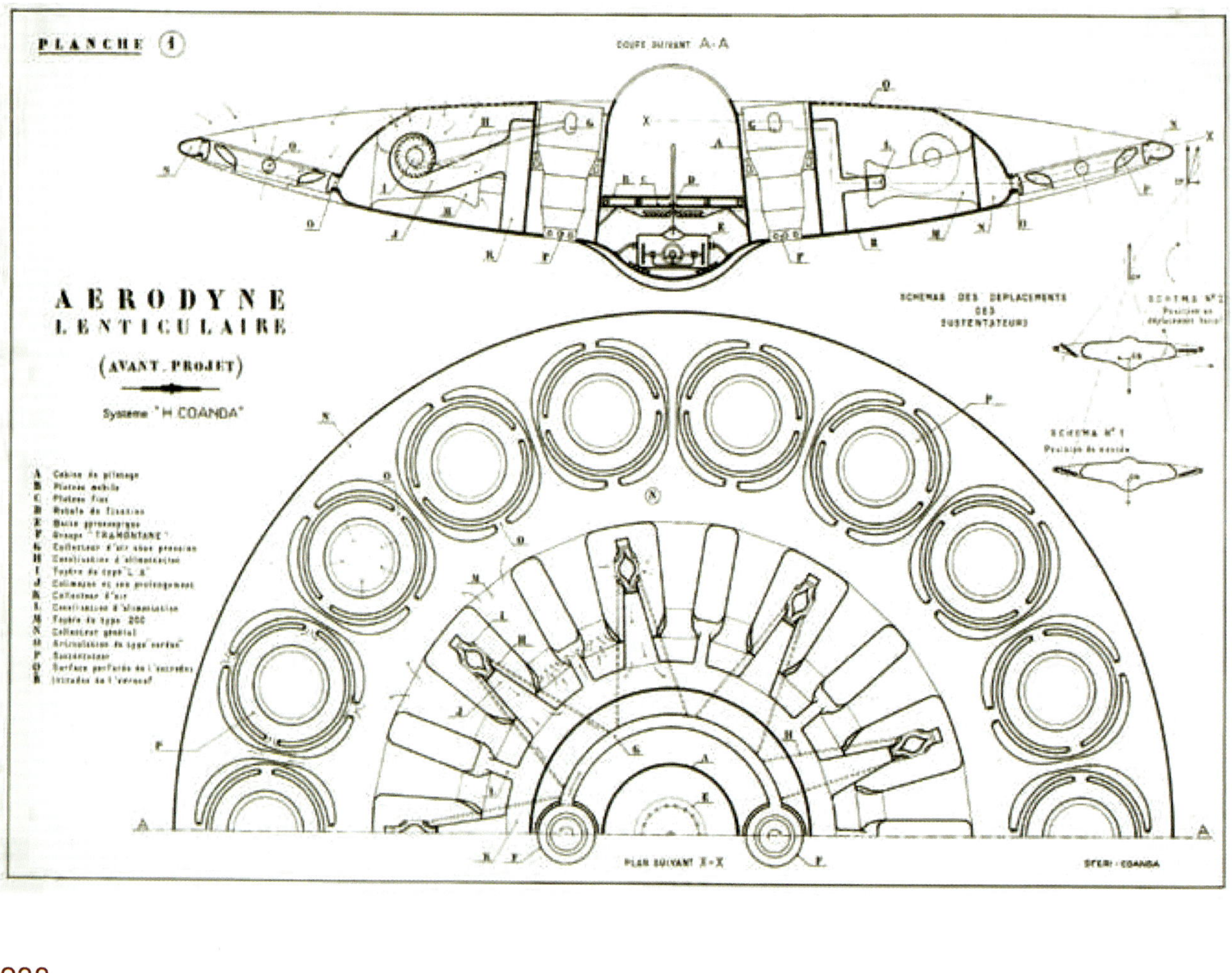

Couzinet RC-360 S1	
Status	3/5th scale mock-up
Span (diameter)	29ft 0in (8.84m)
Gross wing area	236.6sq ft (22sq m) each moving surface, 1,537.6sq ft (143sq m) total
Gross weight	29,762lb (13,500kg)
Powerplant	three Lycoming 135hp (100kW) and one Palas 340lb (1.5kN)
Maximum speed/Height	-

Couzinet RC-360 S2	
Status	project
Span (diameter)	-
Gross wing area	-
Gross weight	-
Powerplant	three Lycoming of 180hp (135kW) and one Marboré 880lb (3.9kN)
Maximum speed/Height	-

Couzinet RC-360 S3	
Status	project
Span (diameter)	44ft 3.5in (13.50m)
Gross wing area	645.2sq ft (60sq m)
Gross weight	29,762lb (13,500kg)
Powerplant	six Lycomings of 180hp (135kW) and one Dassault MD 30 Viper 2,700lb (12kN)
Maximum speed/Height	559mph (900km/h)

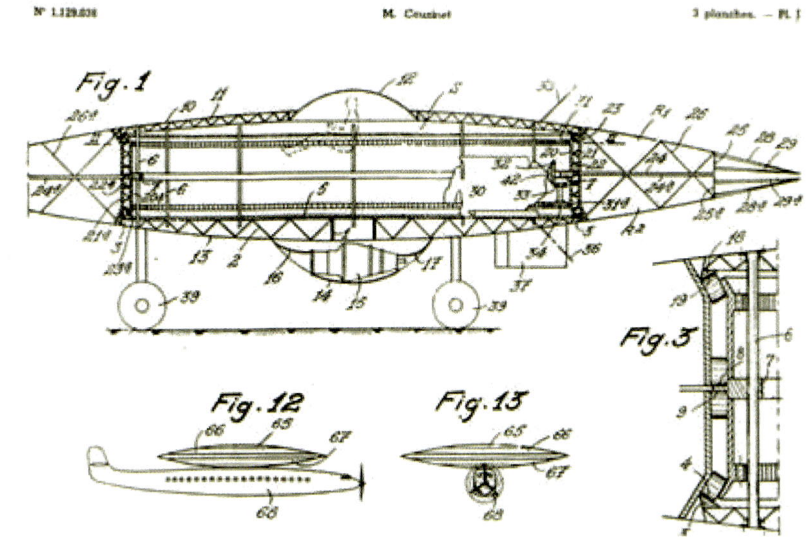

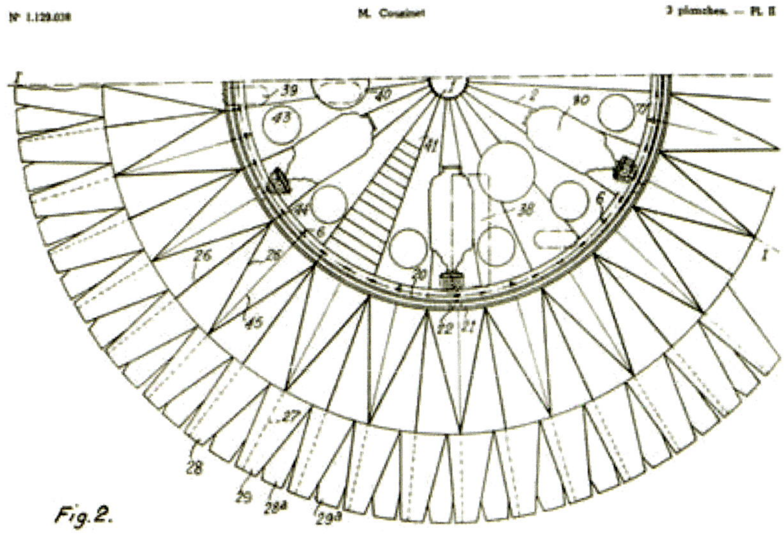

TOP **René Couzinet did build something, although it is uncertain whether it was just an animated mock-up or something capable of flying (which is unlikely). In this cutaway taken from a patent one can see that the demonstrator would have used reciprocating engines for lift and a small turbojet for propulsion. Note that Couzinet intended to apply his lifting wing to an aircraft with a conventional fuselage.** *Author's collection*

ABOVE **The top view of the Couzinet design shows the rotating wings around the disc-shaped fuselage and the need for six in-line engines to power them. This drawing also comes from the Couzinet patent.** *Author's collection*

behind the RC-360 '*Aerodyne à Ailes Multiples*' (Multiple Wing Aircraft) was to rotate a number of small rectangular wings around the main body of the airframe. In fact, there were two concentric assemblies of these wings that rotated in opposite directions to remove any effects of torque. The two sets of wings, each with a total surface area of 236.6sq ft (22sq m), rotated at 2.5 revolutions per second, thereby generating lift and enabling a vertical take-off to be made by the machine. Changes in attitude were achieved by using the variable incidence of the small wings (as controlled by the pilot) and direction control was obtained by rotating the propulsive turbojet installed at the centre of the disc. A 3/5th scale mock-up was built in Coanda's original factory in the île de la Jatte, Levallois, north-west of Paris, and this single-seat machine was to be powered by three Lycoming piston engines (possibly the O-320 for sustentation (lift) and one Turbomeca Palas turbojet (however, other reports have suggested a crew of two with a pilot under the bubble canopy and a flight mechanic inside the body).

Further developments of the original design would have included the S2, which was like the RC-360 and still built in wood but it had three more powerful Lycomings and a Marboré jet. After this, the definitive S3 would have been built in metal and fitted with six 'lift' engines and a Dassault MD 30 Viper turbojet (i.e. the Armstrong Siddeley Viper originally bought by Dassault in 1953 to power the MD 550 Mystère-Delta – see Volume I). The first of these aerodynes was due to fly in July 1956 but it was never to take off.

Apart from their ability to take off vertically, a major advantage of disc-shaped aircraft according to Couzinet was the lower cost incurred when building them using identical quadrant sections. This argument had already been advanced by Zborowski in regard to his annular wing Coléoptère. One small scale model, now the only part of the Couzinet project known to have survived, was tested extensively in a wind tunnel. This differed somewhat from the flying mock-up in that the turbojet pod was positioned above the aircraft and mounted on a raked pylon (and probably fixed), while swept fins were added that probably included rudders; it is likely that this configuration relates to the S3 design. A mock-up also survived for at least a year after the death of its creator because it was still stored in the factory, under wraps, in 1957. The factory itself is now used by Renault.

Payen Pa 61 Novae

The Payen saucer is not well known. Named the Pa 61 Novae (convertible), the project is known only from an artist's illustration, which shows a disc-shaped aircraft with a dome-shaped fuselage that has large

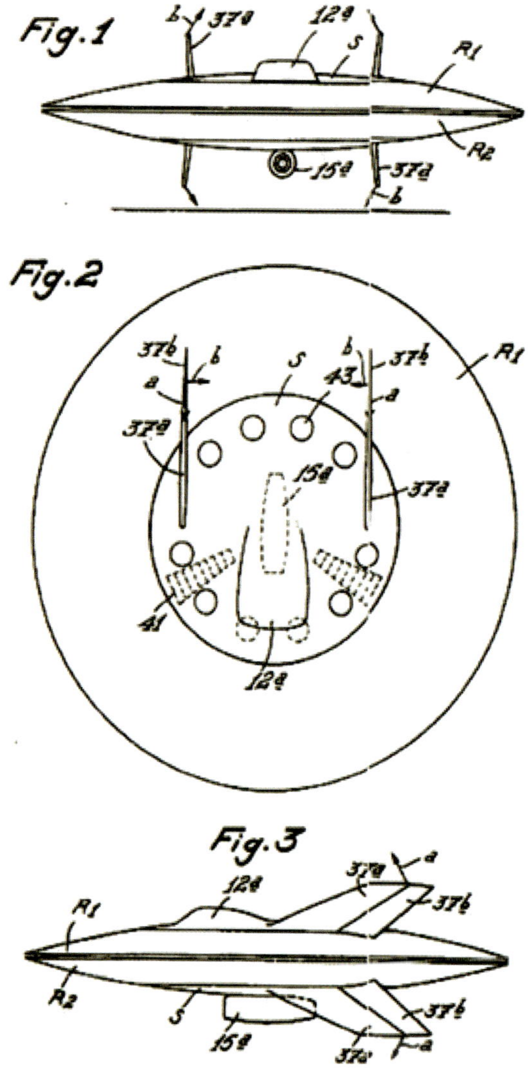

ABOVE RIGHT This three-view drawing from another Couzinet patent shows the final appearance of the designer's saucer, which features a jet engine in an underfuselage pod and twin fins. *Author's collection*

RIGHT René Couzinet looking at a wind tunnel model of the RC-360 Aérodyne Lenticulaire. The spindle-shaped upper pod is the propulsion engine pod (for wind tunnel tests, the inlet and outlet of the jet engine were not represented). *Author's collection*

Payen PA 61 Novae	
Status	project
Span (diameter)	26ft 3in (8.00m)
Gross wing area	-
Gross weight	-
Powerplant	-
Maximum speed/Height	-

windows in the front and a tall spiky tail. The method of propulsion is undefined but it may have employed large blades (the disc wing being composed of four or five large propeller blades). The crew appears to be limited to two people.

SNECMA

In 1958 Michel Poncelet of the YZM department of the Department of Special Studies at SNECMA began working on the application of faired propellers to ring-shaped wings. Inspired by the British Fairey Rotodyne (to which he made a direct reference in his report) he thought of driving the propeller using tip nozzles. In document YZM/5.016 he described '*a concept for a Vertical or Oblique Take-Off Aircraft to which such a propeller could be applied*'. Poncelet calculated that the ring wing was useful only for a short part of its full length/chord – the section in which it acted as a fairing for a ducted propeller. The rest of the length of the wing could be dispensed with and so, instead of a tube-like wing, he ended with a true 'ring' wing. In the end, however, the ring wing was reduced to just an annular leading edge of a flat disc, which was open for most of its surface, and inside this ring was the rotating jet-powered rotor. For

SNECMA saucers (two variants)	
Status	project
Span (diameter)	59ft 0.5in (18.00m) = rotor diameter
Gross wing area	-
Gross weight	61,728lb (28,000kg)
Powerplant	two ATAR 08 9,450lb (42kN)
Maximum speed/Height	-

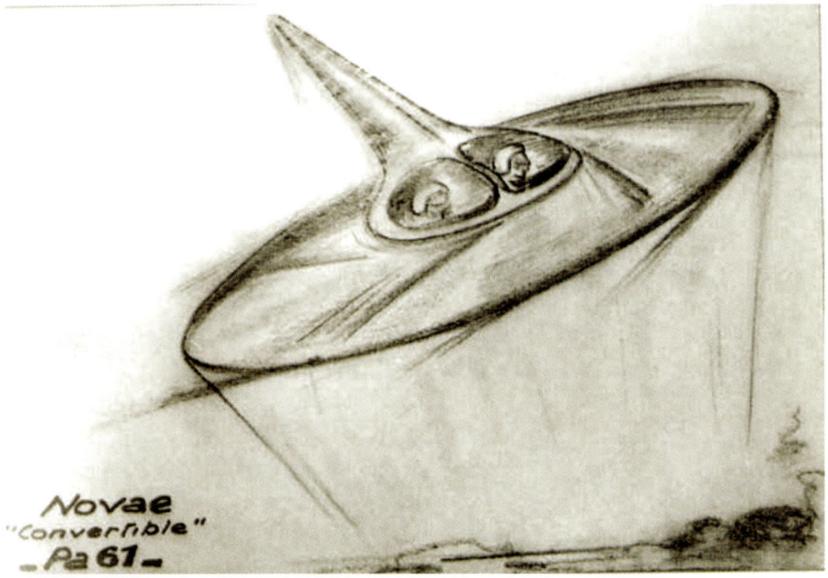

ABOVE **This sketch is the only known illustration depicting Roland Payen's Pa 61 Novae.** *Payen via Gaillard*

BELOW **During the author's research into the C.450 Coléoptère these 'saucer' designs also emerged. Although representing civilian transports, they are well worth including here. This is SNECMA's 'Design A'.** *SNECMA via Poncelet*

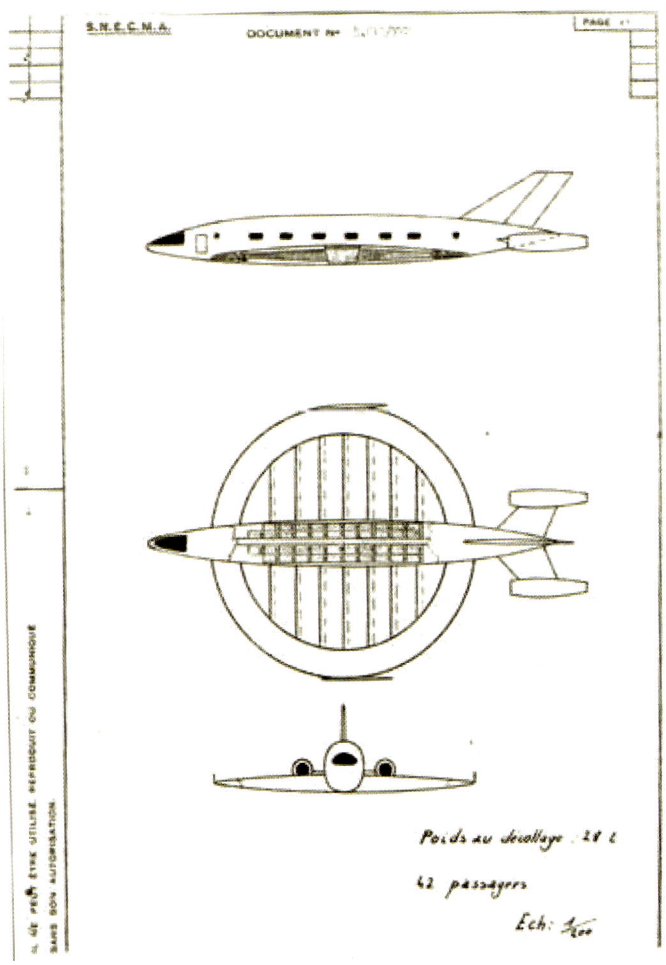

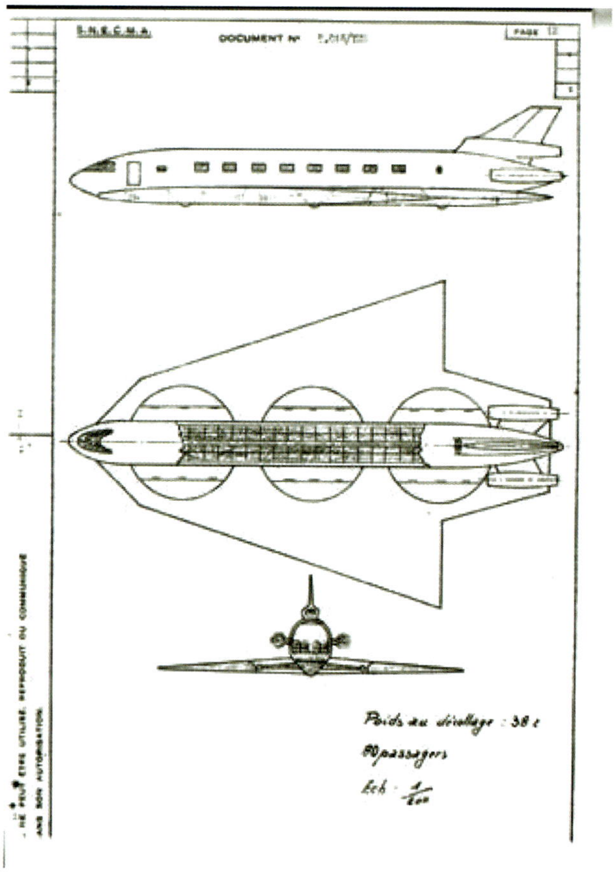

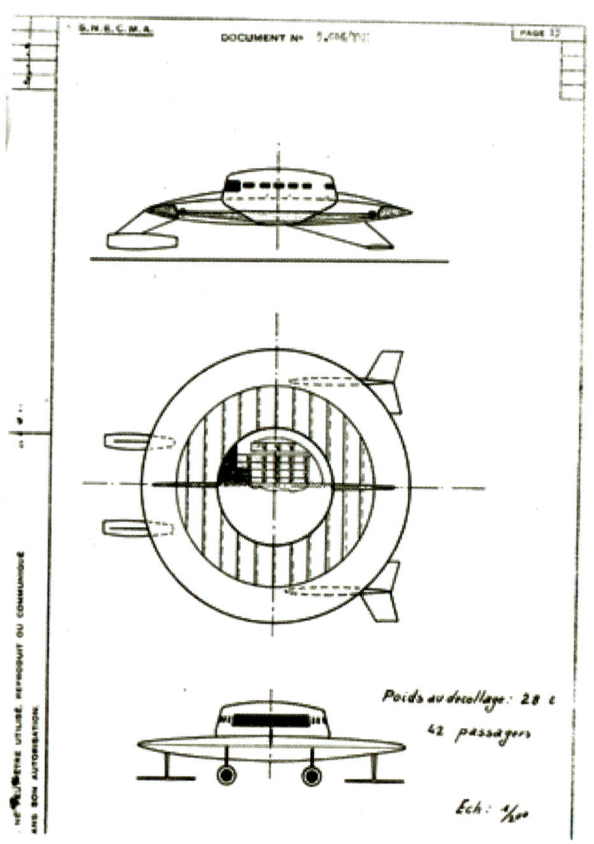

ABOVE LEFT In this alternative design we see the basic rotor-in-wing concept adapted for an aircraft with a conventional fuselage. *SNECMA via Poncelet*

ABOVE RIGHT This third design, again depicting a passenger transport, is possibly the strangest. However, like the other two it resulted from the desire to reduce the annular wing to a shroud encircling a large lift rotor. *SNECMA via Poncelet*

take-off or landing the jet engines fed the nozzles of the rotor, while in level flight these would be used for propulsion (after the rotor had been stopped and hidden behind Venetian shutters, which then restored the aerodynamic profile of the wing). All of this was still purely theoretical and no detailed mechanical studies of the YZM/5.016 aircraft were ever instigated.

The most important element in these designs by Michel Poncelet was that they took off and landed without any change of attitude: '*The Coleoptère's crew had to climb up a ladder and sit on their back; that was OK for a fighter jet but unthinkable for a passenger-carrying aircraft, even though Zborowski himself had proposed it.*' Various combinations of one or two 9,450lb (42kN) thrust ATAR 8 engines were investigated and the results indicated that with a rotor 59ft 0.5in (18m) in diameter and a single turbojet, an aircraft of 44,092lb (20,000kg) weight could lift off, while with two jet engines the load capable of being lifted reached 77,160lb (35,000kg). The report was illustrated with three drawings of aircraft in 1/200 scale, of which two were flying saucers, even though one had a conventional fuselage. No detail was given regarding the arrangement of the landing gear, nor the way the wing panels would fold up or down to free the rotor, but the seating arrangement for the aircraft's forty-two passengers was shown.

Wilbault Gyroptère

Famous even before the war, Michel Wibault emigrated to the USA in 1940 and it was there where in 1953 he patented an '*Aircraft with Enclosed Rotor*', which he called a 'Gyropter' (in English) or '*Gyroptère*' (French). This was the third design to be given this name, after the Papin-Rouilly *Gyroptère* jet-powered helicopter of 1912-15 and the Chappelaine *Gyraptère* flying car of 1929. In this new design, a fan-type rotor, driven by jet nozzle to prevent or reduce torque, was enclosed in a stator, which would then protect it from the influence of the air current flowing over the aircraft. The aeroplane's directional control was achieved by tilting its rim in the desired direction by way of mobile ballast! Thus, Wibault hoped to combine the high speed of an aircraft with the vertical lift and hovering capabilities of a helicopter.

In regard to the aircraft's overall shape, Wibault wrote: *'In the case of a small single rotor aircraft the stator assembly may be in the shape of a disc, thin at the peripheral edges and thickened toward the centre. Alternatively, and more particularly in the case of high speed ships, the stator assembly is preferably in the form of a wing. In such a case, once the aircraft is off the ground and propelled horizontally at sufficient speed, the aerodynamic lift of the wing may be used to supplement the lift of the annular aerofoil, or in some cases may supersede it entirely. In the latter event doors are used to obstruct the air inlet of the rotor in order to prevent any exchange of pressure between the upper and lower part of the stator.'* He also added: *'It will be found more advantageous to utilise multiple rotors rather than attempt to utilise a single rotor of large diameter.'*

His patent illustrated three different designs. The first was a true saucer, single seat, probably of low speed and of small dimensions (the approximate diameter based on referring to the pilot was 26.2ft [8m]). The second was a *'high speed ship'* with a turbojet at its rear for propulsion, it was shaped like a delta wing and the approximate length here, again based on the pilot, was 36.1ft (11m). Finally, the third and last design showed a larger transport aircraft for *'passengers and freight'* and was again shaped in the form of a cambered delta wing. This last design was an example of the use of multiple rotors in a single 'stator' and it would have had an approximate length of 49ft (15m), calculated once more from the size of the pilot.

Wibault was somewhat incorrect when he claimed that in his larger designs *'the wing has a shape of delta wings which are designed for high speed jet aircraft'*, for they all, by construction, use thick delta wings, similar to early Lippisch designs, which NACA aerodynamic testing had proved were inefficient; thin wings being better designed for high speed.

The Curious Case of Dr Pages

Doctor Marcel Pagès (who worked in the field of psychiatry!) made headlines in 1960, including in the serious publication *Aviation Magazine*, with his anti-gravity experiments. He went so far as to patent in 1960 a *'Craft for Cosmic Flight'* using a *'de-gravitational'* effect. Here, around a 13ft to 16.5ft (4m to 5m) diameter sphere, which contained the crew, was installed a *'torus-shaped frame made in an insulating material like plastic'* in which a vacuum was created using a *'molecular pump'*. This torus frame formed a *'particle accelerator'* in which electrons were accelerated up to 183,350mph (295,000km/h) and this apparently would be sufficient to create the *'de-gravitational'* effect, which then allowed the machine to fly. A Magnus effect was created by modifying the course of the electrons through three electric coils and this would enable the pilot to control the direction of the machine.

This may sound like pure Star Trek-like techno-babble, but it is extracted entirely from Pagès' patent, which was dated 5 January 1960! And *Aviation Magazine*, which had Pagès on the cover of its February 1960 issue, seemed to find him credible because one of the publication's regular contributors, Jacques Gambu,

BELOW Michel Wibault, pioneer of tilt nozzle engines, also came up with a scheme that used (in the same way as Michel Poncelet's of SNECMA) a very large lift rotor faired into an airframe. The single-pilot, single-rotor version thus amounted to a flying disc. *Wibault patent in Author's collection*

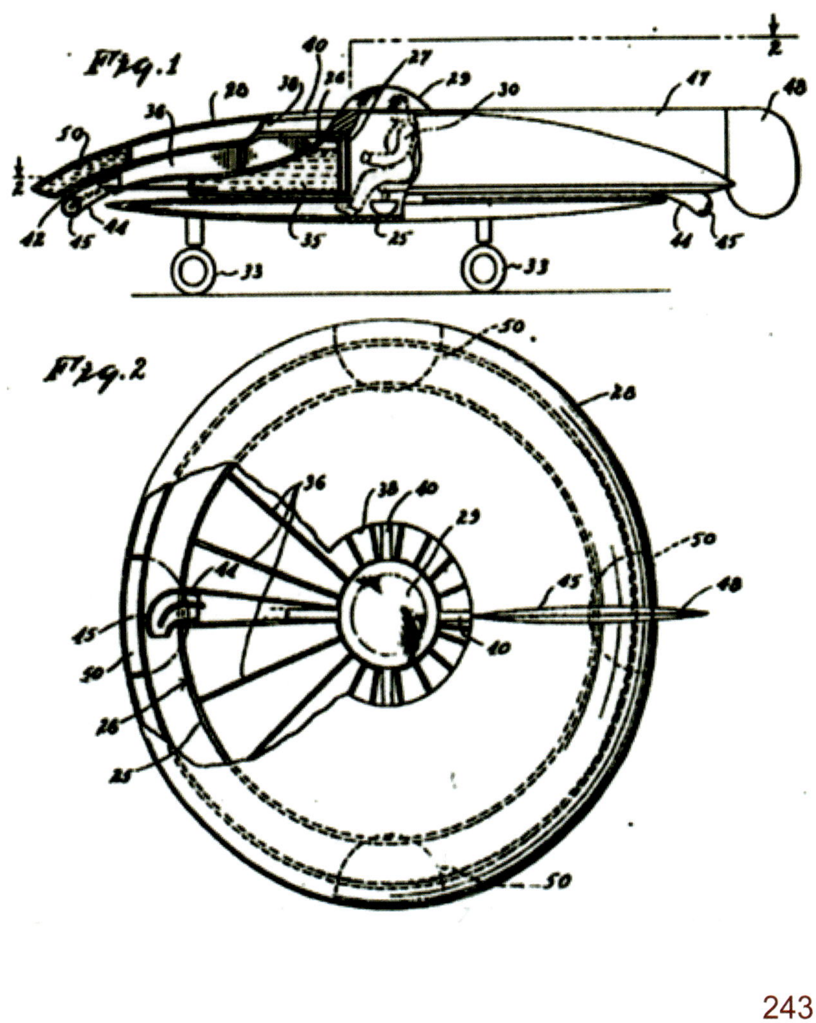

ABOVE **Psychiatric doctor Marcel Pagès managed to get on to the cover of Aviation Magazine with his anti-gravity experiments. Since this was not the 'April Fool' issue, one is led to think that he was considered to be serious in his views (to a degree) to receive this treatment.** *Author's collection*

wrote: '*As it happens, various pieces of information lead us to think this French scientist is nearing the truth, if not touching it, as these elements confirm the interest of the research made by the Doctor from Perpignan.*' According to this article, as a side-effect the device had an acceleration-damping effect, which meant that for the occupants of the saucer '*the machine will become their own local planet and, in the way we do not suffer from the rotation or the movement of our Earth, the passengers will not suffer from the changes of course of the aircraft. In these conditions man will be able to bear without damage accelerations of over 100g for five to six seconds, which is more than necessary for an abrupt change of trajectory*'.

At the end of his article, Gambu concluded: '*Let us think of a few of the processes recommended and verified by Dr Pagès. Anti-gravitation is advancing, that cannot be disputed. And we can imagine vehicles whose realisation is probably nearer than we think.*'

More than fifty years later nothing at all has come from this line of thought and Dr Pagès' theories are well forgotten, so this appears to have been just another dream that lacked any true substance.

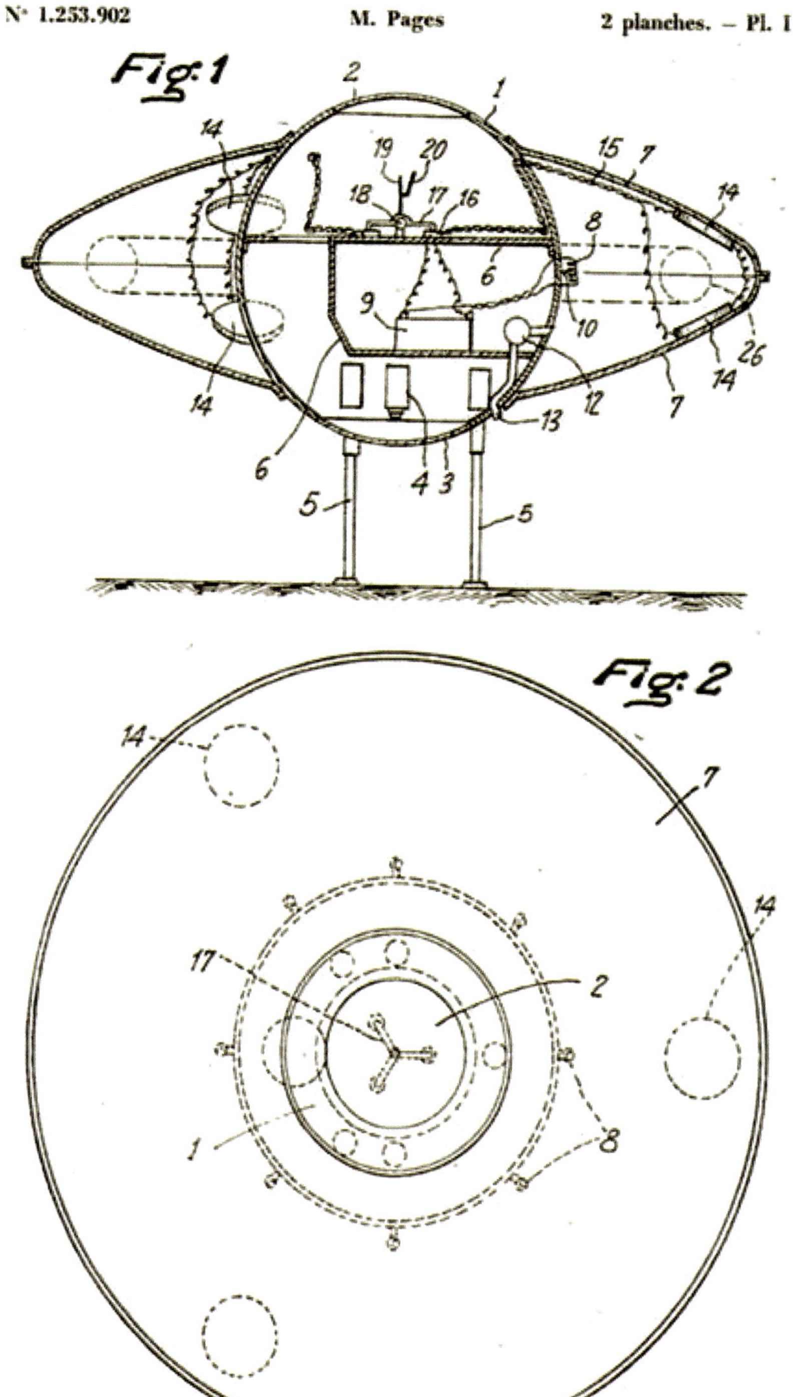

ABOVE **Yet with a patent describing the application of his experiments as an 'Engin Cosmique' (a Cosmos Craft), one may wonder if Pagès was more than just a daydreamer.** *Author's collection*

Chapter Fourteen
Strange Ways

ABOVE The Ludion in flight. *Philippe Ricco*

Beside their conventional VTOL aircraft studies, during the late 1950s and in the 1960s French manufacturers were engaged in research to provide wings to soldiers on the ground. In the late 1950s the STAé asked Nord Aviation to perform a preliminary study into 'flying jeeps' and evaluate the work done by Piasecki, Hiller and others in the USA. The French engineers were somewhat sceptical of the kinaesthetic control trialled by Hiller and so added seats to their version of the flying platform. Nord Aviation's resulting 'flying jeeps' were mere clones of the Piasecki designs, the manufacturer's designers expected stability troubles and so they did not proceed to a prototype. However, they also showed an interest in ducted fans and this research led to the Cadet and Helcade designs in Chapter Eight.

Flying Platforms

Sud Aviation

While Nord Aviation just copied the American Hiller and Piasecki designs, Sud Aviation proposed its very own flying platform designed by Théodore Laufer, a former wartime colleague of Friedrich von Dobloff who had been recruited in France after the war. Laufer began by criticising the Hiller-style platforms, like those that were designed by the competing Nord Aviation, stating: '*It is possible to create flying platforms of rather small diameter, but of a high price because of the cost of the engine and the apparatus required for the compensation of the couple generated by the transmission of power from the engine to the rotary wings.*'

Since the early 1940s Laufer had promoted, first in Germany and then in France, jet-driven rotors and this design was no exception – '*this mode of driving the rotor allows for cheaper machines, but with a wider rotor than on the* [usual] *platforms*'. His design was quite unusual in that it had a long rectangular platform with the large rotor rotating underneath. Laufer stressed the cheaper costs obtained through building the platform out of

Fig.2

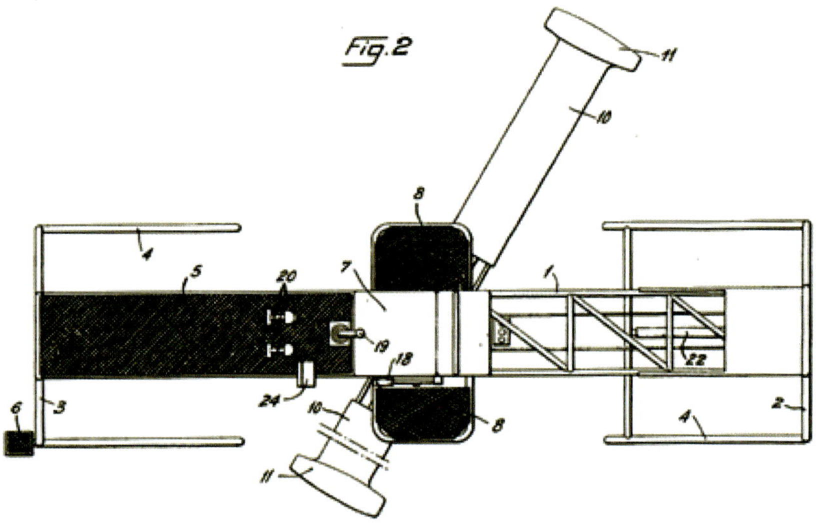

Fig.1

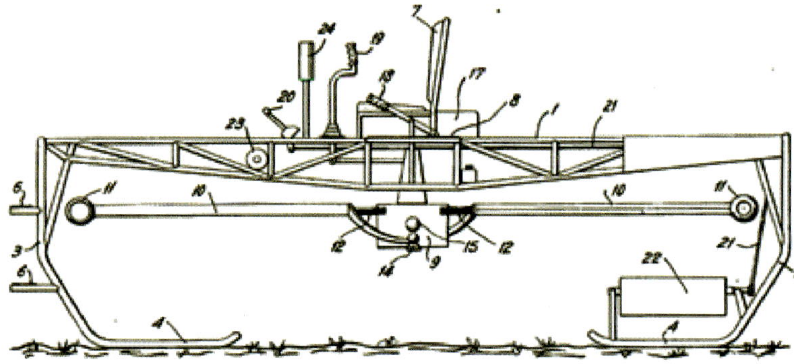

ABOVE **Side and plan view of Theodore Laufer's flying platform for Sud Aviation. Laufer patent.** *Author's collection*

BELOW **Perspective view of Theodore Laufer's flying machine. The jet-driven rotor is well shown. Laufer patent.** *Author's collection*

Fig.3

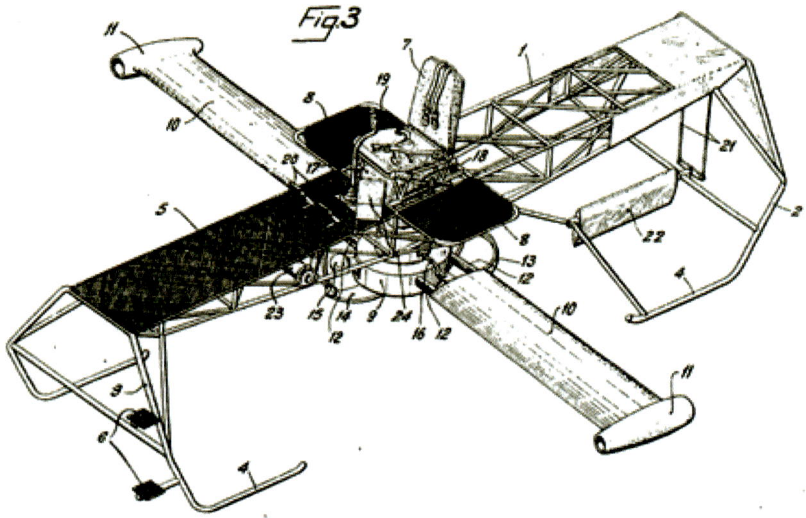

metal tubing; the ease of access for the pilot, who could reach his or her seat even with the rotor in rotation; and the ease of flying in a cluttered environment as the size of the platform helped the pilot to estimate the area swept by the rotor. Finally, the curved landing skids would permit a landing to be made in high grass areas. At the rear, a moving plate was used as rudder. Since the rotor was driven by ramjets or even pulsejets, compressed air (contained in a bottle attached under the platform) was used to initiate the rotation. This novel machine was not built.

Sud Aviation 'Stream Jumper'

Under contract from the *Direction Technique et Industrielle* of the Air Ministry, in 1967-68 Sud Aviation, with the help of the *Société Française d'Entretien et de Réparation de Matériel Aéronautique* (SFERMA) and Bertin, designed a small machine called the Ludion (Ludion is a practical physics experiment in which an object moves up or down in a fluid through pressure differentials). Emulating Bell's 'flying belt', the Sud design enabled an infantryman to fly for a few hundred metres to enable him to cross a river. A notable difference from the American designs was that in the French Ludion the driver (if that is the correct term) was seated instead of standing upright. The initial studies had seen the driver standing on a large ski but the seated arrangement eventually replaced this idea. The concept was a derivative of the Caillette Statodyne concept. The machine flew successfully

Sud Ludion	
Status	prototype
Span (diameter)	4ft 10.5in (1.49m)
Length	6ft 5in (1.95m)
Gross weight	441lb (200kg)
Powerplant	SEPR 178 rocket 405lb (1.8kN)
Maximum speed/Height	62mph (100km/h)
Armament	none

during 1968-69 but failed to find a real operational need and so was subsequently abandoned.

Flying Cars

Bertin

Bertin's proposals in the flying jeep category are not well known. An early 1956 design used two nozzles mounted high above an egg-shaped fuselage with five ranks of seats (meaning probably ten to twelve passengers), and a variant was also proposed with four nozzles. The concept was similar to the later Bertin '*trompe*' idea in which the airflow thrust from a turbojet drove a larger flow of air aspired through a venturi-shaped duct. The same patent also proposed a flat platform-like design intended for use as a flying crane. For the two-nozzle design the turbojets were placed nose to nose and fed by a common intake above the

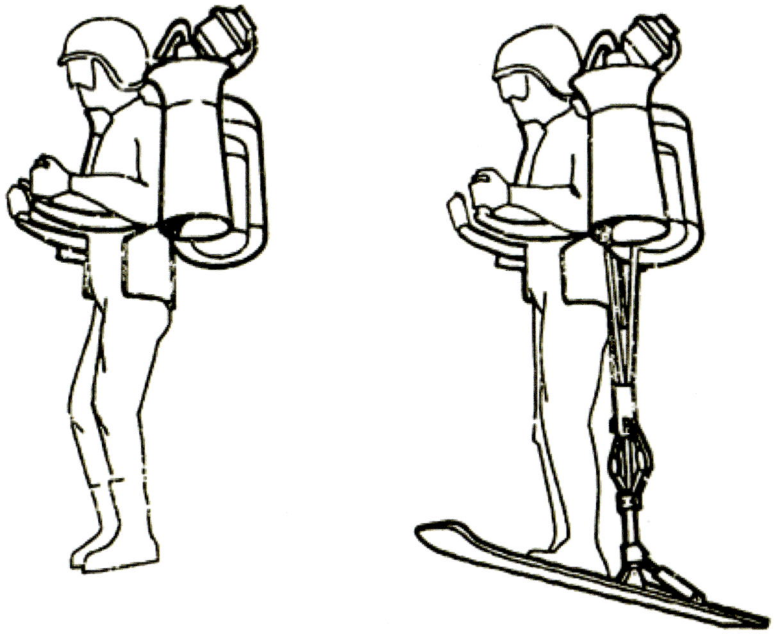

ABOVE Early concept of the Ludion 'Stream Jumper' produced by Sud Aviation. *Sud Aviation, Author's collection*

BELOW A perspective drawing of the Ludion showing its main components. *Sud Aviation, Author's collection*

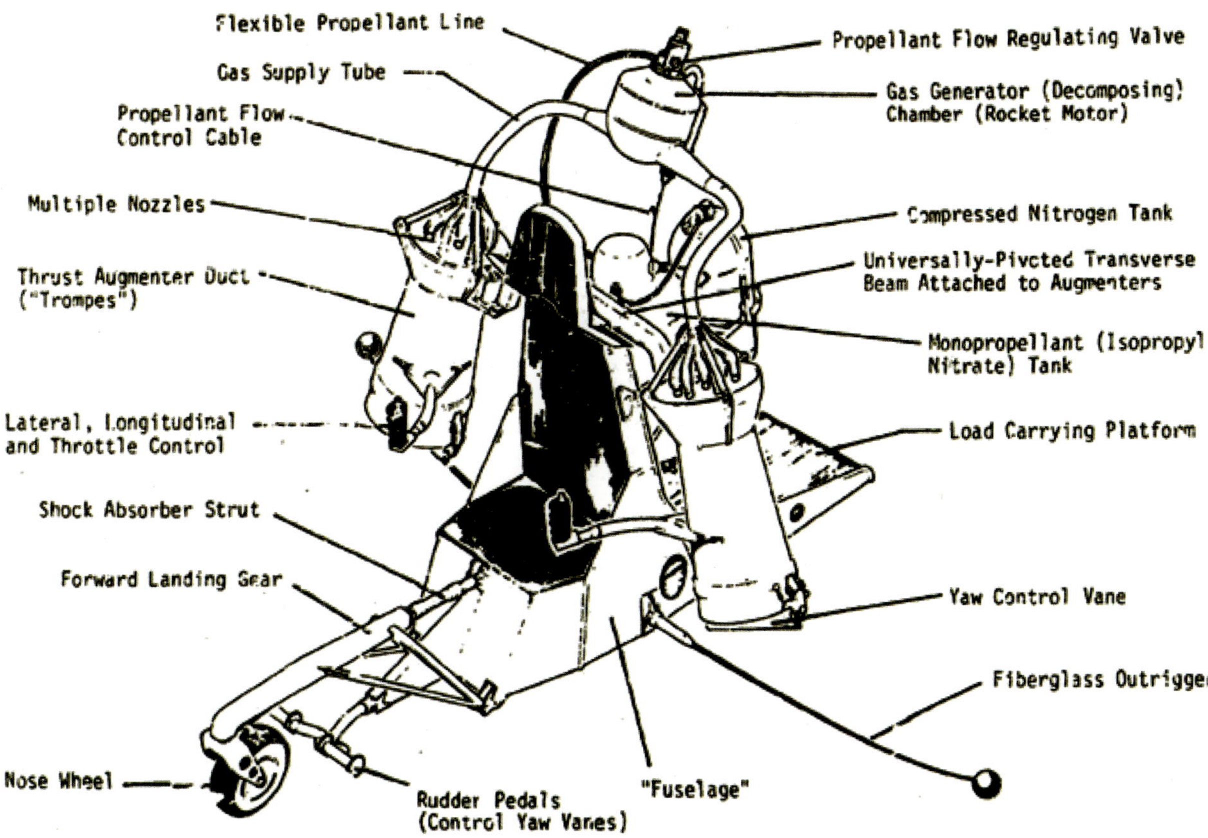

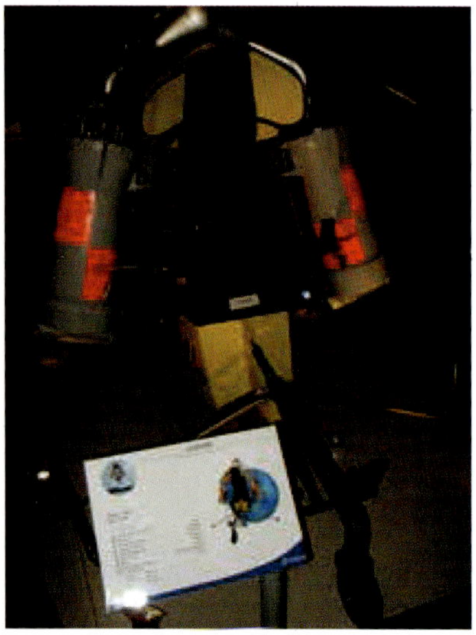

ABOVE The two Ludion prototypes still survive today. This one was photographed during a retro-transport exhibition at the Grand Palais in Paris in 2005. *J.C. Carbonel*

fuselage. The four-nozzle variant had the engines placed laterally, each with its own intake.

Even less is known about some later designs that appeared just as artist's illustrations in the Aladin brochure. The first one appears to have been intended to serve as a technology demonstrator, with four big cylindrical *trompes* positioned vertically behind the single exposed pilot. The other was a more defined design with a large bubble canopy for the pilot and a passenger and with a series of slit-type *trompes* in rank on each side.

Chevrollier Vehicule Volant

Gaston Chevrollier was a Frenchman living in Marylebone Road in London who in the years following the Second World War patented a few designs for flying vehicles. His primary line of thought was to use a turbine either as an engine delivering its power to an axle for propulsion on land or on water, or as a direct thrust turbojet in flight. Chevrollier designed two different cars, one in which its long chord wings folded on to the sides of the vehicle during ground operation, and another in which the wings deployed themselves laterally like on a common variable geometry aeroplane (except that in 1948 variable geometry aircraft were not common!). Chevrollier also applied his propulsion concept to a small motorboat. Besides these designs he was a prolific inventor who patented many improvements to combustion engines, ships and cars, but the author doubts whether he really had the competence to design a true flying machine.

BELOW Gaston Chevrollier beat everyone else with this patent for a flying boat. *Author's collection*

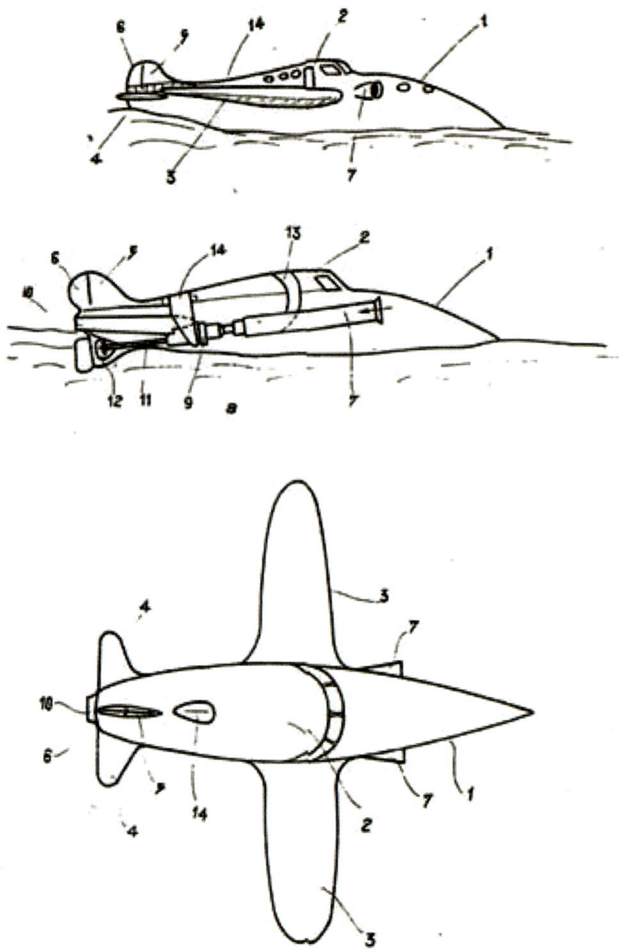

Morane Saulnier MS 850

In parallel with its Statodynes, Morane investigated the design of a flying jeep using lifting fans. The MS 850 was a four-seater in which the pilot and one passenger sat side-by side in the front cockpit, but were separated from the rear cockpit (in which the two other passengers sat facing rearwards) by the duct for two contra-rotating fans driven by an Artouste turbine. The turbine exhausted through a long duct that formed a tail, at the extremity of which were positioned the usual control surfaces. This design was begun in 1958 and a brochure was issued in 1960. An alternative version, ordered by STAé in 1959, used a vertically thrusting turbojet of an

Morane MS 850/1	
Status	project
Width	9ft 6in (2.90m)
Length	20ft 1in (6.12m)
Rotor area	40.9sq ft (3.80sq m)
Gross weight	?
Powerplant	one Artouste 400hp (300kW)
Maximum speed/Height	-
Armament	none

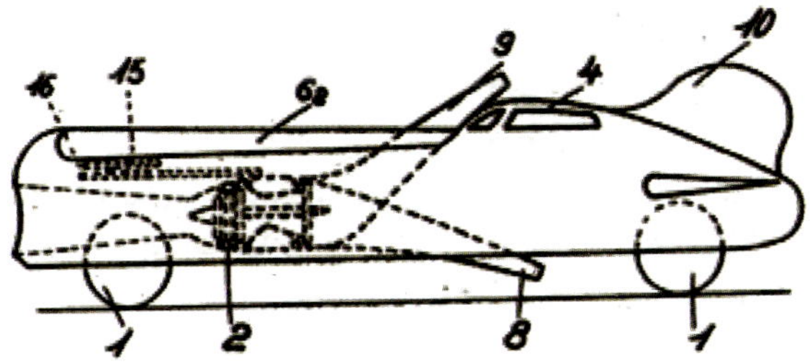

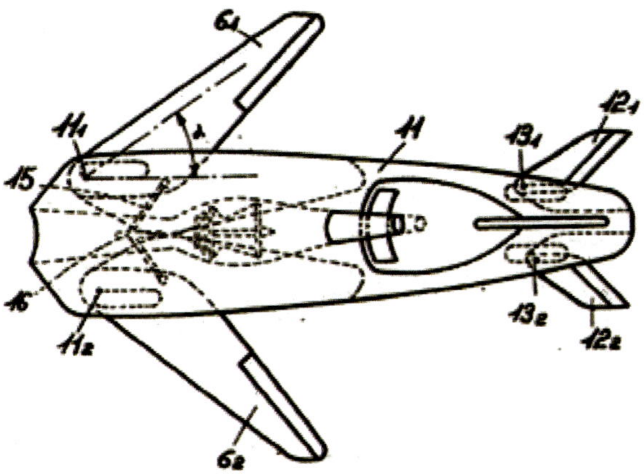

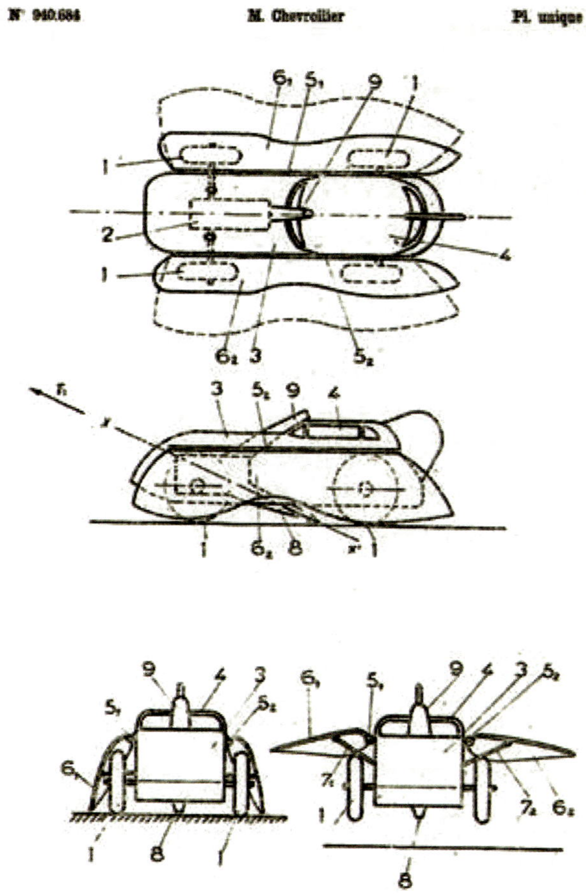

ABOVE LEFT Gaston Chevrollier's flying car project had a jet engine that exhausted above and underneath the hull, plus small retractable wings that appeared too small to provide enough lift for take-off. *Author's collection*

ABOVE RIGHT The second Gaston Chevrollier flying car design used the same exhaust system as before and long chord wings, which again appeared incapable of providing enough lift. *Author's collection*

BELOW The Morane Saulnier MS 850 was a form of flying vehicle built around a ducted fan and with a four-man crew seated under bubbles at front and rear. *Via Lacaze*

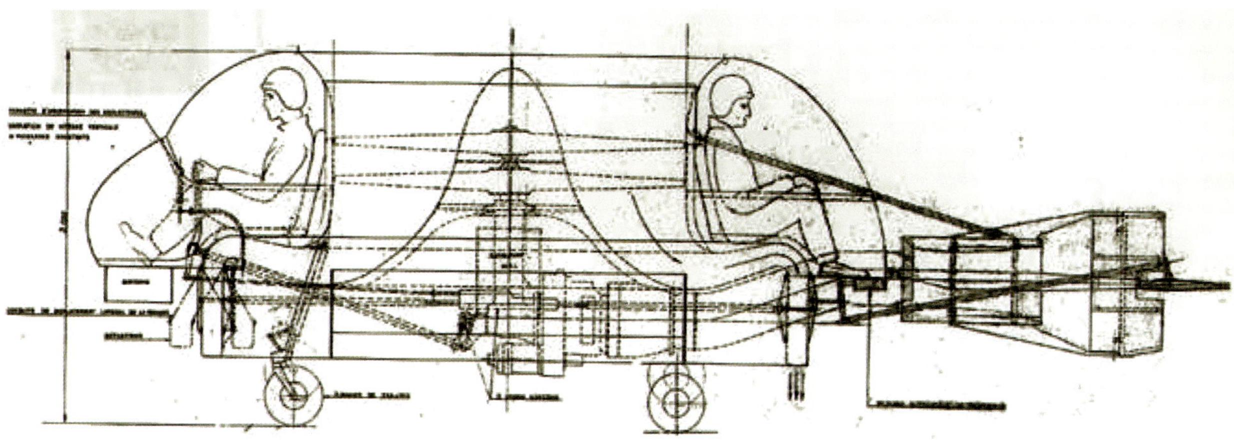

Morane MS 850/2bis	
Status	project
Width	8ft 5.5in (2.58m)
Length	15ft 4in (4.68m)
Rotor area	-
Gross weight	2,429lb (1,102kg)
Powerplant	one Marboré
Maximum speed/Height	31mph (50km/h)
Armament	992lb (450kg) equipment and personnel including pilot

unspecified type (possibly a Marboré) augmented by Bertin *trompes*. In this version the two rear passengers were seated under separate bubbles. It was planned to build a single-seat proof of concept machine using a Marboré turbojet, but in the end nothing came out of this work.

Nord Véhicule Aéroterrestre

The Nord Aviation *Véhicule Aéroterrestre* (air-ground vehicle) was another machine that seems to come from a James Bond movie (or, to keep with the French theme, a Fantomas film) rather than from a serious designer. With an airframe that looked like a bathtub on wheels, the aircraft was fitted with an engine (possibly a car engine) that could drive a rear faired propeller or a two-bladed rotor. There was no mechanical link between the engine and the wheels, so ground propulsion must have come from the propeller, in a similar way to the Leyat car from the 1930s. It is unclear if the engine was intended to drive the rotor continually during flight or if it was only to be used to 'jump-start' the vehicle, with the flight then continuing in autogyro mode. A handlebar was used to control the vehicle on the ground and a mini-joystick provided control during flight, with two front lights provided for driving by night! The time frame in which this machine was designed is uncertain but it probably came from the early 1960s.

Nord Véhicule Aéromobile

Nord went back to the flying car theme in 1967 with the '*Véhicule Aéromobile*'. The aim here was to develop a machine for a '*guerrilla type conflict*', an '*automobile able to take-off vertically and fly away*'. The description added that this was '*a difficult problem as it is not possible to take advantage of the aerodynamic*

BELOW **This Nord Aviation *Véhicule Aéroterrestre* was seen as a 'minimum vehicle' with the ability to operate either on the ground or as a rotary wing flying machine (probably as an autogyro).** *Nord Aviation*

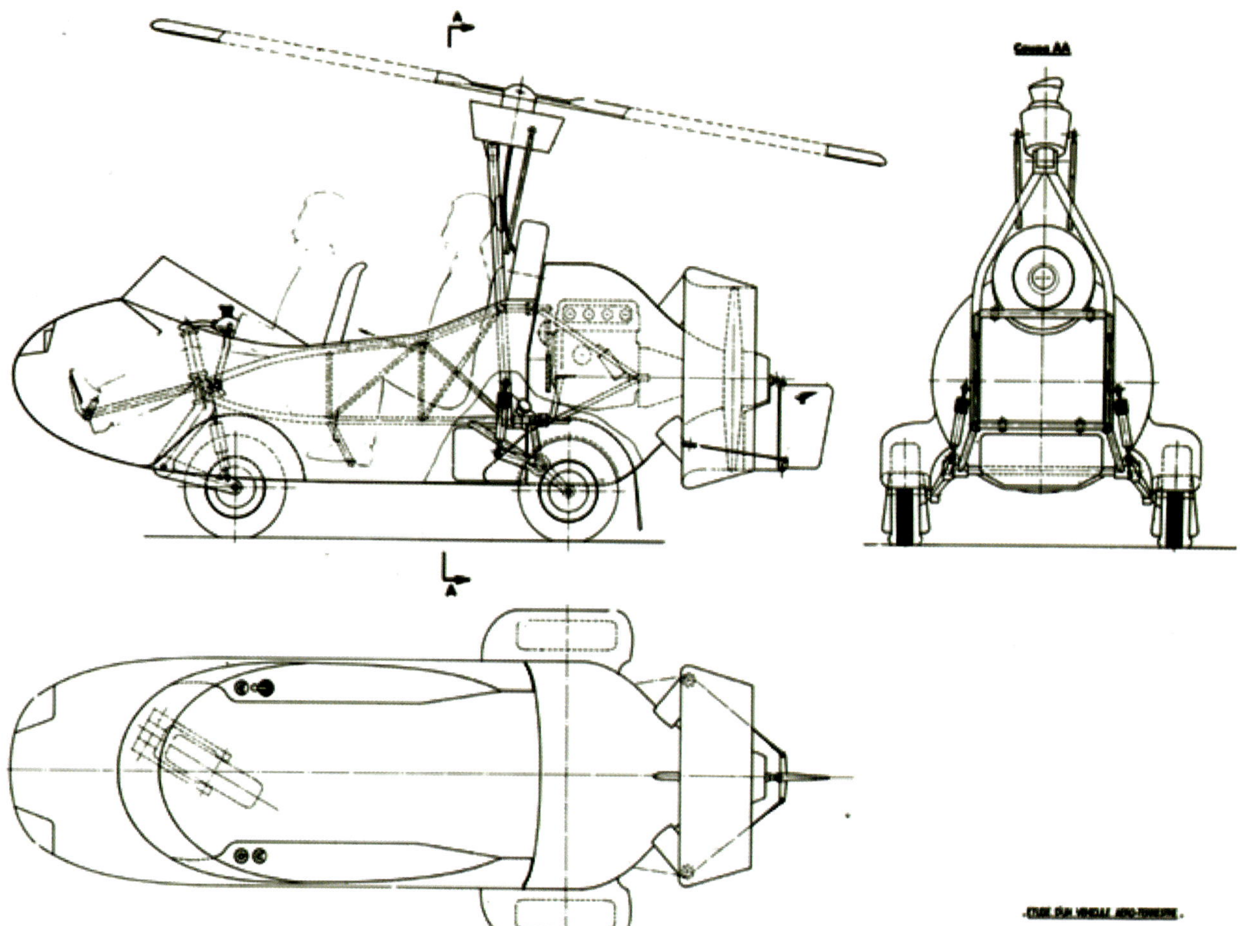

Nord Véhicule Aéromobile

Status	project
Width	6ft 7in (2.00m)
Length	16ft 1in (4.90m)
Gross weight	2,646lb (1,200kg)
Powerplant	one Rover Moreton 126lb (0.56kN)
Maximum speed/Height	81mph (130km/h) in flight; 62mph (100km/h) on the ground
Armament	none

Nord Véhicule Aéromobile

Status	foil
Width	7ft 6.5in (2.30m)
Length	24ft 11in (7.60m)
Gross weight	3,307lb (1,500kg)
Powerplant	one Astazou II 1,870hp (1,395kW) and one Renault-Gordini 103hp (77kW)
Maximum speed/Height	68mph (110km/h) in flight; 71mph (115km/h) on the ground
Armament	none

ABOVE An artist's impression of the Nord Aviation *Véhicule Aéromobile* on the ground. *Nord Aviation*

lift. Since dynamic pressure cannot be used to lift the vehicle, a considerable power must be used to do it'. However, the jet lift that was at the heart of the Norapter (below) was no longer seen as the panacea, rather ducted fans were favoured as Nord was investing a lot of money into the subject with the Nord 500 (see Chapter Eight). However, the use of a turbojet driving a propeller was not seen as a good solution because it required a large diameter rotor to lift the machine, which then meant a large aircraft (for examples of this kind of design see the saucers suggested at SNECMA in Chapter Thirteen). So Nord recommended using lift fans driven by the jet generated from a turbojet, a solution already promoted a few years earlier by Bertin and Breguet (again in Chapter Eight).

A propeller was also promoted for propulsion on the ground rather than having the wheels moved through mechanical means. This had the double advantage of using a single engine for both air and ground propulsion, and it would dispense with weighty mechanical drives. The brochure even evoked the possibility of adding retractable skirts to turn the machine into a type of hovercraft. The vehicle was designed to carry two people and had two lift fans to ease pitch control. The selected turbojet was a Rover Moreton giving 126lb

BELOW To show how its ducted fan was designed as a performance booster, Nord Aviation created this vehicle to the same performance objectives (in terms of speed and carrying ability) as its Aéromobile but using known technology. Designing a 'foil' to promote one's new designs and technology appears to have been a frequent marketing trick for French aircraft manufacturers. For example, SNECMA also used it, comparing a delta fighter to its *Coléoptère* project. *Nord Aviation*

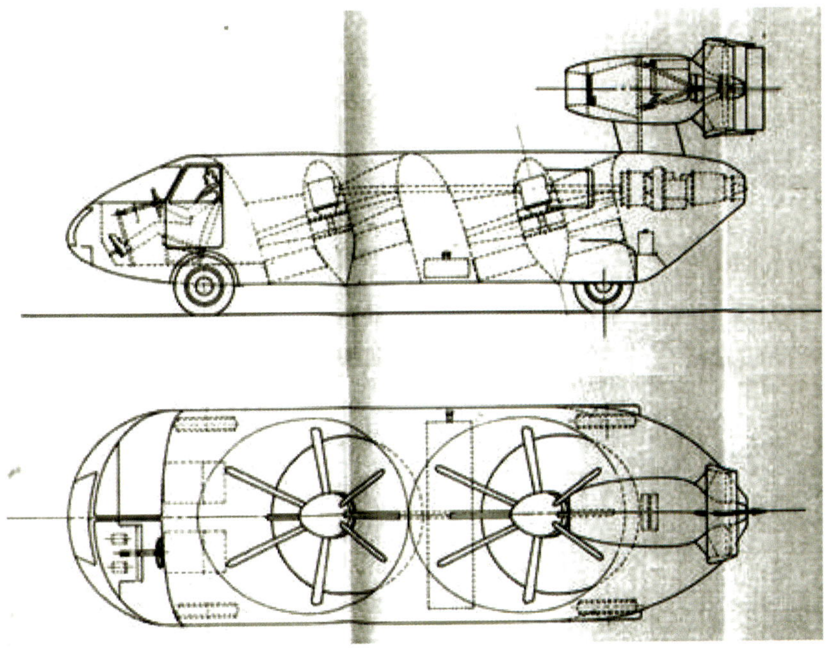

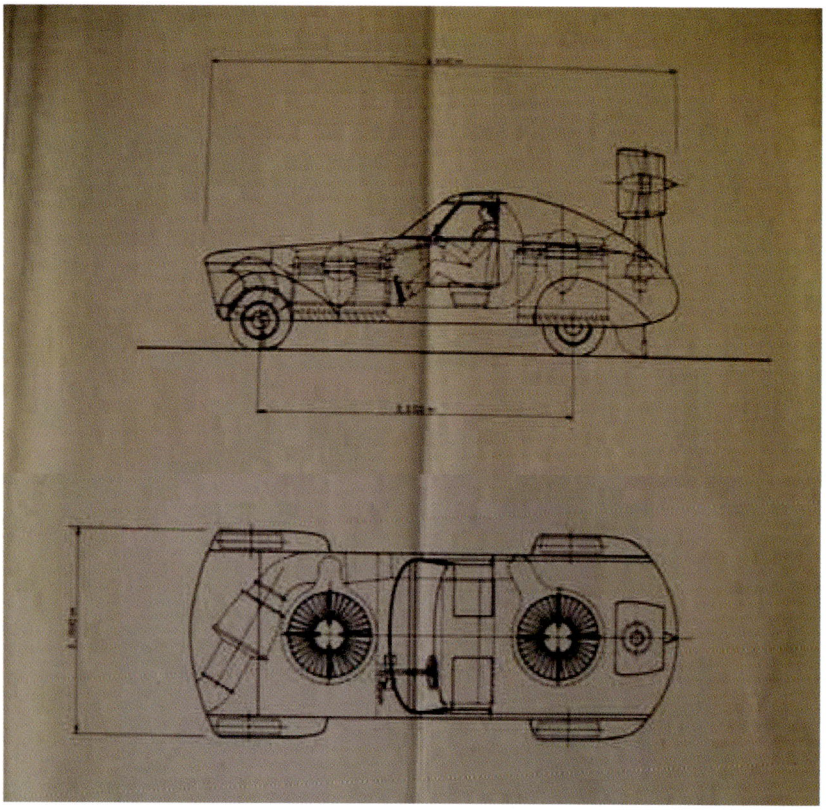

ABOVE The Nord *Aviation Véhicule Aéromobile* actually looked like a car, and it was only the ducted fan at the rear that revealed the intention to fly. *Nord Aviation*

(0.56kN) of thrust and originally designed for the Canadair CL-89 drone. The two lift propellers were 2.72ft (0.83m) in diameter and the propulsion propeller 1.97ft (0.60m) in diameter. The intention was to have the vehicle capable of running for three hours on the ground at a speed of 62mph (100km/h) but also able to take off and fly twice during this period, for five minutes on each occasion.

For comparison, Nord also designed a vehicle having similar characteristics but powered by a Turbomeca Astazou II turboprop driving (through a mechanical transmission) two 5.58ft (1.70m) lift propellers and a 3.28ft (1.00m) diameter propulsion propeller. A Gordini sports car engine was to be used for power on the ground, but in fact this was another case of designing a 'foil' to show how good was your original solution, a practice used repeatedly by the French aircraft industry.

SNECMA

Not wishing to be outdone by the true aircraft manufacturers, engine company SNECMA hired the famous designer of lightweight aircraft Yves Gardan to create its flying jeep. Gardan took the challenge literally and came up with what was essentially a small light car fitted with foldable side rotors! Needless to say, if the result had adhered to the SNECMA brief then the complexity of the design would certainly not have fared well in the field.

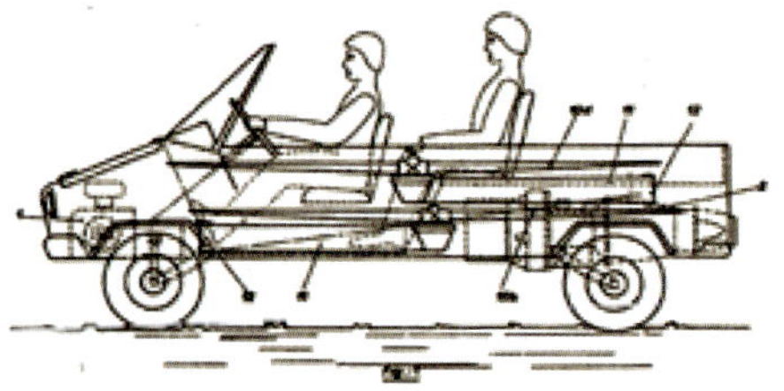

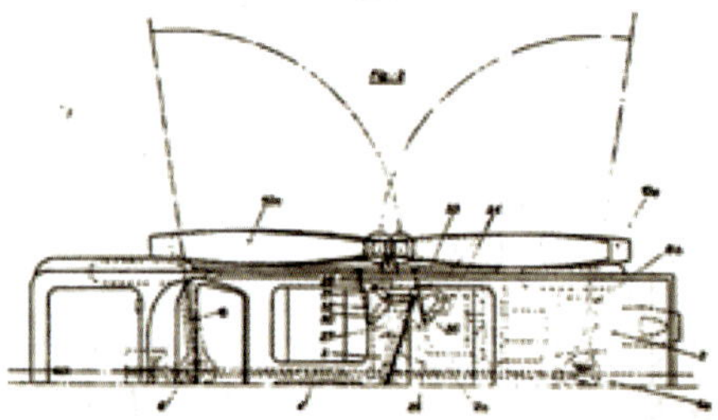

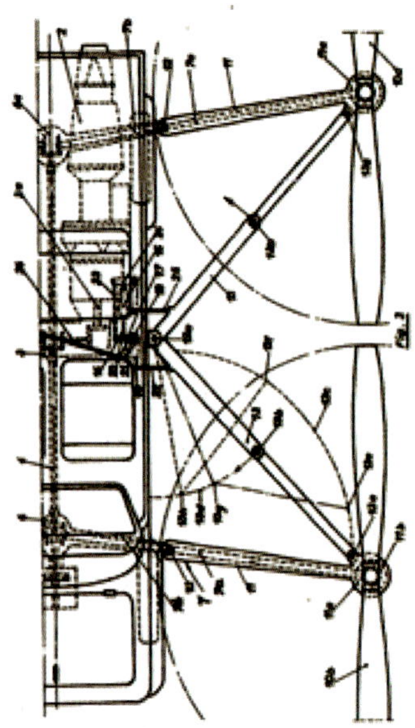

LEFT Working for SNECMA, Yves Gardan took the term 'flying jeep' quite literally with this project, which actually looked like a small car with folding rotors. *Author's collection from SNECMA patent*

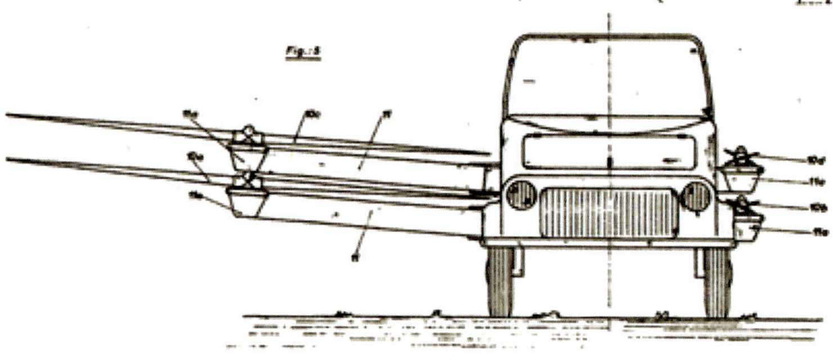

Front view of the SNECMA vehicle showing the extended rotors. It shows the rotors deployed (left) and folded (right). *Author's collection from SNECMA patent*

Flying Armoured Car

Nord Aviation Norapter

Here, with its Norapter concept, Nord really outdid itself. This 1960-62 project was intended to give a conventional reconnaissance armoured car the ability to 'jump' over an obstacle. Jumping here actually meant taking off vertically, flying straight over the obstacle and then landing on the other side! The French Defence Ministry requested the study of such a vehicle to define firstly what was technically feasible, and second the maximum weight of the vehicle based on the thrust of the available engines. This was, therefore, a study intended to prepare a programme for the future but with no immediate concrete technical requirements.

It was intended that if a call for proposals was to be issued then it would be based on the AML (*Auto Mitrailleuse Légère*: Light Armoured Car) currently in service in the French Army. Two types of AML were to be considered – a combat vehicle with a crew of three and an armoured personnel carrier with a crew of two plus ten soldiers. The range on road was to be 622 miles (1,000km) and the new machine had to have the capability to climb those gradients that were acceptable to a conventional armoured car. The ability to do three successive jumps at 490ft (150m) height at a speed of 0.6 miles (1km) in two minutes (i.e. 19mph/30km/h) was requested, but no road speed was specified to Nord. The weight of the vehicle, at 11,905lb (5,400kg), was quite similar to the AML 60, but its size (length 16.1ft, width 9.8ft, height 8.5ft [4.90m × 3.00m × 2.60m]) was quite a bit larger than the Panhard AML (13.6ft × 6.5ft ×

Nord Norapter X.1

Status	project
Width	9ft 5.5in (2.88m)
Length	20ft 4in (6.20m)
Gross weight	10,648lb (4,830kg)
Powerplant	one V8 engine (from truck chassis) and one Pegasus 3
Maximum speed/Height	-
Armament	none

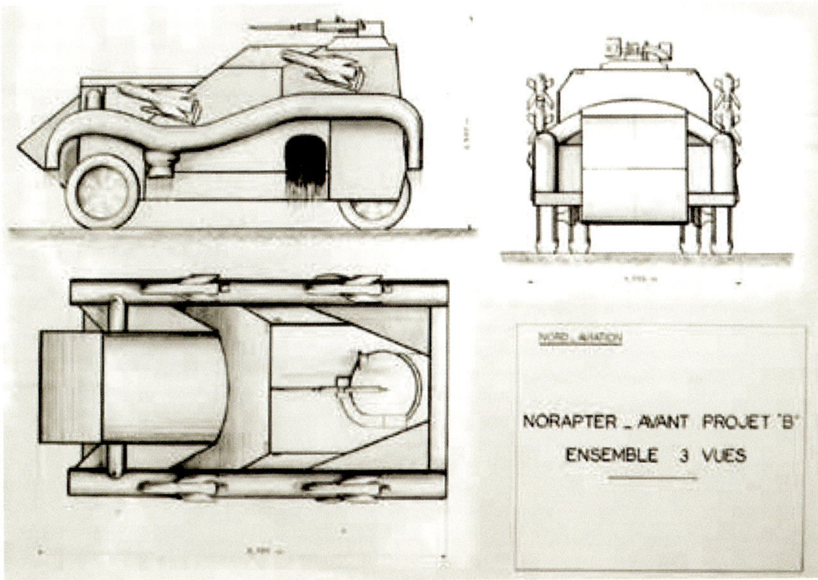

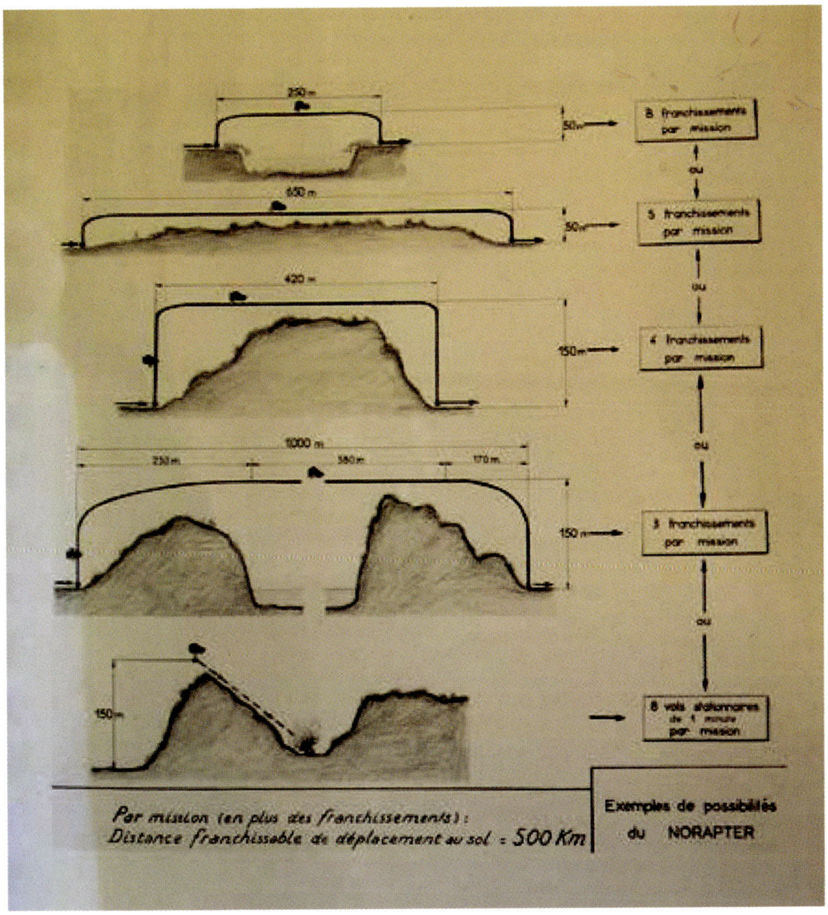

TOP In the early 1960s Nord produced proposals to make armoured cars capable of flight. This was the Norapter project. *Nord Aviation, Author's collection*

ABOVE Schematic drawings showing the Norapter's intended flight path. The craft's ability to fly was limited simply by the elements required to cross a large river. *Nord Aviation, Author's collection*

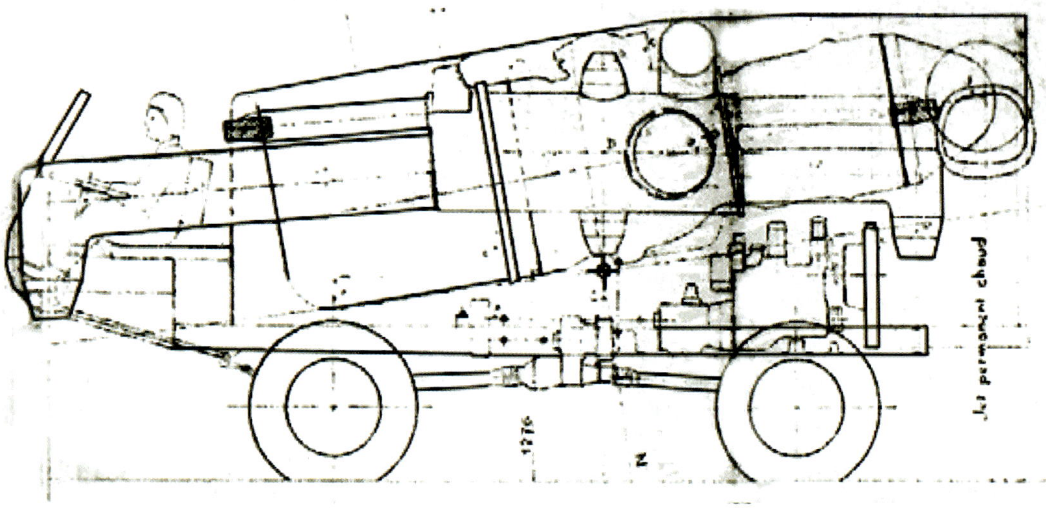

ABOVE To test the feasibility of the Norapter idea Nord Aviation proposed to install a BS.53 engine on a SUMB truck. *Author's from a Nord document*

6.8ft [4.15m × 1.97m × 2.07m]). The armament was given as a 20mm gun, 60mm mortar or SS 11 missiles, and for propulsion a '*Bristol turbojet identical to the one used in the Aptérion project*' (see below) was specified.

On 12 January 1961 Nord Aviation issued a brochure describing the Norapter as an '*off-road armoured car with the ability to cross obstacles through flight*'. Norapter was an appropriate name for the project, taken from the Greek 'A-pteros' – without wing! Moving on the ground required a different engine (a Panhard 4.HD giving 99/108hp [74/81kW]) from the flying part (a Bristol BS.53/5 Pegasus tilt nozzle engine), but they would run on a single type of fuel because the BS.53/5 was supposed to operate satisfactorily on common gasoline. The thrust rating of the BS.53/5 was given as 11,900lb (52.9kN [5,400kg]), which then defined the maximum weight of the vehicle. The project's weight and size faithfully followed the suggestions of the Ministry with the armament being the only option – and that too more or less followed the options offered by Panhard for its AML (the Panhard AML 60 was the then current armoured car of the French Army). The base mission was defined as a ground range of 311 miles (500km) while the distance for the over-obstacle flight was to be 3,280ft (1,000m) at the specified altitude of 490ft (150m). The duration of each 'jump' was calculated to be two minutes for a fuel consumption of 220lb (100kg). For the record, the dimensional data on the drawing attached to the brochure referred to a 'Project B' but without any 'Project A' having been mentioned before.

On 27 May 1962 Nord issued a second brochure that described the 'Aero-Terrestrial Experimental Vehicle Norapter X.1'. This was to be the first phase of the study asked for by the Ministry to validate as quickly as possible the soundness of the concept '*independently of all operational requirements which are still uncertain*'. The chassis would have been taken from the then current off-road truck used by the French army, the Marmon-Herrington MH 600BS, which was built by UNIC from 1964 to 1969 with a Simca-Ford engine and a body designed by Bocquet. In French Army use the truck was called the SUMB for Simca Unic Marmon Bocquet and nearly 7,000 were produced. Attached to the chassis would be a Bristol Siddeley Pegasus 3 (or 5, the brochure is uncertain on this point) and it was hoped that the acquisition of the jet engine would be financed by the MWDP (NATO's Mutual Weapon Development Program). The hot jet exhaust would pass through the rear nozzles in the same way as the Hawker P.1127 V/STOL research aircraft, which used the same engine, while two side ducts would direct the cold jet to the front of the vehicle; however 20% of the flow would be passed to four separate control nozzles. The whole contraption did not have a shape that would provide good aerodynamics simply because of the low translation speed (from vertical to forward flight) under consideration. It was hoped that '*the design of such an experimental vehicle should limit the tests and, being based on two existing and proven elements, should require only minimal cost*'.

Wibault 'Apterion'

Interestingly, a Nord memo refers to a competitor named 'Apterion' that was attributed to 'Wibault-Bristol'. This is a conundrum as the name 'Apterion' is already known to have been used for one (or even two?) Breguet VTOL designs (see Volume I), while nothing along this line of thought is currently known to have come from Wibault. A possibility might have been the Short PD.46 'Prodigal Armoured Car' being proposed to the French authorities by another French manufacturer, but then the Short design used four Rolls-Royce lift engines and not a Bristol rotating-nozzle unit.

Reference Sources and Bibliography

Sources (Books):

Agardographs: various issues

Avions Breguet (Les) 1940-1971 by Jean Cuny and Pierre *Leyvastre, Editions Larivière* 1977

Avions de Combat Français (Les) 1944-1960 Volumes I and II by Jean Cuny, Editions Larivière 1989

Avions Potez (Les) by Jean-Louis Coroller, Editions Lela Presse 2012

Chars de France, Jean Gabriel Jeudy ETAI 1997

Comaéro: various publications

Concorde la Véritable Histoire by Pierre Sparraco, Editions *Larivière 2006*

Dassault 1945-1995: 50 Ans d'Aventure Aéronautique by *Claude Carlier and Luc Berger Editions du Chêne 1996*

Dassault Dossier (A): Aircraft Acquisition in France by *Robert Perry, United States Air Force Project Rand*

Dassault Super Etendard by Frederic Lert, Histoire & Collections 2010

Dictionnaire Fanatique du Trident (Le) by Paul Gauge, Semperfi 2008

Etude du Statoréacteur Supersonique et Hypersonique en France de 1950 à 1974 (Application aux Moteurs Combinés Aérobies) by R. Marguet, P. Berton & F. Hirsinger, Agard 1990

Force de Dissuasion Française (La) by Jacques Villain, Editions Larivière 1987

Gerfaut et Griffon Conquêtes du Statoréacteur et de l'Aile Delta en France by Serge Kaplan and Philippe Ricco, Avia Editions

Histoires Extraordinaires by Philippe Jung, CASP, 2011

Industrie Aéronautique et Spatiale Française 1907-1982, Volumes I, II and III GIFAS 1984

Latécoère Avions et Hydravions by Jean Cuny, Editions Larivière 1992

Matra, la Volonté d'Entreprendre by Claude Carlier, Editions du Chêne, 2003

Mirage et des Hommes (Des). Du Mystère Delta au Mirage III F3 by André Bréand, Volez Editions 2011

Mirage IV (Le) by Hervé Beaumont, Editions Larivière 2003

Mirage F1 (The) Volume 1: Projets et Prototypes by Michel Liebert and Sebastien Buyck, Lela Presse 2007

Morane Saulnier, Ses Avions ses Projets by Henri Lacaze, avec *la* collaboration de Claude Lherbet. Editions Lela Presse 2013

Programme Mirage IV by Jean Cabrière Institut de Stratégie Comparée 1998

René Leduc, Pionnier de la Propulsion à Réaction by Jean Lacroze & Philippe Ricco, Editions Larivière 2000

Saga Etendard (La) by Jean-Marie Gall, Lela Presse 2009

SEPECAT Jaguar by Frédéric Lert, Histoire & Collections 2006

SNECMA, von Zborowski et le Coléoptère (La) by JC Carbonel, Artipresse 2010

SO 4050 Vautour by Alain Crosnier Histoire & Collections 2011

Talisman (Le) Marcel Dassault, Editions Jours de France 1978

X-422 the First Cruise Missile in history by Philippe Jung, Conference at the 48th International Astronautical Congress

Sources (Magazines & Reviews)

Air (L')

Air & Cosmos

Air International

Album du Fanatique de l'Aviation (L')

Aviation Magazine

Aviation Week & Space Technology

Fanatique de l'Aviation (Le)

Flight

Industrie Française Aéronautique et Spatiale, les Matériels

Interavia

Mondaéro

Moniteur Aéronautique (Le)

Pégase

RAF Flying Review

Revue Aéronautique (La)

Technique et Sciences Aéronautiques

Trait d'Union (Le)

On the Net

http://aerophile.over-blog.com

www.hydroretro.net/etudegh/sncase.pdf

http://worldwide.espacenet.com

Index of aircraft types

Reference to three-views drawings are in **bold**

Aérospatiale
- E.650 : 103, 104, **105**
- SA 315 B Lama : 183
- SA 321 Super Frelon : 168, **169**
- SA 321 Flying Crane : 183
- SA 330 Puma : 164, **165,** 168, 170
- SA 330 C : **166**
- SA 330C (attack version) **: 173**
- SA 330 Z : 166SA 330 air cushion landing gear : **167**
- SA 331 : **167**
- SA 340 : 170, 173
- SA 341 Gazelle : **173**
- SA 349 :174
- SA 350 Rotojet : 174, **175**
- SA 360 Dauphin : 175
- SA 365 :170, 175
- SA 365 C : 175
- SA 365 M : 175
- SA 610 Ludion : 245, 247, 248
- SN 600 Diplomate : 233
- X-326A :164
- X-326B : **164**
- X-910 : 157
- EUROFAR : 157, **158**
- Hélicoptère grue : **183**
- Jumbo hélicoptère : 183
- ATR 42 : 212

Alvis Leonides engine : 133, 134, 135

Arado
- Ar 96 : 7
- Ar 234 : 112, 115
- Ar 296 : 7

Armstrong Siddeley
- Mamba turboprop : 130, 227, 230

Arsenal Aéronautique
- Avion d'exploration marine : 213, 214
- Avion de haute mer : 215
- 12H engine : 217

ATAR
- 101 : 13, 29, 38,
- 101B : 13
- 101C : 115
- 101E : 37, 39, 112, 117, 119
- 101G : 39, 47
- 103 : 13
- 8 : 39
- 9 : 46, 47, 49, 51, 52, 54, 56
- Super-Atar : 37, 49, 52, 55

Ateliers Aéronautiques de Suresnes
- AAS-1 : 18

Avro
- Atlantic mk II : 221
- Anson : 123
- Shackleton : 220

BAC
- Nimrod : 221
- TSR-2 : 57

Bertin
- HB 11 : **146**
- HB 12 : **146**, 147
- Flying Jeep : 247, 248

Bloch
- MB161Explorateur : 214

Blohm & Voss
- Bv 138 : 213
- Bv 144 :7

BMW
- 018 :13

Boeing
- B-17 : 213
- B-29 : 19
- C-135 : 59, 60, 62, 85

Breguet
- Br 121 : **94**, 95
- Br 123 : 223, **224, 225**
- Br 126 (TA-501) : 101, **102,** 103
- Br 482 : 18, 19
- Br 760 : 185, **186**
- Br 761 : 185
- Br 762 : 185
- Br 763 Provence : 185
- Br 764 : 185, 215, 216
- Br 765 Sahara : 185, **186**
- Br 766 : 186
- Br 767 : 186
- Br 891 :186, 187, 197
- Br 895 ASW : 216, **217**
- Br 940 : 201, 202
- Br 941 1956 version : **201**
- Br 941 : 202, 203
- Br 941S : 184, **203**,
- Br 941 Z : 204
- Br 942 **: 205**
- Br 943 : 205
- Br 944 : **205**, 206
- Br 945 : **206**, 207, 208
- Br 946 : 207
- Br 947 : 207
- Br 960 : 227
- Br 960 F1: 228
- Br 960 F2 :228
- Br 961 **: 228**, 229, 230
- Br 962 ASW : 230
- Br 963 : 230
- Br 965 : 230
- Br 966 : 230
- Br 1001 Taon : 74
- Br 1005 Taon (ramp launch) : **107**
- Br 1011 Capricorne : 214
- Br 1030 **: 147**
- Br 1050 Alizé : 53, 230, 231
- Br 1050 AEW : **231**
- Br ???? Alizé twin-engine : **232**
- Br 1060 : **126**, 127, 231
- Br 1150 Atlantic : 220
- Br 1160 : 221
- Br 1180 Minerve : 62, 63, 67, 73, 74, **75**
- Br 1190 Minerve : 62, 71, **72**, 73
- Br 1190 Electronic Warfare : **76**
- Br 1191 Veille basse altitude : 221, **222**
- Br 1191 Minerve : 62, 64, 71, 72, 73, **74**
- Br 1191 Transport : **76**
- Br 1250 : **221**
- Br Jaguar : 87
- Br light twin-engine ASW aircraft : **232**
- Br twin-engine ASW : 232
- Br Alphajet : **103**

Breguet-Gyroplane
- G. 20 :161
- G.130 : 163
- G.161 : 161, 163

Bristol
Centaurus engine : 217
Hercules engine : 185, 197, 217, 219, 220
Olympus turbojet :40, 54, 78, 81, 84
Orpheus turbojet : 98, 117, 119, 120, 121
BS.593/3 turbojet : 84
T64 turboprop : 224
BTZ
BTZ Escarbot : **14**
BTZ 324 Dragon : 142, 151
BTZ 511-07 Hanneton **142**
BTZ 511-16 Polyvälent 143
BTZ 511-17 Lucane **143**

Canadian CF-100 : 41
Chance-Vought
F4U Corsair : 123
XF5U Flying Pancake : 156
Chevrollier Véhicule Volant : **248, 249**
Coanda Aerodyne Lenticulaire : 237, **238**
Consolidated
B-24 Liberator: 213
PBY Catalina : 213
Convair B-58 : 81
Couzinet
RC-360 S1 : **239**
RC-360 S2 : 239
RC-360 S3 : 239, **240**

Dassault
Atlantic ANG : 222
Atlantic ATL2 : 222
Atlantic ATL3 : 222
Atlantic M4B : **223**
Balzac : 52
Barougan : 107, 122
Bombardier léger : **51**
Etendard (ramp launch) : **108**
Guardian HU-25 : 233
Lancier : 104
Pétrel : 226
VTX : 103
AMD 188 : 207
MD-30 Viper turbojet : 240
MD 315 Flamant : 123
MD 315B Flamant Rose : **127**
MD 316T SW : 233
MD 410 Spirale : 137, 208
MD 410 Spirale III : **138**
MD 410 Spirale III Early Warning : **233**
MD 410 Spirale IV : 139
MD 415 Communauté : 137
MD ??? Super-Communauté :137
MD 417 : 137
MD 430 : 138
MD 454 Mystère IV : 118
MD 550 : 113
MD 700 : **37**
MD 900 : 51
MD 911 Cavalier : 95,**96**
MD 912 Cavalier II : **96**
MD ??? Cavalier III : 96, **97**
MD 921 : 96
MD 922 : 96
Minerve IV : **80,** 81
Minerve VB : 63, **81**
Minerve VIB : 60, **81, 82,** 83
Minerve / E3 missile : 63
Minerve / E5 missile : **65**
Mirage I (launch ramp) : **108**
Mirage III : 51, 52
Mirage IIIV / X-411 S : 71, **82**, 84
Mirage III O : 57
Mirage IV : 6,44, **51**, 52, 54, 60, 61, 68, 85
Mirage IV A : 52, 53,55, **56**, 62, 63, 78
Mirage IV B : 54, 55
Mirage IV C : 51, 54, 62, **78**
Mirage IV C-2 / Gamma IV : 62, **64**, 76, **78**
Mirage IV C-22 : 63, 77, **78**
Mirage IV C-30 : 62, **79**
Mirage IV E : 55
Mirage IV EX : **58**
Mirage IV F2 : **58**
Mirage IV P . 55, 59
Mirage IV R : 55, 56, **57**,
Mirage IV RJ : 58
Mirage IV / Avon : **57**
Mirage IV / Spey : 57, **58**
Mirage IV/ RB142 : **53,** 55
Mirage IV four-engines : **54**, 55
Mirage IV / Gamma II missile : 62, **65**, 76, **77**
Mirage IV/ Gamma III missile : 65
Mirage IV / Gamma IV missile : **77**
Mirage IV / Sud X-415 : **69**
Super Mirage II : 63, **79**
Super Mirage IV (four engines) : **80**
Super Mirage VI :80

De Havilland DH 100 Vampire : 109
DFS
DFS 332 : **8**
DFS 346 : 13
DOP sled : 110, **111**
Dorand Aile propulsive : 159, **160**
Dornier
Do 24 : 11
Do 335B : 11
P.375 : 101
Douglas
AD-4 Skyraider : 123
B-26 : 37
GAM-87 Skybolt (missile) : 60, 61

English-Electric Lightning : 30
Eurocopter
AS 350 Ecureuil : 176
Attack helicopter : **176**
tiltrotor : **158, 159**

Fairey Swordfish : 213
Fiat G-91 : 101, 121
Fieseler
Fi 103 : 11, 112
Fi 156 : 11, 128
Focke-Achgelis
Fa 61 : 11, 12
Fa 223 : 11, 12, 161
Fa 266 : 11
Fa 284 : **8,** 182
Fa 330 : 11
Focke-Wulf
Fw190 : 11
Fw 200 : 213
Ta 400 : 9
Fouga
CM 10 : 188
CM ??? Centaure : **124**
CM 8-R13 Sylph : 124
CM 82R Lutin : 124
CM 821 : 124
CM 100 : **187**
CM 101 : 187
CM 103 : 189
CM 130 : 87
CM 160 : 88
CM 170 Magister : 87, **88,** 101
CM 170 aile propulsive : 159
CM 170 M Esquif : 88
CM 170 Pamplemousse : 88
CM 170 R : 88, 125
CM 170-2 Super Magister : 88
CM 170-3 Super Magister : 88
CM 171 Makalu : 89

CM 173 : 89, **98,** 99
CM 174 : **88**, 89, 90
CM 175 Zéphyr : 89
CM 175 Sylphe variant : 125
CM 178 : **125**
CM 180 : 89
CM 190 : 89
CM 191 : 89
CM 191 A : 90
CM 191 B : 90
CM 195 : 90
CM 209 : 90
CM 220 : 131
Fouga 90 : 105, 106

General Dynamics F-111 : 58
General Electric
J85 : 95
J79 : 58
Gérin Powered sled : **112**
Gloster Javelin : 41
Gnôme-Rhone 18R : 19
Grumman
E-2 Hawkeye : 224
S-2 Tracker : 139
TBM Avenger : 213

Hawker-Siddeley Kestrel / Harrier : 57
Heinkel
He 162 : 11
He 177 : 19
He 274 : 7, 9, **10,** 18
Henschel Hs 293(missile) : 12, 226, 227
Hispano-Suizo
12Z engine : 18
24Z engine : 18, 19
R800 turbojet : 114
Hurel-Dubois
HD 10 : 188
HD 31 : 188, **189**
HD 32 : 189,190
HD 321 : 191, 219
HD 33 : 191
HD 331 : 191
HD 34 : 191
HD 35 : 192, 219
HD 355 : 219
HD 36 : 192
HD 37 : 192
HD 40 : 192
HD 41 :192
HD 45 : 189
HD 70 : 193
HD 109A : 193
HD 130 : 193, **194**
HD 150 : **194**
HD 151 : 139, 195
Hurel-Gérin assault transport : 195

Illyushin Il-2 Shturmovik : 133

Junkers
Ju 52 : 11
Ju 488 : 10

Kawasaki H6N Emily : 213

Labat Aéroblic : 143, 144
Latécoère
Laté 200 : 226**, 227**
Laté 221 : 217
Laté 222 : 217
Laté 223 : 217
Laté 224 : 217
Laté 225 : 217
Laté 226 : 217
Laté 227 : 218
Laté 228 : **217**, 218
Laté 293 : 226
Laté 631 : 218
Laté 768catapult : 109, **110**
Laté 820 : **123**
Laté 821 : **127**
Laté 853 : 195
Leduc 016 : 9
Lockheed
P2V Neptune : 216
T-33 : 101
Lycoming O-320 : 239

Martin MGM-1 Matador (missile) : 107, 108
Matra
1947 bomber : **20**
511 missile : 47
600 missile : 63, 64, 65, **66,** 67, **72,** 73, 74, **75**, 84
637/638 : 68, 97
Nuclear Martel : 64, 67
R-062 missile : 65
Messerschmitt
Bf108 : 11
Me 163 : 112, 115
Me 164 : 10
Me 208 : 11
Me 262 : 7, **12**, 27
Me 323 : 11
Enzian : 12
McDonnell Douglas
F-4 Phantom II : 52, 57
MD 188 : 204
Morane-Saulnier
MS 470 Vanneau : 87
MS 733 Alcyon :125
MS 735 : 125
MS 750 : 125
MS 751 : 125
MS 752 (two-seater) : 125
MS 752 (single-seater) : 126
MS 753 : 126
MS 755 Fleuret : 90, 126
MS 760 Paris : 108
MS 761 : 126
MS 775 : 128
MS 800 : **113**
MS 801 : 114
MS 802 : 115
MS 850 : 248, **249**
MS 1500 Epervier : **129**
MS 1510 Epervier II : 129
MS 1520 : 129
MS 1530 : **130**
MS 1600 : **130**
MS 2000 : 160
MS 2010 : 160
MS 2015 : 160
Statodyne E1 : **144**
Statodyne E2 : **145**
Statodyne E3 : 141, 145
Statodyne E4 : 145

Nord-Aviation
C-160 Transall : 62, 63, 209
C-160 civilian : **210**
C-160 Astarté : 210
C-160 Gabriel : 210, 211
C-160 Minerve : 85
Nord 500 Cadet : 149, **150**
Nord 500 Démonstrateur, **149**
Nord 500 early design : **148**
Nord 500 Militaire : 151
Nord 501 : 151
Nord 510 : 151, 152, **153**
Nord 511 : **153**
Nord Estocade : 154, 155
Nord Helcade : 153, 154
Nord Rocade : 154
Nord Flying Crane : 182
Nord 1100 Noralpha : 11
Nord 1200 Norécrin : 126
Nord 1405 Gerfaut : 46

Nord 1600 : 35
Nord 1601 : **35**, 36
Nord 1620 : 36
Nord 1700 Norélic : 163
Nord 1750 Norelfe : 163
Nord 1800 : 19
Nord 2100 Norazur : 197
Nord 2500 : 197
Nord 2501 Noratlas : 197
Nord 2501 A :197
Nord 2501 D : 197
Nord 2501 Gabriel : 198
Nord 2501 turboprop : 197
Nord 2501 water bomber : 197
Nord 2501 ASW : 219, **220**
Nord 2502 : 198
Nord 2502 VTOL : 198
Nord 2503 : 198
Nord 2504 : 198, 219
Nord 2505 : 198, 219
Nord 2506 : 198
Nord 2507 : 198
Nord 2508 : 198
Nord 2520 : 199
Nord 2600 : 199
Nord 2700 : 218
Nord 3100 : 199
Nord 2900 : 37
Nord 3300 : 131
Nord 3600 : 96, 97
Nord ???? Norapter : **253, 254**
Mach 2 bomber : 45
Minerve bomber : 63, **84**
Patrouilleur NATO : 225
Véhicule aéroterrestre : **250**
Véhicule aéromobile : 250, **251, 252**
AS-30 missile : 57, 58
North-American
A(5 Vigilante : 82
SM-64 Navajo (missile) : 53
T-6 : 123
T-28 : 123
Northrop F-5 : 99

Orenda turbojet : 55

Pagès Engin Cosmique : 243, **244**
Papin-Rouilly 1915 jet helicopter : 191, 192
Payen
PA 49B Katy : **91**
PA 56 Jockey : 92
PA 57 Aton : **92**
PA 61 Novae : 240, 241
Peenemünde
A4 : 12
Wasserfall : 12
Polikarpov Po-2 : 133
Potez
Potez 75 : 6, 131, 132
Potez 75 hydro : **132**
Potez 91 : 132
Potez P.92 : 98, **99**
Potez P.94 : 99
Potez 840 : 139
Potez 870 : 207, **208**
Potez 880 : 208, **209**
Potez 881 : 208
TOE : **131**
8-D engine : 197
Pratt & Whitney
J75 turbojet : 55
R-1340 Wasp engine : 133, 135, 138
R-1830 engine : 189
R-2800 engine : 185, 216
R-4360 engine : 217
TF-106 turbojet : 5, 84

Rateau SRA-1 : 35
Reims-Cessna FTMA 337 Milirôle : **139**
Renault
6D engine : 197
6Q engine : 11
REP 1954 bomber : **43**
Republic Aviation
F-84G: 107
F-105 : 53
P-47 : 123
Richard Hélicoplane : 155, **156,1 57**
Rolls Royce
Avon turbojet : 38, 40, 57, 193
Conway : turbojet : 186
Dart turboprop : 130, 193, 197
Derwent turbojet : 25, 26, 35
Nene turbojet : 20, 29, 31, 217, 218, 227, 230
RB 142 turbojet :55
RB 172 turbojet : 95, 98, 99
Soar : 116, 117
Spey : 56
Tyne turboprop : 222, 225
Ruhrstahl (missiles) : 12, 226, 227

SEREB Pierres Précieuses : 67, 68
Short
PD 46 Prodigal : 254
Sunderland : 213
Siebel Si204 : 11, 123, 133
SIPA :
S.10 : 7
S.11 : 7
S.111 : 7
S.12 : 7
S.121 : 7
S 200 : **92**
S 300 : 92
1100 : 133
1100B : 133
1120 : 133
1130 : 133
SNCA du Centre
NC-110 : 19
NC-200 : 19
NC-211 : 184, 196
NC-270 : **20, 21**, 26
NC-271 : 9, **22**
NC-701 : 123, 133
NC 2001 Abeille : 162, **163**
NC 2002 Libellule : 162, 163
Skid patent : **113**
SNCASE
SE 116 : 135, 136
SE 117 : **136**
SE 161 Languedoc : 22, 25
SE 200 : 19
SE 210 Caravelle : 85, 193, **199, 200**
SE 212C : 109, **110**
SE 31 Alouette II : 138
SE 535 Mistral (skids) : 111
SE 580 : 30
SE 700 : 161
SE 1010 ASW : 218
SE 1020 : **214**, 215, 218
SE 1400 : 30, 34
SE 1800 : **28**
SE 1801 : **28**
SE 1802 : **29**
SE 1910 powered chariot : 112
SE 2400 :30, 31
SE 2410 : **30, 31**
SE 2411 : 31
SE 2415 : 31, 32
SE 2416 : 32
SE 2417 : 33
SE 2418 : 33
SE 2419 : 33
SE 2420 : **33**
SE 2421 : **34**
SE 2422 : 34
SE 2422R : 34

SE 2423 : 34
SE 2424 : 34
SE 2450 : 34
SE 3000 : 13, 161, 162
SE 3100 : 13, 161, 162
SE 3120 Alouette : 162
SE 3130 Alouette II : 171
SE 3160 Alouette III Navale : **168**
SE 3164 Armed Alouette : 172
SE 316 ? NOTAR : **172**
SE 3200 Frelon : 168
SE 3200 winged version : **168**
SE 4400 missile : 71
SE 5000 Baroudeur : 107, 114, **115**,
SE 5000 w/ Soar booster : **116**
SE 5002 : 117, 121
SE 5003 : 115, **117**, 118
SE 5004 : **118**
SE 5008 : 118
SE 5008 VS : 122
SE 5010 Baroudeur I : 118, 119
SE 5012 : 119
SE 5020 Baroudeur S : **119**
SE 5030 Baroudeur R : **120**
SE 5040 Baroudeur O : 120
SE 50xx Baroudeur A : 120
SE 50xx Baroudeur M : 120
SE 5050 : 121
SE 5091 : 121
SE 5103 : 121
SE X-108 : **218**
SE X-116 : **135**, 136
SE X-223 : 44, 45
SE X-300 : 173
SE X-310 : 171
SE X-315 : 171, 172
SE X-502 : **122**
SNCASO
SO 1100 Ariel : 13, 177, 178
SO 1120 Ariel III : **178**
SO 1220 Djinn : 179
SO 1221 Djinn : 13, 178,179
SO 1300 Farfadet : 180
SO 1310 : 180
SO 1340:180, **181**
SO 1350 : 180
SO 4000 : 20,23, **24**, 25
SO 4000 ASW : 215
SO 4010 :38
SO 4050 Vautour : 6, 39, 53
SO 4050 "robot" : 42
SO 4054 Super-Vautour : 39
SO 4055 : 41
SO 4060 :42, 46, **47**, **48**, 53
SO 4060 B : 49
SO 4060 M : 48, 49
SO 4061 : 48
SO 4062 : 48
SO 5000 : **13**
SO 30 : 197, 200
SO 70 : 19
SO 71 : 19, 20
SO 7100 Dogue : 133, **134**
SO 9000 : 26
SO 9050 : 26, 109
SO 93 : 38
SO M1 : 9, 23, 25
SO M2 : 23, **25**, 26, 112
Deltaviex : 106
SNECMA
AP 508/550 : **49**, **50**
AP 551 : 49, **50**
C-450 Coléoptère : 49, 148
Saucer design A : **241**, 242
Saucer design B: **242**
Saucer design C: **242**
Flying Jeep : **252**
M-36 turbojet : 68
M-45B turbojet : 98
M-46 turbofan : 224
R105 turbojet : 114
12-S engine : 127, 197
14 R engine : 185, 187, 197, 217
14 X engine : 133, 135
Argus 12S engine : 188
TB-1000 turboprop : 201
SOCATA MS 880 Guerrier : **140**
SOCEMA TGAR-1008 : 29, 31, 34
Sud-Aviation
Casseur (missile) : **61**
Cyclone : **42**
SA 125 : 99
X-225 Super-Caravelle / TCS/ PSS : 62, 63
X-225 Super-Caravelle Minerve : 85, **86**
X- ??? Super-Caravelle Nuclear engine : **234**, 235, 236
X-411 S missile : 62, 63, 68, 69
X-412 missile : 68
X-413 missile : 68
X-414 missile : 68, 69, 86
X-415 missile : 68, 69
X-416 missile: 62, 63, 68, 69, 84, 86
X-417 missile : 62, 69, **70**, 71, **74**, 84, 85, 86
X-417 S missile : 70, 72,
X-418 missile : 70
X-419 missile : 69, **70**
X-422 missile : 63, 69, **71**
X-600 : 63
X-??? Attila missile : **236**
X-??? Flying Platform : 245, **246**
Sud-Aviation / Westland
WG-13 : 170, **171**

Turbomeca
Ariel turbojet : 176
Artouste turbojet : 135, 179, 180
Aspin turbojet : 125
Astazou turboprop : 130, 174, 175, 178
Bastan turboprop : 127, 129, 133, 135, 208
Gabizo turbojet : 9
Gourdou turbojet : 89
Macadau turboprop : 128, 180
Marboré turbojet : 87, 88, 89, 109, 124, 125, 188, 219
Ossau turbojet : 89
Palas turbojet : 87, 239
Piméné turbojet : 188
Tourmalet turbojet : 95, 98, 99
Turmo III : 165

Vickers Wellington : 213
Vitrotto RV-1 : 105, **106**

Walter HWK 109-509 rocket engine: 22, 25
Wibault
Aptérion : 254
Gyroptère : 242, **243**
Wright
R1300 engine : 135
R1820 Cyclone engine : 186, 189, 219
R 2600 engine : 218

Yokosuka Judy : 213

Zeppelin ZSO 523 : 11

Index of people and organisations

Companies are listed here where they are quoted in the text or in caption without referring to a specific product.

AIA Clermont-Ferrand : 59
ALAT : 171
Amiot : 19
ANM : 59
Arnold, Kenneth : 237
Arsenal Aéronautique : 13
ASMP : 59
Australian Air Force : 57

BAC : 56, 100
Bastié, Maryse : 197
British European Airways / BEA : 190
Béteille, Roger : 62, 63, 71
Bigand, René : 56
Blériot, Louis : 141
Bomber Command (RAF) : 133
Breguet, Louis : 8, 141, 201
Bruel, André : 163
BTZ : 141

Cabrières, Jean : 49, 51,53, 55
Caillette, Georges : 113, 144, 246
Calvy, Jean : 197
Caneil, Pierre : 90
Cantinieau, Jean : 163
Carlier, Claude : 68
Castello Robert : 87, 124
Caudron : 8
CEA : 58, 234
CEAM : 117
CEV : 201
Charbonnages de France : 69
Chartier, Maurice :162
Chautemps, Claude : 197
CIOS : 7, 9
Coanda, Henri : 7, 237
Coastal Command (RAF) : 220
Collet George : 112
Comité Athena : 60, 61
Comité Coelacanthe : 60,61
Comité Minerve : 60, 61, 85
Cornu, Paul : 161

Dassault, Marcel : 52, 57, 101
Debré, Michel : 62
De Chappedelaine, Jean : 141
De Gaulle, Charles : 61, 63, 67
Demetz André : 184
DERS : 141
Détré, Georges : 132, 197
DGSE : 7
Doblhoff von : 13, 179, 245
Dorand, René : 159, 160, 162
Dornier, Claudius : 101
DTI : 62, 76, 197, 246
Dumez, Raoul : 49

ECAP : 93
ECAT : 93, 94, 100, 101, 124
Eggers, Gerhard : 49
Ernst, Gunther : 49

Fauvel, Charles : 29
Flettner, Anton : 162
Focke Heinrich : 12, 161
Fouga, Gaston : 87
Frédéric-Dupont, Edouard : 55, 136
FAS : 60, 63
FOS : 60
Force de Dissuasion : 60
Force de Frappe : 61, 62, 85, 124

Gabet, Paul : 162
Gaillard, Pierre :22
Gauthier, Gabriel : 101
Gérin, Jacques : 195
GLAM : 200
Glavany, Roland : 53
Grangette, Jacques : 90
Guerre, Marcel : 141

Hawker-Siddeley : 67
Héreil, Georges : 32
Hertel Heinrich : 6, 28, 29
Hurel, Maurice : 186, 195
Hurel-Dubois : 7, 136

IGN : 191

Jacquet, Armand : 149

Kyle, Wallace : 56

Lacroze, Jean : 112
Latécoère : 10
Laufer, Theodor : 13, 179, 245
Lauriol, Marc : 55
Leduc, René : 162, 163
Le Guelinel, ? : 144
Leloup, Robert : 237
Leroy-Finville, Marcel : 190
Letov : 7
Level , Philippe : 133
Lippisch, Alexander : 29
Luftwaffe (BundesLuftwaffe) : 58, 90, 101, 210

Marchal, Raymond : 234
Mauboussin, Pierre : 87, 124
Maulendi, Pierre : 115
Melnik, Constantin : 190
Messerschmitt, Willy : 7, 237
Ministère de l'Air : 18
Messmer, Pierre : 56, 85
Morane-Saulnier : 136
MSBS : 61

Oehmichen, Etienne : 141
Oestrich, Hermann : 13, 29
ONERA : 52, 71, 100, 101, 157

Pagès, Marcel : 243, 244
Parot , Jean-Charles : 23, 39
Payen, Roland : 197, 237
Poncelet , Michel : 241
Puget, Hilarion : 663

RAF : 56, 57, 100, 133, 165
Rastel, Daniel : 23,26
Renollaud , G. : 111
Ricco, Philippe : 112
Richard, Gilbert Camille : 155, 156
Robert, Roger : 20, 109
Rose, Bill : 237

Sänger, Eugen : 13
SAMM : 216
SAUF : 9

SDECE : 7, 190
SEPECAT : 99,100
SEREB : 62, 68
SFERMA : 246
Servanty , Lucien : 63
SNECMA : 13, 14, 55
SNCAN : 9, 11
SNCASO : 11, 53
Soulez-Larivière, Jean : 148, 149, 152, 182
SSBS : 61
STAé : 19, 51, 52, 54, 87, 147, 148
Stehlin, Paul : 62
Steinhoff, Johannes : 101
STO : 11

Thorneycroft, Peter : 56

Villain, Jacques : 60

Wibault, Michel : 141
Witt, Bernard : 220

Zborowski (von), Helmutt : 13, 141, 151, 152, 234
Ziegler, Henri : 235

BELOW **PIctured before 1965 this early Atlantic overflies an Arethuse class conventional-propulsion submarine.** *Breguet-Aviation*

Also Available from Crécy Publishing

French Secret Projects Volume 1
Post War Fighters

Following World War II France made determined efforts to catch-up with other countries in developing high-performance aircraft and designed successful machines to fulfil the needs of the Armée de l'Air, the Marine Nationale and compete in export markets.

For the next twenty years they were the only aircraft manufacturers to investigate with equal effort, turbojet, ramjet and rocket propulsion for manned fighters, either taking advantage of German 'war-booty' technology or using national pre-war research.

A few, such as the Leduc and Griffon ramjet-powered fighters, reached prototype form, the Trident rocket-interceptor advanced to the experimental series (pre-production) stage and the Ouragan, Mystère, Super-Mystère, Mirage III and Etendard were produced in quantity and went on to win export orders.

Later, many attempts were made to design variable-geometry aircraft (including the Mirage G series) and VTOL types (the SNECMA Coléoptère and Dassault Mirage IIIV), and there were even a few flying boat interceptor studies. In the late sixties, in the pursuit of ever-higher speeds, Nord Aviation, Sud Aviation and primarily Avions Marcel Dassault also produced many Mach 3+ proposals.

Period drawings, promotional art, photographs of prototype aircraft, mock-ups, wind tunnel and promotional models are all combined to present, for the first time in the English language, a complete view of French military aircraft design from the Liberation of France to the late twentieth-century.

Jean-Christophe Carbonel
Hardback, 256 pages
978 191080 9006
£27.50 $44.95

British Secret Projects Volume 1
Jet Fighters Since 1950

This completely revised and redesigned second edition takes the original primary source material and adds to it much new material that has come to life in the decades since the original edition was published. Particular emphasis is placed on the tender design competitions and the decisions at the Air Ministry to reject many promising projects, yet allow others to be built and flown. Aircraft types covered include the Hawker P.1103/P.1116/P.1121 series, the extraordinary jet and rocket mixed power-plant interceptors from Saunders-Roe, the equally impressive Fairey 'Delta III' and the origins of today's Hawk and Eurofighter.

Tony Buttler
Hardback, 344 pages
ISBN 9 781910 809051
£27.50 US $44.95

British Secret Projects Volume 5
Britain's Space Shuttle

Even as America and Russia stepped up their efforts in the early 1960s to design ever faster bombers and put men and equipment into space, Britain quietly set to work devising its own hypersonic aircraft and manned space vehicles. This is the story of how, from 1963 to 1966, English Electric/ BAC's Preston works secretly led the world in re-useable spacecraft design.

A huge variety of designs formed the P.42 project with more than 100 proposals for hypersonic interceptors, bombers, reconnaissance aircraft, satellite launchers, spacecraft launchers, orbital spy planes and satellite killers. The end result was the 'Multi-Unit Space Transport And Recovery Device' (MUSTARD), which pre-dated the USA's Space Shuttle programme by six years.

A rare insight into this hitherto little-known chapter in the secret history of the UK manned space flight programme.

Daniel Sharp
Hardback, 224 pages
ISBN 9 781910 809020
£27.50 US $44.95

Japanese Secret Projects Volume 1
Experimental Aircraft of the IJA and IJN 1939-1945

During the final years of World War II, Japan was desperate to combat the threat from America's high-altitude B-29 bombers and the planned invasion of their homeland. As cities were flattened and antiquated aircraft (such as the infamous Zero fighter) fought on only to be shot out of the skies by superior Allied aircraft the Japanese military, like their German counterparts, sought innovative aircraft designs to turn the tide of the war. Japanese Secret Projects volume 1 looks in detail at many of the aeronautical designs and concepts that Japan developed to counter the Allied onslaught.

Edwin M. Dyer III
Hardback, 160 pages
ISBN 9 781857 803173
£24.95 US $42.95

American Secret Projects 1
Fighters, Bombers and Attack Aircraft 1937-1945

By December 7, 1941 almost all the major American combat aircraft of WWII had been designed, selected and in many cases were under production – everything from the P-40 fighter to the huge B-36 'Peacemaker'. Even so, the war years to 1945 saw a dizzying array of new aircraft designs and types being proposed. For example, between 1942 and 1944 Boeing alone submitted no fewer than eight multiengine, intercontinental bomber designs for consideration by the USAAF – every one of which had a wingspan of over 200ft.

American Secret Projects vol 1, includes previously classified files and provides specifications, histories, artist illustrations and 3-view drawings – many redrawn for clarity from the original factory submissions specifically for this book.

Tony Buttler and Alan Griffith
Hardback, 192 pages
ISBN 9 781906 537487
£27.50 US $44.95